Cuba

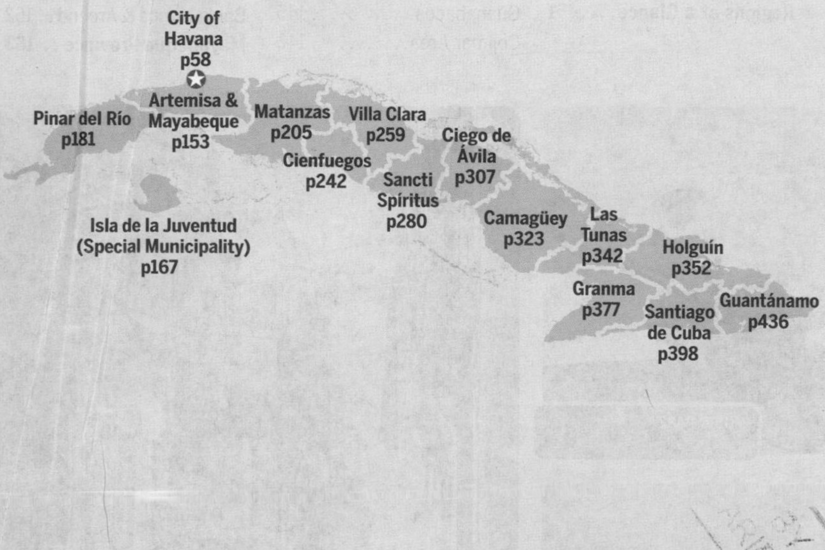

City of
Havana
p58

Pinar del Río
p181

Artemisa &
Mayabeque
p153

Matanzas
p205

Villa Clara
p259

Cienfuegos
p242

Ciego de
Ávila
p307

Sancti
Spíritus
p280

Isla de la Juventud
(Special Municipality)
p167

Camagüey
p323

Las
Tunas
p342

Holguín
p352

Granma
p377

Santiago
de Cuba
p398

Guantánamo
p436

THIS EDITION

Brendan Sainsbury

Luke Waterson

Contents

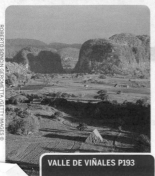

MUSIC P482

VALLE DE VIÑALES P193

ANGELO CAVALLI /GETTY IMAGES ©

MERTEN SNIJDERS /GETTY IMAGES ©

ROBERTO SONCIN GEROMETTA /GETTY IMAGES ©

Contents

HAVANA P58

WALTER BIBIKOW /GETTY IMAGES ©
VARADERO P215

BRENT WINEBRENNER /GETTY IMAGES ©
CIENFUEGOS P243

Contents

TRINIDAD P288

PLAYAS DEL ESTE P147

Contents

FESTIVALS P28

SANTIAGO DE CUBA P401

SPECIAL FEATURES

Welcome to Cuba

Trapped in a time-warp, Cuba is like a prince in a poor man's coat. Behind the sometimes shabby facades, gold dust lingers.

Mildewed Magnificence

There ought to be a banner in the arrivals hall at Havana airport that reads 'Abandon preconceptions, all ye who enter here.' Prepare yourself to be shocked, perplexed, confounded and amazed. Cuba is a country with no historical precedents: economically poor, but culturally rich; visibly mildewed, but architecturally magnificent; infuriating, yet at the same time, strangely uplifting. If the country were a book, it would be James Joyce's *Ulysses;* layered, hard to grasp, serially misunderstood, but – above all – a classic.

Historical Heritage

Halfway between the US to the north and Latin America to the south, Cuba has long struggled to work out where it fits in. Yet, as a former Spanish colony liberally colored with French, African, American, Jamaican, and indigenous Taíno influences, there's no denying the breadth of its historical heritage. When Castro pressed the pause button on economic development in the 1960s, he inadvertently saved many endangered traditions. Though the infrastructure has suffered, important historical heirlooms – forts, palaces, hotels and colonial towns – have survived. Better still, many of them are now being faithfully restored.

Innate Musicality

Most visitors are surprised to arrive in Havana and find, not some grey communist dystopia, but a wildly exuberant place where music emanates from every doorway and even hardened cynics are ensnared by the intrigue and romance. Rhythms and melodies are ubiquitous in this melting pot of African, European and Caribbean cultures. Witness them at the opera and at the ballet; in the corner bar or through the hypnotic drumming of a Santería ceremony; with the trombonist practicing his arpeggios on the seawall, or in the rhythmic gait of the people as they saunter along Havana's musical streets.

Meet the People

That Cuba has survived is a miracle in itself. That it can still enthrall travelers from around the globe with its beaches, bays, mountains, rum, music and impossibly verdant landscapes is an even greater achievement. The key lies in the Cubans themselves: survivors and improvisers, poets and dreamers, cynics and sages. It is the people who have kept the country alive as the infrastructure has crumbled; and it is also they who have ensured that Cuba continues to be the fascinating, perplexing, paradoxical nation it is.

Why I Love Cuba
By Brendan Sainsbury, Author

When I think of Cuba, I always think of my first night back in Havana after a break; the busy atmospheric streets, the snapshots of lives lived out in the open, and the unmistakable aromas: tropical papaya mixed with tobacco leaf, petrol and musty carpets. I love Cuba because it's a forbidden fruit, a complex country of head-scratching contradictions which, however many times you visit, will never adequately answer all your questions. Most of all I love its musicality, its robust culture, its wonderfully preserved history, and the fact that it can frustrate you one minute and unexpectedly inspire you the next.

For more about our authors, see p544.

Above: Avenida Simón Bolívar, Havana (p58)

Cuba

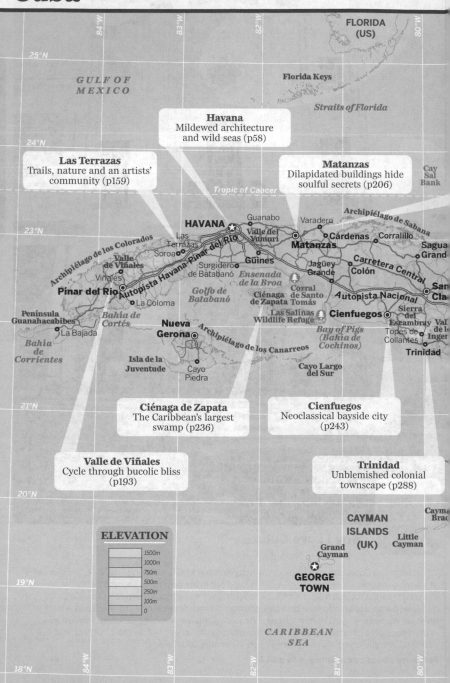

FLORIDA (US)

GULF OF MEXICO

Florida Keys

Straits of Florida

Havana
Mildewed architecture and wild seas (p58)

Las Terrazas
Trails, nature and an artists' community (p159)

Matanzas
Dilapidated buildings hide soulful secrets (p206)

Cay Sal Bank

Tropic of Cancer

Guanabo
Varadero
Archipiélago de Sabana

HAVANA
Las Terrazas
Valle del Yumurí
Cárdenas Corralillo

Soroa
Matanzas

Archipiélago de los Colorados
Valle de Viñales
Surgidero de Batabanó
Güines
Jagüey Grande
Colón
Carretera Central
Sagua Grand

Viñales
Pinar del Río
Autopista Havana-Pinar del Río
Ensenada de la Broa
Corral de Santo Tomás
Autopista Nacional
San Cla

La Coloma
Golfo de Batabanó
Ciénaga de Zapata
Cienfuegos
Sierra del Escambray

Península Guanahacabibes
Bahía de Cortés
Nueva Gerona
Archipiélago de los Canarreos
Las Salinas Wildlife Refuge
Bay of Pigs (Bahía de Cochinos)
Topes de Collantes
Val de la Inger

La Bajada
Bahía de Corrientes
Isla de la Juventude
Cayo Piedra
Cayo Largo del Sur
Trinidad

Ciénaga de Zapata
The Caribbean's largest swamp (p236)

Cienfuegos
Neoclassical bayside city (p243)

Valle de Viñales
Cycle through bucolic bliss (p193)

Trinidad
Unblemished colonial townscape (p288)

CAYMAN ISLANDS (UK)
Cayma Brac
Little Cayman

ELEVATION

	1500m
	1000m
	750m
	500m
	250m
	100m
	0

Grand Cayman
GEORGE TOWN

CARIBBEAN SEA

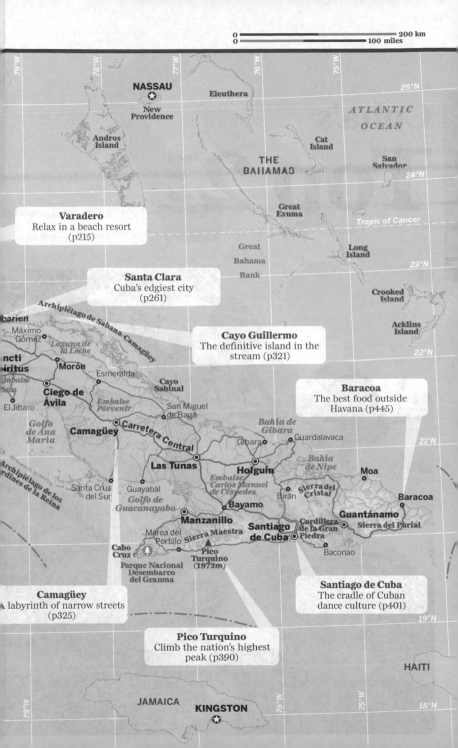

0 ———————— **200 km**
0 ———————— **100 miles**

NASSAU ⭐
New Providence

Eleuthera

ATLANTIC OCEAN

25°N

Andros Island

Cat Island

San Salvador

THE BAHAMAS

24°N

Great Exuma

Tropic of Cancer

Varadero
Relax in a beach resort
(p215)

Great Bahama Bank

Long Island

23°N

Crooked Island

Santa Clara
Cuba's edgiest city
(p261)

Acklins Island

barien
Máximo Gómez

Archipiélago de Sabana-Camagüey

22°N

Laguna de la Leche

Cayo Guillermo
The definitive island in the
stream (p321)

ncti
íritus
Morón

Esmeralda

Cayo Sabinal

mbalse
va

Ciego de Ávila

Embalse Pórvenir

San Miguel de Bagá

El Jibaro

Golfo de Ana María

Camagüey

Carretera Central

Bahía de Gibara

Baracoa
The best food outside
Havana (p445)

Gibara

Guardalavaca

21°N

Las Tunas

Holguín

Bahía de Nipe

Moa

Archipiélago de los rdines de la Reina

Santa Cruz del Sur

Guayabal

Embalse Carlos Manuel de Céspedes

Birán

Sierra del Cristal

Golfo de Guacanayabo

Bayamo

Manzanillo

Cordillera de la Gran Piedra

Guantánamo

Sierra del Purial

Baracoa

Marea del Portillo

Sierra Maestra

Santiago de Cuba

Cabo Cruz

Pico Turquino (1972m)

Baconao

Parque Nacional Desembarco del Granma

Camagüey
A labyrinth of narrow streets
(p325)

Santiago de Cuba
The cradle of Cuban
dance culture (p401)

19°N

Pico Turquino
Climb the nation's highest
peak (p390)

HAITI

JAMAICA

KINGSTON ⭐

18°N

79°W

76°W

75°W

Cuba's
Top 21

1

Live Music Scene

1 In Cuba piped music is considered a cop-out. Here in the land of *son,* salsa, rumba and *trova* everything is spontaneous, live and delivered with a melodic panache. There's the romantic bar-crawling troubadour, the gritty street-based rumba drummer, the bikini-and-feathers cabaret show and the late-night *reggaetón* party. Cuba's musical talent is legendary and rarely comes with the narcissistic 'star status' common in other parts of the world. Matanzas (p213) and Santiago (p420) have the deepest musical roots, Guantánamo (p442) is full of surprises, while Havana (p120) belts out pretty much everything.

Havana's Malecón

2 Only a fool comes to Havana and misses out on the Malecón sea drive (p100), 8km of shabby magnificence that stretches the breadth of the city from Habana Vieja to Miramar and acts as a substitute living room for tens of thousands of cavorting, canoodling, romance-seeking *habaneros.* Traverse it during a storm when giant waves breach the wall, or tackle it at sunset with Benny Moré on your mp3 player, a bottle of Havana Club in your hand and the notion that anything is possible come 10pm. Malecón and Castillo de los Tres Santos Reyes Magnos del Morro

DESIGN PICS / DAVID DUCHEMIN / GETTY IMAGES ©

MARK PAVLOVA / GETTY IMAGES ©

2

Cuba's Casas Particulares

3 Picture the scene: there are two rocking chairs creaking on a polished colonial porch, a half-finished bottle of rum being passed amiably between guest and host, and the sound of lilting music drifting through the humid tropical darkness. It could be any casa particular in any street in any town – they're all the same. Shrugging off asphyxiating censorship and bleak Cold War–style totalitarianism, these private homes reveal Cuba at its most candid. Havana (p103) has the widest selection; Santa Clara's (p266) are the most palatial.

Eclectic Architecture

4 Cuba's architecture reflects its ethnic heritage, with a muscular slice of Spanish baroque, a sprinkling of French classicism, some North American art deco, a hint of European art nouveau and a spark of modernism, all in the lingering shadow of Afro-Cuban slave labor. Sometimes extreme and rarely constant, Cuban architecture yet retains certain binding threads of 'Cuban-ness'. Visit Unesco-listed Havana (p58), Trinidad (p288), Cienfuegos (p243) and Camagüey (p325) to see for yourself.

La Habana Vieja (p62)

3

M G THERIN WEISE / GETTY IMAGES ©

FLAVIO VALLENARI / GETTY IMAGES ©

Idyllic Beach Escapes

5 There's the big showy one in the resort and the wild, windswept one on the north coast; the sheltered palm-fringed one on a paradisical key and the unashamedly nudist one on a secluded island. Cuba's beaches come in all shapes and shades. Search long enough and you're sure to find a slice of nirvana. Big resort areas such as Varadero have hijacked the best strips of sand, but isolated havens remain. Highlights include Playa Pilar (p321) on Cayo Guillermo, Playa Maguana (p453) near Baracoa and Playa Ancón (p301) near Trinidad. Playa Ancón

Bird-Watching

6 Crocodiles aside, Cuba has little impressive fauna, but the paucity of animals is more than made up for by the abundance of birdlife. Approximately 350 species inhabit the shores of this distinct and ecologically weird tropical archipelago, a good two dozen of them endemic. Look out in particular for the colorful *tocororo*, the tiny bee hummingbird, the critically endangered ivory-billed woodpecker and the world's largest flamingo nesting site. The Península de Zapata (p234) and the Sierra del Rosario Bisophere Reserve (p159) are highlights. Green hummingbird

HELENA SMITH / GETTY IMAGES ©

Cuba's Revolutionary Heritage

7 An improbable escape from a shipwrecked yacht, handsome bearded guerrillas meting out Robin Hood–style justice and a classic David versus Goliath struggle that was won convincingly by the underdogs: Cuba's revolutionary war reads like the pages of a movie script. Better than watching it on the big screen is visiting the revolutionary sites in person. Little changed in over 50 years are the disembarkation point of the Granma (p394) and Fidel's wartime HQ at mountaintop Comandancia de la Plata (p388). Plaza de la Revolución (p98), Havana

Diving & Snorkeling in the Caribbean

8 There will be protestations, no doubt, but let's say it anyway: Cuba offers the best diving in the Caribbean (p41). The reasons are unrivaled water clarity, virgin reefs and sheltered waters that teem with millions of fish. Accessibility for divers varies from the swim-out walls of the Bahía de Cochinos (Bay of Pigs; p239) to the hard-to-reach underwater nirvana of the Jardines de la Reina archipelago (p313). For repeat visitors Punta Francés (p171) on Isla de la Juventud – host of an annual underwater photography competition – reigns supreme.

Deep-Sea Fishing Spots

9 When it comes to rating the planet's best deep-sea fishing spots (p44), it's hard to argue with legendary fisherman, Cuba-phile and Nobel Prize–winning author, Ernest Hemingway. Papa adored Cuba for many reasons, not least for the quality of its offshore fishing, enhanced by its location abutting the fast-flowing waters of the Gulf Stream. Cuba's best deep-sea fishing waters hug the abundant north coast keys and few are finer than the archetypal 'island in the stream,' Cayo Guillermo (p321).

Ciénaga de Zapata's Wildlife

10 One of the few parts of Cuba that has never been truly tamed, the Zapata Swamp (p236) is as close to pure wilderness as the country gets. This is the home of the endangered Cuban crocodile, various amphibians, the bee hummingbird and over a dozen different plant habitats. It also qualifies as the Caribbean's largest wetlands, protected in numerous ways, most importantly as a Unesco Biosphere Reserve and Ramsar Convention Site. Come here to fish, bird-watch, hike and see nature at its purest.

Time-Warped Trinidad

11 Soporific Trinidad (p288) went to sleep in 1850 and never really woke up. This strange twist of fate is good news for modern travelers who can explore the perfectly preserved mid-19th-century sugar town. Though it's no secret these days, the time-warped streets still have the power to enchant with their grand colonial homestays, easily accessible countryside and exciting live music scene. But this is also a real working town loaded with all the foibles and fun of 21st-century Cuba. Iglesia Parroquial de la Santísima Trinidad

Labyrinthine Streets of Camagüey

12 Get lost! No, that's not an abrupt put-down; rather it's a recommendation for any traveler passing through the city of *tinajones* (clay pots), churches and erstwhile pirates – aka Camagüey (p325). A perennial rule-breaker, Camagüey was founded on a street grid unlike almost any other Spanish colonial city in Latin America. Here the lanes are as labyrinthine as a Moroccan medina, hiding Catholic churches and triangular plazas, and revealing left-field artistic secrets at every turn.

Cycling Through the Valle de Viñales

13 Cuba is ideal for cycling and there's no better place to do it than the quintessentially rural Valle de Viñales (p193). The valley offers all the ingredients of a tropical Tour de France: craggy *mogotes* (flat-topped hills), impossibly green tobacco fields, bucolic *campesino* huts and spirit-lifting viewpoints at every gear change. The terrain is relatively flat and, if you can procure a decent bike, your biggest dilemma will be where to stop for your sunset-toasting mojito.

Cienfuegos' Classical French Architecture

14 There's a certain *je ne sais quoi* about bayside Cienfuegos (p243), Cuba's self-proclaimed 'Pearl of the South.' Through hell, high water and an economically debilitating Special Period, this city has always retained its poise. The elegance is best seen in the architecture, a homogenous cityscape laid out in the early 19th century by settlers from France and the US. Dip into the cultural life around the center and adjacent Punta Gorda to absorb the Gallic refinement. Casa de la Cultura Benjamin Duarte (p246)

Las Terrazas' Eco-Village

15 Back in 1968, when the fledgling environmental movement was a bolshie protest group for long-haired students in duffel coats, the prophetic Cubans – concerned about the ecological cost of island-wide deforestation – came up with rather a good idea. After saving hectares of denuded forest from an ecological disaster, a group of industrious workers built their own eco-village, Las Terrazas (p159), and set about colonizing it with artists, musicians, coffee growers and the architecturally unique Hotel Moka.

Youthful Energy of Santa Clara

16 Check your preconceived ideas about this country at the city limits. Santa Clara (p261) is everything you thought Cuba wasn't: erudite students, spontaneous nightlife, daring creativity and private homestays in abodes stuffed with more antiques than the local decorative-arts museum. Pop into the drag show at Club Mejunje or hang out for a while with the enthusiastic students in La Casa de la Ciudad. Santa Clara baseball fans celebrating a victory, Parque Vidal

ROBERT HARDING PICTURE LIBRARY LTD / ALAMY ©

Folklórico Dance in Santiago de Cuba

17 There's nothing quite as transcendental as the hypnotic beat of the Santería drums summoning up the spirits of the *orishas* (African deities). But, while most Afro-Cuban religious rites are only for initiates, the drumming and dances of Cuba's *folklórico* troupes are open to all, especially in Santiago de Cuba (p421). Formed in the 1960s to keep the ancient slave culture of Cuba alive, *folklórico* groups enjoy strong government patronage, and their energetic and colorful shows remain spontaneous and grittily authentic.

Unlocking the Secrets of Matanzas

18 Matanzas (p206) is the *Titanic* of Cuba, a sunken liner left to languish in the murky depths, but where flickers of an erstwhile beauty still remain. After manicured Varadero, the city hits you like a slap in the face but, with a little time, its gigantic historical legacy will teach you more about the real Cuba than 20 repeat visits to the resorts. Matanzas' refined culture congregates in the Teatro Sauto, while its African 'soul' manifests itself in the energetic rumba that takes off in Plaza de la Vigía. Puente Calixto García, Matanzas

Baracoa's Spicy Food & Culture

19 Over the hills and far away on the easternmost limb of Guantánamo province lies isolated Baracoa (p445), a small yet historically significant settlement, weird even by Cuban standards for its fickle Atlantic weather, eccentric local populace and unrelenting desire to be – well – different. Watch locals scale coconut palms, listen to bands play *kiribá*, the local take on *son*, and – above all – enjoy the infinitely spicier, richer and more inventive food (p449), starting with the sweet treat *cucuruchu*.

Cuba's Ebullient Festivals

20 Through war, austerity, rationing and hardship, the Cubans have retained their infectious *joie de vivre*. Even during the darkest days of the Special Period, the feisty festivals never stopped, a testament to the country's capacity to put politics aside and get on with the important business of living. The best shows involve fireworks in Remedios (p272), *folklórico* dancing in Santiago de Cuba (p421), movies in Gibara (p365) and every conceivable genre of music in Havana. Arrive prepared.

Pico Turquino – Cuba's Highest Mountain

21 The trek up Cuba's highest mountain, Pico Turquino (p390), is a rare privilege. Guides are mandatory for this tough two- to three-day 17km trek through the steep broccoli-green forests of the Sierra Maestra that acts as a kind of history lesson, nature trail and bird-watching extravaganza all rolled into one. Revolutionary buffs should make a side trip to Fidel's wartime jungle HQ on the way up.

The Sierra Maestra

Need to Know

For more information, see Survival Guide (p501)

Currency
Cuban convertibles (CUC$)

Language
Spanish

Money
Cuba is primarily a cash economy. Credit cards are accepted in resort hotels and work in most ATMs. ATMs don't always accept debit cards.

Visas
A travel card valid for 30 days is usually included in your flight package. US travelers are prohibited from spending money in Cuba.

Cell Phones
Check with your service provider to see if your phone will work (GSM or TDMA networks only). International calls are expensive. You can pre-buy services from the state-run phone company, Cubacel.

Time
Eastern Standard Time (GMT/UTC - five hours)

When to Go

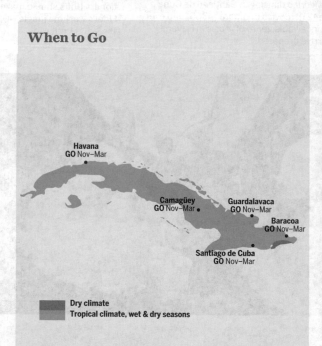

Havana
GO Nov–Mar

Camagüey
GO Nov–Mar

Guardalavaca
GO Nov–Mar

Baracoa
GO Nov–Mar

Santiago de Cuba
GO Nov–Mar

Dry climate
Tropical climate, wet & dry seasons

High Season
(Nov–Mar & Jul–Aug)

➡ Prices are 30% higher and hotels may require advance bookings.

➡ Prices are higher still for two weeks around Christmas and New Year.

➡ Weather is cooler and dryer November to March.

Shoulder
(Apr & Oct)

➡ Look out for special deals outside of peak season.

➡ Watch out for Easter vacation, when prices and crowds increase.

Low Season
(May, Jun & Sep)

➡ Some resort hotels offer fewer facilities or shut altogether.

➡ There's a hurricane risk between June and November and higher chance of rain.

Useful Websites

AfroCuba Web (www.afro cubaweb.com) Everything on Cuban culture.

BBC (www.bbc.co.uk) Interesting correspondent reports on Cuba.

Cuba Absolutely (www.cuba absolutely.com) Art, culture, business and travel.

Cubacasas.net (www.cuba casas.net) Information, photos and contact details for casas particulares.

LonelyPlanet.com (www.lonely planet.com/cuba) Destination information, hotel bookings, traveler forum and more.

Exchange Rates

Argentina	ARS$1	CUC$0.20
Australia	A$1	CUC$1.03
Canada	C$1	CUC$1.00
Europe	€1	CUC$1.34
Japan	¥100	CUC$1.07
Mexico	MXN$1	CUC$0.08
New Zealand	NZ$1	CUC$0.84
UK	£1	CUC$1.57
US	US$1	CUC$1.00

For current exchange rates see www.xe.com

Important Numbers

For details of complicated phone codes, see p510.

Emergency	📞106
Directory assistance	📞113
Police	📞106
Fire	📞105

Daily Costs

Budget: Less than CUC$60

➡ Casas particulares: CUC$20–30

➡ Government-run restaurants: CUC$15–20

➡ Cheap museum entry: CUC$3–6

Midrange: CUC $60–120

➡ Boutique hotels: CUC$35–60

➡ Meals in paladares: CUC$17–22

➡ Travel on Víazul buses

Top End: More than CUC$120

➡ Resort or historic hotel: CUC$150–200

➡ Car hire or taxis: CUC $60–70

➡ Evening cabaret: CUC $35–60

Arriving in Cuba

Aeropuerto Internacional José Martí (Havana) There are no regular buses or trains running direct from the airport into the city center. Taxis cost CUC$20 to CUC$25 and take 30 to 40 minutes to reach most of the city center hotels. You can change money at the bank in the arrivals hall.

Other International Airports Cuba has nine other international airports, but none of them have reliable public transport links; your best bet is always a taxi. Agree fares beforehand.

Getting Around

Buses are the most efficient and practical way of getting around.

Bus The state-run Víazul network links most places of interest to tourists on a regular daily schedule. Cubanacán runs a less comprehensive *conectando* service. Local buses are crowded and have no printed schedules.

Car Rental cars are quite expensive and driving can be challenge due to lack of signposts and ambiguous road rules.

Taxi Taxis are an option over longer distances if you are traveling in a small group. Rates are approximately CUC$0.50 per kilometer.

Train Despite its large train network, Cuban trains are slow, unreliable and lacking in comfort. For stoics only!

Opening Hours

Many four- and five-star hotels in big cities like Havana offer money exchange late into the evening.

Banks 9am to 3pm Monday to Friday

Cadeca Money Exchanges 9am to 7pm Monday to Saturday, 9am to noon Sunday

Pharmacies 8am to 8pm

Post Offices 8am to 5pm Monday to Saturday

Restaurants 10:30am to 11pm

Shops 9am to 5pm Monday to Saturday, 9am to noon Sunday

For much more on transport, see p513

First Time Cuba

For more information, see Survival Guide (p501)

Checklist

➡ Preload credit card with funds in your home country, in case you run out of cash

➡ Bring printed copy of medical insurance to show at airport

➡ Check when booking air ticket that tourist card is included in your flight package

➡ Book some salsa dancing lessons and/or learn basic Spanish

What to Pack

➡ Spanish dictionary/ phrasebook

➡ Plug adaptors for European and US sockets

➡ Good money belt that fits snugly around your waist

➡ Basic first aid, pain killers and any required medications

➡ Insect repellent, sunscreen and sunglasses

➡ Stash of cash in euros, Canadian dollars or sterling

Top Tips for Your Trip

➡ For a glimpse of the real Cuba and a chance to put your money directly into the pockets of individual Cubans, stay in a casa particular (private homestay).

➡ Carry toilet paper and antiseptic hand-wash, and drink bottled water

➡ Roads can be rough and driving can be a challenge. It's cheaper to hire a taxi than a car over longer distances.

➡ Thanks to heavy bureaucracy, answers to simple requests aren't always straightforward. Probe politely and ask at least five different people before you make important decisions.

➡ Cuba is complex, and not always portrayed accurately in the international media. Travel with an open mind and be prepared to be regularly surprised, confused, confounded and astonished.

What to Wear

Cuba is a hot, humid country which, thankfully, has a casual approach to clothing. Locals generally opt for shorts, sandals and T-shirts; women favor tight-fitting lycra, men looser *guayabera* shirts (invented in Cuba). There are only two nude beaches in Cuba, frequented almost exclusively by foreigners. Cinemas and theaters usually have a 'no shorts' rule for men.

Sleeping

There are thousands of casas particulares in Cuba. For the more popular casas, including those in this book, reserve ahead. Book in advance for all-inclusive resorts to avoid expensive rack rates.

➡ **Casas Particulares** Cuban homes renting rooms to foreigners, offering an affordable form of authentic cultural immersion.

➡ **Campismos** Cheap, rustic accommodations in rural areas, usually in bungalows or cabins.

➡ **Hotels** All Cuban hotels are government-owned. Prices and quality range from cheap Soviet-era to high-flying colonial chic.

➡ **Resorts** Large international-standard hotels in resort areas that sell all-inclusive packages.

Money

Cuba has two currencies: convertibles (CUC$) and pesos (*moneda nacional*; MN$). One convertible is worth 25 pesos. Non-Cubans mostly use convertibles.

Cuba is a cash economy; credit cards aren't readily accepted outside international hotels. US-affiliated credit cards aren't accepted at all. Check with your credit company at home.

ATMs are becoming more widespread but often don't accept debit cards; they usually accept credit cards.

For more information, see p508.

Bargaining

Cuba's socialist economy doesn't have a history of bargaining, though there may be some room for maneuver on prices at private enterprise markets.

Tipping

Tipping in Cuba is important. Since most Cubans earn their money in *moneda nacional* (MN$), leaving a small tip of CUC$1 (MN$25) or more can make a huge difference.

➡ **Resorts/Hotels** Tip for good service with bellboys, room maids and bar/restaurant staff.

➡ **Musicians** Carry small notes for the ubiquitous musicians in restaurants. Tip when the basket comes round. It's not obligatory, but if the music is good (it usually is) – why not?

➡ **Restaurants** Standard 10%, or up to 15% if service is excellent.

➡ **Taxis** 10% if you are on the meter, otherwise agree full fare beforehand.

Plaza Vieja (p72), Havana

Etiquette

Cuba is an informal country with few rules of etiquette.

➡ **Greetings** Shake hands with strangers; a kiss or double-cheek kiss is between men-women, women-women who have already met.

➡ **Conversation** Although they can be surprisingly candid, Cubans aren't always keen to discuss politics, especially with strangers and if it involves being openly critical of the government.

➡ **Dancing** Cubans don't harbor any self-consciousness about dancing. Throw your reservations out of the window and let loose on the dance floor.

Eating

➡ **Paladares & Casas Particulares** Private restaurants and homestays offer the best food and service in Cuba, and the portions are invariably huge.

➡ **Hotels & Resorts** All-inclusive resorts offer buffet food of an international standard although after a while it can get a bit bland.

➡ **State-Run Restaurants** Varying food and service from topnotch places in Havana to unimaginative rations in the provinces. Prices are often lower than in paladares.

Language

Cubans working in tourism are usually proficient in English and other European languages including French, Italian and German. Elsewhere, Spanish dominates. The more Spanish you speak, the richer your experience will be.

If You Like...

Amazing Architecture

When Castro pressed the pause button on Cuban economic development in 1959 he inadvertently did his country's colonial buildings a big favor. Protected from modern development, many old architectural heirlooms have survived.

Habana Vieja Like an old attic full of dusty relics, Havana is a treasure chest of eclectic architecture awaiting rediscovery. (p62)

Cienfuegos Cuba's most architecturally homogenous city is a love letter to French neoclassicism, full of elegant cupolas and refined columns. (p243)

Camagüey Unique Unesco-listed Camagüey has an unusual street plan of labyrinthine lanes and baroque spires that hide a devout Catholic soul. (p325)

Trinidad Quite possibly one of the most beguiling and best-preserved towns in the Caribbean, tranquil Trinidad is a riot of colonial baroque. (p288)

Nightlife & Dancing

'Two fatherlands I have: Cuba and the night,' wrote José Martí. He wasn't far wrong. Cuba is a different place after dark, an atmospheric mélange of passion and pathos.

Santa Clara This is the city where the 'next big thing' happens first: drag shows, rock and roll music and everything in between. (p261)

Cabarets Cuba's flamboyant cabarets are one element of opulent prerevolutionary life that refused to die.

Casas de la Trova Cuba's old-fashioned spit-and-sawdust music houses are determined to keep the essence of traditional Cuban music alive.

Uneac Provincial cultural centers full of artistic talent; entry is free and everyone greets you like an old friend.

Subcultures

Cuba is a country of multiple mysteries. To understand some of them you have to lift the lid off a few of its subcultures, many of which inhabit a grey area between what's legal and what's not.

Baseball Fanatics A national obsession that Cubans share with Americans; the hotspot for fans is Havana's *esquina caliente* in Parque Central. (p125)

Gay Culture Gay life is gradually beginning to flower in Cuba, no more so than in the 'liberated' city of Santa Clara. (p261)

Roqueros Once frowned on by the authorities, rock and rollers now display their individuality in Havana on the corner of Calle 23 and Avenida G. (p488)

Abakuá One of a handful of religions of African origin, the secrets of the Abakuá fraternity are best searched for in Matanzas. (p211)

Under the Radar

Sometimes the power fails, the public transport is awful and the buildings look more like demolition jobs than dreamy ruins. Welcome to the real Cuba, where friendships

---

IF YOU LIKE... SANTERÍA

For those interested in Cuban religions of African origin, the best places to do some DIY sleuthing are the cities of Matanzas (p206) and Havana, especially the Regla (p144) and Guanabacoa (p145) neighborhoods.

are forged and ideas exchanged.

Gibara The home of the 'poor man's film festival' is rich in wild, ocean-side scenery and creepy Holguín magic. (p364)

Marea del Portillo Turn right outside the resorts and go for a wander in the magnificent mountains, untouched since the *Granma* yacht ran aground in 1956. (p396)

Matanzas Varadero's outcast sibling lacks sun-lounges and stuff-yourself-silly buffets, but it has soul *socios* – if you're willing to look for them. (p206)

Las Tunas Cuba's least-visited provincial capital defies its 'boring' stereotype on Saturday nights when there's a rodeo in town. (p344)

Holguín *Jinetero*-free streets, an underrated baseball team nicknamed 'the dogs' and a beer-drinking donkey named Pancho. Welcome to Holguín. (p353)

Wildlife-Watching

There are no big land mammals in Cuba, but you *can* get acquainted with the world's smallest hummingbird, the tiniest of all frogs and birds migrating from both North and South America.

Ciénaga de Zapata A microcosm of Cuban wildlife, including the critically endangered Cuban crocodile, in a 66-sq-km swamp. (p236)

Parque Nacional Alejandro de Humboldt Sky-high levels of endemism make Humboldt, home to the world's smallest frog, an ecological rarity. (p453)

Sierra del Chorrillo Non-indigenous exotic animals, including zebra and deer, in a

(Above) World-famous cabaret at the Tropicana Nightclub (p140), Havana

(Below) Colorful Habana Vieja architecture (p62)

quintessentially Cuban grassland setting. (p336)

Río Máximo Behold the largest colony of nesting flamingos in the world on Camagüey's north coast. (p339)

Guanahacabibes Crabs and iguanas do battle with jeep traffic on Cuba's windswept western wilderness. (p191)

Diving & Snorkeling

Diving in Cuba is a trip in its own right. The most pristine spots hug the sheltered Caribbean waters in the south, while the north is kissed by one of the largest coral reefs in the world.

Isla de la Juventud Worth the effort to get there, La Isla is famed for its clear water and hosts an underwater photography competition. (p171)

Jardines de la Reina This heavily protected archipelago has zero infrastructure and safeguards the most unspoiled reefs in the Caribbean. (p313)

María la Gorda Over 50 dive sites and easy access off Cuba's western tip make this small resort 'diver's central'. (p191)

Bahía de los Cochinos Once infamous for another reason, the Bay of Pigs has rediscovered its raison d'être – damn good diving. (p240)

Playa Santa Lucía It's worth braving this rather tacky resort strip to experience the best diving on Cuba's north coast. (p339)

Relaxing at a Resort

Resorts suck up a huge proportion of Cuba's annual visitors. Varadero is the big one, with over 50 hotels. Further east, three more big resort areas hug the northern coast.

Varadero The biggest resort in Cuba isn't to everyone's taste, but it's insanely popular. (p215)

Cayo Coco An island getaway linked to the mainland by a causeway, Cayo Coco is more subtle than Varadero. (p318)

Guardalavaca Three separate enclaves on Holguín's north coast offer different price brackets, with Playa Pesquero selling the poshest packages. (p368)

Cayo Santa María The still-developing *cayos* of Villa Clara province retain a refreshingly tranquil feel. (p276)

Cayo Largo del Sur Cuba's most isolated resort island isn't very Cuban, but its beaches are among Cuba's best. (p177)

White-Sand Beaches

Combine the words 'Caribbean' and 'island' and you'll get more than a hint of Cuba's dazzling beach potential. The best scoops of sand are situated mainly on the north coast.

Playa Pilar Hemingway's favorite is now a much-decorated travel mag photo opportunity

backed by big dunes but – as yet – no hotels. (p321)

Playa Maguana Wind-whipped waves and bruised clouds add to the ethereal ambience of Baracoa's finest beach. (p453)

Playa Pesquero Walk for 200m through clear bathwater-temperature ocean and still only be up to your waist. (p367)

Playa Sirena Huge football-field-sized beach on what is essentially a private tourist island where the dress code is 'bare all'. (p177)

Playa Los Pinos Just you, some driftwood, a good book and perhaps the odd local offering cooked lobster for lunch. (p339)

Pirates & Forts

Cuba was a dangling carrot for pirates in the 16th and 17th centuries, as they regularly terrorized its coastline. Today, the legacy of past battles can be witnessed in a cache of well-preserved forts.

Havana's Forts Four of the finest examples of 16th-century military architecture in the Americas are preserved in their almost original state. (p85)

Camagüey Moved twice to avoid the attentions of pirates, Camagüey redesigned its streets in a labyrinthine pattern to prevent repeat attacks. (p325)

La Roca Two hundred years in the making and never really used for its original purpose as a defensive fort, Santiago's La Roca is today a Unesco World Heritage Site. (p412)

Baracoa The 'first city' has three small but stalwart forts that are today home to a museum, a hotel and a restaurant. (p445)

Matanzas Once breached by the British, Matanzas' little-visited

---

IF YOU LIKE... ZIP-LINING

Cuba's only zip-line catapults vertigo-shunners over the small eco-village of Las Terrazas in Artemisa province, accessible on a day-trip from Havana. (p161)

Idyllic Playa Ancón (p301)

Castillo de San Severino now harbors an interesting slave museum. (p210)

Revolutionary History

Picture January 1959: pistols at dawn, dark shadows descending from the Sierra Maestra and Batista's New Year's party interrupted by a posse of bearded guerrillas. Cuba's revolution continues to resound.

Santa Clara 'Che City' is the home of Guevara's mausoleum, myriad statues and a fascinating open-air museum. (p261)

Bayamo The understated capital of Granma province, where Cuba's first revolution was ignited in 1868. (p379)

Sierra Maestra Flecked with historical significance, including the mountain ridge HQ where Castro directed operations during the revolutionary war. (p388)

Santiago de Cuba The self-proclaimed 'City of Revolutionaries' has potent reminders of past battles on almost every street corner. (p401)

Museo de la Revolución Cuba's most comprehensive museum is an immersion in all things revolutionary. (p94)

Live Music

No introduction required. Cuba hemorrhages music of all types: *son* (Cuba's popular music), salsa, *songo* (fusion of rumba and salsa), *reggaetón* (Cuban hip-hop), opera, classical, jazz – and you could easily plan multiple trips around it.

La Casa de la Música The trendy choice. Casas de la Música mix live music with late-night dancing and pull in big names like Los Van Van. (p121)

Casas de la Trova The traditional choice. *Son* and boleros give an old-fashioned lilt to these cultural houses that characterize every Cuban provincial town.

La Tumba Francesa The esoteric choice. Mysterious *folklórico* dance troupes in Guantánamo and Santiago de Cuba perform musical rites with a Haitian influence. (p442, p421)

Street Rumba Salt-of-the-earth Havana and Matanzas specialize in mesmerizing drumming and dance rituals that can summon up the spirit of the *orishas* (Yoruba gods).

Jazz Cuba's best jazz venues are both in Havana's Vedado district: the Jazz Café (p120) and La Zorra y El Cuervo (p121).

Month by Month

January

The tourist season hits full swing, and the whole country has added buoyancy and life. Cold fronts bring occasionally chilly evenings.

⚜️ Día de la Liberación

As well as seeing in the New Year with roast pork and a bottle of rum, Cubans celebrate January 1 as the triumph of the revolution, the anniversary of Fidel Castro's 1959 victory.

⚜️ Incendio de Bayamo

Bayamo residents remember the 1869 burning of their city with music and theatrical performances in an *espectáculo* (show) culminating in particularly explosive fireworks.

February

The peak tourist season continues and high demand can lead to overbooking, particularly in the rental-car market. Calm seas and less fickle weather promote better water clarity, making this an ideal time to enjoy diving and snorkeling.

⚜️ Feria Internacional del Libro

First held in 1930, the International Book Fair is headquartered in Havana's Fortaleza de San Carlos de la Cabaña, but it later goes on the road to other cities. Highlights include book presentations, special readings and the prestigious Casa de las Américas prize.

⚜️ Festival Internacional de Jazz

The International Jazz Festival is staged in the Karl Marx, Mella and Amadeo Roldán Theaters in Havana and draws in top figures from around the world.

🏃 Diving with Clarity

Calm conditions promote clear water for diving, particularly on Cuba's south coast. The country's prime diving nexus, La Isla de la Juventud, consequently holds the annual Fotosub International Underwater Photography competition.

⚜️ Habanos Festival

Trade fairs, seminars, tastings and visits to tobacco plantations draw cigar aficionados to Havana for this annual cigar festival with prizes, rolling competitions and a gala dinner.

March

Spring offers Cuba's best wildlife-watching opportunities, particularly for migrant birds. With dryer conditions, it is also an ideal time to indulge in hiking, cycling or numerous other outdoor activities.

⚜️ Fiesta de la Toronja

Once famous for its citrus plantations, Isla de la Juventud still celebrates the annual grapefruit harvest with this animated excuse for a party in Nueva Gerona, even though the crop yield is now minimal.

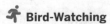 Festival Internacional de Trova

Held since 1962 in honor of *trova* pioneer Pepe Sánchez, this festival invades the parks, streets and music houses of Santiago de Cuba in a showcase of the popular verse/song genre.

Bird-Watching

March is a cross-over period when migrant birds from both North and South America join Cuba's resident endemics en route for warmer or colder climes. There's no better time to polish off your binoculars.

April

Economy-seeking visitors should avoid the Easter holiday, which sees another spike in tourist numbers and prices. Otherwise April is a pleasant month with good fly-fishing potential off the south coast.

Semana de la Cultura

During the first week of April, Baracoa commemorates the landing of Antonio Maceo at Duaba on April 1, 1895 with a raucous Carnaval along the Malecón, expos of its indigenous music *nengon* and *kiribá,* and various culinary offerings.

Festival Internacional de Cine Pobre

Gibara's celebration of low- and no-budget cinema

has been an annual event since 2003, when it was inaugurated by late Cuban film director Humberto Sales. Highlights include film-showing workshops and discussions on movie-making with limited resources.

Bienal Internacional del Humor

You can't be serious! Cuba's unique humor festival takes place in San Antonio de los Baños in out-of-the-way Artemisa province. Head-quartered at the celebrated Museo del Humor, talented scribblers try to outdo each other by drawing ridiculous caricatures. Hilarious!

May

Possibly the cheapest month of all, May is the low point between the foreign crowds of winter and the domestic barrage of summer. Look out for special deals offered by resort hotels and significantly cheaper prices all around.

Romerías de Mayo

This religious festival takes place in the city of Holguín during the first week of May and culminates with a procession to the top of the city's emblematic Loma de la Cruz, a small shrine atop a 275m hill.

Cubadisco

An annual get-together of foreign and Cuban record producers and companies, Cubadisco hosts music concerts, a trade fair and a Grammy-style awards

ceremony that encompasses every musical genre from chamber music to pop.

Hemingway International Marlin Fishing Tournament

Famously won by Fidel in 1960, this annual contest was set up by Ernest Hemingway in 1951 and runs out of the eponymous Havana marina. Teams of up to four use catch-and-release methods.

June

The Caribbean hurricane season begins inauspiciously. A smattering of esoteric provincial festivals keeps June interesting. Prices are still low and, with the heat and humidity rising, travelers from Europe and Canada tend to stay away.

Jornada Cucalambeana

Cuba's celebration of country music, and the witty 10-line *décimas* (stanzas) that go with it, takes place about 3km outside unassuming Las Tunas at Motel Cornito, the former home of erstwhile country-music king, Juan Fajardo 'El Cucalambé.'

Festival Internacional 'Boleros de Oro'

Organized by Uneac (Unión de Escritores y Artistas de Cuba; Union of Cuban Writers and Artists), the Boleros de Oro was created by Cuban composer and music-ologist José Loyola Fernández in 1986 as a celebration of this distinctive Cuban musical genre. Most events take place in Havana's Teatro Mella.

★ Fiestas Sanjuaneras

This feisty carnival in Trinidad on the last weekend in June is a showcase for the local *vaqueros* (cowboys), who gallop their horses through the narrow cobbled streets.

July

High summer is when Cubans vacation; expect the beaches, campismos and cheaper hotels to be mobbed. The July heat also inspires two of the nation's hottest events: Santiago's Carnaval and the annual polemics of July 26.

★ Festival del Caribe, Fiesta del Fuego

The so-called Festival of Caribbean Culture, Fire Celebration in early July kicks off an action-packed month for Santiago with exhibitions, song, dance, poetry and religious-tinged rituals from all around the Caribbean.

★ Día de la Rebeldía Nacional

On July 26 the Cubans 'celebrate' Fidel Castro's failed 1953 attack on Santiago's Moncada Barracks. The event is a national holiday and – in days when he enjoyed better health – Castro was famous for making five-hour speeches. Expect *un poco* (a little) politics and *mucho* (much) eating, drinking and being merry.

★ Carnaval de Santiago de Cuba

Arguably the biggest and most colorful carnival in the Caribbean, the famous Santiago shindig at the end of July is a riot of floats, dancers, rum, rumba and more. Come and join in the very *caliente* (hot) action.

August

While Santiago retires to sleep off its hangover, Havana gears up for its own annual shindig. Beaches and campismos still heave with holidaying Cubans while tourist hotels creak under a fresh influx of visitors from Mediterranean Europe.

★ Festival Internacional 'Habana Hip-Hop'

Organized by the Asociación Hermanos Saíz – a youth arm of Uneac – the annual Havana Hip-Hop Festival is a chance for the island's young musical creators to improvise and swap ideas.

★ Carnaval de la Habana

Parades, dancing, music, colorful costumes and striking effigies – Havana's annual summer shindig might not be as famous as its more rootsy Santiago de Cuba counterpart, but the celebrations and processions along the Malecón leave plenty of other city carnivals in the shade.

September

It's peak hurricane season. The outside threat of a 'big one' sends most Cubaphiles running for cover and tourist numbers hit a second trough. The storm-resistant take advantage of cheaper prices and near-empty beaches. But, beware – some facilities close down completely.

★ Festival Internacional de Música Benny Moré

The Barbarian of Rhythm is remembered in this bi-annual celebration of his suave music, headquartered in the singer's small birth town of Santa Isabel de las Lajas in Cienfuegos province.

★ Fiesta de Nuestra Señora de la Caridad

Every September 8 religious devotees from around Cuba partake in a pilgrimage to the Basílica de Nuestra Señora del Cobre, near Santiago, to honor Cuba's venerated patron saint (and her alter ego, the Santería orisha, Ochún).

October

Continuing storm threats and persistent rain keep all but the most stalwart travelers away until the end of the month. While the solitude can be refreshing in Havana, life in the peripheral resorts can be deathly quiet and lacking in atmosphere.

✨ Festival Internacional de Ballet de la Habana

Hosted by the Cuban National Ballet, this annual festival brings together dance companies, ballerinas and a mixed audience of foreigners and Cubans for a week of expositions, galas, and classical and contemporary ballet. It has been held in even-numbered years since its inception in 1960.

✨ Festival del Bailador Rumbero

During the 10 days following October 10, Matanzas rediscovers its rumba roots with talented local musicians performing in the city's Teatro Sauto.

November

Get ready for the big invasion from the north – and an accompanying hike in hotel rates! Over a quarter of Cuba's tourists come from Canada; they start arriving in early November, as soon as the weather turns frigid in Vancouver and Toronto.

✨ Fiesta de los Bandas Rojo y Azul

Considered one of the most important manifestations of Cuban *campesino* (country person) culture, this esoteric fiesta in the settlement of Majagua, in Ciego de Ávila province, splits the town into two teams (red and blue) that compete against each other in boisterous dancing and music contests.

🏃 Marabana

The popular Havana marathon draws between 2000 and 3000 competitors from around the globe. It's a two-lap course, though there is also a half-marathon and races for 5km and 10km distances.

December

Christmas and the New Year see Cuba's busiest and most expensive tourist spike. Resorts nearly double their prices and rooms sell out fast. The nation goes firework-crazy in a handful of riotous festivals. Book ahead!

✨ Festival Nacional de Changüí

Since 2003, Guantánamo has celebrated its indigenous music in this rootsy music festival held in early December. Look out for Elio Revé Jr and his orchestra.

✨ Festival Internacional del Nuevo Cine Latinoamericano

This internationally renowned film festival, held in cinemas across Havana, illustrates Cuba's growing influence in Latin American cinema around the world.

✨ Procesión de San Lázaro

Every year on December 17, Cubans descend en masse on the venerated Santuario de San Lázaro in Santiago de las Vegas, on the outskirts of Havana. Some come on bloodied knees, others walk barefoot for kilometers to exorcize evil spirits and pay off debts for miracles granted.

☆ Las Parrandas

A firework frenzy that takes place every Christmas Eve in Remedios in Villa Clara province, Las Parrandas sees the town divide into two teams that compete against each other to see who can come up with the most colorful floats and the loudest *bangs!*

☆ Las Charangas de Bejucal

Didn't like Las Parrandas? Then try Bejucal's Las Charangas, Mayabeque province's cacophonous alternative to the firework fever further east. The town splits into the exotically named *Espino de Oro* (Golden Thorn) and *Ceiba de Plata* (Silver Silk-Cotton Tree).

Plan Your Trip
Itineraries

STRAITS OF FLORIDA

HAVANA

Santa Clara

Cienfuegos

Bay of Pigs (Bahía de Cochinos)

Trinidad

Camagüey

Holguín

Baracoa

Bayamo

Santiago de Cuba

CARIBBEAN SEA

18 DAYS The Classic

It's your first time in Cuba and you want to see as many eye-opening sights as possible countrywide. Even better, you don't mind a bit of road travel. This itinerary ferries you between the two rival cities of Havana and Santiago bagging most of the nation's historical highlights on the way. Víazul buses link all of the following destinations.

Fall in love with classic Cuba in **Havana**, with its museums, forts, theaters and rum. Three days is a bare minimum here to get

to grips with the three main neighborhoods of Havana Vieja, Centro Havana and Vedado.

Head southeast next, lingering in the **Bay of Pigs**, scene of an erstwhile Cold War battle, but these days better suited to scuba diving. French-flavored **Cienfuegos**, an architectural monument to 19th-century neoclassicism, deserves a layover. After a night of Gallic style and Cuban music, travel a couple of hours down the road to colonial **Trinidad** with more museums per head than anywhere else in Cuba. The casas particulares (homestays) resemble historical monuments here, so

Parque José Martí, Cienfuegos (p247)

stay three nights. On the second day you can break from the history and choose between the beach (Playa Ancón) or the natural world (Topes de Collantes).

Santa Clara is a rite of passage for Che Guevara pilgrims visiting his mausoleum but also a great place for luxurious private rooms and an upbeat nightlife. Check out Club Mejunje and have a drink in dive-bar La Marquesina. Further east, **Camagüey** invites further investigation with its maze of Catholic churches and giant *tinajones* (clay pots). Skip over Las Tunas, and hightail it to gritty **Holguín** for a slice of workaday Cuba and a salt-of-the-earth

bar scene. Laid-back **Bayamo** is where the Revolution was ignited, and it has an equally sparky street festival called Fiesta de la Cubanía, should you be lucky enough to be there on a Saturday. Allow plenty of time for the cultural nexus of **Santiago de Cuba**, where seditious plans for rebellion have been routinely hatched. The Cuartel Moncada, Cemeterio Ifigenia and Morro Castle will fill a busy two days. Save the best till last with a long, but by no means arduous, journey over the hills and far away to **Baracoa** for two days relaxing with the coconuts, chocolate and other tropical treats.

GULF OF
MEXICO

HAVANA
Varadero
Matanzas
Las
Terrazas
Cárdenas
San Miguel
de los Baños
Colón
Viñales
Boca de Guamá
Ciénaga de
Zapata
Cienfuegos
Playa
Larga

CARIBBEAN
SEA

Escape from Varadero

Varadero has some cheap packages and is a popular gateway into Cuba, but once you've pacified your partner/kids and had your fill of the beach, what else is there for a curious Cuban adventurer to do? Plenty.

Víazul or Conectando buses link all of the following places.

Take a bus west, stopping for lunch in **Matanzas**, where Cuban reality will hit you like a slap to the face. Investigate the Museo Farmacéutico, peek inside the Teatro Sauto and buy a handmade book in Ediciones Vigía. For a slow approach to Havana get on the Hershey train and watch the lush fields of Mayabeque province glide by. Book a night in a fine colonial hotel in **Havana** and spend the next day admiring the copious sights of the old quarter Habana Vieja. Essential stops include the cathedral, the Museo de la Revolución and a stroll along the Malecón.

The next day, head west to **Las Terrazas**, an eco-resort that seems a million miles from the clamorous capital (it's actually only 55km). You can bathe and bird-watch at the same time in the Baños del San Juan and recuperate with a stay over in the Hotel Moka.

Further west is **Viñales**, Cuba's primary tobacco-growing area and a stunningly picturesque Unesco World Heritage Site. Spend a couple of days in a casa particular, eat some of the best roast pork in Cuba, go for a hike or slump into a rocking chair on a rustic colonial porch.

Going back east, keep on the green theme in **Boca de Guamá**, a reconstructed Taíno village and crocodile farm with boat trips to and around a tranquil lake. Procure a night of accommodation at **Playa Larga**, where you can either dive or plan wildlife forays into the **Ciénaga de Zapata**. A couple of hours east lies the city of **Cienfuegos**, an elegant last night stopover with some fine boutique hotels and opportunities for sunset cruises on the bay.

On the leg back to Varadero you can uncover a more secretive Cuba in **Colón**, back in Matanzas province, and a dustier, time-warped one in half-ruined **San Miguel de los Baños**, an erstwhile spa. Last stop before returning to your Varadero sun-lounge is **Cárdenas**, home to three superb museums.

HOLGER LEUE / GETTY IMAGES ©

MERTEN SNIJDERS / GETTY IMAGES ©

Top: Playa Larga (p237)
Bottom: Tobacco plantation in Valle de Viñales (p195)

Around the Oriente

12 DAYS

The Oriente is a different country; they do things differently there, or so they'll tell you in Havana. This circuit allows you to bypass the Cuban capital and focus exclusively on the culturally rich, fiercely independent eastern region. With poor transport links, a hire car could prove useful here.

Make your base in **Santiago de Cuba**, city of revolutionaries, culture and *folklórico* dance troupes. There's tons to do here pertaining to history (Morro castle), music (Cuba's original Casa de la Trova) and religion (Basilica de Nuestra Señora del Cobre). On the second day reserve time to explore east into the Parque Bacanao and the ruined coffee farms around **Gran Piedra**.

Regular buses travel east into the mountains of Guantánamo province. Pass a night in **Guantánamo** to suss out *changüí* music before climbing the spectacular 'Farola' road into **Baracoa** for three days – including beach time at Playa Maguana, a sortie into the Parque Nacional Alejandro de Humboldt and a day absorbing the rhythms of the town.

Heading north via Moa is tough, with taxis or rental cars required to get to **Cayo Saetia**, a wonderful key with a hotel where lonesome beaches embellish a former hunting reserve.

Pinares de Mayarí sits in the pine-clad mountains of the Sierra Crystal amid huge waterfalls and rare flora. Hiking married with some rural relaxation seal the deal at the region's eponymous hotel.

If you have half a day to spare, consider a side trip to **Sitio Histórico de Birán** to see the surprisingly affluent farm community that spawned Fidel Castro.

Take a day off in hassle-free **Bayamo** with its smattering of small-town museums before tackling **Manzanillo**, where Saturday nights in the main square can get feisty. More adventurous transport options will lead you down to Niquero and within striking distance of the largely deserted **Parque Nacional Desembarco del Granma** famous for its uplifted marine terraces and aboriginal remains. Spend your last two nights in one of **Marea del Portillo's** low-key resorts before attempting the spectacular but potholed coast road back to Santiago.

Top: Street music in Santiago de Cuba (p401)
Bottom: Baracoa (p445)

Cuba: Off the Beaten Track

FLORIDA (USA)

GULF OF MEXICO

SIERRA DE JATIBONICO

These little-explored hills in northern Sancti Spíritus province are accessible from the town of Mayajigua. There are paths and guided treks led by Ecotur among rivers, semi-deciduous forest and unusual karst topography. (p306)

CENTRAL MATANZAS

The towns of central Matanzas province – most notably Colón and Jovellanos – are known for their strong Santería traditions and penchant for rumba. Forget the guidebook; this is a place for independent sleuthing. (p233)

Straits of Florida

HAVANA ✪   Matanzas ○

Sagua la Grande

Artemisa ○   Güines ○

○ Pinar del Rio

Colón ○

Santa Clara ○

Bahía de Cortés

Golfo de Batabanó

Bay of Pigs (Bahía de Cochinos)

○ Cienfuegos

Bahía de Corrientes

Isla de la Juventud

Trinidad ○

CARIBBEAN SEA

CAYOS DE SAN FELIPE

A small uninhabited archipelago and national park that is home to birds, turtles, a rare type of tree rat and 22 dive sites. Visit in a diving package with Ecotur. (p176)

CAYMAN ISLANDS (UK)

✪ GEORGE TOWN

THE SOUTHERN ISLA

Cave paintings, wild monkeys, deserted beaches and vast swamps characterize the southern half of La Isla de la Juventud, which is both a military zone and a national park. (p177)

Ⓝ 0 ————— 200 km
0 ————— 100 miles

THE BAHAMAS

ATLANTIC
OCEAN

SIERRA DEL CHORRILLO

Reconnoiter Camagüey province's surprise swathe of serene upland with a stay in a sumptuous old hacienda, a ride on one of Cuba's finest steeds and a foray to find rare birds or rarer-yet petrified trees. (p336)

GIBARA BEACH-BAGGING

Starting in colorful, off-the-radar Gibara, things only get more wild as you voyage via boat or bumpy track to desolate beaches with names like Playa los Bajos or Playa Caletones, where there are also cavern systems to explore. (p365)

○ Caibarién
○ Mayajigua
○ Morón
○ Sancti Spiritus
○ Ciego de Ávila

○ Nuevitas

○ Camagüey

Golfo de Ana María

Bahía de Gibara
○ Gibara

Las Tunas ○
○ Holguín

Santa Cruz del Sur ○

Golfo de Guacanayabo

Baracoa ○

Manzanillo ○
○ Bayamo
Guantánamo ○

Santiago de Cuba ○

SANTA CRUZ DEL SUR

Known mainly for disappearing off the map completely after a 1932 hurricane, this end-of-the-road fishing port, sporting fascinating monuments and a lovely casa, could kick-start a trip to the tranquil cayos of the Jardines de la Reina. (p313)

JAMAICA

BARACOA TO HOLGUIN – THE BACK ROAD

Ever wondered what Cuba's most pristine and bio-diverse protected area (Parque Nacional Alejandro de Humboldt) would look like were it juxtaposed with its ugliest industrial sight (Moa)? Hit this rarely traversed, pothole-ravaged back-road and find out. (p453)

CARIBBEAN SEA

Cycling through Camagüey (p32

Plan Your Trip
Activity Guide

Doubters of Cuba's outdoor potential need only look at the figures: six Unesco Biosphere Reserves, amazing water clarity, thousands of caves, three sprawling mountain ranges, copious bird species, the world's second-largest coral reef, barely touched tropical rainforest and swaths of unspoiled suburb-free countryside.

Helpful Tips

Accessibility

Access to many parks and protected areas in Cuba is limited and can only be negotiated with a prearranged guide or on an organized excursion. If in doubt, consult Ecotur travel agency.

Private Guides

Since the loosening of economic restrictions in 2011, it has become legal for private individuals to set up as outdoor guides in Cuba, though, as yet, there are no full-blown non-government travel agencies. Most private guides operate out of casas particulares or hotels and many are very good (some of the best ones are listed in this book). If you are unsure whether your guide is official, ask to see their government-issued license first.

Prebooking Tours

The following agencies organize outdoor tours from outside Cuba:

Exodus (www.exodus.co.uk) Offers a 15-day walking trip.

Scuba en Cuba (www.scuba-en-cuba.com) Diving trips.

WowCuba (www.wowcuba.com) Specializes in cycling trips.

Outdoor Opportunities

Travelers in search of adventure who've already warmed up on rum, cigars and all-night salsa dancing won't get bored in Cuba. Hit the highway on a bike, fish (as well as drink) like Hemingway, hike on guerrilla trails, jump out of an airplane or rediscover a sunken Spanish shipwreck off the shimmering south coast.

Thanks to the dearth of modern development, Cuba's outdoors is refreshingly green and free of the smog-filled highways and ugly suburban sprawl that infect many other countries.

While not on a par with North America or Europe in terms of leisure options, Cuba's facilities are well established and improving. Services and infrastructure vary depending on what activity you are looking for. The country's diving centers are generally excellent and its instructors are of an international caliber. Naturalists and ornithologists in the various national parks and flora and fauna reserves are similarly conscientious and well qualified. Hiking has traditionally been limited and frustratingly rule-ridden, but opportunities have expanded in recent years, with companies such as Ecotur offering a wider variety of hikes in previously untrodden areas and even some multiday trekking. Cycling is refreshingly DIY, and all the better for it. Canyoning and climbing are new sports in Cuba that have a lot of local support, but little official backing – as yet.

It's possible to hire reasonable outdoor gear in Cuba for most of the activities you will do (cycling excepted). But if you do bring your own supplies, any gear you can donate at the end of your trip to individuals you meet along the way (head lamps, snorkel masks, fins etc) will be greatly appreciated.

Diving

If Cuba has a blue ribbon activity, it is scuba diving. Even Fidel (in his younger days) liked to don a wet suit and escape beneath the iridescent waters of the Atlantic or Caribbean (his favorite dive site was apparently the rarely visited Jardines de la Reina archipelago). Indeed, so famous was the Cuban leader's diving addiction that the CIA allegedly once considered an assassination plot that involved inserting an explosive device inside a conch and placing it on the seabed.

Excellent dive sites are numerous in Cuba. Focus on the area or areas where you want to dive rather than trying to cover multiple sites. The best areas – most notably the Jardines de Reina, María la Gorda and the Isla de la Juventud – are all fairly isolated, requiring travel time (and pre-planning). The more sheltered south coast probably has the edge in terms of water clarity and dependable weather, though the north coast, offering easy access to one of the world's largest reefs, is no slouch.

What makes diving in Cuba special is its unpolluted seas, clear water conditions (average underwater visibility is 30m to 40m), warm seas (mean temperature is 24°C), abundant coral and fish, simple access (including a couple of excellent swimout reefs) and fascinating shipwrecks (Cuba was a nexus for weighty galleons in the 17th and 18th centuries, and rough seas and skirmishes with pirates sunk many).

Diving Centers

In all, Cuba has 25 recognized diving centers spread over 17 different areas. The majority of the centers are managed by **Marlin Náutica y Marinas** (www.nauticamarlin.com), though you'll also find representation from **Gaviota** (☏7-204-5708; gaviota@gaviota.cu; Av 47 No 2833 , btwn Calles 28 & 34, Havana), **Cubanacán Náutica** (☏7-833-4090; www.cubanacan.cu) and **Cubamar** (☏7-833-2523; www.cubamarviajes.cu). Though equipment does vary between installations, you can generally expect safe, professional service with back-up medical support. Environmentally sensitive diving is where things can get wobbly, and individuals should educate themselves about responsible diving. As well as being Scuba Schools International (SSI), American Canadian Underwater Certification (ACUC)

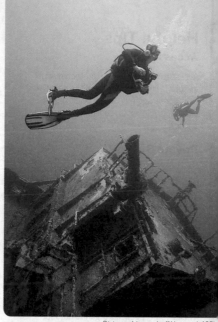

Diving a shipwreck off Havana (p135)

and Confédération Mondiale de Activités Subaquatiques (CMAS) certified, most dive instructors are multilingual, speaking a variety of Spanish, English, French, German and Italian. Because of US embargo laws, Professional Association of Diving Instructors (PADI) certification is generally not offered in Cuba.

Dives and courses are comparably priced island-wide, from CUC$25 to CUC$50 per dive, with a discount after four or five dives. Full certification courses are CUC$310 to CUC$365, and 'resort' or introductory courses cost CUC$50 to CUC$60.

EIGHT REASONS TO GO CYCLING IN CUBA

➡ Light traffic on roads.

➡ Cycling is engrained in the culture and many locals use bikes to get around.

➡ Fierce dogs – the bane of all cyclists – are rare.

➡ *Guarapo* (sugar cane juice mixed with ice and lemon) sold from *guaraperos* (roadside stalls) provides the ultimate natural energy drink.

➡ Ample accommodation can be procured spontaneously in casas particulares.

➡ Dubbed the 'world's best mechanics', the Cubans can help resolve most breakdown problems.

➡ There is an abundance of incredible, unspoiled rural scenery.

➡ You'll meet more local people.

Cycling

Riding a bike in Cuba is *the* best way to discover the island in close-up. Decent and quiet roads, wonderful scenery and the opportunity to get off the beaten track and meet Cubans make cycling here a pleasure, whichever route you take. For less dedicated pedalers, daily bike rental is sometimes available in hotels, resorts and cafes for about CUC$3 to CUC$7 per day, but don't bank on it. The bigger resorts in Varadero

Cuba Diving

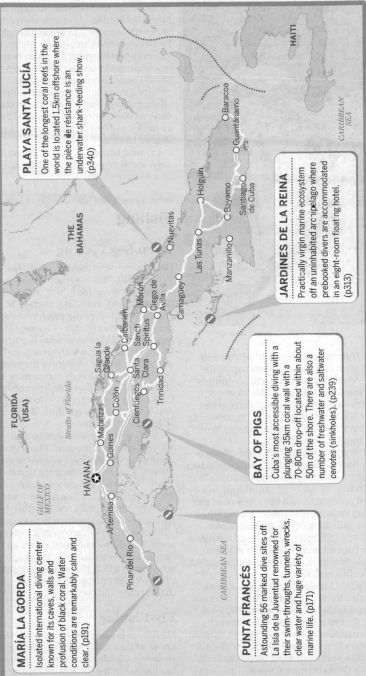

MARÍA LA GORDA

Isolated international diving center known for its caves, walls and profusion of black coral. Water conditions are remarkably calm and clear. (p191)

PUNTA FRANCÉS

Astounding 56 marked dive sites off La Isla de la Juventud renowned for their swim-throughs, tunnels, wrecks, clear water and huge variety of marine life. (p171)

BAY OF PIGS

Cuba's most accessible diving with a plunging 35km coral wall with a 70-80m drop-off located within about 50m of the shore. There are also a number of freshwater and saltwater cenotes (sinkholes). (p239)

JARDINES DE LA REINA

Practically virgin marine ecosystem off an uninhabited archipelago where prebooked divers are accommodated in an eight-room floating hotel. (p313)

PLAYA SANTA LUCÍA

One of the longest coral reefs in the world is located 1.5km offshore where the pièce de résistance is an underwater shark-feeding show. (p340)

Deep-sea fishing

and Guardalavaca are more reliable and will often include bike use as part of the all-inclusive package, though it's unlikely the bikes will have gears. Alternatively, if you're staying in a casa particular, your host will generally be able to rig something together (sometimes quite literally) in order to get you from A to B.

The main problem with Cuban bikes is that they're usually substandard, and when they're combined with poor roads, you'll often feel like you're sitting atop an improvised coat hanger and not a well-oiled machine. Serious cyclists should bring boxed bikes with them on the airplane, along with plenty of spare parts. Since organized bike trips are common here, customs officials, taxi drivers and hotel staff are used to dealing with them.

Cycling highlights include the Valle de Viñales, the countryside around Trinidad, including the flat spin down to Playa Ancón, the quiet lanes that zigzag through Guardalavaca, and the roads out of Baracoa to Playa Maguana (northwest) and Boca de Yumurí (southeast). For a bigger challenge try La Farola between Cajobabo and Baracoa (21km of ascent), the bumpy but spectacular coast road between Santiago and Marea del Portillo – best spread over three days with overnights in Brisas Sierra Mar los Galeones and Campismo la Mula – or, for real wheel warriors, the insanely steep mountain road from Bartolomé Masó to Santo Domingo in Granma province.

With a profusion of casas particulares offering cheap, readily available accommodation, cycle touring is a joy here as long as you keep off the Autopista and steer clear of Havana.

Off-road biking has not yet taken off in Cuba and is generally not permitted.

Fishing

Deep-Sea Fishing

Hemingway wasn't wrong. Cuba's fast-moving Gulf Stream along the north coast supports prime game fishing for sailfish, tuna, mackerel, swordfish, barracuda, marlin and shark pretty much year-round. Deep-sea fishing is a rite of passage for many and a great way to wind down, make friends, drink beer, watch sunsets and generally leave the troubles of the world behind. Not surprisingly, the country has great facilities for sport anglers, and every Cuban boat captain seems to look and talk as if he's walked straight from the pages of a Hemingway classic.

Cuba's best deep-sea fishing center is Cayo Guillermo, the small island that featured in Hemingway's *Islands in the Stream*. Papa may no longer be in residence, but there's still an abundance of fish. Another good bet is Havana, which has two marinas, one at Tarará and the other, better one at Marina Hemingway to the west.

Elsewhere, all of Cuba's main resort areas offer deep-sea-fishing excursions for similar rates. Count on paying approximately CUC$280 per half-day and CUC$450 per full day for four people, including crew and open bar.

Fly-Fishing

Fly-fishing is undertaken mainly on shallow sand flats easily reached from the shoreline. Classic areas to throw a line are Las Salinas in the Ciénaga de Zapata, the protected waters surrounding Cayo Largo

Snorkeling in Cayo Largo del Sur (p177)

el Sur, parts of the Isla de la Juventud and the uninhabited nirvana of the Jardines de la Reina archipelago. The archipelago is a national park and heavily protected. It is not unheard of to catch 25 different species of fish in the same day here.

A 'grand slam' for fly-fishers in Cuba is to bag tarpon, bonefish and permit in the same day; bag a snook as well and they call it a 'superslam'. The best fishing season in this part of Cuba is February to June. The remoteness of the many islands, reefs and sand flats means fishing trips are usually organized on boats that offer on-board accommodations. They are coordinated through a company called Avalon (p313).

The north coast hides a couple of good fly-fishing havens. Most noted are the still uninhabited keys of Cayo Romano and Cayo Cruz in the north of Camagüey province. Trips are coordinated by Ecotur (p46) and are based at an attractive lodge in the mainland town of Brasil.

Freshwater Fishing

Freshwater fishing in Cuba is lesser known than fly-fishing but equally rewarding, and many Americans and Canadians home in on the island's numerous lakes. Fly-fishing is superb in vast Ciénaga de Zapata in Matanzas, where enthusiasts can arrange multiday catch-and-release trips. *Trucha* (largemouth bass) was first introduced into Cuba in the early 20th century by Americans at King's Ranch and the United Fruit Company. Due to favorable environmental protection, the fish are now abundant in many Cuban lakes, and experts believe the next world-record bass (currently 9.9kg) will come from Cuba. Good places to cast a line are the Laguna del Tesoro in Matanzas, the Laguna de la Leche and Laguna la Redonda in Ciego de Ávila province, Embalse Zaza in Sancti Spíritus and Embalse Hanabanilla in Villa Clara – 7.6kg specimens have been caught here! To meet other fisherfolk, head for Hotel Morón in Ciego de Ávila Province, Hotel Zaza in Sancti Spíritus or Hotel Hanabanilla in Villa Clara province.

Snorkeling

You don't have to go very deep to enjoy Cuba's tropical aquarium: snorkelers will feel like divers along the south coast from Playa Larga to Caleta Buena, around Cienfuegos and along the Guardalavaca reef. In Varadero, daily snorkeling tours sailing to Cayo Blanco promise abundant tropical fish and good visibility. If you're not into the group thing, you can don a mask at Playa Coral, 20km away.

Good boat dives for snorkeling happen around Isla de la Juventud and Cayo Largo especially, but also in Varadero and in the Cienfuegos and Guajimico areas. If you intend to do a lot of snorkeling, bring your own gear, as the rental stuff can be tattered and buying it in Cuba will mean you'll sacrifice both price and quality.

Hiking & Trekking

European hikers and North American wilderness freaks take note: while Cuba's trekking potential is enormous, the traveler's right to roam is restricted by several factors, including badly maintained trails, poor signage, a lack of maps and rather draconian restrictions about where you can and cannot go without a guide. Cubans aren't as enthusiastic about hiking for enjoyment as Canadians or Germans. Instead, many park authorities tend to assume that all hikers want to be led by the hand along short, relatively tame trails that are rarely more than 5km or 6km in length. You'll frequently be told that hiking alone is a reckless and dangerous activity, despite the fact that Cuba harbors no big fauna and no poisonous snakes. The best time of year for hiking is outside the rainy season and before it gets too hot (December to April).

USEFUL AGENCIES

....

Ecotur (www.ecoturcuba.co.cu) Runs organized hiking, trekking, fishing and bird-watching trips to some of the country's otherwise inaccessible corners. It has offices in every province and a main HQ in Havana.

Cubamar Viajes (www.cubamarviajes.cu) Runs Cuba's 80+ campismos (rural chalets). It has Reservaciones de Campismo offices in every provincial capital and a helpful head office in Havana.

The dearth of available hikes isn't always the result of nit-picking restrictions. Much of Cuba's trekkable terrain is in ecologically sensitive areas, meaning access is carefully managed and controlled.

Multi-day hiking in Cuba has improved in the last couple of years, and though information is still hard to get, you can piece together workable options in the Sierra Maestra and the Escambray Mountains. The most popular by far is the three-day trek to the summit of Pico Turquino, followed by the overnight San Claudio trail in the Reserva Sierra del Rosario.

More challenging day hikes include El Yunque, a mountain near Baracoa; the Balcón de Iberia circuit in Parque Nacional Alejandro de Humboldt; and some of the hikes around Las Terrazas and Viñales.

Topes de Collantes probably has the largest concentration of hiking trails in its protected zone (a natural park). Indeed, some overseas groups organize four- to five-day treks here, starting near Lago Hanabanilla and finishing in Parque el Cubano. Inquire in advance at the Carpeta Central information office in Topes de Collantes if you are keen to organize something on behalf of a group.

Other, tamer hikes on offer in Cuba include Cueva las Perlas and Del Bosque al Mar on the Península de Guanahacabibes, the guided trail in Parque Natural el Bagá, El Guafe trail in Parque Nacional Desembarco del Granma and the short circuit in Reserva Ecológica Varahicacos in Varadero. Some of these hikes are guided and all of them require the payment of an entry fee.

If you want to hike independently, you'll need patience, resolve and an excellent sense of direction. It's also useful to ask the locals in your casa particular. Try experimenting first with Salto del Caburní or Sendero la Batata in Topes de Collantes or the various hikes around Viñales. There's a beautiful, little-used DIY hike on a good trail near Marea del Portillo and some gorgeous options around Baracoa – ask the locals!

Horseback Riding

Cuba has a long-standing cowboy culture, and horseback riding is available countrywide in both official and unofficial

Boating on Playa Ancón (p301)

capacities. If you arrange it privately, make sure you check the state of the horses and equipment before committing to anything. Riding poorly kept horses is both cruel and potentially dangerous.

The state-owned catering company Palmares owns numerous rustic ranchos across Cuba that are supposed to give tourists a feel for traditional country life. All of these places offer guided horseback riding, usually for around CUC$5 per hour. You'll find good ranchos in Florencia in Ciego de Ávila province and Hacienda la Belén in Camagüey province.

La Guabina is a horse-breeding center near the city of Pinar del Río that offers both horse shows and horseback-riding adventures.

Boating & Kayaking

Kayaking as a sport is pretty low-key in Cuba, where it is treated more as a beach activity in the plusher resorts. Most of the tourist beaches will have *náutica* points that rent out simple kayaks, good for splashing around in but not a lot else. Boat rental is also available on many of the island's lakes. Good options include the Laguna de la Leche and Laguna la Redonda, both in Ciego de Ávila province; Embalse Zaza in Sancti Spíritus province; and the Liberación de Florencia in Ciego de Ávila.

One of Cuba's best rivers is the Río Canímar near Matanzas. You can rent rowboats and head up between the jungle-covered banks of this mini-Amazon.

BEST ECO-LODGES

→ Hotel Moka (p162)
→ Hotel Horizontes El Saltón (p432)
→ Motel la Belén (p336)
→ Villa Pinares del Mayarí (p376)

Rock Climbing

The Valle de Viñales has been described as having the best rock climbing in the Western hemisphere. There are more than 150 routes now open (at all levels of difficulty, with several rated as YDS Class 5.14) and the word is out among the international climbing crowd, who are creating their own scene in one of Cuba's prettiest settings. Independent travelers will appreciate the free rein that climbers enjoy here.

Though you can climb here year-round, the heat can be oppressive, and locals stick to an October-to-April season, with December to January being the optimum months. For more information, visit **Cuba Climbing** (www.cubaclimbing.com) or head straight to Viñales.

It is important to note that, though widely practiced and normally without consequence, climbing in the Valle de Viñales is still not technically legal. You're unlikely to get arrested or even warned, but take extreme care and do not under any circumstances do anything that damages the delicate Parque Nacional Viñales ecosystem.

Caving

Cuba is riddled with caves – more than 20,000 and counting – and cave exploration is available to both casual tourists and professional speleologists. The Gran Caverna de Santo Tomás, near Viñales, is Cuba's largest cavern, with over 46km of galleries; the Cueva de los Peces, near Playa Girón, is a flooded cenote (sinkhole) with colorful snorkeling; and the Cueva de Ambrosio and Cuevas de Bellamar, both in Matanzas, have tours daily.

Caving specialists have virtually unlimited caves from which to choose. With advance arrangements, you can explore deep

Visiting Cueva del Indio by boat (p199)

into the Gran Caverna de Santo Tomás or visit the Cueva Martín Infierno, which has the world's largest stalagmite. Also ask about San Catalina, near Varadero, which has unique mushroom formations. Speleodiving is also possible, but only for those already highly trained. Interested experts should contact Angel Graña, secretary of the **Sociedad Espeleológica de Cuba** (☎7-209-2885; angel@fanj.cult.cu) in Havana.

Plan Your Trip
Travel with Children

Get ready, kids! Cuba is like nothing you've ever seen before. Children on this sundappled Caribbean archipelago are encouraged to talk, sing, dance, think, dream and play, and they are integrated into all parts of society: you'll see them at concerts, restaurants, churches, political rallies (giving speeches even!) and parties.

Cuba for Kids

There are certain dichotomies regarding child facilities in Cuba. On the one hand Cuban society is innately family-friendly, child-loving and tactile. On the other, economic challenges have meant that common 'Western' provisions such as pushchair ramps, changing tables and basic safety measures are often thin on the ground. The one place where you'll find generic international standards of service is in the modern resorts, most of which have dedicated and professionally run 'kid's clubs'.

Children's Highlights

Forts & Castles

➡ **Fortaleza de San Carlos de la Cabaña**
Havana's huge fort has museums, battlements and a nightly cannon ceremony with soldiers in period costume. (p87)

➡ **Castillo de San Pedro de la Roca del Morro**
Santiago's Unesco-listed fort is best known for its exciting pirate museum. (p412)

➡ **Castillo de la Real Fuerza** This centrally located Havana fort has a moat, lookouts and scale models of Spanish galleons. (p66)

Best Regions for Children

Havana

The streets of Habana Vieja can't have changed much since the days of the *Pirates of the Caribbean*, so your kids' imaginations will be allowed to run wild in forts, squares, museums and narrow streets. Havana also has Cuba's largest amusement park (Isla del Coco), and its best aquarium.

Varadero

Cuba's biggest resort has the largest – if most predictable – stash of specifically tailored kids' activities, including nighttime shows, organized sports, beach games and boat trips.

Trinidad

The south coast's southern gem is awash with economic casas particulares, an ideal opportunity for your kids to mix and mingle with Cuban families. Throw in an excellent beach (Playa Ancón), easily accessible snorkeling waters and a profusion of pleasant pastoral activities (horseback riding is popular) and you've got the perfect non-resort family option.

Kids' Playgrounds

➡ **Parque Maestranza** Bouncy castles, fairground rides and sweet snacks overlooking Havana harbor. (p63)

➡ **Isla del Coco** Huge, new-ish, Chinese-funded amusement park in Havana's Playa neighborhood. (p135)

➡ **Parque Lenin** More playground rides, boats, a mini-train and horses for rent in Havana. (p142)

Animal Encounters

➡ **Acuario Nacional** Daily dolphin shows and a decent restaurant are the highlights of the nation's main aquarium in Havana's Miramar district. (p133)

➡ **Criaderos de Cocodrilos** Of the half-dozen croc farms spread across the country, the best is in Guamá, Matanzas province. (p235)

➡ **Horseback riding** Possible all over Cuba and usually run out of rustic fincas in rural areas such as Pinar del Río and Trinidad. (p46)

Festivals

➡ **Las Parrandas** Fireworks, smoke and huge animated floats: Remedios' Christmas Eve party is a blast for kids *and* adults. (p274)

➡ **Carnaval de Santiago de Cuba** A colorful celebration of Caribbean culture with floats and dancing that takes place every July. (p415)

➡ **Carnaval de la Habana** More music, dancing and effigies, this time along Havana's Malecón in August. (p30)

Planning

Travelers with kids are not unusual in Cuba and the trend has proliferated in recent years with more Cuban-Americans visiting their families with offspring in tow; these will be your best sources for on-the-ground information. Aspects of the local culture that parents might find foreign (aside from the material shortages) are the physical contact and human warmth that are so typically Cuban: strangers ruffle kids' hair, give them kisses or take their hands with regularity. Chill, it's all part of the Cuban way.

Your kids shouldn't need any specific pre-trip inoculations for Cuba, though you may want to check with your doctor about individual requirements before departing. Medicines are in short supply in Cuba, so take all you think you might need. Useful stuff to have is acetaminophen, ibuprofen, antinausea medicines and cough drops. Insect repellent is also helpful in lowland areas. Diapers (nappies) and baby formula can be hard to find; bring your own. A copy of your child's birth certificate containing the names of both parents could also prove useful, especially if they use different surnames.

Car seats are not mandatory in Cuba, and taxi and rental-car firms don't carry them. Bring your own if you're planning on renting a car. High chairs in restaurants are also almost nonexistent, though waiters will try to improvise. If you're unsure, bring an easily storable high chair with you. The same goes for travel cribs. Cuba's pavements (sidewalks) weren't designed with pushchairs (strollers) in mind. If your child is small enough, carry him/her in a body harness. Otherwise bring the smallest/lightest pushchair possible, or do without.

Casas particulares are nearly always happy to accommodate families and are exceptionally child-friendly. Resort hotels are family-friendly too.

Eating with Kids

With a dearth of exotic spices and an emphasis on good, plain, non-fancy food, kids in Cuba are often surprisingly well accommodated. The family-orientated nature of life on the island certainly helps. Few eating establishments turn away children, and waiters and waitresses in most cafes and restaurants will, more often than not, dote on your boisterous young offspring and go out of their way to try to accommodate unadventurous or childish tastes. Rice and beans are good staples, and chicken and fish are relatively reliable sources of protein. The main absent food group – though your kid probably won't think so – is a regular supply of fresh vegetables.

Regions at a Glance

Cuba's provinces are splayed end to end across the main island, with the oft-forgotten comma of La Isla de la Juventud hanging off the bottom. All of them have coast access and all are embellished with beautiful beaches, the best hugging the north coast. Equally ubiquitous are the vivid snippets of history, impressive colonial architecture and potent reminders of the 1959 Revolution. The country's highest mountain range, the Sierra Maestra, rises in the east with another significant range, the Escambray, positioned south-central. Cuba's main wilderness areas are the Zapata swamps, the marine terraces of Granma, the tropical forests of Guantánamo and the uninhabited (for now) northern keys. Urban highlights include Havana, Santiago de Cuba, Camagüey and colonial Trinidad.

Havana

Museums
Architecture
Nightlife

Casco Histórico

The capital's 4-sq-km historic center has history wherever you look and museums dedicated to everything from silverware to Simón Bolívar. Kick off with the Museo de la Revolución, garner more cultural immersion in the Museo de la Ciudad and schedule at least half a day for the fine Museo Nacional de Bellas Artes.

Eclecticism

Havana's architecture is not unlike its flora and fauna: hard to categorize and sometimes a little – well – weird. Stroll the streets of Habana Vieja and Centro Havana and choose your own highlights.

Life's a Cabaret

Every Cuban music style is represented in Havana, from street rumba to glitzy cabaret, making it the best place in the country for live concerts, spontaneous busking and racy nightlife.

p58

Artemisa & Mayabeque Provinces

Beaches
Ecotourism
Coffee Ruins

Secret Beach

Rather surprisingly, considering it's stuck on the main highway between Havana and Varadero, Mayabeque province has its own unheralded and delightful beaches, spearheaded by Playa Jibacoa. Get there quick before the golf courses start springing up.

Las Terrazas

This stark white eco-village was practicing environmentally friendly living long before the urgencies of the Special Period or the adoption of eco-practices in the world outside. Today it carries on much as it has always done: quietly, confidently and – above all – sustainably.

Coffee Ruins

Las Terrazas has dozens of them, half-covered by jungle, while Artemisa has its own Antiguo Cafetal Angerona, a larger, more refined, but no-less-weathered ruin that once functioned as a coffee plantation employing 500 slaves.

p153

Isla de la Juventud (Special Municipality)

Diving
Wildlife
History

Into the Blue

Outside the hard-to-access Jardines de la Reina archipelago, La Isla offers the best diving in Cuba and is the main reason many people come here. Ultra-clear water, abundant sea life and a protected marine park at Punta Francés are the highpoints.

Wildlife

If you missed it in the Ciénaga de Zapata, La Isla is the only other place in the world where you can view the Cuban crocodile in its natural state. It has been successfully reintroduced into the Lanier Swamps.

Ex-Prisoners

Not one but two of Cuba's verbose spokesmen were once imprisoned on the archipelago's largest outlying island that also doubled up as a big jail: José Martí and Fidel Castro. Not surprisingly, both their former incarceration sites are riddled with historical significance.

p167

Pinar del Río Province

Diving
Food
Flora & Fauna

Dive Community

Isolated at the westernmost tip of the main island, María la Gorda has long lured travelers for its spectacular diving, enhanced by electrically colored coral, huge sponges and gorgonians, and a knowledgeable but laid-back dive community.

Roast Pork

There's nothing like a true Cuban pork roast and there's no place better to try it than among the *guajiros* (country folk) of Viñales. The *fincas* (farms) and casas particulares that characterize this bucolic village offer up humongous portions of the national dish with trimmings of rice, beans and root vegetables.

Muy Verde

With more protected land than any other province, Pinar is a green paradise. Go hiking in Parque Nacional Viñales, spot a sea turtle in Parque Nacional Península de Guanahacabibes or train your binoculars on the feathered action around Cueva de los Portales.

p181

Matanzas Province

Diving
Flora & Fauna
Beaches

Accessible Dives

Bahía de Cochinos (Bay of Pigs) might not have Cuba's best diving, but it certainly has its most accessible. You can glide off from the shore here and be gawping at coral-encrusted drop-off walls within a few strokes. There's more impressive shore diving from Playa Coral, on the north coast.

Swamp Life

In contrast to the resort frenzy on the north coast, Matanzas' southern underbelly is one of Cuba's last true wildernesses and an important refuge for wildlife, including Cuban crocodiles, manatees, bee hummingbirds and tree rats.

Varadero

Even if you hate resorts, there's still one reason to go to Varadero – an unbroken 20km ribbon of golden sand that stretches the whole length of the Península de Hicacos. It's arguably the longest and finest beach in Cuba.

p205

Cienfuegos Province

Architecture
Music
Diving

French Classicism

Despite its position as one of Cuba's newer cities, founded in 1819, Cienfuegos retains a remarkably homogenous urban core full of classical facades and slender columns that carry the essence of 19th-century France, where it drew its inspiration.

Benny Moré

Benny Moré, Cuba's most adaptable and diverse musician, who ruled the clubs and dance halls in the 1940s and '50s, once called Cienfuegos the city he liked best. Come and see if you agree and, on the way, visit the village where he was born.

Guajimico

Welcome to one of Cuba's least-discovered diving spots, run out of a comfortable *campismo* (camping installation) on the warm, calm south coast and renowned for its coral gardens, sponges and scattered wrecks.

p242

Villa Clara Province

Beaches
History
Nightlife

Spectacular Keys

Cuba's newest resorts on the keys off the coast of hide some stunning and still relatively uncrowded beaches, including the publicly accessible Las Salinas on Cayo las Brujas and the more-refined Playa el Mégano and Playa Ensenachos on Cayo Ensenachos.

Che Guevara

Love him or hate him, his legacy won't go away, so you might as well visit Santa Clara to at least try to understand what made the great *guerrillero* (person) tick. The city hosts Che's mausoleum, a museum cataloguing his life and the historic site where he ambushed an armored train in 1958.

Student Scene

The city of Santa Clara has the edgiest and most contemporary nightlife scene in Cuba, where local innovators are constantly probing for the next big thing.

p259

Sancti Spíritus Province

Museums
Hiking
Music

Revolution to Romance

Trinidad has more museums per square meter than anywhere outside Havana, and they're not token gestures either. Themes include history, furniture, counterrevolutionary wars, ceramics, contemporary art and romance.

Topes is Tops

Topes de Collantes has the most comprehensive trail system in Cuba and showcases some of the best scenery in the archipelago, with waterfalls, natural swimming pools, precious wildlife and working coffee plantations. Further trails can be found in the less-heralded Alturas de Banao and Jobo Rosado reserves.

Spontaneous Sounds

In Trinidad – and to a lesser extent Sancti Spíritus – music seems to emanate out of every nook and cranny, much of it spontaneous and unrehearsed. Trinidad, in particular, has the most varied and condensed music scene outside Havana.

p280

Ciego de Ávila Province

Fishing
Beaches
Festivals

Hemingway's Haunts

Cayo Guillermo has all the makings of a fishing trip extraordinaire: a warm tropical setting; large, abundant fish; and the ghost of Ernest Hemingway to follow you from port to rippling sea and back. Pack a box of beer and follow the Gulf Stream.

Pilar Paradise

Colorados, Prohibida, Flamingo and Pilar – the beaches of the northern keys lure you with their names as much as their reputations and, when you get there, there's plenty of room for everyone.

Fiestas & Fireworks

No other province has such a varied and – frankly – weird stash of festivals. Ciego is home to an annual cricket tournament, rustic country dancing, strange voodoo rites and explosive fireworks.

p307

Camagüey Province

Diving
Architecture
Beaches

Feeding Sharks

OK, the resorts aren't exactly refined luxury, but who cares when the diving's this good? Playa Santa Lucía sits astride one of the largest coral reefs in the world and is famous for its shark-feeding show.

Urban Maze

Camagüey doesn't conform to the normal Spanish colonial building manual when it comes to urban layout, but that's part of the attraction. Lose yourself in Cuba's third-largest city that, since 2008, has been a Unesco World Heritage Site.

Limitless Sand

The beaches on the province's north coast are phenomenal. There's 20km-long Playa Santa Lucía, the Robinson Crusoe–like Playa Los Pinos on Cayo Sabinel, and the shapely curve of Playa los Cocos at the mouth of the Bahía de Nuevitas.

p323

Las Tunas Province

Beaches
Art
Festivals

Eco-Beaches

Hardly anyone knows about them, but they're still there. Las Tunas' northern eco-beaches are currently the preserve of local Cubans, seabirds and the odd in-the-know outsider. Come and enjoy them before the resort-building bulldozers wreck the tranquility.

City of Sculptures

The city of Las Tunas' sculpture isn't of the grandiose, in-your-face Florentine variety, but scout around the congenial streets of the provincial capital and you'll uncover an esoteric collection of revolutionary leaders, two-headed Taíno chiefs and oversized pencils crafted in stone.

Country Music

The bastion of country music in Cuba, Las Tunas hosts the annual Cucalambeana festival, where songwriters from across the country come to recite their quick-witted satirical *décimas* (verse).

p342

Holguín Province

Beaches
Ecotourism
Archaeology

Unknown Beaches

Most tourists gravitate to the well-known beaches of Playa Pesquero and Guardalavaca that are now backed by big resorts. Less touted, but equally *linda* (pretty), are Playa Caleta near Gibara and Las Morales near Banes.

Mountains & Keys

Weirdly, for a province that hosts Cuba's largest and dirtiest industry (the Moa nickel mines), Holguín has a profusion of green escapes tucked away in pine-clad mountain retreats or hidden on exotic keys. Discover Cayo Saetia and visit Pinares de Mayarí.

Pre-Columbian Culture

Holguín preserves Cuba's best stash of archaeological finds. The region's long-lost pre-Columbian culture is showcased at the Museo Chorro de Maita and its adjacent reconstructed Taíno village. There are more artifacts on display at the Museo Indocubano Baní in nearby Banes.

p352

Granma Province

History
Hiking
Festivals

Revolutionary Sites

History is never as real as it is in Cuba's most revolutionary province. Here you can hike up to Castro's 1950s mountaintop HQ, visit the sugar mill where Céspedes first freed his slaves or ponder the poignant spot where José Martí fell in battle.

Bagging a Peak

With the Sierra Maestra overlaying two national parks, Granma has tremendous hiking potential, including the trek up to the top of the nation's highest peak, Pico Turquino.

Street Parties

Granma is famous for its street parties. Towns such as Bayamo and Manzanillo have long celebrated weekly alfresco shindigs with whole roast pork, chess tournaments and music provided by old-fashioned street organs.

p377

Santiago de Cuba Province

Dance
History
Festivals

Folklórico Groups

As magical as they are mysterious, Santiago's *folklórico* (Afro-Cuban folkdance) troupes are a throwback to another era when slaves hid their traditions behind a complex veneer of singing, dancing and syncretized religion.

Historical Sites

Cuba's hotbed of sedition has inspired multiple rebellions and many key sites can still be visited. Start at Moncada Barracks and head south through the birth houses of local heroes Frank País and Antonio Maceo, to the eerily named Museo de la Lucha Clandestina (Clandestine War Museum).

Caribbean Culture

Santiago has a wider variety of annual festivals than any other Cuban city. July is the top month, with the annual Carnaval preceded by the Festival del Caribe, celebrating the city's rich Caribbean culture.

p398

Guantánamo Province

Flora & Fauna
Hiking
Food

Endemism

Guantánamo's historical isolation and complex soil structure has led to high levels of endemism, meaning you're likely to see plant and animal species here that you'll see nowhere else in the archipelago. Aspiring botanists should gravitate towards Parque Nacional Alejandro de Humboldt.

Growing Potential

As Baracoa grows as an ecological center, hiking possibilities are opening up. Try the long-standing treks up El Yunque or into Parque Nacional Alejandro de Humboldt, or tackle newer trails around the Duaba River or to the beaches near Boca de Yumurí.

Coconuts, Coffee & Cocoa

What do you mean you didn't come to Cuba for the food? Baracoa is waiting to blow away your culinary preconceptions with a sweet-and-spicy mélange of dishes concocted from the locally ubiquitous cocoa, coffee, coconuts and bananas.

p436

On the Road

Havana

♪ 7 / POP 2,130,431

Best Places to Eat

➡ Doña Eutimia (p110)

➡ Casa Miglis (p113)

➡ Paladar La Fontana (p139)

Best Places to Stay

➡ Hotel Los Frailes (p104)

➡ Hotel Iberostar Parque Central (p107)

➡ Hostal Conde de Villanueva (p104)

Why Go?

Close your eyes for a moment and imagine you are there.

Waves crashing against a mildewed sea wall; a young couple cavorting in a dark, dilapidated alley; guitars and voices harmonizing over a syncopated drum rhythm; sunlight slanting across rotten peeling paintwork; a handsome youth in a *guayabera* shirt leaning against a Lada; the smell of car fumes and cheap aftershave; tourists with Hemingway beards; Che Guevara on a billboard, a banknote, a key-ring, a T-shirt...

No one could have invented Havana. It's too audacious, too contradictory, and – despite 50 years of withering neglect – too damned beautiful. How it does it, is anyone's guess. Maybe it's the swashbuckling history, the survivalist spirit, or the indefatigable salsa energy that ricochets off walls and emanates most emphatically from the people. Don't come here looking for answers. Just arrive with an open mind and prepare yourself for a long, slow seduction.

When to Go

➡ One of Havana's most outstanding music festivals is the Festival Internacional de Jazz, which is held each year in February. Don't miss it!

➡ Havana's summer heat can be stifling. To avoid it, come in October, a wonderfully quiet month when there's still plenty to do – such as enjoy the annual Festival Internacional de Ballet.

➡ Busier (for a reason) is December, when people line up for the Festival del Nuevo Cine Latinoamericano, Cuba's premiere movie shindig.

History

In 1514 San Cristóbal de La Habana was founded on the south coast of Cuba near the mouth of the Río Mayabeque by Spanish conquistador Pánfilo de Narváez. Named after the daughter of a famous Taíno chief, the city was moved twice during its first five years due to mosquito infestations and wasn't permanently established on its present site until December 17, 1519. According to local legend, the first Mass was said beneath a ceiba tree in present day Plaza de Armas.

Havana is the most westerly and isolated of Diego Velázquez' original villas, and life was hard in the early days. Things didn't get any better in 1538 when French pirates and local slaves razed the city.

It took the Spanish conquest of Mexico and Peru to swing the pendulum in Havana's favor. The town's strategic location, at the mouth of the Gulf of Mexico, made it a perfect nexus for the annual treasure fleets to regroup in its sheltered harbor before heading east. Thus endowed, its ascension was quick and decisive, and in 1607 Havana replaced Santiago as the capital of Cuba.

The city was sacked by French pirates led by Jacques de Sores in 1555; the Spanish replied by building La Punta and El Morro forts between 1558 and 1630 to reinforce an already formidable protective ring. From 1674 to 1740, a strong wall around the city was added. These defenses kept the pirates at bay but proved ineffective when Spain became embroiled in the Seven Years' War with Britain.

On June 6, 1762, a British army under the Earl of Albemarle attacked Havana, landing at Cojímar and striking inland to Guanabacoa. From there they drove west along the northeastern side of the harbor, and on July 30 they attacked El Morro from the rear. Other troops landed at La Chorrera, west of the city, and by August 13 the Spanish were surrounded and forced to surrender. The British held Havana for 11 months.

When the Spanish regained the city a year later in exchange for Florida, they began a building program to upgrade the city's defenses in order to avoid another debilitating siege. A new fortress, La Cabaña, was built along the ridge from which the British had shelled El Morro, and by the time the work was finished in 1774 Havana had become the most heavily fortified city in the New World, the 'bulwark of the Indies.'

The British occupation resulted in Spain opening Havana to freer trade. In 1765 the city was granted the right to trade with seven Spanish cities instead of only Cádiz, and from 1818 Havana was allowed to ship its sugar, rum, tobacco and coffee directly to any part of the world. The 19th century was an era of steady progress: first came the railway in 1837, followed by public gas lighting (1848), the telegraph (1851), an urban transport system (1862), telephones (1888) and electric lighting (1890).

By 1902 the city, which had been physically untouched by the devastating wars of independence, boasted a quarter of a million inhabitants. It had expanded rapidly west along the Malecón and into the wooded glades of formerly off-limits Vedado. There was a large influx of rich Americans at the start of the Prohibition era, and the good times began to roll with abandon; by the 1950s Havana was a decadent gambling city frolicking amid the all-night parties of American mobsters and scooping fortunes into the pockets of various disreputable hoods such as Meyer Lansky.

For Fidel Castro, it was an aberration. On taking power in 1959, the new revolutionary government promptly closed down all the casinos and sent Lansky and his henchmen back to Miami. The once-glittering hotels were divided up to provide homes for the rural poor. Havana's long decline had begun.

Today the city's restoration is ongoing and a stoic fight against the odds in a country where shortages are part of everyday life and money for raw materials is scarce. Since 1982 City Historian Eusebio Leal Spengler has been piecing Habana Vieja back together street by street and square by square with the aid of Unesco and a variety of foreign investors. Slowly but surely, the old starlet is starting to reclaim her former greatness.

DOWNTOWN HAVANA

For simplicity's sake downtown Havana can be split into three main areas: Habana Vieja, Centro Habana and Vedado, which between them contain the bulk of the tourist sights. Centrally located Habana Vieja is the city's atmospheric historic masterpiece; dense Centro Habana, to the west, provides an eye-opening look at the real-life Cuba in close-up; and the more majestic spread-out Vedado is the once-notorious Mafia-run

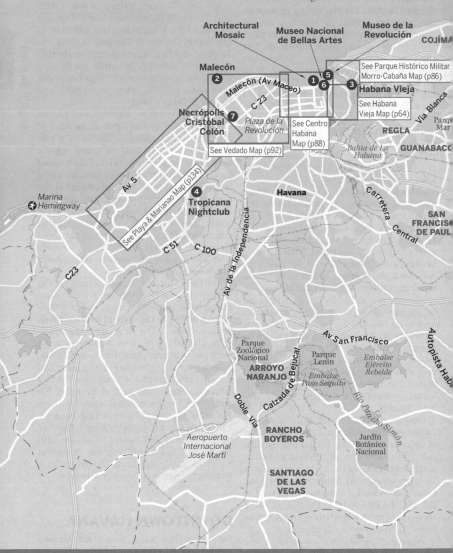

Havana Highlights

1 Stroll through Havana's mosaic of art deco, colonial baroque and neoclassical **architecture** (p87).

2 Take in the dramatic sweep of the **Malecón** (p100) at sunset.

3 See how tourist money has helped to rehabilitate **Habana Vieja** (p62).

4 Rediscover kitsch at the **Tropicana Nightclub** (p140).

5 Storm the gates of the **Museo de la Revolución** (p94).

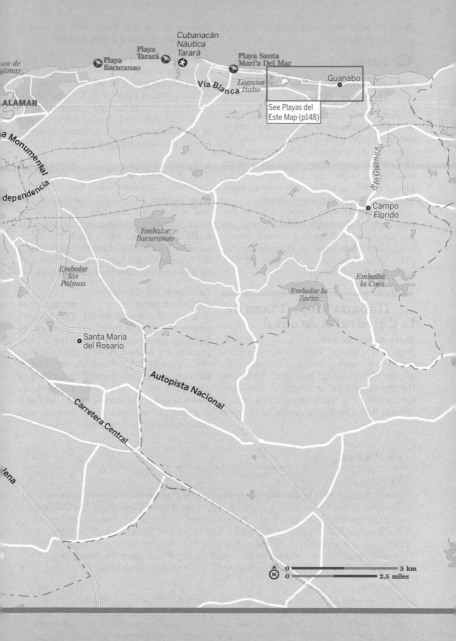

6 Trace the history of Cuban painting in the **Museo Nacional de Bellas Artes** (p91).

7 Try not to get spooked in the strangely beautiful **Necrópolis Cristóbal Colón** (p99).

district replete with hotels, restaurants and a pulsating nightlife.

Sights

◉ Habana Vieja

Studded with architectural jewels from every era, Habana Vieja offers visitors one of the finest collections of urban edifices in the Americas. At a conservative estimate, the Old Town alone contains over 900 buildings of historical importance, with myriad examples of illustrious architecture ranging from intricate baroque to glitzy art deco.

For a whistle-stop introduction to the best parts of the neighborhood, check out the illustrated walking tour or stick closely to the four main squares: Plaza de Armas, Plaza Vieja, Plaza de San Francisco de Asís and Plaza de la Catedral.

◉ Habana Vieja: Plaza de la Catedral & Around

Plaza de la Catedral   SQUARE
(Map p64) Habana Vieja's most uniform square is a museum to Cuban baroque with all the surrounding buildings, including the city's beguiling asymmetrical cathedral, dating from the 1700s. Despite this homogeneity, it is actually the newest of the four squares in the Old Town, with its present layout dating from the 18th century.

Palacio de los Marqueses de Aguas Claras   NOTABLE BUILDING
(Map p64; San Ignacio No 54) Situated on the western side of Plaza de la Catedral is this majestic one-time baroque palace completed in 1760 and widely lauded for the beauty of its shady Andalucian patio. Today it houses the Restaurante el Patio.

Casa de Lombillo   NOTABLE BUILDING
(Map p64; Plaza de la Catedral) Right next door to Catedral de San Cristóbal de la Habana this *palacio* was built in 1741 and once served as a post office (a stone-mask ornamental mailbox built into the wall is still in use). Since 2000 it has functioned as an office for the City Historian. Next door is the equally resplendent Palacio del Marqués de Arcos, which dates from the same era.

Palacio de los Condes de Casa Bayona   NOTABLE BUILDING
(Map p64; San Ignacio No 61) The square's southern aspect is taken up by its oldest building, constructed in 1720. Today it functions as the **Museo de Arte Colonial** (Map p64; unguided CUC$2; ⊙9am-6:30pm), a small museum displaying colonial furniture and decorative arts. Among the finer exhibits are pieces of china with scenes of colonial Cuba, a collection of ornamental flowers, and many colonial-era dining-room sets.

HAVANA IN...

Two Days
Explore Habana Vieja by strolling the streets between the four main colonial squares. There is a plethora of museums, so you'll want to weed out the good ones. The Museo de la Ciudad (p65) is a highlight in the colonial core, while in Centro Habana don't miss the Museo de la Revolución (p94) and the dual-site Museo Nacional de Bellas Artes (p91). You can cover a lot of ground on Havana's open-topped bus tour, although the Malecón (p100) sea drive is best plied on foot. For nightlife, soak up the nocturnal essence of Habana Vieja, dipping into bars on Calle Obispo and Plaza Vieja.

Four Days
With two extra days, make sure you check out the 1950s-era kitsch of the Vedado neighborhood. Essential stops are the Hotel Nacional (p97) for a mojito on the alfresco terrace and Plaza de la Revolución (p98) for a look at the Che mural and the Memorial a José Martí. Stick around in the evening for some excellent nightlife in jazz clubs, lounge bars and cabarets.

One Week
Three more days gives you time to get out to suburban sights such as the Museo Hemingway (p144), the historic colonial forts on the east side of the harbor and the Aquarium (p133) in Miramar.

Catedral de San Cristóbal de la Habana
CHURCH

(Map p64; cnr San Ignacio & Empedrado; ⊙ until noon) Dominated by two unequal towers and framed by a theatrical baroque facade designed by Italian architect Francesco Borromini, Havana's incredible cathedral was once described by novelist Alejo Carpentier as 'music set in stone.' The Jesuits began construction of the church in 1748 and work continued despite their expulsion in 1767.

When the building was finished in 1787, the diocese of Havana was created and the church became a cathedral, and is one of the oldest in the Americas. The remains of Columbus were interred here from 1795 to 1898, when they were moved to Seville. The best time to visit is during Sunday Mass (10:30am).

Centro Wifredo Lam
CULTURAL BUILDING

(Map p64; cnr San Ignacio & Empedrado; admission CUC$3; ⊙ 10am-5pm Mon-Sat) On the corner of Plaza de la Catedral, this cultural center contains the Cafe Amarillo and an exhibition center named after the island's most celebrated painter, but which usually displays the works of more modern painters.

Taller Experimental de Gráfica
CULTURAL BUILDING

(Map p64; Callejón del Chorro No 6; admission free; ⊙ 10am-4pm Mon-Fri) Easy to miss at the end of a short cul-de-sac, but ignore it at your peril. This is Havana's most cutting-edge art workshop, which also offers the possibility of engraving classes. Come and see the masters at work.

Parque Maestranza
PARK

(Map p64; Av Carlos Manuel de Céspedes; admission CUC$1) Small-scale but fun kids' playground (children under four years only) with inflatable castles and other games overlooking the harbor.

◉ Habana Vieja: Plaza de Armas & Around

Plaza de Armas
SQUARE

Havana's oldest square was laid out in the early 1520s, soon after the city's foundation, and was originally known as Plaza de Iglesia after a church – the Parroquial Mayor – that once stood on the site of the present-day Palacio de los Capitanes Generales.

The name Plaza de Armas (Square of Arms) wasn't adopted until the late 16th century, when the colonial governor, then housed in the Castillo de la Real Fuerza, used the site to conduct military exercises. Today's plaza, along with most of the buildings around it, dates from the late 1700s.

In the center of the square, which is lined with royal palms and hosts a daily (except Sundays) secondhand book market, is a marble statue of Carlos Manuel de Céspedes (Map p64), the man who set Cuba on the road to independence in 1868. The statue replaced one of unpopular Spanish king, Ferdinand VII, in 1955.

Also of note on the square's eastern aspect is the late-18th-century Palacio de los Condes de Santovenia (Map p64; Calle Baratillo No 9), today the five-star, 27-room Hotel Santa Isabel.

HAVANA STREET NAMES

OLD NAME	NEW NAME
Av de los Presidentes	Calle G
Av de Maceo	Malecón
Av del Puerto	Av Carlos Manuel de Céspedes
Av de Rancho	Av de la Independencia Boyeros (Boyeros)
Belascoaín	Padre Varela
Cárcel	Capdevila
Carlos III (Tercera)	Av Salvador Allende
Cristina	Av de México
Egido	Av de Bélgica
Estrella	Enrique Barnet
Galiano	Av de Italia
La Rampa	Calle 23
Monserrate	Av de las Misiones
Monte	Máximo Gómez
Paseo del Prado	Paseo de Martí
Paula	Leonor Pérez
Reina	Av Simón Bolívar
San José	San Martín
Someruelos	Aponte
Teniente Rey	Brasil
Vives	Av de España
Zulueta	Agramonte

Habana Vieja

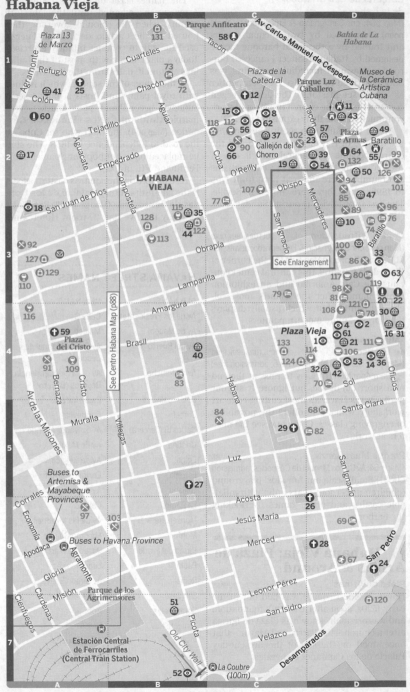

(Map p64)

Museo el Templete
MUSEUM

(Map p64; Plaza de Armas; admission CUC$2; ⏲8:30am-6pm) The tiny neoclassical Doric chapel on the east side of Plaza de Armas was erected in 1828 at the point where Havana's first Mass was held beneath a ceiba tree in November 1519. A similar ceiba tree has now replaced the original. Inside the chapel are three large paintings of the event by the French painter Jean Baptiste Vermay (1786–1833).

Museo Nacional de Historia Natural
MUSEUM

(Map p64; Obispo No 61; admission CUC$3; ⏲10am-5:30pm Wed-Sun, 1:30-5pm Tue) An average museum that contains examples of Cuba's flora and fauna, and overlooks Plaza de Armas.

Museo de la Ciudad
MUSEUM

(Map p64; Tacón No 1; admission CUC$3; ⏲9:30am-6pm) Filling the whole west side of Plaza de Armas, this museum is housed in the **Palacio de los Capitanes Generales** (Map p64), dating from the 1770s. Built on the site of Havana's original church, it's a textbook example of Cuban baroque architecture hewn out of rock from the nearby San Lázaro quarries and has served many purposes over the years.

From 1791 until 1898 it was the residence of the Spanish captains general. From 1899 until 1902, the US military governors were based here, and during the first two decades of the 20th century the building briefly became the presidential palace. Since 1968 it has been home to the City Museum, one of Havana's most comprehensive and interesting. City Museum wraps its way regally around a splendid central courtyard adorned with a white marble statue of Christopher Columbus (1862). Artifacts include period furniture, military uniforms and old-fashioned 19th-century horse carriages, while old photos vividly recreate events from Havana's roller-coaster history, such as the 1898 sinking of US battleship *Maine* in the harbor. It's better to body-swerve the pushy attendants and wander around at your own pace.

Palacio del Segundo Cabo
HISTORIC BUILDING

(Map p64; O'Reilly No 4; admission CUC$1; ⏲Sala Galería Raúl Martínez 9am-6pm Mon-Sat) Wedged into the square's northwest corner, this building was constructed in 1772 as the headquarters of the Spanish vice-governor. After several reincarnations as a post office,

Habana Vieja

the palace of the Senate, the Supreme Court, the National Academy of Arts and Letters and the seat of the Cuban Geographical Society, the building is today a well-stocked bookstore.

Pop-art fans should take a look at the palace's Sala Galería Raúl Martínez. The building was being renovated at the time of writing.

Gabinete de Arqueología   MUSEUM
(Map p64; Tacón No 12; ☉ 9am-5pm Tue-Sat, 9am-2:30pm Sun) FREE See the rainbow of influ-

ences on Cuba's colonial culture from everyday artifacts dug up nearby. Of particular interest are the ceramics which demonstrate a 17th- and 18th-century penchant for English china, Chinese porcelain and Mexican ceramics among the Spanish-Cuban aristocracy. Upstairs rooms are dedicated to older pre-Columbian finds.

Castillo de la Real Fuerza   FORT
(Map p64) On the seaward side of Plaza de Armas is one of the oldest existing forts in the Americas, built between 1558 and 1577

on the site of an earlier fort destroyed by French privateers in 1555. The west tower is crowned by a copy of a famous bronze weather vane called **La Giraldilla**.

The original was cast in Havana in 1632 by Jerónimo Martínez Pinzón and is popularly believed to be of Doña Inés de Bobadilla, the wife of gold explorer Hernando de Soto. The original is now kept in the Museo de la Ciudad, and the figure also appears on the Havana Club rum label. Imposing and indomitable, the castle is ringed by an impressive moat and today shelters the **Museo de Navegación** (Map p64; admission CUC$3; ⊙9am-5pm), which opened in 2008 and displays interesting exposés on the history of the fort and Old Town, and its connections with the erstwhile Spanish Empire. Look out for the huge scale model of the *Santíssima Trinidad* galleon.

Museo de Transporte Automotor MUSEUM (Map p64; Oficios No 13; admission CUC$1.50; ⊙9am-5pm Tue-Sun, 9am-1pm Sun) Few miss the irony of this vaguely surreal museum stuffed with ancient Thunderbirds, Pontiacs and Ford Model Ts, most of which appear to be in better shape than the dinosaurs that ply the streets outside.

★**Calle Mercaderes** STREET

Cobbled, car-free Calle Mercaderes (Merchant's Street) has been extensively restored by the City Historian's Office and is an almost complete replica of its splendid 18th-century high-water mark. Interspersed with the museums, shops and restaurants are some real-life working social projects, such as a maternity home and a needlecraft co-operative. Most of the myriad museums are free, including the Casa de Asia (Map p64; Mercaderes No 111; ⊙10am-6pm Tue-Sat, 9am-1pm Sun), with paintings and sculpture from China and Japan; the Armería 9 de Abril (Map p64; Mercaderes No 157; ⊙10am-6pm Mon-Sat), an old gun shop (now museum) stormed

by revolutionaries on the said date in 1958; and the Museo de Bomberos (Map p64; cnr Mercaderes & Lamparilla; ⊙10am-6pm Mon-Sat), which has antediluvian fire equipment dedicated to 19 Havana firemen who lost their lives in an 1890 railway fire.

Just off Mercaderes down Obrapía, it's worth slinking into the gratis Casa de África (Map p64; Obrapía No 157; admission free; ⊙9:30am-5pm Tue-Sun, 9:30am-1pm Sun), which houses sacred objects relating to Santería and the secret Abakuá fraternity collected by ethnographer Fernando Ortíz.

The corner of Mercaderes and Obrapía has an international flavor, with a bronze statue of Simón Bolívar (Map p64), the Lat-

---

HISTORICAL JIGSAW

Never in the field of architectural preservation has so much been achieved by so many with so few resources.

You hear plenty about the sterling performance of the Cuban education and health-care systems in the international press, but relatively little about the remarkable work that has gone into preserving the country's valuable but seriously endangered historical legacy, most notably in Habana Vieja.

A work-in-progress since the late 1970s, the piecing back together of Havana's 'old town' after decades of neglect has been a foresighted and startlingly miraculous process considering the economic odds stacked against it. The genius behind the project is Eusebio Leal Spengler, Havana's celebrated City Historian who, unperturbed by the tightening of the financial screws during Cuba's Special Period, set up Habaguanex in 1994, a holding company that earns hard currency through tourism and re-invests it in a mix of historical preservation and city-wide urban regeneration. The process has reaped multiple benefits since its inception. By safeguarding Havana's historical heritage, Leal and his cohorts have attracted more tourists to the city and earned a bigger slice of revenue for Habaguanex to plough back into further restoration work and much-needed social projects.

Eschewing the temptation to turn Havana's old quarter into a historical theme-park, Leal has sought to re-build the city's urban jigsaw as an authentic 'living' center that provides tangible benefits for the neighborhood's 700,000 inhabitants. As a result, schools, neighborhood committees, care-homes for seniors, and centres for children with disabilities sit seamlessly alongside the cleaned-up colonial edifices. This local-tourist juxtaposition is both commendable and unique. Sip an alfresco mojito in gorgeous Plaza Vieja and you will be sharing the space with children from the Angela Landa School that abuts the square. Stroll around the 17th-century Convento Belén and you will be rubbing shoulders with Havana's senior citizens in a convalescent home. In essence, every time you put your money into a Habaguanex hotel, museum or restaurant, you are contributing, not just to the quarter's continued restoration, but to a whole raft of social projects that directly benefit the local population.

Today, Habaguanex splits its annual tourist income (reported to be in excess of US$160 million) between further restoration (45%) and social projects in the city (55%), of which there are now over 400. The company is renowned for its meticulous attention-to-detail using old texts, drawings, history books and – where available – photos archived in the Fototeca museum in Plaza Vieja in its restoration projects. So far, one quarter of Habana Vieja has been returned to the height of its colonial-era splendor with ample tourist attractions including 20 Habaguanex-run hotels, four classic forts and over 30 museums.

in America liberator, and across the street you'll find the Museo de Simón Bolívar (Map p64; Mercaderes No 160; donations accepted; ☺9am-5pm Tue-Sun) dedicated to Bolívar's life. The Casa de México Benito Juárez (Map p64; Obrapía No 116; admission CUC$1; ☺10:15am-5:45pm Tue-Sat, 9am-1pm Sun) exhibits Mexican folk art and plenty of books, but not a lot on Señor Juárez (Mexico's first indigenous president) himself. Just east is the Casa Oswaldo Guayasamín (Map p64; Obrapía No 111; donations accepted; ☺9am-2:30pm Tue-Sun), now a museum, but once the studio of the great Ecuadorian artist who painted Fidel in numerous poses.

Mercaderes is also characterized by its restored shops, including a perfume store and a spice shop. Wander at will.

Maqueta de La Habana Vieja   MUSEUM
(Map p64; Mercaderes No 114; admission CUC$1.50; ☺9am-6:30pm) Herein lies a 1:500 scale model of Habana Vieja complete with an authentic soundtrack meant to replicate a day in the life of the city. It's incredibly detailed and provides an excellent way of geographically acquainting yourself with the city's historical core.

The on-site Cinematógrafo Lumière (admission CUC$2) is a small cinema that shows nostalgia movies for senior citizens, and educational documentaries about the restoration for visitors.

Casa de la Obra Pía   NOTABLE BUILDING
(Map p64; Obrapía No 158; admission CUC$1.50; ☺9am-4:30pm Tue-Sat, 9:30am-12:30pm Sun) One of the more muscular sights on Calle Mercaderes is this typical Havana aristocratic residence originally built in 1665 and rebuilt in 1780. Baroque decoration – including an intricate portico made in Cádiz, Spain – covers the exterior facade.

In addition to its historical value, the house today contains a sewing and needle-craft cooperative that has a workshop inside and a small shop selling clothes and textiles on Calle Mercaderes.

☺ Habana Vieja: Plaza de San Francisco de Asís & Around

Plaza de San Francisco de Asís   SQUARE
(Map p64) Facing Havana harbor, the breezy Plaza de San Francisco de Asís first grew up in the 16th century when Spanish galleons stopped by at the quayside on their passage through the Indies to Spain. A market took root in the 1500s, followed by a church in 1608, though when the pious monks complained of too much noise the market was moved a few blocks south to Plaza Vieja.

The Plaza de San Francisco underwent a full restoration in the late 1990s and is most notable for its uneven cobblestones and the white marble Fuente de los Leones (Map p64) (Fountain of Lions) carved by the Italian sculptor Giuseppe Gaginni in 1836. A more modern statue outside the square's famous church depicts El Caballero de París (Map p64), a well-known street person who roamed Havana during the 1950s, engaging passers-by with his philosophies on life, religion, politics and current events. On the eastern side of the plaza stands the Terminal Sierra Maestra cruise terminal, which dispatches shiploads of weekly tourists, while nearby the domed Lonja del Comercio (Map p64; Plaza de San Francisco de Asís) is a former commodities market erected in 1909 and restored in 1996 to provide office space for foreign companies with joint ventures in Cuba.

Iglesia y Monasterio de
San Francisco de Asís   MUSEUM
(Map p64; Oficios, btwn Amargura & Brasil; Museo de Arte Religioso unguided/guided CUC$2/3; ☺concert hall from 5pm or 6pm, Museo de Arte Religioso 9am-6pm) Built in 1739, this church/convent ceased to have a religious function in the 1840s. In the late 1980s crypts and religious objects were dug up during excavations, and many of them were later incorporated into the Museo de Arte Religioso that opened on the site in 1994. Since 2005, part of the old monastery has functioned as a children's theater for the neighborhood's young residents. Classical concerts are hosted here.

Il Genio di Leonardo da Vinci   MUSEUM
(Map p64; Churruca, btwn Oficios & Av del Puerto; admission CUC$2; ☺9:30am-4pm Tue-Sat) A new permanent exposition in the Convento de San Francisco de Asís' Salón Blanco (use separate entrance on the church's south side behind the Coche Mambí) that has cleverly built mock-ups of many of Leonardo's famous drawings – gliders, odometers, bikes, parachutes and tanks – the antecedents to pretty much half the inventions in the modern world.

It's beautifully laid out with explanations in six languages, including Russian.

Habana Vieja

WALKING TOUR OF OLD HAVANA

This easy 'four plaza' walking tour, though less than 2km in length, could fill a day with its museums, shops, bars and street theater. It highlights Havana's unique historical district, built up around four main squares. Start at **Catedral de San Cristóbal de la Habana 1** which anchors the Plaza de la Catedral. This compact square has bags of atmosphere and is always awash with interesting characters. Then take Calle Empedrado followed by Calle Mercaderes to Plaza de Armas, once used for military exercises and still guarded by the **Castillo de la Real Fuerza 2**. The fort's museum is worth a quick look. Worth more time is the Museo de la Ciudad in the **Palacio de los Capitanes Generales 3**; eschew the on-site guides and wander alone. Walk up **Calle Obispo 4** next, Havana's busy main drag, before turning left into **Calle Mercaderes 5**, where old shops and several museums make ambling a pleasure. Turn left on Calle Amargura and dive into Plaza de San Francisco de Asís, dominated by **Iglesia y Monasterio de San Francisco de Asís 6**. Make a note of upcoming classical concerts (great acoustics!) and try to take in one of the church's two museums (Il Genio di Leonardo da Vinci is best). Turn right on Calle Brasil and you'll enter **Plaza Vieja 7**, home to a planetarium and several museum-galleries. And when you're museumed-out, crash at Factoria Plaza Vieja for a smooth microbrewed beer.

MUSEUMS

Dip into some of the museums you will pass on the way (in order):

➡ **Museo de Arte Colonial** Colonial furniture

➡ **Museo de Navegación** Maritime history

➡ **Museo de la Ciudad** City history

➡ **Museo de Pintura Mural** Frescos

➡ **Maqueta de la Habana Vieja** Scale model of Havana

➡ **Museo de Naipes** Playing cards

Catedral de San Cristóbal de la Habana

The cathedral's interior was originally baroque, like its main facade. However, in the early 19th century, a renovation project redecorated the church's inner sanctum in a more sober classical tone.

Calle Obispo

The lower section of Obispo is an architectural crossroads. The row of buildings on the south are the oldest townhouses in Havana, dating from the 1570s. Opposite is the Hotel Ambos Mundos, Hemingway's 1930s hangout.

Castillo de la Real Fuerza

The highlight of this fort's onsite maritime museum is a 4m-long model of the *Santissima Trinidad*, a ship built in Havana in the 1760s that fought at the Battle of Trafalgar in 1805.

MARK LEWIS/GETTY ©

Palacio de los Capitanes Generales

An interesting feature of this sturdy building is the marine fossils embedded in its limestone walls. The street outside is lined with wooden bricks designed to deaden the sound of horses' hooves.

BRENT WINEBRENNER/GETTY ©

DANITA DELIMONT/GETTY ©

Iglesia y Monasterio de San Francisco de Asís

Once Havana's tallest building, the bell tower of this former church/monastery was originally topped by a statue of St Francis of Assisi; the figurine fell off during an 1846 hurricane.

← **Plaza de Armas**

Barillo

Cuba tacon

3

4

Oficios

Baratillo

5

Mercaderes

Plaza de San Francisco de Asís

6

Obispo

Obrapía

San Ignacio

Lamparilla

Amargura

7

Cuba

teniel

Muralla

Sol

Calle Mercaderes

Pedestrian-friendly 'Market Street' is notable for its esoteric shops. On the corner of Calle Obrapía sits the Casa de la Obra Pía, one of the first renovation projects of city historian Eusebio Leal in 1968.

RICK RUDNICKI/GETTY ©

Plaza Vieja

Plaza Vieja's buildings were constructed as private residences rather than municipal buildings. They housed some of Havana's richest families, who would gather to watch the plaza's gory public spectacles, including executions.

WALTER BIBIKOW/GETTY ©

Museo Alejandro Humboldt
MUSEUM

(Map p64; cnr Oficios & Muralla; ⊗9am-5pm Tue-Sat) FREE Often referred to as the 'second discoverer' of Cuba, German scientist, Alejandro Humboldt's huge Cuban legacy goes largely unnoticed by outsiders. This small museum displays a historical trajectory of his work collecting scientific and botanical data across the island in the early 1800s. Nearby is the Coche Mambí (Map p64; admission free; ⊗9am-2pm Tue-Sat), a train carriage built in the US in 1900 and brought to Cuba in 1912.

Museo del Ron
MUSEUM

(Map p64; San Pedro No 262; admission incl guide CUC$7; ⊗9am-5:30pm Mon-Thu, 9am-4:30pm Fri-Sun) You don't have to be an Añejo Reserva quaffer to enjoy the Museo del Ron in the Fundación Havana Club, but it probably helps. The museum, with its trilingual guided tour, shows rum-making antiquities and the complex brewing process. A not overgenerous measure of rum is included in the price.

There's a bar and shop on site, but the savvy reconvene to Bar Dos Hermanos next door. The museum sits opposite Havana harbor.

Aquarium
AQUARIUM

(Map p64; Brasil No 9, btwn Mercaderes & Oficios; admission CUC$1.50; ⊗9:30am-5pm Mon-Sat, 9:30am-1pm Sun) Indoor freshwater fish in tanks make this small aquarium of interest to children.

◉ Habana Vieja: Plaza Vieja & Around

★Plaza Vieja
SQUARE

(Map p64) Laid out in 1559, Plaza Vieja (Old Square) is Havana's most architecturally eclectic square, where Cuban baroque nestles seamlessly next to Gaudí-inspired art nouveau. Originally called Plaza Nueva (New Square), it was initially used for military exercises and later served as an open-air marketplace.

During the Batista regime an ugly underground parking lot was constructed here, but this monstrosity was demolished in 1996 to make way for a massive renovation project. Sprinkled liberally with bars, restaurants and cafes, Plaza Vieja today has its own micro-brewery, the Angela Landa primary school, a beautiful fenced-in fountain and, on its west side, some of Havana's finest *vitrales* (stained-glass windows).

Cámara Oscura
LANDMARK

(Map p64; Plaza Vieja; admission CUC$2; ⊗9am-5pm Tue-Sat, 9am-1pm Sun) On the northwestern corner of Plaza Vieja is this clever optical device providing live, 360-degree views of the city from atop a 35m-tall tower. Explanations are in Spanish and English.

Fototeca de Cuba
GALLERY

(Map p64; Mercaderes No 307; ⊗10am-5pm Tue-Fri, 9am-noon Sat) FREE A photographic archive of Old Havana since the early 20th century that was started by former City Historian, Emilio Roig de Leuchsenring in 1937. There are an estimated 14,000 photos inside, and they have been instrumental in providing the graphic pointers for the current restoration.

Museo de Naipes
MUSEUM

(Map p64; Muralla No 101; ⊗9am-6pm Tue-Sun) FREE Encased in Plaza Vieja's oldest building is this quirky playing-card museum with a 2000-strong collection that includes rock stars, rum drinks and round cards.

La Casona Centro de Arte
GALLERY

(Map p64; Muralla No 107; ⊗10am-5pm Mon-Fri, 10am-2pm Sat) FREE Housed in one of Plaza Vieja's most striking buildings (note the sturdy colonial overtones), this gallery/shop has great solo and group shows by up-and-coming Cuban artists.

Palacio Cueto
NOTABLE BUILDING

(Map p64; cnr Muralla & Mercaderes) Kissing the southeast corner of Plaza Vieja is this distinctive Gaudí-esque building, which remains Havana's finest example of art nouveau. Its outrageously ornate facade once housed a warehouse and a hat factory before it was rented by José Cueto in the 1920s as the Palacio Vienna hotel. Habaguanex, the commercial arm of the City Historian's Office, is in the process of restoring the building, which was constructed in 1906 and has lain empty and unused since the early 1990s.

Planetario
PLANETARIUM

(Map p64; Mercaderes; admission CUC$10; ⊗9:30am-5pm Wed-Sat, 9:30am-12:30pm Sun) Built with the help of Japanese investment and opened in December 2009, Havana's planetarium is only accessible by guided tours booked in advance. Tours take place Wednesday to Sunday and can be booked on Monday and Tuesday. There are four tours daily and two on Sunday.

Exhibits include a scale reproduction of the solar system inside a giant orb, a simulation of the Big Bang, and a theater that allows viewing of over 6000 stars. All pretty exciting stuff.

Centro Cultural Pablo
de la Torriente Brau   CULTURAL BUILDING
(Map p64; www.centropablo.cult.cu; Muralla No 63; ⊙9am-5:30pm Tue-Sat) FREE Tucked away behind Plaza Vieja, the 'Brau' is a leading cultural institution that was formed under the auspices of the Unión de Escritores y Artistas de Cuba (Uneac; Union of Cuban Writers and Artists) in 1996. The center hosts expositions, poetry readings and live acoustic music. Its Salón de Arte Digital is renowned for its groundbreaking digital art.

⊙ Habana Vieja: Calle Obispo & Around

Calle Obispo   STREET
Narrow, car-free Calle Obispo (Bishop's Street), Habana Vieja's main interconnecting artery, is packed with art galleries, shops, music bars and people. Four- and five-story buildings block out most of the sunlight, and the swaying throng of people seems to move in time to the all-pervading live music.

Museo de Numismático   MUSEUM
(Map p64; Obispo, btwn Aguiar & Habana; admission CUC$1.50; ⊙9am-5pm Tue-Sat, 9:30am-12:45pm Sun) This numismatist's heaven brings together various collections of medals, coins and banknotes from around the world, including a stash of 1000 mainly American gold coins (1869–1928) and a full chronology of Cuban banknotes from the 19th century to the present.

Museo 28 Septiembre de los CDR   MUSEUM
(Map p64; Obispo, btwn Aguiar & Habana; admission CUC$2; ⊙9am-5:30pm) A venerable building on Obispo that dedicates two floors to a rather biased dissection of the nationwide Comites de la Defensa de la Revolución (CDR; Committees for the Defense of the Revolution). Commendable neighborhood-watch schemes, or grassroots spying agencies? Sift through the propaganda and decide.

Museo de Pintura Mural   MUSEUM
(Map p64; Obispo, btwn Mercaderes & Oficios; ⊙10am-6pm) FREE A simple museum that exhibits some beautifully restored original frescoes in the Casa del Mayorazgo de Recio, popularly considered to be Havana's oldest surviving house.

Edificio Santo Domingo   MUSEUM
(Map p64; Mercaderes, btwn Obispo & O'Reilly) FREE On Obispo is the site of Havana's original university, which stood here between 1728 and 1902. It was originally part of a convent; the contemporary modern office block was built by Habaguanex in 2006 over the skeleton of an uglier 1950s office, the roof of which had been used as a helicopter landing pad. The building has now been ingeniously refitted with the convent's original bell tower and baroque doorway, providing an interesting juxtaposition of old and new.

Many of the university's arts faculties have now moved back here, and a small museum/art gallery displays a scale model of the original convent and various artifacts that were rescued from it.

Plaza del Cristo & Around   SQUARE
Habana Vieja's fifth (and most overlooked) square lies at the west end of the neighborhood, a little apart from the historical core, and has yet to benefit from the City Historian's makeover. It's worth a look for the **Parroquial del Santo Cristo del Buen Viaje** (Map p64), a church dating from 1732, although there has been a Franciscan hermitage on this site since 1640.

Still only partially renovated, the building is most notable for its intricate stained-glass windows and brightly painted wooden ceiling. The Plaza del Cristo also hosts a primary school (hence the noise) and a microcosmic slice of everyday Cuban life without tourists.

Museo de la Farmacia Habanera   MUSEUM
(Map p64; cnr Brasil & Compostela; ⊙9am-5pm) FREE A few blocks east from Plaza del Cristo, this museum-store founded in 1886 by Catalan José Sarrá still acts as a working pharmacy for Cubans. The small museum section displays an elegant mock-up of an old drugstore with some interesting historical explanations.

continued on page 84

HAVANA SIGHTS

Architecture

There is nothing pure about Cuban architecture. Rather like its music, the nation's buildings exhibit an unashamed assortment of styles, ideas and background influences. The result is a kind of architectural 'theme and variations', that has absorbed a variety of imported genres and shaped them into something that is uniquely Cuban.

ECCLESIAL ARCHITECTURE

Cuba's earliest townscapes were dominated by ecclesial architecture, reflected initially in the noble cloisters of Havana's Convento de Santa Clara, built in 1632, and culminating a century or so later in the magnificent Catedral de San Cristóbal, considered by many to be the country's most outstanding baroque monument. Gothic – a dominant architectural style in Europe – is unusual in Cuba, where churches are normally baroque or neoclassical in design. Rare examples can be seen at Iglesia del Sagrado Corazón de Jesús in Havana and its namesake church in the nation's most devoutly religious city, Camagüey.

Styles & Trends

Emerging relatively unscathed from the turmoil of three revolutionary wars and buffered from modern globalization by Cuba's peculiar economic situation, the nation's well-preserved cities have survived into the 21st century with the bulk of their colonial architectural features intact. The preservation has been helped by the nomination of Havana Vieja, Trinidad, Cienfuegos and Camagüey as Unesco World Heritage Sites, and aided further by foresighted local historians who have created a model for self-sustaining historical preservation that might well go down as one of the revolutionary government's greatest achievements.

Cuba's classic and most prevalent architectural styles are baroque and neoclassicism. Baroque designers began sharpening their quills in the 1750s; neoclassicism gained the ascendency in the 1820s and continued, amid numerous revivals, until the 1920s.

Trademark buildings of the American era (1902–59) exhibited art deco and, later on, modernist styles. Art nouveau played a cameo role during this period influenced by Catalan modernisme; recognizable art nouveau curves and embellishments can be seen on pivotal east–west axis streets in Centro Havana. Ostentatious eclecticism, courtesy of the Americans, characterized Havana's rich and growing suburbs from the 1910s onwards.

Building styles weren't all pretty. Cuba's brief flirtation with Soviet architectonics in the 1960s and '70s threw up plenty of breeze-block apartments and ugly utilitarian hotels that sit rather jarringly alongside the beautiful relics of the colonial era. Havana's Vedado neighborhood maintains a small but significant cluster of modernist 'skyscrapers' constructed during a 10-year pre-revolutionary building boom in the 1950s.

1. Streets of Havana (p58) 2. Catedral de San Cristóbal de la Habana (p63), Havana

Coastal Fortifications

While European kings were hiding from the hoi polloi in muscular medieval castles, their Latin American cousins were building up their colonial defenses in a series of equally colossal renaissance forts.

The protective ring of fortifications that punctuates Cuba's coastline stretching from Havana in the west to Baracoa in the east forms one of the finest ensembles of military architecture in the Americas. The construction of these sturdy stone behemoths by the Spanish in the 16th, 17th and 18th centuries reflected the colony's strategic importance on the Atlantic trade routes and its vulnerability to attacks by daring pirates and competing colonial powers.

As Cuban capital and the primary Spanish port in the Caribbean, Havana was the grand prize to ambitious would-be raiders. The sacking of the city by French pirate, Jacques de Sores, in 1555 exposed the weaknesses of the city's meager defenses and provoked

the first wave of fort building. Havana's authorities called in Italian Military architect Giovanni Bautista Antonelli to do the job and he responded with aplomb, reinforcing the harbor mouth with two magnificent forts, the Morro and San Salvador La Punta. The work, which started in the 1580s, was slow but meticulous; the forts weren't actually finished until after Antonelli's death in the 1620s. Antonelli also designed the Morro Castle in Santiago, started around the same time but, thanks to ongoing attacks most notoriously by British buccaneer Henry Morgan in 1662, not finished until 1700.

More forts were added in the 18th century, most notably at Jagua (near present-day Cienfuegos) on the south coast and Matanzas in the north. Baracoa in the far east was encircled with a bulwark of three small fortifications, all of which survive.

With their thick walls, and polygon layout designed to fit in with the coastal topography, Cuba's forts were built to last (all still survive) and largely served

1. Colonial buildings of Camagüey (p325) 2. Buildings of Trinidad's Plaza Mayor (p290)

their purpose at deterring successive invaders until 1762. In that year the British arrived during the Seven Years War, blasting a hole in San Severino in Matanzas and capturing Havana after a 44-day siege of the Morro Castle. Spain's response when it got back Havana from the British in 1763 was to build the humungous La Cabaña, the largest fort in the Americas. Not surprisingly, its heavy battlements were never breached.

In the 1980s and '90s, Havana's and Santiago's forts were named Unesco World Heritage Sites.

Theatrical Architecture

Attend a dance or play in a provincial Cuban theater and you might find your eyes flicking intermittently between the artists on the stage and the equally captivating artistry of the building.

As strong patrons of music and dance, the Cubans have a tradition of building iconic provincial theaters and most cities have an historic venue where you can view the latest performances. By popular consensus, the most architecturally accomplished Cuban theaters are the Teatro Sauto (p205) in Matanzas, the Teatro la Caridad (p261) in Santa Clara, and the Teatro Tomás Terry (p243) in Cienfuegos. All three gilded buildings were constructed in the 19th century (in 1863, 1885 and 1890 respectively) with sober French neoclassical facades overlaying more lavish Italianate interiors. A generic defining feature is the U-shaped three-tiered auditoriums which display a profusion of carved wood-paneling and wrought iron, and are crowned by striking ceiling frescos. The frescos of angelic cherubs in the Caridad and Tomás Terry were painted by the same Philippine artist, Camilo Salaya, while the Sauto's was the work of the theater's Italian architect, Daniele Dell'Aglio. Other features include ornate chandeliers, gold-leafed mosaics and striking marble statues: the Sauto's statues are of Greek goddesses, while the Tomás Terry sports a marble recreation of its eponymous financier, a Venezuelan-born sugar baron.

Philanthropy played a major part in many Cuban theaters in the 19th century, none more so than Santa Clara's Caridad (the name means 'charity') which was paid for by local benefactor, Marta Abreu. In an early show of altruism, Abreu, who donated to many social and artistic causes, ensured that a percentage of the theater's ongoing profits went to charity.

Lack of funds in recent times has left many Cuban theaters in dire need of repair. Some buildings haven't survived. The Colesio, Cuba's earliest modern theater built in 1823 in Santiago de Cuba was destroyed by fire in 1846. The **Teatro Brunet** in Trinidad built in 1840 is now a ruin used as an atmospheric social center. Havana's oldest theater, the **Tacón** survives, but was overlaid by a Spanish social center (the Centro Gallego) in the 1910s. Pinar del Río's recently refurbished **Teatro Milanes** (1838) has a lovely Sevillan patio, while the neoclassical **Teatro Principal** (1850) in Camagüey is home of Cuba's most prestigious ballet company.

Cuban Baroque

Baroque architecture arrived in Cuba in the mid 1700s, via Spain, a good 50 years after its European high-water mark. Fueled by the rapid growth of the island's nascent sugar industry, nouveau riche slave-owners and sugar merchants ploughed their juicy profits into grandiose urban buildings. The finest examples of baroque in Cuba adorn the homes and public buildings of Habana Vieja, although the style didn't reach its zenith until the late-1700s with the construction of the Catedral de San Cristóbal de la Habana and the surrounding Plaza de la Catedral.

Due to climatic and cultural peculiarities, traditional baroque (the word is taken from the Portuguese noun *barroco*, which means an 'elaborately shaped pearl') was quickly 'tropicalized' in Cuba, with local architects adding

TRINIDAD'S COLONIAL ARCHITECTURE

Trinidad is one of the best-preserved colonial towns in the Americas. Most of its remarkably homogenous architecture dates from the early 19th century when Trinidad's sugar industry reached its zenith. Typical Trinidad houses are large one-storey buildings with terracotta-tiled roofs held up by wooden beams. Unlike in Havana, the huge front doors usually open directly into a main room rather than a vestibule. Other typical Trinidadian features include large glass-less windows fronted with wooden (or iron) bars, wall frescos, verandas, and balconies with wooden balustrades raised above the street. Larger Trinidad houses have mudéjar-style courtyards with trademark *aljibes* (storage wells).

1. Havana's Plaza Vieja (p72) **2.** Interior, Museo de la Revolución (p94), Havana **3.** View over Trinidad (p288)

their own personal flourishes to the new municipal structures that were springing up in various provincial cities. Indigenous features included: *rejas*, metal bars secured over windows to protect against burglaries and allow for a freer circulation of air; *vitrales*, multicolored glass panes fitted above doorways to pleasantly diffuse the tropical sun rays; *entresuelos*, mezzanine floors built to accommodate live-in slave families; and *portales*, galleried exterior walkways that provided pedestrians with shelter from the sun and the rain. Signature baroque buildings, such as the Palacio de los Capitanes Generales in Plaza de Armas in Havana were made from hard local limestone dug from the nearby San Lázaro quarries and constructed using slave labor. As a result, the intricate exterior decoration that characterized baroque architecture in Italy and Spain was noticeably toned down in Cuba, where local workers lacked the advanced stonemasonry skills of their more accomplished European cousins.

Some of the most exquisite baroque buildings in Cuba are found in Trinidad and date from the early decades of the 19th century when designs and furnishings were heavily influenced by the haute couture fashions of Italy, France and Georgian England.

Neoclassicism

Neoclassicism first evolved in the mid-18th century in Europe as a reaction to the lavish ornamentation and gaudy ostentation of baroque. Conceived in the progressive academies of London and Paris, the movement's early adherents advocated sharp primary colors and bold symmetrical lines, coupled with a desire to return to the perceived architectural 'purity' of ancient Greece and Rome. The style eventually reached Cuba at the beginning of the 19th century, spearheaded by groups of French émigrés who had fled west from Haiti following a violent slave rebellion in 1791. Within a couple of decades, neoclassicism

....

1. Capitolio Nacional (p77), Havana **2.** Colonial style in Cienfuegos (p243)

had established itself as the nation's dominant architectural style.

By the mid-19th century sturdy neoclassical buildings were the norm among Cuba's bourgeoisie in cities such as Cienfuegos and Matanzas, with striking symmetry, grandiose frontages and rows of imposing columns replacing the decorative baroque flourishes of the early colonial period.

Havana's first true neoclassical building was El Templete, a diminutive Doric temple constructed in Habana Vieja in 1828 next to the spot where Father Bartolomé de las Casas is said to have conducted the city's first Mass. As the city gradually spread westward in the mid-1800s, outgrowing its 17th-century walls, the style was adopted in the construction of more ambitious buildings, such as the famous Hotel Inglaterra overlooking Parque Central. Havana grew in both size and beauty during this period, bringing into vogue new residential design features such as spacious classical courtyards and rows of imposing street-facing colonnades, leading seminal Cuban novelist Alejo Carpentier to christen it the 'city of columns'.

A second neoclassical revival swept Cuba at the beginning of the 20th century, spearheaded by the growing influence of the US on the island. Prompted by the ideas and design ethics of the American Renaissance (1876–1914), Havana underwent a full-on building explosion, sponsoring such gigantic municipal buildings as the Capitolio Nacional and the Universidad de la Habana. In the provinces, the style reached its high-water mark in a series of glittering theaters.

Art Deco

Art deco was an elegant, functional and modern architectural movement that originated in France at the beginning of the 20th century and reached its apex in America in the 1920s and '30s. Drawing from a vibrant mix of Cubism, futurism and primitive African art, the genre promoted lavish yet streamlined buildings with sweeping curves and

HAVANA'S PARISIAN INFLUENCE

French landscape architect, Jean-Claude Forestier added a Parisian flavor to Havana's modern urban layout in the 1920s. Fresh from high profile commissions in the French capital, Forestier arrived in Havana in 1925 where he was invited to draw up a master-plan to link the city's disparate urban grid. He spent the next five years sketching broad tree-lined boulevards, Parisian-style squares and a harmonious city landscape designed to accentuate Havana's iconic monuments and lush tropical setting. Forestier's plans were unhinged by the Great Depression, but his Parisian vision was ultimately realized 30 years later with the construction of Plaza de la Revolución and its radiating avenues.

exuberant sun-burst motifs such as the Chrysler building in New York and the architecture of the South Beach neighborhood in Miami.

Brought to Cuba via the United States, the nation quickly acquired its own clutch of 'tropical' art deco buildings with the lion's share residing in Havana. One of Latin America's finest examples of early art deco is the Edifico Bacardí in Habana Vieja, built in 1930 to provide a Havana headquarters for Santiago de Cuba's world-famous rum-making family. Another striking creation was the 14-story Edificio López Serrano in Vedado, constructed as the city's first real *rascacielo* (skyscraper) in 1932, using New York's Rockefeller Center as its inspiration. Other more functional art deco skyscrapers followed, including the Teatro América on Av de la Italia, the Teatro Fausto on Paseo de Martí and the Casa de las Américas on Calle G. A more diluted and eclectic interpretation of the genre can be seen in the famous Hotel Nacional, whose sharp symmetrical lines and decorative twin Moorish turrets dominate the view over the Malecón.

1. A mint-hued facade, Trinidad (p288) **2.** Palacio de Valle (p247), Cienfuegos

Eclecticism

Eclecticism is the term often applied to the non-conformist and highly experimental architectural zeitgeist that grew up in the United States during the 1880s. Rejecting 19th-century ideas of 'style' and categorization, the architects behind this revolutionary new genre promoted flexibility and an open-minded 'anything goes' ethos, drawing their inspiration from a wide range of historical precedents.

Thanks to the strong US presence in the decades before 1959, Cuba quickly became a riot of modern eclecticism, with rich American and Cuban landowners constructing huge Xanadu-like mansions in burgeoning upper-class residential districts. Expansive, ostentatious and, at times, outlandishly kitschy, these fancy new homes were garnished with crenellated walls, oddly shaped lookout towers, rooftop cupolas and leering gargoyles. For a wild tour of Cuban eclecticism, head to Miramar in Havana, Alegre Vista in Santiago de Cuba and the Punta Gorda neighborhood in Cienfuegos.

BEST EXAMPLES OF ARCHITECTURAL STYLES

Early Colonial Museo de Pintura Mural (p73)

Baroque Catedral de San Cristóbal de la Habana (p63)

Neoclassical Capitolio Nacional (p77)

Art Deco Edificio Bacardí (p74)

Art Nouveau Palacio Cueto (p72)

Eclectic Palacio de Valle (p245)

Modernist Edificio Focsa (p87)

Gothic Iglesia del Sagrado Corazón de Jesús (p87)

continued from page 73

⊙ Habana Vieja: Southern Habana Vieja

Iglesia y Convento de Santa Clara CONVENT
(Map p64; Cuba No 610; admission CUC$2; ⊙ 9am-4pm Mon-Fri) South of Plaza Vieja is Havana's largest and oldest convent built between 1638 and 1643, though since 1920 it has served no religious purpose. For a while it housed the Ministry of Public Works, and today part of the Habana Vieja restoration team is based here. It was being renovated at the time of research.

**Iglesia y Convento de
Nuestra Señora de Belén** CONVENT
(Map p64; Compostela, btwn Luz & Acosta; ⊙ 9am-5pm Mon-Fri) This huge building was completed in 1718 and functioned first as a convalescent home and later as a Jesuit convent. It was abandoned in 1925 and fell into a disrepair exacerbated in 1991 by a damaging fire.

The City Historian reversed the decline in the late 1990s, using tourist coffers to make this splendid old building into an active community center for families, young people, the physically and mentally impaired, and the elderly (there are 18 permanent apartments for senior citizens here).

**Iglesia y Convento de
Nuestra Señora de la Merced** CHURCH
(Map p64; Cuba No 806; ⊙ 8am-noon & 3-5:30pm) Built in 1755, this hemmed-in church was reconstructed in the 19th century. Beautiful gilded altars, frescoed vaults and a number of old paintings create a sacrosanct mood; there's a quiet cloister adjacent. Two blocks away is the rather neglected **Iglesia Parroquial del Espíritu Santo** (Map p64; Acosta 161; ⊙ 8am-noon & 3-6pm), Havana's oldest surviving church, built in 1640 and rebuilt in 1674.

Iglesia de San Francisco de Paula CHURCH
(Map p64; cnr Leonor Pérez & Desamparados) One of Havana's most attractive churches, this building was fully restored in 2000. It is all that remains of the San Francisco de Paula women's hospital from the mid-1700s. Lit up at night for concerts, the stained glass, heavy cupola and baroque facade are romantic and inviting.

**Catedral Ortodoxa
Nuestra Señora de Kazán** CHURCH
(Map p64; Av Carlos Manuel de Céspedes, btwn Sol & Santa Clara) One of Havana's newest buildings, this beautiful gold-domed Russian Orthodox church was built in the early 2000s and consecrated at a ceremony attended by Raúl Castro in October 2008. The church was part of an attempt to reignite Russian-Cuban relations after they went sour in 1991.

Museo-Casa Natal de José Martí MUSEUM
(Map p64; Leonor Pérez No 314; admission CUC$1.50, camera CUC$2; ⊙ 9am-5pm Tue-Sat) Opened in 1925, this tiny museum bivouacked in the house where the apostle of Cuban independence was born on January 28, 1853 is considered to be the oldest in Havana. The City Historian's Office took the house over in 1994, and its succinct stash of exhibits devoted to Cuba's national hero continues to impress.

Old City Wall HISTORIC SITE
(Map p64) In the 17th century, anxious to defend the city from attacks by pirates and overzealous foreign armies, Cuba's paranoid colonial authorities drew up plans for the construction of a 5km-long city wall. Built between 1674 and 1740, the wall on completion was 1.5m thick and 10m high, running along a line now occupied by Av de las Misiones and Av de Bélgica.

Among the wall's myriad defenses were nine bastions and 180 big guns aimed toward the sea. The only way in and out of the city was through 11 heavily guarded gates that closed every night and opened every morning to the sound of a solitary gunshot. The walls were demolished starting in 1863, but a few segments remain, the largest of which stands on Av de Bélgica close to the train station.

⊙ Habana Vieja: Avenida de las Misiones

Edificio Bacardí LANDMARK
(Bacardí Building; Map p64; Av de las Misiones, btwn Empedrado & San Juan de Dios; ⊙ hours vary) Finished in 1929, the magnificent Edificio Bacardí is a triumph of art deco architecture with a whole host of lavish finishings that somehow manage to make kitsch look cool. Hemmed in by other buildings, it's hard to get a full kaleidoscopic view of the structure from street level, though the opulent bell tower can be glimpsed from all over Havana.

There's a bar in the lobby, and for CUC$1 you can travel up to the tower for an eagle's-eye view.

Iglesia del Santo Angel Custodio CHURCH
(Map p64; Compostela No 2; ⊙ during Mass 7:15am Tue, Wed & Fri, 6pm Thu, Sat & Sun) Originally constructed in 1695, this church was pounded by a ferocious hurricane in 1846, after which it was entirely rebuilt in neo-Gothic style. Among the notable historical and literary figures that have passed through its handsome doors are 19th-century Cuban novelist Cirilo Villaverde, who set the main scene of his novel *Cecilia Valdés* here, and Félix Varela and José Martí, who were baptized in the church in 1788 and 1853 respectively.

The church has been recently renovated, as have the pretty colonial houses facing Plazuela de Santo Ángel at the back.

◉ Parque Histórico Militar Morro-Cabaña

The sweeping views of Havana from the other side of the bay are spectacular, and a trip to the two old forts of the Parque Histórico Militar Morro-Cabaña is a must. Despite their location on the opposite side of the harbor, both forts are included in the Habana Vieja Unesco World Heritage Site. Sunset is a good time to visit when you can stay over for the emblematic *cañonazo* ceremony.

To get to the forts, use the P-15, P-8 or P-11 metro buses (get off at the first stop after the tunnel), but make sure you're near an exit as very few other people get out there. Otherwise, a metered tourist taxi from Habana Vieja should cost around CUC$4. Another alternative is via the Casablanca ferry, which departs from Av Carlos Manuel de Céspedes in Habana Vieja. From the Casablanca landing follow the road up to the huge Estatua de Cristo (Christ Statue), where you bear left and traverse another road past the Área Expositiva Crisis de Octubre. The entrance to La Cabaña is on your left.

Área Expositiva Crisis de Octubre
MONUMENT
(Map p86; admission CUC$1) Looking surprisingly innocuous today, the missiles that nearly caused World War III are laid out on a grassy knoll behind the Cabaña fort put there on the 50th anniversary of the Cuban Missile Crisis in 2012. Here you can ponder the Soviet R-12 nuclear rocket with a range of 2100km that was stationed in Pinar del Río in 1962 and caused the Kennedy

---

A BRITISH INTERLUDE

In 1762 Spain, hedging its bets in one of Europe's great colonial conflicts, joined on the side of France against the British in what became known as the Seven Years' War. For their important colony of Cuba it turned out to be a fatal omen. The mighty British Navy, sensing an opportunity to disrupt trade in Spain's economically lucrative Caribbean empire, promptly turned up uninvited off the coast of Havana on June 6, 1762 with over 50 ships and 20,000 men (the largest cross-Atlantic fleet ever amassed), intending to breach the supposedly impregnable El Morro castle and hence make both the city and Cuba a cricket-playing, Yorkshire pudding-eating colony of Britain.

Under the command of the 3rd Earl of Albemarle, the British caught the Spanish off-guard, landing 12,000 men near the village of Cojímar without the loss of a single British life and marching on nearby Guanabacoa where they established an important base and food supply. After a seaborne attack of El Morro failed (the castle was too high for the British cannons), Albemarle decided to attack the castle from the rear and had his army build bastions on the woefully unprotected Cabaña hill on the harbor's eastern side. From here the British fired relentlessly on the thick castle walls until, 44 days into the siege, the plucky but demoralized Spanish raised a white flag. With El Morro gone, it was only a matter of time before the walled city of Havana fell. From the captured castle, the British lobbed cannonballs across the harbor at La Punta fort until the city finally signaled it was ready to surrender, on August 13, 1762. Victory couldn't have come soon enough. Although Britain's military casualties were light, they had lost over 4000 men to tropical disease, mainly yellow fever.

The British occupation turned out to be brief but incisive. Within 11 months, with the Seven Years' War brought to an end by the Treaty of Paris, the British elected to swap Cuba for the Spanish colony of Florida, which would act as an important buffer for their American colonies to the north. Oh, how history could have been so different.

Parque Histórico Militar Morro-Cabaña

Parque Histórico Militar Morro-Cabaña

◎ Top Sights

◎ Sights

⊗ Eating

◎ Drinking & Nightlife

administration and the rest of the world plenty of sleepless nights.

Also on show is the wing of an American U2 spy plane shot down over Holguín province on October 27, 1962.

Castillo de los Tres Santos Reyes Magnos del Morro
FORT

(Map p86; El Morro; admission CUC$6) This imposing fort was erected between 1589 and 1630 in order to protect the entrance to Havana harbor from pirates and foreign invaders (the French corsair Jacques de Sores had sacked the city in 1555). Perched on a rocky bluff high above the Atlantic, the fort's irregular polygonal shape, 3m-thick walls and deep protective moat represent a classic example of Renaissance military architecture.

For more than a century the fort withstood numerous attacks by French, Dutch and English privateers, but in 1762, after a 44-day siege, a British force captured El Morro by attacking from the landward side. The Castillo's famous lighthouse was added in 1844.

Aside from the fantastic views over the sea and the city, El Morro also hosts a **maritime museum** (Map p86) that includes a riveting account of the fort's siege and eventual surrender to the British in 1762 using words (in English and Spanish) and paintings. To climb to the top of the **lighthouse** (admission CUC$2; ⊗8am-8pm) is an additional CUC$2.

★ **Fortaleza de San Carlos de la Cabaña** FORT

(Map p86; admission day/night CUC$6/8; ⊘ 8am-11pm) This 18th-century colossus was built between 1763 and 1774 on a long, exposed ridge on the east side of Havana harbor to fill a weakness in the city's defenses. In 1762 the British had taken Havana by gaining control of this strategically important ridge, and it was from here that they shelled the city mercilessly into submission.

In order to prevent a repeat performance, the Spanish King Carlos III ordered the construction of a massive fort that would repel future invaders. Measuring 700m from end to end and covering a whopping 10 hectares, it is the largest Spanish colonial fortress in the Americas.

The impregnability of the fort meant that no invader ever attacked it, though during the 19th century Cuban patriots faced firing squads here. Dictators Machado and Batista used the fortress as a military prison, and immediately after the Revolution Che Guevara set up his headquarters inside the ramparts to preside over another catalog of grisly executions (this time of Batista's officers).

These days the fort has been restored for visitors, and you can spend at least half a day checking out its wealth of attractions. As well as bars, restaurants, souvenir stalls and a cigar shop (containing the world's longest cigar), La Cabaña hosts the **Museo de Fortificaciones y Armas** (Map p86) and the engrossing **Museo de Comandancia del Che** (Map p86). The nightly 9pm **cañonazo ceremony** (Map p86) is a popular evening excursion in which actors dressed in full 18th-century military regalia reenact the firing of a cannon over the harbor. You can visit the ceremony independently or as part of an organized excursion.

⊙ Centro Habana

Capitolio Nacional LANDMARK

(Map p88; unguided/guided CUC$3/4; ⊘ 9am-8pm) The incomparable Capitolio Nacional is Havana's most ambitious and grandiose building, constructed after the 'Dance of the Millions' had gifted the Cuban government a seemingly bottomless treasure box of sugar money. Similar to the US Capitol Building in Washington, DC, but (marginally) taller and much richer in detail, the work was initiated by Cuba's US-backed dictator Gerardo Machado in 1926 and took 5000 work-ers three years, two months and 20 days to build at a cost of US$17 million.

Formerly it was the seat of the Cuban Congress, but since 1959 it has housed the Cuban Academy of Sciences and the National Library of Science and Technology.

Constructed with white Capellanía limestone and block granite, the entrance is guarded by six rounded Doric columns atop a staircase that leads up from the Prado. Looking out over the Havana skyline is a 62m stone cupola topped with a replica of 16th-century Florentine sculptor Giambologna's bronze statue of Mercury in the Palazzo de Bargello. Set in the floor directly below the dome is a copy of a 24-carat diamond. Highway distances between Havana and all sites in Cuba are calculated from this point.

The entryway opens up into the **Salón de los Pasos Perdidos** (Room of the Lost Steps; so named because of its unusual acoustics), at the center of which is the statue of the republic, an enormous bronze woman standing 11m tall and symbolizing the mythic Guardian of Virtue and Work.

The Capitolio has been undergoing lengthy renovations for two years and should open again in late 2013. Admission prices may change.

Real Fábrica de Tabacos Partagás HISTORIC BUILDING

(Map p88; Industria No 520, btwn Barcelona & Dragones; tours CUC$10; ⊘ tours every 15min 9-10:15am & noon-1:30pm) One of Havana's oldest and most famous cigar factories, the landmark neoclassical Real Fábrica de Tabacos Partagás was founded in 1845 by Spaniard Jaime Partagás. Today some 400 workers toil for up to 12 hours a day in here rolling such famous cigars as Montecristos and Cohibas. As far as tours go, Partagás is the most popular and reliable factory to visit.

Tour groups check out the ground floor first, where the leaves are unbundled and sorted, before proceeding to the upper floors to watch the tobacco get rolled, pressed, adorned with a band and boxed. Though interesting in an educational sense, the tours here are often rushed and a little robotic. Still, if you have even a passing interest in tobacco and/or Cuban work environments, it's probably worth a peep.

The factory was being renovated at the time of research, but was due to reopen 2013. You could visit it at its temporary location on the corner of Calles San Carlos and Penalver in Centro Habana.

Centro Habana

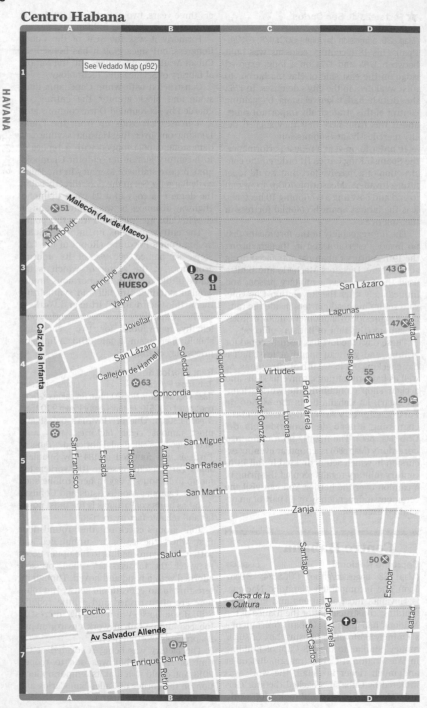

See Vedado Map (p92)

Malecón (Av de Maceo)

51

44 Humboldt

Principe

CAYO HUESO

Vapor

23 11

San Lázaro

43

Lagunas

Jovellar

Ánimas

47

Legaltad

San Lázaro

Callejón de Hamel

63

Soledad

Oquendo

Virtudes

Padre Varela

Gervasio

55

Concordia

Marqués Gonzáz

Lucena

29

65

Neptuno

San Francisco

Espada

Hospital

Aramburu

San Miguel

San Rafael

San Martín

Zanja

Salud

Santiago

50

Escobar

Pocito

Casa de la Cultura

Padre Varela

San Carlos

9

Av Salvador Allende

75

Enrique Barnet

Retiro

Lealtad

Calz de la Infanta

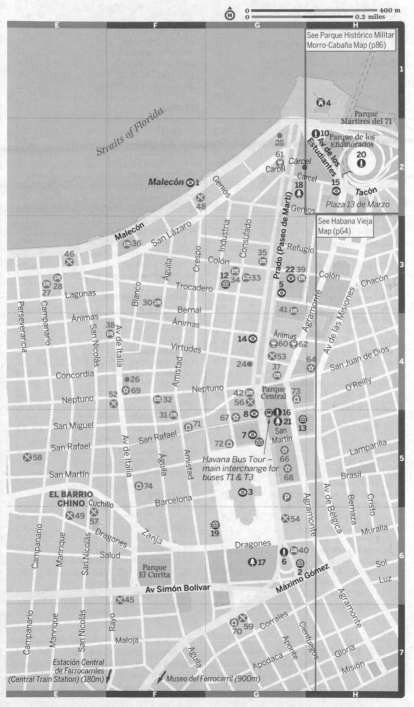

See Parque Histórico Militar Morro-Cabaña Map (p86)

See Habana Vieja Map (p64)

Straits of Florida

Malecón ◉ 1

Malecón

San Lázaro

Genios

Prado (Paseo de Martí)

Parque Mártires del 71

Parque de los Enamorados

Av de los Estudiantes

Tacón

Plaza 13 de Marzo

Cárcel

Refugio

Colón

Chacón

Av de las Misiones

Perseverancia

Campanario

San Nicolás

Av de Italia

Amistad

Agustín

Lagunas

Ánimas

Concordia

Neptuno

San Miguel

San Rafael

San Martín

EL BARRIO CHINO

Cuchillo

Dragones

Salud

Zanja

Barcelona

Parque El Curita

Av Simón Bolívar

Maloja

Crespo

Colón

Trocadero

Blanco

Bernal

Ánimas

Virtudes

Neptuno

San Rafael

Industria

Consulado

Parque Central

Ánimas

San Juan de Dios

O'Reilly

Lamparilla

Brasil

Muralla

Sol

Luz

Agramonte

Av de Bélgica

Bernaza

Cristo

Máximo Gómez

Dragones

Av de la Misiones

Havana Bus Tour – main interchange for buses T1 & T3

San Martín

Campanario

Manrique

San Nicolás

Rayo

Aguila

Corrales

Aponte

Cienfuegos

Apodaca

Agramonte

Gloria

Misión

Estación Central de Ferrocarriles (Central Train Station) (180m)

Museo del Ferrocarril (900m)

Centro Habana

Parque de la Fraternidad   PARK
(Map p88) Leafy Parque de la Fraternidad was established in 1892 to commemorate the fourth centenary of the Spanish landing in the Americas. A few decades later it was remodeled and renamed to mark the 1927 Pan-American Conference. The name is meant to signify American brotherhood, hence the many busts of Latin and North American leaders that embellish the green

areas, including one of US president **Abraham Lincoln**.

Today the park is the terminus of numerous metro bus routes, and is sometimes referred to as 'Jurassic Park' because of the plethora of photogenic old American cars now used as *colectivos* (collective taxis) that congregate here.

The **Fuente de la India** (Map p88; Paseo de Martí), on a traffic island across from the park, is a white Carrara marble fountain, carved by Giuseppe Gaginni in 1837 for the Count of Villanueva. It portrays a regal Indian woman adorned with a crown of eagle's feathers and seated on a throne surrounded by four gargoyle-like dolphins. In one hand she holds a horn-shaped basket filled with fruit, in the other a shield bearing the city's coat of arms.

**Asociación Cultural
Yoruba de Cuba**   MUSEUM
(Map p88; Paseo de Martí No 615; admission CUC$10; ⊘9am-4pm Mon-Sat) A museum that provides a worthwhile overview of the Santería religion, the saints and their powers, although some travelers have complained that the exhibits don't justify the price. There are *tambores* (Santería drum ceremonies) on alternate Fridays at 4:30pm. Note that there's a church dress code for the *tambores* (no shorts or tank tops). For groups of two or more entry is CUC$6 each.

Parque Central & Around   PARK
(Map p88) Diminutive Parque Central is a scenic haven from the belching buses and roaring taxis that ply their way along the Prado. The park, long a microcosm of daily Havana life, was expanded to its present size in the late 19th century after the city walls were knocked down. The marble statue of José Martí (Map p88) (1905) at its center was the first of thousands to be erected in Cuba.

Raised on the 10th anniversary of the poet's death, the monument is ringed by 28 palm trees planted to signify Martí's birth date: January 28. Hard to miss over to one side is the group of baseball fans who linger 24/7 at the famous **Esquina Caliente**, discussing form, tactics and the Havana teams' prospects in the play-offs.

Gran Teatro de la Habana   THEATER
(Map p88; Paseo de Martí No 458; guided tours CUC$2; ⊘9am-6pm) 'A style without style that in the long run, by symbiosis, by amalgamation, becomes baroquism.' So wrote

Cuban novelist and sometime architectural dabbler, Alejo Carpentier, of the ornate neo-baroque **Centro Gallego** erected as a Galician social club between 1907 and 1914. The Centro was built around the existing Teatro Tacón, which opened in 1838 with five masked Carnaval dances.

This connection is the basis of claims by the present 2000-seat theater that it's the oldest operating theater in the Western hemisphere. History notwithstanding, the architecture is brilliant, as are many of the weekend performances.

The theater was being renovated at the time of writing with performances switched to the Teatro Nacional in Plaza de la Revolución.

Hotel Inglaterra   NOTABLE BUILDING
(Map p88; Paseo de Martí No 416) Havana's oldest hotel first opened its doors in 1856 on the site of a popular bar called El Louvre (the hotel's alfresco bar still bears the name). Facing leafy Parque Central, the building exhibits the neoclassical design features in vogue at the time, although the interior decor is distinctly Moorish. At a banquet here in 1879, José Martí made a speech advocating Cuban independence, and much later US journalists covering the Spanish-Cuban-American War stayed at the hotel.

Just behind lies **Calle San Rafael**, a riot of peso stalls, 1950s department stores and local cinemas, which gives an immediate insight into everyday life in economically challenged Cuba.

★**Museo Nacional de Bellas Artes** MUSEUM
Cuba has a huge art culture, and at this dual-site art museum you can spend a whole day viewing everything from Greek ceramics to Cuban pop art.

Arranged inside the fabulously eclectic Centro Asturianas (a work of art in its own right), the **Museo Nacional de Bellas Artes (Arte Universal)** (Map p88) exhibits international art from 500 BC to the present day on three separate floors. Highlights include an extensive Spanish collection (with a canvas by El Greco), some 2000-year-old Roman mosaics, Greek pots from the 5th century BC and a suitably refined Gainsborough canvas (in the British room).

The **Museo Nacional de Bellas Artes (Arte Cubano)** (Map p64; Trocadero, btwn Agramonte & Av de las Misiones; adult/under 14yr CUC$5/free; ⊘9am-5pm Tue-Sat, 10am-2pm Sun) displays purely Cuban art and, if

Vedado

Straits of Florida

Malecón

C 1

C 3

C 5

37

34

56

50

23

Calzada

Casa de
la Cultura
de Plaza

Línea

24

C 11

C 4

C 6

C 8

C 10

C 12

C 14

C 16

C 18

C 20

C 22

C 24

C 26

C 28

Río Almendares

Río Almendares

C 23

Calz de Zapata

C 2

Paseo

C A

C B

C C

C D

C E

C 13

C 17

C 19

C 21

C 35

C Loma

58

44

88

75

68

73

82

60

85

93

95

81

72

94

55

77

98

99

63

71

12

3

38

36

48

Necrópolis
Cristóbal Colón

19

See Playa & Marianao
Map (p134)

San Antonio
Chiquito

NUEVO
VEDADO

C 26

La Torre

C 24

Viazul (1km)

51

19 de
Noviembre
(200m)

Protestantes

Bellavista

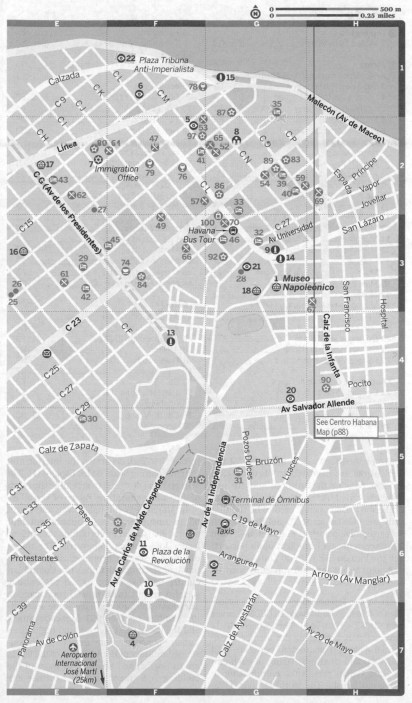

0 — 500 m
0 — 0.25 miles

22 Plaza Tribuna Anti-Imperialista

Calzada

C K
CL
6
CM
78
15

C 9
C J
C I
35

5
53
87
8

C H
97
65
CO
CP

Línea
47
52

80 61
7
Immigration Office
79
41
89 83

17
76
54 39 59
40
69

43
86

62
C L
57
33

27
Espada
Príncipe
Vapor
Jovellar
San Lázaro

49
100 70
C 27
Av Universidad

C 15
Havana — Bus Tour
46
32
9
14

16
45
74
66
92
21

29
28
1 Museo Napoleónico

26
61
84
18

25
42
67

C 23

C F

13

90
Pocito

20

Av Salvador Allende

See Centro Habana Map (p88)

C 25

C 27

C 29
30

Calz de Zapata

C 31

C 33
91
31

C 35
Pozos Dulces
Bruzón
Luaces

Paseo
Terminal de Ómnibus

C 37
96
Taxis
C 19 de Mayo

Protestantes

11
Plaza de la Revolución
Aranguren

2
Arroyo (Av Manglar)

10

C 39

Panorama

4

Av de Colón
Aeropuerto Internacional José Martí (25km)

Calz de Ayestarán

Av 20 de Mayo

Av de Carlos de Máde Céspedes

Av de la Independencia

Malecón (Av de Maceo)

C G (Av de los Presidentes)

C N

C L

Hospital

San Francisco

Calz de la Infanta

Vedado

you're pressed for time, is the better of the duo. Works are displayed in chronological order starting on the 3rd floor and are surprisingly varied. Artists to look out for are Guillermo Collazo, considered to be the first truly great Cuban artist; Rafael Blanco with his cartoonlike paintings and sketches; Raúl Martínez, a master of 1960s Cuban pop art; and the Picasso-like Wifredo Lam.

A joint ticket for both museums can be purchased for CUC$8.

Museo de la Revolución   MUSEUM
(Map p64; Refugio No 1; admission CUC$6, camera extra CUC$2; ◎9am-5pm) The Museo de la Revolución is housed in the former Presidential Palace, constructed between 1913 and 1920 and used by a string of cash-embezzling Cuban presidents, culminating in Fulgencio Batista. The world-famous Tiffa-

ny's of New York decorated the interior, and the shimmering Salón de los Espejos (Hall of Mirrors) was designed to resemble the room of the same name at the Palace of Versailles.

In March 1957 the palace was the target of an unsuccessful assassination attempt against Batista led by revolutionary student leader José Antonio Echeverría. The museum itself descends chronologically from the top floor starting with Cuba's pre-Columbian culture and extending to the present-day socialist regime (with *mucho* propaganda). The downstairs rooms have some interesting exhibits on the 1953 Moncada attack and the life of Che Guevara, and highlight a Cuban penchant for displaying blood-stained military uniforms. Most of the labels are in English and Spanish. In front of the building is a fragment of the former city wall, as well as an SAU-100 tank used by Castro during the 1961 battle of the Bay of Pigs.

In the space behind the museum you'll find the Pavillón Granma (Map p64), a memorial to the 18m yacht that carried Fidel Castro and 81 other revolutionaries from Tuxpán, Mexico, to Cuba in December 1956. It's encased in glass and guarded 24 hours a day, presumably to stop anyone from breaking in and making off for Florida in it. The pavilion is surrounded by other vehicles associated with the Revolution and is accessible from the Museo de la Revolución.

Prado (Paseo de Martí) STREET

Construction of this stately European-style boulevard – the first street outside the old city walls – began in 1770, and the work was completed in the mid-1830s during the term of Captain General Miguel Tacón (1834–38).

The original idea was to create a boulevard as splendid as any found in Paris or Barcelona (Prado owes more than a passing nod to Las Ramblas). The famous bronze lions that guard the central promenade at either end were added in 1928.

Notable Prado buildings include the neo-Renaissance Palacio de los Matrimonios (Map p88; Paseo de Martí No 302), the streamline-modern Teatro Fausto (Map p88; cnr Paseo de Martí & Colón) and the neoclassical Escuela Nacional de Ballet (Map p88; cnr Paseo de Martí & Trocadero), Alicia Alonso's famous ballet school.

Statue of General Máximo Gómez MONUMENT

(Map p88; Malecón cnr Paseo de Martí) On a large traffic island overlooking the mouth of the harbor is a rather grand statue on the right-hand side. Gómez was a war hero from the Dominican Republic who fought tirelessly for Cuban independence in both the 1868 and 1895 conflicts against the Spanish. The impressive statue of him sitting atop a horse was created by Italian artist Aldo Gamba in 1935 and faces heroically out to sea.

Museo Lezama Lima   MUSEUM
(Map p88; Trocadero No 162, cnr Industria; unguided/guided CUC$1/2; ⊙9am-5pm Tue-Sat, 9am-1pm Sun) The modest book-filled house of the late Cuban man of letters, José Lezama Lima, is an obligatory pit stop for anyone attempting to understand Cuban literature beyond Hemingway. Lima's magnus opus was the rambling classic, *Paradiso,* and he wrote most of it here.

Parque de los Enamorados   PARK
(Map p88) Preserved in Parque de los Enamorados (Lovers' Park), surrounded by streams of speeding traffic, lies a surviving section of the colonial Cárcel or Tacón Prison, built in 1838, where many Cuban patriots including José Martí were imprisoned.

A brutal place that sent unfortunate prisoners off to perform hard labor in the nearby San Lázaro quarry, the prison was finally demolished in 1939 with this park dedicated to the memory of those who had suffered so horribly within its walls. Two tiny cells and an equally minute chapel are all that remain. The beautiful wedding cake-like building (art nouveau with a dash of eclecticism) behind the park, flying the Spanish flag, is the old Palacio Velasco (Map p88) (1912), now the Spanish embassy.

Beyond that is the Memorial a los Estudiantes de Medicina (Map p88), a fragment of wall encased in marble marking the spot where eight Cuban medical students were shot by the Spanish in 1871 as a reprisal for allegedly desecrating the tomb of a Spanish journalist (in fact, they didn't do it).

Castillo de San Salvador de la Punta   FORT
(Map p88; museum admission CUC$6; ⊙museum 10am-6pm Wed-Sun) One in a quartet of forts defending Havana harbor, La Punta was designed by the Italian military engineer Giovanni Bautista Antonelli and built between 1589 and 1600. During the colonial era a chain was stretched 250m to the castle of El Morro every night to close the harbor mouth to shipping.

The castle's museum displays artifacts from sunken Spanish treasure fleets, a collection of model ships and information on the slave trade.

El Barrio Chino   NEIGHBORHOOD
One of the world's more surreal Chinatowns, Havana's Barrio Chino is notable for its gaping lack of Chinese people, most of whom left as soon as a newly inaugurated Fidel Castro uttered the word *'socialismo.'* Nevertheless, it's worth a wander on the basis of its novelty and handful of decent restaurants.

The first Chinese arrived as contract laborers on the island in the late 1840s to fill in the gaps left by the decline of the transatlantic slave trade. By the 1920s Havana's Chinatown had burgeoned into the biggest Asian neighborhood in Latin America, a bustling hub of human industry that spawned its own laundries, pharmacies, theaters and grocery stores. The slide began in the early 1960s when thousands of business-minded Chinese relocated to the US. Recognizing the tourist potential of the area in the 1990s, the Cuban government invested money and resources into rejuvenating the district's distinct historical character with bilingual street signs, a large pagoda-shaped arch at the entrance to Calle Dragones, and incentives given to local Chinese businesspeople to promote restaurants. Today most of the action centers on the narrow Calle Cuchillo and its surrounding streets.

⊙ Vedado

Vedado (known officially as the municipality of 'Plaza de la Revolution') is Havana's commercial hub and archetypal residential district, older than Playa but newer than Centro Habana. The first houses penetrated this formerly protected forest reserve in the 1860s, with the real growth spurt beginning in the 1920s and continuing until the 1950s.

Laid out in a near-perfect grid, Vedado has more of a North American feel than other parts of the Cuban capital, and its small clutch of *rascacielos* (skyscrapers) – which draw their inspiration from the art deco giants of Miami and New York – are largely a product of Cuba's 50-year dance with the US.

During the 1940s and 1950s, Vedado was a louche and tawdry place where Havana's prerevolutionary gambling party reached its heady climax. The Hotel Nacional once boasted a Las Vegas–style casino, the ritzy

Hotel Riviera was the former stomping ground of influential mobster Meyer Lansky, while the now empty Hotel Capri was masterfully managed by Hollywood actor (and sometime mob associate) George Raft. Everything changed in January 1959 when Fidel Castro rolled into town with his army of bearded rebels in tow and set up shop on the 24th floor of the spanking-new Havana Hilton hotel (promptly renamed Hotel Habana Libre).

Today, Vedado has a population of approximately 175,000, and its leafy residential pockets are interspersed with myriad theaters, nightspots, paladares (privately run restaurants) and restaurants. Bisected by two wide Parisian-style boulevards, Calle G and Paseo, its geometric grid is embellished by a liberal sprinkling of pleasant parks and the gargantuan Plaza de la Revolución laid out during the Batista era in the 1950s.

Iglesia del Sagrado Corazón de Jesús   CHURCH

(Map p88; Av Simón Bolívar, btwn Gervasio & Padre Varela) A little out on a limb but well worth the walk is this inspiring marble creation with a distinctive white steeple – it's one of Cuba's few Gothic buildings. The church is rightly famous for its magnificent stained-glass windows, and the light that penetrates through the eaves first thing in the morning (when the church is deserted) gives the place an ethereal quality.

Hotel Nacional   NOTABLE BUILDING

(Map p92; cnr Calles O & 21) Built in 1930 as a copy of the Breakers Hotel in Palm Beach, Florida, the eclectic art deco/neoclassical Hotel Nacional is a national monument and one of Havana's 'postcard' sights.

The hotel's notoriety was cemented in October 1933 when, following a sergeant's coup by Fulgencio Batista that toppled the regime of Gerardo Machado, 300 aggrieved army officers took refuge in the building hoping to curry favor with resident US ambassador, Sumner Wells, who was staying there. Much to the officers' chagrin, Wells promptly left, allowing Batista's troops to open fire on the hotel, killing 14 of them and injuring seven. More were executed later, after they had surrendered.

In December 1946 the hotel gained notoriety of a different kind when US mobsters Meyer Lansky and Lucky Luciano used it to host the largest ever get-together of the North American Mafia, who gathered here under the guise of a Frank Sinatra concert.

These days the hotel maintains a more reputable face and the once famous casino is long gone, though the kitschy Parisién cabaret is still a popular draw. Nonguests are welcome to admire the Moorish lobby, stroll the breezy grounds overlooking the Malecón and examine the famous photos of past guests on the walls inside.

Hotel Habana Libre   NOTABLE BUILDING

(Map p92; Calle L, btwn Calles 23 & 25) This classic modernist hotel – the former Havana Hilton – was commandeered by Castro's revolutionaries in 1959 just nine months after it had opened, and promptly renamed the Habana Libre. During the first few months of the Revolution, Fidel ruled the country from a luxurious suite on the 24th floor.

A 670-sq-meter Venetian tile mural by Amelia Peláez is splashed across the front of the building, while upstairs Alfredo Sosa Bravo's *Carro de la Revolución* utilizes 525 ceramic pieces. There are some good shops here and an interesting photo gallery inside, displaying snaps of the all-conquering *barbudas* (literally 'bearded ones') lolling around with their guns in the hotel's lobby in January 1959.

Edificio Focsa   LANDMARK

(Focsa Building; Map p92; cnr Calles 17 & M) Unmissable on the Havana skyline, the modernist Edificio Focsa was built between 1954 and 1956 in a record 28 months using pioneering computer technology. In 1999 it was listed as one of the seven modern engineering wonders of Cuba. With 39 floors housing 373 apartments, it was, on its completion in June 1956, the second-largest concrete structure of its type in the world, constructed entirely without the use of cranes.

Falling on hard times in the early 1990s, the upper floors of the Focsa became nests for vultures, and in 2000 an elevator cable snapped, killing one person. Rejuvenated once more after a restoration project, this skyline-dominating Havana giant nowadays contains residential apartments and – in the shape of top-floor restaurant La Torre – one of the city's most celebrated eating establishments.

Hotel Capri   RUIN

(Map p92; Calle 21, cnr Calle N) Some cities sport Roman ruins. Havana, on the other hand, has 1950s ruins. The not-so-ancient Capri was built in modernist style with Mafia money in 1957. In its (brief) heyday, the hotel was owned by mobster Santo Trafficante who used American actor George Raft as his debonair front-man. When Castro's guerrillas came knocking in January 1959, Raft allegedly told them where to stick it and slammed the door in their faces.

The hotel, with its rooftop pool has featured in two movies: Carol Reed's *Our Man in Havana* and Mikhael Kalatazov's *Soy Cuba*. It was also the setting for Michael Corleone's meeting with Hyman Roth in *The Godfather: Part II,* though, due to the embargo, Coppola shot the scenes in the Dominican Republic. Closed in 2003, the Capri is now a 19-story ruin getting ready for its second coming.

Universidad de la Habana   UNIVERSITY
(Map p92; cnr Calle L & San Lázaro) Founded by Dominican monks in 1728 and secularized in 1842, Havana University began life in Habana Vieja before moving to its present site in 1902. The existing neoclassical complex dates from the second quarter of the 20th century, and today some 30,000 students follow courses in social sciences, humanities, natural sciences, mathematics and economics here.

Perched on a Vedado hill at the top of the famous *escalinata* (stairway), near the **Alma Mater statue**, the university's central quadrangle, the Plaza Ignacio Agramonte, displays a tank captured by Castro's rebels in 1958. Directly in front is the **Librería Alma Mater** (library) and, to the left, the **Museo de Historia Natural Felipe Poey** (Map p92; admission CUC$1; ⊗9am-noon & 1-4pm Mon-Fri Sep-Jul), the oldest museum in Cuba, founded in 1874 by the Royal Academy of Medical, Physical and Natural Sciences. Many of the stuffed specimens of Cuban flora and fauna date from the 19th century. Upstairs is the **Museo Antropológico Montané** (Map p92; admission CUC$1; ⊗9am-noon & 1-4pm Mon-Fri Sep-Jul), established in 1903, with a rich collection of pre-Columbian Indian artifacts including the wooden 10th-century Ídolo del Tabaco.

Monumento a Julio Antonio Mella   MONUMENT
(Map p92; cnr Neptuno & San Lázaro) At the bottom of the university steps there is a monument to the student leader who founded the first Cuban Communist Party in 1925. In 1929 the dictator Machado had Mella assassinated in Mexico City. More interesting than the monument itself are the black-and-white **Mella portraits** (Map p92) permanently mounted on the wall in the little park across San Lázaro.

★**Museo Napoleónico**   MUSEUM
(Map p92; San Miguel No 1159; unguided/guided CUC$3/5; ⊗9am-4:30pm Tue-Sat) Without a doubt, one of the best museums in Havana and, by definition, Cuba, this magnificently laid out collection of 7000 objects associated with the life of Napoleon Bonaparte was amassed by Cuban sugar baron Julio Lobo and politician Orestes Ferrera.

Highlights include sketches of Voltaire, paintings of the battle of Waterloo, china, furniture, an interesting recreation of Napoleon's study and bedroom, and one of several bronze Napoleonic death masks made two days after the emperor's death by his personal physician, Dr Francisco Antommarchi. It's set over four floors of a beautiful Vedado mansion next to the university and has stunning views from its 4th-floor terrace.

Museo de Artes Decorativas   MUSEUM
(Map p92; Calle 17 No 502, btwn Calles D & E; admission CUC$2; ⊗11am-7pm Tue-Sat) Worth checking out if you're in the neighborhood (it's a little out of the way) is this decorative arts museum with its fancy rococo, oriental and art deco baubles. Perhaps more interesting is the building itself, of French design, commissioned in 1924 by the wealthy Gómez family (who built the Manzana de Gómez shopping center in Centro Habana).

Museo de Danza   MUSEUM
(Map p92; Línea No 365; admission CUC$2; ⊗10am-6pm Tue-Sat) A dance museum in Cuba – well, there's no surprise there. This longstanding place in an eclectic Vedado mansion collects objects from Cuba's rich dance history, including some personal effects of ex-ballerina, Alicia Alonso.

Plaza de la Revolución   SQUARE
Conceived by French urbanist Jean Claude Forestier in the 1920s, the gigantic Plaza de la Revolución (known as Plaza Cívica until 1959) was part of Havana's 'new city,' which grew up between 1920 and 1959. As the nexus of Forestier's ambitious plan, the square was built on a small hill (the Loma de los Catalanes) in the manner of Paris' Place de Étoile, with various avenues fanning out toward the Río Almendares, Vedado and the Parque de la Fraternidad in Centro Habana.

Surrounded by gray, utilitarian buildings constructed in the late 1950s, the square today is the base of the Cuban government and a place where large-scale political rallies are held. In January 1998, one million people (nearly one-tenth of the Cuban population) crammed into the square to hear Pope Jean Paul II say Mass.

The ugly concrete block on the northern side of the plaza is the **Ministerio del Interior** (Map p92; Plaza de la Revolución), well known for its huge mural of Che Guevara (a copy of Alberto Korda's famous photograph taken in 1960) with the words Hasta la Victoria Siempre (Always Toward Victory) emblazoned underneath. In 2009 a similarly designed image of Cuba's other heroic *guerrillero*, Camilo Cienfuegos, was added on the adjacent telecommunications building.

On the eastern side is the 1957 **Biblioteca Nacional José Martí** (Map p92; admission free; ☺8am-9:45pm Mon-Sat), which has a photo exhibit in the lobby, while on the west is the Teatro Nacional de Cuba (p102).

Tucked behind the Martí Memorial are the governmental offices housed in the heavily guarded **Comité Central del Partido Comunista de Cuba** (Map p92; Plaza de la Revolución).

Memorial a José Martí   MONUMENT
(Map p92; admission CUC$5; ☺9:30am-5pm Mon-Sat) Center-stage in Plaza de la Revolución is this monument, which at 138.5m is Havana's tallest structure. Fronted by an impressive 17m marble statue of a seated Martí in a pensive *Thinker* pose, the memorial houses a **museum** – the definite word on Martí in Cuba – and a 129m lookout (reached via a small CUC$2 lift) with fantastic city views.

Quinta de los Molinos   LANDMARK
(Map p92; cnr Av Salvador Allende & Luaces) The former stately residence of General Máximo Gómez, the Quinta sits amid lush botanical gardens on land that once belonged to Havana University. The residence and grounds seem to be stuck in a perennial renovation project, with promises of a new museum and touched-up botanical gardens in the ever-distant future. The potential is huge.

Necrópolis Cristóbal Colón   CEMETERY
(Map p92; admission CUC$5; ☺8am-5pm) Once described as an 'exercise in pious excesses,' this cemetery (a national monument) is renowned for its striking religious iconography and elaborate marble statues. Far from being eerie, a walk through these 56 hallowed hectares can be an educational and emotional stroll through the annals of Cuban history. A guidebook with a detailed map (CUC$5) is for sale at the entrance.

It's one of the largest cemeteries in the Americas. After entering the neo-Romanesque **northern gateway** (1870), there's the tomb of independence leader **General Máximo Gómez** (1905) on the right (look for the bronze face in a circular medallion). Further along past the first circle, and also on the right, are the **monument to the firefighters** (1890) and the neo-Romanesque **Capilla Central** (1886) in the center of the cemetery. Just northeast of this chapel is the graveyard's most celebrated (and visited) tomb, that of **Señora Amelia Goyri** (cnr Calles 1 & F), better known as La Milagrosa (the miraculous one), who died while giving birth on May 3, 1901. The marble figure of a woman with a large cross and a baby in her arms is easy to find due to the many flowers piled on the tomb and the local devotees in attendance. For many years after her death, her heartbroken husband visited the grave several times a day. He always knocked with one of four iron rings on the burial vault and walked away backwards so he could see her for as long as possible. When the bodies were exhumed some years later, Amelia's body was uncorrupted (a sign of sanctity in the Catholic faith) and the baby, who had been buried at its mother's feet, was allegedly found in her arms. As a result, La Milagrosa became the focus of a huge spiritual cult in Cuba, and thousands of people come here annually with gifts in the hope of fulfilling dreams or solving problems. In keeping with tradition, pilgrims knock with the iron ring on the vault and walk away backwards when they leave.

Also worth seeking out is the tomb of Orthodox Party leader **Eduardo Chibás** (Calle 8, btwn Calles E & F). During the 1940s and early 1950s Chibás was a relentless crusader against political corruption, and as a personal protest he committed suicide during a radio broadcast in 1951. At his burial ceremony a young Orthodox Party activist named Fidel Castro jumped atop Chibás' grave and made a fiery speech denouncing the old establishment – the political debut of the most influential Cuban of the 20th century.

Also worth looking out for are the graves of novelist Alejo Carpentier (1904–80), scientist Carlos Finlay (1833–1915), the Martyrs of Granma and the Veterans of the Independence Wars.

★ **Malecón** STREET

(Map p88) The Malecón, Havana's evocative 8km-long sea drive, is one of the city's most soulful and quintessentially Cuban thoroughfares. Long a favored meeting place for assorted lovers, philosophers, poets, traveling minstrels, fishermen and wistful Florida-gazers, the Malecón's atmosphere is most potent at sunset when the weak yellow light from creamy Vedado filters like a dim torch onto the buildings of Centro Habana, lending their dilapidated facades a distinctly ethereal quality.

Laid out in the early 1900s as a salubrious ocean-side boulevard for Havana's pleasure-seeking middle classes, the Malecón expanded rapidly eastward in the century's first decade with a mishmash of eclectic architecture that mixed sturdy neoclassicism with whimsical art nouveau. By the 1920s the road had reached the outer limits of burgeoning Vedado, and by the early 1950s it had metamorphosed into a busy six-lane highway that carried streams of wave-dodging Buicks and Chevrolets from the gray hulk of the Castillo de San Salvador de la Punta to the borders of Miramar. Today the Malecón remains Havana's most authentic open-air theater, a real-life 'cabaret of the poor' where the whole city comes to meet, greet, date and debate.

Fighting an ongoing battle with the corrosive effects of the ocean, many of the thoroughfare's magnificent buildings now face decrepitude, demolition or irrevocable damage. To combat the problem, 14 blocks of the Malecón have been given special status by the City Historian's Office in an attempt to stop the rot.

The Malecón is particularly evocative when a cold front blows in and massive waves crash thunderously over the sea wall. The road is often closed to cars at these times, meaning you can walk right down the middle of the empty thoroughfare and get very wet.

Monumento a Antonio Maceo MONUMENT

(Map p88) Lying in the shadow of Hospital Nacional Hermanos Ameijeiras, a Soviet-era 24-story hospital built in 1980, is this bronze representation of the *mulato* general who cut a blazing trail across the entire length of Cuba during the First War of Independence. The nearby 18th-century **Torreón de San Lázaro** (Map p88; cnr Malecón & Vapor) is a watchtower that quickly fell to the British during the invasion of 1762.

Monumento a las Víctimas del Maine MONUMENT

(Map p92; Malecón) West beyond Hotel Nacional is a monument to the victims of USS *Maine*, the battleship that blew up mysteriously in Havana harbor in 1898. Once crowned by an American eagle, the monument (first raised during the American-dominated period in 1926) was decapitated during the 1959 Revolution.

US Interests Section LANDMARK

(Map p92; Calzada, btwn Calles L & M) The modern seven-story building with the high security fencing at the western end of this open space is the US Interests Section, first set up by the Carter administration in the late 1970s. Surrounded by hysterical graffiti, the building is the site of some of the worst tit-for-tat finger-wagging on the island.

Facing the office front is **Plaza Tribuna Anti-Imperialista** (also known as Plaza de la Dignidad), built during the Elián González saga in 2000 to host major protests under the nose of the Americans. The mass of flag-poles were put up by the Cubans to block out an electronic message board mounted on the Interests Section that flashed up messages, or propaganda, depending on which side you're on (yawn!).

Edificio López Serrano LANDMARK

(Map p92; Calle L, btwn Calles 11 & 13) Tucked away behind the US Interests Section is this art deco tower, which looks like the Empire State with the bottom 70 floors chopped off. One of Havana's first *rascacielos* when it was built in 1932, the López Serrano building now houses apartments.

Av de los Presidentes STREET

Statues of illustrious Latin American leaders line the Las Ramblas–style Calle G (officially known as Av de los Presidentes), including Salvador Allende (Chile), Benito Juárez (Mexico) and Simón Bolívar. At the top of the avenue is a huge marble **Monumento a José Miguel Gómez** (Map p92), Cuba's second president. At the other end, the monument to his predecessor – Cuba's first president – Tomás Estrada Palma (long considered a US puppet) has been toppled, and all that remains are his shoes on a **plinth**.

Guarding the entrance to Calle G on the Malecón is the equestrian **Monumento a Calixto García** (Map p92; cnr Malecón & Calle G), paying homage to the valiant Cuban general who was prevented by US military leaders in Santiago de Cuba from attending the Spanish surrender in 1898. Twenty-four bronze plaques around the statue provide a history of García's 30-year struggle for Cuban independence.

Casa de las Américas　　CULTURAL BUILDING
(Map p92; www.casa.cult.cu; cnr Calles 3 & G; ⊙10am-4:40pm Tue-Sat, 9am-1pm Sun) **FREE** Just off the Malecón at the ocean end of Calle G, this cultural institution was set up by Moncada survivor Haydee Santamaría in 1959 and awards one of Latin America's oldest and most prestigious literary prizes. Inside there's an art gallery, a bookstore and an atmosphere of erudite intellectualism.

Gran Synagoga Bet Shalom　　SYNAGOGUE
(Map p92; Calle I No 251, btwn Calles 13 & 15) Cuba has three synagogues servicing a Jewish population of approximately 1500. The main community center and library are located here, where the friendly staff would be happy to tell interested visitors about the fascinating and little-reported history of the Jews in Cuba.

Museo del Ferrocarril　　MUSEUM
(cnr Av de México & Arroyo; admission CUC$2; ⊙9am-5pm) A peripheral museum housed in the old Cristina train station built in 1859. There's a big collection of signaling and communication gear here plus old locos and an overview of Cuba's pioneering railway history. Train rides are possible by prior appointment.

 Activities

Havana's two marinas, which offer numerous fishing, diving and boating opportunities, lie in its outer suburbs (p132).

Havana, with its spectacular Malecón sea drive, possesses one of the world's most scenic municipal jogging routes. The path from the Castillo de San Salvador de la Punta to the outer borders of Miramar measures 8km, though you can add on a few extra meters for holes in the pavement, splashing waves, veering *jineteros* (touts) and old men with fishing lines. The recent upsurge in fume-belching traffic has meant that the air along the Malecón has become increasingly polluted. If you can handle it, run first thing in the morning.

Boxing enthusiasts should check out **Gimnasio de Boxeo Rafael Trejo** (Map p64; ☑862-0266; Cuba No 815, btwn Merced & Leonor Pérez, Habana Vieja). At this boxing gym you

---

VAS BIEN, FIDEL
· ·

Conscientious students who paid attention in school history lessons will already be well-acquainted with Che Guevara whose famous visage decorates the Ministerio del Interior building in the Plaza de la Revolución. But non-Cubans could be forgiven for scratching their heads at the identity of the square's other humungous mural: that of Camilo Cienfuegos, with the words 'Vas bien, Fidel' inscribed beneath it.

Cienfuegos is one of history's 'what if?' figures. A leading commander in the revolutionary war he was second only to Fidel in popularity when the victorious rebels swarmed into Havana in January 1959. During Fidel's first public speech in Camp Columbia, it was Camilo who stood behind the pontificating *comandante* on the podium. At one point during his two-hour oration, Fidel turned around to Cienfuegos and asked, 'Voy bien Camilo?' (Am I doing OK, Camilo?), to which a smiling Camilo replied 'Vas bien Fidel' (You're doing OK, Fidel). The phrase quickly became a rallying cry for the revolution and was reinforced when someone in the crowd released a cage of white doves, one of which landed on Fidel's shoulder (in the Santería religion white doves represent Otabalá, the *orisha* of peace and intellect which to the superstitious Cubans seemed to give Castro a divine calling).

Though a loyal revolutionary and leftist, Cienfuegos was less dogmatic than Guevara and Castro in his political views. How he would have handled the leftward drift of the revolution post-1960 can never be verified. Cienfuegos was killed in a plane crash in October 1959 on his way to Havana from Camagüey. If he were alive today he would be 81. One can only guess how he might answer Fidel today if the old warrior shuffled around and said, 'Voy bien, Camilo?'

can see fights on Friday at 7pm (CUC$1), or drop by any day after 4pm to watch the training. Travelers interested in boxing can find a trainer here. Enquire within; they're very friendly.

Courses

Aside from Spanish-language courses, Havana offers a large number of learning activities for aspiring students. Private lessons can be arranged by asking around locally – try your casa particular. Your casa particular can also probably point you in the direction of dance classes. If your owner says he (or she) can't dance, he's either lying or not endowed with sufficient Cuban blood!

Other places to check out Spanish courses include the following:

Universidad de la Habana LANGUAGE
(Map p92; ☎ 832-4245, 831-3751; www.uh.cu; Calle J No 556, Edificio Varona, 2nd fl, Vedado) The university offers Spanish courses 12 months a year, beginning on the first Monday of each month. Costs start at CUC$100 for 20 hours (one week), including textbooks, and all levels from beginners through to advanced are offered. You must first sit a placement test to determine your level. Aspiring candidates can sign up in person at the university or reserve beforehand via email or phone.

Uneac LANGUAGE
(Map p92; ☎ 832-4551; cnr Calles 17 & H, Vedado) The pulse of the Cuban arts scene, this place is the first point of call for anyone with more than a passing interest in poetry, literature, art and music.

Cubamar Viajes LANGUAGE
(Map p92; ☎ 830-1220; www.cubamarviajes.cu; Av 3, btwn Calle 12 & Malecón, Vedado; ⊙ 8:30am-5pm Mon-Sat)

Teatro América DANCE
(Map p88; ☎ 862-5416; Av de Italia No 253, btwn Concordia & Neptuno, Centro Habana) Next to the Casa de la Música, it can fix you up with both a class and a partner for approximately CUC$8 per hour.

Conjunto Folklórico Nacional de Cuba DANCE
(Map p92; ☎ 830-3060; www.folkcuba.cult.cu; Calle 4 No 103, btwn Calzada & Calle 5, Vedado) Teaches highly recommended classes in *son*, salsa, rumba, mambo and more. It also teaches percussion. Classes start on the third Monday in January and the first Monday in July, and cost CUC$500 for a 15-day course. An admission test places students in classes of four different levels.

Centro Hispano Americano de Cultura CULTURE
(Map p88; ☎ 860-6282; Malecón No 17, btwn Paseo de Martí & Capdevila, Centro Habana; ⊙ 9am-5pm Tue-Sat, 9am-1pm Sun) Has all kinds of facilities, including a library, cinema, internet cafe and concert venue. Pick up its excellent monthly brochure and ask about the literature courses.

Paradiso CULTURE
(Map p92; ☎ 832-9538; www.paradiso.cu; Calle 19 No 560, Vedado) A cultural agency that can arrange courses of between four and 12 weeks on history, architecture, music, theater, dance and more.

Teatro Nacional de Cuba YOGA
(Map p92; ☎ 879-6011; cnr Paseo & Calle 39, Vedado) Look for the class schedule by the box office.

Centro Andaluz MUSIC
(Map p88; ☎ 863-6745; Paseo de Martí, btwn Virtudes & Neptuno, Centro Habana) Typically, Cubans perform flamenco as well as the Spanish, and you can take dance classes or even enquire about the possibility of taking guitar lessons here.

Taller Experimental de Gráfica ART
(Map p64; ☎ 862-0979; Callejón del Chorro No 6, Habana Vieja) Offers classes in the art of engraving. Individualized instruction lasts one month, during which the student creates an engraving with 15 copies; longer classes can be arranged. It costs around CUC$250.

Tours

Most general agencies offer the same tours, with some exceptions noted below. The regular tour diet includes a four-hour city tour (CUC$15), a specialized Hemingway tour (from CUC$20), a *cañonazo* ceremony (the shooting of the cannons at the Fortaleza de San Carlos de la Cabaña; without/with dinner CUC$15/25), a Varadero day trip (from CUC$35) and, of course, excursions to Tropicana Nightclub (starting at CUC$65). Other options include tours to Boca de Guamá crocodile farm (CUC$48), Playas del Este (CUC$20 including lunch), Viñales (CUC$44), Cayo Largo del Sur (CUC$137) and a Trinidad–Cienfuegos overnight

(CUC$129). Children usually pay a fraction of the price for adults, and solo travelers get socked with a CUC$15 supplement. Note that if the minimum number of people don't sign up, the trip will be cancelled. Any of the following agencies can arrange these tours and more:

Infotur is based at the **airport** (☑642-6101; Terminal 3 Aeropuerto Internacional José Martí; ⊗24hr) and in **Habana Vieja** (☑863-6884; cnr Obispo & San Ignacio; ⊗10am-1pm & 2-7pm).

Havanatur   GUIDED TOUR
(☑835-3720; www.havanatur.cu; Calle 23, cnr M, Vedado) All of Habana's main travel agencies offer a Hemingway tour, and the packages are much the same. The itinerary (CUC$20) includes a visit to the author's house, La Finca Vigía, a side trip to the fishing village of Cojímar (where Papa moored his boat), plus an opportunity to down copious cocktails in Hemingway's favorite watering holes, the overhyped Bodeguita del Medio and El Floridita.

Paradiso   CULTURAL TOUR
(Map p92; ☑832-9538; Calle 19 No 560, Vedado) Offers tours with an emphasis on art. Tours depart from many cities and are in several languages. Check out Martí's Havana or special concert tours.

🛏 Sleeping

With literally thousands of private houses letting out rooms, you'll never struggle to find accommodations in Havana. Casas particulares go for anywhere between CUC$20 and CUC$40 per room, with Centro Habana offering the best bargains. Rock-bottom budget hotels can match casas for price, but not comfort. There's a dearth of decent hotels in the midrange price bracket, while Havana's top-end hotels are plentiful and offer oodles of atmosphere, even if the overall standards can't always match facilities elsewhere in the Caribbean.

Many of Havana's hotels are historic monuments in their own right. Worth a look, even if you're not staying over, are Hotel Sevilla and Hotel Saratoga (in Centro Habana), the Raquel, Hostal Condes de Villanueva and Hotel Florida (all in Habana Vieja), and the iconic Hotel Nacional (in Vedado).

🛏 Habana Vieja

Greenhouse   CASA PARTICULAR $
(Map p64; ☑862-9877; San Ignacio No 656, btwn Merced & Jesús María; r CUC$30-40; ☒) Fabulous Old Town casa run by Eugenio and Fabio who have added superb design features to their huge colonial home (check out the terrace fountain and the backlit model of Havana on the stairway). There are five rooms in this virtual hotel all with modern private bathrooms.

Hostal Peregrino El Encinar CASA PARTICULAR $
(Map p64; ☑860-1257; Chacón No 50 Altos, btwn Cuba & Aguiar; s/d/tr CUC$30/35/40; ☒) This outpost of Centro Habana's Hostal Peregrino is probably the closest Cuba has yet come to a private hotel. Four rooms (with four more

---

DON'T MISS

HAVANA'S BEST CITY TOURS

For the best tours in the city, sign up with San Cristóbal Agencia de Viajes (p129), the official travel agency of the City Historian's Office, Habaguanex. The agency's unique excursions encourage small groups (there is no minimum), offer decent prices, and provide well-versed, interested guides who are true experts in their field. Trips can be booked in any Habaguanex Hotel.

Conservation (from CUC$20) – A tour of Habana Vieja's pioneering social projects, including a convalescent home and a needlecraft cooperative, that have been financed through tourist money.

Architecture (from CUC$20) – Part walking tour, part driving tour through Havana's amazing assemblage of eclectic architecture.

Art & Culur (CUC$12) – Take in art galleries, learn about Cuban painters, and visit the two-site Museo Nacional de Bellas Artes.

Religion (from CUC$22) – A look at some of Havana's restored churches, and a peep into the mysterious rites of Santería, including a visit to the suburb of Regla.

on the way) all with private bathrooms are approaching boutique standard with fine tilework, hairdryers, TVs and mini-bars. The delightful roof terrace overlooks the bay with views toward La Cabaña fort.

Noemi Moreno
CASA PARTICULAR $

(Map p64; ✆ 862-3809; Cuba No 611 apt 2, btwn Luz & Santa Clara; r CUC$25-30; ✿) Offering two nicely renovated, clean rooms sharing a bathroom, Noemi has a great location behind the Santa Clara convent. If full, there are five more apartments in the same building that also rent.

Casa de Pepe & Rafaela
CASA PARTICULAR $

(Map p64; ✆ 862-9877; San Ignacio No 454, btwn Sol & Santa Clara; r CUC$30) One of Havana's better casas: antiques and Moorish tiles throughout, two rooms with balconies and gorgeous new bathrooms, excellent location and great hosts.

Pablo Rodríguez
CASA PARTICULAR $

(Map p64; ✆ 861-2111; pablo@sercomar.telemar. cu; Compostela No 532, btwn Brasil & Muralla; r CUC$30) A lovely old colonial classic, this place has some original frescoes partially uncovered on the walls. It would be worth millions elsewhere, but here you can rent one of venerable Pablo's three rooms with bathrooms (one en suite, two private but separate), fan and fridge for a giveaway CUC$30 per night.

Mesón de la Flota
HOTEL $$

(Map p64; ✆ 863-3838; Mercaderes No 257, btwn Amargura & Brasil; s/d incl breakfast CUC$88/145; ✿) Habana Vieja's smallest hotel is an old Spanish tavern decked out with maritime motifs and located within spitting distance of gracious Plaza Vieja. Five individually crafted rooms contain all of the modern comforts and amenities, while downstairs a busy restaurant serves up delicious tapas.

★ Hotel Los Frailes
HISTORIC HOTEL $$$

(Map p64; ✆ 862 9383; Brasil No 8, btwn Oficios & Mercaderes; s/d CUC$88/145; ✿@) There's nothing austere about Los Frailes (the friars), despite the monastic theme (the staff wears hooded robes) inspired by the nearby San Francisco de Asís convent. Instead, this is the kind of hotel you'll look forward to coming back to at the end of a long day to recline in large, historical rooms in your monkish dressing gown with candlelight flickering on the walls.

An added perk is the resident woodwind quartet in the lobby; the musicians are so good that they regularly lure passing tour groups for impromptu concerts.

★ Hostal Conde de Villanueva
HOTEL $$$

(Map p64; ✆ 862-9293; Mercaderes No 202; s/d CUC$108/175; ✿@) If you want to splash out on one night of luxury in Havana, check out this highly lauded colonial gem. Restored under the watchful eye of the City Historian in the late 1990s, the Villanueva has been converted from a grandiose city mansion into a thoughtfully decorated hotel with nine bedrooms spread around an attractive inner courtyard (complete with resident peacock).

Upstairs suites contain stained-glass windows, chandeliers, arty sculptures and – in one – a fully workable whirlpool bathtub.

Hotel San Felipe y Santiago de Bejúcal
HOTEL $$$

(Map p64; ✆ 864-9191; cnr Oficios & Amargura; s/d CUC$150/240; ✿@⍏) Cuban baroque meets modern minimalist in Habaguanex's newest offering, and the results are something to behold. Spreading 27 rooms over six floors in the blustery Plaza de San Francisco de Asís, this place is living proof that Habaguanex's delicate restoration work is getting better and better. If the Americans really are coming, they're going to be impressed.

Hotel Florida
HOTEL $$$

(Map p64; ✆ 862-4127; Obispo No 252; s/d incl breakfast CUC$108/175; ✿@) They don't make them like this anymore. The Florida is an architectural extravaganza built in the purest colonial style, with arches and pillars clustered around an atmospheric central courtyard. Habaguanex has restored the 1836 building with loving attention to detail: the amply furnished rooms retain their original high ceilings and wonderfully luxurious finishes.

Anyone with even a passing interest in Cuba's architectural heritage will want to check out this colonial jewel, complemented with an elegant cafe and a popular bar-nightspot (from 8pm).

Hotel Raquel
HOTEL $$$

(Map p64; ✆ 860-8280; cnr Amargura & San Ignacio; s/d CUC$108/175; ✿@) Encased in a dazzling 1908 palace (that was once a bank), the Hotel Raquel takes your breath away with its grandiose columns, sleek marble statues and intricate stained-glass ceiling. Painstakingly restored in 2003, the reception area in this marvelous eclectic building is a tourist sight in its own right – it's replete with priceless antiques and intricate art nouveau flourishes.

Behind its impressive architecture, the Raquel offers well-presented if noisy rooms, a small gym/sauna, friendly staff and a great central location.

Hotel Santa Isabel   HOTEL $$$
(Map p64; ☎860-8201; Baratillo No 9; s/d incl breakfast CUC$150/240; ❄ @) Considered one of Havana's finest hotels, as well as one of its oldest (it first began operations in 1867), the Hotel Santa Isabel is housed in the Palacio de los Condes de Santovenia, the former crash pad of a decadent Spanish count. In 1998 this three-story baroque beauty was upgraded to five-star status, and the Santa Isabel actually comes close to justifying the billing.

The 17 regular rooms have bundles of historic charm and are all kitted out with attractive Spanish colonial furniture as well as paintings by contemporary Cuban artists. No small wonder ex-US president Jimmy Carter stayed here during his historic 2002 visit.

Hostal Valencia   HOTEL $$$
(Map p64; ☎867-1037; Oficios No 53; s/d incl breakfast CUC$108/175; ❄ @) The Valencia is decked out like a Spanish *posada* (inn), with hanging vines, doorways big enough to ride a horse through and a popular on-site paella restaurant. You can almost see the ghosts of Don Quixote and Sancho Panza floating through the hallways. Slap-bang in the middle of the historic core, and one of the cheapest offerings in the Habaguanex stable, this hotel is an excellent old-world choice, with good service and plenty of atmosphere.

Hostal Palacio O'Farrill   HOTEL $$$
(Map p64; ☎860-5080; Cuba No 102-108, btwn Chacón & Tejadillo; s/d CUC$108/175; ❄ @) Not an Irish joke, but one of Havana's most impressive period hotels, the Palacio O'Farrill is a staggeringly beautiful colonial palace that once belonged to Don Ricardo O'Farrill, a Cuban sugar entrepreneur who was descended from a family of Irish nobility. Taking the Emerald Isle as its theme, there's plenty of greenery in the plant-filled 18th-century courtyard.

The 2nd floor, which was added in the 19th century, provides grandiose neoclassical touches, while the 20th-century top floor merges seamlessly with the magnificent architecture below.

Hostal Beltrán de la Santa Cruz   HOTEL $$$
(Map p64; ☎860-8330; San Ignacio No 411, btwn Muralla & Sol; s/d incl breakfast CUC$88/145; ❄ @) Excellent location, friendly staff and plenty of old-world authenticity make this compact inn just off Plaza Vieja a winning combination. Housed in a sturdy 18th-century building and offering just 11 spacious rooms, intimacy is assured and the standard of service has been regularly lauded by both travelers and reviewers.

Hotel Ambos Mundos   HOTEL $$$
(Map p64; ☎860-9529; Obispo No 153; s/d CUC$108/175; ❄ @) Hemingway's Havana hideout and the place where he is said to have penned his seminal guerrilla classic *For Whom the Bell Tolls* (Castro's bedtime reading during the war in the mountains). The pastel-pink Ambos Mundos is a Havana institution and an obligatory pit stop for anyone on a world tour of 'Hemingway-once-fell-over-in-here' bars.

Small, sometimes windowless rooms suggest overpricing, but the lobby bar is classic enough (follow the romantic piano melody) and drinks in the rooftop restaurant one of the city's finest treats.

Hotel el Comendador   HOTEL $$$
(Map p64; ☎867-1037; cnr Obrapía & Baratillo; s/d incl breakfast CUC$108/175; ❄ @) Situated in the historic quarter, the El Comendador offers exquisite colonial digs for an excellent rate.

Centro Habana

★ Hostal Peregrino   CASA PARTICULAR $
(Map p88; ☎861-8027; www.hostalperegrino.com; Consulado No 152, btwn Colón & Trocadero; s/d/tr CUC$30/35/40; ❄) Julio Roque is a pediatrician who, along with his wife Elsa, has expanded his former two-room casa particular into a growing web of accommodations. His HQ, Hostal Peregrino, offers three rooms just a block from Prado with another two-bed apartment available a few doors away. Both Julio and Elsa are super-helpful, fluent in English, and are mines of local information.

Extra services include airport pickup, internet, laundry and cocktail bar. The family offers two more places (one in Habana Vieja, the other in Calle Lealtad) both bookable through the same number.

★ Casa 1932
CASA PARTICULAR $

(Map p88; ☑ 863-6203, 05-264-3858; www.casa-habana.net; Campanario 63, btwn San Lázaro & Lagunas; r CUC$20-35; ✳) The charismatic Luis Miguel is an art deco fanatic who offers his house as both comfy private homestay and museum to the 1930s when his preferred architectural style was in vogue. Collectibles, including old signs, mirrors, toys, furniture and stained glass, will make you feel like you've just walked into a Clark Gable movie. The three rooms and services are also excellent.

Check the pancakes and peanut butter on the breakfast table, or ask Luis Miguel to take you on an art deco architectural tour of the city.

Casa Amada
CASA PARTICULAR $

(Map p88; ☑ 862-3924; www.casaamada.net; Lealtad No 262 Altos, btwn Neptuno & Concordia; r CUC$25-30; ✳) A huge house with gracious hosts offering four rooms (with private bathrooms) and a communal roof terrace. An enclosed balcony out front overlooks the gritty cinematic street life that is Centro Habana.

Casa 1940
CASA PARTICULAR $

(Map p88; ☑ 863-6203; San Lázaro No 409; r CUC$25-30; ✳) Casa 1940 is a house whose furnishings come from the era when art deco style gave way to modernism.

Esther Cardoso
CASA PARTICULAR $

(Map p88; ☑ 862-0401; esthercv2551@cubarte.cult.cu; Águila No 367, btwn Neptuno & San Miguel; r CUC$30-35) Esther is an actress (quite well-known in Havana), and this little palace shines like an oasis in Centro Habana's dilapidated desert, with tasteful decor, funky posters, spick-and-span bathrooms and a spectacular roof terrace. Book early, as this place is well known.

Eumelia & Aurelio
CASA PARTICULAR $

(Map p88; Consulado No 157, btwn Colón & Trocadero; CUC$25-30; ✳) Brand-new bathrooms, minibars and digitally controlled air-con feature in this pleasant house close to El Prado with two rooms with a shared terrace.

Lourdes Cervantes
CASA PARTICULAR $

(Map p88; ☑ 879-2243; lourdescervantesparades@yahoo.es; Calzada de la Infanta No 17, btwn 23 & Humboldt; CUC$25-30; ✳) On the border of Vedado and Centro Habana a stone's throw from the Hotel Nacional, this 1st-floor apartment offers two large rooms with balconies. The bathroom is large but shared. Lourdes, the hostess, is fluent in English and French.

Casa de Lourdes & José
CASA PARTICULAR $

(Map p88; ☑ 863-9879; Águila 168B, btwn Ánimas & Trocadero; r CUC$25; ✳) Reader recommended house in the midst of Centro with en suite rooms, set-you-up-for-the-day breakfasts and friendly owners.

Dulce Hostal – Dulce María González
CASA PARTICULAR $

(Map p88; ☑ 863-2506; Amistad No 220, btwn Neptuno & San Miguel; r CUC$20; ✳) The Dulce (sweet) Hostal on Amistad (friendship) St sounds like a good combination, and sweet and friendly is what you get in this beautiful colonial house with tile floors, soaring ceilings and a gregarious, helpful hostess.

Hotel Lincoln
HOTEL $

(Map p88; ☑ 862-8061; Av de Italia, btwn Virtudes & Ánimas; s/d CUC$24/38; ✳) This peeling nine-story giant on busy Galiano (Av de Italia) was the second-tallest building in Havana when it was built in 1926. Overshadowed by taller opposition these days, it still offers 135 air-con rooms with bathroom and TV in an atmosphere that is more 1950s than 2010s.

Notoriety hit in 1958 when Castro's 26th of July Movement kidnapped motor racing world champion Carlos Fangio from the lobby on the eve of the Cuban Grand Prix. A small 'museum' on the 8th floor records the event for posterity. Otherwise, the facilities are best described as timeworn.

Hotel Caribbean
HOTEL $

(Map p88; ☑ 860-8233; Paseo de Martí No 164, btwn Colón & Refugio; s/d CUC$31/50; ✳) Cheap but not always so cheerful, the Caribbean offers aspiring Cuban renovators a lesson in how not to decorate. Rooms are a tad dark and pokey. Bargain-basement seekers only.

Hotel Park View
HOTEL $$

(Map p88; Colón No 101; s/d CUC$59/95; ✳ @) Built in 1928 with American money, the Park View's reputation as a poor man's 'Sevilla' isn't entirely justified. Its location alone (within baseball-pitching distance of the Museo de la Revolución) is enough to consider this mint-green city charmer a viable option. Chuck in friendly doormen, modern furnishings and a perfectly poised 7th-floor restaurant and you have a rare midrange bargain.

Hotel Deauville
HOTEL $$

(Map p88; ☑866-8812; Av de Italia No 1, cnr Malecón; s/d/tr CUC$52/72/103; Ⓟ✳@☒) A long-term fixture on the Malecón, this former Mafia gambling den doesn't quite match up to the stellar views. Currently reborn in sea-blue and already showing the effects of the corrosive sea water, the Deauville's handy facilities (money exchange and car rental) and reasonably priced restaurant are ever popular with the mid-priced tour-circuit crowd. Savvy independents hit the casas particulares.

★Hotel Iberostar Parque Central
HOTEL $$$

(Map p88; ☑860-6627; www.iberostar.com; Neptuno, btwn Agramonte & Paseo de Martí; s/d CUC$200/300; Ⓟ✳@☎☒) If you have a penchant for hanging out in expensive five-star hotel lobbies sipping mojitos, the Parque Central could fill a vacuum. Reserving a room is another (more expensive) matter. Outside Havana's two Meliás, the Iberostar is, without a doubt, Havana's best international-standard hotel, with service and business facilities on a par with top-ranking five-star facilities elsewhere in the Caribbean.

Although the fancy lobby and classily furnished rooms may lack the historical riches of the Habaguanex establishments, the ambience here is far from antiseptic. Bonus facilities include a full-service business center, a rooftop swimming pool/fitness center/Jacuzzi, an elegant lobby bar, the celebrated El Paseo restaurant, plus excellent international telephone and internet links. Two of the bedrooms are wheelchair-accessible. In 2009 the Parque Central opened an even swankier new wing across Calle Virtudes, connected to the rest of the hotel by means of an underground tunnel. As well as state-of-the-art rooms, the addition includes its own luxurious restaurant, cafe and reception area.

Hotel Terral
BOUTIQUE HOTEL $$$

(Map p88; ☑860-2100; Malecón, cnr Lealtad; s/d CUC$108/175; ✳@) At last, Havana's semi-ruined sea drive gets a boutique hotel that can look out across the water at Florida and compare notes. Despite being built (and run) by the City Historian's Office, Terral is not historic. On the contrary, the 14 ocean-facing rooms are chic, clean-lined and minimalist. A sinuous glass-fronted cafe/bar downstairs offers inviting sofas and great coffee.

Hotel Saratoga
HOTEL $$$

(Map p88; ☑868-1000; Paseo de Martí No 603; s/d CUC$225/310; Ⓟ✳@☎☒) The glittering Saratoga is an architectural work-of-art that stands imposingly at the intersection of Prado and Dragones with fantastic views over toward the Capitolio. Sharp, if officious, service is a feature here, as are the extra-comfortable beds, power showers and a truly decadent rooftop swimming pool.

Not surprisingly, there's a price for all this luxury. The Saratoga is Havana's most expensive hotel, and while its facilities impress, its service can't quite match other, often marginally cheaper, hotels.

Hotel Sevilla
HOTEL $$$

(Map p88; ☑860-8560; Trocadero No 55, btwn Paseo de Martí & Agramonte; s/d incl breakfast CUC$150/210; Ⓟ✳@☒) Al Capone once hired out the whole 6th floor, Graham Greene used room 501 as a setting for his novel *Our Man in Havana* and the Mafia requisitioned it as operations centre for their prerevolutionary North American drugs racket. Now run in partnership with the French Sofitel group, the Moorish Sevilla still drips with history as countless old black-and-white photos of past celebrity guests testify.

Rooms are spacious and equipped with comfortable beds, and the ostentatious lobby could have been ripped straight out of the Alhambra.

Hotel Telégrafo
HOTEL $$$

(Map p88; ☑861-4741, 861-1010; Paseo de Martí No 408; s/d CUC$108/175; ✳@) This bold royal-blue Habaguanex beauty on the northwest corner of Parque Central juxtaposes old-style architectural features (the original building hails from 1888) with futuristic design flourishes; these include shiny silver sofas, a huge winding central staircase and an intricate tile mosaic emblazoned on the wall of the downstairs cafe. The rooms are equally spiffy.

Hotel Inglaterra
HOTEL $$$

(Map p88; ☑860-8595; Paseo de Martí No 416; s/d CUC$96/154; Ⓟ✳@) It was José Martí's one-time Havana hotel of choice and it's still playing on the fact – which says something about the current state of affairs. Despite a recent renovation, the Inglaterra remains a better place to hang out in than stay in, with its exquisite Moorish lobby and crusty colonial interior easily outshining the lackluster and often viewless rooms.

The rooftop bar is a popular watering hole, and the downstairs foyer is a hive of bustling activity where there's always live music blaring. Beware the streets outside, which are full of overzealous hustlers waiting to pounce.

Vedado

★ Marta Vitorte
CASA PARTICULAR $

(Map p92; ☑ 832-6475; martavitorte@hotmail.com; Calle G No 301 apt 14, btwn Calles 13 & 15; r CUC$35-40; P ❋) Marta has lived in this sinuous apartment on Av de los Presidentes since the 1960s. One look at the view and you'll see why – the glass-fronted wrap-around terrace that soaks up 270 degrees of Havana's stunning panorama makes it seem as if you're standing atop the Martí monument. Not surprisingly, her four rooms are deluxe with lovely furnishings, minibars and safes.

Then there are the breakfasts, the laundry, the parking space, the lift attendant... Get the drift? Marta also rents a self-contained apartment with garage nearby (CUC$70 to US$80).

Flora & Osvaldo
CASA PARTICULAR $

(Map p92; ☑ 833-9151; Calle B No 705, btwn Zapata & 29; r CUC$25-30; ❋) Forget the out-of-the-way location. This palatial detached home with two modern rooms could be worth the commute. The Plaza de la Revolución is almost around the corner and the English-speaking owners have been enthusiastically recommended by readers.

Mercedes González
CASA PARTICULAR $

(Map p92; ☑ 832-5846, 52-91-76-85; mercylupe@hotmail.com; Calle 21 No 360 apt 2A, btwn Calles G & H; r CUC$30-35; ❋) One of the most welcoming hosts in Havana, Mercedes comes highly recommended by readers, fellow travelers, other casa owners, you name it. Her lovely art deco abode is a classic Vedado apartment with two fine rooms, an airy terrace and top-notch service.

Eddy Gutiérrez Bouza
CASA PARTICULAR $

(Map p92; ☑ 832-5207; Calle 21 No 408, btwn Calles F & G; r CUC$30; P ❋) Eddy is a fantastic host with a great knowledge of Havana, and his huge colonial house has hosted many visitors over the years. It's an inviting abode with a well-kept garden, a grand exterior and Eddy's 1974 Argentinian-made Dodge parked in the driveway.

Guests are accommodated out back in comfortable quarters, and one of the three rooms comes equipped with a kitchenette.

Nelsy Alemán Machado
CASA PARTICULAR $

(Map p92; ☑ 832-8467; Calle 25 No 361 apt 1, btwn Calles K & L; r CUC$25) Nelsy is one of two renters in this house up by the university and a stone's throw from the Hotel Habana Libre. Geographically, it's one of Vedado's better options: it's safe and secure, but close to most of the action.

Melba Piñada Bermudez
CASA PARTICULAR $

(Map p92; ☑ 832-5929; lienafp@yahoo.com; Calle 11 No 802, btwn Calles 2 & 4; r CUC$30) This 100-year-old villa in a shady Vedado street would be a millionaire's pad anywhere else. Here in Havana, it's a casa particular with two large rooms and decent meals.

Luis Suávez Fiandor
CASA PARTICULAR $

(Map p92; ☑ 832-5213; Calle F No 510 Altos, btwn Calles 21 & 23; r CUC$35; ❋) Welcome to another clean, safe Vedado option with gracious hosts and two upstairs rooms with private bathrooms and a terrace overlooking the weathered Havana rooftops.

Hotel Colina
HOTEL $

(Map p92; ☑ 836-4071; cnr Calles L & 27; s/d CUC$34/42; ❋ @) The friendliest and least fussy of Vedado's cheaper options, the 80-room Colina is situated directly outside the university and is a good choice if you're here for a Spanish course.

Hotel Bruzón
HOTEL $

(Map p92; ☑ 877-5684; Bruzón No 217, btwn Pozos Dulces & Av de la Independencia; s/d CUC$22/31; ❋) There are only two reasons to stay here: you've got an early bus to catch (the terminal's 400m away), or everywhere else is full. Otherwise, the claustrophobic rooms aren't worth it.

Hotel Victoria
HOTEL $$

(Map p92; ☑ 833-3510; Calle 19 No 101; s/d incl breakfast CUC$70/90; P ❋ @ ❋) A well-heeled and oft-overlooked Vedado option, the diminutive five-story Victoria is a venerable Gran Caribe establishment housed in an attractive neoclassical building dating from 1928. It contains a swimming pool, a bar and a small shop. A sturdy midrange choice (if you can get in – it's invariably full).

Hotel Paseo Habana
HOTEL $$

(Map p92; ☑ 836-0808; Calle 17, cnr A; s/d CUC$55/70; ❋) First things first. The new

Hotel Paseo Habana is not actually in Paseo, rather it's one block east on the corner of Calle A. If you can overlook this and a couple of other small foibles (dodgy water pressure, missing light fittings), this is a veritable Havana bargain. Relax on one of the terrace rocking chairs and count your savings.

Hotel Vedado
HOTEL **$$**

(Map p92; ☑ 836-4072; Calle O No 244, btwn Calles 23 & 25; s/d CUC$46/73; ✳ @ ☀) Ever popular with the tour-bus crowd, the Hotel Vedado's regular refurbishments never quite break the three-star barrier despite an OK pool (rare in Havana), passable restaurant and not unpleasant rooms.

Elsewhere the patchy service, perennially noisy lobby and almost total lack of character will leave you wondering if you wouldn't have been better off staying in a local casa particular – for half the price.

Hotel St John's
HOTEL **$$**

(Map p92; ☑ 833-3740; Calle O No 216, btwn Calles 23 & 25; s/d incl breakfast CUC$46/73; ✳ @ ☀) A fair-to-middling Vedado option, St John's has a rooftop pool, clean bathrooms, reasonable beds and the ever-popular Pico Blanco nightclub on the 14th floor. If wall-vibrating Cuban discos aren't your thing, you might get more peace at another similarly priced hotel.

Hotel Nacional
HOTEL **$$$**

(Map p92; ☑ 836-3564; cnr Calles O & 21; s/d CUC$132/187; P ✳ @ ☀ ☀) The cherry on the cake of Cuban hotels and a flagship of the government-run Gran Caribe chain, the neoclassical/neocolonial/art deco (let's call it eclectic) Hotel Nacional is as much a city monument as it is an international accommodations option. Even if you haven't got the money to stay here, chances are you'll find yourself sipping at least one minty mojito in its exquisite ocean-side bar.

Steeped in history and furnished with plaques that advertise details of illustrious past occupants, this towering Havana landmark sports two swimming pools, a sweeping manicured lawn, a couple of lavish restaurants and its own top-class nighttime cabaret, the Parisién. While the rooms might lack fancy gadgets, the ostentatious communal areas and the erstwhile ghosts of Winston Churchill, Frank Sinatra, Lucky Luciano and Errol Flynn that haunt the Moorish lobby make for a fascinating and unforgettable experience.

Hotel Meliá Cohiba
HOTEL **$$$**

(Map p92; ☑ 833-3636; Paseo, btwn Calles 1 & 3; s/d CUC$235/280; P ✳ @ ☀ ☀) Cuba's sharpest and best-quality city hotel is an ocean-side concrete giant built in 1994 (it's the only building from this era on the Malecón) that will satisfy the highest of international expectations with its knowledgeable, consistent staff and modern, well-polished facilities. After a few weeks in the Cuban outback, you'll feel like you're on a different planet here.

For workaholics there are special 'business-traveler rooms' and 59 units have Jacuzzis. On the lower levels gold-star facilities include a shopping arcade, one of Havana's plushest gyms and the ever-popular Habana Café.

Hotel Habana Libre
HOTEL **$$$**

(Map p92; ☑ 834-6100; Calle L, btwn Calles 23 & 25; d/ste incl breakfast CUC$204/240; P ✳ @ ☀) Havana's biggest and boldest hotel opened in March 1958 on the eve of Batista's last waltz. Once part of the Hilton chain, in January 1959 it was commandeered by Castro's rebels, who put their boots over all the plush furnishings and turned it into their temporary HQ.

Now managed by Spain's Meliá chain as an urban Tryp Hotel, this skyline-hogging giant has all 574 rooms kitted out to international standard, though the lackluster furnishings could do with a makeover. The tour desks in the lobby are helpful for out-of-town excursions and the 25th-floor Cabaret Turquino is a city institution.

Hotel Riviera
HOTEL **$$$**

(Map p92; ☑ 836-4051; cnr Paseo & Malecón; s/d incl breakfast CUC$63/106; P ✳ @ ☀) Meyer Lansky's magnificent Vegas-style palace has leapt back into fashion with its gloriously retro lobby almost unchanged since 1957 (when it was the height of modernity). It isn't hard to imagine all the old Mafia hoods congregating here with their Cohiba cigars and chauffer-driven Chevrolets parked outside.

The trouble for modern-day visitors are the rooms (there are 354 of them), which, though luxurious 50 years ago, are now looking a little rough around the edges and struggle to justify their top-end price tag. You can dampen the dreariness in the fabulous '50s-style pool, the good smattering of restaurants or the legendary Copa Room cabaret, which is far cheaper than Tropicana. The location on a wild and wave-lashed section of the Malecón is spectacular, although a good bus or taxi ride from the Old Town.

Hotel ROC Presidente HOTEL $$$
(Map p92; ☑ 55-18-01; cnr Calzada & Calle G; s/d CUC$90/140; P❋@☎) Fully restored in 2000, this art deco influenced hotel wouldn't be out of place on a street just off Times Sq in New York. Built the same year as the Victoria (1928), the Presidente is similar but larger, with gruffer staff. Unless you're a walker or fancy getting some elbow exercise on Havana's crowded bus system, the location can be awkward.

Eating

Habana Vieja

Havana's Old Town has the most consistent stash of government-run restaurants in Cuba, most of them competently operated by the City Historian's agency, Habaguanex. Experimenting beyond the usual *comida criolla,* you'll find decent ethnic places here (eg Italian, Arabic and Chinese), albeit run primarily by Cubans. Habana Vieja's paladares are some of the city's most ambitious and are often housed in plush colonial digs.

Café Lamparilla INTERNATIONAL $
(Map p64; Lamparilla, btwn Mercaderes & San Ignacio; ⊙ noon-midnight) Crowding out the cobbled street with its alfresco tables, the Lamparilla is perennially popular – your best bet for a seat is in the air-conditioned refinement of the sinuous art deco bar. Most people drop by for a beer or a cocktail, but the food is surprisingly good and plentiful, and the prices economical.

Café Santo Domingo CAFE $
(Map p64; Obispo No 159, btwn San Ignacio & Mercaderes; ⊙ 9am-9pm) Tucked away above Habana Vieja's best bakery – and encased in one of its oldest buildings – this laid-back cafe is aromatic and light on the wallet. Check out the delicious fruit shakes, huge *sandwich especial,* or smuggle some cakes upstairs to enjoy over a steaming cup of *café con leche* (coffee with warm milk).

Cafetería Torre la Vega CARIBBEAN $
(Map p64; Obrapía No 114A, btwn Mercaderes & Oficios; ⊙ 9am-9pm) This is the flop-down lunchtime place that everyone hits in the middle of a sightseeing tour. It's perfectly placed in the middle of the Old Town, with tables spilling onto the street and into a little park opposite. Diners sit with their noses in guidebooks

chomping on 'spag bol,' pizza, chicken and sandwiches, none of it particularly expensive.

Hanoi INTERNATIONAL $
(Map p64; cnr Brasil & Bernaza; ⊙ noon-11pm) The name might suggest solidarity with 'communist' Vietnam, but don't get too excited – you won't find any Saigon-flavored spring rolls here. Instead, what you get is straight-up Creole cuisine, with a couple of fried-rice dishes thrown in to justify the (rather misleading) name.

One of the only fully restored buildings in untouristy Plaza del Cristo, the Hanoi is a backpacker favorite, where the foreign clientele usually has its communal nose in a guidebook.

Restaurante Puerto de Sagua SEAFOOD $
(Map p64; Av de Bélgica No 603; ⊙ noon-midnight) This nautical-themed eating joint in Habana Vieja's grittier southern quarter is characterized by its small porthole-style windows. It serves mostly seafood at reasonable prices.

★ Doña Eutimia CUBAN $$
(Map p64; Callejón del Chorro 60c; mains CUC$7-9) Keep it simple. The secret at new paladar Dona Eutemia is there *is* no secret. Just serve decent-sized portions of incredibly tasty Cuban food (the *ropa vieja* – shredded beef – and minced beef *picadillo* both deserve mentions) from a pretty spot next to the cathedral and charge highly reasonable prices. The rest is history – or it soon will be.

Mama Inés CUBAN $$
(Map p64; ☑ 862-2669; Obrapía No 62; mains CUC$8-11) Fidel Castro, Jane Fonda, Jack Nicholson, Jimmy Carter, Hugo Chávez; executive chef, Erasmo, has cooked for a who's who of celebrity 'lefties.' Joining the culinary revolution, he's recently chucked his hat in the paladar ring, opening a restaurant in gorgeous colonial digs just off Calle Oficios. Erasmo impresses with fine renditions of what the Cubans do best: *ropa vieja,* breaded prawns and roast pork, at decidedly uncelebrity prices.

Nao Bar Paladar SEAFOOD $$
(Map p64; ☑ 867-3463; Obispo No 1; mains CUC$6-12) No 1 in Havana's main drag and not too far behind in its food ranking, Nao opened in March 2012 in a 200-year building near the docks that plays on its seafaring theme. The small upstairs space is good for main courses (seafood dominates), the downstairs bar and outdoor seating excels in snacks

including what must be the best warm baguettes in Cuba. Try one stuffed with cured *jamón serrano*.

Mesón de la Flota   TAPAS $$

(Map p64; Mercaderes No 257, btwn Amargura & Brasil; tapas CUC$3-6) This nautically themed tapas bar/restaurant might have been transported from Cádiz's Barrio de Santa María, so potent is the atmosphere. Old-world tapas include *garbanzos con chorizo* (chickpeas with sausage), calamari and tortilla, but there are also more substantial seafood-biased *platos principales* (main meals).

For music lovers the real drawcard is the nightly *tablaos* (flamenco shows), the quality of which could rival anything in Andalusia. Sit back and soak up the intangible spirit of *duende* (climactic moment in a flamenco concert inspired by the fusion of music and dance).

El Mercurio   INTERNATIONAL $$

(Map p64; Plaza de San Francisco de Asís; mains CUC$5-10; ⊙24hr) An elegant indoor-outdoor cafe/restaurant, with cappuccino machines, intimate booths and waiters in black ties, that serves cheap lunches (Cuban sandwich) and more substantial dinners (lobster and steak tartare).

Al Medina   MIDDLE EASTERN $$

(Map p64; Oficios No 12, btwn Obrapía & Obispo; mains CUC$5-10; ⊙noon-midnight; ✐) Havana takes on the Middle East in this exotic restaurant, appropriately situated in one of the city's 17th-century *mudéjar*-style buildings. Tucked into a beautiful patio off Calle Oficios, Al Medina is where you can dine like a Moroccan sheik on lamb couscous, chicken tagine and Lebanese sumac with a spicy twist.

It's especially recommended for its voluminous vegetarian platter, which comes

---

VIVA THE CULINARY REVOLUTION!

Goodbye iron rations, hello nouveau cuisine (or should that be *nueva cocina*?). In the last few years, eating in Havana has entered a whole new universe with a raft of nascent private restaurants taking advantage of more liberal laws governing private enterprise. In a city where veterans of WWII rationing once risked unpleasant flashbacks, gastronomes now compare eggplant caviar recipes and talented chefs battle to prepare the best duck *à la orange*.

The key lies in the more 'open' business environment. Until 2011, paladares (privately run restaurants), first legalized by Fidel Castro in 1995, faced draconian restrictions. Seating was capped at 12 people per restaurant, taxes were set high and proprietors were only allowed to serve rather mundane dishes such as pork and chicken. After an initial surge of new private restaurants in the mid-1990s, few people could muster the resources to attempt a business start-up, while plenty of the existing paladares were forced to close; and when the poster child of Cuban paladares, La Guarida, closed temporarily in 2009, it looked as if the game was well and truly over.

All that changed in January 2011 when Raúl Castro's new privatization laws ushered in an era of economic 'glasnost' unmatched since the bearded ones took power in 1959. Restaurants can now seat up to 50 people, employ nonfamily staff, and serve previously unheard of luxuries such as lobster, beef, prawns and wine.

Culinary creativity, pent up for decades and stifled by lack of ingredients during the Special Period, began to flourish, and surprised tourists realized that much-maligned Cuban food (rice, beans, root vegetables, plantain and succulent roast pork) was not so bad after all. Eager to lure in sophisticated foreign gastronomes raised on Italian risotto or French foie gras, Havana's racier chefs started fusing basic *comida criolla* (Creole food) with myriad foreign influences. Swept up in the experimentation, the capital sprouted its first Indian restaurant (Bollywood), a fine Cuban-Swedish paladar (Casa Miglis) and numerous authentic Italian eateries dishing up homemade pasta.

While the phenomenon has spread quickly across the nation, the paladar explosion remains most evident in Havana where, by 2013, new eating establishments were opening almost weekly. You can literally taste the excitement in the medley of cautiously ambitious sports bars, cafes, dive-bars, fine dining and homespun family-run restaurants that now pepper the capital. The country is in the midst of a new revolution, but this time it is more about food than Fidel.

with hummus, tabouleh, dolma, pilaf and falafel.

Restaurante la Dominica ITALIAN $$
(Map p64; O'Reilly No 108; mains CUC$10-18; ⊙noon-midnight) Despite a tendency to be a little overgenerous with the olive oil, La Dominica – with its wood-fired pizza oven and al dente pasta – could quite legitimately stake a claim as Havana's finest Italian restaurant. Located in an elegantly restored dining room with alfresco seating on Calle O'Reilly, the menu offers Italy's 'usual suspects,' augmented by shrimp and lobster.

Professional house bands serenade diners with a slightly more eclectic set than the obligatory Buena Vista Social Club staples.

Restaurante la Paella SPANISH $$
(Map p64; cnr Oficios & Obrapía; paella CUC$10; ⊙noon-11pm) Known for its paella, this place attached to the Hostal Valencia has an authentic ambience and tries hard to emulate its Spanish namesake (the birthplace of Spain's famous rice dish). Food can be variable, but on a good day you'll be scraping the rice off the bottom of your serving pan with relish.

Restaurante el Patio CARIBBEAN $$
(Map p64; San Ignacio No 54; meals CUC$15-20; ⊙noon-midnight) When the hustlers stay away, El Patio is one of the most romantic settings on the planet: the mint stalks in your mojito are pressed to perfection and the band breaks spontaneously into your favorite tune. This place in the Plaza de la Catedral must be experienced at night alfresco, when the atmosphere is almost otherworldly. The food doesn't quite match the setting.

La Mina CARIBBEAN $$
(Map p64; Obispo No 109, btwn Oficios & Mercaderes; ⊙24hr) A mediocre menu, but with a top-class location, La Mina graces a scenic corner of Plaza de Armas, meaning every tourist in Havana walks past it at some point. The food options – displayed on a stand in the street outside and backed up by an army of verbose waiters – include chicken, pork and prawns cooked in a variety of different ways, but lack culinary panache.

There's a tempting *heludería* (ice-cream parlor) around the corner in Calle Oficios.

La Torre de Marfil CHINESE $$
(Map p64; Mercaderes No 111, btwn Obispo & Obrapía; ⊙noon-10pm Mon-Thu, noon-midnight Fri-Sun) Where have all the punters gone? Chinatown, perhaps? You feel sorry for the Marfil. Perfectly placed in Calle Mercaderes with smiling wait staff and an inviting interior, it somehow always seems to be three-quarters empty. Brave the deserted interior and you'll find that the chop suey and chow mein plates – *when* they arrive – are fresh, crisp and huge.

★ Restaurante el Templete SEAFOOD $$$
(Map p64; Av del Puerto No 12; meals CUC$15-30; ⊙noon-11pm) Welcome to a rare Cuban breed: a restaurant that could compete with anything in Miami – and a government-run one at that! The Templete's specialty is fish, and special it is: fresh, succulent and cooked simply without the pretensions of celebrity chef-obsessed America. Sure, it's a little *caro* (expensive), but it's worth every last *centivo*.

Paladar Los Mercaderes CUBAN $$$
(Map p64; ☎861-2437; Mercaderes No 207; mains CUC$10-17) This new restaurant in a historic building has to be one of Cuba's most refined paladares for ambience, service *and* food, both Cuban and international. Follow a staircase strewn with flower petals to a luxurious first floor dining room where musicians strum and fine international dishes combine meat with exotic sauces. *Muy romántico!*

Café del Oriente CARIBBEAN, FRENCH $$$
(Map p64; Oficios 112; mains CUC$20-30; ⊙noon-11pm) Havana suddenly becomes posh when you walk through the door at this choice establishment on breezy Plaza de San Francisco de Asís. Smoked salmon, caviar (yes, caviar!), goose liver pâté, lobster thermidor, steak au poivre, cheese plate and a glass of port. Plus service in a tux, no less. There's just one small problem: the price. But what the hell?

La Imprenta INTERNATIONAL $$$
(Map p64; Mercaderes No 208; mains CUC$10-15; ⊙noon-midnight) This Habaguanex restaurant has a resplendent interior filled with memorabilia from the building's previous incarnation as a printing works. The food isn't quite as spectacular although service is thorough and the menu offers previously unheard-of Cuban innovations such as al dente pasta, creative seafood medleys and a stash of decent wines.

Self-Catering

Harris Brothers SUPERMARKET $
(Map p64; O'Reilly No 526; ☺9am-9pm Mon-Sat)
The best-stocked grocery store in Habana
Vieja sells everything from fresh pastries to
baby's nappies. It's just off Parque Central
and is open until late.

Agropecuario Belén MARKET $
(Map p64; Sol, btwn Habana & Compostela) Vieja's
local farmers market.

✗ Parque Histórico Militar Morro-Cabaña

Restaurante los Doce
Apóstoles CARIBBEAN $$
(Map p86; ☺noon-11pm) Parts of the fortresses
have been converted into good restaurants
and atmospheric bars including this one be-
low El Morro. The restaurant is so named
(*doce* means '12') because of the battery of 12
cannons atop its ramparts. The restaurant
serves *comida criolla,* and it's a better-than-
average government-run kitchen with fair
prices.

Restaurante la
Divina Pastora INTERNATIONAL $$$
(Map p86; ☺noon-11pm) Near the Dársena de
los Franceses and a battery of 18th-century
cannons lies one of the big guns of Cuban
cooking. Eschewing the iron rations of yore,
La Divina Pastora offers homemade pasta,
sun-dried tomatoes, pesto-doused vegetables and excellent seafood. To top it off,
there are waiters with *savoir faire* and a
credible wine list.

Paladar Doña Carmela CUBAN $$$
(Map p86; ☑867-7472; Calle B No 10; CUC$15-35;
☺noon-11pm) A private eating option near
Havana's forts that offers quality dishes such
as octopus in garlic and whole roast pork
cooked in a wood oven. Tables are arranged
in a very pleasant garden. Makes for a good
dinner before or after the *cañonazo.*

✗ Centro Habana

Centro offers scanter fare than Habana
Vieja, though a handful of outstanding
paladares now punctuate its dense grid.
Look out for Spanish clubs run by the Cen-
tro Asturiano and dip into the restaurant
strip on Calle Cuchillo in the Barrio Chino
(Chinatown).

Café Neruda INTERNATIONAL $
(Map p88; Malecón No 203, btwn Manrique & San
Nicolás; ☺11am-11pm) Barbecued Chilean ox,
Nerudian skewer, Chilean turnover? Poor
old Pablo Neruda would be turning in his
grave if this weren't such an inviting place
on the mildewed Malecón. Spend a poetic
afternoon watching the waves splash over
the sea wall.

Pastelería Francesa CAFE $
(Map p88; Parque Central No 411; ☺8am-11pm)
This cafe has all the ingredients of a
Champs-Élysées classic: a great location in
Parque Central, waiters in waistcoats and
delicate pastries displayed in glass cases. But
the authentic French flavor is diminished by
grumpy staff and the swarming *jineteras*
(female touts) who roll in with Hans from
Hamburg or Marco from Milano for ciga-
rettes and strong coffee.

★ Casa Miglis SWEDISH $$
(Map p88; ☑864-1486; www.casamiglis.com;
Lealtad No 120, btwn Ánimas & Lagunas; mains
CUC$6-12; ☺noon-1am) There's a place for every-
thing in Havana these days, even Swedish-
Cuban fusion food. Emerging improbably
from a kitchen in the battle-scarred tene-
ments of Centro Habana, comes toast ska-
gen, ceviche, couscous, and the *crème de la
crème:* melt-in-your-mouth meatballs with
mashed potato.

The owner's Swedish (no surprise) and
the decor (empty picture frames, and chairs
attached to the wall) has a touch of Ikea
minimalism about it.

Castropol SPANISH $$
(Map p88; Malecón 107, btwn Genios & Crespo;
mains CUC$6-12; ☺6pm-midnight) Run by the
local Spanish Asturianas society, this re-
cently expanded place has added downstairs
seating to its upstairs space where a balcony
overlooks Havana's dreamy 8km sea drive.
Formerly frequented mainly by Cubans,
word about the tasty and remarkably cheap
Spanish and Caribbean food has got out.

Go for the paella, *garbanzos fritos* (fried
chickpeas), prawns in a tangy sauce and
generous portions of lobster pan-fried in
butter.

Los Nardos SPANISH $$
(Map p88; Paseo de Martí No 563; mains from
CUC$4; ☺noon-midnight) An open secret
opposite the Capitolio, but easy to miss (look
out for the queue), Los Nardos is a semi-
private restaurant operated by the Spanish

Asturianas society. Touted in some quarters as one of the best eateries in the city, the dilapidated exterior promises little, but the leather/mahogany decor and astoundingly delicious dishes suggest otherwise.

The menu includes lobster in a Catalan sauce, garlic prawns with sautéed vegetables and an authentic Spanish paella. Portions are huge, service is attentive and the prices, for what you get, are mind-bogglingly cheap.

Flor de Loto   CHINESE $$
(Map p88; Salud No 303, btwn Gervasio & Escobar; mains CUC$6-8) Popularly considered to be Havana's best Chinese restaurant, as the queues outside will testify. Camouflaged beneath Centro Habana's decaying facades, it serves up extra-large portions of lobster, fried rice and sweet and sour sauce in a frigidly air-conditioned interior.

Restaurante Tien-Tan   CHINESE $$
(Map p88; Cuchillo No 17, btwn Rayo & San Nicolás; mains from CUC$3; ⊗ 11am-midnight) One of the Barrio Chino's best authentic Chinese restaurants, Tien-Tan (the 'Temple of Heaven') is run by a Chinese-Cuban couple and serves up an incredible 130 different dishes.

Try chop suey with vegetables, or chicken with cashew nuts and sit outside in action-packed Cuchillo, one of Havana's most colorful and fastest-growing 'food streets.'

Los Gijones   SPANISH $$
(Map p88; Paseo de Martí No 309; mains from CUC$5; ⊗ noon-midnight) Melancholy Mozart serenades you here, causing you to weep helplessly into your *ropa vieja*. Dry your eyes and you'll find that you're in another Spanish mutual-aid society, this time the Centro Asturiano, whose dark mahogany dining room is frequented by a charming resident violinist.

Chi Tack Tong   CHINESE $$
(Map p88; Dragones No 356, btwn San Nicolás & Manrique; mains CUC$6-9; ⊗ noon-midnight) Upstairs in Calle Dragones, this place is famous for being one of the few cheap restaurants in Havana where you won't hear the words *'No hay'* (we don't have it) when you place your order. The menu is a little limited, but portion sizes are huge. Box up your leftovers.

San Cristóbal   CUBAN $$$
(Map p88; ☎ 867-9109; San Rafael, btwn Campanario & Lealtad; mains CUC$8-15; ⊗ noon-midnight) At San Cristóbal you can sit down in front of a Catholic/*santería* altar

flanked by pictures of Maceo and Martí and give thanks for extraordinarily good food. Located in the thick of Centro Habana, the menu and decor share Cuban, African and Spanish influences. Admire the Hemingway-esque animal skins while enjoying a generous starter plate of *jamón serrano* and six different cheeses.

Paladar la Guarida   INTERNATIONAL $$$
(Map p88; ☎ 866-9047; Concordia No 418, btwn Gervasio & Escobar; ⊗ noon-3pm & 7pm-midnight) On the top floor of a spectacularly dilapidated Havana tenement, La Guarida's lofty reputation rests on its movie-location setting (*Fresa y chocolate* was filmed in this building) and a clutch of swashbuckling newspaper reviews (including the *New York Times* and the *Guardian*).

The food is up there with Havana's best, shoehorning its captivating blend of Nueva Cocina Cubana into dishes such as sea bass in a coconut reduction, and chicken with honey and lemon sauce. Reservations required.

Self-Catering

Supermercado Isla de Cuba   SUPERMARKET $
(Map p88; cnr Máximo Gómez & Factoría; ⊗ 10am-6pm Mon-Sat, 9am-1pm Sun) On the southern side of Parque de la Fraternidad, with yogurt, cereals, pasta etc. You have to check your bag outside, to the right of the entrance.

Almacenes Ultra   SUPERMARKET $
(Map p88; Av Simón Bolívar No 109; ⊗ 9am-6pm Mon-Sat, 9am-1pm Sun) A decent supermarket in Centro Habana, at the corner of Rayo, near Av de Italia.

La Época   SUPERMARKET $
(Map p88; cnr Av de Italia & Neptuno; ⊗ 9am-9pm Mon-Sat, 9am-noon Sun) A hard-currency department store with a supermarket in the basement. Check your bags outside before entering this epic Havana emporium.

Mercado Agropecuario Egido   MARKET $
(Map p64; Av de Bélgica, btwn Corrales & Apodaca) For fresh produce hit this free-enterprise market.

✕ Vedado

Vedado's culinary scene has been transformed in the last three years by a cavalcade of new paladares.

Toke Infanta y 25
SNACK BAR **$**

(Map p92; Infanta cnr 25; snacks CUC$2-4; ⊘7am-midnight) Plush, slick, minimalist, economical and above all tasty, recently opened Toke is a Havana success story that was waiting to happen, filling a huge gap between insipid state-run joints and more formal paladares. It sits pretty amid the bruised edifices of Calzada de la Infanta on the cusp of Vedado and Centro Habana luring enamored *habaneros* (and tourists) with cool neon, smart color accents and excellent *hamberguesas* (hamburgers) and chocolate brownies.

La Chucheria
SNACKS **$**

(Map p92; Calle 1, btwn Calles C & D, snacks CUC$2-7; ⊘7am-midnight) Clinging to its perch close to the Malecón, this sleek new sports bar owned by a Cuban comedian looks as if it floated mockingly across the straits from Florida like a returning exile. The diminutive interior with its clear plastic chairs and flat-screen TVs replaying Messi's latest match-winner, demonstrates how the line between *socialismo* and *capitalismo* is becoming ever more blurred.

Forget about politics momentarily as you contemplate pizza toppings and ice-cream milkshakes so thick you can stand your straw up in them.

Waoo Snack Bar
SNACK BAR **$**

(Map p92; Calle L No 414, cnr Calle 25; snacks CUC$2-4; ⊘noon-midnight) Wow! The Waoo snack bar truly impresses with its wooden wraparound bar, happening locale close to 23 and L (Vedado's metaphoric G-spot) and quick dishes you might want to savour – think carpaccio, cheese plates and coffee with accompanying desserts.

Dulcinea
BAKERY **$**

(Map p92; Calle 25 No 164, btwn Infanta & Calle O; ⊘8am-midnight) Formerly part of the small but precious Pain de París chain, this cake shop cum bakery can still cut it with good pastries, coffee and space to sit down. There's a **24-hour branch** (Map p92) on Línea, adjacent to the Trianón cinema.

Café TV
FAST FOOD **$**

(Map p92; cnr Calles N & 19; ⊘10am-9pm) Hidden in the bowels of Edificio Focsa, this TV-themed cafe is a funky dinner/performance venue lauded by those in the know for its cheap food and hilarious comedy nights. If you're willing to brave the frigid air-con and rather foreboding underground entry tunnel, head here for fresh burgers, healthy salad, pasta and chicken cordon bleu.

Cafetería Sofía
FAST FOOD **$**

(Map p92; Calle 23 No 202; ⊘24hr) Late-night hair-of-the-dog seekers meet annoyingly chirpy early risers at this 24-hour institution on La Rampa (Calle 23).

Infanta Cafetería
ICE CREAM **$**

(Map p88; cnr Calle 23 & Infanta, Vedado; ⊘11am-11pm) Phenomenally creamy stuff in flavors like coffee, condensed milk (sounds gross, tastes great) and rum raisins; pay in convertibles.

Coppelia
ICE CREAM **$**

(Map p92; cnr Calles 23 & L, Vedado; ⊘10am-9:30pm Tue-Sat) Havana's celebrated ice-cream parlor housed in a flying saucerlike

---

FOOD TO GO

There are some great peso places sprinkled about, though few have names; look for the streets. Some of the most outstanding **peso pizza** (Map p92) is at San Rafael just off Infanta (look for the lines). Av de la Italia (Galiano to anyone who lives there) also has some holes-in-the-wall. Also try around Calles H and 17, where there are clusters of **peso stalls** (Map p92) and Calle 21 between Calles 4 and 6; this area is close to the hospital, so there's great variety and long hours.

Cajitas (takeout meals in cardboard boxes) usually cost about CUC$1. Some boxes have cutout spoons on the lid, but most don't, so you'll have to supply your own fork (or use part of the box itself as a shovel). You can usually buy *cajitas* at *agropecuarios* (vegetable markets); Chinatown is known for its *cajitas*.

The latest Cuban street food craze is *churros* (long fried doughnuts sprinkled with sugar). Vendors set up all over town. The best permanent stall is on Calle Muralla next to the Factoría Plaza Vieja. It offers toppings of chocolate or honey.

Cubans haven't really caught onto the idea of coffee 'to go,' so you'll get baffled looks if you ask for a coffee *para llevar* (take-out).

structure in a park in Vedado is as celebrated for its massive queues as much as it is for its ice cream. Join the line and share a table with the locals.

Bollywood INDIAN $$

(Map p92; ☑883-1216; www.bollywoodhavana.com; Calle 35 No 1361, btwn La Torre & 24; mains CUC$6-11; ⊙noon-midnight) Cuba's first and – as yet – only Indian restaurant is the brainchild of Cedric Fernando, a Brit of Sri Lankan parents who has set himself the pioneering task of converting the spice-starved Cubans to tikka masala, roti and other Indian delicacies.

Located out in Nuevo Vedado, Bollywood is worth the taxi ride (or hike), not least for its delicious almond-flavored butter chicken. The decor is subtly Asian (silk scarves and tropical fish) and the service spot on, with the loquacious Cedric working the tables like a pro.

Castas y Tal CUBAN $$

(Map p92; ☑833-1425; Calle E 158B, btwn 9 & Calzada; mains CUC$5-8; ⊙noon-7pm) A homely old-style paladar that'll make you feel more like a guest at a house party than a dollar sign in a restaurant. Castas and Tal is run out of an 11th-floor apartment off Línea by a couple of young imaginative Vedado-ites who have added nouveau touches to a traditional Cuban base.

Ride up the painfully slow elevator to enjoy wraparound views of Havana as you tuck into inspired creations such as chicken in orange sauce, prawn and fruit *brochetas* with peanut dip, and creamy carrot soup.

El Idilio CUBAN $$

(Map p92; ☑830-7921; Av de los Presidentes, cnr Calle 15; mains CUC$5-9; ⊙noon-midnight) New, bold, adventurous – Idilio epitomises the Cuban culinary scene as it spreads its wings and flies. Anything goes here: pasta, ceviche and Cuban standards, or opt for the seafood medley peeled freshly off the BBQ before your very eyes.

Paladar Mesón Sancho Panza MEDITERRANEAN $$

(Map p92; ☑831-2862; Calle J No 508, btwn Calles 23 & 25; mains CUC$4-10; ⊙noon-11pm) Appropriately situated next to Parque Don Quijote, Paladar Mesón Sancho Panza doesn't let down its loyal literary *compañero*. Fine Spanish-influenced food is served in a lovely semi-alfresco restaurant adorned with ponds, planet-covered trellises and there's

a cake case that could make skipping dessert difficult. Set yourself up with paella (CUC$12 to CUC$16), lasagna or *brochetas* first.

Paladar los Amigos CUBAN $$

(Map p92; Calle M No 253; mains CUC$8-11; ⊙noon-midnight) Anthony Bourdain's paladar of choice while making his 2011 episode of *No Reservations,* Los Amigos sticks to the basics, offering traditional Cuban fare with lashings of rice and beans. The snarky one was suitably impressed, so they must be doing something right.

El Gringo Viejo CUBAN $$

(Map p92; ☑831-1946; Calle 21 No 454, btwn Calles E & F; mains CUC$10-12; ⊙noon-11pm) The Gringo offers a good atmosphere and large portions of invariably brilliant food. Locals and visitors love it for its speedy service, fine wine list and big portions of more adventurous fusion plates, such as smoked salmon with olives and Gouda, or crabmeat in red sauce.

Centro Vasco CARIBBEAN $$

(Map p92; Calle 3, cnr Calle 4; mains CUC$5-8; ⊙noon-midnight) This outpost of Havana's Basque society, near the Hotel Meliá Cohiba, has a decent restaurant and a 24-hour bar/cafe. The Caribbean food has Spanish inflections.

★Café Laurent INTERNATIONAL $$$

(Map p92; ☑832-6890; Calle M No 257, btwn 19 & 21; mains CUC$8-15) Talk about a hidden gem. The strangely underadvertised Café Laurent (there's no sign) is a sophisticated new restaurant encased, incongruously, in a glaringly ugly 1950s apartment block next to the Focsa building. Take the rickety lift to the 5th floor, open the door and jump hungrily into a new post-Fidel Castro reality.

Starched white tablecloths, polished glasses and fancy drapes furnish the bright modernist interior, while lamb stew laced with mint, and meatballs with sesame seeds headline the menu. Viva the culinary revolution!

Atelier CUBAN $$$

(Map p92; ☑836-2025; Calle 5 No 511 Altos, btwn Paseo & Calle 2; mains CUC$12-25) The first thing that hits you at Atelier is the stupendous wall art – huge, thought-provoking, religious-tinged paintings. The second is the antique wooden ceiling, terrace, and general old-school elegance. At some point you'll get around to the food – Cuban with a French influence – and it doesn't falter. Try the duck (the specialty) or the exotic (for Cuba) salmon and aubergine.

Paladar le Chansonnier   FRENCH $$$
(Map p92; ☑ 832-1576; Calle J No 257, btwn Calles 13 & 15) A great place to dine if you can find it (there's no sign) hidden in a faded mansion-turned-paladar whose revamped interior is dramatically more modern than the front facade. It's not just the name of this place that's French; French wine and French flavors show their colors in house specialties such as rabbit in red-wine sauce, caviar made from aubergine, and octopus with garlic and onions.

Opening times can be sporadic and it's often busy. Phone ahead.

La Torre   FRENCH, CARIBBEAN $$$
(Map p92; ☑ 838-3088; Edificio Focsa, cnr Calles 17 & M; mains from CUC$15; ⊙ 11:30am-12:30am) One of Havana's tallest and most talked-about restaurants is perched high above downtown Vedado atop the skyline-hogging Focsa building. A colossus of both modernist architecture and French/Cuban haute cuisine, this lofty fine-dining extravaganza combines sweeping city views with a progressive French-inspired menu that serves everything from artichokes to foie gras to *tarte amandine* (almond tart).

The prices are as distinctly non-Cuban as the ingredients, but with this level of service, it might be worth it.

Decameron   ITALIAN $$$
(Map p92; ☑ 832-2444; Línea No 753, btwn Paseo & Calle 2; meals CUC$12-15; ⊙ noon-midnight; ☑) Ugly from the outside, but far prettier within, the Decameron is an intimate Italian-influenced restaurant where you can order from the varied menu with abandon. Veggie pizza, lasagna bolognese, steak au poivre and a divine *calabaza* (pumpkin) soup – it's all good. On top of that, there's a decent wine selection and the kitchen is sympathetic to vegetarians.

Self-Catering

Supermercado Meridian   SUPERMARKET $
(Map p92; Galerías de Paseo, cnr Calle 1 & Paseo; ⊙ 10am-5pm Mon-Fri, 10am-2pm Sun) Across the street from the Hotel Meliá Cohiba, this supermarket has a good wine and liquor selection, lots of yogurt, cheese and crisps.

Agropecuario 17 & K   MARKET $
(Map p92; cnr Calles 17 & K) A 'capped' market with cheap prices, but limited selection.

Agropecuario 19 & A   MARKET $
(Map p92; Calle 19, btwn Calles A & B) Havana's 'gourmet' market, with cauliflower, fresh herbs and rarer produce during shoulder seasons.

Agropecuario 21 & J   MARKET $
(Map p92; cnr Calles 21 & J) Good selection, including potted plants.

🍷 Drinking & Nightlife

Bars

★ La Factoria Plaza Vieja   BAR
(Map p64; cnr San Ignacio & Muralla, Habana Viejo; ⊙ 11am-midnight) Havana's only microbrewery is on a boisterous corner of Plaza Vieja. Established by an Austrian company in 2004, it sells smooth, cold homemade beer at sturdy wooden benches set up outside on the cobbles or indoors in an atmospheric beer hall. Gather a group together and you'll get the amber nectar in a tall plastic tube drawn from a tap at the bottom. There's also an outside grill.

El Chanchullero   BAR
(Map p64; www.el-chanchullero.com; Brasil, btwn Bernaza & Christo, Habana Vieja; ⊙ 1pm-midnight) *Aqui jamás estuvo Hemingway* (Hemingway was never here) reads the blackboard outside roguish Chanchullero, expressing more than a hint of irony. It had to happen. While rich tourists toast Hemingway in the Bodeguita del Medio, poorer Cubans and foreign backpackers pay peanuts (CUC$2) for cocktails in their own boho alternative.

It's a small, clamorous, graffiti-ridden dive-bar where the music rocks in 4/4 time rather than 6/8. Stuff that in your cigar and smoke it, Ernesto!

Café Madrigal   BAR
(Map p92; Calle 17 No 302, btwn Calles 2 & 4, Vedado; ⊙ 6pm-2am Tue-Sun) Vedado flirts with bohemia in this dimly lit romantic bar that might have materialized serendipitously from Paris' Latin Quarter in the days of Joyce and Hemingway. Order a *tapita* (small tapa) and a cocktail, and retire to the atmospheric art nouveau terrace where the buzz of nighttime conversation competes with the noise of Yank tanks rattling in the street below.

La Bodeguita del Medio   BAR

(Map p64; Empedrado No 207, Habana Viejo; ☉11am-midnight) Made famous thanks to the rum-swilling exploits of Ernest Hemingway (who by association instantly sends the prices soaring), this is Havana's most celebrated bar. A visit here has become *de rigueur* for tourists who haven't yet cottoned on to the fact that the mojitos are better and (far) cheaper elsewhere.

Past visitors have included Salvador Allende, Fidel Castro, Nicolás Guillén, Harry Belafonte and Nat King Cole, all of whom have left their autographs on La Bodeguita's wall – along with thousands of others (save for the big names, the walls are repainted every few months). These days the clientele is less luminous, with package tourists from Varadero outnumbering beatnik bohemians. Purists claim the CUC$4 mojitos have lost their Hemingway-esque shine in recent years. Only one way to find out...

Bar Dos Hermanos   BAR

(Map p64; San Pedro No 304, Habana Viejo; ☉24hr) This once seedy, now polished bar down by the docks broadcasts a boastful list of former celebrity rum-sluggers on a plaque by the door, Federico Lorca, Marlon Brando, Errol Flynn and, of course, Hemingway among them. With its long wooden bar and salty seafaring atmosphere, it still spins a little magic.

El Floridita   BAR

(Map p64; Obispo No 557, Habana Viejo; ☉11am-midnight) Promoting itself as the 'cradle of the daiquirí,' El Floridita was a favorite of expat Americans long before Hemingway dropped by in the 1930s (hence the name, which means 'little Florida'). A bartender named Constante Ribalaigua invented the daiquirí soon after WWI, but it was Hemingway who popularized it, and ultimately the bar christened a drink in his honor: the Papa Hemingway Special (a grapefruit-flavored daiquirí).

His record – legend has it – was 13 doubles in one sitting. Any attempt to equal it at the current prices (CUC$6 and up for a shot) will cost you a small fortune – and a huge hangover.

La Lluvia de Oro   BAR

(Map p64; Obispo No 316, Habana Viejo; ☉24hr) It's on Obispo and there's always live music belting through the doorway, so it's always crowded. But with a higher-than-average *jinetero/jinetera* to tourist ratio, it might not be your most intimate introduction to Havana. Small snacks are available and the musician's 'hat' comes round every three songs.

La Dichosa   BAR

(Map p64; cnr Obispo & Compostela, Habana Viejo; ☉10am-midnight) It's hard to miss rowdy La Dichosa on busy Calle Obispo. Small and cramped with at least half the space given over to the resident band, this is a good place to sink a quick mojito.

Café Taberna   BAR

(Map p64; cnr Brasil & Mercaderes, Habana Viejo) Founded in 1772 and still glowing after a 21st-century makeover, this drinking and eating establishment is a great place to prop up the (impressive) bar and sink a few cocktails before dinner. The music, which gets swinging around 8pm, doffs its cap, more often than not, to one-time resident mambo king Benny Moré. Skip the food.

Café París   BAR

(Map p64; Obispo No 202, Habana Viejo; ☉24hr) Things never stand still at this rough-hewn Habana Vieja dive-bar, known for its live music and gregarious tourist-heavy atmosphere. On good nights, the rum flows and spontaneous dancing erupts.

Monserrate Bar   BAR

(Map p64; Obrapía No 410, Habana Viejo; ☉noon-midnight) A couple of doors down from El Floridita, Monserrate is a Hemingway-free zone, meaning the daiquirís are half the price.

Prado & Animas   BAR

(Map p88; Paseo de Martí, cnr Ánimas No 12, Centro Habana; ☉9am-9pm) Another good old-fashioned Prado place. The cafe also serves simple food and coffee, but it's best for a beer, sitting at one of the window tables beneath the baseball memorabilia (including a picture of a *pelota*-playing Fidel).

Prado No 12   BAR

(Map p88; Paseo de Martí No 12, Centro Habana; ☉noon-11pm) A slim flat-iron building on the corner of Prado and San Lázaro that serves drinks and simple snacks; Prado No 12 still resembles Havana in a 1950s time-warp. Soak up the atmosphere of this amazing city here after a sunset stroll along the Malecón.

Bar-Club Imágenes   BAR

(Map p92; Calzada No 602, Vedado; ☉9pm-5am) This upscale piano bar attracts something of an older crowd with its regular diet of *boleros* (ballads) and *trova,* though there are sometimes comedy shows; check the schedule posted outside. Affordable meals are available (minimum CUC$5).

3D Café
BAR

(Map p92; ☑ 863-0733; Calle 1 No 107, btwn Calles C & D, Vedado; ☺ 3pm-late) The ice-cool new place to see and be seen, this tiny but super slick bar/club close to the Malecón is full of dry ice and beautiful people enjoying nightly humor and live music shows. Food comes in small tapas and cocktails are *de rigeuer*. Call by or phone ahead as it has a reservation policy.

Bar el Polvorín
BAR

(Map p86; ☺ 10am-4am) Situated just below El Morro fort in the Parque Histórico Militar Morro-Cabaña, this bar offers drinks and light snacks on a patio overlooking the bay. It's surprisingly lively after dark.

Cafes

Museo del Chocolate
CAFE

(Map p64; cnr Amargura & Mercaderes, Habana Viejo; ☺ 9am-10pm) Chocolate addicts beware, this unmissable place in the heart of Habana Vieja is a lethal dose of chocolate, truffles and yet more chocolate (all made on the premises). Situated – with no irony intended – in Calle Amargura (literally, Bitterness Street), the sweet-toothed establishment is more a cafe than a museum, with a small cluster of marble tables set amid a sugary mélange of chocolate paraphernalia. Not surprisingly, everything on the menu contains one all-pervading ingredient: have it hot, cold, white, dark, rich or smooth – the stuff is divine, whichever way you choose.

Café el Escorial
CAFE

(Map p64; Mercaderes No 317, cnr Muralla, Habana Viejo; ☺ 9am-9pm) Opening onto Plaza Vieja and encased in a finely restored colonial mansion, there's something definitively European about El Escorial. Among some of the best caffeine infusions in the city served here are *café cubano, café con leche,* frappé, coffee liquor and even *daiquirí de café.* There's also a sweet selection of delicate cakes and pastries.

Café de las Infusiones
CAFE

(Map p64; Mercaderes, btwn Obispo & Obrapía, Habana Viejo; ☺ 8am-11pm) Wedged into Calle Mercaderes, this Habaguanex coffee house is a caffeine addict's heaven. You can order more than a dozen different cuppas here, including Irish coffee, punch coffee, mocha and cappuccino.

El Reloj Cuervo y Sobrinos
CAFE

(Map p64; cnr Oficios & Muralla, Habana Viejo; ☺ 10am-7pm Mon-Sat, 10am-1pm Sun) A new art deco coffee bar set in a restored watch

HAVANA DRINKING & NIGHTLIFE

THE LONG-AWAITED RETURN OF SLOPPY JOE'S

In 1919, young Spanish immigrant José García (aka 'Joe') opened a humble bar on the corner of Calles Agramonte (Zulueta) and Ánimas. Not over-fussy about the finer points of hygiene, José's joint quickly became notorious for its sloppy lack of sanitation, but its cocktails were abundant and cheap, and, by the end of the decade, 'Sloppy Joe's', as punters had humorously taken to calling the burgeoning establishment, had become something of a nexus for a thirsty contingent of Americans who frequented Havana during the prohibition era. The bar's reputation continued to grow in the 1930s and 1940s when the US Mafia moved in, bringing prostitution and gambling to the Caribbean capital. To satisfy their around-the-clock appetites, Joe added some culinary snacks, inventing a soggy sandwich filled with Cuban *ropa vieja* (shredded beef), known appropriately as the 'Sloppy Joe.' Celebrities and celebrity sycophants kept pouring in, 90% of them non-Cuban, and in 1937 a copycat bar opened up in Key West, Florida. Hemingway often stopped at Sloppy Joe's on his way between the Floridita and the Bodeguita del Medio, and he probably crossed paths at some time or other with Frank Sinatra and Graham Greene, both of whom were clients. The bar even featured in the 1959 film version of Greene's book, *Our Man in Havana.*

Sloppy Joe's (Map p88; Agramonte, cnr Ánimas), along with most of Havana's tawdry nightlife, fell on hard times after the Revolution when it really did start to look sloppy, and closed completely in the early 1960s after a fire gutted the interior. The noble neoclassical facade survived, however, and in 2013, after years of on-off rumors, it reopened as a fancier, cleaner version of its sloppy predecessor and a favorite with a new generation of tourists.

shop that belonged to an erstwhile Swiss watchmaker in the 1880s. Time your air-conditioned sightseeing break over a strong *café cubano*.

Café Literario del 'G'   CAFE
(Map p92; Calle 23, btwn Av de los Presidentes & Calle, Vedado) If Havana has a proverbial Left Bank, this is it: an unkempt student hangout full of arty wall scribblings and coffee-quaffing intellectuals discussing the merits of Guillén over Lorca. Relax in the airy front patio among the green plants and dusty books and magazines (available to read, lend and buy), and keep an ear out for one of the regular *trova* (traditional music), jazz and poetry presentations.

Café Fresa y Chocolate   CAFE
(Map p92; Calle 23, btwn Calles 10 & 12, Vedado; ☺9am-11pm) No ice cream here, just movie memorabilia. This is the HQ of the Cuban Film Institute and a nexus for coffee-quaffing students and art-house movie addicts. You can debate the merits of Almodóvar over Scorsese on the pleasant patio before disappearing to the film institute for a film preview.

Nightclubs
Café Cantante   NIGHTCLUB
(Map p92; ☑879-0710; cnr Paseo & Calle 39, Vedado; admission CUC$10; ☺9pm-5am Tue-Sat) Below the Teatro Nacional de Cuba (side entrance), this is a hip disco that offers live salsa music and dancing, as well as bar snacks and food. The clientele is mainly 'yummies' (young urban Marxist managers) and ageing male tourists with their youthful Cuban girlfriends. The cafe tends to get a little feisty.

Musically, there are regular appearances from big-name singers such as Haila María Mompie. No shorts, T-shirts or hats may be worn, and no under-18s are allowed.

Piano Bar Delirio Habanero   NIGHTCLUB
(Map p92; cnr Paseo & Calle 39, Vedado; admission CUC$5; ☺from 6pm Tue-Sun) This suave lounge upstairs in the Teatro Nacional de Cuba hosts everything from young *trovadores* to smooth, improvised jazz. The deep red couches abut a wall of glass overlooking the Plaza de la Revolución – it's stunning at night with the Martí Memorial alluringly backlit. Come up for air here when the adjoining nightclub gets too hot.

Cabaret Las Vegas   NIGHTCLUB
(Map p92; Infanta No 104, btwn Calles 25 & 27, Vedado; admission CUC$5; ☺10pm-4am) Rough and slightly seedy local music dive (with a midnight show) where a little rum and a lot of *No moleste, por favor* will help you withstand the overzealous entreaties of the hordes of haranguing *jineteras*.

Pico Blanco   NIGHTCLUB
(Map p92; Calle O, btwn Calles 23 & 25, Vedado; admission CUC$5-10; ☺9pm) An insanely popular nightclub, the Pico Blanco is on the 14th floor of the Hotel St John's in Vedado and kicks off nightly at 9pm. The program can be hit or miss. Some nights it's karaoke and cheesy *boleros;* another it's jamming with some rather famous Cuban musicians.

Club la Red   NIGHTCLUB
(Map p92; cnr Calles 19 & L, Vedado; admission CUC$3-5) Mixed convertible peso disco in Vedado.

Karachi Club   NIGHTCLUB
(Map p92; cnr Calles 17 & K, Vedado; admission CUC$3-5; ☺10pm-5am) Ferociously *caliente* (hot).

Discoteca Amanecer   NIGHTCLUB
(Map p92; Calle 15 No 12, btwn Calles N & O, Vedado; admission CUC$3-5; ☺10pm-4am) Fun if your budget is blown.

Club Tropical   NIGHTCLUB
(Map p92; cnr Línea & Calle F, Vedado; ☺4pm-2am) Relaxed evening cafe that turns into a hot local club after 10pm. Friday and Saturday nights are best.

☆ Entertainment

Nightlife exists in the Old Town, but it's more of the live-music-in-a-bar variety. Don't forget the excellent flamenco shows in Mesón de la Flota and – occasionally – Hostal Valencia. Although it may have lost its prerevolutionary reputation as a ritzy casino quarter, Vedado is still the place for nightlife in Havana while Centro's nightlife is edgier and more local than Vedado's.

Live Music
Jazz Café   LIVE MUSIC
(Map p92; top fl, Galerías de Paseo, cnr Calle, Vedado 1 & Paseo; cover after 8pm CUC$10; ☺noon-late) This upscale joint, located improbably in a shopping mall overlooking the Malecón, is a kind of jazz supper club, with dinner tables and a decent menu. At night, the club

swings into action with live jazz, *timba* and, occasionally, straight-up salsa. It attracts plenty of big-name acts.

Basílica Menor de
San Francisco de Asís CLASSICAL MUSIC
(Map p64; Plaza de San Francisco de Asís, Habana Vieja; tickets CUC$3-8; ☉ from 6pm Thu-Sat) Plaza de San Francisco de Asís' glorious church, which dates from 1738, has been reincarnated as a 21st-century museum and concert hall. The old nave hosts choral and chamber music two to three times a week (check the schedule at the door) and the acoustics inside are excellent. It's best to bag your ticket at least a day in advance.

Callejón de Hamel LIVE MUSIC
(Map p88; ☉ from noon Sun) Aside from its funky street murals and psychedelic art shops, the main reason to come to Havana's high temple of Afro-Cuban culture in Centro Habana is for the frenetic rumba music that kicks off every Sunday at around noon. For aficionados, this is about as raw and hypnotic as it gets, with interlocking drum patterns and lengthy rhythmic chants powerful enough to summon up the spirit of the *orishas* (Santería deities).

Due to a liberal sprinkling of tourists these days, some argue that the Callejón has lost much of its basic charm. Don't believe them. This place can still deliver.

Jazz Club la Zorra y El Cuervo LIVE MUSIC
(Map p92; cnr Calles 23 & O, Vedado; admission CUC$5-10; ☉ 10pm) Havana's most famous jazz club (The Vixen and the Crow) is on La Rampa, and opens its doors nightly at 10pm to long lines of committed music fiends. Enter through a red English phonebox and descend into a cramped, smoky basement. The freestyle jazz here is second to none, and in the past the club has hosted such big names as Chucho Valdés and George Benson.

La Casa de la Música
Centro Habana LIVE MUSIC
(Map p88; Av de Italia, btwn Concordia & Neptuno, Centro Habana; admission CUC$5-25) One of Cuba's best and most popular (check the queues) nightclubs and live-music venues. All the big names play here, from Bamboleo to Los Van Van – and you'll pay peanuts to see them. Of the city's two Casas de la Música, this Centro Habana version is a little edgier than its Miramar counterpart (some say it's too edgy), with big salsa bands and little space. Price varies depending on the band.

El Hurón Azul LIVE MUSIC
(Map p92; cnr Calles 17 & H, Vedado) If you want to rub shoulders with some socialist celebrities, hang out at Hurón Azul, the social club of Uneac. Replete with priceless snippets of Cuba's under-the-radar cultural life, most performances take place outside in the garden. Wednesday is the Afro-Cuban rumba, Saturday is authentic Cuban *boleros*, and alternate Thursdays there's jazz and *trova*. You'll never pay more than CUC$5.

Casa de la Amistad LIVE MUSIC
(Map p92; Paseo No 416, btwn Calles 17 & 19, Vedado) Housed in a beautiful rose-colored mansion on leafy Paseo, the Casa de la Amistad mixes traditional *son* sounds with suave Benny Moré music in a classic Italian Renaissance-style garden. Buena Vista Social Club luminary, Compay Segundo, was a regular here before his death in 2003, and there is a weekly 'Chan Chan' night in his honor.

Other perks include a restaurant, a bar, a cigar shop and the house itself – an Italianate masterpiece.

El Gato Tuerto LIVE MUSIC
(Map p92; Calle O No 14, btwn Calles 17 & 19, Vedado; drink minimum CUC$5; ☉ noon-6am) Once the HQ of Havana's alternative artistic and sexual scene, the 'one-eyed cat' is now a nexus for karaoke-crazy baby-boomers who come here to knock out rum-fuelled renditions of traditional Cuban *boleros*. It's hidden just off the Malecón in a quirky two-story house with turtles swimming in a front pool.

The upper floor is taken up by a restaurant, while down below late-night revelers raise the roof in a chic nightclub.

Conjunto Folklórico
Nacional de Cuba TRADITIONAL DANCE
(Map p92; Calle 4 No 103, btwn Calzada & Calle 5, Vedado; admission CUC$5; ☉ 3pm Sat) Founded in 1962, this high-energy ensemble specializes in Afro-Cuban dancing (all of the drummers are Santería priests). See them perform, and dance along during the regular Sábado de Rumba at El Gran Palenque. This group also performs at Teatro Mella. A major festival called **FolkCuba** unfolds here biannually during the second half of January.

Casa del Alba Cultural LIVE MUSIC

(Map p92; Línea, btwn Calles C & D, Vedado) This venue was designed to strengthen cultural solidarity between the ALBA nations (Cuba, Venezuela, Bolivia, Ecuador, Nicaragua), but in reality it hosts a variety of artistic and music-based shows and expos. It was opened in December 2009 with Raúl Castro, Daniel Ortega and Hugo Chávez in attendance.

La Madriguera LIVE MUSIC

(Map p92; cnr Salvador Allende & Luaces, Vedado; admission 5-10 pesos) Locals bill it as a 'hidden place for open ideas,' while outsiders are bowled over by its musical originality and artistic innovation. Welcome to La Madriguera, home to the Hermanos Saíz organization, the youth wing of Uneac. This is where the pulse of Cuba's young musical innovators beats the strongest.

Come here for arts, crafts, spontaneity and the three Rs: *reggaetón* (Cuban hip-hop), rap and rumba.

Theater

★ Gran Teatro de la Habana THEATER

(Map p88; ☎ 861-3077; cnr Paseo de Martí & San Rafael, Centro Habana; per person CUC$20; ⊙ box office 9am-6pm Mon-Sat, to 3pm Sun) The amazing neobaroque theater across from Parque Central is the seat of the acclaimed Ballet Nacional de Cuba, founded in 1948 by Alicia Alonso. It is also the home of the Cuban National Opera.

A theater since 1838, the building contains the grandiose Teatro García Lorca, along with two smaller concert halls: the Sala Alejo Carpentier and the Sala Ernesto Lecuono – where art films are sometimes shown. For upcoming events enquire at the ticket office. Backstage tours of the theater leave throughout the day (CUC$2).

Teatro América THEATER

(Map p88; Av de Italia No 253, btwn Concordia & Neptuno, Centro Habana) Housed in a classic art deco *rascacielo* on Galiano (Av de Italia), the América seems to have changed little since its theatrical heyday in the 1930s

GAY HAVANA

The Revolution had a hostile attitude toward homosexuality in its early days. While the Stonewall riots were engulfing New York City, Cuban homosexuals were still being sent to re-education camps by a government that was dominated by macho, bearded ex-guerrillas dressed in military fatigues.

But, since the 1990s, the tide has been turning, spearheaded somewhat ironically by Fidel's combative niece Mariela (the daughter of current president, Raúl Castro), the director of the Cuban National Center for Sex Education in Havana. In May 2013, Mariela was granted a visa by the American government to travel to the US in order to accept an award from Equality Forum for her gay rights advocacy.

An important landmark for the LGBT community was the 1993 release of the Oscar-nominated film *Fresa y chocolate*, a tale of homosexual love between a young communist student and a skeptical Havana artist. A decade later, gay characters hit the headlines again in a popular government-sponsored Cuban soap opera called *La cara oculta de la luna* (The Dark Side of the Moon).

The unprecedented happened in June 2008 when the Cuban government passed a law permitting free sex-change operations to qualifying citizens courtesy of the country's famously far-sighted health system. And in November 2012, Cuba elected its first transgender person to public office when Adela Hernanadez (a woman) won a municipal seat in Villa Clara province.

Though Cuba still has no 'official' gay clubs, there are plenty of places where a 'gay scene' has taken root. Havana is the obvious focus, with the busy junction of Calles 23 and L in Vedado outside the Cine Yara serving as the main nighttime cruising spot. Other meeting places include the Malecón below the Hotel Nacional and the beach at Boca Ciega in Playas del Este.

Hang around at these places in the evening to get word of spontaneous gay parties in private houses, or bigger shindigs in venues such as Parque Lenin. You can now also enjoy gay film nights at the Icaic headquarters on the corner of Calles 23 and 12 and, since 2009, an annual gay parade along Calle 23 in mid-May. Legally, lesbians enjoy the same rights as gay men, though there is a less evident lesbian 'scene'.

and 1940s. It plays host to vaudeville variety, comedy, dance, jazz and salsa; shows are normally staged on Saturdays at 8:30pm and Sundays at 5pm. You can also enquire about dance lessons here.

Teatro Fausto
THEATER
(Map p88; Paseo de Martí No 201, Centro Habana) Rightly renowned for its side-splitting comedy shows, Fausto is a streamlined art deco theater on Prado.

Teatro Nacional de Cuba
THEATER
(Map p92; ☑ 879-6011; cnr Paseo & Calle 39, Vedado; per person CUC$10; ☺ box office 9am-5pm & before performances) One of the twin pillars of Havana's cultural life, the Teatro Nacional de Cuba on Plaza de la Revolución is the modern rival to the Gran Teatro in Centro Habana. Built in the 1950s as part of Jean Forestier's grand city expansion, the complex hosts landmark concerts, foreign theater troupes, La Colmenita children's company and the Ballet Nacional de Cuba.

The main hall, Sala Avellaneda, stages big events such as musical concerts or plays by Shakespeare, while the smaller Sala Covarrubias along the back puts on a more daring program (the seating capacity of the two halls combined is 3300). The 9th floor is a rehearsal and performance space where the newest, most experimental stuff happens. The ticket office is at the far end of a separate single-story building beside the main theater.

Teatro Amadeo Roldán
THEATER
(Map p92; ☑ 832-1168; cnr Calzada & Calle D, Vedado; per person CUC$10) Constructed in 1922 and burnt down by an arsonist in 1977, this wonderfully decorative neoclassical theater was rebuilt in 1999 in the exact style of the original. Named after the famous Cuban composer and the man responsible for bringing Afro-Cuban influences into modern classical music, the theater is one of Havana's grandest with two different auditoriums.

The Orquesta Sinfónica Nacional plays in the 886-seat Sala Amadeo Roldán, while soloists and small groups are showcased in the 276-seat Sala García Caturla.

Teatro Mella
THEATER
(Map p92; Línea No 657, btwn Calles A & B, Vedado) Occupying the site of the old Rodi Cinema on Línea, the Teatro Mella offers one of Havana's most comprehensive programs, including an international ballet festival,

comedy shows, theater, dance and intermittent performances from the famous Conjunto Folklórico Nacional. If you have kids, come to the children's show Sunday at 11am.

Sala Teatro Hubert de Blanck
THEATER
(Map p92; Calzada No 657, btwn Calles A & B, Vedado) This theater is named for the founder of Havana's first conservatory of music (1885). The Teatro Estudio based here is Cuba's leading theater company. You can usually see plays in Spanish on Saturday at 8:30pm and on Sunday at 7pm. Tickets are sold just prior to the performance.

Sala Teatro el Sótano
THEATER
(Map p92; Calle K No 514, btwn Calles 25 & 27, Vedado; ☺5-8:30pm Fri & Sat, 3-5pm Sun) If you understand Spanish, it's well worth attending some of the cutting-edge contemporary theater that's a staple of Grupo Teatro Rita Montaner at this venue near the Habana Libre.

Café Teatro Brecht
THEATER
(Map p92; cnr Calles 13 & I, Vedado) Varied performances take place. Your best bet is 10:30pm on a Saturday (tickets go on sale one hour before the performance).

Teatro Nacional de Guiñol
THEATER
(Map p92; Calle M, btwn Calles 17 & 19, Vedado) This venue has quality puppet shows and children's theater.

Cabaret
Habana Café
CABARET
(Map p92; Paseo, btwn Calles 1 & 3, Vedado; admission CUC$10; ☺from 9:30pm) A hip and trendy nightclub cum cabaret show at the Hotel Meliá Cohiba laid out in 1950s American style. After 1am the tables are cleared and the place rocks to 'international music' until the cock crows. Excellent value.

Cabaret Parisién
CABARET
(Map p92; ☑ 836-3564; cnr Calles 21 & O, Vedado; admission CUC$35; ☺9pm) One rung down from Marianao's Tropicana, in both price and quality, the nightly Cabaret Parisién in the Hotel Nacional is still well worth a look, especially if you're staying in or around Vedado. It's the usual mix of frills, feathers and semi-naked women, but the choreography is first class and the whole spectacle has excellent kitsch value.

Copa Room
CABARET
(Map p92; ☑ 836-4051; cnr Paseo & Malecón, Vedado; admission CUC$20; ☺9pm) Doormen in

tuxes and an atmosphere that's pure 1950s retro make the refurbished Copa Room in Meyer Lansky's Hotel Riviera look like a nostalgic walk through *The Godfather: Part II*.

Cabaret Turquino
CABARET

(Map p92; Calle L, btwn Calles 23 & 25, Vedado; admission CUC$15; ⊗ from 10pm) Spectacular shows in a spectacular setting on the 25th floor of the Hotel Habana Libre.

Cultural Centers

Fundación Alejo Carpentier
CULTURAL CENTER

(Map p64; Empedrado No 215, Habana Vieja; ⊗8am-4pm Mon-Fri) Near the Plaza de la Catedral. Check for cultural events at this baroque former palace of the Condesa de la Reunión (1820s) where Carpentier set his famous novel *El Siglo de las Luces*.

Instituto Cubano de Amistad con los Pueblos
CULTURAL CENTER

(ICAP; Map p92; ☎ 830-3114; Paseo No 416, btwn Calles 17 & 19, Vedado; ⊗11am-11pm) Rocking cultural and musical events in an elegant mansion (1926); there's also a restaurant, bar and cigar shop.

Casa de las Américas
CULTURAL CENTER

(Map p92; ☎ 838-2706; cnr Calles 3 & G, Vedado) Powerhouse of Cuban and Latin American culture, with conferences, exhibitions, a gallery, book launches and concerts. The casa's annual literary award is one of the Spanish-speaking world's most prestigious. Pick up a schedule of weekly events in the library.

Cinemas

There are about 200 cinemas in Havana. Most have several screenings daily, and every theater posts the *Cartelera Icaic*, which lists show times for the entire city. Tickets are usually CUC$2; queue early. Hundreds of movies are screened throughout Havana during the Festival Internacional del Nuevo Cine Latinoamericano in late November/ early December. Schedules are published daily in the *Diario del Festival*, available in the morning at big theaters and the Hotel Nacional. Here are the best movie houses:

Cine Infanta
CINEMA

(Map p88; Infanta No 357, Centro Habana) Newly renovated Infanta is possibly Havana's plushest cinema. It's an important venue during the International Film Festival.

Cine Actualidades
CINEMA

(Map p88; Av de las Misiones No 262, btwn Neptuno & Virtudes, Centro Habana) Timeworn place centrally located behind the Hotel Plaza.

Cine Charles Chaplin
CINEMA

(Map p92; Calle 23 No 1157, btwn Calles 10 & 12, Vedado) An art-house cinema adjacent to the Icaic HQ. Don't miss the poster gallery of great Cuban classic films next door or the movie grapevine that is the Café Fresa y Chocolate opposite.

Cine la Rampa
CINEMA

(Map p92; Calle 23 No 111, Vedado) Ken Loach movies, French classics, film festivals – catch them all at this Vedado staple which houses the Cuban film archive.

Cine Payret
CINEMA

(Map p88; Paseo de Martí No 505, Centro Habana) Opposite the Capitolio, this is Centro Habana's largest and most luxurious cinema, erected in 1878. Plenty of American movies play here.

Cine Riviera
CINEMA

(Map p92; Calle 23 No 507, btwn Calles G & H, Vedado) Big pop, rock and sometimes rap concerts happen here. The movies are a mix of Latin American, European and North American, and the audience has a strong student demographic.

Cine Trianón
CINEMA

(Map p92; Línea No 706, Vedado) Movies or live theater in a salubrious setting.

Cine Yara
CINEMA

(Map p92; cnr Calles 23 & L, Vedado) One big screen and two video *salas* (cinemas) here at Havana's most famous cinema. The venue for many a hot date.

Cinecito
CINEMA

(Map p88; San Rafael No 68, Centro Habana) Films for kids behind the Hotel Inglaterra. There's another one next to Cine Chaplin on Calles 23 and 12.

Sports

Ciudad Deportiva
SPORT

(cnr Av de la Independencia & Vía Blanca, Vedado; admission 5 pesos) 'Sport City' is Cuba's premier sports training center and big basketball, volleyball, boxing and track contests happen at the coliseum here. The P-2 metro bus from the corner of Línea and Av de los Presidentes (Calle G) stops across the street.

LOCAL KNOWLEDGE

BASEBALL CALIENTE

For a no-holds-barred initiation into Havana's baseball passion, visit the **Esquina Caliente** (literally, 'hot corner') in Parque Central, where an almost permanent bevy of boisterous *habaneros* loudly discuss baseball around the clock. Even better, go to a game. Havana's two teams, Los Industriales (the proverbial Manchester United) and the Metropolitanos (the perennial underachievers) alternate fixtures at the **Estadio Latinoamericano** (Zequiera No 312, Vedado; tickets CUC$2). Games are 7:30pm Tuesday, Wednesday and Thursday, and 1:30pm Saturday and Sunday.

Sala Polivalente Ramón Fonst SPORT
(Map p92; Av de la Independencia, Vedado; admission 1 peso) Basketball and volleyball games are held at this tatty-looking stadium opposite the main bus station.

Kid Chocolate SPORT
(Map p88; Paseo de Martí, Centro Habana) A boxing club directly opposite the Capitolio, which usually hosts matches on Friday at 7pm.

🛍 Shopping

Shopping isn't Havana's big draw – this, after all, is a city where disposable income is something of an oxymoron. That said, there are some decent outlets for travelers and tourists, particularly if you're after the standard Cuban shopping triumvirate of rum, cigars and coffee. Art is another lucrative field. Havana's art scene is cutting edge and ever changing, and collectors, browsers and admirers will find many galleries in which to while away hours. There are at least a dozen studios in Calle Obispo alone. For gallery events, look for the free *Arte en La Habana,* a triquarterly listings flyer (the San Cristóbal agency on Plaza de San Francisco de Asís usually has them).

🏛 Habana Vieja

⭐ **Centro Cultural Antiguos Almacenes de Deposito San José** ARTS & CRAFTS
(Map p64; cnr Av Desamparados & San Ignacio; ⊘10am-6pm Mon-Sat) In November 2009 Havana's open-air handicraft market moved under the cover of this old shipping warehouse in Av del Puerto. Check your socialist ideals at the door. Herein lies a hive of free-enterprise and (unusually for Cuba) haggling. Possible souvenirs include paintings, *guayabera* shirts, woodwork, leather items, jewelry and numerous apparitions of the highly marketable El Che.

There are also snacks, clean-ish toilets and a tourist information representative from the San Cristóbal agency. It's as popular with Cubans as it is with tourists.

Palacio de la Artesanía SOUVENIRS
(Map p64; Cuba No 64; ⊘9am-7pm) A former 18th-century colonial palace turned into a shopping mall! Gathered around a shaded central patio it is one-stop shopping for souvenirs, cigars, crafts, musical instruments, CDs, clothing and jewelry at fixed prices. Join the gaggles of tour-bus escapees and fill your bag.

Longina Música MUSIC
(Map p64; Obispo No 360, btwn Habana & Compostela; ⊘10am-7pm Mon-Sat, 10am-1pm Sun) This place on the pedestrian mall has a good selection of CDs, plus musical instruments such as bongos, guitars, maracas, *guiros* (gourds) and *tumbadoras* (conga drums). It often places loudspeakers in the street outside to grab the attention of passing tourists.

Casa de Carmen Montilla ART
(Map p64; Oficios No 164; ⊘10:30am-5:30pm Tue-Sat, 9am-1pm Sun) An important art gallery named after a celebrated Venezuelan painter who maintained a studio here until her death in 2004. Spread across three floors, the house exhibits the work of Montilla and other popular Cuban and Venezuelan artists. The rear courtyard features a huge ceramic mural by Alfredo Sosabravo.

Plaza de Armas Secondhand Book Market BOOKS
(Map p64; cnr Obispo & Tacón; ⊘9am-7pm Tue-Sun) A book market stocking old, new and rare books, including Hemingway, some weighty poetry and plenty of written pontifications from Fidel. It's all here under the leafy boughs in Plaza de Armas. Browse to your heart's content.

Habana 1791
PERFUME

(Map p64; Mercaderes No 156, btwn Obrapía & Lamparilla) A specialist shop that sells perfume made from tropical flowers, Havana 1791 retains the air of a working museum. Floral fragrances are mixed by hand – you can see the petals drying in a laboratory out the back.

Gallery Estudio Medina Photos
PHOTOGRAPHY

(Map p64; Muralla No 166, btwn Cuba & San Ignacio) Extremely accomplished photographer selling color and black-and-white shots of Havana life; some of them are reduced onto CUC$2.50 postcards.

Fayad Jamás
BOOKS

(Map p64; Obispo, btwn Habana & Aguiar; ⊘9am-7pm Mon-Sat, 9am-1pm Sun) Havana's newest bookstore is actually a throwback to the 1920s refurbished to fit in with its Old Town surroundings. Editions are mainly in Spanish, but there are some interesting cultural magazine including *Temas*.

Librería la Internacional
BOOKS

(Map p64; Obispo No 526; ⊘9am-7pm Mon-Sat, 9am-3pm Sun) Good selection of guides, photography books and Cuban literature in English; next door is Librería Cervantes, an antiquarian bookseller.

Estudio Galería los Oficios
ART

(Map p64; Oficios No 166; ⊘10am-5:30pm Mon-Sat) Pop into this gallery to see the large, hectic but intriguing canvases by Nelson Domínguez, whose workshop is upstairs.

Taller de Serigrafía René Portocarrero ART

(Map p64; Cuba No 513, btwn Brasil & Muralla; ⊘9am-4pm Mon-Fri) Paintings and prints by young Cuban artists are exhibited and sold here (from CUC$30 to CUC$150). You can also see the artists at work.

Moderna Poesía
BOOKS

(Map p64; Obispo 525; ⊘10am-8pm) Perhaps Havana's best spot for Spanish-language books is this classic art deco building at the western end of Calle Obispo.

🔒 Centro Habana

Galería la Acacia
ART

(Map p88; San Martín No 114, btwn Industria & Consulado; ⊘10am-3:30pm Mon-Fri, 10am-1pm Sat) This gallery behind the Gran Teatro de La Habana has paintings by leading artists such as Zaida del Río, plus antiques. Export permits are arranged.

El Bulevar
MARKET

(Map p88; San Rafael, btwn Paseo de Martí & Av de Italia) This is the pedestrianized part of Calle San Rafael near the Hotel Inglaterra. Come here for peso snacks and surprises and 1950s shopping nostalgia.

La Manzana de Gómez
SHOPPING CENTER

(Map p88; cnr Agramonte & San Rafael) Talk about faded glory! This once-elegant European-style covered shopping arcade was built in 1910. Today it's full of shabby, half-empty stores, including an improbable adidas outlet.

Area de Vendedores por Cuenta Propia
MARKET

(Map p88; Máximo Gómez No 259; ⊘9am-5pm Mon-Sat) This is a permanent flea market where you can pick up Santería beads, old books, leather belts etc.

Librería Luis Rogelio Nogueras
BOOKS

(Map p88; Av de Italia No 467, btwn Barcelona & San Martín) Literary magazines and Cuban literature in Spanish at one of Centro's best bookstores.

🔒 Vedado

Galería de Arte Latinoamericano
ART

(Map p92; cnr Calles 3 & G; admission CUC$2; ⊘10am-4:30pm Tue-Sat, 9am-1pm Sun) Situated inside the Casa de las Américas and featuring art from all over Latin America.

Instituto Cubano del Arte e Industria Cinematográficos
SOUVENIRS

(Map p92; Calle 23, btwn Calles 10 & 12; ⊘10am-5pm) Best place in Havana for rare Cuban movie posters and DVDs. The shop is inside the Icaic (Cuban Film Institute) building and accessed through the Café Fresa y Chocolate.

Feria de la Artesanía
SOUVENIRS

(Map p92; Malecón, btwn Calles D & E; ⊘from 10:30am, closed Wed) This artisan market is a pale imitation of Habana Vieja's Antiguos Almacenes, with a few handmade shoes and sandals, and some old stamps and coins thrown in for good measure.

ARTex
SOUVENIRS

(Map p92; cnr Calles 23 & L) A fabulous selection of old movie posters, antique postcards, T-shirts and, of course, all the greatest Cuban films on videotape are sold at this shop inside the Cine Yara.

WHERE TO BUY RUM, CIGARS & COFFEE

Shops selling Cuba's top three homegrown products are relatively common in Havana. All are government-run. As a rule of thumb, never buy cigars off the street, as they will almost always be damaged and/or substandard. Havana's prime factory-outlet cigar shop is at the **Real Fábrica de Tabacos Partagás** (Map p88; Industria No 520, btwn Barcelona & Dragones; ⊙9am-7pm) and is always well stocked. Another excellent option is La Casa del Habano (p141) in Miramar, which has an air-conditioned smoking room and a reputable bar/restaurant. While many top hotels stock cigars, the best shop is in the **Hostal Condes de Villanueva** (Map p64; Mercaderes No 202). There's an equally good option just down the street in the **Museo del Tabaco** (Map p64; Mercaderes No 120).

For rum, look no further than the **Fundación Havana Club shop** (Map p64; San Pedro No 262; ⊙9am-9pm) at the Museo de Ron in Habana Vieja.

Coffee is sold at all of the above places, but for a bit more choice and a decent taster cup pop into **La Casa del Café** (Map p64; Baratillo, cnr Obispo; ⊙9am-5pm) just off Plaza de Armas in Habana Vieja.

Galerías de Paseo   SHOPPING CENTER
(Map p92; cnr Calle 1 & Paseo; ⊙9am-6pm Mon-Sat, 9am-1pm Sun) Across the street from the Hotel Meliá Cohiba, this place is an upscale (for Cuba) shopping center with some designer labels and even a car dealership. It sells well-made clothes and other consumer items to tourists and affluent Cubans.

Plaza Carlos III   SHOPPING CENTER
(Map p88; Av Salvador Allende, btwn Arbol Seco & Retiro; ⊙10am-6pm Mon-Sat) After Plaza América in Varadero, this is probably Cuba's flashiest shopping mall – and there's barely a foreigner in sight. Step in on a Saturday and see the double economy working at a feverish pitch.

Librería Centenario del Apóstol   BOOKS
(Map p92; Calle 25 No 164; ⊙10am-5pm Mon-Sat, 9am-1pm Sun) Great assortment of used books with a José Martí bias in downtown Vedado.

Librería Rayuela   BOOKS
(Map p92; cnr Calles 3 & G; ⊙9am-4:30pm Mon-Fri) This small but respected store bivouacked in the bookish Casa de las Américas building is great for contemporary literature, compact discs and some guidebooks.

La Habana Sí   SOUVENIRS
(Map p92; cnr Calles 23 & L; ⊙10am-10pm Mon-Sat, 10am-7pm Sun) This shop opposite the Hotel Habana Libre has a good selection of CDs, cassettes, books, crafts and postcards.

⊕ Information

EMERGENCY
Asistur (⌨866-4499, emergency 866-8527; www.asistur.cu; Paseo de Martí No 208, Centro Habana; ⊙8:30am-5:30pm Mon-Fri, 8am-2pm Sat) Someone on staff should speak English; the alarm center here is open 24 hours.
Fire Service (⌨105)
Police (⌨106)

INTERNET ACCESS
Havana doesn't have any private internet cafes. Your best bet outside the Etecsa Telepuntos is the posher hotels. Most Habaguanex hotels in Habana Vieja have internet terminals and sell scratch cards (CUC$6 per hour) that work throughout the chain. You don't have to be a guest to use them.

You could also try the Hotel Business Centers at: **Hotel Habana Libre** (Calle L, btwn Calles 23 & 25, Vedado); **Hotel Inglaterra** (Paseo de Martí No 416, Centro Habana); **Hotel Nacional** (cnr Calles O & 21, Vedado); Hotel Iberostar Parque Central (p107). Costs vary at these places.

For wi-fi you can purchase a password for CUC$8 per hour for use in the lobby of Hotel Iberostar Parque Central, Hotel Saratoga or Hotel Meliá Cohiba.
Etecsa Telepunto (Habana 406; ⊙9am-7pm) Six terminals in a back room. Cost is CUC$6 per hour.

MEDIA
Cuba has a fantastic radio culture, where you'll hear everything from salsa to Supertramp, plus live sports broadcasts and soap operas. Radio is also the best source for listings on concerts, plays, movies and dances.
Radio Ciudad de La Habana (820AM & 94.9FM) Cuban tunes by day, foreign pop at night; great '70s flashback at 8pm on Thursday and Friday.
Radio Metropolitana (910AM & 98.3FM) Jazz and traditional *boleros* (music in 3/4 time); excellent Sunday afternoon rock show.

Radio Musical Nacional (590AM & 99.1FM) Classical.

Radio Progreso (640AM & 90.3 FM) Soap operas and humor.

Radio Rebelde (640AM, 710AM & 96.7FM) News, interviews, good mixed music, plus baseball games.

Radio Reloj (950AM & 101.5FM) News, plus the time every minute of every day.

Radio Taíno (1290AM & 93.3FM) National tourism station with music, listings and interviews in Spanish and English. Nightly broadcasts (5pm to 7pm) list what's happening around town.

MEDICAL SERVICES

Most of Cuba's specialist hospitals offering services to foreigners are based in Havana; see www.cubanacan.cu for details. The Playa and Marianao areas also have international clinics and pharmacies.

There are hotel pharmacies at **Hotel Habana Libre** (☑ 831-9538; Calle L, btwn Calles 23 & 25, Vedado), where products are sold in convertibles, and **Hotel Sevilla** (☑ 861-5703; Prado, cnr Trocadero, Habana Vieja).

Centro Oftalmológico Camilo Cienfuegos (☑ 832-5554; cnr Calle L No 151 & Calle 13, Vedado) Head straight here with eye problems; also has an excellent pharmacy.

Farmacia Taquechel (☑ 862-9286; Obispo No 155, Habana Vieja; ☺ 9am-6pm) Next to the Hotel Ambos Mundos. Cuban wonder drugs such as anticholesterol medication PPG sold in pesos here.

Hospital Nacional Hermanos Ameijeiras (☑ 877-6053; San Lázaro No 701, Centro Habana) Special hard-currency services, general consultations and hospitalization. Enter via the lower level below the parking lot off Padre Varela (ask for CEDA in Section N).

MONEY

Banco de Crédito y Comercio Vedado (cnr Línea & Paseo); Vedado (☑ 870-2684; Calle 23, Airline Bldg) Expect lines.

Banco Financiero Internacional Habana Vieja (☑ 860-9369; cnr Oficios & Brasil); Vedado (Calle L, Hotel Habana Libre, btwn Calles 23 & 25)

Banco Metropolitano Centro Habana (☑ 862-6523; Av de Italia No 452, cnr San Martín); Vedado (☑ 832-2006; cnr Línea & Calle M)

Cadeca Centro Habana (cnr Neptuno & Agramonte; ☺ 9am-noon & 1-7pm Mon-Sat); **Habana Vieja** (cnr Oficios & Lamparilla; ☺ 8am-7pm Mon-Sat, 8am-1pm Sun); **Vedado** (Calle 23, btwn Calles K & L; ☺ 7am-2:30pm & 3:30-10pm); **Vedado** (Calle 19, btwn Calles A & B, Mercado Agropecuario; ☺ 7am-6pm Mon-Sat,

8am-1pm Sun); **Vedado** (cnr Malecón & Calle D) Cadeca gives cash advances and changes traveler's checks at 3.5% commission Monday to Friday (4% weekends).

Cambio (Obispo No 257, Habana Vieja; ☺ 8am-10pm) The best opening hours in town and an ATM.

POST

DHL can be found at two locations in **Vedado** (☑ 832-2112; Calzada No 818, btwn Calles 2 & 4; ☺ 8am-5pm Mon-Fri) and **Vedado** (☑ 836-3564; Hotel Nacional, cnr Calles O & 21).

Post offices include those in: **Centro Habana** (Gran Teatro, cnr San Martín & Paseo de Martí); **Habana Vieja** (Oficios No 102, Plaza de San Francisco de Asís); **Habana Vieja** (Obispo No 518, Unidad de Filatelia; ☺ 9am-7pm); **Vedado** (cnr Línea & Paseo; ☺ 8am-8pm Mon-Sat); **Vedado** (cnr Calles 23 & C; ☺ 8am-6pm Mon-Fri, 8am-noon Sat); **Vedado** (Av de la Independencia, btwn Plaza de la Revolución & Terminal de Ómnibus; ☺ stamp sales 24hr). The Independencia branch one has many services, including photo developing, a bank and a Cadeca. The **Museo Postal Cubano** (☑ 870-5581; admission CUC$1; ☺ 10am-5pm Sat & Sun) here has a philatelic shop. The post office at Obispo, Habana Vieja, also has stamps for collectors.

TELEPHONE

Etecsa Telepuntos (Aguilar No 565; ☺ 8am-9:30pm). There's a **Museo de las Telecomunicaciones** (☺ 9am-6pm Tue-Sat) here if you get bored waiting. Another office is in **Habana Vieja** (Habana 406).

TOILETS

Havana isn't over-endowed with clean and available public toilets. Most tourists slip into upscale hotels if they're caught short. Make sure you tip the lady at the door.

Hotel Ambos Mundos (Obispo No 153, Habana Vieja) Tip the attendant.

Hotel Iberostar Parque Central (Neptuno, btwn Agramonte & Paseo de Martí) Bear left inside the entrance and behind the staircase.

Hotel Nacional (cnr Calles O & 21, Vedado) Right in the lobby and left past the elevators.

Hotel Sevilla (Trocadero No 55, btwn Paseo de Martí & Agramonte, Centro Habana) Turn right inside the lobby.

TOURIST INFORMATION

Infotur is based at the **airport** (☑ 642-6101; Terminal 3 Aeropuerto Internacional José Martí; ☺ 24hr) and in **Habana Vieja** (☑ 863-6884; cnr Obispo & San Ignacio; ☺ 10am-1pm & 2 7pm). It books tours and sells maps and phone cards.

TRAVEL AGENCIES

Many of the following agencies also have offices at the airport, in the international arrivals lounge of Terminal 3.

Cubamar Viajes (☑ 833-2523, 833-2524; www.cubamarviajes.cu; Calle 3, btwn Calle 12 & Malecón, Vedado; ☺ 8:30am-5pm Mon-Sat) Travel agency for Campismo Popular cabins countrywide.

Cubanacán (☑ 873-2686; www.cubanacan. cu; Hotel Nacional, cnr Calles O & 21, Vedado; ☺ 8am-7pm) Very helpful; head here if you want to arrange fishing or diving at Marina Hemingway; also in Hotel Iberostar Parque Central, Hotel Inglaterra and Hotel Habana Libre.

Cubatur (☑ 835-4155; cnr Calles 23 & M, Vedado; ☺ 8am-8pm) Below Hotel Habana Libre. This agency pulls a lot of weight and finds rooms where others can't, which goes a long way toward explaining its slacker attitude. It has desks in most of the main hotels.

Ecotur (☑ 649-1055; www.ecoturcuba.co.cu; Av Independencia No 116, cnr Santa Catalina, Cerro) Sells all kinds of naturalistic excursions.

San Cristóbal Agencia de Viajes (☑ 861-9171, 861-9172; www.viajessancristobal.cu; Oficios No 110, btwn Lamparilla & Amargura, Habana Vieja; ☺ 8:30am-5:30pm Mon-Fri, 8:30am-2pm Sat, 9am-noon Sun) Habaguanex agency operating Habana Vieja's classic hotels; income helps finance restoration. It offers the best tours in Havana.

ℹ Getting There & Away

AIR

Cubana Airlines (☑ 834-4446; Calle 23 No 64, cnr Infanta, Vedado; ☺ 8:30am-4pm Mon-Fri, 8:30am-noon Sat) head office is at the Malecón end of the Airline Building on La Rampa. International or domestic tickets. It's often packed.

Aerocaribbean (☑ 832-7584; Calle 23 No 64, Airline Bldg, Vedado) is another airline with domestic services.

BOAT

Buses connecting with the hydrofoil service to Isla de la Juventud leave at 9am from the **Terminal de Ómnibus** (☑ 878-1841; cnr Av de la Independencia & 19 de Mayo, Vedado), near the Plaza de la Revolución, but they're often late. You'll be told to arrive at least an hour early to buy your ticket; heed this advice. Bus/boat combo tickets are sold at the kiosk marked 'NCC' between gates 9 and 10, and we found the staff quite unhelpful. Tickets cost CUC$50 for the boat and CUC$0.25 for the bus. Bring your passport.

BUS

Víazul (☑ 881-1413, 881-5652; www.viazul.com; cnr Calle 26 & Zoológico, Nuevo Vedado) covers most destinations of interest to travelers, in deluxe, air-conditioned coaches. All buses are direct except those to Guantánamo and Baracoa; for these destinations you must change in Santiago de Cuba. You board all Víazul buses at the inconveniently located terminal 3km southwest of Plaza de la Revolución. This is where you'll

---

HAVANA SCAMS

Tourist scams are the bane of travelers in many countries, and Cuba is no exception, although places like Havana rates more favorably than plenty of other Latin American cities. Some Cuban con tricks are familiar to anyone who has traveled internationally. Agree on taxi fares before getting in a cab, don't change money on the street and always check your bill and change in restaurants. Cuba's professional tricksters are called *jineteros* (literally, jockeys). They are particularly proficient in Havana where their favorite pastime is selling knock-off cigars to unsuspecting tourists.

Cuba's dual currency invites scammers. Although the two sets of banknotes look very similar, there are actually 25 *moneda nacional* (MN$; sometimes called Cuban pesos) to every Cuban convertible (CUC$). Familiarize yourself with the banknotes early on (most banks have pictorial charts) and double-check all money transactions to avoid being left seriously out of pocket.

Casas particulares (private homestays) attract jineteros who prey on both travelers and casa owners. An increasingly common trick is for a *jinetero* to pose falsely as a reputed casa particular owner who a traveler has booked in advance (often ones listed in this book), and then proceed to lead you to a different house where they will extract CUC$5 to $CUC10 commission (added to your room bill). On some occasions, travelers are not aware they have been led to the wrong home. There have even been reports of people writing bad reviews on Tripadvisor for the wrong casas.

If you've prebooked a casa, or are using this book to find one, make sure you turn up without a commission-seeking *jinetero*.

also have to come to buy tickets in the Venta de Boletines office. You can get full schedules on the website or at Infotur. Some casa particular owners may offer help with prearranging bus tickets. Ask.

Havana-bound, you *might* be able to get off the Víazul bus from Varadero/Matanzas in Centro Habana right after the tunnel (check with the driver beforehand), but if you arrive from most other points you'll be let out at the Nuevo Vedado terminal. Buses from the Nuevo Vedado terminal to the city are unreliable unless you want to do a bit of walking. A taxi will cost you a rip-off CUC$10, unless you negotiate extra hard.

A newer alternative to the increasingly crowded Víazul buses is Conectando run by Cubanacán which offers six itineraries linking Havana with Viñales, Trinidad, Varadero and Santiago de Cuba.The smaller buses which run daily pick up from various hotels and charge similar prices to Víazul. Tickets can be reserved at Infotur or with any Cubanacán hotel rep.

Buses to points in the Artemisa and Mayabeque provinces leave from Apodaca No 53, off Agramonte, near the main train station in Habana Vieja. They go to Güines, Jaruco, Madruga, Nueva Paz, San José, San Nicolás and Santa Cruz del Norte, but expect large crowds and come early to get a peso ticket.

TAXI

Small Lada taxis, operated by Cubataxi, park on Calle 19 de Mayo beside the Terminal de Ómnibus. They charge approximately CUC$0.50 per kilometer. This translates as CUC$70 to Varadero, CUC$80 to Pinar del Río, CUC$140 to Santa Clara, CUC$125 to Cienfuegos and CUC$165 to Trinidad. Up to four people can go for the price. It's worth considering in a pinch and is perfectly legal.

TRAIN

Trains to most parts of Cuba depart **Estación Central de Ferrocarriles** (Central Train Station; 861-8540, 862-1920; cnr Av de Bélgica & Arsenal) on the southwestern side of Habana Vieja. Foreigners must buy tickets in convertibles at **La Coubre station** (cnr Av del Puerto & Desamparados, Habana Vieja; 9am-3pm Mon-Fri). If it's closed, try the Lista de Espera office adjacent, which sells tickets for trains leaving immediately. Kids under 12 travel half price.

Cuba's best train, the *Tren Francés* (an old French SNCF train), runs every third day between Havana and Santiago stopping in Santa Clara (CUC$21) and Camagüey (CUC$40). It leaves Havana at 6:27pm and arrives in Santiago the following morning at 9am. There are no sleeper cars, but carriages are comfortable and air-conditioned, and there's a snack service. Tickets cost CUC$62 for 1st class and CUC$50 for 2nd class.

Slower *coche motor* (cross-island train) services run to Santiago, stopping in smaller stations such as Matanzas (CUC$4), Sancti Spíritus (CUC$13), Ciego de Ávila (CUC$16), Las Tunas (CUC$23), Bayamo (CUC$26), Manzanillo (CUC$28) and Holguín (CUC$27). One train goes as far as Guantánamo (CUC$32). There are separate branch lines to Cienfuegos (CUC$11) and Pinar del Río (CUC$6.50).

The above information is only a rough approximation; services are routinely delayed or canceled (including the Tren Francés, which was temporarily out of service at the time of writing). Always double-check scheduling and which terminal your train will leave from.

Getting Around

TO/FROM THE AIRPORT

Aeropuerto Internacional José Martí is at Rancho Boyeros, 25km southwest of Havana via Av de la Independencia. There are four terminals here. Terminal 1, on the southeastern side of the runway, handles only domestic Cubana flights. Three kilometers away, via Av de la Independencia, is Terminal 2, which receives flights and charters from Miami and New York and to and from the Cayman Islands. All other international flights use Terminal 3, a well-ordered, modern facility at Wajay, 2.5km west of Terminal 2. Charter flights on Aerocaribbean, Aerogaviota, Aerotaxi etc to Cayo Largo del Sur and elsewhere all use the Caribbean Terminal (also known as Terminal 5), situated at the northwestern end of the runway, 2.5km west of Terminal 3 (Terminal 4 hasn't been built yet.) Check carefully ahead of time which terminal you'll be using.

Public transport from the airport into central Havana is practically nonexistent. A standard taxi will cost you approximately CUC$20 to CUC$25 (40 minutes). You can change money at the bank in the arrivals hall.

True adventurers with light luggage and a tight budget can chance their arm on the P-12 metro bus from the Capitolio or the P-15 from the Hospital Hermanos Ameijeiras on the Malecón, both of which go to Santiago de las Vegas, stopping close to the airport (about 1.5km away) on Av Boyeros. This is a lot easier for departing travelers, who will have better knowledge of local geography.

TO/FROM THE BUS TERMINAL

The Víazul bus terminal is in the suburb of Nuevo Vedado, and taxis will charge between CUC$5 and CUC$10 for the ride to central Havana. There are no direct metro buses from central Havana. If you take the P-14 from the Capitolio, you'll have to get off on Av 51 and walk the last 500m or so.

BICI-TAXI

Two-seater bici-taxis will take you anywhere around Centro Habana for CUC$1/2 for a short/long trip, after bargaining. It's a lot more than a Cuban would pay, but cheaper and more fun than a tourist taxi.

BOAT

Passenger **ferries** (☎ 867-3726) shuttle across the harbor to Regla and Casablanca, leaving every 10 or 15 minutes from Muelle Luz, at the corner of San Pedro and Santa Clara, on the southeast side of Habana Vieja. The fare is a flat 10 centavos, but foreigners are often charged CUC$1. Since the ferries were hijacked to Florida in 1994 and again in 2003 (the hijackers never made it outside Cuban waters), security has been tightened. Expect bag searches and airport-style screening.

CAR

There are lots of car-rental offices in Havana, so if you're told there are no cars or there isn't one in your price range, just try another office or agency. All agencies have offices at Terminal 3 at Aeropuerto Internacional José Martí. Otherwise, there's a car-rental desk in any three-star (or higher) hotel. Prices for equivalent models are nearly always the same between the companies; it's called *socialismo*.

Cubacar (☎ 835-0000) has desks at most of the big hotels, including Meliá Cohiba, Meliá Habana, Iberostar Parque Central, Habana Libre and Sevilla.

Rex Rent a Car (☎ 836-7788; cnr Línea & Malecón, Vedado) rents fancy cars for extortionate prices.

Servi-Cupet gas stations are in Vedado at Calles L and 17; Malecón and Calle 15; Malecón and Paseo, near the Riviera and Meliá Cohiba Hotels; and on Av de la Independencia (northbound lane) south of Plaza de la Revolución. All are open 24 hours a day.

Guarded parking is available for approximately CUC$1 all over Havana, including in front of the Hotel Sevilla, Hotel Inglaterra and Hotel Nacional.

VÍAZUL BUS DEPARTURES FROM HAVANA

Check for the most up-to-date departure times on www.viazul.com.

DESTINATION	COST (CUC$)	DURATION (HR)	DEPARTURE TIMES
Bayamo	44	13	7:40am, 3:15pm, 10pm
Camagüey	33	9	7:40am, 8:40am, 3:15pm, 6pm, 8:30pm, 10pm
Ciego de Ávila	27	7	7:40am, 3:15pm, 8:30pm, 10pm
Cienfuegos	20	4	8:15am, 11:05am, 1pm
Holguín	44	12	8:40am, 3:15pm, 8:30pm
Las Tunas	39	11½	7:40am, 3:15pm, 8:30pm, 10pm
Matanzas	7	2	8am, 10am, noon, 5:40pm
Pinar del Río	11	3	9am, 2pm
Sancti Spíritus	23	5¾	8:40am, 9:30am, 3:15pm, 8:30pm, 10pm
Santa Clara	18	3¾	7:40am, 3:15pm, 8:30pm, 10pm
Santiago de Cuba	51	15	7:40am, 3:15pm, 6pm, 10pm
Trinidad	25	6	8:15am, 11:05am, 1pm
Varadero	10	3	8am, 10am, noon, 5:40pm
Viñales	12	4	9am, 2pm

PUBLIC TRANSPORTATION

The handy new hop-on/hop-off **Havana Bus Tour** (☑ 831-7333; Calle L No 456, btwn Calles 25 & 27) runs on two routes, numbers T1 and T3 (route T2 had been suspended at time of research). The main stop is in Parque Central opposite the Hotel Inglaterra. This is the pickup point for bus T1, which runs from Habana Vieja via Centro Habana, the Malecón, Calle 23 and Plaza de la Revolución to La Cecilia at the west end of Playa; and bus T3, which runs from Centro Habana to Playas del Este (via Parque Histórico Militar Morro-Cabaña). Bus T1 is an open-top double-decker. Bus T3 is an enclosed single-decker. All-day tickets are CUC$5. Services run from 9am to 9pm and routes and stops are clearly marked on all bus stops. Beware; these bus routes and times have been known to change. Check latest route maps at the bus stop in Parque Central.

Havana's bus service has improved immensely in recent years with the introduction of a brand-new fleet of Chinese-made 'bendy' buses that replaced the famously crowded and dirty *camellos* (the city's former metro buses) in 2007. These buses run regularly along 14 different routes, connecting most parts of the city with the suburbs. Fares are 20 centavos (five centavos if you're using convertibles), which you deposit into a small slot in front of the driver when you enter.

Cuban buses are crowded and little used by tourists. Beware of pickpockets and guard your valuables closely.

All bus routes have the prefix P before their number:

P-1 Diezmero – Playa (via Virgen del Camino, Vedado, Línea, Av 3)

P-2 Diezmero – Línea y G (via Vibora and Ciudad Deportiva)

P-3 Alamar – Túnel de Línea (via Virgen del Camino and Vibora)

P-4 San Agustín – Terminal de Trenes (via Playa, Calle 23, La Rampa)

P-5 San Agustín – Terminal de Trenes (via Lisa, Av 31, Línea, Av de Puerto)

P-6 Calvario – La Rampa (via Vibora)

P-7 Cotorro – Capitolio (via Virgen del Camino)

P-8 Calvario – Villa Panamericano (via Vibora, Capitolio and harbor tunnel)

P-9 Vibora – Lisa (via Cuatro Caminos, La Rampa, Calle 23, Av 41)

P-10 Vibora – Playa (via Altahabana and Calle 100)

P-11 Alamar – G y 27 (via harbor tunnel)

P-12 Santiago de las Vegas – Capitolio (via Av Boyeros)

P-13 Santiago de las Vegas – Vibora (via Calabazar)

P-14 San Agustín – Capitolio (via Lisa and Av 51)

P-15 Santiago de las Vegas – Hermanos Ameijeiras (via Av Boyeros and Calle G)

P-16 Hospital Naval – Playa (via Calle 100 and Lisa)

Older buses still run along some cross-town routes (eg bus 400 to Playas del Este), but there are no printed timetables or route maps. Individual services have been mentioned where appropriate.

TAXI

Metered tourist taxis are readily available at all of the upscale hotels, with the air-conditioned Nissan taxis charging higher tariffs than the non-air-con Ladas. The cheapest official taxis are operated by **Panataxi** (☑ 55-55-55), with a CUC$1 starting fare, then CUC$0.50 per kilometer. Tourist taxis charge CUC$1 per kilometer and can be ordered from **Havanautos Taxi** (☑ 73-22-77) and **Transgaviota** (☑ 206-9793). **Taxi OK** (☑ 204-0000, 877-6666) is based in Miramar. Drivers of the tourist taxis are government employees who work for a peso salary.

The cheapest taxis are the older yellow-and-black Ladas, many of which are privately owned these days. Agree on the fare before getting into the car, and carry exact change. There are usually classic-car taxis parked around Parque Central.

WALKING

Yes, walking! It's what the gas-starved *habaneros* have been doing for decades. Most parts of Habana Vieja, Centro Habana and Vedado can be easily navigated on foot if you're energetic and up for some exercise. You'll see a lot more of of the local street life in the process.

OUTER HAVANA

Splaying out on three sides from the downtown district, Havana's suburbs are full of quirky and easy-to-reach sights and activities that can make interesting day and half-day trips from the city center. Playa boasts a decent aquarium, top-class conference facilities and Cuba's best restaurants; Guanabacoa and Regla are famous for their Afro-Cuban religious culture; and the bayside forts of La Cabaña and El Morro exhibit some of the island's most impressive military architecture.

Playa & Marianao

The municipality of Playa, west of Vedado across the Río Almendares, is a paradoxical mix of prestigious residential streets and tough proletarian housing schemes.

Gracious Miramar is a leafy neighborhood of broad avenues and weeping laurel trees, where the traffic moves more sedately and diplomats' wives – clad in sun visors and Lycra leggings – go for gentle afternoon jogs along Av Quinta (Fifth Ave). Many of Havana's foreign embassies are housed here in old pre-Revolution mansions, and business travelers and conference attendees flock in from around the globe to make use of some of Cuba's grandest and most luxurious facilities. If you're interested primarily in sightseeing and entertainment, commuting to Vedado or Habana Vieja is a nuisance and an expense. However, some of the best salsa clubs, discos and restaurants are out this way and the casas particulares are positively luxurious.

Cubanacán plays host to many of Havana's business or scientific fairs and conventions, and it is also where several specialized medical institutes are situated. Despite the austerity of the *período especial* (Special Period), vast resources have been plowed into biotechnological and pharmaceutical research institutes in this area. Yachties, anglers and scuba divers will find themselves using the Marina Hemingway at Playa's west end.

Marianao is world-famous for the Tropicana Nightclub, but locally it's known as a tough, in parts rough neighborhood with a powerful Santería community and a long history of social commitment.

◉ Sights

◉ Miramar

★ Fundación Naturaleza y El Hombre   MUSEUM
(☑ 204-0438; Av 5B No 6611, btwn Calles 66 & 70, Playa; admission CUC$2; ⊘ 8:30am-3pm Mon-Fri) This fascinating museum displays artifacts from the 17,422km canoe trip from the Amazon source to the sea, led by Cuban intellectual and anthropologist Antonio Nuñez Jiménez in 1987. Other exhibits in an astounding collection include one of Cuba's largest photography collections, books written by the prolific Nuñez Jiménez, and the famous Fidel portrait by Guayasamín.

'The glass house' displays glass cases containing all kinds of intriguing ephemera from the founder's life. The museum

is a foundation and one of Havana's most rewarding.

Pabellón para la Maqueta de la Capital   MUSEUM
(Calle 28 No 113, btwn Avs 1 & 3; admission CUC$3; ⊘ 9:30am-5pm Tue-Sat) If you thought the Maqueta de La Habana Vieja was impressive, check out this ultramodern pavilion containing a huge 1:1000 scale model of the whole city (being renovated at time of research). The model was originally created for urban-planning purposes, but is now a tourist attraction.

Nearby, the two **parks** on Av 5, between Calles 24 and 26, with their immense banyan trees and dark lanes, are an atmospheric pocket.

★ Acuario Nacional   AQUARIUM
(cnr Av 3 & Calle 62; adult/child CUC$10/7; ⊘ 10am-6pm Tue-Sun) Founded in 1960, the national aquarium is a Havana institution and it gets legions of visitors annually, particularly since it underwent a revamp in 2002. Despite its rather scruffy appearance, this place leaves most of the other Cuban *acuarios* (aquatic centers) in the shade (which isn't saying much). Miami it certainly isn't.

Saltwater fish are the specialty, but there are also sea lions, dolphins and running-around room for kids. Dolphin performances are almost hourly from 11am, with the final show at 9pm; admission price includes the show.

Russian Embassy   LANDMARK
(Av 5 No 6402, btwn Calles 62 & 66, Playa) In case you were wondering, that huge Stalinist obelisk that dominates the skyline halfway down Av Quinta is the Russian (formerly Soviet) embassy, testament to the days when Castro was best mates with Brezhnev et al.

Iglesia Jesús de Miramar   CHURCH
(cnr Av 5 & Calle 82, Playa) Despite its modernity, Playa cradles Cuba's second-largest church. The Jesús is an aesthetically pleasing neo-Romanesque structure topped by a giant dome. Built in 1948, it protects Cuba's largest pipe-organ and unusual murals depicting the Stations of the Cross.

Parque Almendares   PARK
Running along the banks of the city's Río Almendares, below the bridge on Calle 23, is this wonderful oasis of greenery and fresh air in the heart of chaotic Havana. The park

Playa & Marianao

has been undergoing a slow restoration (and clean-up) for more than a decade: benches now line the river promenade and plants grow profusely.

There are also many facilities here, including an antiquated **miniature golf course**, the **Anfiteatro Parque Almendares** (a small outdoor performance space) a playground and – the most recent addition – a **dinosaur park** contained stone reproductions of the monstrous reptiles. There are several good places to eat.

⊙ Marianao

Museo de la Alfabetización　　MUSEUM
(cnr Av 29E & Calle 76; ☉ 8am-noon & 1-4:30pm Mon-Fri, 8am-noon Sat) **FREE** The former Cuartel Colombia military airfield at Marianao is now a school complex called **Ciudad Libertad**. Pass through the gate to visit this inspiring museum, which describes the 1961 literacy campaign, when 100,000 youths aged 12 to 18 spread out across Cuba to teach reading and writing to farmers, workers and the aged.

In the center of the traffic circle, opposite the entrance to the complex, is a tower in the form of a syringe in memory of Carlos Juan Finlay, who discovered the cause of yellow fever in 1881.

⊙ Cubanacán

Instituto Superior de Arte　　CULTURAL BUILDING
(ISA; Calle 120 No 1110) The leading art academy in Cuba was established in the former Havana Country Club in 1961 and elevated to the status of institute in 1976. The cluster of buildings – some unfinished, some half-restored, but all gloriously graceful due to the arches, domes and red brick – was the brainchild of Che Guevara and a team of architects.

Among them was Ricardo Porro, who designed the striking Facultad de Artes Plásticas (1961), which has long curving passageways and domed halls in the shape of a reclining woman. Some 800 students study here, and foreigners can too.

Palacio de las Convenciones　　NOTABLE BUILDING
(Calle 146, btwn Avs 11 & 13) Also known as the Havana Convention Center, this is one of Cuba's most dramatic modern buildings. Built for the Nonaligned Conference in 1979, the four interconnecting halls contain a state-of-the-art auditorium with 2101 seats and 11 smaller halls. The 589-member National Assembly meets here twice a year, and the complex hosts more than 50,000 conference attendees annually.

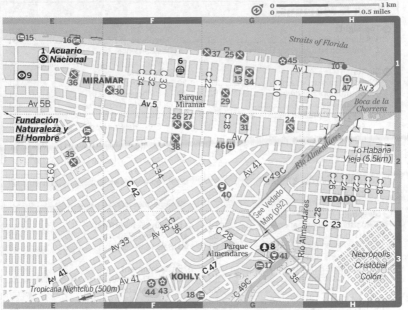

Not far from here is **Pabexpo** (cnr Av 17 & Calle 180), 20,000 sq meters of exhibition space in four interconnecting pavilions that hosts about 15 trade shows a year.

Isla del Coco   AMUSEMENT PARK
(Av 5 & Calle 112, Playa) A huge new Chinese-built amusement park in Playa with big wheels, bumper cars, roller coasters, the works.

🏃 Activities

Marlin Náutica   WATER SPORTS
(cnr Av 5 & Calle 248, Barlovento) There are many water activities available at Marina Hemingway in Barlovento, 20km west of central Havana. Fishing trips can be arranged at Marlin Náutica from CUC$150 for four anglers and four hours of bottom fishing, and CUC$280 for four anglers and four hours of deep-sea fishing.

Included are a captain, a sailor, an open bar and tackle. Marlin season is June to October. Scuba packages for CUC$35 per dive and tours of Havana's littoral (CUC$60 in a catamaran) can also be arranged.

La Aguja Marlin Diving Center   DIVING
(☑ 204-5088; cnr Av 5 & 248, Barlovento) Between Cubanacán Náutica and the shopping center, this center offers scuba diving for CUC$30 per dive, plus CUC$5 for gear. It has one morning and one afternoon departure. A diving excursion to Varadero or Playa Girón can also be arranged. Reader reviews have been favorable.

🛏 Sleeping

🛏 Miramar

Casa de Cuca   CASA PARTICULAR $
(☑ 205-4082; Calle 11 No 7406, btwn Calles 74 & 76; r CUC$40; 🅿 ✳ 🏊) Casa de Cuca? More like Palacio de Cuca! You'll feel as if you're staying in the house of a well-off friend at this luxury Playa house with four rooms with king-sized beds, private bathrooms and, yes, a swimming pool.

Complejo Cultural La Vitrola   HOTEL $
(☑ 202-7922; Calle 18 No 103, btwn Avs 1 & 3; r CUC$30; ✳) Imagine staying at London's Abbey Road recording studios. Well, this is the Cuban equivalent. The Egrem studios – working space for Cuba's top musical artists – now has a lovely on-site hotel whose five rooms (named *bolero*, *son*, *chachachá*, rumba and *trova*) have bright interiors with song lyrics painted on the wall. Hang around in the downstairs Bar Bilongo and you might even bump into Silvio Rodríguez.

Playa & Marianao

Hotel el Bosque
HOTEL $

(☑204-9232; Calle 28A, btwn Calles 49A & 49B, Kohly; s/d CUC$36/48; ❄@) Economical and often underrated, El Bosque is the better and less costly arm of the Gaviota-run Kohly-Bosque *complejo* (complex). Clean and friendly, the hotel lies on the banks of the Río Almendares surrounded by the Bosque de La Habana – the city's green lungs – and is a good (and rare) midrange choice in this neck of the woods.

Marta Rodríguez
CASA PARTICULAR $

(☑203-8596; Calle 42 No 914; r CUC$40; P) There aren't many casas in Miramar, but Marta's is one that could be worth the trip, offering art deco beds, TV, VCR, a music system and lots of space.

Aparthotel Montehabana
HOTEL $$

(☑206-9595; Calle 70, btwn Avs 5A & 7, Playa; s/d/tr CUC$75/85/120; P❄@🛜🏊) This modern Gaviota giant opened in 2005 with the promise of offering something a little different. Of the rooms here, 101 are apartments that have living rooms and fully equipped kitchens, providing a great opportunity to stock up in the Havana markets and find out how Cubans cook. Kitchens are well supplied with microwaves, refrigerators, toasters and coffee machines – even your own cutlery.

If you're not up to cooking, the restaurant does a CUC$8 breakfast and a CUC$15 dinner buffet. Elsewhere the facilities are comprehensive, if a little utilitarian. Guests share the gym, pool and tennis courts with the Hotel Occidental Miramar next door.

Hotel Chateau Miramar
HOTEL $$

(📞204-0224; Av 1, btwn Calles 60 & 70, Playa; s/d CUC$67/84; P ❄ @ ☁) It's marketed as a 'boutique hotel,' but read between the lines – this *château* ain't no Loire Valley retreat. Still, techno addicts will appreciate the free internet, flat-screen TV and direct international phone service that come with the otherwise mediocre rooms.

Hotel Kohly
HOTEL $$

(📞204-0240; cnr Calles 49A & 36, Kohly; s/d CUC$47/63; ❄ @ ☁) The Kohly makes up for its utilitarian exterior with an inviting swimming pool and an excellent pizza restaurant.

Hotel Copacabana
HOTEL $$

(📞204-1037; Av 1, btwn Calles 44 & 46; s/d CUC$72/104; P ❄ @ ☁) Right on the beach, the Copacabana is back in business after a lengthy 2009–10 refurbishment, though there's still a dankness about the whole establishment, despite its fine ocean-side location.

★Hotel Meliá Habana
HOTEL $$$

(📞204-8500; Av 3, btwn Calles 76 & 80; s/d CUC$200/260; P ❄ @ 🛜 ☁) Ugly outside but beautiful within, Miramar's gorgeous Hotel Meliá Habana, which opened in 1998, is one of the city's best-run and best-equipped accommodation options. The 409 rooms (four of which are wheelchair-accessible) are positioned around a salubrious lobby with abundant hanging vines, marble statues and gushing water features.

Outside, Cuba's largest and most beautiful swimming pool stands next to a desolate, rocky shore. Throw in polite service, an excellent buffet restaurant and the occasional room discount, and you could be swayed.

Quinta Avenida Habana
HOTEL $$$

(📞214-1470; Av 5, btwn Calles 76 & 80, Miramar; s/d CUC$110/130; ❄ @ 🛜 ☁) One of Playa's newer hotels, this concrete colossus was opened in 2010. It completes a trio of plush accommodations set behind the Miramar Trade Center. While the facilities claim a high star-rating with expansive rooms (all with separate showers and bathtubs) and a good on-site restaurant, the place suffers from the usual foibles of humungous chain-run establishments: a cold, generic feel and a weirdly un-Cuban lack of personality.

Occidental Miramar
HOTEL $$$

(📞204-3583, 204-3584; cnr Av 5 & Calle 74; s/d CUC$100/130; P ❄ 🛜 ☁) Formerly the Novotel, this 427-room colossus was taken over by Gaviota a few years back and has benefited as a result. Professional staff, great business facilities and high standards of service throughout are par for the course here.

There are also plenty of sporty extras if the isolated location starts to grate, including tennis courts, swimming pool, sauna, gym and games room.

H10 Habana Panorama
HOTEL $$$

(📞204-0100; cnr Av 3 & Calle 70; s/d CUC$100/135; P ❄ @ ☁) This flashy 'glass cathedral' on Playa's rapidly developing hotel strip opened in 2003. The rather strange aesthetics – acres of blue-tinted glass – improve once you step inside the monumental lobby where space-age elevators whisk you promptly up to one of 317 airy rooms, which offer great views over Miramar and beyond.

Extra facilities include a business center, a photo shop, numerous restaurants and a spacious and shapely swimming pool. But the Panorama is almost too big: its scale makes you feel small and gives the place a rather deserted and antiseptic feel.

🛏 Cubanacán

There is one hotel in this neighborhood, where you might end up if you're here for an organized activity/conference.

Hotel Palco
HOTEL $$$

(📞204-7235; Calle 146, btwn Avs 11 & 13; s/d CUC$91/111; P ❄ ☁) Two kilometers to the north and attached to the Palacio de las Convenciones, the Palco is a business hotel normally block-booked by foreigners in town to attend a conference/symposium/product launch.

🛏 Marina Hemingway

Hotel Club Acuario
HOTEL $$

(📞204-6336; cnr Aviota & Calle 248; s/d CUC$79/108; ❄) You really shouldn't come to Marina Hemingway for the hotels. With the El Viejo y el Mar perennially on hiatus, the only real option for foreign travelers is the strung-out Acuario, splayed between two of the harbor channels and infested with cheap out-of-date furnishings.

If you're booked for an early morning diving excursion, this place might just qualify; otherwise stay in Havana and commute.

✗ Eating

Playa has been a bastion of some of Cuba's best paladares since the 1990s and many of the old stalwarts continue to impress despite an abundance of new competition. There are also some surprisingly good state-run restaurants. It's worth the CUC$5 to CUC$10 taxi fare from the city center to eat out here.

✗ Miramar

Chaplin's Café   CAFE $
(Calle 8 No 518, btwn Avs 5 & 5B; tapas CUC$2-7; ⊙9am-midnight) Charlie Chaplin's humor has always been a great cultural leveler, and no more so than in Cuba (there's even a Havana cinema named after him). This diminutive new bar/restaurant set up by a Chaplin fanatic in 2012 blends smart black and white Chaplin imagery with decent food. Hit the giant sofa for tapas snacks or the chicer tables for dinner.

Le Garage   FAST FOOD $
(Av 3, cnr 60; snacks CUC$2-4; ⊙noon-2am, till 6am Fri-Sun) Not actually a garage but a small private fast-food joint with some indoor booths and an outdoor patio where you can stop for milkshakes, burgers and onion rings – all rare pickings in Cuba until recently. Note the generous opening hours.

Pan.com   FAST FOOD $
(☑204-4232; cnr Av 7 & Calle 26; snacks CUC$1-4; ⊙10am-midnight) Not an internet cafe but a haven of Havana comfort food with hearty sandwiches, fantastic burgers and ice-cream milkshakes to die for. Join the diplomats under the airy front canopy.

Supermercado 70   SUPERMARKET $
(cnr Av 3 & Calle 70; ⊙9am-6pm Mon-Sat, 9am-1pm Sun) Still known as the 'Diplomercado' from the days when only diplomats came here, this place is large by Cuban standards and has a wide selection.

★ El Aljibe   CARIBBEAN $$
(☑204-1584, 204-1583; Av 7, btwn Calles 24 & 26; mains CUC$12; ⊙noon-midnight) On paper a humble Palmares restaurant, but in reality a rip-roaring culinary extravaganza, El Aljibe has been delighting both Cuban and foreign diplomatic taste buds for years. The furore surrounds the gastronomic mysteries of just one dish, the obligatory *pollo asado* (roast chicken), which is served up with as-much-as-you-can-eat helpings of white rice, black beans, fried plantain, French fries and salad. The accompanying bitter orange sauce is said to be a state secret.

La Carboncita   ITALIAN $$
(Av 3 No 3804, btwn Calles 38 & 40; pasta & pizza CUC$7-8; ⊙noon-midnight) The food appears mysteriously from the garage of this Miramar house-turned-Italian-restaurant with both indoor and outdoor front porch seating, but there's nothing mechanical about the flavors. On the contrary, the pasta's homemade by the Italian owner and you can choose from a multitude of authentic sauces including pesto. The thin-crust pizzas are good too.

La Corte del Principe   ITALIAN $$
(cnr Calles 9 & 74; pasta CUC$7-8; ⊙noon-3pm & 7-11pm) Dig the new breed! Possibly the most Italian of Havana's new Italian restaurants, La Corte prints its menu in Italiano, takes a siesta (3pm to 7pm) and doesn't serve pizza. Call them snooty purists if you like, but the pasta here is Torino-good and the basket of plump purple aubergines they stick outside the door is hard to walk past.

Paladar Vista Mar   SEAFOOD $$
(☑203-8328; Av 1, btwn Calles 22 & 24; mains CUC$8-15; ⊙noon-midnight) The Paladar Vista Mar in Miramar is in the 2nd-floor family-room-turned-restaurant of a private residence, which faces the sea. The oceanside ambience is embellished by a beautiful swimming pool that spills its water into the sea. If enjoying delicious seafood dishes overlooking the crashing ocean sounds enticing, this could be your bag.

Casa Española   SPANISH $$
(☑206-9644; cnr Calle 26 & Av 7; mains CUC$7-12; ⊙noon-midnight) A medieval parody built in the Batista-era by the silly-rich Gustavo Guitérrez y Sánchez, this crenellated castle in Miramar has found new life as a Spanish-themed restaurant cashing in on the Don Quixote legend. The ambience is rather fine, if you don't mind suits of armor watching you as you tuck into paella, Spanish omelet or *lanja cerdo al Jerez* (pork fillet).

Bom Apetite   INTERNATIONAL $$
(Calle 11 No 7210, btwn Calles 72 & 74; mains CUC$5-10; ⊙noon-midnight) Way out in eastern Playa, Bom Apetite is all about the setting, which is refined and upscale in a quiet private house with its own separate bar. The food

mixes Cuban favorites with North American staples such as filet mignon, and throws in some strong Italian inflections with pasta and pizza.

Dos Gardenias
CARIBBEAN $$

(cnr Av 7 & Calle 28; ⊘noon-midnight) You can choose from a grill or a pasta restaurant in this complex, which is famous as a *bolero* hot spot. Stick around to hear the singers belting out ballads later on.

La Casa del Habano
CARIBBEAN $$

(cnr Av 5 & Calle 16; mains CUC$8-15) Most head here for its reputation as Havana's best cigar store, but repeat visitors come back for the food in the adjoining restaurant.

Paladar la Cocina de Lilliam
FUSION $$$

(☑209-6514; Calle 48 No 1311, btwn Avs 13 & 15; mains CUC$15-25; ⊘noon-midnight) Slick service, secluded ambience and freshly cooked food to die for, La Cocina de Lilliam has all the ingredients of a prize-winning restaurant. Set in an illustrious villa in Miramar and surrounded by a garden with trickling fountains and lush tropical plants, diners can tuck into such Cuban rarities as chicken mousse and tuna bruschetta in an atmosphere more European than Caribbean. Not a cheese-and-ham sandwich in sight!

★ Paladar la Fontana
BARBECUE $$$

(☑202-8337; Av 3A No 305; mains CUC$12-20; ⊘noon-midnight) Huge portions of meat and fish are served up in this recently renovated villa-cum-paladar, so go easy on the starters, which include crab mixed with eggplant, quail eggs and fried chickpeas. La Fontana specializes in just about everything you'll never see elsewhere in Cuba, from lasagna to huge steaks.

Big-shot reviews from the *Cigar Aficionado* and the *Chicago Tribune* testify to a longstanding legend.

La Esperanza
INTERNATIONAL $$$

(☑202-4361; Calle 16 No 105, btwn Avs 1 & 3; ⊘7-11pm Mon-Sat) An old-school paladar that still makes the cut, the unassuming Esperanza was being gastronomically creative long before the 2011 reforms made life for chefs a lot easier. While unspectacular from the street, the interior of this vine-covered house is a riot of quirky antiques, old portraits and refined 1940s furnishings.

The food, which is produced in a standard-sized family kitchen, includes such exquisite dishes as *pollo luna de miel* (chicken flambéed in rum), fish marinated in white wine, lemon and garlic, and a lamb brochette.

Doctor Café
CUBAN $$$

(☑203-4718; Calle 28, btwn Avs 1 & 3) Exotic dishes such as ceviche, red snapper and grilled octopus served in a fern-filled patio or cooler indoor dining area for eating; this doctor is obviously getting the treatment spot on. The menu is from all over the globe, and there are numerous rarities you'll find at few other places in Cuba. Bypass the turtle, if offered.

Don Cangrejo
SEAFOOD $$$

(Av 1 No 1606, btwn Calles 16 & 18; crab CUC$15; ⊘noon-midnight) On the seafront, this unique seafood restaurant, a favorite of the diplomatic crowd, is run by the Ministry of Fisheries and scores high points for atmosphere and service. Fresh fish dishes include red snapper, grouper and prawns, while the lobster comes from a pit on the terrace.

El Tocororo
CARIBBEAN $$$

(☑202-4530; Calle 18 No 302; meals CUC$12-35; ⊘noon-midnight) Once considered (along with El Aljibe) to be one of Havana's finest government-run restaurants, El Tocororo has lost ground to its competitors in recent years and is often criticized for being overpriced. Nonetheless, the candlelit tables and inviting garden are still worth a visit, while the unprinted menu, with such luxuries as lobster's tail and (occasionally) ostrich, still has the ability to surprise.

El Tocororo also has a small attached sushi bar and restaurant called **Sakura**.

✕ Cubanacán

El Palenque
INTERNATIONAL $$

(☑208-8167; cnr Av 17A & Calle 190, Siboney; mains CUC$3-10; ⊘10am-10pm) A huge place, next to the Pabexpo exhibition center, that sprawls beneath a series of open-sided thatched *bohíos* (traditional Cuban huts), the Palenque offers an extensive menu at prices cheap enough to attract both Cubans and foreigners. The cuisine is Cuban/Italian, with pizzas, steak and fries and lobster *mariposa*.

La Cecilia
CARIBBEAN $$$

(☑204-1562; Av 5 No 11010, btwn Calles 110 & 112; mains CUC$12-20; ⊘noon-midnight) This classy place is up there with El Aljibe in terms of food quality (check out the *ropa vieja*), but trumps all comers with its big-band music, which blasts out on weekend nights inside its large but atmospheric courtyard.

La Ferminia
CARIBBEAN $$$

(☑273-6786; Av 5 No 18207, Flores; mains from CUC$15; ☺noon-midnight) Havana gets swanky at this memorable restaurant set in an elegant converted colonial mansion in the leafy neighborhood of Flores. Dine inside in one of a handful of beautifully furnished rooms, or outside on a glorious garden patio – it doesn't matter. The point is the food. Try the mixed grill, pulled straight from the fire, or lobster tails pan-fried in breadcrumbs.

There's a strict dress code here: no shorts or sleeveless T-shirts (guys). It's one of the few places where Fidel Castro has dined in public.

✕ Marina Hemingway

Restaurante la Cova
ITALIAN $$

(cnr Av 5 & Calle 248; mains CUC$8; ☺noon-midnight) Part of the Pizza Nova chain, this place also does fish, meat and rigatoni à la vodka. The pepperoni topping is purportedly flown in from Canada.

Papa's Complejo Turístico
CARIBBEAN, CHINESE $$

(cnr Av 5 & Calle 248; ☺noon-3am) There's all sorts of stuff going on here, from beer-swilling boatmen to warbling *American Idol* wannabes hogging the karaoke machine. The eating options are equally varied, with a posh Chinese place (with dress code) and an outdoor *ranchón* (rural restaurant). Good fun if there's enough people.

Drinking & Nightlife

Casa de la Música
NIGHTCLUB

(☑202-6147; Calle 20 No 3308, cnr Av 35, Miramar; admission CUC$5-20; ☺10pm Tue-Sat) Launched with a concert by renowned jazz pianist Chucho Valdés in 1994, this Miramar favorite is run by national Cuban recording company, Egrem, and the programs are generally a lot more authentic than the cabaret entertainment you see at the hotels.

Platinum players such as NG la Banda, Los Van Van and Aldaberto Álvarez y Su Son play here regularly; you'll rarely pay more than CUC$20. It has a more relaxed atmosphere than its Centro Habana namesake.

Salón Chévere
NIGHTCLUB

(Parque Almendares, cnr Calles 49C & 28A, Miramar; admission CUC$6-10; ☺from 10pm) One of Havana's most popular discos, this alfresco place in a lush park setting hosts a good mix of locals and tourists.

Sala de Fiesta Macumba Habana
NIGHTCLUB

(cnr Calle 222 & Av 37, La Lisa; admission CUC$10-20; ☺10pm) Cocooned in a residential neighborhood southwest of Cubanacán is Macumba, one of Havana's biggest venues for live salsa. The outdoor setting is refreshing and the sets are long, so you'll get a lot of dancing in.

This is a great place to catch jazz-salsa combos and *timba* music, a modern extension of salsa mixed with jazz and rap and championed by NG la Banda (who perform here regularly). You can also dine at La Giradilla in the same complex.

☆ Entertainment

Teatro Karl Marx
LIVE MUSIC

(☑203-0801, 209-1991; cnr Av 1 & Calle 10, Miramar) Size-wise the Karl Marx puts other Havana theaters in the shade with a seating capacity of 5500 in a single auditorium. The very biggest events happen here, such as the closing galas for the jazz and film festivals and rare concerts by *trovadores* like Silvio Rodríguez.

Tropicana Nightclub
CABARET

(☑267-1871; Calle 72 No 4504, Marianao; ☺10pm) A city institution since it opened in 1939, the world-famous Tropicana was one of the few bastions of Havana's Las Vegas-style nightlife to survive the clampdowns of the Revolution. Immortalized in Graham Greene's 1958 classic *Our Man in Havana*, this open-air cabaret show is little changed since its 1950s heyday – a bevy of scantily clad señoritas climbs nightly down from the palm trees to dance Latin salsa amid flashing lights on stage. Tickets go for a slightly less than socialistic CUC$75.

Salón Rosado Benny Moré
LIVE MUSIC

(El Tropical; ☑206-1281; cnr Av 41 & Calle 46, Kohly; admission 10 pesos-CUC$10; ☺9pm-late) For something completely different, check out the very *caliente* action at this outdoor venue. The Rosado (aka El Tropical) packs in hot, sexy Cuban youths dancing madly to Los Van Van, Pupi y Su Son Son or Habana Abierta. It's a fierce scene and female travelers should expect aggressive come-ons. Friday to Sunday is best.

Some travelers pay pesos, others dollars – more of that Cuban randomness for you.

Circo Trompoloco   CIRCUS
(cnr Av 5 & Calle 112, Playa; admission CUC$10; ⊘7pm Thu-Sun) Havana's permanent 'Big Top' with a weekend matinee.

Estadio Pedro Marrero   STADIUM
(cnr Av 41 & Calle 46, Kohly) Football – or is it soccer in Cuba? Come over on weekends at 3pm to this 15,000-seat stadium and watch them dance down the wings.

 Shopping

La Casa del Habano   CIGARS
(Av 5, cnr Calle 16, Miramar; ⊘10am-6pm Mon-Sat, 10am-1pm Sun) Smokers and souvenir seekers will like La Casa, arguably Havana's top cigar store. You'll find a comfy smoking lounge and a decent restaurant here as well.

La Maison   CLOTHING
(Calle 16 No 701, Miramar) The Cuban fashion fascination is in high gear at this place, with a large boutique selling designer clothing, shoes, handbags, jewelry, cosmetics and souvenirs. They also hold regular fashion shows.

Egrem Tienda de Música   MUSIC
(Calle 18 No 103, Miramar; ⊘9am-6pm Mon-Sat) There's a small CD-outlet here hidden in leafy Miramar at the site of Havana's most celebrated recording studios.

Casa de la Música   MUSIC
(Calle 20 No 3308, cnr Av 35, Miramar; ⊘10am-10pm) A small musical outlet graces Miramar's famous music venue.

Miramar Trade Center   SHOPPING CENTER
(Av 3, btwn Calles 76 & 80) Cuba's largest and most modern shopping and business center houses myriad stores, airline offices and embassies.

La Puntilla   SHOPPING CENTER
(Calle A, cnr Av 1) Decade-old shopping center spread over four floors at the Vedado end of Miramar; fairly comprehensive by Cuban standards.

ⓘ Information

INTERNET ACCESS
Hotel Business Centers (Av 3, Hotel Meliá Habana, btwn Calles 76 & 80, Miramar) Meliá

Habana charges CUC$7 an hour for wi-fi. Most other hotels have terminals for similar prices.

MEDICAL SERVICES
Clínica Central Cira García (☑204-2811; Calle 20 No 4101, cnr Av 41, Playa; ⊘9am-4pm Mon-Fri, emergencies 24hr) Emergency, dental and medical consultations for foreigners (consultations CUC$25 to CUC$35).

Farmacia Internacional Miramar (☑204-4350; cnr Calles 20 & 43, Playa; ⊘9am-5:45pm) Across the road from Clínica Central Cira García.

Pharmacy (☑204-2880; Calle 20 No 4104, cnr Calle 43, Playa; ⊘24hr) In Clínica Central Cira García; one of the city's best.

MONEY
There are Banco Financiero Internacional branches in **Miramar** (Sierra Maestra Bldg, cnr Av 1 & Calle 0, Miramar) and **Playa** (cnr Av 5 & Calle 92, Playa).

Cadeca is also located in **Miramar** (Av 5A, btwn Calles 40 & 42) and **Playa** (☑204-9087; Playa, cnr Av 3 & Calle 70).

POST
DHL (cnr Av 1 & Calle 26, Miramar; ⊘8am-8pm) For important mail, you're better off using DHL.

Post Office (Calle 42 No 112, btwn Avs 1 & 3, Miramar; ⊘8am-11:30am & 2-6pm Mon-Fri, 8am-11:30am Sat)

TOURIST INFORMATION
Infotur (cnr Av 5 & Calle 112, Playa; ⊘8:30am-5pm Mon-Sat, 8:30am-noon Sun) Oddly located but informative office.

TRAVEL AGENCIES
The following agencies also sell organized tours.
Cubanacán (☑204-8500) Desk in Hotel Meliá Habana.

Gaviota (☑204-4411; www.gaviota-grupo.com)

ⓘ Getting There & Away

The best way to get to Playa from Havana is on the Havana Bus Tour, which plies most of the neighborhoods' highlights all the way to La Cecilia on Av 5 cnr Calle 110. Plenty of metro buses make the trip, though they often detour around the more residential neighborhoods.

ⓘ Getting Around

Cubacar (☑204-1707) has offices at the Chateau Miramar and the Meliá Habana hotels. Rental is around CUC$70 per day with insurance.

Vía Rent a Car (☑204-3606; cnr Avs 47 & 36, Kohly) has an office opposite the Hotel el Bosque.

There are Servi-Cupet gas stations at Av 31 between Calles 18 and 20 in Miramar, on the corner of Calle 72 and Av 41 in Marianao (near the Tropicana), as well as on the traffic circle at Av 5 and Calle 112 in Cubanacán. The Oro Negro gas station is at Av 5 and Calle 120 in Cubanacán. All are open 24 hours.

Parque Lenin Area

Parque Lenin, off the Calzada de Bejucal in Arroyo Naranjo, 20km south of central Havana, is the city's largest recreational area. Constructed between 1969 and 1972 on the orders of Celia Sánchez, a long-time associate of Fidel Castro, it is one of the few developments in Havana from this era. The 670 hectares of green parkland and beautiful old trees surround an artificial lake, the Embalse Paso Sequito, just west of the much larger Embalse Ejército Rebelde, which was formed by damming the Río Almendares.

Although the park itself is attractive enough, the mishmash of facilities inside has fallen on hard times since the onset of the Special Period. Taxi drivers will wax nostalgic about when 'Lenin' was an idyllic weekend getaway for scores of pleasure-seeking Havana families, though these days the place retains more of a neglected and surreal air. Fortunately, help is on the way. New management and millions of pesos of Chinese investment are currently financing a major renovation project, but it's a big job that's still a long way from completion.

◉ Sights

Parque Lenin PARK
The main things to see in the park are south of the lake, including the **Galería de Arte Amelia Peláez** (admission CUC$1). Up the hill there's a dramatic white marble **monument to Lenin** (1984) by the Soviet sculptor LE Kerbel, and west along the lake is an overgrown **amphitheater** and an **aquarium** (admission CUC$2; ⊘ 10am-5pm Tue-Sun, closed Mon) with freshwater fish and crocodiles. The 1985 bronze **monument to Celia Sánchez**, who was instrumental in having Parque Lenin built, is rather hidden beyond the aquarium. A **ceramics workshop** is nearby.

Most of these attractions are open 9am to 5pm Tuesday to Sunday, and admission to the park itself is free. You can sometimes rent a **rowboat** on the Embalse Paso Sequito from a dock behind the **Rodeo Nacional**, an arena where some of Cuba's best rodeos take place (the annual **Cattlemen's fair** is also held here). A 9km **narrow-gauge railway** with four stops operates inside the park from 10am to 3pm Wednesday to Sunday.

ExpoCuba EXHIBITION HALL
(admission CUC$1; ⊘ 9am-5pm Wed-Sun) A visit to Parque Lenin can be combined with a trip to ExpoCuba at Calabazar on the Carretera del Rocío in Arroyo Naranjo, 3km south of Las Ruinas restaurant. Opened in 1989, this large permanent exhibition showcases Cuba's economic and scientific achievements in 25 pavilions based on themes such as sugar, farming, apiculture, animal science, fishing, construction, food, geology, sports and defense.

Cubans visiting ExpoCuba flock to the amusement park at the center of the complex, bypassing the rather dry propaganda displays. **Don Cuba** (⌀ 57-82-87), a revolving restaurant, is atop a tower. The Feria Internacional de la Habana, Cuba's largest trade fair, is held at ExpoCuba in the first week of November. Parking is available at Gate E, at the south end of the complex (CUC$1).

Jardín Botánico Nacional GARDENS
(admission CUC$3; ⊘ 10am-4pm Wed-Sun) Across the highway from ExpoCuba is this 600-hectare botanical garden. The **Pabellones de Exposición** (1987), near the entry gate, is a series of greenhouses with cacti and tropical plants, while 2km beyond is the garden's highlight, the tranquil **Japanese Garden** (1992). Nearby is the celebrated Restaurante el Bambú, where a vegetarian buffet is served (a rare treat in Cuba).

The **tractor train ride** around the park departs four times a day and costs CUC$3, gardens admission included. Parking costs CUC$2.

Parque Zoológico Nacional ZOO
(adult/child CUC$3/2; ⊘ 9am-3:30pm Wed-Sun) Let's face it: you don't come to Cuba to see elephants and lions, do you? The Special Period was particularly tough on the island's zoo animals, and a visit to this park on Av Zoo-Lenin in Boyeros, 2km west of the Parque Lenin riding school, only bears out this fact.

Though the zoo grounds are extensive and some fauna such as rhinos and hippos roam relatively free, the park is hardly the Serengeti, and many of the animals languish in cramped cages. A trolley bus tours the grounds all day (included in admission price).

✦ Activities

Centro Ecuestre — HORSEBACK RIDING
(Parque Lenin; ⊙9am-5pm) The stables in the northwestern corner of Parque Lenin are run by environmental agency, Flora y Fauna. At the time of writing they were offering all-day horseback riding lessons at their equestrian center for CUC$45. For more casual rides through the park, you'll have to use the boys who gather at the park entrance.

Horce Riding — HORSEBACK RIDING
Legalized under Raúl Castro's reforms, the *chicos* who gallop around Park Lenin's northeast entrance on horseback offer their mounts for more relaxed excursions ($4/8 half/full hour). Check the state of your horse before mounting (and the offical license of your hirer).

Club de Golf la Habana — GOLF
(Carretera de Venta, Km 8, Reparto Capdevila, Boyeros; ⊙8am-8pm, bowling alley noon-11pm) The club lies between Vedado and the airport. Poor signposting makes it hard to find and most taxi drivers get lost looking: ask locals for directions to the *golfito* or Dilpo Golf Club. Originally titled the Rover's Athletic Club, it was established by a group of British diplomats in the 1920s, and the diplomatic corps is largely the clientele today.

There are nine holes with 18 tees to allow 18-hole rounds. Green fees start at CUC$20 for nine holes and CUC$30 for 18 holes, with extra for clubs, cart and caddie. In addition, the club has five tennis courts and a bowling alley. Fidel and Che Guevara played a round here once as a publicity stunt soon after the Cuban missile crisis in 1962. The photos of the event are still popular. Che won – apparently.

✕ Eating

Restaurante el Bambú — VEGETARIAN $
(Jardín Botánico Nacional; meals CUC$1; ⊙noon-5pm, closed Mon; 🖉) This is the first and finest example of vegetarian dining in Havana, and has been a leading advocate for the benefits of a meatless diet (a tough call in the ration-card economy of Cuba). The all-you-can-eat lunch buffet is served alfresco, deep in the botanical gardens, with the natural setting paralleling the wholesome tastiness of the food.

For MN$15 you can gorge on soups and salads, root vegetables, tamales and eggplant caviar.

Las Ruinas — CARIBBEAN $
(Cortina de la Presa; meals CUC$6; ⊙11am-midnight Tue-Sun) Once celebrated for its architecture (a modernist structure that incorporates the ruins of an old sugar mill), Las Ruinas is now, like much else in Parque Lenin, a ruin itself, although it still tries to pass itself off as a restaurant. While the eye-catching stained glass by Cuban artist René Portocarrero impresses, the food, ambience and service don't. Not that you've got much choice out this way.

❶ Getting There & Away
Your public transport choices to Parque Lenin are bus, car or taxi. The bus isn't easy. The P-13 will get you close, but to catch it you have to first get to Vibora. The best way to do this is to get on the P-9 at Calles 23 and L. Havana taxi drivers are used to this run and it should be easy to negotiate a rate with stops for CUC$25 and up.

❶ Getting Around
There's a Servi-Cupet gas station on the corner of Av de la Independencia and Calle 271 in Boyeros, north of the airport. It's accessible only from the northbound lane and is open 24 hours a day.

Santiago de las Vegas Area
While not exactly brimming with tourist potential, downbeat and dusty Santiago de las Vegas offers a fleeting glimpse of Cuba that isn't featured in coffeetable photo spreads. Visitors, if they come here at all, usually encounter this settlement – a curious amalgamation of small town and sleepy city suburb – every December during the 5000-strong devotional crawl to the Santuario de SanLázaro (named after a Christian saint known for his ministrations to lepers and the poor) in the nearby village of El Rincón.

◉ Sights

Mausoleo de Antonio Maceo — MONUMENT
Located on a hilltop at El Cacahual, 8km south of Aeropuerto Internacional José Martí and reached via Santiago de las Vegas, is the little-visited mausoleum of the hero of Cuban independence, General Antonio Maceo, who was killed in the Battle of San Pedro near Bauta on December 7, 1896. An open-air pavilion next to the Antonio Maceo mausoleum shelters a historical exhibit.

Santuario de San Lázaro CHURCH
(Carretera San Antonio de los Baños) The focus of Cuba's biggest annual pilgrimage lacks ostentation and is tucked away in the rustic village of El Rincón. The saint inside the church is San Lázaro (also known as *Babalú Ayé;* an *orisha* in the Santería religion), the patron saint of healing and the sick. Hundreds come to lights candles and lay flowers daily.

There's a small museum displaying a raft of previous offerings to San Lázaro in a chapel next door.

ⓘ Getting There & Away

To get here, take bus P-12 from the Capitolio or bus P-16 from outside Hospital Hermanos Ameijeiras just off the Malecón.

Regla

POP 42,390

The old town of Regla, just across the harbor from Habana Vieja, is an industrial port town known as a center of Afro-Cuban religions, including the all-male secret society Abakúa. Long before the triumph of the 1959 Revolution, Regla was known as the Sierra Chiquita (Little Sierra, after the Sierra Maestra) for its revolutionary traditions. This working-class neighborhood is also notable for a large thermoelectric power plant and shipyard. Regla is almost free of tourist trappings, and makes an easily reachable afternoon trip away from the city; the skyline views from this side of the harbor offer a different perspective.

◎ Sights

Iglesia de Nuestra Señora de Regla CHURCH
(◎ 7:30am-6pm) As important as it is diminutive, Iglesia de Nuestra Señora de Regla, which lies just behind the boat dock in the municipality of Regla, has a long and colorful history. Inside on the main altar you'll find La Santísima Virgen de Regla.

The virgin, represented by a black Madonna, is venerated in the Catholic faith and associated in the Santería religion with Yemayá, the *orisha* of the ocean and the patron of sailors (always represented in blue). Legend claims that this image was carved by St Augustine 'The African' in the 5th century, and that in AD 453 a disciple brought

---

WORTH A TRIP

MUSEO HEMINGWAY

There's only one reason to visit the mundane if tranquil Havana suburb of San Francisco de Paula – the **Museo Hemingway** (admission CUC$5, guide CUC$5; ◎ 10am-5pm Mon-Sat, 10am-1pm Sun). In 1939 US novelist Ernest Hemingway rented the Finca la Vigía villa on a hill here, 15km southeast of central Havana. A year later he bought the house (1888) and property and lived there continuously until 1960, when he moved back to the United States.

The villa's interior has remained unchanged since the day Hemingway left (there are lots of stuffed trophies), and the wooded estate is now a museum. Hemingway left his house and its contents to the 'Cuban people,' and his house has been the stimulus for some rare shows of US-Cuban cooperation. In 2002 Cuba agreed to a US-funded project to digitalize the documents stored in the basement of Finca la Vigía, and in May 2006 sent 11,000 of Hemingway's private documents to the JFK Presidential Library in America for digitalization. This literary treasure trove (including a previously unseen epilogue for *For Whom the Bell Tolls*) was finally made available online in January 2009.

To prevent the pilfering of objects, visitors are not allowed inside the house, but there are enough open doors and windows to allow a proper glimpse into Papa's universe. There are books everywhere (including beside the toilet), a large Victrola and record collection, and an astounding number of knickknacks. Don't come when it's raining as the house itself will be closed. A stroll through the garden is worthwhile to see the surprisingly sentimental dog cemetery, Hemingway's fishing boat *El Pilar* and the pool where actress Ava Gardner once swam naked. You can chill out here on a chaise lounge below whispering palms and bamboo.

To reach San Francisco de Paula, take metro bus P-7 (Cotorro) from the Capitolio in Centro Habana. Tell the driver you're going to the museum. You get off in San Miguel del Padrón.

the statue to Spain to safeguard it from barbarians. The small vessel in which the image was traveling survived a storm in the Strait of Gibraltar, so the figure was recognized as the patron of sailors. These days rafters attempting to reach the US also evoke the protection of the Black Virgin.

To shelter a copy of the image, a hut was first built on this site in 1687 by a pilgrim named Manuel Antonio. But this structure was destroyed during a hurricane in 1692. A few years later a Spaniard named Juan de Conyedo built a stronger chapel, and in 1714 Nuestra Señora de Regla was proclaimed patron of the Bahía de la Habana. In 1957 the image was crowned by the Cuban Cardinal in Havana cathedral. Every year on September 8 thousands of pilgrims descend on Regla to celebrate the saint's day, and the image is taken out for a procession through the streets.

The current church dates from the early 19th century and is always busy with devotees from both religions stooping in silent prayer before the images of the saints that fill the alcoves. In Havana, there is probably no better (public) place to see the layering and transference between Catholic beliefs and African traditions.

Museo Municipal de Regla   MUSEUM
(Martí No 158; admission CUC$2; ⊙9am-5pm Mon-Sat, 9am-1pm Sun) If you've come across to see the church, you should also check out this quirky museum, which is spread over two sites, one adjacent to the church and the other (better half) a couple of blocks up the main street from the ferry recording the history of Regla and its Afro-Cuban religions.

There's an interesting, small exhibit on Remigio Herrero, first *babalawo* (priest) of Regla, and a bizarre statue of Napoleon with his nose missing. Price of admission includes both museum outposts and the Colina Lenin exhibit.

Colina Lenin   MONUMENT
From the museum, head straight (south) on Martí past Parque Guaicanamar, and turn left on Albuquerque and right on 24 de Febrero, the road to Guanabacoa. About 1.5km from the ferry you'll see a high metal stairway that gives access to Colina Lenin, one of two monuments in Havana to Vladimir Ilyich Ulyanov (better known to his friends and enemies as Lenin).

The monument was conceived in 1924 by the socialist mayor of Regla, Antonio Bosch, to honor Lenin's death (in the same year). Above a monolithic image of the man is an olive tree planted by Bosch, surrounded by seven lithe figures. There are fine harbor views from the hilltop.

ⓘ Getting There & Away

Regla is easily accessible on the passenger ferry that departs every 15 minutes (CUC$0.25) from Muelle Luz at the intersection of San Pedro and Santa Clara, in Habana Vieja. Bicycles are readily accepted via a separate line that boards first.

Bus 29 runs to Guanabacoa from Parque Maceo between the ferry terminal and the Museo Municipal de Regla.

Guanabacoa

POP 106.374

Guanabacoa is the little village that got swallowed up by the big city. In spite of this, the settlement's main thoroughfare, diminutive Parque Martí, still retains a faintly bucolic small-town air. Locals call it *el pueblo embrujado* (the bewitched town) for its strong Santería traditions, though there are indigenous associations too. In the 1540s the Spanish conquerors concentrated the few surviving Taínos at Guanabacoa, 5km east of central Havana, making it one of Cuba's first official *pueblos Indios* (Indian towns). A formal settlement was founded in 1607, and this later became a center of the slave trade. In 1762 the British occupied Guanabacoa, but not without a fight from its mayor, José Antonio Gómez Bulones (better known as Pepe Antonio), who attained almost legendary status by conducting a guerrilla campaign behind the lines of the victorious British. José Martí supposedly gave his first public speech here, and it was also the birthplace of the versatile Cuba singer Rita Montaner (1900–58), after whom the Casa de la Cultura is named.

Today, Guanabacoa is a sleepy yet colorful place that can be tied in with an excursion to nearby Regla (easily accessible by ferry).

⊙ Sights

Iglesia de Guanabacoa   CHURCH
(cnr Pepe Antonio & Adolfo del Castillo Cadenas; ⊙parochial office 8-11am & 2-5pm Mon-Fri) The church, on Parque Martí in the center of

town, is also known as the Iglesia de Nuestra Señora de la Asunción, and was designed by Lorenzo Camacho and built between 1721 and 1748 with a Moorish-influenced wooden ceiling.

The gilded main altar and nine lateral altars are worth a look, and there is a painting of the *Assumption of the Virgin* at the back. In typical Cuban fashion, the main doors are usually locked; knock at the **parochial office** out back if you're keen.

Museo Municipal de Guanabacoa MUSEUM (Martí No 108; admission CUC$2; ⊙10am-6pm Mon & Wed-Sat, 9am-1pm Sun) The town's main sight is the renovated museum two blocks west of Parque Martí. Founded in 1964, it tracks the development of the neighborhood throughout the 18th and 19th centuries and is famous for its rooms on Afro-Cuban culture, slavery and the Santería religion, with a particular focus on the *orisha* Elegguá.

The museum has another arm further west along Calle Martí in the **Museo de Mártires** (Martí No 320; admission free; ⊙10am-6pm Tue-Sat, 9am-1pm Sun), which displays material relevant to the Cuban Revolution.

✖ Eating

★**Centro Cultural Recreativo los Orishas** CARIBBEAN $$
(cnr Martí & Lamas; admission CUC$3; ⊙10am-midnight) Situated in the hotbed of Havana's Santería community, this funky bar-restaurant hosts live rumba music at weekends, including regular visits from the Conjunto Folklórico Nacional. The pleasant garden bar is surrounded by colorful Afro-Cuban sculptures that depict various Santería deities such as Babalou Aye, Yemayá and Changó.

Well off the beaten track and hard to get to at night, this quirky music venue is usually visited by foreigners in groups. It also does a good selection of food from a CUC$1 pizza to CUC$20 lobster.

Los Ibelly Heladería ICE CREAM $
(Adolfo del Castillo Cadenas No 5a; ⊙10am-10pm) As close as Guanabacoa gets to the Coppelia, with quick-serve ice cream.

❶ Getting There & Away

Bus P-15 from the Capitolio in Centro Habana goes to Guanabacoa via Av del Puerto. Alternatively, you can walk uphill from Regla, at which the Havana ferry docks, to Guanabacoa (or vice versa) in about 45 minutes, passing Colina Lenin on the way.

Cojímar Area

Situated 10km east of Havana is the little port town of Cojímar, famous for harboring Ernest Hemingway's fishing boat *El Pilar* in the 1940s and 1950s. This picturesque, if slightly run-down, harbor community served as the prototype for the fishing village in Hemingway's novella *The Old Man and the Sea*, which won him the Nobel Prize for Literature in 1954. The settlement was founded in the 17th century at the mouth of the Río Cojímar. In 1762 an invading British army landed here on its way through to take Havana; in 1994 thousands of 'rafters' split from the sheltered but rocky bay, lured across to Florida by US radio broadcasts and promises of political asylum.

To the southwest of Cojímar just off the Vía Blanca is the rather ugly sporting complex and athletes' village built when Cuba staged the 1991 Pan-American Games.

◉ Sights

Estadio Panamericano STADIUM
The huge 55,000-seat stadium on the Vía Monumental between Havana and Cojímar, was built for the 1991 Pan-American Games and is already looking prematurely dilapidated. There are also tennis courts, Olympic-sized swimming pools and other sporting facilities nearby.

Torreón de Cojímar FORT
Overlooking the harbor is an old Spanish fort (1649) presently occupied by the Cuban Coast Guard. It was the first fortification taken by the British when they attacked Havana from the rear in 1762. Next to this tower and framed by a neoclassical archway is a gilded **bust of Ernest Hemingway**, erected by the residents of Cojímar in 1962.

Alamar NEIGHBORHOOD
East across the river from Cojímar is a large housing estate of prefabricated apartment blocks built by *micro brigadas* (small armies of workers responsible for building much of the postrevolutionary housing), beginning in 1971. This is the birthplace of Cuban rap and the annual hip-hop festival is still centered here.

🛏 Sleeping

Hostal Marlin   CASA PARTICULAR $
(☑ 766-6154; Real No 128 btwn Santo Domingo &
Chacón; r CUC$30) Chilled apartment with a
sea view and a terrace on the roof that offers a potential escape from the tumult of
Havana. There's a kitchenette, a separate
entrance and plenty of privacy.

Hotel Panamericano   HOTEL $
(☑ 95-10-10,   95-10-00;   s/d incl breakfast
CUC$20/44; 🅿 ♿ ☀) This four-story ugly
duckling was used as the accommodations
for the 1991 Pan-American Games (thank
goodness, Havana isn't hosting the Olympics). The decent swimming pool and cable
TV are small mercies.

✗ Eating

Restaurante la Terraza   SEAFOOD $$$
(Calle 152 No 161; ◷ noon-11pm) Another photo-
adorned shrine to the ghost of Hemingway,
La Terraza specializes in seafood and does a
roaring trade from the hordes of Papa fans
who pour in daily. The terrace dining room
overlooking the bay is pleasant. More at-
mospheric, however, is the old bar out front,
where mojitos haven't yet reached El Florid-
ita rates. The food is surprisingly mediocre.
Just down from the Hotel Panamericano is
a **bakery** (Hotel Panamericano; ◷ 8am-8pm).
Across the Paseo Panamericano is a grocery
store, the **Mini-Super Caracol** (◷ 9am-8pm),
and a clean and reasonably priced Italian
restaurant **Allegro** (◷ noon-11pm), which of-
fers lasagna, risotto, spaghetti and pizza, all
for under CUC$5.

ℹ Information

Bandec (◷ 8:30am-3pm Mon-Fri, 8:30-11am
Sat), on Paseo Panamericano, changes
traveler's checks and gives cash advances.

ℹ Getting There & Away

Metro bus P-8 goes to the Villa Panamericano
from the Capitolio in Centro Habana. From the
hotel it's around 2km downhill through the vil-
lage to the Hemingway bust.

Casablanca

Casablanca, just across the harbor from
Habana Vieja and in the shadow of La
Cabaña fort, is a small village surrounded
by urbanization. It's dominated by a white
marble **Estatua de Cristo** (statue of Christ),
created in 1958 by Jilma Madera. It was
promised to President Batista by his wife
after the US-backed dictator survived an at-
tempt on his life in the Presidential Palace in
March 1957, but was (ironically) unveiled on
Christmas Day 1958 one week before the dic-
tator fled the country. As you disembark the
Casablanca ferry, follow the road uphill for
about 10 minutes until you reach the statue.
The views from up here are stupendous and
it is a favorite nighttime hangout for locals.
Behind the statue is the **Observatorio Na-
cional** (closed to tourists).

Passenger ferries to Casablanca depart
Muelle Luz, on the corner of San Pedro
and Santa Clara in Habana Vieja, about
every 15 minutes (CUC$0.25). Bicycles are
welcome. The **Casablanca train station**,
next to the ferry wharf, is the western ter-
minus of the only electric railway in Cuba.
In 1917 the Hershey Chocolate Company of
the US state of Pennsylvania built this line
to Matanzas. Trains still depart for Matan-
zas three times a day (at 4:45am, 12:21pm
and 4:35pm). You'll travel via Guanabo
(CUC$0.75, 25km), Hershey (CUC$1.40,
46km), Jibacoa (CUC$1.65, 54km) and
Canasí (CUC$1.95, 65km) to Matanzas
(CUC$2.80, 90km) and dozens of smaller
stations. No one on a tight schedule should
use this train; it usually leaves Casablanca
on time but often arrives an hour late.
Bikes aren't officially allowed. It's a scenic
four-hour trip (on a good day), and tickets
are easily obtainable at the station.

Playas del Este

In Cuba you're never far from an idyl-
lic beach. Havana's very own pine-fringed
Riviera, Playas del Este, begins just 18km to
the east of the capital at the small resort of
Bacuranao, before continuing east through
Tarará, El Mégano, Santa María del Mar
and Boca Ciega to the town of Guanabo.
Although none of these places has so far
witnessed the kind of megadevelopment
redolent of Cancún or Varadero, Playas del
Este is still a popular tourist drawcard. Dur-
ing the summer months of July and August,
all of Havana comes to play and relax on
the soft white sands and clear aquamarine
waters of the beautiful Atlantic coastline.

While the beaches might be postcard-
perfect, Playas del Este can't yet boast the
all-round tourist facilities of other Cuban
resorts such as Varadero and Cayo Coco,

Playas del Este

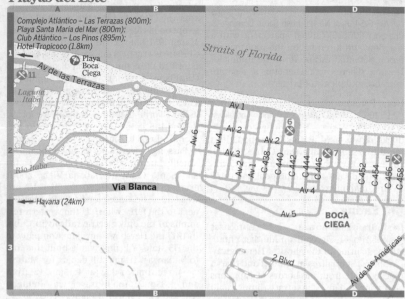

Complejo Atlántico – Las Terrazas (800m);
Playa Santa María del Mar (800m);
Club Atlántico – Los Pinos (895m);
Hotel Tropicoco (1.8km)

Straits of Florida

Playa Boca Ciega

Av de las Terrazas

Laguna Itabo

Av 1

Av 2

Av 2

Av 6

Av 4

Av 4

Av 2

Av 3

C-438

C-440

C-442

C-444

C-446

C-452

C-454

C-456

C-458

Río Itabo

Av 2

Av 1

Vía Blanca

Havana (24km)

Av 4

Av 5

BOCA CIEGA

2 Blvd

Av de las Américas

Playas del Este

Sleeping

Eating

Entertainment

much less the all-out luxury of celebrated Caribbean getaways. Come here in winter and the place often has a timeworn and slightly abandoned air, and even in summer, seasoned beach bums might find the tatty restaurants and ugly Soviet-style hotel piles more than a little incongruous.

But for those who dislike modern tourist development or are keen to see how Cubans

get out and enjoy themselves at weekends, Playas del Este is a breath of fresh air.

Each of the six beaches that dot this 9km stretch of attractive coastline has its own distinctive flavor. Tarará is a yacht and diving haven, Santa María del Mar is where the largest concentration of resorts (and foreigners) can be found, Boca Ciega is popular with gay couples, while Guanabo is the rustic Cuban end of the strip, with shops, a nightclub and plenty of cheap casas particulares.

🏃 Activities

Yacht charters, deep-sea fishing and scuba diving are offered by **Cubanacán Náutica Tarará** (☑ 96-15-08, 96-15-09; VHF channels 16 & 77; cnr Av 8 & Calle 17, Tarará), 22km east of Havana. Ask about this at your hotel tour desk.

There are a number of **Club Náutica** points spaced along the beaches. The most central is outside Club Atlántico in the middle of Playa Santa María del Mar. Here you can rent pedal boats (CUC$6 per hour; four to six people), banana boats (CUC$5 per five minutes; maximum five people), one-/two-person kayaks (CUC$2/4 per hour), snorkel gear (CUC$4) and catamarans (CUC$12 per hour; maximum four people plus lifeguard). A paddle around the coast exploring the mangrove-choked canals is a pleasure.

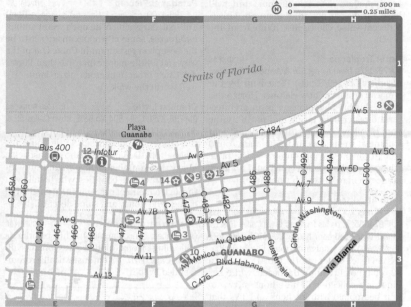

Beach toys such as sailboards, water bikes and badminton gear may also be available; ask. Many people rent similar equipment all along the beach to Guanabo, but check any water vessels and gear carefully, as we've received complaints about faulty equipment. Consider leaving a deposit instead of pre-paying in full, should anything go awry.

🛏 Sleeping

🛏 Guanabo

Guanabo has dozens of casas particulares and one passable hotel.

Elena Morina CASA PARTICULAR $
(☑796-7975; Calle 472 No 7B11, btwn Avs 7B & 9; r CUC$25-30; ✽) *Hay Perro* reads the sign, but don't worry, the pit bull that lives here is friendly (really), as is the hostess Elena, who once lived in Italy. The chatty host makes great coffee and rents two decent rooms with a leafy patio a few blocks back from the beach.

Pablo M Durán Jubiel CASA PARTICULAR $
(☑796-5281; Calle 476 No 905, btwn Avs 9 & 9B; r CUC$25-30; P✽) A little house near the beach with a kitchen and patio; there are also rooms at Nos 906 and 9B01 nearby.

Castellanos o Angela CASA PARTICULAR $
(☑796-3755; Calle 462 No 1306; r CUC$25-30; P✽) Up a hill and set back a bit from the beach, this place does have a decent view and a small swimming pool. Basic rooms have plenty of space and the whole floor can be rented as a self-contained apartment.

Villa Playa Hermosa HOTEL $
(☑796-2774; Av 5D, btwn Calles 472 & 474; s/d with shared bathroom CUC$20/25; P✽@✉) This unpretentious villa has 47 rooms in small bungalows with shared bathroom and TV. It's a popular spot, so expect music, dancing and drinking to all hours; Playa Hermosa is 300m away.

🛏 Santa María del Mar

None of Santa María's hotels is a knockout and some are downright ugly.

Complejo Atlántico – Las Terrazas APARTMENT, HOTEL $$
(☑797-1494; Av de las Terrazas, btwn Calles 11 & 12; 1-/2-/3-bedroom apt CUC$50/75/88; P✽✉) An amalgamation of two old *aparthotels*, this place offers 60 or so apartments (with kitchenettes) that are mainly the preserve of families. The two-bedroom units sleep four people and the three-bedrooms

accommodate six. Ask if your unit will have a fridge, as not all of them do. This is a decent-value choice just 100m from the beach.

Hotel Tropicoco
RESORT **$$**

(☎ 797-1371; btwn Av del Sur & Av de las Terrazas; all-incl s/d CUC$69/99; ✥) Picked up by Cubanacán from the now defunct Horizontes chain, this big blue monster is an architectural disaster both inside and out. Pity the poor travelers who book this online without looking at the photos first. The main (only) benefit for the terribly unfussy is the price (cheap) and the location (you could hit a big home run onto the beach from here).

Club Atlántico – Los Pinos
APARTMENT, HOTEL **$$$**

(☎ 797-1085; Av de las Terrazas, btwn Calles 11 & 12; all-incl s/d/2-bedroom house CUC$105/150/160; P✳@✥) An amalgamation of two of Playas del Este's better resorts, the Atlántico is a 92-room hotel right on the beach, while Los Pinos is a collection of little houses (two to four bedrooms) with kitchens and TVs that were holiday homes before the Revolution. Collectively, they're one of the resort's best bets.

Extra facilities include tennis courts, a swimming pool, cabaret and a Club Náutica point renting boats etc on the beach.

🛏 Bacuranao

Villa Bacuranao
HOTEL **$**

(☎ 65-76-45; s/d CUC$38/44) On the Vía Blanca, 18km east of Havana, this is the closest beach resort to Havana. There's a long sandy beach between the resort and mouth of the Río Bacuranao, across which is the old Torreón de Bacuranao (inside the compound of the military academy and inaccessible).

The beach here isn't as attractive as its more easterly counterparts, but the price is nice.

✕ Eating

Surprise! Playas del Este does some good pizza.

✕ Guanabo

Pan.com
FAST FOOD **$**

(Av 5 No 47802; ⊘24hr) Lackluster outlet of the sometimes good local snack chain. Try the milkshakes.

Paladar el Piccolo
ITALIAN **$$**

(☎ 796-4300; cnr Av 5 & Calle 502; ⊘noon-11pm) This paladar is a bit of an open secret among *habaneros,* some of whom consider it to be the best pizza restaurant in Cuba. Out of the way and a little more expensive than Playas del Este's other numerous pizza joints, it's well worth the walk.

Chicken Little
INTERNATIONAL **$$**

(☎ 796-2351; Calle 504 No 5815, btwn Calles 5B & 5C; mains CUC$5-8; ⊘noon-11pm) Forgive them the kitschy name, Chicken Little could yet make it big. Defying Guanabo's ramshackle image they staff their deluxe restaurant with polite waiters in bow ties who'll talk you through a menu of pesto chicken, chicken in orange and honey and some decent fish.

Restaurante Maeda
CUBAN **$$**

(Av Quebec; ⊘noon-midnight) This paladar is still going strong, hidden away on the hill (near Calle 476). It's enthusiastically recommended by locals.

✕ Boca Ciega

Los Caneyes
CARIBBEAN **$**

(Av 1, btwn Calles 440 & 442; ⊘10am-10pm) A *rancho*-style restaurant just steps from the east end of Boca Ciega beach with a thatched roof and open sides. The food is pretty traditional, but the fish dishes taste better with the sea breeze lapping round your nostrils.

El Cubano
CUBAN **$$**

(☎ 796-4061; Av 5, btwn Calles 456 & 458; ⊘11am-midnight) This is a spick-and-span place almost in Guanabo, with a full wine rack (French and Californian), checkered tablecloths and a good version of chicken cordon bleu.

✕ Santa María del Mar

Don Pepe
SEAFOOD **$**

(Av de las Terrazas; ⊘10am-11pm) When the Guanabo pizza gets too much, head to this thatched-roof, beach-style restaurant about 50m from the sand. It specializes in seafood.

Restaurante Mi Cayito
CARIBBEAN **$$**

(☎ 797-1339; ⊘10am-6pm) On a tiny island in the Laguna Itabo, this place serves lobster, shrimp and grilled fish in an open-air locale. There's a live show here every Saturday and Sunday at 3pm that you can enjoy for the price of a drink.

Restaurante Mi Casita de Coral   SEAFOOD $$
(cnr Av del Sur & Calle 8; ☉10am-11pm) Tucked just off the roundabout by the international clinic. This secluded little place is surprisingly upscale for this neck of the woods. Serves good seafood at reasonable prices.

Self-Catering
Among the many small grocery stores in and around Santa María del Mar are **Minisuper la Barca** (cnr Av 5 & Calle 446; ☉9:15am-6:45pm Mon-Sat, 9:15am-2:45pm Sun); **Mini-Super Santa María** (cnr Av de las Terrazas & Calle 7; ☉9am-6:45pm), located opposite Hotel Tropicoco; and **Tienda Villa los Pinos** (Av del Sur, btwn Calles 5 & 7; ☉9am-6:45pm).

El Mégano

Pizzería Mi Rinconcito   ITALIAN $
(cnr Av de las Terrazas & Calle 4; pizzas CUC$2-3; ☉noon-9:45pm) Located near Villa los Pinos, this place contains a surprisingly delicious pizza-fest, plus cannelloni, lasagna, salads and spaghetti.

☆ Entertainment

Cabaret Guanimar   CABARET
(cnr Av 5 & Calle 468, Guanabo; per couple CUC$10; ☉9pm-3am Tue-Sat) An outdoor club with a show at 11pm; if you want to be in the front rows, it's CUC$16 for a couple.

Teatro Avenida   THEATER
(Av 5 No 47612, btwn Calles 476 & 478, Guanabo) General theater with children's matinees at 3pm Saturday and Sunday.

Cine Guanabo   CINEMA
(Calle 480, Guanabo; ☉5:30pm except Wed) Just off Av 5, this movie house shows mainly action flicks.

Playas del Este's gay scene revolves around a couple of beach bars on Playa Boca Ciega near Restaurante Mi Cayito, at the east end of Santa María del Mar.

ⓘ Information

INTERNET ACCESS & TELEPHONE
Etecsa Telepunto (Av de las Terrazas, Edificio los Corales, btwn Calles 10 & 11, Santa María del Mar)

MEDICAL SERVICES
Clínica Internacional Habana del Este (☏96-18-19; Av de las Terrazas No 36, Santa María del Mar) Open 24 hours; doctors can make hotel visits. There's also a well-stocked pharmacy on-site. This clinic was being renovated at the time of writing.
Farmacia (cnr Av 5 & Calle 466, Guanabo)

MONEY
Banco Popular de Ahorro (Av 5 No 47810, btwn Calles 478 & 480, Guanabo) Changes traveler's checks.

Cadeca is at **Guanabo** (Av 5 No 47612, Guanabo, btwn Calles 476 & 478) and **Santa María del Mar** (Av de las Terrazas, Santa María del Mar, Edificio los Corales, btwn Calles 10 & 11).

POST
Post Office (Av 5, btwn Calles 490 & 492, Guanabo)

TOURIST INFORMATION
Infotur is at **Guanabo** (Av 5, btwn Calles 468 & 470, Guanabo) and **Santa María del Mar** (Av de las Terrazas, Edificio los Corales, btwn Calles 10 & 11).

TRAVEL AGENCIES
Cubatur and Havanatur both have desks at Hotel Tropicoco, between Av del Sur and Av de las Terrazas in Santa María del Mar. Their main business is booking bus tours, though they might be willing to help with hotel reservations.

ⓘ Getting There & Away

BUS
The Havana Bus Tour runs a regular (hourly) service from Parque Central out to Playa Santa María, stopping at Villa Bacuranao, Tarará, Club Mégano, Hotel Tropicoco and Club Atlántico. It doesn't go as far as Guanabo. All-day tickets cost CUC$3.

Bus 400 to Guanabo leaves every hour or so from Calle Agramonte in Centro Habana and stops near the central train station in Habana Vieja. Going the other way, it stops all along Av 5, but it's best to catch it as far east as possible. Bus 405 runs between Guanabacoa and Guanabo.

TAXI
A **Taxis OK** (☏796-6666) tourist taxi from Playas del Este to Havana will cost around CUC$20.

TRAIN
One of the most novel ways to get to Guanabo is on the Hershey Train (p163), which leaves five times a day from either Casablanca train station or Matanzas. The train will drop you at Guanabo station, approximately 2km from the far eastern end of Guanabo. It's a pleasant walk along a quiet road to the town and beaches.

❶ Getting Around

A large guarded parking area is off Calle 7, between Av de las Terrazas and Av del Sur, near Hotel Tropicoco (CUC$1 a day from 8am to 7pm). Several other paid parking areas are along Playa Santa María del Mar.

You can find Cubacar branches at **Club Atlántico** (☑797-1650; Club Atlántico), **Hotel Blau Club Arenal** (☑797-1272; Hotel Blau Club Arenal) and in **Guanabo** (☑796-6997; cnr Calle 478 & Av 9, Guanabo). Rents average-sized cars for far from average prices – bank on CUC$70 a day with insurance.

There are Servi-Cupet gas stations in **Guanabo** (cnr Av 5 & Calle 464, Guanabo) and west of **Bacuranao** (Vía Blanca, west of Bacuranao). Both have snack bars and are open 24 hours. The gas station west of Bacuranao is opposite the military academy.

Artemisa & Mayabeque Provinces

47 / POP 885,544

Best Hiking

➡ La Rosita (p158)

➡ Sendero La Serafina (p160)

➡ El Contento (p160)

➡ Parque Escaleras de Jaruco (p165)

Best Swimming

➡ Baños del San Juan (p161)

➡ Salto del Arco Iris (p158)

➡ Baños del Bayate (p161)

➡ Playa Jibacoa (p163)

Why Go?

Leap-frogged by almost everyone on an organized 'itinerary,' Cuba's two smallest provinces, created by dividing Havana province in half in 2010, deal with more everyday topics – like growing half of the crops that feed the nation, for example. But in among the patchwork of citrus and pineapple fields lie a smattering of small towns that will satisfy the curious and the brave. The most interesting corner is Las Terrazas and Soroa, Cuba's most successful eco-project and an increasingly important nexus for trekking and birdwatching; while, east of Havana, Jibacoa's beaches are the domain of a small trickle of Varadero-avoiding tourists who guard their secret jealously.

Wander elsewhere and you'll be in mainly Cuban company (or none at all) contemplating sugar plantation ruins, weird one-of-a-kind museums, and improbably riotous festivals. For a kaleidoscope of the whole region take the ridiculously slow Hershey train through the nation's proverbial backyard and admire the view.

When to Go

➡ The provinces' big attractions vary considerably climate-wise. Because of their unique geographical situation, Soroa and Las Terrazas have a microclimate: more rain and minimum monthly temperatures 2°C to 3°C colder than Havana.

➡ As it gets hotter later here than elsewhere in the region, February through May is the optimum time to visit, being warm without being significantly wet.

➡ April sees the provinces' premier festival, the International Humor Festival in San Antonio de los Baños.

➡ December through April is best for the beaches at Playa Jibacoa.

Artemisa & Mayabeque Provinces Highlights

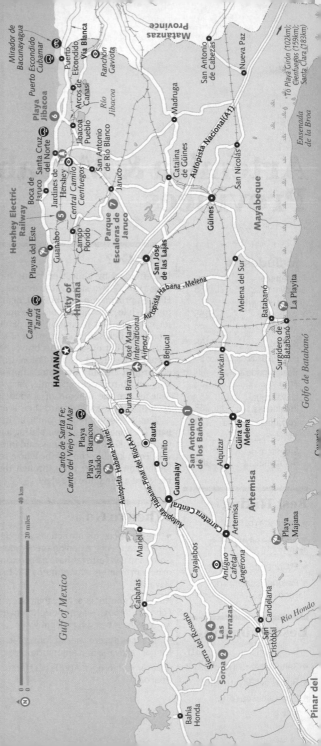

1 Try to suppress giggles at San Antonio de los Baños' **Museo del Humor** (p155).

2 Hike the hills above verdant **Soroa** (p158).

3 Go green at Cuba's primary eco-village where the slopes have been replanted with trees, orchids, painters and poets in **Las Terrazas** (p159).

4 Breathe easier at the country's first and best eco-hotel, **Hotel Moka** (p162).

5 Escape the tourist trails on the historic **Hershey Electric Railway** (p163).

6 Bag a beach retreat beside alluring Playa Jibacoa at the elegant **Superclub Breezes** (p165).

7 Feast with a view and with weekending Havana folk at scenic **Parque Escaleras de Jaruco** (p165).

History

Havana was originally founded on the site of modern-day Surgidero de Batabanó in 1515 but rapidly relocated; the region's role in the shaping of Cuba was to become an almost exclusively agricultural one. Coffee and sugar were the key crops cultivated. Western Artemisa was the center of the country's short-lived coffee boom from 1820 until 1840, when sugar took over as the main industry. Large numbers of slaves were recruited to work on the plantations during the second half of the 19th century when Cuba became the center of the Caribbean slave trade and, as such, the area became a focus for the events leading up to the abolition of slavery in the 1880s.

The success of the sugar industry swept over into the 20th century: sweets mogul Milton S Hershey turned to Mayabeque as a dependable source for providing sugar for his milk chocolate in 1914. This lucrative industry would later suffer under Fidel Castro, once the Americans and then the Russians ceased to buy Cuba's sugar at over-the-odds prices. The region was hard-hit economically, and this deprivation was perhaps best epitomized by the 1980 Mariel Boatlift, when a port on the coast west of Havana became the stage for a Castro-sanctioned (and Jimmy Carter–endorsed) mass exodus of Cubans to Florida.

A major step against the area's downturn was taken in 1968. Neglected land in Western Artemisa province, around the very coffee plantations that had once sustained it, was reforested and transformed into a pioneering eco-village – now one of the region's economic mainstays through the tourism it has generated.

ARTEMISA PROVINCE

In many ways a giant vegetable patch for Havana, Artemisa province's fertile delights include the verdant eco-village of Las Terrazas and the outdoor action on offer among the scenic forested slopes of the Sierra del Rosario mountain range. Then there are myriad mystery-clad coffee plantation ruins and the ever-inventive town of San Antonio de los Baños, which has spawned an internationally renowned film school as well as some of Cuba's top artists. On the north coast, good beaches and great back roads entice the adventurous.

San Antonio de los Baños

POP 35.979

Full of surprises, artsy San Antonio de los Baños, 35km southwest of central Havana, is Cuba on the flip side, a hard-working municipal town where the local college churns out wannabe cinematographers and the museums are more about laughs than crafts.

Founded in 1986 with the help of Nobel Prize–winning Colombian novelist Gabriel García Márquez, San Antonio's Escuela Internacional de Cine y TV invites film students from around the world to partake in its excellent on-site facilities, including an Olympic-sized swimming pool for practicing underwater shooting techniques. Meanwhile, in the center of town, an unusual humor museum makes a ha-ha-happy break from the usual stuffed animal/revolutionary artifact double act.

San Antonio is also the birthplace of *nueva trova* music giant Silvio Rodríguez, born here in 1946. Rodríguez went on to write the musical soundtrack to the Cuban Revolution almost single-handedly. His best-known songs include *Ojalá, La Maza* and *El Necio*.

⊙ Sights & Activities

San Antonio de los Baños has several attractive squares. Most resplendent is the square at the intersection of Calles 66 and 41, which boasts an impressive early 19th-century church. With its twin towers and porthole windows, it is one of the largest and grandest religious buildings in Artemisa and Mayabeque.

Museo Municipal   MUSEUM
(Calle 66 No 4113, btwn Calles 41 & 43) This museum is closed for refurbishment until late 2013, but houses important works by local-born painter Eduardo Abela (1899–1965), a modernist who studied in Paris and from his self-imposed exile rediscovered his homeland with nostalgia.

Museo del Humor   MUSEUM
(cnr Calle 60 & Av 45; admission CUC$2; ⊙10am-6pm Tue-Sat, 9am-1pm Sun) Unique in Cuba is this fun selection of cartoons, caricatures and other entertaining ephemera. Among the drawings exhibited in a neoclassical colonial house are saucy cartoons, satirical scribblings and the first known Cuban caricature, dating from 1848.

Look out for the work of Cuba's foremost caricaturist, Carlos Julio Villar Alemán, a member of Unión de Escritores y Artistas de Cuba (Uneac) and a one-time judge at the International Humor Festival, which is still held here every April (entries remain on display for several weeks during this period).

More local artwork is displayed at **Galería Provincial Eduardo Abela** (Calle 58 No 3708, cnr Calle 37; admission free; ⊘ noon-8pm Mon-Sat, 8am-noon Sun).

Hiking

A footbridge across the river next to La Quintica restaurant leads to a couple of **hiking trails** around the leafy banks.

Boating

Boat trips on the Río Ariguanabo take off from a boat dock at the Hotel Las Yagrumas. A motor boat will take you on an 8km spin for CUC$2. Rowing boats go for CUC$1 an hour.

🛏 Sleeping & Eating

The main shopping strip is Av 41, and there are numerous places to snack on peso treats along this street. The **pizzeria** in the rose-pink building opposite Banco de Crédito y Comercio at Av 41 No 6004 is popular.

Hotel Las Yagrumas   HOTEL $
(⏰38-44-60; s/d from CUC$20/30; 🅿❄✹🛍) A hotel of untapped potential, Las Yagrumas, 3km north of San Antonio de los Baños, overlooking the picturesque but polluted Río Ariguanabo, ought to be a town highlight, but suffers from a familiar lack of government investment.

Its 120 rooms with balcony and terrace (some of which face the river) are popular with peso-paying Cubans as opposed to foreign tourists, but a dearth of maintenance money means many fixtures are falling apart. Sports facilities are better; there's table tennis and a gigantic pool (cover charge for nonguests CUC$6). Boat trips take off on the nearby river.

Don Oliva   CUBAN $
(Calle 62 No 3512, btwn Calles 33 & 35; mains CUC$3-5; ⊘ noon-11pm Tue-Sun) Quite possibly the cheapest lobster in Cuba is served on Don Oliva's secluded covered patio; the price coming in at less than CUC$5, and it's not bad either. Not surprisingly this is a refreshingly untouristed new paladar with prices displayed in *moneda nacional*. Opt for the seafood.

🍷 Drinking & Nightlife

Taberna del Tío Cabrera   NIGHTCLUB
(Calle 56 No 3910, btwn Calles 39 & 41; ⊘ 2-5pm Mon-Fri, 2pm-1am Sat & Sun) An attractive garden nightclub that puts on occasional humor shows (organized in conjunction with the museum). The clientele is a mix of townies, folk from surrounding villages and film-school students.

ℹ Getting There & Away

Hard to get to without a car, San Antonio is supposedly connected to Havana's Estación 19 de Noviembre (four trains a day), but check well ahead. Otherwise, a taxi should cost CUC$30 one way from central Havana.

Artemisa

POP 57,159

Becoming the capital of Artemisa province is unlikely to ever transform Artemisa into a tourist mecca: this farming town's days of affluence and appeal lie firmly embedded in the past. Having once attracted notables such as Ernest Hemingway and the famed Cuban poet Nicolás Guillén, and having grown wealthy on the back of 19th-century sugar and coffee booms, Artemisa's importance declined when the bottom fell out of the sugar and coffee industries. It's known today as the Villa Roja (Red Town), or the Jardín de Cuba (Garden of Cuba) for the famous fertility of its soil, which still yields a rich annual harvest of tobacco, bananas and some sugarcane.

Artemisa has no accommodations for foreigners: Soroa is the nearest option. As if in compensation, several stalls at the town end of the road to Antigua Cafetal Angerona do mean peso pizza.

◉ Sights

If you're passing, Artemisa contains two national monuments, along with a restored section of the **Trocha Mariel-Majana**, a defensive wall erected by the Spanish during the Wars of Independence.

Mausoleo a los Mártires de Artemisa   MAUSOLEUM
(⏰36-32-76; Av 28 de Enero; admission CUC$1; ⊘ 9am-5pm Tue-Sun) Revolution buffs may want to doff a cap to the Mausoleo a los Mártires de Artemisa. Of the 119 revolutionaries who accompanied Fidel Castro in the 1953 assault on the Moncada Barracks, 28

were from Artemisa or this region. Fourteen of the men presently buried below the cube-shaped bronze mausoleum died in the actual assault or were killed soon after by Batista's troops. The other Moncada veterans buried here died later in the Sierra Maestra. There's a small subterranean museum containing photos and personal effects of the combatants.

Antiguo Cafetal Angerona   HISTORIC SITE
The Antiguo Cafetal Angerona, 5km west of Artemisa on the road to Cayajabos and the Autopista Habana–Pinar del Río (A4), was one of Cuba's earliest *cafetales* (coffee farms). It is now a national monument. Erected between 1813 and 1820 by Cornelio Sauchay, Angerona once employed 450 slaves tending 750,000 coffee plants. Behind the ruined mansion lie the slave barracks and an old watchtower, from which the slaves were monitored. The estate is mentioned in novels by Cirilo Villaverde and Alejo Carpentier, and James A Michener devotes several pages to it in *Six Days in Havana*. It's a quiet and atmospheric place that has the feel of a latter-day Roman ruin. Look for the stone-pillared gateway on the right as you leave Artemisa.

❶ Getting There & Away

The **Artemisa train station** (Av Héroes del Moncada) is four blocks east of the bus station. There are supposed to be two trains a day from Havana at noon and midnight, but don't bank on it.

The bus station is on the Carretera Central in the center of town.

North of Artemisa

The coastline north of Artemisa is visited, though rarely, for its beaches and the little-used back road from Havana to Bahía Honda and the northern coast of Pinar del Río

---

TRAINSPOTTING

Mention rail travel to the average Cuban and they'll probably roll their eyes and tell you you're better off hitchhiking. But, while Cuba's contemporary trains are unkempt, tardy (if they arrive at all) and move at an average pace of 40kmh, their historical legacy is gigantic.

The nation's first pioneering train chugged into action in November 1837, long before any other country in Latin America had a rail network and – ironically – 11 years before colonial overlord, Spain. The inaugural line ran for 27.5km and connected Havana with the provincial town of Bejucal in Mayabeque province. Its opening came little more than a decade after Britain's Stockton and Darlington railway (the world's first), and it was soon followed by an 80km line from Camagüey to the port of Nuevitas on Cuba's north coast. By 1848 tramways were crisscrossing the streets of Havana, before any European city outside of Paris.

Until the beginning of the 20th century, 80% of Cuban railways were associated with the sugar industry. It wasn't until 1902 that the west–east passenger network was joined for the first time by US-Canadian railway magnate William Van Horne (builder of the first Canadian transcontinental railway), creating a line that stretched 1100km from Guane in Pinar del Río province to Guantánamo in the east.

After the Revolution and the US trade embargo that ensued, Cuba's once groundbreaking rail network struggled to find new rolling stock and fuel. Most of what you see today is borrowed from 'friendly' countries such as Britain, Canada, Mexico and, more recently, China. Cuba's only vaguely reliable train, the Tren Francés, which runs every three days between Havana and Santiago de Cuba, uses secondhand coaches from the Trans-Europe Express (Paris–Amsterdam) that were shipped to Cuba in 2001. In common with its automobiles, most of Cuba's trains are antediluvian. Current locomotives are predominantly from the US (pre-1959) and the former Soviet Union, with more recent additions from France, Canada and China. Tourist steam trains ply routes in the Valle de los Ingenios near Trinidad and the Patria O Muerte sugar factory near Moron using old British and American trains from the 1910s.

Trainspotters can probe Cuba's train history further at railway museums in Havana and Bejucal and at the Museo de Agroindustria Azucarero Marcelo Salado near Remedios.

province. Beaches are stony more often than sandy and pollution is rife in places. The monstrous main settlement here, Mariel, is Cuba's second-most polluted town after Moa in Holguín province. Mariel, 45km west of Havana, is best known for the 125,000 Cubans who left here for Florida in April 1980. Once you see it, you'll want to flee, too, but Mariel has a redeeming feature: namely its proximity to a couple of good (and non-polluted) beaches.

Twenty-two kilometers east on the Autopista is **Playa Salado**, a largely deserted beach with some 15 dive sites lying offshore, mostly accessed via excursion groups from Havana. The more developed **Playa Baracoa** is a few kilometers further east. Big dudes near the shoreline lean on old American cars sipping beer while fishers throw lines from the rocky shore. A couple of basic beach shacks sell food.

Soroa

Known appropriately as the 'rainbow of Cuba,' Soroa, a gorgeous natural area and tiny settlement 95km southwest of Havana, is the closest mountain resort to the capital. Located 8km north of Candelaria in the Sierra del Rosario, the easternmost and highest section of the Cordillera de Guaniguanico, the region's heavy rainfall (more than 1300mm annually) promotes the growth of tall trees and orchids. The area gets its name from Jean-Pierre Soroa, a Frenchman who owned a 19th-century coffee plantation in these hills. One of his descendants, Ignacio Soroa, created the park as a personal retreat in the 1920s, and only since the Revolution has this luxuriant region been developed for tourism. This is a great area to explore by bike.

◎ Sights & Activities

All Soroa's sights are conveniently near Hotel & Villas Soroa, where you can also organize horseback riding and a couple of hikes into the surrounding forest. For an average hourly rate of CUC$6, you can arrange several guided hikes through the Hotel & Villas Soroa.

Other trails lead to a rock formation known as **Labyrinth de la Sierra Derrumbada** and an idyllic bathing pool, the **Poza del Amor** (Pond of Love). Ask at the hotel.

Orquideario Soroa   GARDENS
(admission CUC$3, camera CUC$2; ⊙ 8:30am-4:30pm) Tumbling down a landscaped hillside garden next door to Hotel & Villas Soroa is a labor of love built by Spanish lawyer Tomás Felipe Camacho in the late 1940s in memory of his wife and daughter. Camacho traveled round the world to amass his collection of 700 orchid species (the largest in Cuba), including many endemic plants.

Though he died in the 1960s, the Orquideario, connected to the University of Pinar del Río, lives on with guided tours in Spanish or English.

La Rosita   VILLAGE
🌿 The most exciting trail in Soroa is to the eco-village of La Rosita, perched in the hills beyond the Hotel & Villas Soroa. Besides great bird-watching en route, the focus is on spending time at this pioneering eco-community established in 1997, meeting the people, finding out about their way of life and tasting the coffee cultivated on the plantations.

It's one of the all too rare, hands-on opportunities to experience rural life as Cubans do – without the gimmicks and the 'acting up' to tourists. La Rosita is accessed via the El Brujito path; the route is 5km or 17km, depending on your preference. Organize guides at Hotel & Villas Soroa.

Castillo de las Nubes   CASTLE
(Castle of the Clouds) A romantic castle with a circular tower on a hilltop 1.5km up a rough road beyond the Orquideario, the Castillo de las Nubes makes for a good leg stretch. There are stunning views of the Valle de Soroa and the coastal plain from the ridge beyond the bar, but the interior – formerly a restaurant – is currently undergoing a refurbishment and will soon re-emerge as a boutique hotel.

Salto del Arco Iris   WATERFALL
(admission CUC$3) This is a 22m waterfall on the Arroyo Manantiales. The entrance to the park encompassing it is to the right just before the hotel. The falls are at their most impressive in the May-to-October rainy season; otherwise it's a trickle. You can swim here.

Baños Romanos   SWIMMING
(per hr CUC$5) On the opposite side of the stream from the waterfall car park is a stone bathhouse with a pool of cold sulfurous water. Ask at the hotel about the baths and massage treatments.

★ El Mirador
HIKING

Starting at the Baños Romanos, take the signposted well-trodden path 2km uphill to the Mirador, a rocky crag with an incredible sweeping panorama of all Soroa and the coastal flats beyond. Hungry turkey vultures circle below you.

Bird-Watching

This part of the Sierra del Rosario is one of the best bird-watching sites in western Cuba after the Ciénaga de Zapata. You don't have to venture far from the Hotel & Villas Soroa to see species such as the Cuban trogan and the entertaining Cuban tody. Guided tours, arranged through the hotel, are CUC$6 per hour.

🛏 Sleeping & Eating

Several signposted houses on the road from Candelaria to Soroa, 3km below the Hotel & Villas Soroa, rent rooms and concoct meals. These are also worth considering as bases for visiting Las Terrazas.

Don Agapito
CASA PARTICULAR $

(☑ 51-21-59; Carretera a Soroa Km 8; r CUC$20-25; P ❋) Two fantastic well-lit, super-clean rooms and some professional touches, including a personalized giant map of the province, make a stopover at this Soroa casa particular right next to the Orquideario a real pleasure. The food is equally marvelous.

Maité Delgado
CASA PARTICULAR $

(☑ 52-27-00-69; Carretera a Soroa Km 7; r CUC$20-25; P ❋) This accommodation is within easy walking distance of the Soroa sights, the family is pleasant and there are kitchen privileges. If it's full, the owners will point you down the road in the direction of a few other houses.

Hotel & Villas Soroa
RESORT $$

(☑ 52-35-34; s/d all-incl CUC$51/72; P ❋ 🐾) You can't knock the setting of this place nestled in a narrow valley amid stately trees and verdant hills (though you might wonder about the juxtaposition of these scattered blocklike cabins against such a breathtaking natural backdrop).

Isolated and tranquil, there are 80 rooms in a spacious complex, along with an inviting pool, a small shop and an ordinary restaurant. The forest is just shouting distance from your front door.

Restaurante el Salto
CARIBBEAN $

(⊗ 9am-7pm) This simple place next to the Baños Romanos is your only eating option outside the hotel.

❶ Getting There & Away

The Havana–Viñales Víazul bus stops in Las Terrazas, but not Soroa; you can cover the last 16km in a taxi for approximately CUC$8. If staying at a casa particular, ask about lifts. Transfer buses (not to be depended upon) sometimes pass through Soroa between Viñales and Havana. Inquire at Hotel & Villas Soroa, or at Havanatur in Viñales or Havana.

The only other access to Soroa and the surrounding area is with your own wheels: car, bicycle or moped. The Servi-Cupet gas station is on the Autopista at the turn-off to Candelaria, 8km below Villas Soroa.

Las Terrazas
POP 1200

The pioneering eco-village of Las Terrazas dates back to a reforestation project in 1968. Today it's a Unesco Biosphere Reserve, a burgeoning activity center (with Cuba's only canopy tour) and the site of the earliest surviving coffee plantations in Cuba. Not surprisingly, it attracts day-trippers from Havana by the busload.

Overnighters can stay in the community's sole hotel, the mold-breaking Hotel Moka, an upmarket eco-resort built between 1992 and 1994 by workers drawn from Las Terrazas to attract foreign tourists. Close by, in the picturesque whitewashed village that overlooks a small lake, there's a vibrant art community with open studios, woodwork and pottery workshops. But the region's biggest attraction is its verdant natural surroundings, which are ideal for hiking, relaxing and bird-watching.

⊙ Sights

The Las Terrazas area supported 54 coffee estates at the height of the Cuban coffee boom in the 1820s and '30s. However, today coffee is barely grown at all, but you can discover the jungle-immersed ruins of at least half a dozen old *cafetales* in the area.

Looming in the fecund forest and only accessible by hiking trails are the Santa Serafina, the San Idelfonso and El Contento coffee-estate ruins (see p160).

Cafetal Buenavista   HISTORIC SITE

About 1.5km up the hill from the Puerta las Delicias (eastern) gate, and accessible by road, are the restored ruins of Cuba's oldest coffee plantation, built in 1801 by French refugees from Haiti. The huge *tajona* (grindstone) out the back once extracted the coffee beans from their shells. Next the beans were sun-dried on huge platforms.

Ruins of the quarters of some of the 126 slaves held here can be seen alongside the driers. The attic of the master's house (now a restaurant) was used to store the beans until they could be carried down to the port of Mariel by mule. There are decent views from here.

Hacienda Unión   HISTORIC SITE

About 3.5km west of the Hotel Moka access road, the Hacienda Unión is another partially reconstructed coffee-estate ruin that features a country-style restaurant, a small flower garden known as the **Jardín Unión** and horseback riding (CUC$6 per hour).

San Pedro & Santa Catalina   HISTORIC SITE

These 19th-century coffee-estate ruins are down a branch road at **La Cañada del Infierno** (Trail to Hell), midway between the Hotel Moka access road and the Soroa side entrance gate. A kilometer off the main road, and just before the ruins of the San Pedro coffee estate, a bar overlooks a popular swimming spot. After this it's another kilometer to Santa Catalina.

A trail leads on from here to Soroa.

Peña de Polo Montañez   MUSEUM

(⊘ Tue-Sun) **FREE** The former lakeside house of local *guajiro* musician Polo Montañez is now a small museum containing various gold records and assorted memorabilia. It's right in the village overlooking the lake.

Polo's most famous songs include 'Guajiro Natural' and 'Un Monton de Estrellas'; they captured the heart of the nation between 2000 and 2002 with simple lyrics about love and nature, during which time Montañez came to be regarded as one of Cuba's finest-ever folk singers. His stardom was short-lived, however: he died in a car accident in 2002.

Galleria de Lester Campa   GALLERY

(⊘ 24hr) **FREE** Several well-known Cuban artists are based at Las Terrazas, including Lester Campa, whose work has been exhibited internationally. Pop into his lakeside studio-gallery, on the right-hand side a few houses after Peña de Polo Montañez.

La Plaza   PLAZA

(⊘ 24hr) In the village, the area just above Hotel Moka encompasses a cinema, a library and an absorbing museum. All are generally open throughout the day, or can become so if you ask.

Activities

Hiking

The Sierra del Rosario has some of the best hikes in Cuba. However, they're all guided, ie you can't officially do any of them on your own (nonexistent signposting deters all but the hardiest from trying). On the upside, most of the area's guides are highly trained, which means you'll emerge from the experience both fitter and wiser. The cost of the hikes varies depending on the number of people and the length of the walk. Bank on anything between CUC$15 and CUC$25 per person. Book at the Oficinas del Complejo or Hotel Moka.

San Claudio   HIKING

The biosphere's toughest hike is a 20km trail traversing the hills to the northwest of the community, and culminating in the 20m-high San Claudio waterfall. It was once offered as an overnighter (with opportunities to camp out in the forest), but hurricane damage had curtailed this at last research.

El Contento   HIKING

This 7.6km ramble takes you through the reserve's foothills between the Campismo el Taburete (for Cubans only) and the Baños del San Juan, taking in two coffee-estate ruins: San Idelfonso and El Contento.

El Taburete   HIKING

This hike (5.6km) has the same start and finish point as El Contento, but follows a more direct route over the 452m Loma el Taburete where a poignant **monument** is dedicated to the 38 Cuban guerrillas who trained in these hills for Che Guevara's ill-fated Bolivian adventure.

Sendero la Serafina   HIKING

The easy 6.4km La Serafina loop starts and finishes near the Rancho Curujey. It's a well-known paradise for bird-watchers (there are more than 70 species on show). Halfway through the walk you will pass the ruins of the Cafetal Santa Serafina, one of the first coffee farms in the Caribbean.

Sendero las Delicias   HIKING

This 3km route runs from Rancho Curujey to the Cafetal Buenavista, incorporating some fantastic views.

Bajo del Corte del Tocororo   HIKING

A newly developed 6km hike that ventures out from the village, traverses the skirts of Loma El Salón, and finishes at Hacienda Unión. It is ideal for spotting Cuba's national bird, the tocororo.

Swimming

Baños del San Juan   SWIMMING

(admission with/without lunch CUC$10/4) It's hard to envisage more idyllic natural swimming pools than those situated 3km to the south of Hotel Moka down an undulating paved road. These *baños* (baths) are surrounded by naturally terraced rocks, where the clean, bracing waters cascade into a series of pools.

Riverside, there are a handful of open-air eating places, along with changing rooms, showers and overnight cabins, though the spot still manages to retain a sense of rustic isolation.

Baños del Bayate   SWIMMING

(admission CUC$3) More natural baths; these offer a relaxed idyll on the Río Bayate near the San Pedro coffee-estate ruins.

Cycling

A 30km guided cycling tour takes in most of the area's highlights for CUC$22. Inquire at Hotel Moka, which hires bicycles out for CUC$2 per hour.

Ziplining

Cuba's only **canopy tour** (per person CUC$25) maintains three zip lines that catapult you over Las Terrazas village and the Lago del San Juan like an eagle in flight. The total 'flying' distance is 800m. The professional instructors here maintain high safety standards.

🛏 Sleeping & Eating

Through the Moka you can also book five rustic cabins 3km away in Río San Juan (single/double CUC$15/25) or arrange tent camping (CUC$12). There are also three villas (single/double CUC$60/85) available for rent in the village.

You'll find other *ranchónes* (rural farms) at Cafetal Buenavista, Baños del Bayate and Baños del San Juan.

Villa Duque   CASA PARTICULAR $

(☑ 53-22-14-31; Carretera a Cayajabos Km 2, Finca San Andres; r CUC$20; ℗ ❄) Eco-tourism doesn't have to come at a cost. Those on a budget might wish to check out this

ARTEMISA & MAYABEQUE PROVINCES LAS TERRAZAS

NEW MODEL VILLAGE

Back in 1968, when Al Gore was still cramming at Harvard and the nascent environmental movement was a prickly protest group for renegades with names like 'Swampy,' the forward-thinking Cubans – concerned about the ecological cost of island-wide deforestation – came up with an idea.

The plan involved taking a 5000-hectare tract of degraded land in Cuba's mountainous west around the remains of some old French *cafetales* (coffee farms) and reforesting it on terraced, erosion-resistant slopes. In 1971, with the first phase of the plan completed, the workers on the project created a reservoir and on its shores constructed a groundbreaking model village to provide much-needed housing for the area's disparate inhabitants.

The result was Las Terrazas, Cuba's first eco-village, a thriving community of 1200 inhabitants whose self-supporting, sustainable settlement includes a hotel, myriad artisan shops, a vegetarian restaurant and small-scale organic farming techniques. The project was so successful that, in 1985, the land around Las Terrazas was incorporated into Cuba's first Unesco Biosphere Reserve, the Sierra del Rosario.

In 1994, as the tourist industry was expanded to counteract the economic effects of the Special Period, Las Terrazas opened Hotel Moka, an environmentally congruous hotel designed by minister of tourism and green architect Osmani Cienfuegos, brother of the late revolutionary hero Camilo.

Now established as Cuba's most authentic eco-resort, Las Terrazas operates on guiding principles that include energy efficiency, sustainable agriculture, environmental education and a sense of harmony between buildings and landscape. The area is also home to an important ecological research center.

farmhouse 2km before the eastern entrance of Las Terrazas, which has one spick-and-span room, a fridge full of beer, a wraparound balcony and breakfast included in the price. The fresh country smells come free of charge, too.

★**Hotel Moka**   RESORT **$$**
(☑ 57-86-00; Las Terrazas; s/d all-inclusive CUC$80/110; P ❄ ❅) * Cuba's only *real* eco-hotel might not qualify for the four stars it advertises, but who's arguing? With its trickling fountains, blooming flower garden and resident tree growing through the lobby, Moka would be a catch in any country. The 26 bright, spacious rooms have fridges, satellite TV and bathtubs with a stupendous view (there are blinds for the shy).

Equipped with a bar, restaurant, shop, pool and tennis court, the hotel also acts as an information center for the reserve and can organize everything from hiking to fishing.

★**Patio de María**   CAFE **$**
(Las Terrazas; ⊙ 9am-11pm) * Patio de María is a small, brightly painted coffee bar that might just qualify for the best brew in Cuba. The secret comes in the expert confection (María lives upstairs) and the fact that the beans are grown about 20m away from your cup in front of the flowery terrace.

El Romero   VEGETARIAN **$**
(Las Terrazas; ⊙ noon-9pm; ☑) * The most interesting place to grab a bite, this full-blown eco-restaurant specializes in vegetarian fare. El Romero uses solar energy and home-grown organic vegetables and herbs, and keeps its own bees. You'll think you've woken up in San Francisco when you browse the menu replete with hummus, bean pancake, pumpkin and onion soup, and extra-virgin olive oil.

Rancho Curujey   CARIBBEAN **$**
(⊙ 9am-6pm) Recently refurbished, this *ranchón*-style set-up offers beer and snacks under a small thatched canopy overlooking Lago Palmar.

Casa del Campesino   CARIBBEAN **$**
(Las Terrazas; ⊙ 9am-9pm) Of the *ranchón*-style restaurants dotted around, this one adjacent to the Hacienda Unión is a visitor favorite.

❶ Information

Las Terrazas is 20km northeast of Hotel & Villas Soroa and 13km west of the Havana–Pinar del Río Autopista at Cayajabos. There are toll gates at both entrances to the reserve (CUC$3 per person). The eastern toll gate, Puerta las Delicias, is a good source of information on the park, while the best place to get information and arrange excursions is at the **Oficinas del Complejo** (☑ 57-87-00, 57-85-55), adjacent to Rancho Curujey, or on the other side of the road at Hotel Moka; both places act as nexus points for the reserve. None of these information points should be confused with the Centro de Investigaciones Ecológicas, a research station approached via a separate driveway east of Rancho Curujey.

❶ Getting There & Away

Two Víazul buses a day currently stop at the Rancho Curujey next door to Las Terrazas; one at around 10am from Havana to Pinar del Río and Viñales, the other at 4pm heading in the opposite direction. Occasional transfer buses pass through bound for Havana or Viñales. Inquire at Hotel Moka or contact the Viñales office of Havanatur.

❶ Getting Around

The Essto station is 1.5km west of the Hotel Moka access road. Fill up here before heading east to Havana or west to Pinar del Río. Most excursions organize transport. Otherwise, you'll have to rely on hire car, taxi or your own two feet to get around.

Bahía Honda & Around

The wild, whirling road north from Soroa along the coast to either Bahía Honda and the north of Pinar del Río province (west) or Havana (east) is surprisingly low-key and bucolic. You'll feel as if you're 1000km from the busy capital here. Forested hills give way to rice paddies in the shaded river valleys as you breeze past a picturesque succession of thatched farmhouses, craning royal palms and machete-wielding *guajiros* (rural workers). It makes a tough but highly rewarding cycling route.

Bahía Honda itself is a small bustling town with a pretty church. Despite its relative proximity to Havana, you'll feel strangely isolated here, particularly as the road deteriorates after Soroa.

Your nearest accommodations options are Soroa to the southeast and Playa Mulata to the west.

MAYABEQUE PROVINCE

Tiny Mayabeque, now the country's smallest province, is a productive little place, cultivating citrus fruit, tobacco, grapes for wine and the sugarcane for Havana Club rum, the main distillery of which is also here. Tourists, predominantly Cubans, come here principally for the sandy coast in the northeast, drawn by the good-value resorts that back onto beautiful beaches for a fraction of the price of a Varadero vacation. Inland amid the workaday agricultural atmosphere lie some luxuriant scenic treats: landscaped gardens, the picturesque protected area of Jaruco, Cuba's best bridge and a classic Cuban train journey transecting the lot.

Playa Jibacoa Area

Playa Jibacoa is the Varadero that never was, or the Varadero yet to come – depending on your hunch. For the time being it's a mainly Cuban getaway with an all-inclusive resort, a hotel-standard campismo (cheap rustic accommodation in bungalows) and several other scenic sleeping options thrown in for good measure. Punctuated by a series of small but splendid beaches and blessed with good offshore snorkeling, Jibacoa is backed by a lofty limestone terrace overlooking the ocean. The terrace offers excellent views and some short DIY hikes.

Travelers with children will find interesting things to do in the surrounding area, and the popularity of the region with Cuban families means fast friends are made wherever you go. The Vía Blanca, running between Havana and Matanzas, is the main transport artery in the area, although few buses make scheduled stops here, making Playa Jibacoa a more challenging pit stop than it should be. Just inland are picturesque farming communities and tiny time-warped hamlets linked by the Hershey Electric Railway.

⊙ Sights

Puente de Bacunayagua　　　BRIDGE
Marking the border between Havana and Matanzas provinces, this is Cuba's longest (314m) and highest (103m) bridge. Begun in 1957 and finally opened by Fidel Castro in September 1959, the bridge carries the busy

ARTEMISA & MAYABEQUE PROVINCES PLAYA JIBACOA AREA

WORTH A TRIP

THE HERSHEY TRAIN

'Cow on the line,' drawls the bored-looking ticket seller. 'Train shut for cleaning' reads a scruffy hand-scrawled notice. To *habaneros*, the catalog of daily transport delays is tediously familiar. While the name of the antique Hershey Electric Railway might suggest a sweet treat to most visitors, in Cuba it signifies a more bitter mix of bumpy journeys, hard seats and interminable waits.

Built in 1921 by US chocolate 'czar' Milton S Hershey (1857–1945), the electric-powered railway line was originally designed to link the American mogul's humungous sugar mill in eastern Havana province with stations in Matanzas and the capital. Running along a trailblazing rural route, it soon became a lifeline for isolated communities cut off from the provincial transport network.

In 1959 the Hershey factory was nationalized and renamed Central Camilo Cienfuegos after Cuba's celebrated rebel commander. But the train continued to operate, clinging unofficially to its chocolate-inspired nickname. In the true tradition of the postrevolutionary 'waste not, want not' economy, it also clung to the same tracks, locomotives, carriages, signals and stations.

While a long way from *Orient Express*–style luxury, an excursion on today's Hershey train is a captivating journey back in time to the days when cars were for rich people and sugar was king. For outsiders, this is Cuba as the Cubans see it. It's a microcosm of rural life at the sharp end, with all its daily frustrations, conversations, foibles and – er – fun.

The train seemingly stops at every house, hut, horse stable and hillock between Havana and Matanzas. Getting off is something of a toss-up. Beach bums can disembark at Guanabo and wander 2km north for a taste of Havana's rustic eastern resorts. History buffs can get off at Central Camilo Cienfuegos and stroll around the old Hershey sugar mill ruins. The rest can choose between Playa Jibacoa, Arcos de Canasí and the beautiful Valle de Yumurí. For information on times and fares, see p147.

HAVANA CLUB'S HUB

Some 30km west of the province-spanning bridge, Santa Cruz del Norte is a quiet town that's home to a famous rum factory: the Ronera Santa Cruz, producer of Havana Club rum and one of the biggest plants of its kind in Cuba. Havana Club, founded in 1878 by the Arrechabala family of Cárdenas, opened its first distillery at Santa Cruz del Norte in 1919, and in 1973 a new factory was built with the capacity to produce 30 million liters of rum annually. No tours are currently run, but Havana Club is widely available throughout the country.

Vía Blanca across a densely wooded canyon that separates the Valle de Yumurí from the sea.

There is a restaurant and observation deck on the Havana side of the bridge where you can sink some drinks in front of one of Cuba's most awe-inspiring views. Imagine dark, bulbous hills, splashes of blue ocean and hundreds upon hundreds of royal palm trees standing like ghostly sentries in the valley haze. The bridge restaurant is a favorite stopping-off point for tour buses and taxis.

Central Camilo Cienfuegos LANDMARK
Five kilometers south of Santa Cruz del Norte is this former sugar mill, once one of Cuba's largest and a testimony to the country's previous production clout. Known as Central Hershey until 1959, the mill, which opened in 1916, once belonged to the Philadelphia-based Hershey Chocolate Company, which used the sugar to sweeten its world-famous chocolate.

The Hershey Electric Railway used to transport produce and workers between Havana, Matanzas and the small town that grew up around the mill. While the train still runs three times a day, the mill was closed in July 2002. It now stands disused on a hilltop like a huge rusting iron skeleton (see also boxed text, p163).

Jardines de Hershey GARDENS
The gardens here are on a tract of land formerly owned by the famous American chocolate tycoon, Milton Hershey, who ran the nearby sugar mill. They're pretty wild these days, with attractive paths, plenty of green foliage and a beautiful river, and this essentially is their charm.

There are a couple of thatched-roof restaurants on-site. It's a serene spot for lunch and a stroll. The gardens are approximately 1km north of Camilo Cienfuegos train station on the Hershey train line. Alternatively, if you're staying in Playa Jibacoa, it's approximately 4km south of Santa Cruz del Norte. The road is quiet and it makes a nice hike if you're up to it.

🏃 Activities

There is good snorkeling from the beach facing Campismo los Cocos; heading westward along the coast you'll find unpopulated pockets where you can don a mask or relax under a palm.

Ranchón Gaviota HORSEBACK RIDING, KAYAKING
(☑ 61-47-02; admission incl meal CUC$8; ⊙ 9am-6pm) This activities center, 12km inland from Puerto Escondido, is usually incorporated into day trips from Matanzas and Varadero. It's approached via a pretty drive through the palm-sprinkled countryside of the Valle de Yumurí. The hilltop ranch itself overlooks a reservoir and offers such delights as horseback riding, kayaking and cycling, plus a massive feast of *ajiaco* (meat stew), roasted pork, *congrí* (rice with beans), salad, dessert and coffee.

To get to the *ranchón,* take the inland road for 2km to Arcos de Canasí and turn left at the fork for another 10km to the signpost.

🛏 Sleeping & Eating

Eating is a grim prospect over this way unless you're in a hotel. You could try the Puente de Bacunayagua restaurant; otherwise there are a couple of bars around selling microwave pizza.

Campismo los Cocos CAMPISMO $
(☑ 29-52-31, 29-52-32; r CUC$18; P ✳ 🏊 🚼)
The newest and, arguably, the plushest of Cubamar's 80 or more campismo sites, Los Cocos has facilities to match a midrange hotel and a beachside setting that emulates the big shots in Varadero. Ninety self-contained, supermodern cabins are clustered around a pool set in the crook of the province's low steplike cliffs.

Facilities include a small library, a medical post, an à la carte restaurant, a games room, rooms for travelers with disabilities and walking trails. Note that amenities are showing their age and there's often blaring poolside music to contend with.

Cameleón Villas Jibacoa   RESORT $$
(📞 29-52-05; s/d all-incl CUC$70/100; P ❄ @ ☎) This friendly, well-landscaped resort with great snorkeling and large (if dated) rooms offers good bang for your buck. It's marketed as a three-star and is popular with package tourists from Canada.

★ SuperClub Breezes   RESORT $$$
(📞 29-51-22; s/d all-incl CUC$76/135; P ❄ @ ☎) Who knew? One of Cuba's best all-inclusive resorts isn't in Varadero (or any other resort strip for that matter), but in the more tranquil confines of Jibacoa. The secret? The 250-room Breezes doesn't try too hard. The trickling fountains, 24-hour pool and narrow but idyllic beach are elegantly unpretentious.

Then there's the joy of the surf and turf surroundings – boat trips from the shore and trekking into the uplifted terraces just inland. Children under 16 are not accepted. Coming from Matanzas, the turn-off is 13km west of the Puente de Bacunayagua.

❶ Getting There & Away

The best – some would say the only – way to get to Playa Jibacoa is on the Hershey Electric Railway from Casablanca train station in Havana to Jibacoa Pueblo (see boxed text, p163). There's no bus to the beach from the station and traffic is sporadic, so bank on hiking the last 5km – a not unpleasant walk if you don't have too much gear. The electric train also stops at Arcos de Canasí, but that's still 6km from the beach and it's not a good walking road.

One other option is to take crowded thrice-daily bus 669 from outside La Coubre Station (p130), just south of Havana's Estación Central, to Santa Cruz del Norte, still 9km from Jibacoa. Another alternative is to go to the Havana bus station and take any bus headed for Matanzas along the Vía Blanca. Talk to the driver to arrange a drop-off at Playa Jibacoa, just across a long bridge from Villa Loma de Jibacoa.

Jaruco
POP 18,107

Jaruco, set back from the coast between Havana and Matanzas, is a good day trip for travelers with a car, moped or bike who want to give the beaches a body-swerve and instead sample quintessential rural Cuba.

Jaruco village is a wash of pastel-hued houses bunched along steeply pitching streets that wouldn't look amiss in the Peruvian Andes. The **Parque Escaleras de Jaruco**, 6km west via hushed unmarked lanes, is a protected area featuring forests, caves and strangely shaped limestone cliffs similar to the *mogotes* of the Viñales valley. *Habaneros* come here for bucolic weekend breaks, but otherwise the park is a forgotten oasis with outstanding *miradors* (viewpoints) over Mayabeque province. A handful of restaurants open up from Thursday to Sunday and blare out cheesy music, which can disrupt the serenity. The best of these is the pleasant *ranchón*-style **El Criollo** (⊙11:30am-5pm), where you'll pay in pesos for various pork- and fish-focused offerings.

ARTEMISA & MAYABEQUE PROVINCES JARUCO

OFF THE BEATEN TRACK

LAS CHARANGAS DE BEJUCAL

The journeyman town of Bejucal, like many settlements in Mayabeque province, is not exactly overflowing with interesting things to do – unless you time your visit to coincide with **Las Charangas** on December 24, which compete with Las Parrandas of Remedios and Santiago's Carnival as Cuba's most cacophonous and colorful festival. As in Remedios, the town splits into two competing groups, the *Ceiba de Plata* (Silver Ceiba) and the *Espina de Oro* (Golden Thorn) who hit the streets laughing, dancing and singing among outrageously large, dazzling floats and the famous Bejucal *tambores* (drums). The climax comes with the building of 20m-high towers made of brightly lit artistic displays in the main plaza to the accompaniment of the music of the traditional conga. The displays mix tradition with topical news stories referencing everything from Santería deities to global warming. Las Charangas dates back to the early 1800s when the parading groups were split between creoles and black slaves (the racial discriminations no longer exist), making it one of Cuba's oldest festivals.

There's no real accommodation in town for travelers, but at 25 miles from Havana, Bejucal is within easy reach of the city.

It's 32km to Jaruco from Guanabo in a southeasterly direction via Campo Florido, and you can make it a loop by returning through Santa Cruz del Norte, 18km northeast of Jaruco via Central Camilo Cienfuegos. A taxi from Havana costs CUC$30 one way.

Surgidero de Batabanó

POP 22,313

Spanish colonizers founded the original settlement of Havana on the site of Surgidero de Batabanó on August 25, 1515, but quickly abandoned it in favor of the north coast. Looking around the decrepit town today, with its ugly apartment blocks and grubby beachless seafront, it's not difficult to see why. The only reason you're likely to end up in this fly-blown port is during the purgatorial bus-boat trip to the Isla de la Juventud. Should there be unforeseen delays, either staying within the port confines or cabbing it back to Havana, however depressing, are preferable to spending any time in the town itself.

Fidel Castro and the other Moncada prisoners disembarked here on May 15, 1955, after Fulgencio Batista granted them amnesty.

❶ Getting There & Away

The ferry from Surgidero de Batabanó to Isla de la Juventud is supposed to leave daily at noon with an additional sailing at 3:30pm on Wednesday, Friday and Sunday (CUC$55, two hours). It is advisable to buy your bus-boat combo ticket in Havana from the office at the main Astro bus station rather than turning up and doing it here. More often than not convertible tickets are sold out to bus passengers.

There's a **Servi-Cupet gas station** (Calle 64 No 7110, btwn Calles 71 & 73) in Batabanó town. The next Servi-Cupet station east is in Güines.

Isla de la Juventud (Special Municipality)

POP 86,420

Best Beaches

➡ Playa Sirena (p177)

➡ Cayo Rico (p178)

➡ Playa Larga (p177)

➡ Punta Francés (p171)

Best Places to Stay

➡ Sol Cayo Largo (p179)

➡ Playa Blanca Beach Resort (p179)

➡ Villa Choli – Ramberto Pena Silva (p171)

➡ Hotel Colony (p176)

Why Go?

An enigma even by Cuban standards, the metaphoric comma of land off mainland Cuba's southwest coast is the sixth largest island in the Caribbean. Amply stocked with pine trees, fruit plantations, prisons masquerading as museums and the odd disheveled beach or three, La Isla's attractions are defiantly esoteric. The Cayman Islands, this most certainly isn't. If you thought 'mainland' Cuba was stuck in a time warp, try blowing the dust off Nueva Gerona where the main street doubles up as a baseball diamond, and the food 'scene' is still stuck in the Special Period. Of the small trickle of people that make it this far, the majority come to dive in some of the most pristine reefs in the Caribbean. Others revel in the becalmed island ambience and hospitable locals.

Further east, Cayo Largo de Sur is La Isla's polar opposite, a manufactured tourist enclave renowned for its wide (nudist) beaches beloved by package tourists.

When to Go

➡ The beach life, diving and snorkeling are highlights of La Isla, Cayo Largo or any of the other mini-paradises in the Archipiélago de los Canarreos. The hottest times are the best: July to August along with the cooler-but-balmy high season in December to April.

➡ Anglers may wish to flock to Cayo Largo's September fishing tournaments.

Isla de la Juventud Highlights

1 Meditate on revolutionary days gone by at the hacienda home of José Martí, **Museo Finca el Abra** (p170).

2 Get the lowdown on local life in petite, sleepy **Nueva Gerona** (p169).

3 Explore the ominous prison where Fidel Castro was once incarcerated at **Presidio Modelo** (p174).

4 Investigate an important crocodile conservation project at the Isla's **Criadero Cocodrilo** (p176).

5 Dive amid wrecks, walls, coral gardens and caves at **Punta Francés** (p171), *the* best place to dive in Cuba.

6 Watch turtles nesting on the moonlit beaches of **Cayo Largo del Sur** (p177).

7 Trek along the wide, white (sometimes nudist) beaches to Cayo Largo del Sur's **Playa Sirena** (p177).

History

La Isla's first settlers were the Siboneys, a pre-ceramic civilization who came to the island around 1000 BC via the Lesser Antilles and settled down as hunters and fishermen. They named their new-found homeland Siguanea and created a fascinating set of cave paintings, which still survive in Cueva de Punta del Este.

By the time Columbus arrived on these shores in June 1494, the Siboney had long departed (either dying out or returning to the mainland). The intrepid navigator promptly renamed the island Juan el Evangelista, claiming it for the Spanish crown. But the Spanish did little to develop their new possession, which was knotted with mangroves and surrounded by a circle of shallow reefs.

Instead La Isla became a hideout for pirates, including Francis Drake and Henry Morgan. They called it Parrot Island, and their exploits are said to have inspired Robert Louis Stevenson's novel *Treasure Island*.

In December 1830 the Colonia Reina Amalia (now Nueva Gerona) was founded, and throughout the 19th century the island served as a place of imposed exile for independence advocates and rebels, including José Martí. Twentieth-century dictators Gerardo Machado and Fulgencio Batista followed this Spanish example by sending political prisoners – Fidel Castro included – to the island, which had by then been renamed a fourth time and was known as Isla de Pinos (Isle of Pines).

Aside from its Spanish heritage, La Isla has had its dose of English and American influences. In the 19th century families from the British colony of the Cayman Islands settled on the south coast. The infamous 1901 Platt Amendment included a proviso placing Isla de Pinos outside the boundaries of the 'mainland' part of the archipelago, and subsequently some 300 US colonists established themselves here.

The Americans stayed, worked the citrus plantations and built the efficient infrastructure that survives today. During WWII, the Presidio Modelo was used by the US to inter Axis prisoners, and by the 1950s La Isla had become a favored vacation spot for rich Americans, who flew in daily from Miami. Fidel Castro abruptly ended the decadent party in 1959.

Before the Revolution, Isla de Pinos was sparsely populated. In the 1960s and 1970s, however, thousands of young people from across the developing world volunteered to study here at specially built 'secondary schools'. In 1978 their role in developing the island was officially recognized when the name was changed for the fifth time to Isla de la Juventud (Isle of Youth).

ISLA DE LA JUVENTUD

🔊 46

Large, detached and set to a slow metronome, La Isla is both historically and culturally different to the rest of the Cuban archipelago. Mass sugar and tobacco production never existed here and, until the Castro revolution, the island yielded to a greater American influence. Eclectic expat communities, which call on Cayman Island, American and Japanese ancestry, have even thrown up their own musical style, a subgenre of Cuban *son* known as *sucu sucu*. Today the island, bereft of the foreign students that once populated its famous schools, is a sleepy, laid-back place. The opportunities for getting (way) off the beaten track will appeal to escape artists, adventurers and committed contrarians.

Nueva Gerona

POP 47,038

Flanked by the Sierra de las Casas to the west and the Sierra de Caballos to the east, Nueva Gerona is a small, unhurried town that hugs the left bank of the Río las Casas, the island's only large river. It's a little-visited, cheap and incredibly friendly place with a surprisingly lively entertainment scene, and you could easily find that you're the only foreign face around.

◎ Sights

This is a good area to discover on bicycle, with beaches, Museo Finca el Abra and the Presidio Modelo all only a few kilometers from Nueva Gerona. The folk at Villa Choli organize bike rental.

Museo Casa Natal Jesus Montané MUSEUM
(Calle 24, cnr Calle 45; ⊗9:30am-5pm Tue-Sat, 8:30am-noon Sun) **FREE** A recently refurbished museum in a freshly painted green house that documents the life of revolutionary, Jesús Montané who was born here. Montané took part in the Moncada Barracks

attack in 1953, fought alongside Fidel in the Sierra Maestra, and served in the post-1959 government. It's a small but fascinating place and well worth 30 minutes of your time.

Museo de Historia Natural   MUSEUM
(Calle 41, cnr Calle 52; admission CUC$1; ⊘ 8am-5pm Tue-Sat, to noon Sun) Realistically, this is a dusty heap of stuffed animals well past their sell-by date and crying out for some government investment. It's worth visiting only if you are passing on your way to Finca El Abra.

There used to be a planetarium here, but questions about reopening were invariably met with sighs and shakes of the head from staff. It's just before the distinctive tower of the Archivo Histórico on the Hotel Colony road.

El Pinero   MONUMENT
(Calle 28, btwn Calle 33 & river) Two blocks east of Parque Guerrillero Heroico, you'll see a tatty black-and-white ferry set up as a memorial next to the river. This is El Pinero, the original boat used to transport passengers between La Isla and the main island. On May 15, 1955, Fidel and Raúl Castro, along with the other prisoners released from Moncada, returned to the main island on this vessel.

These days it is a meeting point for young *reggaetón* (Cuban hip-hop) fanatics (read: very loud music).

Nuestra Señora de los Dolores   CHURCH
(Calle 28, cnr Calle 39) On the northwest side of Parque Central, this dinky, Mexican colonial-style church was built in 1926, after the original was destroyed by a hurricane. In 1957 the parish priest, Guillermo Sardiñas, left Nueva Gerona to join Fidel Castro in the Sierra Maestra, the only Cuban priest to do so.

★ Museo Finca el Abra   MUSEUM
(Carretera Siguanea Km 2; admission CUC$1; ⊘ 9am-5pm Tue-Sun) The teenage José Martí arrived at Finca el Abra on October 17, 1870, to spend nine weeks of exile on this farm, prior to his deportation to Spain. Legend has it that the revolutionary's mother forged the shackles he wore here into a ring, which Martí wore to his death. The old hacienda is directly below the Sierra de las Casas, and it's worth coming as much for the surroundings as for the museum.

Cuban oaks and eucalyptus trees line the access road, and a huge ceiba tree stands next to the museum. The adjacent house is still occupied by descendants of Giuseppe Girondella, who hosted Martí here.

This museum is 3km southwest of Nueva Gerona, off the road to La Demajagua (the continuation of Calle 41). A sign indicates the access road. Let an enthusiastic on-site guide show you around as they will be able to flesh out the scant but important exhibits with interesting anecdotes.

A dirt road just before the museum leads north to the island's former marble quarry, clearly visible in the distance. The quarry is moderately interesting (if you like big holes in the ground), but the real attraction is the climb up the hill, from where there are lovely **views**. After descending, continue north between a garbage dump and several rows of pig pens to Calle 54 on the right. This street will bring you back into town via the Museo de Historia Natural, six blocks to the east.

Museo Municipal   MUSEUM
(Calle 30, btwn Calles 37 & 39; admission CUC$1; ⊘ 8am-1pm & 2-5pm Mon-Fri, to 4pm Sat, to noon Sun) In the former Casa de Gobierno (1853), the Museo Municipal houses a small historical collection that begins with a huge wall-mounted map of La Isla and continues through themed salas relating to aboriginals, pirates, US occupiers and some local art.

🏃 Activities

Sierra de las Casas   HIKING
Behold the view! It's possible to climb the northernmost face of the craggy Sierra de las Casas from the west end of Calle 22. A few hundred meters along a dirt track, you will see a sinuous trail on the left heading toward the hills. At the very foot of the hill is a deep cave with a concrete stairway leading down to the local **swimming hole**.

A **trail** beyond here leads up steeply to the mountaintop (warning: the last bit is closer to rock scrambling than hiking). The view from the summit is amazing, taking in half the island with the noises from the town clearly audible below.

🎉 Festivals & Events

Fiesta de la Toronja   CARNAVAL
The Grapefruit Festival is held on La Isla every March. Since a plague killed off most of the grapefruit crop a few years back it's become an excuse for a general carnival.

🛏 Sleeping

Casas particulares are your only town centre options and will provide meals; the owners will invariably meet arriving ferries. Nueva Gerona's two run-down state-run hotels are south of town.

★ Villa Choli –
Ramberto Pena Silva   CASA PARTICULAR $
(☑ 32-31-47; Calle C No 4001A, btwn Calles 6 & 8; r CUC$20-25; P ❋ @) Two large, modern 1st-floor rooms with TV, internet access, secure parking space, delicious food and – possibly the highlight – a great terrace with a hammock. You'll receive attentive treatment at this reader-recommended place. There are bicycles for rent, and port pickup/tickets can be arranged.

Villa Mas –
Jorge Luis Mas Peña   CASA PARTICULAR $
(☑ 32-35-44; Calle 41 No 4108 apt 7, btwn Calles 8 & 10; r CUC$20-25; ❋) Forget the rather ugly apartment-block setting; there are two above-average rooms here with recently refurbished full marble bathrooms. Jorge and his partner are formidable cooks and will serve you dinner on their refreshing rooftop terrace. It's in the northern part of town behind the hospital.

Villa Peña   CASA PARTICULAR $
(☑ 32-23-45; Calle 10, cnr 37; CUC$15-20; ❋) A comfortable, secure option near the hospital with two clean rooms and meals, if the other two places are full.

Motel el Rancho el Tesoro   HOTEL $
(☑ 32-30-35; Autopista Nueva Gerona-La Fe Km 2; s/d CUC$18/24; P ❋) This lackluster motel with a castellated frontage that lies in a wooded area near the Río las Casas, 3km south of town, has seen better days – and they were a long time ago. There are 34 sizeable rooms, with cable TV and a paltry state restaurant.

Villa Isla de Juventud   HOTEL $
(☑ 32-32-90; Autopista Nueva Gerona-La Fe Km 1; s/d incl breakfast CUC$6/11; P ❋ ❋) About 5km from the airport and 2.5km from Nueva Gerona, this hotel has 20 rooms with ridiculously low prices, though it's probably all they're worth. Despite its pleasant location, the complex suffers from tatty fittings, ubiquitous 'out of order' signs and uninterested staff. But if budget's your main priority...

🍴 Eating

As far as food goes, La Isla is still living in the 1990s. Weight-watchers could open a club here. After one night of fruitless searching most travelers sensibly elect to dine in their casa particular. Small sandwich and churros vendors set up on Martí (Calle 39) and peso ice-cream sellers appear spontaneously in various windows.

INTO THE BLUE

Protected from sea currents off the Gulf of Mexico and blessed with remarkable coral and marine life, Isla de la Juventud offers some of the Caribbean's best diving: 56 buoyed dive sites here include everything from caves and passages to vertical walls and coral hillocks. Wreck diving is also possible further east where the remains of 70 ships have been found in an area known as **Bajo de Zambo**.

International Diving Center (☑ 46-39-81-81, 46-39-82-82), run from the Marina Siguanea just south of Hotel Colony on the island's west coast, is the center of diving operations. The establishment has a modern on-site recompression chamber along with the services of a dive doctor. It's from here that you can be transported out to the National Maritime Park at **Punta Francés**.

Boat transfers to Punta Francés take an hour and deliver you to a gorgeous stretch of white-sand beach (there's a restaurant, but it was closed at the time of research), from which most main dive sites are easily accessible. Cream of the crop are **Cueva Azul** (advanced) and **Pared de Coral Negro** (intermediate), where you'll see lots of fish, including tarpon, barracuda, groupers, snooks and angelfish, along with the odd sea turtle.

Diving costs start at CUC$36. Nondivers can get to the wonderful Punta Francés beach for CUC$12. Enquire at **Hotel Colony** (☑ 39-81-81) about diving and other nautical activities on offer first.

Nueva Gerona

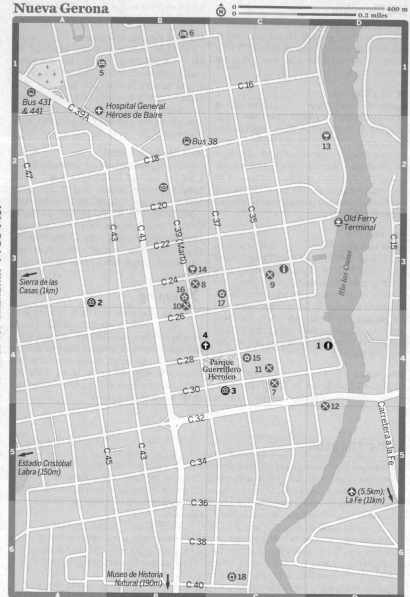

N

0   400 m
0   0.2 miles

Bus 431 & 441

C 39A

Hospital General Héroes de Baire

C 16

Bus 38

13

C 47

C 18

C 20

Old Ferry Terminal

C 43

C 41

C 39 (Martí)

C 22

C 37

C 35

C 15

Río las Casas

Sierra de las Casas (1km)

C 24

14

8

16

9

2

C 26

10

17

4

C 28

15

11

Parque Guerrillero Heroico

1

C 30

3

7

C 32

12

C 45

C 43

C 34

Carretera a la Fe

Estadio Cristóbal Labra (150m)

C 36

(5.5km); La Fe (11km)

C 38

Museo de Historia Natural (190m)

C 40

18

Mesón La Mitta

CUBAN $

(Calle 39 No 2416, btwn 24 & 26; mains CUC$2-4; ⊗ noon-10pm) A new paladar (privately owned restaurant) where the tablecloths already look 50 years old, but at least these guys are making a stab of it in the private sector. The best thing is the 1st-floor terrace. The second best is the *tostones* (fried plantain).

Nueva Gerona

Restaurante Río   SEAFOOD $
(Calle 32, btwn Calle 33 & river; ⊗noon-10pm)
This is a dog-eared establishment located
by the river that gets varied reviews from
the locals. On a good day it serves fresh
river and sea fish (one of the few places in
Cuba where you can eat both), and you'll
pay in *moneda nacional*. It has an outside
terrace with a stereo that blasts out the
latest Cuban pop and an air-conditioned
interior.

El Cochinito   CARIBBEAN $
(Calle 39, cnr 24; ⊗noon-10pm Thu-Tue) The ominously named 'little pig' offers *desperados*
various pork concoctions in a fly-blown
interior.

Pizzería la Góndola   ITALIAN $
(cnr Calles 30 & 35; ⊗noon-10pm) It's a long
way from Italy, in both geography and the
quality of the pizzas, but if you're really sick
of pork...

Self-Catering

Mercado Agropecuario   MARKET $
(cnr Calles 24 & 35) Try this large market for
fresh vegetables and meat.

Cubalse Supermarket   SUPERMARKET $
(Calle 35, btwn Calles 30 & 32; ⊗9:30am-6pm Mon-
Sat) Sells life-saving Pringles and biscuits.

🍷 Drinking & Nightlife

Call it pent-up boredom, but Nueva Gerona
likes a party.

La Rumba   NIGHTCLUB
(Calle 24, btwn Calles 37 & 39; ⊗10pm-2am) Buy
your drinks in the cagelike bar next door
then head to the courtyard and hectic disco
round the corner. If you don't dance hard,
you'll stand out here.

El Pinero   NIGHTCLUB
(Calle 28, btwn Calle 33 & river) Extremely loud
music along with most of the town's teenagers and 20-somethings converge by the
historic boat for alfresco dancing. Drink and
snack stalls also set up shop.

Disco la Movida   NIGHTCLUB
(Calle 18; ⊗from 11pm) For a little atmospheric
booty shaking, join the throngs of locals
dancing in an open-air locale hidden among
the trees near the river.

☆ Entertainment

Live music is sometimes staged outside the
Cine Caribe.

Uneac   CULTURAL CENTER
(Calle 37 btwn 24 & 26) Your best bet for a non-
reggaetón night out is this nicely renovated
colonial house with patio, bar and suave live
music.

Sucu Sucu   LIVE MUSIC
(Calle 39, btwn Calles 24 & 26) A joint with live
music and theater: there's a board out front
with upcoming events. When nothing else
is on, it serves as an intimate drinking spot.

Cine Caribe   CINEMA
(cnr Calles 37 & 28) Surprisingly colorful and
happening cinema right on Parque Central.

Estadio Cristóbal Labra   SPORT
(cnr Calles 32 & 53) Nueva Gerona's baseball stadium, Estadio Cristóbal Labra is
seven blocks west of Calle 39. Ask at your
local casa particular for details of upcoming
games (staged from October to April).

ISLA DE LA JUVENTUD (SPECIAL MUNICIPALITY) NUEVA GERONA

🛍 Shopping

Calle 39, also known as Calle Martí, is a pleasant pedestrian mall interspersed with small parks.

Centro Experimental de
Artes Aplicadas   ARTS & CRAFTS
(Calle 40, btwn 39 & 37; ⊘8am-4pm Mon-Fri, 8am-noon Sat) Centro Experimental de Artes Aplicadas, near the Museo de Historia Natural, makes artistic ceramics.

ℹ Information

Banco de Crédito y Comercio (Calle 39 No 1802; ⊘8am-3pm Mon-Fri) Has an ATM.
Cadeca (Calle 39 No 2022; ⊘8:30am-6pm Mon-Sat, to 1pm Sun) Has an ATM.
Ecotur (☑32-71-01; Calle 24 btwn 31 & 33; ⊘8am-4pm Mon-Fri) Organizes trips into the militarized zone and to Punta Francés.
Etecsa Telepunto (Calle 41 No 2802, btwn Calles 28 & 30; ⊘8:30am-7:30pm) Three internet terminals at usual prices.
Farmacia Nueva Gerona (☑32-60-84; cnr Calles 39 & 24; ⊘8am-11pm Mon-Sat)
Hospital General Héroes de Baire (☑32-30-12; Calle 39A) Has a recompression chamber.
Post Office (Calle 39 No 1810, btwn Calles 18 & 20; ⊘8am-6pm Mon-Sat)
Radio Caribe Broadcasts varied music programs on 1270AM.
Victoria Local paper published on Saturday.

ℹ Getting There & Away

AIR
The most hassle-free and (often) the cheapest way to get to La Isla is to fly. Unfortunately, most people have cottoned onto this, so flights are usually booked out at least a week in advance.

Rafael Cabrera Mustelier Airport (airport code GER) is 5km southeast of Nueva Gerona.
Cubana Havana (p129), **Nueva Gerona** (☑32-25-31; Calle 39 No 1415, btwn Calles 16 & 18, Nueva Gerona) Flies here from Havana twice daily from as little as CUC$35 one way. There are no international flights.

There are no regular flights from Isla de la Juventud to Cayo Largo del Sur.

ℹ Getting Around

TO/FROM THE AIRPORT
From the airport, look for the bus marked 'Servicio Aéreo,' which will take you into town for one peso. To get to the airport, catch this bus in front of Cine Caribe. A taxi to town will cost about CUC$5, or CUC$25 to CUC$30 to the Hotel Colony.

BUS
Ecotur can organize trips/transfers from Nueva Gerona to the diving areas and into the militarized zone. A taxi (easily arranged through your casa or hotel) from Nueva Gerona to Hotel Colony should cost approximately CUC$25 to CUC$30. There are less reliable local buses: buses 431 to La Fe (26km) and 441 to the Hotel Colony (45km) leave from a stop opposite the cemetery on Calle 39A, just northwest of the hospital.

Bus 38 leaves from the corner of Calles 18 and 37, departing for Chacón (Presidio Modelo), Playa Paraíso and Playa Bibijagua, about four times a day.

CAR
Cubacar (☑32-44-32; cnr Calles 32 & 39; ⊘7am-7pm) rents cars from CUC$65 with insurance and can arrange transport into the military zone.

The Servi-Cupet gas station is at the corner of Calles 30 and 39 in the center of town.

HORSE CART
Horse *coches* (carts) often park next to the Cubalse supermarket on Calle 35. You can easily rent one at CUC$10 per day for excursions to the Presidio Modelo, Museo Finca el Abra, Playa Bibijagua and other nearby destinations. If you've got the time, you can be sure the driver will.

East of Nueva Gerona

⦿ Sights

★**Presidio Modelo**   NOTABLE BUILDING
(admission CUC$1) Welcome to the island's most impressive yet depressing sight. Located near Reparto Chacón, 5km east of Nueva Gerona, this striking prison was built between 1926 and 1931, during the repressive regime of Gerardo Machado. The four rather scary-looking six-story, yellow circular blocks were modeled after those of a notorious penitentiary in Joliet, Illinois, and could hold 5000 prisoners at a time.

During WWII, assorted enemy nationals who happened to find themselves in Cuba (including 350 Japanese, 50 Germans and 25 Italians) were interned in the two rectangular blocks at the north end of the complex.

The Presidio's most famous inmates, however, were Fidel Castro and the other Moncada rebels, who were imprisoned here from October 1953 to May 1955. They were held separately from the other prisoners, in

GETTING TO THE ISLA BY BOAT: A BEGINNER'S GUIDE

The over-bureaucratic, typically Cuban experience of getting to La Isla de la Juventud by boat isn't the piece of cake it ought to be. To do it you'll need eight hours (if you're lucky), decent supplies of food (breakfast and lunch at least) and saintly amounts of patience. A reasonable command of Spanish, though not a prerequisite, will minimize confusion.

It is highly advisable to reserve and pay for your ticket at least a day in advance at the **Naviera Cubana Caribeña (NCC) kiosk** (☎ 07-878-1841; ⏰ 7am-noon) in Havana's main Terminal de Ómnibus (not the Víazul terminal). The best time to do this is between 9am and noon. You'll need your passport and CUC$50. Plump for the earlier ferry as the later one (supposedly running Wednesday, Friday and Sunday) is less reliable.

On the day of departure you'll need to turn up at 7:30am to reserve your bus transfer ticket ($5 in *moneda nacional*). The bus leaves from bay 9 of the Terminal de Ómnibus at around 9:30 and trundles slowly to the disheveled port in Surgidero de Batabanó where you'll have to join the lengthy, disorderly queues to reconfirm your boat ticket to Nueva Gerona. You'll then be ushered through airport-style security into a waiting room for a likely period of one to two hours before the boat departs.

The crossing by catamaran takes about 2½ hours; there are no printed schedules. If you take the early bus/boat and all goes well you'll be on La Isla at 4pm (total journey time eight hours, total ticket cost CUC$50.25).

Refreshments on this trip are either basic (a can of coke) or not available as it's mostly Cubans traveling. Furthermore, the air-con on the *Iris* catamaran is arctic and the unrelenting 'action' films deafening. Unfortunately, there's no escape. Access above deck is barred.

Do not show up independently in Batabanó with the intention of buying a ferry ticket direct from the dock. Although technically possible, a number of travelers have come unstuck here, being told that the tickets have been sold out through the NCC kiosk in Havana. Furthermore, bedding down overnight in Batabanó holds little appeal for travelers.

The return leg is equally problematic. Procure your ticket the day before you wish to travel in Nueva Gerona's **NCC ferry terminal** (☎ 46-32-49-77, 46-32-44-15; cnr Calles 31 & 24), beside the Río las Casas. The **ticket office** (⏰ Mon-Fri) is across the road. The ferry leaves for Surgidero de Batabanó daily at 8am (CUC$50), but you'll need to get there at least two hours beforehand to tackle the infamous queues. A second boat is supposed to leave at noon (with a check-in time of 9:30am).

Don't take anything as a given until you have booked your ticket. Isla boat crossings, rather like Cuban trains, have a tendency to be late, break down or get cancelled altogether.

Traveling in either direction, you'll need to show your passport.

the hospital building at the south end of the complex.

In 1967 the prison was closed and the section where Castro stayed was converted into a museum. There is one room dedicated to the history of the prison and another focusing on the lives of the Moncada prisoners. Admission includes a tour, but cameras/videos are CUC$3/25 extra. Bring exact change. Admission to the circular blocks (the most moving part of the experience) is free.

Cementerio Colombia   CEMETERY

The cemetery here contains the graves of Americans who lived and died on the island

during the 1920s and 1930s. It's about 7km east of Nueva Gerona and 2km east of Presidio Modelo. Bus 38 passes by.

Beaches   BEACH

About 2km north of Chacón (about 6km northeast of Nueva Gerona), **Playa Paraíso** is a dirty brown beach with good currents for water sports. The wharf was originally used to unload prisoners heading to the Presidio Modelo. There is a small bar here.

A better beach, **Playa Bibijagua**, lies 4km to the east of Chacón. Here there are pine trees, a peso restaurant and plenty of

OFF THE BEATEN TRACK

CAYOS DE SAN FELIPE

Technically, they're in Pinar del Río province, but, as yet, the only way to get to the almost virgin Cayos de San Felipe is with an organized excursion arranged through Hotel Colony on La Isla de la Juventud. One of Cuba's 14 national parks, this small necklace of keys approximately 30km south of Pinar del Río and 30km northwest of La Isla are uninhabited save for the odd environmental researcher. The Cayos are (were?) home to a rare subspecies of the tree rat called the Little Earth Jutia, but the rodent hasn't been seen since 1978 when black rats were introduced to the archipelago. The flat mangrove-infested isles also support turtles and numerous bird species.

Fauna aside, the main reason to come here is to dive in 22 Columbus-era-quality **dive sites** that see little or no dive traffic. The trip starts in Pinar del Río before transferring by bus to the fishing village of Coloma where a boat takes you out to the Cayos for diving. After lunch on board, you will be spirited over the sea to Hotel Colony on La Isla without having to suffer the purgatory of the crowded Iris ferry.

This trip was new at the time of research. Inquire at Hotel Colony for rates and availability. Ecotur (p174) is another good information portal.

low-key Cuban ambience. Nondrivers can catch bus 38 from Nueva Gerona.

South of Nueva Gerona

◉ Sights & Activities

The main reason to come here is for the diving at Punta Francés, but there are a couple of other diversions for those who have time.

La Jungla de Jones   GARDENS
(admission CUC$3; ⊘24hr) Situated 6km west of La Fe in the direction of Hotel Colony, this is a botanical garden containing more than 80 tree varieties. Bisected by shaded trails and punctuated by a cornucopia of cacti and mangoes, this expansive garden was established by two American botanists, Helen and Harris Jones, in 1902.

The highlight is the aptly named Bamboo Cathedral, an enclosed space surrounded by huge clumps of craning bamboo that only a few strands of sunlight manage to penetrate.

Criadero Cocodrilo   CROCODILE FARM
(admission CUC$3; ⊘7am-5pm) ✔ This farm has played an important part in crocodile conservation in Cuba over the last few years and the results are interesting to see. Harboring more than 500 crocodiles of all shapes and sizes, the *criadero* (hatchery) acts as a breeding center, similar to the one in Guamá in Matanzas, although the setting here is infinitely wilder.

Taken care of until they are seven years old, the center releases groups of crocs back

into the wild when they reach a length of about 1m. To get to the criadero turn left 12km south of La Fe just past Julio Antonio Mella.

🛏 Sleeping & Eating

★**Hotel Colony**   HOTEL $$
(☎39-81-81; all-incl s/d CUC$36/56; P❄) The Colony, 46km southwest of Nueva Gerona, originated in 1958 as part of the Hilton chain, but was confiscated by the revolutionary government before it began operating. Today the main building is a bit run-down, but the newer bungalows are clean, bright and airy. You might save a few cents by taking a package that includes meals and scuba diving.

The water off the hotel's white-sand beach is shallow, with sea urchins littering the bottom. Take care if you decide to swim. A safer bet is the Colony's convivial pool. A long wharf (with a bar perfect for sunset mojitos) stretches out over the bay, but the snorkeling in the immediate vicinity of the hotel is mediocre. The diving, however, is to die for. A car-rental office is located at the hotel.

❶ Getting There & Away

Transport is tough on La Isla, and bus schedules make even the rest of Cuba seem efficient. Try bus 441 from Nueva Gerona. Otherwise, your best bet to get to the hotel is by taxi (approximately CUC$35 from the airport), moped or rental car.

The Southern Military Zone

The entire area south of Cayo Piedra is a military zone, and to enter you must first procure a one-day pass (CUC$15) from Ecotur in Nueva Gerona. The company will provide you with a Spanish-/English-/German-/French-/Italian-speaking guide, but it is up to you to find your own 4WD transport for within the zone itself. This can be organized with Cubacar in Nueva Gerona. Traveling in the military zone is not possible without a guide or an official pass, so don't arrive at the Cayo Piedra checkpoint without either. As the whole excursion can wind up being rather expensive, it helps to split the transport costs with other travelers. For more up-to-date advice on the region inquire at Hotel Colony or Ecotur in Nueva Gerona.

The southern Isla is replete with unusual wildlife. Look out for monkeys, deer, crocodiles (three types), lizards and turtles.

Cueva de Punta del Este

The Cueva de Punta del Este, a national monument 59km southeast of Nueva Gerona, has been called the 'Sistine Chapel' of Caribbean Indian art. Long before the Spanish conquest (experts estimate around AD 800), Indians painted some 235 pictographs on the walls and ceiling of the cave. The largest has 28 concentric circles of red and black, and the paintings have been interpreted as a solar calendar. Discovered in 1910, they're considered the most important of their kind in the Caribbean. There's a small **visitor center** and meteorological station. The long, shadeless white beach nearby is another draw (for you and the mosquitoes – bring repellent).

Cocodrilo

A potholed road runs south from Cayo Piedra to the gorgeous white-sand beach of **Playa Larga**, then west 50km to the friendly village of Cocodrilo. Barely touched by tourism, and with a population of just 750, Cocodrilo was formerly known as Jacksonville, and was colonized in the 19th century by families from the Cayman Islands. You still occasionally meet people here who can converse in English. Through the lush vegetation beside the potholed road one catches glimpses of cattle, birds, lizards and beehives. The rocky coastline, sporadically gouged by small, white sandy beaches lapped by crystal-blue water, is magnificent.

Sea Turtle Breeding Center TURTLE FARM (admission CUC$1; ⊗8am-6pm) One kilometer west of Cocodrilo, the breeding center does an excellent job in conserving one of Cuba's rarest and most endangered species. Rows of green-stained glass tanks teem with all sizes of turtles.

CAYO LARGO DEL SUR
☑45

If you came to Cuba to witness historic colonial cities, exotic dancers, asthmatic Plymouths and peeling images of Che Guevara, then 38-sq-km Cayo Largo del Sur, 114km east of Isla de la Juventud, will hugely disappoint. If, instead, you booked tickets while dreaming of glittering white beaches, teeming coral reefs, fabulous all-inclusive resorts and lots of fleshy Canadians and Italians wandering around naked, then this small mangrove-covered tropical paradise is undeniably the place for you.

No permanent Cuban settlement has ever existed on the Cayo. Instead, the island was developed in the early 1980s purely as a tourism enterprise. Cayo Largo del Sur (Cayo Largo for short) is largely frequented by Italian tourists – one resort caters exclusively for them. The other all-inclusives are less picky. The heavenly beaches (26km of them) surpass most visitors' expectations of Caribbean paradise and are renowned for their size, emptiness and – during summer – nesting turtles. There's also a profusion of iguanas and birdlife, including cranes, *zunzuncitos* (bee hummingbirds) and flamingos.

The island can be visited as an expensive day trip from Havana, but most people come here on prebooked packages for a week or two.

In 2001, Hurricane Michelle (category 4) caused a storm surge that inundated the whole of Cayo Largo del Sur. It took the island years to recover. In the interim many of the tourists defected to the newly developed Cayo Santa María on Cuba's north coast.

Sights

Playa Sirena BEACH
Cayo Largo's (and, perhaps, Cuba's) finest beach is the broad westward-facing Playa

Cayo Largo del Sur

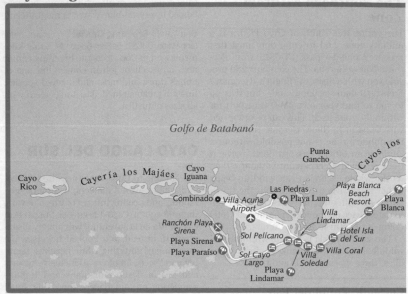

Sirena, where 2km of powdery white sand is wide enough to accommodate a couple of football pitches. Tourists on day trips from Havana and Varadero are often brought here, and the usual nautical activities (kayaks, catamarans) are available. Set back from the beach there's a *ranchón*-style bar and restaurant along with showers and toilets.

Just southeast is **Playa Paraíso**, a narrower and less shady but nonetheless wonderful strip of sand, serviced by a small bar.

Granja de las Tortugas   TURTLE FARM
(Combinado; admission CUC$1; ⊘ 7am-noon & 1-6pm) A small, often-closed complex on the northwest end of the island beyond the airstrip in the settlement of Combinado. From May to September guides here can organize nighttime **turtle watching** on the Cayo's beaches.

Playa los Cocos   BEACH
You can head up the island's east coast via this beach, where there is good snorkeling (the paved road gives out after Playa Blanca).

Playa Tortuga   BEACH
Beyond Playa los Cocos at the far end of the island is this beach, where sea turtles lay their eggs in the sand in the summer.

★**Cayo del Rosario & Cayo Rico**   ISLANDS
The other big day-trip destinations are these islands between Cayo Largo and Isla de la Juventud. Boat excursions to these beaches from the hotels cost around CUC$56 per person.

Cayo Iguana   ISLAND
Off the northwest tip of Cayo Largo, Cayo Iguana is home to, that's right, hundreds of iguanas. A yacht trip with **snorkeling** will cost you CUC$44.

🏃 Activities

The island's best (and only) hike is from Playa Sirena round to Sol Cayo Largo along the beach (7km) or vice versa. A broken path follows the dune ridge for much of the way if the tide is high. You can also procure a bicycle if you're staying in one of the resorts and head east beyond the Playa Blanca Beach Resort to some of the island's remoter beaches.

Other activities available on the island include snorkeling (from CUC$19), windsurfing, sailing and tennis. Added recently is a boat adventure in the mangroves (CUC$37) and swimming with a couple of dolphins (CUC$90) near Playa Sirena. You can also organize day trips to Havana and Trinidad

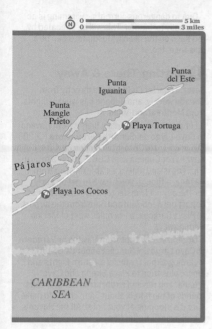

(approximately CUC$150 to CUC$160). Ask at the hotels.

Marina Internacional Cayo Largo DIVING, FISHING
(☑ 24-81-33; Combinado) Just beyond the turtle farm in Combinado, this is the departure point for deep-sea fishing trips (CUC$325 for four hours and eight people) and diving (CUC$39 for one immersion including hotel transfer). Prices are more expensive here because you can't shop around. The marina also organizes two international fishing tournaments held here in September.

🛏 Sleeping

All of Cayo Largo del Sur's hotels face the 4km beach on the south side of the island. Though largely shadeless, the beach here is gorgeous and rarely crowded (as no one lives here). If you're on a day trip, a day pass to the Sol resorts is CUC$35 including lunch.

Sandwiched between Sol Pelicano and Hotel Isla del Sur there is also the 55-room **Villa Coral** (Gran Caribe; ☑ 34-81-11; s/d CUC$100/140), with 10 two-story, faux-colonial buildings and a swimming pool, and finally the drabber 24-room **Villa Soledad** (Gran Caribe; ☑ 34-81-11; s/d CUC$100/140), looking more like a displaced retirement village than a dream Caribbean

getaway. The other hotel here, Villa Lindamar, is actually the best, but it caters exclusively for Italian tourists who book through agencies back home.

★**Sol Cayo Largo** RESORT $$$
(☑ 24-82-60; all-incl s/d CUC$160/270; P ❋ @ ☒)
Sol Meliá's best property is the four-star Sol Cayo Largo, with its Greek-temple-like lobby and trickling Italianate fountains. The beach out here is fantastic (and nudist) and the brightly painted (but not luxurious) rooms all have terraces with sea views. To date, it's Cayo Largo's most exclusive resort and great if you want to escape the families and poolside bingo further east.

Check out the on-site spa and gym – a trip to Shangri-La.

Playa Blanca Beach Resort RESORT $$$
(☑ 24-80-80; all-incl s/d CUC$102/170; P ❋ @ ☒ 👪) Cayo Largo's newest resort is set apart from the rest on an expansive stretch of Playa Blanca. Rather drab architecture is augmented by three different dining options and an impressive array of sporting activities. There's an individual touch, too.

Artworks by leading Cuban artist Carlos Guzmán decorate the public areas, and the suites in the upper echelons with their mezzanine sleeping areas could hold their own in Greenwich Village. Well, nearly. Some shade wouldn't go amiss, though.

Sol Pelícano RESORT $$$
(☑ 24-82-33; all-incl s/d CUC$112/180; P ❋ @ ☒ 👪) This Spanish-style resort, flush on the beach 5km southeast of the airport, has 203 rooms in a series of three-story buildings and two-story duplex *cabañas* (cabins) built in 1993. This is the island's largest resort but it's open only in high season. Facilities include a nightclub and plenty of family-friendly concessions.

Hotel Isla del Sur & Eden Village Complex RESORT $$$
(☑ 34-81-11; all-incl s/d CUC$80/120; P ❋ ☒) The Isla del Sur, the first hotel on Cayo Largo, is now the hub of the Eden Village complex, known as Eden Viaggi to its predominantly Italian guests, or El Pueblito due to the fact it does indeed resemble a small town (one with nightmarish architecture). Most resort facilities are concentrated around 59-room Isla del Sur, a long two-story building close to the slightly tacky nightly poolside entertainment.

✕ Eating

Of the all-inclusives, the Sol Cayo Largo serves the best food.

Restaurante el Torreón   CARIBBEAN $$
(☺ noon-midnight) In Cayo Largo's Combinado settlement, and encased in a stone fortlike building by the marina, El Torreón serves Cuban food with a glint of imagination, along with several Spanish surprises (and wine).

★ **Ranchón Playa Sirena**   SEAFOOD $$$
(☺ 9am-5pm) A rather fetching beach bar amid the Playa Sirena palm trees, with Latino Tom Cruises tossing around the cocktail glasses. Good food is also served here and a buffet (CUC$20) happens if enough tourists are around. It offers no-nonsense, salt-of-the-earth *comida criolla* (Creole food) and good grilled *pargo* (red snapper) for CUC$12.

🍸 Drinking & Nightlife

Taberna el Pirata   NIGHTCLUB
(☺ 24hr) About the only non-all-inclusive option, Taberna el Pirata is primarily a haunt for boat-hands, resort workers and the odd escaped tourist alongside Marina Internacional Cayo Largo.

ℹ Information

There's a **Cubatur** (☎ 24-82-58) in the Sol Pelícano and further information offices in the Sol Cayo Largo and Playa Blanca Resorts. You can change money at the hotels; otherwise Combinado houses the island's main bank, **Bandec** (☺ 8:30am-noon & 2-3:30pm Mon-Fri, 9am-noon Sat & Sun). Adjacent is a **Casa del Tabaco** (☎ 24-82-11; ☺ 8am-8pm) cigar shop and a **Clínica Internacional** (☎ 24-82-38; ☺ 24hr) medical clinic. Euros are accepted at tourist installations here.

Due to dangerous currents, swimming is occasionally forbidden. This will be indicated by red flags on the beach. Mosquitoes can be a nuisance, too.

ℹ Getting There & Away

Several charter flights arrive directly from Canada weekly, and Cubana has weekly flights from Montreal and Milan.

For pop-by visitors, daily flights from Havana to Cayo Largo del Sur with **Aerogaviota** (☎ 203-8686; Av 47 No 2814, btwn Calles 28 & 34, Kohly, Havana) or Cubana cost CUC$129 for a return trip. The island makes a viable day trip from Havana, although you'll have to get up early for the airport transfer (all Cayo Largo flights depart between 7am and 8am from the airport at Playa Baracoa, a few miles west of Marina Hemingway).

Organized day trips from Havana or Varadero to Cayo Largo del Sur cost about CUC$150, including airport transfers, return flights and lunch, plus trips to Playa Sirena and Cayo Iguana. The Havana airport transfer starts its rounds of the hotels about 5am; check to make sure it's stopping at your hotel. All the Havana travel agencies offer this.

ℹ Getting Around

Getting around Cayo Largo shouldn't present too many challenges. A taxi or transfer bus can transport you the 5km from the airport to the hotel strip. From here a mini bus-train (the *trencito*) carts tourists out to Playa Paraíso (6km) and Playa Sirena (7km). The train returns in the afternoon, or you can hike back along the beach. The tiny settlement of Combinado is 1km north of the airport and 6km from the nearest resort. For taxis hang around outside the hotels and airport.

Pinar del Río Province

48 / POP 594,279

Best Tobacco Tours

➡ Alejandro Robaina Tobacco Plantation (p189)

➡ Fábrica de Tabacos Francisco Donatien (p185)

Best Nature Excursions

➡ Cabo de San Antonio Excursion (p192)

➡ Cocosolo Palmarito (p199)

➡ Los Aquáticos (p198

Why Go?

If you love green you'll love Pinar del Río province whose all-pervading emerald sheen protects more land than any other province of Cuba. Joint jewels in the crown are the Península de Guanahacabibes, a Unesco Biosphere Reserve, and the Valle de Viñales, a Unesco World Heritage Site. This is also the best place in the world to grow tobacco, a blessing that fosters one of Cuba's most quintessential landscapes: fertile, rust-red, oxen-furrowed fields guarded by thatched tobacco-drying houses and sombrero-wearing *guajiros*.

The tough but gentle *guajiros* are one of Cuba's classic regional stereotypes, amiable rural farmers almost too generous for their own good. Appropriately, their spiritual home is Viñales, a serene, hassle-free village ringed by craggy hills and Van Gogh-like rustic beauty.

Beyond the countryside, Pinar's highlights are the idyllic sandy beaches of Cayo Jutías and Cayo Levisa, along with María la Gorda in the remote west where over 50 dazzling dive sites await offshore.

When to Go

➡ Come from May through August to see prized wildlife, such as the Guanahacabibes turtles.

➡ October through March is best for bird-watching.

➡ December through March for the best beach weather.

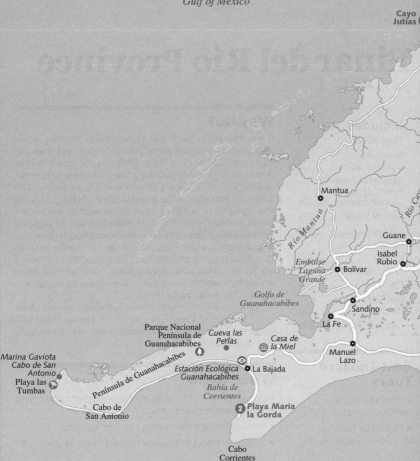

Gulf of Mexico

Cayo
Jutías

Mantua

Río Cuya...

Guane

Río Mantua

Isabel
Rubio

Embalse
Laguna
Grande

Bolívar

Golfo de
Guanahacabibes

Sandino

La Fe

Parque Nacional
Península de
Guanahacabibes

Cueva las
Perlas

Casa de
la Miel

Manuel
Lazo

Marina Gaviota
Cabo de San
Antonio

Estación Ecológica
Guanahacabibes

La Bajada

Playa las
Tumbas

Península de Guanahacabibes

Bahía de
Corrientes

Cabo de
San Antonio

Playa María
la Gorda

Cabo
Corrientes

Pinar del Río Province Highlights

① Get in touch with the region's cosmopolitan side with a walk around **Pinar del Río** (p184).

② Experience scuba diving at translucent **Playa María la Gorda** (p191).

③ Get out of the tour bus and see, smell and taste the agricultural beauty of **Valle de Viñales** (p193).

④ Mount a horse and take a ride with the *guajiros* into the Valle de Palmarito in **Parque Nacional Viñales** (p198).

⑤ Get gobsmacked by the grottos and caves of **Gran**

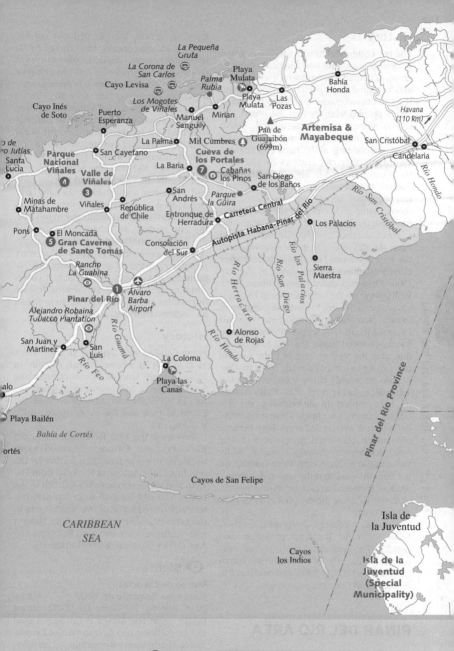

Caverna de Santo Tomás (p201), one of Latin America's largest subterranean systems.

6 Recharge your batteries on dreamy **Cayo Jutías** (p201).

7 See where Che Guevara played chess during the Cuban Missile Crisis in **Cueva de los Portales** (p204).

History

The pre-Columbian history of western Cuba is synonymous with the Guanahatabeys, a group of nomadic Indians who lived in caves and procured their livelihood largely from the sea. Less advanced than the other indigenous peoples who lived on the island, the Guanahatabeys were a peaceful and passive race whose culture had developed more or less independently of the Taíno and Siboney cultures further east. Extinct by the time the Spanish arrived in 1492, little firsthand documentation remains on how the archaic Guanahatabey society was structured, although some archaeological sites have been found on the Península de Guanahacabibes.

Post-Columbus the Spanish left rugged Pinar del Río largely to its own devices, and the area developed lackadaisically only after Canary Islanders began arriving in the late 1500s. Originally called Nueva Filipina (New Philippines) for the large number of Filipinos who came to the area to work the burgeoning tobacco plantations, the region was renamed Pinar del Río in 1778, supposedly for the pine forests crowded along the Río Guamá. By this time the western end of Cuba was renowned for its tobacco, already home to what is now the world's oldest tobacco company, Tabacalera, dating from 1636. Cattle ranching also propped up the economy. The fastidious farmers who made a living from the delicate and well-tended crops here became colloquially christened *guajiros*, a native word that means – literally – 'one of us.' By the mid-1800s, Europeans were hooked on the fragrant weed and the region flourished. Sea routes opened up and the railway was extended to facilitate the shipping of the perishable product.

These days tobacco, along with tourism, keeps Pinar del Río both profitable and popular. The region has more or less fully recovered from the two catastrophic hurricanes that hit during 2008, and continues to fly the flag as Cuba's eco-epicenter.

PINAR DEL RÍO AREA

Pinar del Río

POP 191,660

Surrounded by beautiful verdant countryside and given an economic boost by its proximity to the world's best tobacco-growing terrain, the city of Pinar del Río emits a strange energy, exacerbated by its famous *jineteros* (hustlers) who can wear down the most thick-skinned traveler. As a result, the place probably has more detractors than fans, especially since the bucolic *jinetero*-free paradise of Viñales is so close by. But a stopover here needn't be purgatorial. There's a tobacco factory to visit, some weirdly interesting architecture, and a hot, frenetic after-dark scene if you're up for it.

Pinar del Río was one of the last provincial capitals on the island to take root, and still seems a tad stuck in the slow lane. Overlooked by successive central governments who preferred sugarcane to tobacco, the city became an urban backwater and the butt of countless jokes about the supposedly easy-to-fool *guajiros* who were popularly portrayed as simple-minded rural hicks. But the city fought back. It's overcome neglect, derision and several furious hurricanes and is busily trying to overturn its negative connotations.

History

Pinar del Río was founded in its current form in 1774 by a Spanish army captain. In 1896 General Antonio Maceo brought the Second War of Independence to Pinar del Río in an ambitious attempt to split the island in two, and the town rallied to his wake-up call.

Following the 1959 Revolution Pinar del Río's economic fortunes improved exponentially; this was facilitated further by the building of the Autopista Nacional from Havana and the development of tourism in the 1980s. The city baseball team has also historically reared some of the best players in the country after the big boys from Havana and Santiago: many, like Alexi Ramíerez and José Contreras, have defected to the US.

◉ Sights

Museo de Ciencias
Naturales Sandalio de Noda   MUSEUM
(Martí Este No 202; admission CUC$1, camera CUC$1; ⊙9am-5pm Mon-Fri, to 1pm Sun) A mad but magnificent neo-Gothic-meets-Moorish-meets-Hindu-meets-Byzantium mansion built by local doctor and world traveler Francisco Guasch in 1914. Once you've got over shock of the whimsical exterior (gargoyles, turrets and sculpted seahorses), you'll realize it's now a natural history museum with

everything from a stuffed baby giraffe to a giant stone T-rex in the rear garden.

Museo Provincial de Historia
MUSEUM

(Martí Este No 58, btwn Colón & Isabel Rubio; admission CUC$1; ⊙ 8:30am-6:30pm Mon-Fri, 9am-1pm Sat) A museum collecting the history of the province from pre-Columbian times to the present, including Enrique Jorrín ephemera (Jorrín was the creator of the *chachachá*). It was closed for renovation at time of research.

Teatro José Jacinto Milanes
CULTURAL BUILDING

(✍ 75-38-71; Martí No 160, btwn Colón & Isabel Rubio) Often included in a set of seven classic 19th-century Cuban provincial theaters, the 540-seat Milanés dates from 1845 – making it one of Cuba's oldest. It reopened in 2006 after lengthy renovations and, with its three-tiered auditorium, antique seats, and Spanish-style patio and cafe, is well worth a look.

Palacio de los Matrimonios
NOTARI F BUILDING

(Martí, btwn Rafael Morales & Plaza de la Independencia) **FREE** West on Martí, the grand neoclassical facades give way to the outlandishly opulent in the shape of this building, primarily a wedding venue and dating from 1924. That said, the amiable guards will let you look around the lavish interior which includes a plethora of artwork, much of it Chinese in origin.

Fábrica de Tabacos Francisco Donatien
CIGAR FACTORY

(Maceo Oeste No 157; admission CUC$5; ⊙ 9am-noon & 1-4pm Mon-Fri) You can observe people busily rolling some of Pinar's (read: the world's) finest cigars in this factory, which was a jail until 1961 but is now tobacco central on the tourist circuit.

Smaller than the Partagás factory in Havana, you get a more intimate insight here, though the foibles are the same – robotic guides, rushed tours and the nagging notion that it's all a bit voyeuristic. There's an excellent cigar shop opposite.

Catedral de San Rosendo
CHURCH

(Maceo Este No 3) The city's understated cathedral is four blocks southeast of the cigar factory. It dates from 1883 and its pastel-yellow exterior seems to get a more regular paint job than the rest of the city's buildings. As with most Cuban churches, the interior is often closed. Slip inside for a peek during Sunday morning service.

Fábrica de Bebidas Casa Garay
BRANDY FACTORY

(Isabel Rubio Sur No 189, btwn Ceferino Fernández & Frank País; admission CUC$1; ⊙ 9am-3:30pm Mon-Fri, to 12:30pm Sat) Workers here use a secret recipe to distill sweet and dry versions of the city's signature liquor, Guayabita del Pinar guava brandy. Whistle-stop 15-minute multilingual factory tours are topped off with a taste of the brew in the sampling room. There's a shop adjacent.

Centro Provincial de Artes Plásticas Galería
GALLERY

(Antonio Guiteras; ⊙ 8am-9pm Mon-Sat) **FREE** Across the plaza, this is a top-notch Pinar gallery, housing many local works.

🎊 Festivals & Events

Carnaval
CARNIVAL

Carnaval in early July features a procession of *carrozas* (carriages) through the streets with couples dancing between the floats. It's a big, drunken dance party.

🛏 Sleeping

Villa Aguas Claras
CABIN $

(✍ 77-84-27; s/d incl breakfast CUC$36/40; [P] [≋]) This plush campismo lies 8km north of town on the Carretera a Viñales (off Rafael Morales) and has the facilities of a midrange hotel. The 50 bungalows with hot showers sleep two (10 have air-con). The rooms are adequate, the landscaping lush and the staff congenial. Besides an OK restaurant, the Villa Aguas Claras also offers horseback riding and day trips.

Insect repellent is essential here. Aguas Claras is accessible from Pinar del Río by bus several times a day.

PINAR DEL RÍO STREET NAMES

Locals stick to the old street names; this chart should help.

OLD NAME	NEW NAME
Calzada de la Coloma	Rafael Ferro
Caubada	Comandante Pinares
Recreo	Isabel Rubio
Rosario	Ormani Arenado
San Juan	Rafael Morales
Vélez Caviedes	Gerardo Medina
Virtudes	Ceferino Fernández

Pinar del Río

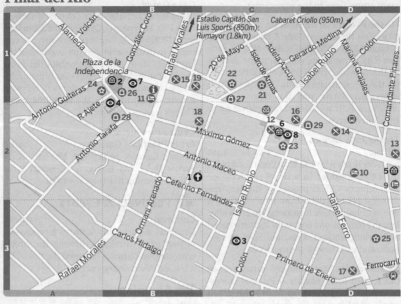

Pinar del Río

⦿ Sights

⬤ Sleeping

✖ Eating

⦿ Drinking & Nightlife

⦿ Entertainment

⦿ Shopping

Gladys Cruz Hernández   CASA PARTICULAR **$**
(📞77-96-98; casadegladys@gmail.com; Av Comandante Pinares Sur No 15, btwn Martí & Máximo
Gómez; r CUC$20; ❄) A splendid house with
tasteful colonial furnishings situated near
the train station; there are two rooms with

bathrooms and fridges, a TV and an attractive rear patio.

Hostal Sr Handy Santalla   CASA PARTICULAR **$**
(📞72-12-22; Calle Máximo Gómez No 169A, btwn
Ciprián Valdés & Av Pinares; r CUC$20-25) Keen
young owner giving it a shot in the new

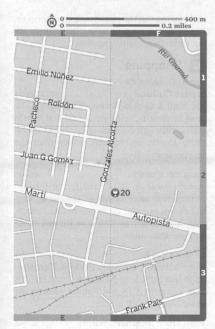

economy with two small 1st-floor rooms with brand new bathroom fittings, and a patio and garage downstairs.

Hotel Vueltabajo HOTEL **$$**
(☑75-93-81; cnr Martí & Rafael Morales; s/d CUC$35/55; ☒) Stylishly colonial with high ceilings and striped Parisian window awnings, the rooms at this fabulous hotel are so spacious you almost think they must have run out of furniture. Old-fashioned shutters open onto the street and downstairs there's an OK bar-restaurant; a reasonable breakfast is included in the price.

✖ Eating

El Mesón CUBAN **$**
(☑75-28-67; Martí Este 205; meals CUC$4-6; ☺11am-11pm) A private enterprise that has gone through various hostal/paladar reincarnations, but is now firmly a paladar (privately owned restaurant), and a rather good one at that. Expect liberal helpings of simple *comida criolla* heavy on the rice and beans, with plenty of Cuban company.

La Casona CUBAN **$**
(cnr Martí & Colón; mains CUC$5; ☺8am-3pm & 4-11pm) Hard to believe, but this is Pinar's best government-run restaurant outside Rumayor. Encouragingly there are tablecloths

and wine glasses, along with steak, chicken and pasta on the menu, but positioned unstrategically on the town's busiest nexus the hissing hustlers are never far away. Get a seat away from the door.

El Marino SEAFOOD **$**
(Martí, cnr Isabel Rubio; mains MN$25-30; ☺noon-3pm & 6-9:15pm) Pay in pesos for tasty paella and other fish dishes, and let the pleasant nautical decor enhance the experience.

Heladería ICE CREAM **$**
(cnr Martí & Rafael Morales; ☺9am-9pm) A substantial *tres gracias* (three scoops) at this clean, cheerful place is the price of half a teaspoon's worth of Haagen Daas.

El Pedregal CUBAN **$$**
(Azcuy No 143E; mains CUC$5-8; ☺noon-11pm) Around the back of another paladar (called Don Fabio), Pedregal isn't exactly Havana quality, but the food's simple and plentiful if you can brave the *jineteros*.

Rumayor CUBAN **$$**
(☑76-80-07; Carretera a Viñales Km 1; mains CUC$10; ☺noon-midnight) Some of Pinar's best food can be found at Rumayor, 2km north of the town center off the Carretera a Viñales. Justly famous for its succulent *pollo ahumado* (smoked chicken), you'll pay a little extra here, but it is definitely worth it. It's also one of Pinar's premier cabaret spots in the evening.

Self-Catering

Mercado Agropecuario MARKET **$**
(Rafael Ferro; ☺8am-6pm Mon-Sat, to 1pm Sun) Pinar del Río's colorful open-air market is almost on top of the tracks near the train station. You'll see the odd tour group tramping through here getting a grip on Special Period economics.

Panadería Doña Neli BAKERY **$**
(cnr Gerardo Medina Sur & Máximo Gómez; ☺7am-7pm) Gives you each day your daily bread.

Supermercado el Comercio SUPERMARKET **$**
(cnr Martí Oeste & Arenado; ☺9am-5pm Mon-Sat, to noon Sun) One of the best supermarkets in town.

☕ Drinking & Entertainment

Disco Azul NIGHTCLUB
(cnr Gonzales Alcorta & Autopista; admission CUC$5; ☺from 10pm Tue-Sun) A drab hotel, but a kicking disco – this glittery nightclub in Hotel Pinar del Río, on the edge of town

coming from the Autopista, is the city's most popular.

Rumayor
CABARET

(☑76-30-51; Carretera a Viñales Km 1; cover charge CUC$5; ⊙noon-midnight) Besides serving very good food, this place undergoes a metamorphosis at night from Tuesday through Sunday to a kitschy cabaret with a fantastic floor show that starts at 11pm. It's not the Tropicana, but it ain't half bad.

Café Pinar
LIVE MUSIC

(Gerardo Medina Norte No 34; admission CUC$3; ⊙10am-2am) This spot gets the local youth vote and is also the best place to meet other travelers. Situated on a lively stretch of Calle Gerardo Medina there are live bands at night on the open patio, and light menu items such as pasta, chicken and sandwiches during the day.

La Piscuala
CULTURAL CENTER

(cnr Martí & Colón) With the Teatro José Jacinto Milanés back in business you'd be foolish to miss this theatrical patio alongside the real deal. Check the schedule posted outside for nightly cultural activities.

Cabaret Criollo
CABARET

(Carretera Central Km 1, btwn Av Aeropuerto & Carretera a Viñales; ⊙9pm-2am Mon-Sat) The musical half of an eponymous restaurant, locals rate this nightly cabaret in an enormous open-air patio rather highly.

Casa de la Música
LIVE MUSIC

(Gerardo Medina Norte No 21; admission CUC$1; ⊙concerts start at 9pm nightly) After warming up at Café Pinar, many revelers cross the street for more live music here.

Teatro Lírico Ernesto Lecuona
THEATER

(Antonio Maceo Oeste No 163) Near the cigar factory, this theater is best for classical music and opera.

Uneac
CINEMA

(Antonio Maceo 178) In addition to the venues listed above, try Uneac (Unión de Escritores y Artistas de Cuba) near the train station for nightly film screenings and occasional live music.

Estadio Capitán San Luis Sports
SPORT

(☑75-38-95; admission 1 peso; ⊙matches 7pm Tue-Thu & Sat, 4pm Sun) From October to April, exciting baseball games happen at this stadium on the north side of town. Pinar del Río is one of the country's best teams, often

challenging the Havana–Santiago monopoly. Pop by in the evening to see the players going through a training session.

 Shopping

Fondo Cubano de Bienes Cultural
ARTS & CRAFTS

(cnr Martí & Gerardo Medina; ⊙9am-5pm) The most interesting selection of regional handicrafts, although revenue goes almost exclusively to the government rather than the makers themselves.

Casa del Habano
CIGARS

(Antonio Maceo No 162) Opposite the tobacco factory, this store is one of the better outlets of this popular government cigar chain, with a patio bar and air-conditioned shop, and smoking room.

La Casa del Ron
ARTS & CRAFTS, RUM

(Antonio Maceo Oeste No 151; ⊙9am-4:30pm Mon-Fri, to 1pm Sat & Sun) Near the cigar factory, sells souvenirs, CDs and T-shirts, plus plenty of the strong stuff.

Todo Libro Internacional
BOOKS

(cnr Martí & Colón; ⊙8am-noon & 1:30-6pm Mon-Fri, 8am-noon & 1-4pm Sat) Selection of maps, books and office supplies in same building as the Cubanacán office.

ℹ Information

DANGERS & ANNOYANCES

For a relatively untouristed city Pinar del Río has had its fair share of unsolicited touts or *jineteros*. The majority are young men who hang around on Calle Martí, offering everything from paladar meals to 'guided tours' of tobacco plantations. Most will back off at your first or second '*no me moleste, por favor*' but bolder ones have been known to mount bicycles and accost tourist cars (identifiable by their purple/brown number plates) when they stop at traffic lights. Although they're generally nonaggressive, it's best to be firmly polite from the outset and not invite further attention.

INTERNET ACCESS & TELEPHONE

Etecsa Telepunto (cnr Gerardo Medina & Juan Gómez; per hr CUC$6; ⊙8:30am-7:30pm) You can also check your email here.

MEDIA

Guerrillero is published on Friday. Radio Guamá airs on 1080AM or 90.2FM.

MEDICAL SERVICES

Farmacia Martí (Martí Este No 50; ⊙8am-11pm)

Hospital Provincial León Cuervo Rubio
(☑75-44-43; Carretera Central) Two kilometers north of town.

MONEY

Banco Financiero Internacional (Gerardo Medina Norte No 46; ☻8:30am-3:30pm Mon-Fri) Opposite Casa de la Música.
Cadeca (Martí No 46; ☻8:30am-5:30pm Mon-Sat)

POST

Post Office (Martí Este No 49; ☻8am-8pm Mon-Sat)

TOURIST INFORMATION

Infotur (☑72-86-16; ☻9am-5.30pm Mon-Fri) At the Hotel Vueltabajo, and one of the city's most helpful sources of information.

TRAVEL AGENCIES

Cubanacán (☑77-01-04, 750-1078; Martí No 109) Has moped rental.

ⓘ Getting There & Away

BUS

The city's **bus station** (Adela Azcuy, btwn Colón & Comandante Pinares) is conveniently close to the center. Pinar del Río is well-served by the Víazul network, with all services to Havana and destinations east originating in Viñales. There are departures to Havana at 8:25am and 2:55pm (CUC$11, 2½ hours). The afternoon Havana bus also stops in Las Terrazas while the morning bus continues to Cienfuegos and Trinidad. Buses to Viñales leave at 12:10pm and 5pm (CUC$6, 45 minutes).

Conectando buses running most days offer services to Havana and a direct service to Viñales bypassing Havana. You'll need to book ahead with Cubanacán. Ask here about other transfers to Cayo Levisa, Cayo Jutías and María la Gorda.

TAXI

Private taxis hanging around outside the bus station will offer prices all the way to Havana. Sometimes these are worth considering. A fare to José Martí International Airport, for example, could cost around CUC$60 compared to the standard CUC$25 just from Havana.

Colectivos (collective taxis) congregate at the start of the Carretera a Viñales outside the hospital north of town, offering the scenic Viñales jaunt for CUC$1.

TRAIN

Before planning any train travel, check the station blackboards for canceled/suspended/rescheduled services. From the **train station** (☑75-57-34; cnr Ferrocarril & Comandante Pinares Sur; ☻ticket window 6:30am-noon & 1-6:30pm) there's a painfully slow train to Havana (CUC$7, 5½ hours) every other day. You can buy your ticket for this train the day of departure; be at the station a good hour before departure. Local trains go southwest to Guane via Sábalo (CUC$2, two hours). This is the closest you can get by train to the Península de Guanahacabibes.

ⓘ Getting Around

Cubacar (☑75-93-81) has a car-rental office at Hotel Vueltabajo and **Havanautos** (☑77-80-15) has one at Hotel Pinar del Río. Mopeds can be rented from Cubanacán.

Servicentro Oro Negro is two blocks north of the Hospital Provincial on the Carretera Central. The Servi-Cupet gas station is 1.5km further north on the Carretera Central toward Havana; another is on Rafael Morales Sur at the south entrance to town.

Horse carts (one peso) on Isabel Rubio near Adela Azcuy go to the Hospital Provincial and out onto the Carretera Central. Bici-taxis cost five pesos around town.

If you are up for cadging a ride to Viñales Cuban-style, trudge north to the junction of the Carretera a Viñales with the Carretera Central and get talking to the *amarillo* (traffic organizer).

Southwest of Pinar del Río

If Cuba is the world's greatest tobacco producer and Pinar del Río its proverbial jewel box, then the verdant San Luis region southwest of the provincial capital is the diamond in the stash. Few deny that the pancake-flat farming terrain around the smart town of **San Juan y Martínez** churns out the *crème de la crème* of the world's tobacco and the rural scenery is typically picturesque. Further on, there are a couple of little-visited southern beaches and the freshwater **Embalse Laguna Grande**, stocked with largemouth bass.

⊙ Sights

Alejandro Robaina Tobacco Plantation   FARM
(☑79-74-70; admission CUC$2; ☻9am-5pm) This is the only real opportunity in Cuba to tour a working tobacco plantation – so take it! The famous Robaina *vegas* (fields), in the rich Vuelta Abajo region southwest of Pinar del Río, have been growing quality tobacco since 1845, but it wasn't until 1997 that a new brand of cigars known as Vegas Robaina was first launched to wide international acclaim.

LOCAL KNOWLEDGE

ROBAINA TOBACCO

Long considered Cuba's finest tobacco grower and one of the few private farmers to remain in operation during the Fidel Castro years, Alejandro Robaina was the 'godfather' of the Cuban cigar industry until his death in 2010. Ninety per cent of Robaina's lovingly harvested leaves are used in cigars (compared with 20% elsewhere in Cuba), mainly in the outer wrappers, and in 1997 he was given the honor of having a brand of cigars named after him, *Vegas Robainas*. Deemed medium-strong with an almondy, nutty flavor, they come in five *vitolas* (sizes) and are rolled exclusively in Havana's H Upmann factory. Robaina's secret lies in his farm's rich San Luis soil, 150 years of family business experience, minute attention to detail and, in the minds of some, Robaina's stoic desire to stick to his own economic model.

This made Alejandro Robaina the only contemporary Cuban with a brand of cigars named after him. Yet, although the 'Godfather' of Cuban tobacco passed away in April 2010 the show must go on, and does at the plantation today: it's been unofficially open to outside visitors for some years. With a little effort and some deft navigational skills, you can roll up at the farm and get the lowdown on the tobacco-making process from delicate plant to aromatic wrapper. There's a small on-site cafe and all guests receive a souvenir *puro* (cigar).

To get there, take the Carretera Central southwest out of Pinar del Río for 12km, turn left toward San Luis and left again after approximately 3km at the Robaina sign. This rougher track continues for 1.5km to the farm. Do not hire a *jinetero* (hustler) to lead you, as they often take you to the wrong farm. Tours are available every day. The tobacco-growing season runs from October to February and this is obviously the best time to visit.

Rancho la Guabina   RANCH
(📞 75-76-16; Carretera de Luis Lazo Km 9.5) A former Spanish farm spread over 1000 hectares of pasture, forest and wetlands, the Rancho la Guabina is a jack of all trades and a master of at least one. You can partake in horseback riding here, go boating on a lake or enjoy a scrumptious Cuban barbecue.

The big drawcard for most, though, is the fantastic horse shows. The *rancho* is a long-standing horse-breeding center that raises fine Pinto Cubano and Apaloosa horses, and mini-rodeo-style shows run on Monday, Wednesday and Friday from 10am to noon and from 4pm to 6pm. Agencies in Viñales and Pinar del Río run excursions here starting at CUC$29, or you can arrive on your own. It's a great place to enjoy the peaceful *guajiro* life. Limited accommodations are available.

Playa Bailén   BEACH
The beach life here can't match the alluring north coast; still, this makes a pleasant, sandy deviation on the way out west.

🛏 Sleeping & Eating

The best places to try for casas particulares are bright San Juan y Martínez and Sandino, 6km from the Laguna Grande turnoff. There are rough cabins for rent around Playa Bailén.

Villa Laguna Grande   CABIN $
(📞 84-34-53; Carretera a Ciudad Bolívar; r from CUC$23) Something of an anomaly, this rough-around-the-edges fishing resort, 29km southwest of Guane and 18km off the highway to María la Gorda, is Islazul's most isolated outpost. The 12 rather scruffy thatched cabins sit in woodland directly below the Embalse Laguna Grande, a reservoir stocked with bass where locals come to fish.

Rancho La Guabina   HOSTEL $$
(📞 75-76-16; Carretera de Luis Lazo Km 9.5; r CUC$65; 🅿 ❄) Just outside Pinar del Río, this expansive farm offers eight rooms, five in a cottage-style house and three in separate cabins. It's a charming and unhurried place with excellent food and friendly staff.

❶ Getting There & Away

Two trains a day travel between Pinar del Río and Guane stopping at San Luis, San Juan y Martínez, Sábalo and Isabel Rubio (two hours). Passenger trucks run periodically between Guane and Sandino but, southwest of there, public transport is sparse, apart from the sporadic Havanatur transfer. Fill your tank up at the Servi-

Cupet gas station in Isabel Rubio if you intend to drive to Cabo de San Antonio, as this is the last gasp for gas.

PENÍNSULA DE GUANAHACABIBES

As the island narrows at its western end, you fall upon the low-lying and ecologically rich Península de Guanahacabibes. One of Cuba's most isolated enclaves, it once provided shelter for its earliest inhabitants, the Guanahatabeys. A two-hour drive from Pinar del Río, this region lacks major tourist infrastructure, meaning it feels far more isolated than it is. There are two reasons to come here: a national park (also a Unesco Biosphere Reserve) and the international-standard diving center at María la Gorda.

Parque Nacional Península de Guanahacabibes

Flat and deceptively narrow, the elongated Península de Guanahacabibes begins at La Fe, 94km southwest of Pinar del Río. In 1987, 1015 sq km of this uninhabited sliver of idyllic coastline was declared a Biosphere Reserve by Unesco – one of only six in Cuba. The reasons for the protection measures were manifold.

First, the reserve's submerged coastline features a wide variety of different landscapes including broad mangrove swamps, low-scrub-thicket vegetation and an up-lifted shelf of alternating white sand and coral rock. Second, the area's distinctive limestone karst formations are home to a plethora of unique flora and fauna including 172 species of bird, 700 species of plant, 18 types of mammal, 35 types of reptiles, 19 types of amphibian, 86 types of butterfly and 16 orchid species. Sea turtles, including loggerhead and green turtles, come ashore at night in summer to lay their eggs – the park is the only part of mainland Cuba where this happens.

Another curiosity is the swarms of *cangrejos colorados* (red and yellow crabs) that crawl across the peninsula's rough central road only to be unceremoniously crushed under the tires of passing cars. The stench of the smashed shells is memorable.

The area is thought to shelter at least 100 important archaeological sites relating to the Guanahatabey people.

◉ Sights

Casa de la Miel MUSEUM
(⊙8:30am-3:30pm Mon-Sat) About to open at the time of research, the latest attraction in the reserve is just before the park entrance, an eco-museum telling the tale of the area's agriculture and selling honey straight from the on-site hives. Inquire at the visitor center.

🏃 Activities

Península de Guanahacabibes is a paradise for divers, eco-travelers, conservationists and bird-watchers – or, at least, it ought to be. However, thanks to strict park rules (you can't go anywhere without a guide), some travelers have complained that the experience is too limiting. Feathered species on display here include parrots, *tocororos*, woodpeckers, owls, tody flycatchers and *zunzuncitos* (bee hummingbirds) and, with no official settlements, the peninsula is one of Cuba's most untouched.

Centro Internacional de Buceo DIVING
(⌨77-13-06; María la Gorda) Diving is María la Gorda's *raison d'être* and the prime reason people come to Cuba's western tip. The nerve center is this well-run base next to the eponymous hotel at the Marina Gaviota. Good visibility and sheltered offshore reefs are highlights, plus the proximity of the 32 dive sites to the shore.

Couple this with the largest formation of black coral in the archipelago and you've got a recipe for arguably Cuba's best diving reefs outside the Isla de la Juventud.

A dive here costs a reasonable CUC$35 (night diving CUC$40), plus CUC$7.50 for equipment. The center offers a full CMAS (Confédération Mondiale des Activités Subaquatiques; World Underwater Activities Federation) scuba certification course (CUC$365, four days) and snorkelers can hop on the dive boat for CUC$12. The dive center also offers four hours of deep-sea fishing for CUC$200 for up to four people and line fishing/trolling at CUC$30 per person, four maximum.

Among the 50 identified dive sites in the vicinity, divers are shown El Valle de Coral Negro, a 100m-long black-coral wall, and El Salón de María, a cave 20m deep containing

TURTLE-WATCHING

Guanahacabibes is still a park in tentative development, but it has recently introduced turtle-monitoring opportunities to its limited stash of organized excursions. The turtle program has been running for several years under the direction of environmental researchers and with involvement from the local population (primarily schoolchildren), but for the first time outsiders are being allowed to participate. Green turtles lay their eggs on half a dozen of the peninsula's south-facing beaches between June and August, and willing participants are invited to observe, monitor and aid in the process. To take part, inquire in advance at the park office at La Bajada. Tours take place nightly between 10pm and 2am in season. The release of baby turtles begins in mid-September.

feather stars and brilliantly colored corals. The concentrations of migratory fish can be incredible. The furthest entry is only 30 minutes by boat from shore.

Marina Gaviota Cabo de San Antonio   DIVING
(✆ 75-01-18) Cuba's most westerly located boat dock is on Playa las Tumbas at the end of the Península Guanahacabibes. The marina has fuel, boat mooring, a small restaurant, shop and easy access to 27 diving sites. The Villa Cabo San Antonio is nearby.

Cueva las Perlas   HIKING
(3km; admission CUC$8) The three-hour trek to the 'pearl cave' traverses deciduous woodland replete with a wide variety of birds, including *tocororos, zunzuncitos* and woodpeckers. After 1.5km you come to the cave itself, where you can spy (and hear) screech owls: it's a multi-gallery cavern with a lake of which 300m is accessible to hikers.

Del Bosque al Mar   HIKING
(1.5km; admission CUC$6) Leaving from near the eco-station, this trail passes a lagoon where you can view resident birdlife, and takes in some interesting flora including orchids, as well as a *cenote* (a kind of water-submerged cave) for swimming.

At 90 minutes it's rather short for such an immense park, but the guides are highly

trained and informed, and tours can be conducted in Spanish, English or Italian.

Tours

Cabo de San Antonio Excursion   WILDLIFE TOUR
(CUC$10) The visitor center can arrange guides, specialized visits and a five-hour tour to the park's (and Cuba's) western tip at Cabo de San Antonio. The responsibility is yours to supply transport, sufficient gas, water, sunscreen, insect repellent and food, which makes the task a little more difficult for travelers without their own wheels.

During most of the 120km round-trip you'll have dark, rough *diente de perro* (dog's teeth) rock on one side and the brilliant blue sea on the other. Iguanas will lumber for cover as you approach and you might see small deer, *jutías* (tree rats) and lots of birds. Beyond the lighthouse is deserted Playa las Tumbas where you'll be given 30 minutes for a swim. Thanks to the freshly renovated road surface, any hire car can make this trip. The five-hour excursion costs CUC$10 per person, plus the CUC$80 or so you'll need to hire a car (there's car rental at Hotel María la Gorda). Besides the diving, the beaches and the chance to see turtles, the wealth of lesser-known activities (such as exploring caves and viewing rare wildlife like the fish eagle) at Cabo San Antonio makes staying out here worthwhile.

🛏 Sleeping & Eating

Hotel María la Gorda   HOTEL $$
(✆ 77-30-67, 77-81-31; s/d/tr incl breakfast CUC$39/58/84; 🅟 ❄) This is the most remote hotel on the main island of Cuba and the isolation has its advantages. The adjoining palm-fringed beach is pretty (if a little rocky), but 90% of people come here to dive; reefs and vertical drop-offs beckon just 200m from the hotel. María la Gorda (literally 'Maria the Fatso') is on the Bahía de Corrientes, 150km southwest of Pinar del Río.

Room-wise you get a choice of three pink-concrete, motel-type buildings or 20 newer cabins set back from the beach. The latter are more comfortable and private. Far from being a posh resort, María la Gorda is an easygoing place where hammocks are strung between palm trees, cold beers are sipped at sunset and dive talk continues into the small hours.

Buffet meals cost CUC$15 for lunch or dinner; reports on the food vary. A small shop sells water and basic provisions. There's a rip-off CUC$10 (including a sandwich) charge to visit Hotel María la Gorda and its adjoining 5km beach for nonguests (making it Cuba's most expensive sandwich)!

Villa Cabo San Antonio CABINS $$
(☑ 75-76-76, 75-01-18; Playa las Tumbas; r CUC$65; 🌐) 🏊 A 16-villa complex on the almost-virgin Península de Guanahacabibes, set 3km from the Faro Roncali (Roncali Lighthouse) and 4km from the Gaviota Marina, this environmentally friendly and surprisingly well-appointed place has satellite TV, car rental, bike hire and a small cafe.

ℹ️ Information

Although the park border straddles the tiny community of La Fe, the reserve entrance is at La Bajada. Some 25km before the reserve proper, Manuel Lazo has the last accommodations for budget-conscious travelers.

It's advisable to phone the **visitor center** (☑ 75-03-66; osmanibf@yahoo.es; ⏰ 8.30am-3pm) at La Bajada to arrange park activities before showing up at the park entrance, as with limited resources there are often not the staff to arrange impromptu guided tours.

The visitor center, adjacent to the Estación Ecológica Guanahacabibes, has interpretive displays on the local flora and fauna. English is spoken. You can arrange to meet guides here for all activities except the diving, which is organized from Hotel María la Gorda. Just beyond the center the road splits with the left-hand branch going south to María la Gorda (14km along a deteriorating coastal road) and the right fork heading west toward the end of the peninsula.

It's a 120km round-trip to Cuba's westernmost point from here. The lonesome Cabo de San Antonio is populated by a solitary lighthouse, the Faro Roncali, inaugurated by the Spanish in 1849, and Gaviota Marina and villa. Four kilometers northwest is Playa las Tumbas, an idyllic beach where visitors to the park are permitted to swim.

ℹ️ Getting There & Away

A transfer bus (return CUC$35) operates between Viñales and María la Gorda most days, but check and book ahead. It is scheduled to leave Viñales at 7am and arrive at the peninsula at 9:30am. The return leg leaves María la Gorda at 5pm and arrives in Viñales at 7pm. Single/return costs CUC$25/35. Reserve at Cubanacán in Viñales or Infotur in Pinar del Río.

Via Gaviota (☑ 77-81-31) has an office at Hotel María la Gorda, offering car hire for the usual steep prices.

VALLE DE VIÑALES

Embellished by soaring pine trees and scattered with bulbous limestone cliffs that teeter like giant haystacks above placid tobacco plantations, Parque Nacional Viñales is one of Cuba's most magnificent natural settings. Wedged spectacularly into the Sierra de los Órganos mountain range, this 11km-by-5km valley was declared a Unesco World Heritage Site in 1999 for its dramatic rocky outcrops (known as *mogotes*), coupled with the vernacular architecture of its traditional farms and villages.

Once upon a time the whole region was several hundred meters higher. Then, during the Cretaceous period 100 million years ago, underground rivers ate away at the limestone bedrock, creating vast caverns. Eventually the roofs collapsed, leaving only the eroded walls we see today. It is the finest example of a limestone karst valley in Cuba and contains the Gran Caverna de Santo Tomás, the island's largest cave system.

Rock studies aside, Viñales also offers opportunities for fine hiking, history, rock climbing and horseback trekking. On the accommodations front it boasts first-class hotels and some of the best casas particulares in Cuba. Despite drawing in daytrippers by the busload, the area's well-protected and spread-out natural attractions have somehow managed to escape the frenzied tourist circus of other less well-managed resorts, while the atmosphere in and around the town remains refreshingly hassle-free.

Viñales

POP 27,806

The moment you spot a cigar chewing *guajiro* driving his oxen and plough through a rust-colored tobacco field, you know that you must be within striking distance of Viñales. Despite its longstanding love affair with tourism, this slow, relaxed, wonderfully traditional settlement is a place that steadfastly refuses to put on a show. What you see here is what you get – a tiny agricultural town that just happens to occupy one of Cuba's most beautiful natural corners. Grab a comfortable rocking chair, sit back on a rustic porch and enjoy a slice of the real Cuba.

◎ Sights

Founded in 1875, Viñales is more about setting than sights with most of its activities of a lung-stretching outdoor nature.

Viñales

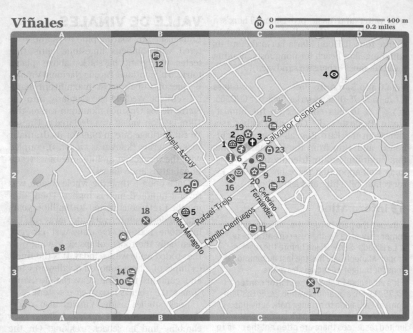

0 ——————— 400 m
0 ——————— 0.2 miles

Viñales

Nevertheless the town has some engaging architecture and a lively main square backed by the sturdy colonial **Casa de la Cultura** (Map p194), one of the oldest structures in the valley. Next door is a tiny **art gallery** (Map p194) while nearby is an equally diminutive (and recently restored) **church** (Map p194).

Museo Municipal   MUSEUM
(Map p194; Salvador Cisneros No 115; admission CUC$1; ⊙8am-10pm Mon-Sat, to 4pm Sun)

Positioned halfway down Cisneros, Viñales' pine-lined main street, the Museo Municipal occupies the former home of independence heroine Adela Azcuy (1861–1914) and tracks the local history. Five different hikes leave from here daily.

El Jardín de Caridad   GARDENS
(Map p194; donations accepted; ⊙8am-5pm) Just opposite the Servi-Cupet gas station as the road swings north out of town, you'll spot

an outlandish, vine-choked gate beckoning you in. This is the entrance to a sprawling garden almost a century in the making. Cascades of orchids bloom alongside plastic doll heads, thickets of orange lilies grow in soft groves and turkeys run amok.

Knock on the door of the Little Red Riding Hood cottage and one of the elderly owners will probably show you around.

La Casa del Veguero FARM
(Carretera a Pinar del Río Km 24; ⊙10am-5pm) To learn about the local tobacco-growing process, stop by just outside Viñales on the road to Los Jazmines at this tobacco plantation and see a fully operating *secadero* (drying house) in which tobacco leaves are cured from February to May. The staff gives brief explanations and you can buy loose cigars at discount prices. There's a restaurant here too.

🏃 Activities

While most of the activities in Viñales are located outside town, there's a handful – including some climbing routes – within easy walking distance. Even if you're staying in a casa, it's worth strolling the 2km uphill to the lovely La Ermita where you can swim (CUC$7, including bar cover) in the gorgeous pool or book a massage (CUC$20 to CUC$35). Los Jazmines has an equally amazing pool (CUC$7, including bar cover) though the ubiquitous tour buses can sometimes kill the tranquility.

Cycling
Despite the hilly terrain, Viñales is one of the best places in Cuba to cycle (most roads follow the valleys and are relatively flat). Traffic on the roads is still light. Agencies in town offer valley cycling tours.

Bike Rental Point CYCLING
(Map p194; bike hire 1/8 hours CUC$1/6, 1 week CU$25) There is a new Bike Rental Point offering modern Chinese-made bikes with gears in Viñales' main plaza. Alternatively, some casa particular owners now rent bikes.

👉 Tours

Yoan & Yarelis Reyes HIKING, CYCLING
(Map p194; ☑79-33-17, 0152-74-17-34; Salvador Cisneros No 206C) Yoan and Yarelis are adept at being able to rustle up all number of activities, including walks, cycling tours, horseback riding, massage, salsa lessons and visits to a nearby farm and tobacco plantation **Finca Raúl Reyes**, run by Yoan's father, where you can enjoy fruit, coffee, puros and a dose of throat-warming rum.

The two highlight trips are the 'Sunrise tour' to Los Aquaticos and the 'Sunset tour' to the wonderfully peaceful Valle del Silencio.

Cubanacán GUIDED TOUR
(Map p194; ☑79-63-93; Salvador Cisneros No 63C; ⊙9am-7pm Mon-Sat) Cubanacán organizes perennially popular day trips to Cayo Levisa (CUC$29), Cayo Jutías (CUC$22), Gran Caverna de Santo Tomás (CUC$21) and María la Gorda (CUC$35). There's an organized valley bike tour for CUC$20 and horseback riding from CUC$5. Official park hikes leave from here daily (CUC$8).

🛏 Sleeping

Almost every house rents rooms in Viñales, giving you well over one hundred to choose from (you'll always find space somewhere). Most are good, but those listed here stand out from the crowd. The two hotels within walking distance of Viñales village are both spectacularly located gems.

★**Villa Los Reyes** CASA PARTICULAR $
(Map p194; ☑79-33-17; joanmanuel2008@yahoo. es; Salvador Cisneros No 206C; r CUC$20-25; P🅿❄@) A great modern house with two rooms, all amenities and a secluded patio for dining; the talented owners can organize multiple extra-curricular activities. Hostess, Yarelis, is a biologist at the national park and host, Yoan, has Viñales running through his veins. A taxi service and other excursions are offered.

Villa Pitín & Juana CASA PARTICULAR $
(Map p194; ☑79-33-38; emilitin2009@yahoo.es; Carretera a Pinar del Río No 2 Km 25; r CUC$25; P❄) With three wonderful rooms on separate floors (the top floor with the private double patio is the classic traveler retreat) and a fantastic family atmosphere, this place also benefits from scrumptious home cooking. No wonder this is one of the longest-running casas in town.

Hostal Doña Hilda CASA PARTICULAR $
(Map p194; ☑79-60-53; flavia@correodecuba.cu; Carretera a Pinar del Río No 4 Km 25; r CUC$20-25; ❄) One of the first houses in town on the road from Pinar del Río, Hilda's (Chichi to her friends) house is small, unpretentious and classic Viñales – just like the perennially smiling hostess – with truly wonderful food.

The mojitos are among Cuba's very best. Ask here about dance classes.

El Balcón
CASA PARTICULAR $

(Map p194; ☑ 69-67-25; el_balcon2005@yahoo.es; Rafael Trejo No 48; r CUC$20-30; ✺ ✺) Situated a block south of the plaza, El Balcón has four private rooms (two of them brand new), a street-facing balcony (of course), and a huge roof terrace where fine food is served. Friendly owners Mignelys and Juanito speak English.

Oscar Jaime Rodríguez
CASA PARTICULAR $

(Map p194; ☑ 69-55-16; Adela Azcuy No 43; r CUC$20-25) Oscar's something of a local legend for his role as the king of climbing in Viñales. Consequently his casa (with two private rooms) doubles up as a nexus for climbers who want to mix, mingle and plan sorties up the *mogotes*.

Villa Cafetal
CASA PARTICULAR $

(Map p194; ☑ 533-11752; Adela Azcuy Final; r CUC$15-20; ✺) The owners of this reader-recommended house are experts on climbing and have a shed stacked with equipment: appropriately, since the best climbs in Viñales are on their doorstep. Ensconced in a resplendent garden which cultivates its own coffee (yes, you get it for breakfast) you can practically taste the mountain air here as you swing on the hammock.

Villa Nelson
CASA PARTICULAR $

(Map p194; ☑ 79-61-94; villanelson@correodecuba.cu; Camilo Cienfuegos No 4; r CUC$20; ✺) Loquacious Nelson has been around for ages, having survived Gustav, Ike, high taxes and more. He still offers a prized local cocktail known as Ochún (rum, honey and orange juice) in his homely backyard along with two recently renovated rooms with baths.

Villa Purry & Isis
CASA PARTICULAR $

(Map p194; ☑ 69-69-21; Salvador Cisneros No 64; r CUC$20-25) This expansive colonial casa with two rooms on offer has a column-bedecked front terrace with rocking chairs to watch the world trundle by, and a rear patio too. It's a stone's throw from the plaza.

★ Hotel los Jazmines
HOTEL $$

(☑ 79-64-11; Carretera a Pinar del Río; s/d CUC$61/92; P ✺ ✺) Prepare yourself: the vista from this pastel-pink colonial-style hotel is one of the best and most quintessential in Cuba. Open the shutters of your classic valley-facing room and drink in the shimmering sight of magnificent *mogotes*,

oxen-ploughed red fields and palm frond-covered tobacco drying houses.

While no five-star palace, Los Jazmines benefits from its unrivaled location, gloriously inviting swimming pool and a host of handy extras such as international clinic, massage room and small shop/market. The setting comes at a cost: bus tours stop off here every hour or two, thus eroding some of the ethereal ambience. The hotel is walkable from Viñales: 4km south on the Pinar del Río road. The Viñales tour bus stops here.

La Ermita
HOTEL $$

(☑ 79-62-50; Carretera de La Ermita Km 1.5; s/d incl breakfast CUC$61/92; P ✺ ✺) While Los Jazmines might edge the prize for best view, La Ermita takes top honors for architecture, interior furnishings and all-round services and quality. It's also a lot less frenetic, thanks to the absence of any tour buses. Among a plethora of extracurricular attractions are an excellent pool, skillfully mixed cocktails, tennis courts, a shop, horseback riding and massage.

Rooms with views are housed in handsome two-story colonial edifices and the restaurant is an ideal perch for breakfast. You can walk the 2km downhill to the village or take the Viñales tour bus.

✗ Eating & Drinking

Viñales home-cooking is some of the best in Cuba – eat at your casa particular! As with many tourist towns, there has been an explosion of new paladares over the last two years including few good ones.

★ El Olivo
MEDITERRANEAN $

(Map p194; Salvador Cisneros No 89; pasta CUC$3-4; ◷ noon-11pm) Maybe you didn't come to Viñales to eat Mediterranean food, but there are exceptions to every rule – and you should make one for Olivo. The chef once worked in Italy and knocks out tremendous lasagna and pasta dishes backed up by other Med classics such as duck *à la orange* and gazpacho.

The joker in the pack is rabbit with herbs in a dark chocolate sauce. Service is slick with bread baskets and a free taster appetizer. Desserts go down nicely with a cappuccino.

Balcón del Valle
CUBAN $$

(meals CUC$6-8; ◷ noon-midnight) Never was a restaurant so aptly named as this one which really is a 'balcony over the valley' with three deftly constructed wooden decks overhanging a panorama of tobacco fields, drying houses and craggy *mogotes*.

With views like this, the food better be good, and the Balcón doesn't disappoint. The unwritten menu gives a four-way choice between chicken, pork, fish and lobster all prepared country-style with copious trimmings.

Restaurant Fernan-2 INTERNATIONAL $$
(Map p194; ☎ 60 66 28; Carretera a la Ermita Km 1; mains CUC$6-8; ☺ noon-midnight) Perched like a treehouse, Fernan-2 (the name is a pun on the Cuban way of saying two – 'do'), run by the ever-obliging Fernan-do, is a collection of fine details. Check out the water features made with old bottles and the terraced gardens and ponds. The food – which is plentiful, with an emphasis on rustic flavors – is equally splendid.

Restaurante la Casa de Don Tomás CUBAN, INTERNATIONAL $$
(Map p194; Salvador Cisneros No 140; mains around CUC$10; ☺ 10am-11pm) The oldest house in Viñales was once its best restaurant by default, but with new private competition, its mantle has slipped. Nonetheless, the casa, with its terra-cotta roof and exuberant flowering vines, remains a salubrious place to try *las delicias de Don Tomás*: rice, lobster, fish, pork, chicken and sausage with an egg on top (CUC$10).

☆ Entertainment

Centro Cultural Polo Montañez LIVE MUSIC
(Map p194; cnr Salvador Cisneros & Joaquin Pérez; admission after 9pm CUC$1) Named for the late Pinar del Río resident-turned-*guajiro* hero, Polo Montañez, this open-to-the-elements patio off the main plaza is a bar-restaurant with a full-blown stage and lighting rig that comes alive after 9pm.

Patio del Decimista LIVE MUSIC
(Map p194; Salvador Cisneros No 102; ☺ music at 9pm) Smaller than Centro Cultural Polo Montañez but equally ebullient is this long-standing place that serves live music, cold beers, snacks and great cocktails.

Cine Viñales CINEMA
(Map p194; cnr Ceferino Fernández & Rafael Trejo) The settlement's only cinema is a block south of the main square.

⬜ Shopping

Artex SOUVENIRS
(Map p194; Salvador Cisneros No 102) You can get postcards, T-shirts and CDs here. It's attached to the Patio del Decimista.

La Vega CIGARS, RUM
(Map p194; ☎ 79-60-80; Salvador Cisneros No 57; ☺ 9am-9pm) A hot selection of cigars – many made right on-site – and rum to go with it.

ⓘ Information

INTERNET ACCESS & TELEPHONE

Etecsa Telepunto (Ceferino Fernández No 3; internet per hr CUC$6; ☺ 8:30am-4:30pm) One of Cuba's tiniest Telepunto offices was being refurbished at last visit.

MEDICAL SERVICES

Farmacia Internacional (☎ 79-64-11) In Hotel los Jazmines.

MONEY

Banco de Crédito y Comercio (Salvador Cisneros No 58; ☺ 8am-noon & 1:30-3pm Mon-Fri, 8-11am Sat)

Cadeca (cnr Salvador Cisneros & Adela Azcuy; ☺ 8:30am-4pm Mon-Sat) Gives cash advances and changes traveler's checks at higher commissions than banks.

POST

Post Office (cnr Salvador Cisneros & Ceferino Fernández; ☺ 9am-6pm Mon-Sat) Relocated to a small booth near the park post Hurricane Gustav.

TOURIST INFORMATION

Infotur (Salvador Cisneros No 63B; ☺ 9:30am-5:30pm)

TRAVEL AGENCIES

Cubanacán (p195) arranges tours, excursions and transfer buses.

ⓘ Getting There & Around

BUS

The well-ordered **Víazul ticket office** (Salvador Cisneros No 63A; ☺ 8am-noon & 1-3pm) is opposite the main square in the same building as Cubataxi. The daily Víazul bus for Havana via Pinar del Río departs at 7:30am and 2pm (CUC$12). The morning bus continues to Cienfuegos (CUC$32, eight hours) and Trinidad (9½ hours). At the time of research only the second bus stopped in Las Terrazas.

Conectando buses run by Cubanacán have daily transfers to Havana (CUC$15), as well as Trinidad (CUC$37) via Cienfuegos. Book a day ahead. You may also be able to pick up transfers to Soroa and Las Terrazas. To get to Cayo Levisa or Cayo Jutías take the day-trip buses. A bus runs to María la Gorda (one way/return CUC$25/35; six minimum) if enough people book. It leaves Viñales at 7am and María La Gorda at 5pm.

CAR & MOPED

To reach Viñales from the south, take the long and winding road from Pinar del Río; the roads from the north coast are not as sinuous, but are pretty drives. The remote mountain road from the Península de Guanahacabibes through Guane and Pons is one of Cuba's most spectacular routes. Allow a lot of travel time.

Car hire can be arranged at **Cubacar** (⌂79-60-60; Salvador Cisneros No 63C; ⊙9am-7pm) in the Cubanacán office and **Havanautos** (⌂76-63-30; Salvador Cisneros final) opposite the Servi-Cupet gas station at the northeast end of Viñales town.

Mopeds can be rented for CUC$24 a day at Restaurante la Casa de Don Tomás.

TAXI

Cubataxi (⌂79-31-95; Salvador Cisneros No 63A) shares an office with Víazul. Drivers hanging around outside will take you to Pinar del Río for approximately CUC$15, Palma Rubia (for the boat to Cayo Levisa) for CUC$28 or Gran Caverna de Santo Tomás for CUC$13. Good value at around CUC$60 are the cabs to José Martí

DON'T MISS

VALLE DEL SILENCIO
....

When you've had your fill of the big city therapist, decamp to Viñales and book a stint in the Valle del Silencio for an alternative cure. This is the park's gentlest, least explored and – arguably – most picturesque valley, where the lion's share of the municipality's tobacco is grown. It gets its name from... well, sit on a rocking chair on a rustic porch at sunset at one of the valley's beautiful rustic *fincas* (farms) and you'll soon deduce how it got its name. Golden silence.

You can go it alone in the valley or hitch up with an organized excursion. Yoan and Yarelis Reyes in Viñales arrange a sublime sunset trip that ends at a beautiful eco-farm where you can banter with local farmers and share life-changing views of the sun's orb slipping behind the *mogotes* (limestone monoliths).

International Airport: the ride from Havana to the airport alone costs CUC$25.

For cheaper travel to Pinar, head to the intersection of the Carretera a Pinar del Río and Salvador Cisneros, just down from Restaurante la Casa de Don Tomás: old 1950s *colectivo* taxis splutter along the route for CUC$1 per seat.

VIÑALES BUS TOUR

The Viñales Bus Tour is a hop-on/hop-off minibus that runs nine times a day between the valley's spread-out sites. Starting and finishing in the town plaza, the whole circuit takes an hour and five minutes with the first bus leaving at 9am and the last at 4:50pm. There are 18 stops along the route, which runs from Hotel los Jazmines to Hotel Rancho San Vicente, and all are clearly marked with route maps and timetables. All-day tickets cost CUC$5 and can be purchased on the bus.

Parque Nacional Viñales

Parque Nacional Viñales' extraordinary cultural landscape covers 150 sq km and supports a population of 25,000 people. A mosaic of *mogote*-studded settlements grow coffee, tobacco, sugarcane, oranges, avocados and bananas on some of the oldest landscapes in Cuba.

⊙ Sights

Mural de la Prehistoria   RUIN
(admission incl drink CUC$3) Four kilometers west of Viñales village on the side of Mogote Dos Hermanas is a 120m-long painting designed in 1961 by Leovigildo González Morillo, a follower of Mexican artist Diego Rivera (the idea was hatched by Celia Sánchez, Alicia Alonso and Antonio Núñez Jiménez).

On a cliff at the foot of the 617m-high Sierra de Viñales, the highest portion of the Sierra de los Órganos, this massive mural took 18 people four years to complete. The huge snail, dinosaurs, sea monsters and humans on the cliff symbolize the theory of evolution and are either impressively psychedelic or monumentally horrific, depending on your point of view. You don't really have to get up close to appreciate the artwork, but the admission fee is waived if you take the delicious, if a little overpriced, CUC$15 lunch at the site restaurant. Horses are usually available here (CUC$5 per hour) for various excursions.

Los Aquáticos   VILLAGE
A kilometer beyond the turn-off to Dos Hermanas, a dirt road leads toward the mountain

community of Los Aquáticos, founded in 1943 by followers of visionary Antoñica Izquierdo, who discovered the healing power of water when the *campesinos* of this area had no access to conventional medicine. They colonized the mountain slopes and two families still live there. Los Aquáticos is accessible only by horse or on foot. Guided trips can be organized in Viñales.

You can also go it alone. Although there are no signs marking the path, there are plenty of homesteads en route where you can ask the way. From the main road follow a dirt road for approximately 400m before branching left and heading crosscountry. You should be able to pick out a blue house halfway up the mountain ahead of you. This is your goal. Once there, you can admire the view, procure drinks and chat to the amiable owners about the water cure. After your visit, you can make a loop by returning via Campismo Dos Hermanas and the cliff paintings; it's a wonderfully scenic route (the complete Los Aquáticos–Dos Hermanas circuit totals 6km from the main highway).

Cueva del Indio
CAVE

(admission CUC$5; ⊙9am-5:30pm) In a pretty nook 5.5km north of Viñales village, this cave is very popular with tourists. An ancient indigenous dwelling, it was rediscovered in 1920. Motor boats now ply the underground river through the electrically lit cave.

Cueva de San Miguel
CAVE

(admission CUC$1; ⊙9am-5:30pm) This is a small cave at the jaws of the Valle de San Vicente, the entrance of which is a bar/nightspot. Your entrance fee gets you into a gaping cave that engulfs you for five minutes or so before dumping you a tad cynically in the El Palenque de los Cimarrones restaurant on the other side.

🏃 Activities

Hiking

The Parque Nacional Viñales has four official hikes (five if you count the Gran Caverna de Santo Tomás) and others continually under 'consideration.' All of them can be arranged directly at the visitor center, the Museo Municipal or the town's tour agencies. The cost is CUC$6 to CUC$8 per person.

Below are just the official hikes. There are many more unofficial treks available and asking around at your casa particular will elicit further suggestions. Try the hike to Los Aquáticos with its incredible vistas; the

Valle de Viñales

Map of Valle de Viñales showing: El Ranchón (5km); Puerto Esperanza (18km); Hotel Rancho San Vicente; Cueva del Indio; Valle de San Vicente; Underground Trail; Sierra la Guasasa; Cueva de San Miguel; Underground River; Mogote la Esmeralda; Valle de la Guasasa; Mogote; Valle del Silencio; Valle de Palmarito; Mogote Dos Hermanas (400m); Mogote del Valle (402m); See Viñales Map (p194); Mogote Coco Solo; Mural de la Prehistoria; Campismo Dos Hermanas; VIÑALES; La Ermita; Valle de Viñales; La Casa del Veguero; El Naranjo (7.5km); Balcón del Valle; Parque Nacional Viñales Visitors Center; Hotel los Jazmines; Pinar del Río (26km)

See Viñales Map (p194)

Cueva de la Vaca, a cave that forms a tunnel through the *mogotes* and is easily accessible (1.5km) from Viñales village; and the **Valle de Palmarito**, infamous among in-the-know locals for its high-stakes cockfights.

Cocosolo Palmarito
HIKING

This walk starts on a spur road just before La Ermita hotel and progresses for 8km taking in the Valle del Silencio, the Coco Solo and Palmarito *mogotes* and the Mural de la Prehistoria. There are good views and plenty of opportunities to discover the local flora and fauna including a visit to a tobacco *finca* (farmhouse; ask about lunch with one of the families there).

It returns you to the main road back to Viñales.

Maravillas de Viñales
HIKING

A 5km loop beginning 1km before El Moncada and 13km from the Dos Hermanas turnoff, this hike takes in endemic plants,

CLIMBING IN VIÑALES

You don't need to be Reinhold Messner to recognize the unique climbing potential of Viñales, Cuba's mini-Yosemite. Sprinkled with steep-sided *mogotes* (limestone monoliths) and blessed with whole photo-albums' worth of stunning natural vistas, climbers from around the world have been coming here for over a decade to indulge in a sport that has yet to be officially sanctioned by the Cuban government.

Thanks to the numerous gray areas, Viñales climbing remains very much a word-of-mouth affair. There are no printed route maps and no official on-the-ground information (indeed, most state-employed tourist reps will deny all knowledge of it). If you are keen to get up onto the rock face, your first points of reference should be the comprehensive website of Cuba Climbing (p48) along with the book *Cuba Climbing* by Anibal Fernandez and Armando Menocal (2009). Once on the ground, the best nexus for climbers are Oscar Jaime Rodríguez and the Villa Cafetal casas in Viñales.

Viñales has numerous well-known climbing routes, including the infamous 'Wasp Factory,' and a handful of skillful Cuban guides, but there's no reliable equipment hire (bring your own) and there are no adequate safety procedures in place. Everything you do is at your own risk, and this includes any sticky situations you may encounter with the authorities, who don't officially condone climbing (although they generally tend to turn a blind eye). Also bear in mind that unregulated climbing in a national park area has the potential to damage endangered flora and ecosystems. Proceed with caution and care.

orchids and the biggest ant-cutter hive in Cuba (so they say).

San Vicente/Ancón   HIKING
The trail around the more remote Valle Ancón enables you to check out still-functioning coffee communities in a valley surrounded by *mogotes:* it's an 8km loop.

Cueva El Cable   HIKING
The park's newest hiking excursion is a 3.5km hike into a local cave typical of Viñales' karst topography.

Horseback Riding
The hills and valleys (and the *guajiros*) around town lend themselves to horseback riding, particularly the Valle de Palmarito and the route to Los Aquáticos. Ask at Villa los Reyes or the Mural de la Prehistoria.

Swimming
It is possible to swim in a natural pool at **La Cueva de Palmarito** in the Valle de Palmarito. This place is a doable hike/horseback ride from Viñales. Ask the locals for directions.

🛏 Sleeping

Campismo Dos Hermanas   CAMPISMO $
(Cubamar; ☎ 79-32-23; s/d CUC$9.5/13) Trapped between the sheer-sided jaws of the Dos Hermanas (literally 'two sisters') *mogotes* and in view of the Mural de la Prehistoria is one of Cubamar's best international campismos. Bonuses include a restaurant, pool

and horseback riding, and a couple of trails starting just outside the gate. The only incongruity is the loud music that spoils the tranquil ambience of this beautiful valley.

Hotel Rancho San Vicente   HOTEL $$
(☎ 79-62-01; Carretera a Esperanza Km 33; s/d CUC$55/80; P ❄ ☀) After Viñales' two spectacularly located hotels, you probably thought it couldn't get any better, but Rancho San Vicente does a good job trying. Situated 7km north of the village, this highly attractive hotel nestled in a grove with two dozen or more wooden cabins is lush and – for once – the interior furnishings match the magnificent setting.

There's a restaurant, pool, massage facility and short bird-watching hike on-site.

🍴 Eating & Drinking

★ El Ranchón   CUBAN $$
(Carretera a Esperanza Km 38; meals CUC$11; ⊙ 8am-5pm) Eat here! You won't forget the experience. The set meal, which is (judging by the crowds) a proverbial rite of passage on the tour bus circuit, is melt-in-your-mouth delicious. You pay CUC$11 for a huge traditional spread of roast pork and all the trimmings.

Restaurante Mural
de la Prehistoria   CUBAN, INTERNATIONAL $$
(set lunch CUC$15; ⊙ 8am-7pm) Steep but almost worth it, the Mural's humungous set

lunch – tasty pork roasted and smoked over natural charcoal – ought to keep you going at least until tomorrow's breakfast.

❶ Information

The park is administered through the highly informative **Parque Nacional Viñales Visitors Center** (☐79-61-44; Carretera a Pinar del Río Km 22; ☺8am-6pm) on the hill just before you reach Hotel los Jazmines. Inside, colorful displays (in Spanish and English) map out the park's main features. Hiking information and guides are also on hand.

❶ Getting Around

Bike, car, moped or the Viñales Bus Tour; take your pick.

West of Viñales

El Moncada, a pioneering post revolutionary workers' settlement lies 14km west of Dos Hermanas and 1.5km off the road to Minas de Matahambre. Here you'll find the greatest of Cuba's caves.

◉ Sights

Gran Caverna de Santo Tomás CAVES
(admission CUC$10; ☺8:30am-3pm) Welcome to Cuba's largest cave system and the second-largest on the American continent. There are over 46km of galleries on eight levels, with a 1km section accessible to visitors. There's no artificial lighting, but headlamps are provided for the 90-minute guided tour. Highlights include bats, stalagmites and stalactites, underground pools, interesting rock formations and a replica of an ancient native Indian mural.

Wear suitable shoes and be aware that the cave requires some steep climbs and scrambling over slippery rocks. Most people visit the cave on an organized trip from Viñales (CUC$21).

El Memorial 'Los Malagones' MONUMENT
Los Malagones, from the community of El Moncada, comprised the first rural militia in Cuba formed from 12 men who rooted out a counterrevolutionary band from the nearby mountains in 1959. A mausoleum and memorial fountain inaugurated in 1999 contains niches dedicated to the 12 militiamen (all but two are now dead).

It is crowned by a stone recreation of a famous photo of their leader, Leandro Rodríguez Malagón, taken by photographer Raúl Corrales in the early 1960s.

Museum MUSEUM
(admission CUC$1; ☺10am-10pm) The visitor center by the cave contains a small museum with ephemera relating to Cuban scientist Antonio Núñez Jiménez who studied Santo Tomás in depth.

THE NORTHERN COAST

Considering their relative proximity to Havana, Pinar del Río province's northern shores are remote and largely unexplored. Facilities are sparse and roads are rutted on the isolated Gulf of Mexico coast, though visitors who take the time to make the journey out have reported memorable DIY adventures and famously hospitable locals.

Cayo Jutías

Pinar del Río's most discovered 'undiscovered' beach is the 3km-long blanket of sand that adorns the northern coast of Cayo Jutías, a tiny mangrove-covered key situated approximately 65km northwest of Viñales and attached to the mainland by a short *pedraplén* (causeway). Jutías – named for its indigenous tree rats – vies with Cayo Levisa to the east for the title of the province's most picturesque beach and, while the latter might be prettier, the former has less crowds and more tranquility.

The serenity is thanks to the lack of any permanent accommodations (unlike Levisa). The only facilities on the island are the thatched oceanside **Restaurante Cayo Jutías** (☺11am-5pm), specializing in local seafood, and a small **dive center** that rents out kayaks for CUC$1 per hour, runs boat trips and snorkeling trips for CUC$12, and organizes diving from CUC$37 for one immersion (there are seven dive sites nearby). Beyond the initial arc of sand the beach continues for 3km; you can hike barefoot through the mangroves. The cayo's access road starts about 4km west of Santa Lucía. Four kilometers further on you'll come to a control post at the beginning of the causeway where you'll need to pay a CUC$5 per person entry fee. Ten minutes later the **Faro de Cayo Jutías** appears; this metal lighthouse was built by the US in 1902. The route ends at the white Jutías beach caressed by crystal-clear water, 12.5km from the coastal highway.

Tours from Viñales (basically just transport and a snack lunch) cost CUC$22 and will give you an adequate six hours' beach time. Otherwise you will have to make your own transport arrangements. The fastest, and by far the prettiest, route is via Minas de Matahambre, through rolling pine-clad hills.

Puerto Esperanza

Puerto Esperanza (Port of Hope), 6km north of San Cayetano and 25km north of Viñales, is a sleepy fishing village visited sometimes by yachts sailing around the country and, mostly, by absolutely no one. According to town lore, the giant mango trees lining the entry road were planted by slaves in the 1800s. A long pier pointing out into the bay is decent for a jump in the ocean. Otherwise the clocks haven't worked here since…oh…1951.

☉ Sights & Activities

This is the kind of low-key sort of place where it's more fun to unravel the social life on your own. Discover some weirdly transcendental Santería ritual or take a spontaneous tour around your neighbor's tobacco plantation in search of pungent peso cigars.

⏣ Sleeping & Eating

Teresa Hernández Martínez CASA PARTICULAR $
(☑ 79-37-03; Calle 4 No 7; r CUC$15.20) The charismatic Teresa is as colorful as her three bright and clean rooms furnished unsubtly in lurid pink, blue and green. She also runs a paladar in a jungle-like garden out back where fish headlines the menu.

Villa Leonila Blanco CASA PARTICULAR $
(☑ 79-39-49; Frank País No 52A, cnr Hermanos Caballeros; r CUC$15-20; ❄) Two big rooms with bathrooms, garage and meals.

❶ Getting There & Away

There's a handy Servi-Cupet gas station at San Cayetano. The road to Santa Lucía and Cayo Jutías deteriorates to dirt outside of San Cayetano: expect a throbbing backside if you're on a bike or moped.

Cayo Levisa

More frequented than Cayo Jutías but equally splendid, Cayo Levisa sports a beach-bungalow-style hotel, basic restaurant and fully equipped diving center, yet still manages to feel relatively isolated. Separation from the mainland obviously helps. Unlike other Cuban keys, there's no causeway here, and visitors must make the 35-minute journey by boat from Palma Rubia. It's a well worthwhile trip: 3km of sugar-white sand and sapphire waters earmark Cayo Levisa as Pinar del Río's best beach. American writer Ernest Hemingway first 'discovered' the area, part of the Archipiélago de los Colorados, in the early 1940s after he set up a fishing camp on Cayo Paraíso, a smaller coral island 10km to the east. These days Levisa attracts up to 100 visitors daily as well as the 50-plus hotel guests. While you won't feel like an errant Robinson Crusoe here, you should find time (and space) for plenty of rest and relaxation.

☉ Sights & Activities

Levisa has a small marina offering scuba diving for CUC$40 per immersion, including gear and transport to the dive site. Fourteen dive sites are peppered off the coast, including towering coral *mogotes* and the popular **Corona de San Carlos** (San Carlos' Crown), the formation of which allows divers to get close to turtles and the like unobserved. Snorkeling plus gear costs CUC$12 and a sunset cruise goes for the same price. Kayaking and aqua biking are also possible.

⏣ Sleeping & Eating

Hotel Cayo Levisa HOTEL $$
(☑ 75-65-03; cabins from CUC$90; ❄) With an idyllic tropical beach just outside your front door, you won't worry about the slightly outdated *cabañas* (cabins) and dull food choices here. Expanded to a 40-room capacity in 2006, the Levisa's newer wooden cabins (all with bathroom) are an improvement on the old concrete blocks and the service has pulled its socks up too. Book ahead as this place is understandably popular.

❶ Getting There & Away

The landing for Cayo Levisa is around 21km northeast of La Palma or 40km west of Bahía Honda. Take the turnoff to Mirian and proceed 4km through a large banana plantation to reach the coast-guard station at Palma Rubia, where there is a snack bar (open 10am to 6pm) and the departure dock for the island. The Cayo Levisa boat leaves at 10am and returns at 5pm, and costs CUC$25 per person round-trip (CUC$10 one way) including lunch. From the Cayo Levisa dock you cross the mangroves on a wooden walkway to the resort and gorgeous beach along the island's north side. If you are without a car, the easiest way to get here is via a day excursion from Viñales, good value at CUC$29 including the boat and lunch.

SAN DIEGO DE LOS BAÑOS & AROUND

Halfway between Viñales and Soroa, San Diego de los Baños is a famous spa town but there's more to this area than mud baths and massages. Stop by for some memorable wildlife-watching and to discover one of Che Guevara's old hideaways.

San Diego de los Baños

Sitting 130km southwest of Havana, this nondescript town just north of the Carretera Central is popularly considered the country's best spa location. As with other Cuban spas, its medicinal waters were supposedly 'discovered' in the early colonial period when a sick slave stumbled upon a sulfurous spring, took a revitalizing bath and was miraculously cured. Thanks to its proximity to Havana, San Diego's fame spread quickly and a permanent spa was established here in 1891. During the early 20th century American tourists flocked here, leading to the development of the current hotel-bathhouse complex in the early 1950s.

Sitting beside the Río San Diego, the village enjoys an attractive natural setting, with the Sierra del Rosario to the east, the Sierra de Güira to the west, and a nature reserve with pine, mahogany and cedar forests. It's a favorite spot for bird-watchers. The town, despite numerous possibilities for tourism, has been long due an overhaul by the authorities, who have let it slump into an amiable, leafy lethargy.

👁 Sights & Activities

Balneario San Diego   THERMAL BATHS
(⊙8am-5pm) Undergoing refurbishment until late 2013 (at least!), the Balneario is a decrepit-looking bathing complex where thermal waters of 30°C to 40°C are used to treat muscular and skin afflictions. The sulfurous waters of these mineral springs are potent and immersions of only 20 minutes per day are allowed. Mud from the Río San Diego is also used here for revitalizing mud baths.

Other health services include massage and a 15-day course of acupuncture; don't expect fluffy towels and complimentary cups of coffee. The Balneario San Diego is more like a Moroccan hammam than a five-star hotel facility, though it's perennially popular with Cubans undergoing courses of medical treatment, plus the odd curious tourist.

If you're looking for cold water, you can swim at the Hotel Mirador **pool** (admission CUC$1; ⊙9am-6pm).

Bird-Watching & Hiking
Bird-watching and hiking trips into Parque la Güira can be organized at Hotel Mirador with qualified guide, **Julio César Hernández** (📞54-89-46; carpeta@mirador.sandiego.co.cu). All-day excursions start at CUC$10 but you'll need your own wheels.

OFF THE BEATEN TRACK

MIL CUMBRES

On the eastern flank of the Cordillera de Guaniguanico lies Mil Cumbres, a protected area of 'managed resources' that is being tentatively opened up to tourism. Little visited as yet, the region abuts Parque la Güira and contains western Cuba's highest peak, the distinctive 699m-high **Pan de Guajaibón** which you can climb (with a guide). A bust of Independence War general, Antonio Maceo, and an abandoned radar station are perched on the summit. Other possible trails include the short **Regreso al Jurásico** (Return to the Jurassic era), so-named for the cork palms that grow amid ancient geological formations. The metal-rich soils here have led to a high level of floral endemism (there's a wild orchid farm and a pine forest nearby) which, in turn, attracts multiple bird species. The reserve's nexus is a field station bivouacked in an old wooden coffee planter's house situated approximately 20km east of the town of La Palma. Rustic accommodations are available in a series of double rooms and cabins. Inquire ahead of time with **Ecotur** (📞79-61-20; ecoturpr@enet.cu).

🛏 Sleeping & Eating

Hotel Mirador   HOTEL $
(📞 54-88-66, 77-83-38; s/d CUC$23/36, grill meals under CUC$8; 🅿 ❋ ⛱) The Mirador is a low-key stopoff. Predating the Revolution by five years, the hotel was built in 1954 to accommodate spa-seekers headed for the adjacent Balneario San Diego. Well-tended terraced gardens slope up to rooms which match the pretty exterior: crisp, cozy and looking for the most part onto balconies with garden and *balneario* views.

Downstairs there's a pleasant swimming pool and an outdoor grill that does whole roast pig on a spit. There's also a proper restaurant *con una vista* (with a view) inside serving Cuban cuisine.

Villa Julio & Cary   CASA PARTICULAR $
(📞 54-80-37; Calle 29 No 4009; r CUC$20-25) The town's only casa is a not unpleasant nook with a small garden, colorful mural and porches (with rockers) guarding clean, tidy rooms, all within spitting distance of Hotel Mirador.

Parque la Güira

With rough roads and precious little accommodations, the untamed Sierra de Güira, a medley of limestone karst cliffs and swooping pockets of forest west of San Diego de los Baños, is off the tourist radar. This didn't prevent it becoming a retreat for the Revolution's most renowned figures in the past and, to this day, a host of rare birdlife.

◉ Sights

Hacienda Cortina   RUIN
Five kilometers west of San Diego de los Baños sprawls surreal Parque la Güira, an abandoned – and vaguely spooky – country mansion surrounded by 219-sq-km of protected parkland.

Known formerly as the Hacienda Cortina, this rich-man's-fantasy-made-reality was built in the style of a giant urban park during the 1920s and 1930s by wealthy lawyer José Manuel Cortina who plunked a stately home in its midst. Various remnants of the estate remain – most notably the grand crenellated entry gate, along with a gatehouse, the ruins of a Chinese pavilion and huge clusters of bamboo. Wander around to soak up the atmosphere; the complex behind the unimpressive state-operated restaurant (1km beyond the gate and closed at the time of research) is reserved for vacationing military personnel. You'll need your own wheels to get here. Isolation has allowed the park to become an important refuge for birds like the olive-capped warbler and Cuban solitaire: the Hotel Mirador in San Diego de los Baños runs tours.

Cabañas los Pinos   HISTORIC SITE
Twelve kilometers west of San Diego de los Baños via Parque la Güira is the Cabañas los Pinos, an abandoned mountain retreat used by Castro's secretary Celia Sánchez in the 1960s. The cabins are built like tree houses above the ground with Sánchez' circular abode standing in the center of the eerie complex.

It's another rather surreal curiosity that gets few visitors but is worth a spare hour or two of silent contemplation. Ask at Hotel Mirador for directions.

Cueva de los Portales   CAVE
(admission CUC$1) During the October 1962 Cuban Missile Crisis, Ernesto 'Che' Guevara transferred the headquarters of the Western Army to this rather spectacular cave, 11km west of Parque la Güira and 16km north of Entronque de Herradura on the Carretera Central. The cave is set in a beautiful remote area among steep-sided vine-covered *mogotes* and was declared a national monument in the 1980s.

A small outdoor museum contains a few of Che's roughshod artifacts including his bed and the table where he played chess (while the rest of the world stood at the brink of nuclear Armageddon). Three other caves called El Espejo, El Salvador and Cueva Oscura are up on the hillside. Again, this area is brilliant bird-watching turf: trips can be arranged at the Hotel Mirador, or you can ask the staff at the cave entrance. There's a campismo and small restaurant outside the cave. Both have been closed since Hurricanes Gustav and Ike.

❶ Getting Around

Ask the Havana–Pinar del Río Víazul drivers nicely and they may stop at the Carretera Central turnoff 10km from town. The walk isn't too bad. There's a Servi-Cupet gas station at the entrance to San Diego de los Baños from Havana. The road across the mountains from Cabañas los Pinos and Che Guevara's cave is beautiful, but precariously narrow and full of potholes. That said; a brave driver or super fit (and careful) cyclist should make it.

Matanzas Province

📞 45 / POP 692,536

Best Outdoor Adventures

➜ Wildlife-watching on Río Hatiguanico (p237)

➜ Diving in the Bahía de Cochinos (p239)

➜ Boat trip on Río Canímar (p210)

Best Casas Particulares

➜ Hostal Azul (p212)

➜ Hostal Luis (p240)

➜ Hostal Ida (p231)

➜ El Caribeño (p238)

Why Go?

With a name translating as 'massacres,' Matanzas province conceals an appropriately tumultuous past beneath its modern-day reputation for glam all-inclusive holidays. In the 17th century pillaging pirates ravaged the region's prized north coast, while three centuries later, more invaders grappled ashore in the Bahía de Cochinos (Bay of Pigs) under the dreamy notion that they were about to liberate the nation.

The Bahía de Cochinos attracts more divers than mercenaries these days, while sunbathers rather than pirates invade the northern beaches of Varadero, the vast Caribbean resort and lucrative economic 'cash cow' that stretches 20km along the sandy Península de Hicacos.

Providing a weird juxtaposition is the scruffy city of Matanzas, the mildewed but music-rich provincial capital that has gifted the world with rumba, *danzón* and countless grand neoclassical buildings. Santería is rife both here and in other nearby cities where tourists are scant but soulful, only-in-Cuba experiences are surprisingly abundant.

When to Go

➜ December through April the all-inclusive hotels in the province's tourist set-piece, Varadero, hike prices for the *temporada alta* (high season).

➜ High season is the best time for beach-basking: the hurricane season is over and the weather is hot without being unbearable.

➜ Hit Matanzas city around October 10 for the annual rumba festival.

NORTHERN MATANZAS

Home to Cuba's largest resort area (Varadero) and one of its biggest ports (Matanzas), the northern coastline is also the province's main population center and a hub for industry and commerce. Despite this, the overriding feel is distinctly green, and most of the region is undulating farmland – think a cross between North American prairie and the UK's Norfolk Broads – occasionally rupturing into lush, dramatic valleys like the Valle de Yumurí.

Matanzas

POP 152,408

Once radiant and beautiful, Matanzas has aged terribly since the Revolution; now its

Matanzas Province Highlights

❶ Unlock the buried secrets of dusty **Matanzas**, the 'Athens of Cuba' (p206).

❷ Check out a performance at Matanzas' resplendent **Teatro Sauto** (p213).

❸ Immerse yourself in the crystalline waters of **Playa Coral** (p211) for a spot of snorkeling.

❹ Go tandem skydiving over diamond-dusted **Varadero** (p215).

❺ Admire forgotten grandeur in **San Miguel de los Baños** (p233).

❻ Explore the vast, varied vegetation zones of the **Ciénaga de Zapata** (p236).

❼ Discover the plunging drop-offs and colorful coral walls while diving off **Playa Larga** (p237).

outward countenance seems to belie four centuries of illustrious history when, thanks to a gigantic literary and musical heritage, it was regularly touted as the 'Athens of Cuba.' With its battle-scarred buildings and cars belching out asphyxiating diesel fumes, contemporary Matanzas is a long way from the vacation glitter of Varadero; though there's dignity amid the dilapidation. If the city were a character it would be the fisherman, Santiago, in Hemingway's *The Old Man and the Sea*. 'thin and gaunt with deep wrinkles' yet, irrepressibly 'cheerful and undefeated.'

Two pivotal Cuban musical forms, *danzón* and rumba, were hatched here among Matanzas' erstwhile splendor, along with various religions of African origin, including Arará, Regla de Ocha (Santería) and the secret Abakuá fraternity (see boxed text, p211). Matanzas is also the home of Cuba's finest provincial theater (the Sauto), and was the birthplace of some its most eloquent poets and writers. Today, the city offers little in the way of standard sights, but plenty of under-the-radar pleasures. Join a spontaneous game of dominoes in Plaza Libertad, or listen to some *bembe* drummers in the Marina neighborhood, and you'll quickly ascertain that Matanzas' greatest strength is its people, a proud, poetic populace infused with the spirit of stoic survivors. Welcome to the real Cuba, *asere*.

History

In 1508 Sebastián de Ocampo sighted a bay that the indigenous population called Guanima. Now known as the Bahía de Matanzas, it's said the name recalls the *matanza* (massacre) of a group of Spaniards during an early indigenous uprising. In 1628 the Dutch pirate Piet Heyn captured a Spanish treasure fleet carrying 12 million gold florins, ushering in a lengthy era of smuggling and piracy. Undeterred by the pirate threat, 30 families from the Canary Islands arrived in 1693, on the orders of King Carlos III of Spain, to found the town of San Carlos y Severino de Matanzas; the first fort went up in 1734. In 1898 the bay saw the first engagement of the Spanish-American War.

In the late 18th and 19th centuries, Matanzas flourished through the building of numerous sugar mills and coffee exporting. In 1843, with the laying of the first railway to Havana, the floodgates for prosperity were opened. The second half of the 19th century became a golden age: the city set new cul-

MATANZAS STREET NAMES

Matanzas residents ignore the numbering system of their streets and continue to use the old colonial street names. However, here we have used the numbers because that's what you'll see on street corners.

OLD NAME	NEW NAME
Contreras	Calle 79
Daoíz	Calle 75
Maooo	Callo 77
Medio/Independencia	Calle 85
Milanés	Calle 83
San Luis	Calle 298
Santa Teresa	Calle 290
Zaragoza	Calle 202

tural benchmarks with the development of a newspaper, a public library, a high school, a theater and a philharmonic society. Due to the large number of writers and intellectuals living in the area, Matanzas became known as the 'Athens of Cuba' with a cultural scene that dwarfed even Havana.

It was then that African slaves, imported to meet burgeoning labor demands, began to foster another reputation for Matanzas as the spiritual home of rumba. In tandem, and from the same roots, spread a network of Santería *cabildos* (associations) – brotherhoods of those from slave descent who came together to celebrate the traditions and rituals of their African ancestors. Both rumba and *cabildos* flourish here to this day.

Other landmarks in Matanzas' history include staging Cuba's first *danzón* performance (1879); later the city produced nationally important poets Cintio Vitier and Carilda Oliver Labra.

Sights & Activities

City Center

Teatro Sauto THEATER
(24-27-21; Plaza de la Vigía) The defining symbol of the city according to Mexican painter (and admirer) Diego Rivera, the Teatro Sauto (1863) on the plaza's south side is one of Cuba's finest theaters and famous for its superb acoustics. The lobby is graced by marble Greek goddesses and the ceiling in the main hall bears paintings of the muses.

Three balconies enclose this 775-seat theater, which features a floor that can

Matanzas

N

0 — 500 m
0 — 0.25 miles

VERSALLES

Iglesia de
Monserrate (900m)

Carretera Yumurí

Río Yumurí

C 278

C 57

C 266

C 270

Hershey Train
Station

C 67

C 71

Castillo de San
Severino (1.7km)

**MATANZAS
ESTE**

C 278

C 300

C 298

C 294

C 292

C 290

C 288

C 282

C 280

Puente de la
Concordia

C 61

Bahía de
Matanzas

C 77

C 276

C 79

2 18 27

14

25

C 272

MATANZAS

C 83

Parque
Libertad

9

1

19

8

Puente
Calixto
García

C 85

16 15

7

3

20

26

13

10

12

C 91

21

Bus 12 to Iglesia
de Monserrate &
Cuevas de Bellamar

23

5

Plaza de
la Vigía

C 93

17

Puente Calixto
García

C 95

22

Río San Juan

4

24

Vía Blanca

C 97

C 97

C 105

C 109

Costa Bella (2km);
Río Canímar (8km)

C 115

Estadio Victoria
de Girón (600m)

C 117

C 272

C 268

C 264

Av Martín Dihigo

C 298

**PUEBLO
NUEVO**

Las Palmas (300m)

C 127

C 171

C 131

National
Bus Station

C 226

11

C 171

C 276

be raised to convert the auditorium into a ballroom. The original theater curtain is a painting of Matanzas' very own Puente de la Concordia, and notables like Soviet dancer Anna Pavlova have performed here. Much-needed restoration work was ongoing as of early 2013. Performances are generally Friday and Saturday nights and Sunday afternoons.

Puente Calixto García BRIDGE
If you've only got time to see *one* bridge (there are 21 in total) in Cuba's celebrated 'city of bridges,' gravitate toward this impressive steel structure built in 1899, spanning the Río San Juan with its kayaks floating lazily by. Just south is an eye-catching **Che Mural** while the northern side leads directly into Plaza de la Vigía.

Plaza de la Vigía SQUARE
The original Plaza de Armas still remains as Plaza de la Vigía (literally 'lookout place'), a reference to the threat from piracy and smuggling that the first settlers faced. This diminutive square was where Matanzas was founded in the late 17th century and numerous historical buildings still stand guard.

Ediciones Vigía CULTURAL BUILDING
(Plaza de la Vigía, cnr Calle 91; ⊙9am-6pm) To the southwest of Plaza de la Vigía is a unique book publisher, founded in 1985 that produces high-quality handmade paper and first-edition books on a variety of topics. The books are typed, stenciled and pasted in editions of 200 copies. Visitors are welcome in the Dickensian workshop where they can purchase numbered and signed copies (CUC$5 to CUC$15).

Museo Histórico Provincial MUSEUM
(cnr Calles 83 & 272; admission CUC$2; ⊙10am-6pm Tue-Fri, 1-7pm Sat, 9am-noon Sun) Also known as Palacio del Junco (1840), this double-arched edifice on the Plaza de la Vigía showcases the full sweep of Matanzas' history from 1693 to the present. Cultural events are also held here.

Museo Farmacéutico MUSEUM
(Calle 83 No 4951; admission CUC$3; ⊙10am-6pm Mon-Sat, 8am-noon Sun) On Parque Libertad – Matanzas' modern nexus with a bronze statue (1909) of José Martí in its center – you'll find Museo Farmacéutico, one of the city's showcase sights. Founded in 1882 by the Triolett family, the antique pharmacy was the first of its type in Latin America. The fine displays include all the odd bottles, instruments and suchlike used in the trade.

Biblioteca Gener y Del Monte NOTABLE BUILDING
(cnr Calles 79 & 290) Matanzas' library, formerly the Casino Español, is on the northern side of Parque Libertad beside the grandiose peach facade of Hotel Velazco. The library was where the first performance of the *danzonete* (ballroom dance) *Rompiendo la Rutina,* by Anceto Díaz, took place.

Catedral de San Carlos Borromeo   CHURCH

(Calle 282, btwn Calles 83 & 85; donation welcome; ⊙8am-noon & 3-5pm Mon-Sat, 9am-noon Sun) Standing back from the disorganized melée of Calle 83 behind shady Plaza de la Iglesia, this once-great, perennially shut, neoclassical cathedral was constructed in 1693 and contains some of Cuba's most famous frescoes, suffering terribly after years of neglect.

Archivo Histórico   NOTABLE BUILDING

(Calle 83 No 28013, btwn Calles 280 & 282) The city archives are housed in the former residence of local poet José Jacinto Milanés (1814–63). A bronze statue of Milanés stands on the nearby Plaza de la Iglesia in front of the cathedral.

Palacio de Gobierno   NOTABLE BUILDING

(Calle 288, btwn Calles 79 & 83) Dating from 1853, this muscular building dominates the east side of Parque Libertad; these days it's the seat of the Poder Popular (Popular Power), the local government.

Palacio de Justicia   NOTABLE BUILDING

(Plaza de la Vigía & Calle 85) This is another impressive construction on the Plaza de la Vigía opposite the Teatro Sauto, first erected in 1826 and rebuilt between 1908 and 1911.

Palmar del Junco   SPORTS VENUE

(Calle 171) Baseball fans can make the pilgrimage to the south of the city, the site of Cuba's first baseball field (1904) and a source of much civic pride.

⊙ Versalles & the North

North of the Río Yumurí, Versalles is the birthplace of rumba (see boxed text p214). From the Plaza de la Vigía you enter the *barrio* (neighborhood) by taking Calle 272 across graceful **Puente de la Concordia**.

Castillo de San Severino   FORT

(☑28-32-59; Av del Muelle; ⊙10am-7pm Tue-Sat, 9am-noon Sun) Northeast of Versalles lies this formidable crenellation built by the Spanish in 1735 as part of Cuba's defensive ring. Slaves were offloaded here in the 18th century and, later, Cuban patriots were imprisoned within the walls – and sometimes executed. San Severino remained a prison until the 1970s and in more recent times has become the scantly populated slavery-themed **Museo de la Ruta de los Esclavos** (admission CUC$2; ⊙10am-6pm).

The castle itself, with its well-preserved central square, has great views of the Bahía de Matanzas. A taxi from the city center costs CUC$2.

Iglesia de Monserrate   CHURCH

For a view of mildewed Matanzas and the broccoli green Valle de Yumurí, climb 1.5km northeast of the center up Calle 306 to the recently renovated church dating from 1875. The lofty bastion perched high above the city was built by colonists from Catalonia in Spain as a symbol of their regional power.

The **lookout** near here has a couple of *ranchón*-style restaurants good for skull-splitting music and basic refreshments.

Iglesia de San Pedro Apóstol   CHURCH

(cnr Calles 57 & 270) In the heart of Versalles, this neoclassical church is another Matanzas jewel that has recently benefited from a full renovation.

⊙ Outside Town

Cuevas de Bellamar   CAVE

(☑25-35-38, 26-16-83; admission CUC$8, camera CUC$5; ⊙9am-5pm) Cuba's oldest tourist attraction, according to local propaganda, lies 5km southeast of Matanzas and is 300,000 years old. There are 2500m of caves here, discovered in 1861 by a Chinese workman in the employ of Don Manual Santos Parga. A 45-minute Cuevas de Bellamar visit leaves almost hourly starting at 9:30am.

Well-maintained, well-lit paths mean it's easy for kids to imbibe the stupendous geology, too. The caves on show include a vast 12m stalagmite and an underground stream; cave walls glitter eerily with crystals. The entrance is through a small museum. Outside the Cuevas de Bellamar are two restaurants and a playground. To get there, take bus 12 from Plaza Libertad or use the Matanzas Bus Tour connecting to Varadero.

Río Canímar & Around   RIVER

Boat trips on the Río Canímar, 8km east of Matanzas, are a truly magical experience. Gnarly mangroves dip their jungle-like branches into the ebbing water and a warm haze caresses the regal palm trees as your boat slides silently 12km upstream from an insalubrious start beneath the Vía Blanca bridge.

Cubamar in Varadero offers this wonderful excursion with lunch, horseback riding, fishing and snorkeling for CUC$25, or you can chance it by showing up at the landing below the bridge on the east side. Rowboats

(CUC$2 per hour) are also available for rent from Bar Cubamar though not to Cubans (on the pretext that they might use them to emigrate).

Castillo del Morrillo   CASTLE
(admission CUC$1; ☺9am-5pm Tue-Sun) On the Matanzas side of the Río Canímar bridge, a road runs 1km down to a cove presided over by the four guns of this yellow-painted castle (1720). The castle is now a museum dedicated to the student leader Antonio Guiteras Holmes (1906–35), who founded the revolutionary group Joven Cuba (Young Cuba) in 1934.

After serving briefly in the post-Machado government, Guiteras was forced out by army chief Fulgencio Batista and shot on May 8, 1935. A bronze bust marks the spot where he was executed.

Playa Coral   BEACH
With no reefs accessible from the coast in Varadero, your closest bet for a bit of shore **snorkeling** is the aptly named Playa Coral on the old coastal road (about 3km off the Vía Blanca) halfway between Matanzas and Varadero. Although you can snorkel solo from the beach itself, it's far better (and safer) to enter via the **Laguna de Maya** (open 8am to 5pm).

At the **Flora and Fauna Reserve**, 400m east of the beach, professional Ecotur guides rent snorkeling gear and take you out to the reef at a bargain CUC$5 for one hour plus CUC$2 equipment hire. There are a reported 300 species of fish here and visibility is a decent 15m to 20m. Diving is on offer too. The Laguna de Maya also incorporates a snack bar-restaurant by the eponymous lake nearby with boat rental and horseback-riding opportunities. A package including

ABAKUÁ

A secret all-male society, a language understood only by initiates, a close-knit network of masonic-like lodges and the symbolic use of the African leopard to denote power: the mysterious rites of Abakuá read like a Cuban Da Vinci Code.

In a country not short on foggy religious practices, Abakuá is perhaps the least understood. It's a complicated mixture of initiations, dances, chants and ceremonial drumming that testifies to the remarkable survival of African culture in Cuba since the slave era.

Not to be confused with Santería or other syncretized African religions, Abakuá's traditions were brought to Cuba by enslaved Efik people from the Calabar region of southeastern Nigeria in the 18th and 19th centuries. Organizing themselves into 'lodges' or *juegos*, the first of which was formed in the Havana suburb of Regla in 1836, Abakuá acted as a kind of African mutual aid society made up primarily of black dock workers whose main goal was to help buy their tribal brethren out of slavery.

In the early days, Abakuá lodges were necessarily anti-slavery and anti-colonialist and were suppressed by the Spanish. Nonetheless, by the 1860s, the lodges were increasingly admitting white members and finding that their strength lay in their secretiveness and invisibility.

Today, there are thought to be over 100 Abakuá lodges in Cuba, some up to 600-strong, based primarily in Havana, Matanzas and Cárdenas (the practice never penetrated central or eastern Cuba). Initiates are known as *ñáñigos* and their intensely secret ceremonies take place in a temple known as a *famba*. Although detailed information about the brotherhood is scant, Abakuá is well-known to the outside world for its masked dancers called *Ireme* (devils) who showcase their skills in various annual carnivals and were instrumental in the development of the *guaguancó* style of rumba. Cuba's great abstract artist, Wifredo Lam, used Abakuá masks in his paintings, and composer, Amadeo Roldán, incorporated its rhythms into classical music.

While there is a strong spiritual and religious element to the brotherhood (forest deities and the leopard symbol are important), it differs from the more widespread Santería religion in that it is does not hide its deities behind Catholic saints. Cuban anthropologist, Fernando Ortíz, once referred to Abakuá societies as a form of 'African masonry' while other researchers have suggested it acts like a separate state within a nation with its owns laws and language. The casual Cuban word '*asere*' meaning 'mate' is actually derived from the Abakuá term for 'ritual brother.'

MATANZAS PROVINCE MATANZAS

all the activities is offered for CUC$25. Most of the coast hereabouts is a gray-white coral shelf but there are beaches just west of Playa Coral.

Cuevas de Santa Catalina
CAVE

(combined admission with Cuevas de Bellamar CUC$15; ☉9am-5pm) A less-visited cave system off the Matanzas–Varadero highway near Boca de Camarioca, where highlights include Amerindian cave paintings. Organize trips at the Cuevas de Bellamar or ask at one of the Varadero all-inclusive accommodations (see p221).

Cueva Saturno
CAVE

(☏25-32-72; admission incl snorkel gear CUC$5; ☉8am-6pm) One kilometer south of the Vía Blanca, near the airport turnoff, is the freshwater Cueva Saturno, a highly popular (read: crowded) subterranean cave with a pool billed as a **snorkeling** and/or **swimming** spot. The water's about 20°C and the maximum depth is 22m, though there are shallower parts. There's a snack bar and equipment rental post on-site.

🎓 Courses

Casa del Danzón
DANCING

(Calle 85, btwn Calle 280 & Plaza de la Vigía) If you fancy learning some local dance steps, enquire here as it offers weekend *danzón* classes.

🎉 Festivals & Events

Festival del Bailador Rumbero
MUSIC

During the 10 days following October 10, Matanzas rediscovers its rumba roots with talented local musicians at the Festival del Bailador Rumbero, taking place in the Teatro Sauto. This coincides with the anniversary of the city's founding (October 12), a multiday party which includes celebrations of luminaries who have made the city what it is (or was).

Carnaval
CARNIVAL

Carnaval in Matanzas every August doesn't quite reach the dizzying heights of Santiago but it's still a lively affair.

🛏 Sleeping

🛏 City Center

Matanzas complements its one period hotel with a handful of equally retro casas particulares.

★ Hostal Azul
CASA PARTICULAR $

(☏24-24-49; hostalazul.cu@gmail.com; Calle 83 No 29012, btwn Calles 290 & 292; r CUC$20-25; ❄) With a front door large enough to ride an elephant through, this handsome blue house dating from the 1890s is a veritable palace with original tiled floors, an antique wooden spiral staircase and four castle-sized rooms set around a spacious alfresco patio.

Even better, multilingual owner, Joel, is a true gent and happy to offer his sturdy 1984 Lada for taxi duty.

Hostal Alma
CASA PARTICULAR $

(☏29-08-57; hostalalma@gmail.com; Calle 83 No 29008, btwn Calles 290 & 292; r CUC$20-25; ❄) A house with *mucha alma* (soul), Mayra's place has Seville-invoking *azulejos* (tiles), relaxing rocking chairs, and rainbow *vitrales* (stained glass) that refract colored light across the tiled floors. You can enjoy a welcome cocktail on one of its two terraces while surveying Matanzas' semi-ruined rooftops. There are three spiffy rooms.

Hostal Río
CASA PARTICULAR $

(☏24-30-41; hostalrio.cu@gmail.com; Calle 91 No 29018, btwn Calles 290 & 292; r CUC$20-25; ❄) A new renter, this house is owned by the parents of Joel, star of Hostal Azul, so it comes with good recommendations. There are two comfortable rooms in a good location. Meals are served at Hostal Azul.

Evelio & Isel
CASA PARTICULAR $

(☏24-30-90; Calle 79 No 28201, btwn Calles 282 & 288; r CUC$20-25; P❄) Rooms at this 2nd-floor apartment have TV, security boxes, balconies and underground parking. The owner is an expert on the local music scene.

Hotel Velazco
HOTEL $$

(☏25-38-80; Calle 79, btwn Calles 290 & 288; s/d/ste CUC$41/58/80; ❄@☏) If this is a taste of things to come in Matanzas, bring it on! After years of desolation, the city has got back a hotel it deserves restored in its original 1902 fin de siècle style and blending seamlessly with the horses, carts and antediluvian autos in the square outside.

A beautiful mahogany bar lures you in; 16 elegant rooms (with flat-screen TVs and wifi) practically force you to stay.

🛏 Outside Town

Hotel Canimao
HOTEL $

(☏26-10-14; s/d CUC$21/25; P❄🌊) Perched above the Río Canímar 8km east of Matanzas, the Canimao has 160 comfortable rooms with little balconies. It's handy for Río Canímar excursions, the Cuevas de Bellamar or to visit the Tropicana Matanzas, but otherwise you're isolated here. There are two restaurants: one Cuban and one Italian. Matanzas Bus Tour stops on the main road.

Eating

Ⅹ City Center

Matanzas' once scant dining scene is improving – slowly.

Plaza la Vigía CAFE $
(cnr Plaza de la Vigía & Calle 85; snacks CUC$2-3; ⊙10am-midnight) Burgers and draft beer rule the menu, while young student types dominate the clientele in this throwback bar that looks like a scene from a Parisian art nouveau poster, circa 1909. The ultimate anti-Varadero escape!

Café Atenas CARIBBEAN $
(Calle 83 No 8301; ⊙10am-11pm) Settle down here in the clean, bland interior or out on the *terraza* (terrace) with the local students, taxi drivers and hotel workers on a day off, and contemplate everyday life on Plaza de la Vigía. Decent sandwiches, grilled meats and fish fillets are available.

Restaurante Teni CARIBBEAN $
(cnr Calles 129 & 224; mains CUC$5; ⊙noon-10:45pm) A large, thatched-roof affair alongside the beach in Reparto Playa, this ambient place offers substantial set *comida criolla* meals, with rice, root vegetables, salad and meat. There's live music on weekends.

Restaurante Paladar Mallorca INTERNATIONAL $$
(🖉28-32-82; Calle 334, btwn Calles 77 & 79; mains CUC$8-14; ⊙11am-11pm) Run by an ex-Meliá hotel chef, the Mallorca out in the Los Mangos neighborhood northwest of the center impresses immediately with one of the finest piña coladas in Cuba along with adventurous dishes such as fish in balsamic cream glaze.

The food presentation is very *nouveau* and there are surprise touches such as a kids' menu, handwash brought to your table and live minstrel music.

Self-Catering
Cadena Cubana del Pan BAKERY $
(Calle 83, btwn Calles 278 & 280; ⊙24hr) Bread shop for beach picnics.

Centro
Variedades Commercial SUPERMARKET $
(Calle 85, btwn Calles 288 & 290; ⊙9am-6pm) For groceries and (upstairs) great cakes.

Mercado la Plaza MARKET $
(cnr Calles 97 & 298) Near the Puente Sánchez Figueras; for produce/peso stalls.

Ⅹ Outside Town

El Marino SEAFOOD $
(⊙noon-9pm) On the main Varadero road next to the Hotel Canimao turnoff, El Marino specializes in seafood, namely lobster and shrimp.

El Ranchón Bellamar CARIBBEAN $$
(⊙noon 8:30pm) If you're visiting the Cuevas de Bellamar, you'd do well to grab a *comida criolla* lunch at this *ranchón*-style restaurant before heading back into town. Good pork or chicken meals with the trimmings go for between CUC$7 and CUC$8.

☐ Drinking & Nightlife

Ruinas de Matasiete BAR
(cnr Vía Blanca & Calle 101; ⊙24hr) The city's famed drinking hole is a frenetic (too frenetic for some) place housed in the ruins of a 19th-century, bay-facing warehouse. Drinks and grilled meats are served on an open-air terrace, but a better reason to come here is to hear live music (9pm Friday to Sunday; cover charge CUC$3).

☆ Entertainment

★**Teatro Sauto** THEATER
(🖉24-27-21) Across Plaza de la Vigía, Teatro Sauto is a national landmark and one of Cuba's premier theaters. Performances have been held here since 1863, and you might catch the Ballet Nacional de Cuba or the Conjunto Folklórico Nacional de Cuba if it's recovered from a lengthy renovation. Performances are at 8:30pm with Sunday matinees at 3pm.

Centro Cultural Comunitario Nelson Barrera CULTURAL CENTER
(Calle 276, cnr 77; ⊙9am-5pm Tue-Sun) A good starting point for anyone interested in Matanzas' Afro-Cuban history lies in this Marina neighborhood cultural center. Inquire at the office about upcoming events and you could get lucky with religious processions, drum sessions, or just shooting the breeze with some *hombres* from the *barrio*.

DON'T MISS

STREET RUMBA

'Without rumba there is no Cuba and without Cuba there is no rumba,' goes a wise old Cuban saying. To see the music in its gritty authenticity, come to Matanzas where the highly spiritual drumming and chanting was born. The best place for live alfresco rumba performances is in Plaza de la Vigía outside the Museo Histórico Provincial at 4pm on the third Friday of every month (check the museum's noticeboard for more details).

Tropicana Matanzas CABARET
(🕿 26-53-80; admission CUC$35; ⊘10pm-2am Tue-Sat) Capitalizing on its success in Havana and Santiago de Cuba, the famous Tropicana cabaret has a branch 8km east of Matanzas, next to the Hotel Canimao. You can mingle with the Varadero bus crowds and enjoy the same entertaining formula of lights, feathers, flesh and frivolity in the open air. Rain stops play if the weather cracks.

Museo Histórico Provincial CULTURAL CENTER
(cnr Calles 83 & 272; admission CUC$2; ⊘10am-6pm Tue-Fri, 1-7pm Sat & 9am-noon Sun) Check the board outside this building (also known as Palacio del Junco) for events ranging from theater to *danzón* performances to rumba, with listings for the month ahead.

Teatro Velazco CINEMA
(cnr Calles 79 & 288) On Parque Libertad, this is Matanzas' main movie house.

Las Palmas LIVE MUSIC
(cnr Calles 254 & 127; admission CUC$1; ⊘noon-midnight Mon-Wed, to 2am Fri-Sun) A good starlit night out for a fraction of the price of the Tropicana shindig can be had at this ARTex place.

Estadio Victoria de Girón SPORTS
(Av Martín Dihigo) From October to April, baseball games take place at this stadium 1km southwest of the market. Once one of the country's leading teams, the local Los Cocodrilos (Crocodiles) aren't as snappy as their name suggests and struggle to beat La Isla de la Juventud these days.

Shopping

Bad luck, shopaholics: checking out the stores (what stores?) in Matanzas makes a car boot sale look like Hollywood Boulevard.

Ediciones Vigía BOOKS
(Plaza de la Vigía; ⊘8am-4pm Mon-Fri) Browse here for beautiful handmade books, each one unique.

Information

Banco Financiero Internacional (cnr Calles 85 & 298) ATM.

Cadeca (Calle 286, btwn Calles 83 & 85; ⊘8am-6pm Mon-Sat, 8am-noon Sun) Two portable money-exchange kiosks behind the cathedral.

Etecsa Telepunto (cnr Calles 83 & 282; per hr CUC$6; ⊘8:30am-7:30pm) Internet terminals

Post Office (Calle 85 No 28813) On the corner of Calle 290.

Servimed (🕿 25-31-70; Hospital Faustino Pérez, Carretera Central Km 101) Clinic just southwest of town.

Getting There & Away

AIR

Matanzas is connected to the outside world through Juan Gualberto Gómez International Airport, aka Varadero airport, 20km east of town.

BICYCLE

Matanzas is reachable by bike from Varadero. The 32km road is well-paved and completely flat, bar the last 3km into the city starting at the Río Canímar bridge (a relatively easy uphill climb if you're heading east). Bike hire is available at some Varadero all-inclusive hotels.

BUS

All buses, long distance and provincial, use the **National Bus Station** (🕿 91-64-45) in the old train station on the corner of Calles 131 and 272 in Pueblo Nuevo south of the Río San Juan. Matanzas has decent connections to the rest of the country, although for destinations like Cienfuegos and Trinidad you need to change at Varadero. Practically, this means taking the first Varadero bus of the day then waiting for the afternoon Varadero–Trinidad bus. **Víazul** (www.viazul.com) has four daily departures to Havana (CUC$7, two hours, 9am, 12:35pm, 4:35pm and 7pm) and Varadero (CUC$6, one hour, 10:35am, 12:15pm, 2:15pm and 7:55pm). The first three Varadero departures also call at the airport (CUC$6, 25 minutes).

Matanzas Bus Tour

Matanzas Bus Tour is a hop on/hop off tourist bus linking Varadero with Matanzas and its various outlying sights. It stops at all of the main hotels in Varadero frequented by the similar Varadero Bus Tour as well as Río Canímar, Cuevas del Bellmar, Iglesia de Monserrate and central Matanzas. It runs four times daily (with some low-season hiccups). All-day tickets cost CUC$10. Schedules are sometimes cancelled in low season.

TRAIN

The **train station** (☑ 29-16-45; Calle 181) is in Miret, at the southern edge of the city. Foreigners usually pay the peso price in convertibles to the *jefe de turno* (shift manager). Most trains between Havana and Santiago de Cuba stop here (except the fast Tren Francés). In theory, there are eight daily trains to Havana (CUC$3, 1½ hours). The daily Santiago de Cuba train (CUC$27) should leave in the evening at around 11pm stopping at Santa Clara, Ciego de Ávila, Camagüey and Las Tunas. Other eastbound trains reach Sancti Spíritus. Cuban trains are notoriously fickle. Always check ahead, preferably in person at the station.

Latest train information is plastered on pieces of paper stuck to a billboard on the far wall of the waiting room. Get here well in advance to beat the bedlam.

The **Hershey Train Station** (☑ 24-48-05; cnr Calles 55 & 67) is in Versalles, an easy 10-minute walk from Parque Libertad. There are three trains a day to Casablanca station in Havana (CUC$2.80, four hours) via Canasí (CUC$0.85), Jibacoa (CUC$1.10, 1½ hours; for Playa Jibacoa), Hershey (CUC$1.40, two hours; for Jardines de Hershey) and Guanabo (CUC$2). Departure times from Matanzas are 4:39am, 12:09am (an express service that should take three hours) and 4:25pm.

Ticket sales begin an hour before the scheduled departure time and, except on weekends and holidays, there's no problem getting aboard. Bicycles may not be allowed (ask). The train usually leaves on time, but often arrives in Havana's Casablanca station (just below La Cabaña fort on the east side of the harbor) one hour late. This is the only electric railway in Cuba. It's a scenic trip if you're not in a hurry, and a great way of reaching the little-visited attractions of Mayabeque province.

❶ Getting Around

Bus 12 links Plaza Libertad with the Cuevas del Bellamar and the Iglesia de Monserrate. You can also use the handy hop on/hop off Matanzas Bus Tour to get to Cuevas del Bellamar and Canímar.

The Oro Negro gas station is on the corner of Calles 129 and 210, 4km outside the city of Matanzas on the Varadero road. The Servi-Cupet gas station and **Havanautos** (☑ 25-32-94; cnr Calles 129 & 210) are a block further on. If you're driving to Varadero, you will pay a CUC$2 highway toll between Boca de Camarioca and Santa Marta (no toll between Matanzas and the airport).

Bici-taxis congregate next to the Mercado la Plaza and can take you to most of the city's destinations for one to two Cuban pesos. A taxi to Varadero town should cost around CUC$25.

Varadero

POP 27,630

Varadero, located on the sinuous 20km-long Hicacos peninsula, stands at the vanguard of Cuba's most important industry – tourism. As the largest resort in the Caribbean, it guards a huge, unsubtle and constantly evolving stash of hotels (over 50), shops, banks, water activities and poolside entertainment; though its trump card is its beach, an uninterrupted 20km stretch of blond sand, undoubtedly one of the best in the Caribbean. But, while this large, tourist-friendly mega-resort may be essential to the Cuban economy, it offers little in the way of unique Cuban experiences. For these you'll need to escape the crowds from Canada and Europe and dip into the readily accessible hinterland for nearby 'reality checks' in Matanzas, Cárdenas or Bahía de Cochinos.

Most Varadero tourists buy their vacation packages overseas and are content to idle for a week or two enjoying the all-inclusiveness of their resort (and why not?). However, if you're touring Cuba independently, and want to alternate your esoteric rambles with some less stressful beach life, Varadero can provide a few nights of well-earned sloth after a dusty spell on the road. For the best prices book online before you leave home, though there are plenty of economical hotels and casas particulares in the western end of the town that can be bagged on-the-spot.

◉ Sights

For art and history, you're in the wrong place, but there are a few sights worth checking out if the beach life starts to bore you.

**Parque Central & Parque
de las 8000 Taquillas**   PARK
(btwn Calles 44 & 46) Standing together between Calles 44 and 46, these parks were once the center of the town's social life, but became neglected during the 1990s as bigger resorts sprouted up further east.

Varadero Town – East

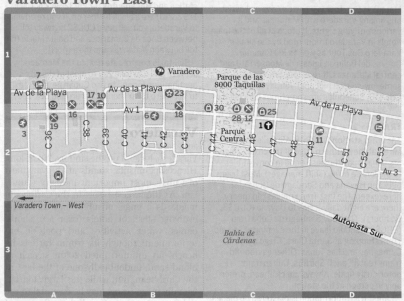

Varadero Town – East

Redeveloped in 2008, Parque de las 8000 Taquillas now has a small subterranean shopping center beneath the ever-popular Coppelia ice-cream parlor.

Museo Municipal de Varadero MUSEUM
(Map p216; Calle 57; admission CUC$1; ⊙10am-7pm) Walking up the beach from Hotel Acuazul Varazul, you'll see many typical

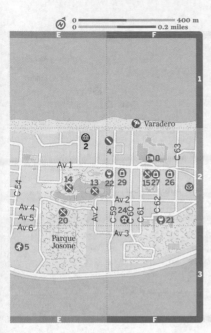

wooden beach houses with elegant wraparound porches. The most attractive of the bunch, Varadero's Museo Municipal, has been turned into a balconied chalet displaying period furniture and a snapshot of the resort's history. It's more interesting than you'd think.

Parque Josone
PARK

(cnr Av 1 & Calle 58; ⊙ 9am-midnight) This green oasis is more enclosed and much prettier than Parque Central. The gardens date back to 1940, taking their name from the former owners, José Fermín Iturrioz y Llaguno and his wife Onelia, who owned the Arrechabala rum distillery in nearby Cárdenas and built a neoclassical mansion here: the Retiro Josone.

Expropriated after the Revolution, the mansion became a guesthouse for visiting foreign dignitaries. The park is now a public space for the enjoyment of all – you may see Cuban girls celebrate their *quinciñeras* (15th-birthday celebrations) here. Josone's expansive, shady grounds feature a lake with rowboats (CUC$0.50 per person per hour), atmospheric eateries, resident geese, myriad tree species and a mini-train. There's a public swimming pool (admission CUC$2) in the south of the park and the odd ostrich

lurking nearby. Good music can be heard nightly.

Mansión Xanadú
NOTABLE BUILDING

(Map p ☑ 66-84-82; Av las Américas, Km 3; all-incl s/d CUC$166/240; ⓟ ❄ @) Everything east of the small stone water tower (it looks like an old Spanish fort, but was built in the 1930s), next to the Restaurant Mesón del Quijote, once belonged to the Du Pont family. Here the millionaire American entrepreneur, Irenée built the three-story Mansión Xanadu.

It's now an upscale hotel atop Varadero's 18-hole golf course with a top-floor bar conducive for sipping sunset cocktails.

Cueva de Ambrosio
CAVE

(Map p???; admission CUC$3; ⊙ 9am-4:30pm) Beyond Marina Chapelín, Varadero sprawls east like a displaced North American suburb with scrubby mangroves interspersed with megahotel complexes, the odd iron crane and a dolphin show. Pass all this and 500m beyond the Club Amigo Varadero on the Autopista Sur, you'll find this cave, interesting for its 47 pre-Columbian drawings, discovered in a 300m recess in 1961.

The black-and-red drawings feature the same concentric circles seen in similar paintings on the Isla de la Juventud, perhaps a form of solar calendar. The cave was also used as a refuge by escaped slaves.

Reserva Ecológica Varahicacos
PARK

(Map p222; www.varahicacos.cu; 45min hiking trails CUC$3; ⊙ 9am-4:30pm) A few hundred meters beyond Cueva de Ambrosio is the entrance to Varadero's nominal green space and a wildlife reserve that's about as 'wild' as New York's Central Park. Bulldozers have been chomping away at its edges for years. There are three underwhelming trails but the highlight is the **Cueva de Musalmanes** with its 2500-year-old human remains.

Cayo Piedras del Norte
MARINE PARK

Five kilometers north of Playa las Calaveras (one hour by boat), Cayo Piedras del Norte has been made into a 'marine park' through the deliberate sinking of an assortment of vessels and aircraft in 15m to 30m of water during the late 1990s.

Scuttled for the benefit of divers and glass-bottom boat passengers are a towboat, a missile-launching gunboat (with missiles intact), an AN-24 airplane and the yacht Coral Negro.

Varadero Town – West

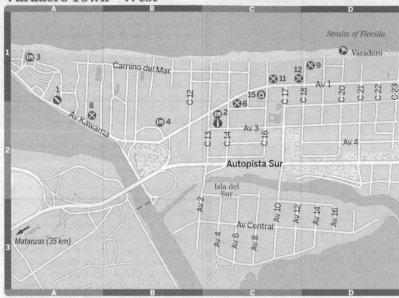

Straits of Florida

Varadero

Camino del Mar

Av Kawama

Autopista Sur

Isla del Sur

Av Central

Matanzas (35 km)

Iglesia de Santa Elvira　　　　CHURCH
(Map p216; cnr Av 1 & Calle 47) Just east of Parque Central is this tiny colonial-style building resembling a displaced alpine chapel.

🏃 Activities

Diving & Snorkeling

Varadero has four excellent dive centers, although, this being tourist-ville, the prices are double those in the Bahía de Cochinos on the province's south coast. All of the 21 dive sites around the Península de Hicacos require a boat transfer of approximately one hour. Highlights include reefs, caverns, pitchers and a Russian patrol boat sunk for diving purposes in 1997. The nearest shore diving is 20km west at Playa Coral (p211). The centers also offer day excursions to superior sites at the Bahía de Cochinos (one/two immersions CUC$50/70, with transfer).

Barracuda Diving Center　　　DIVING
(Map p216; 📞 61-34-81; cnr Av 1 & Calle 59; ⊙ 8am-7pm) Varadero's top scuba facility is the mega-friendly, multilingual Barracuda Diving Center. Diving costs CUC$50 per dive with equipment, cave diving is CUC$60 and night diving costs CUC$55. Packages of multiple dives work out cheaper.

Barracuda conducts introductory resort courses for CUC$70, and ACUC (American Canadian Underwater Certifications) courses starting at CUC$220, plus many advanced

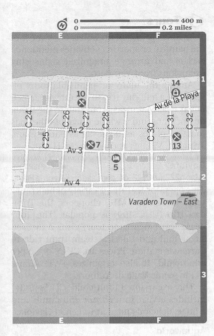

0 — 400 m
0 — 0.2 miles

14
10
Av de la Playa
C-24 C-25 C-26 C-27 C-28 Av 2 Av 3 7 C-30 C-31 C-32 13
5
Av 4

Varadero Town – East

courses. Snorkeling with guide is CUC$30. A brand-new recompression facility is on site and there's also a training pool, resident doctor and popular seafood restaurant on the premises, Barracuda Grill. Barracuda has a daily capacity for 70 divers in three 12m boats.

Acua Diving Center DIVING
(Map p218; ☑ 66-80-63; Av Kawama, btwn Calles 2 & 3; ☺ 8am-5pm) Backing up Barracuda Diving is this secondary option in western Varadero near the Hotel Kawama. It charges much the same prices as Barracuda, but doesn't have quite the facilities, or volume.

When a north wind is blowing and diving isn't possible in the Atlantic, you can be transferred to the Caribbean coast in a minibus (90-minute drive); this costs a total of CUC$55/75 for one/two dives. Popular trips include Cueva Saturno for diving and Playa Coral for snorkeling and diving.

Marina Gaviota DIVING
(Map p222; ☑ 66-47-22; Autopista Sur y Final) Another professional outfit at the eastern end of Autopista Sur, this has slightly cheaper scuba diving/snorkeling excursions both locally and at the Bahía de Cochinos.

Aquaworld Diving Center DIVING
(☑ 66-75- 50; Autopista Sur Km 12) At the Marlin Marina Chapelín, Aquaworld also organizes diving/snorkeling trips for the same prices.

Fishing

Varadero has three marinas, all of which offer a similar variety of nautical activities and facilities.

Marlin Marina Chapelín FISHING
(Map p222; ☑ 66-75-50) Situated close to the entrance to Hotel Riu Turquesa, five hours of deep-sea fishing here costs CUC$290 for four people (price includes hotel transfers, open bar and licenses; nonfishing companions pay CUC$30).

Marina Gaviota FISHING
(☑ 66-47-22) At the eastern end of Autopista Sur and in the midst of some massive condo development, this place has similar packages to Marlin Marina Chapelín.

Skydiving
Centro Internacional de Paracaidismo SKYDIVING
(☑ 66-72-60, 66-72-56) For those with a head for heights, Varadero's greatest thrill has to be skydiving at this base at the old airport just west of Varadero. The terminal is 1km up a dirt road, opposite Marina Acua. Skydivers take off in an Antonov AN-2 biplane of WWII design (don't worry, it's a replica) and jump from 3000m using a two-harness parachute with an instructor strapped in tandem on your back.

After 35 seconds of free fall the parachute opens and you float tranquilly for 10 minutes down onto Varadero's white sandy beach. The center also offers less spectacular (but equally thrilling) ultralight flights at various points along the beach. Prices for skydiving are CUC$180 per person with an extra CUC$45 for photos and CUC$60 for video. Ultralight flights start at CUC$30 and go up to CUC$300 depending on the duration of the flight. If you are already a qualified skydiver, solo jumps are available on production of the relevant certification.

A day's notice is usually required for skydiving (which many hotels can book on your behalf), and jumps are (obviously) weather dependent. Since opening in 1993 the center has reported no fatalities.

MATANZAS PROVINCE VARADERO

Golf

Varadero Golf Club
GOLF
(Map p222; ☑ 66-77-88; www.varaderogolfclub.com; Mansión Xanadú; green fees 9/18 holes CUC$48/70; ⏱ 7am-7pm) While it's no Pebble Beach, golfers can have a swinging session at this uncrowded and well-landscaped club: Cuba's first 18-hole course. The original nine holes created by the Du Ponts are between Hotel Bella Costa and Dupont's Mansión Xanadú; another nine holes added in 1998 flank the southern side of the three Meliá resorts.

Bookings for the course (par 72) are made through the pro shop next to the Mansión Xanadú (now a cozy hotel with free, unlimited tee time). Bizarrely, golf carts (CUC$30 per person) are mandatory.

El Golfito
MINIGOLF
(Map p216; cnr Av 1 & Calle 42; per person CUC$3; ⏱ 24hr) Golf neophytes can play the miniature version here.

Other Activities

There are **sailboards** available for rent at various points along the public beach (CUC$10 per hour), as are small catamarans, banana boats, sea kayaks etc. The upmarket resorts usually include these water toys in the all-inclusive price.

Centro Todo En Uno
BOWLING
(Map p216; cnr Calle 54 & Autopista Sur; per game CUC$2.50; ⏱ 24hr) Bowling alleys are popular in Cuba and the *bolera* here, including a small shopping/games complex on Autopista Sur, is usually full of Cuban families who also come to enjoy the adjacent kids' playground and fast-food joints.

🍴 Courses

Many of Varadero's all-inclusive hotels lay on free Spanish lessons for guests. If you're staying in cheaper digs, ask at the reception of one of these larger hotels and see if you can find your way onto an in-house language course by offering to pay a small fee.

Academia Baile en Cuba
DANCING
(Map p216; cnr Av 1 & Calle 34) A new dance school aimed at tourists located in Varadero's Casa de la Cultura and run by cultural agency Paradiso. You can organize lessons in various genres of Cuban dance at your hotel or directly at the venue for approximately CUC$5 an hour. Drum and language lessons are promised in the future.

Tours

Tour desks at the main hotels book most of the nautical or sporting activities mentioned earlier and arrange organized sightseeing excursions from Varadero.

Among the many off-peninsula tours offered are a half-day trip to the Cuevas de Bellamar near Matanzas, a bus tour to the Bahía de Cochinos and a whole range of other bus tours to places as far away as Santa Clara, Trinidad, Viñales and, of course, Havana.

Gaviota
HELICOPTER TOUR
(Map p222; ☑ 61-18-44; cnr Calle 56 & Av de la Playa) This operator features a variety of helicopter tours in Russian M1-8 choppers; the Trinidad trip (CUC$199) is popular. The Tour de Azúcar (sugarcane tour) visits a disused sugar mill and takes a steam train ride to Cárdenas station. Prices are CUC$39/30 per adult/child. It also organizes 4WD safaris to the scenic Valle de Yumurí.

The excursion (adult/child CUC$45/34) includes a visit to a *campesino* family and a huge, delicious meal at Ranchón Gaviota.

Aquaworld
Marina Chapelín
BOAT TRIPS, WATER SPORTS
(Map p222; ☑ 66-75-50; Autopista Sur Km 12) Aquaworld Marina Chapelín organizes Varadero's nautical highlight in the popularity stakes: the **Seafari Cayo Blanco**, a seven-hour sojourn (CUC$101) from Marina Chapelín to nearby Cayo Blanco and its idyllic beach. The trip includes an open bar, lobster lunch, two snorkeling stops, live music and hotel transfers.

There's also a shorter CUC$45 catamaran tour with snorkeling, open bar and a chicken lunch. The **Fiesta en el Cayo** is a sunset cruise (CUC$41) to Cayo Blanco with dinner, music and more free-flowing rum at the key.

Boat Adventure Boat Trip
BOAT TRIPS
(Map p222; ☑ 66-84-40; per person CUC$39; ⏱ 9am-4pm) This two-hour guided trip, also leaving from the Marina Chapelín, is a speedy sortie through the adjacent mangroves on two-person jet skis or motorboats to view myriad wildlife including friendly crocs. Bookings for all these watery excursions can also be made at most of the big hotels.

✨ Festivals & Events

Golf tournaments are held at the Varadero Golf Club in June and October and the annual regatta is in May. Varadero also hosts the annual tourism convention in the first week in May when accommodations are tight and some places are reserved solely for conference participants.

🛌 Sleeping

Varadero is huge – there are at least 50 hotels. For budget travelers turning up impromptu, hunting down bargain rooms is a sport akin to marathon running. Book ahead or concentrate your efforts on the peninsula's southwest end where hotels are cheaper and the town retains a semblance of Cuban life.

Since January 2011 it has been legal to rent private rooms in Varadero. Between 20 and 30 casas particulares have so far taken root.

All-inclusive hotel packages booked through travel agents in your home country may have differing (cheaper) rates to those given here.

Club Herradura HOTEL $
(Map p216; ☑61-37-03; Av de la Playa, btwn Calles 35 & 36; low season s/d incl breakfast CUC$30/44; ❄️🐾) Plain from the front, but infinitely more attractive on the oceanside, this four-story, crescent-shaped hotel is within wave-lapping distance of a recently replenished section of the beach. Accommodations are ample, if a little dog-eared, with timeless wicker furniture and good balcony view

rooms facing the beach. A pleasant all-round unpretentious vibe.

Hotel Pullman HOTEL $$
(Islazul; Map p216; ☑61-27-02, 66 71 61; Av 1, btwn Calles 49 & 50; s/d incl breakfast CUC$30/48) In a turreted castle-like building with heavy wooden furniture and rocking chairs on the front porch overlooking the street, Hotel Pullman has Old-fashioned but comfortable rooms including a quadruple.

Hotel Dos Mares HOTEL $
(Map p216; ☑61-27-02; cnr Av 1 & Calle 53; s/d incl breakfast CUC$30/48) ISituated in a modern three-story building that is 70m from a cracking niche of beach. Rooms are cozy, if dark.

Villa la Mar HOTEL $
(Map p218; ☑61-45-15; Av 3, btwn Calles 28 & 30; all-incl s/d CUC$49/76; ❄️) At no-frills, no-pretensions Villa la Mar you'll dine on fried chicken, mingle with peso-paying Cuban tourists and fall asleep to the not-so-romantic sound of the in-house disco belting out the Cuban version of Britney Spears.

Hotel los Delfines RESORT $$
(Map p216; ☑66-77-20; cnr Av de la Playa & Calle 39; all-incl s/d from CUC$80/120; ❄️🐾) Hotel chain Islazul goes (almost) all-inclusive in this friendlier, cozier copy of the big resorts further northeast. The 100 rooms come packed

VARADERO'S HOTELS IN A NUTSHELL

Varadero's confusingly large hotel zone can, for simplicities sake, be broken into four broad segments.

The accommodations in the small Cuban town at the west end of the peninsula consist of older budget hotels wedged in among the banks, bars and vintage beachhouses. Since 2011, town residents have been able to legally rent out rooms to foreigners and over 20 casas particulars have now taken root.

The section from Calle 64 northeast to the golf course is punctuated by a thin strip of hodgepodge architecture, from kitschy Holiday Camp to bloc-style Sovietesque. Selling cheap packages to mainly foreign tourists, many of these hotels are already looking dated after only three or four decades in operation.

East of the Mansión Xanadú is a cluster of large single structure hotels with impressive lobbies and multiple stories built mostly in the early 1990s. The tallest is the spectacular 14-story Blau Varadero.

The nearer you get to the end of the peninsula, the more it starts to look like a Florida suburb. Contemporary Cuban all-inclusive resorts favor detached one-to-three story blocks that are laid out like mini-towns and spread over multiple acres. Most of these sprawling resorts have been built since 2000 and it is here that you'll find Varadero's largest (the 1025-room Memories Varadero), most luxurious (the CUC$360-a-night Paradisus Varadero) and modern (Ocean Varadero El Patriarca; opened October 2012) accommodations. The peninsula's other new attraction is a giant condo development being built at the rapidly expanding Marina Gaviota.

Varadero Hotel Zone

Varadero Hotel Zone

with additional extras such as satellite TV, minibar and safe deposit box, and there's a lovely scoop of wide protected beach.

Hotel Tuxpán
RESORT $$
(Map p222; ☎66-75-60; Av las Américas, Km 2; all-incl s/d from CUC$70/120; P ❄ @ ☒) Concrete-block architecture and palm-fringed beaches make jarring bedfellows that are all too common in Varadero. But the Tuxpán is famous for other reasons, such as its disco, La Bamba, purportedly one of the resort's hottest. For those not enamored with Soviet architectonics, the beautiful beach is never far away.

Hotel Acuazul Varazul
RESORT $$
(Map p218; ☎66-71-32; Av 1, btwn Calles 13 & 14; s/d all-incl CUC$58/92, Varazul s/d CUC$49/78; ❄ @ ☒) You can't knock the Acuazul for trying. Every year it is reborn with a different paint-job. The eye-watering pink and blue was recently replaced by a slightly more subtle lemon and blue while inside they've polished the colorful stained-glass windows, turned the music down around the pool, and tarted up the all-inclusive buffet.

It's still a far cry from Cancún-style luxury, but it cheerfully retains an inkling of Cubaness.

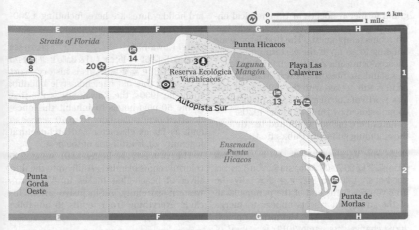

★**Blau Varadero** RESORT $$$
(Map p222; ☑66-75-45; Carretera de las Morlas, Km 15; all-incl r CUC$200; P❄@☎) Suspend your judgment on Varadero's tallest and most architecturally unsubtle resort. Trying hard to imitate an Aztec pyramid from the outside (why?), the interior is nothing short of spectacular; a 14-story enclosed courtyard embellished by hundreds of hanging plants, some falling for over 80m.

Huge rooms are surgically clean and the higher ones have the best views in Varadero. Downstairs, you're in resort land, so expect loquacious poolside entertainers, beer in plastic cups and iffy Michael Jackson theme nights.

Meliá Paradisus Varadero HOTEL $$$
(☑66-87-00; Punta Rincón Francés; s/d CUC$250/360; P❄@☎) Fort Knox style security characterizes Varadero's most refined and luxurious resort, so don't even think of sneaking in with the wrong colored wristband. The wallet-lightening prices promise romance, elegance and exclusivity, especially if you pay extra for the so-called 'royal service' where formal butlers will treat you like Marie Antoinette.

The decor has a desert island feel with open-sided thatched shelters, pillars, pools and lush tropical plants.

Sandals Royal Hicacos RESORT $$$
(Map p222; ☑66-88-51, 66-88-44; Punta Hicacos; all-incl r CUC$160-190; P❄@☎) Having a more understated look (and more personable service) than many of its neighbors has helped Sandals Royal Hicacos immeasurably and made it one of the most appealing resorts on the end-point of the peninsula with vast *ranchón*-style public areas and babbling water features lending a mellifluous air.

Bedrooms, done up in sunny yellows and oranges, have their own reception areas and huge bathrooms.

Meliá Las Américas RESORT $$$
(Map p222; ☑66-76-00; Autopista Sur Km 7; all-incl s/d CUC$250/400; P❄@☎) The smaller, more grown-up alternative to the Meliá Varadero next door, Las Américas has a no-kids policy, a nice slice of palm tree embellished beach, fancy chandeliers and a Japanese restaurant. With 225 rooms, it's too large to be intimate, though there's a more refined ambience here than in the other resort giants nearby.

It's also the nearest hotel to Varadero golf course.

Meliá Varadero RESORT $$$
(Map p222; ☑66-70-13; Autopista Sur Km 7; all-incl d $360; P❄@☎☎) Twice as big as its sister Meliá hotel (Las Américas) and happy to cater to families, the 490-room Meliá Varadero immediately impresses with its cylindrical vine-draped lobby. Perched on a small rocky promontory, the beach is set to one side and offers plenty of shade.

Unlike many of its Varadero brethren the Meliá offers free bike hire for guests and wifi that (usually) works.

Mansión Xanadú RESORT $$$
(Map p222; ☑66-84-82; Av las Américas, Km 3; all-incl s/d CUC$166/240; P❄@) Varadero's most intriguing and intimate lodging is in the

grand former residence of US chemical entrepreneur Irenée Du Pont, where eight lavish rooms tempt guests. The first large-scale building to go up at the eastern end of the Hicacos peninsula and an outstanding jewel in a bland architectural desert, Mansión Xanadú is still decked with the millions of dollars' worth of Cuban marble and furnishings commissioned by Du Pont in the 1930s.

Rates here include unlimited tee time at the adjoining golf club (Cuba's first).

Memories Varadero RESORT $$$
(Map p222; ☑ 66-70-09; Autopista Sur Km 8; all-incl standard s/d CUC$195/242; P⊠@≋) By the time you reach the end of the peninsula all of the strung-out resorts appear to merge into one – this one. The Memories (opened 2008, changed its name 2012) is a kind of identikit of a modern beach hotel: 1025 rooms, international cuisine, wall-to-wall entertainment and lots of sunburned Europeans whizzing around on golf-carts.

Blau Marina Palace RESORT $$$
(Map p222; ☑ 66-99-66; Autopista Sur Final; all-incl s/d CUC$150/240, cayo s/d CUC$185/310; P⊠@≋) The last stop on the peninsula before Florida and looking a lot like it, Marina Blau (until recently called the Barceló) follows the modern Varadero resort trend, ie spread-out low-rise units, lush spacious grounds and exemplary service. There's an imitation lighthouse, acres of swimming pools and a fine strip of adjacent beach.

For added luxury (and irony) you can plump for the 'royal' upgrade on a small adjoining island, Cayo Libertad, connected by a bridge where butlers cater for your every need. Ah...*socialismo!*

Tryp Península Varadero RESORT $$$
(Map p222; ☑ 66-88-00; Reserva Ecológica Varahicacos; all-incl r from CUC$180; P⊠@≋) Some may revel in Tryp's four-star luxuries. The facilities here are admittedly plush, but there's not much cross-fertilizing with the real Cuba.

Sol Palmeras RESORT $$$
(☑ 66-70-09; Carretera de las Morlas; all-incl s/d CUC$160/220; ⊠@≋) This mid-ranking, middle-of-the-peninsula all-inclusive built in 1990 avoids the architectural catastrophes of many of its predecessors while shunning the nagging pretensions of the more modern competition to the east. There may not be many wow factors, but all the standard holiday lures are here, including a 200-unit bungalow village next door.

Hotel Kawama RESORT $$$
(Map p218; ☑ 61-44-16; cnr Av 1 & Calle 1; all-incl s/d CUC$84/128; P⊠@≋) This is history – sort of. A venerable old hacienda-style building from the 1930s, the Kawama was the first of the 50-plus hotels to inhabit this once-deserted peninsula more than 70 years ago and, as far as character and architectural ingenuity go, it's still one of the best.

The property is huge, with some 235 colorful rooms blended artfully into the thin sliver of beach that makes up Varadero's western extremity. All-inclusive prices include everything from tennis to aquabike usage.

Hotel Varadero Internacional RESORT $$$
(Map p222; ☑ 66-70-38; Av las Américas, Km 1; all-incl s/d CUC$100/140; P⊠@≋) Opened in December 1950 as a sister hotel to Miami's Fontainebleau, the four-story Internacional regularly lured golf club-wielding celebrities before the Revolution canceled Hollywood's summer vacation plans. While once it looked agreeably retro, now it just looks 10 years past its last scheduled refurbishment. Nonetheless, extensive facilities include tennis courts, massages and Varadero's best cabaret.

Unlike some of Varadero's more sprawling options it's also right on the beach. Bonuses at the Internacional include cool art (there's a large René Portocarrero mural in the lobby) and superfriendly staff.

Hotel ROC Barlovento RESORT $$$
(Map p218; ☑ 66-71-40; Av 1, btwn Calles 10 & 12; all-incl s/d CUC$133/190; P⊠@≋) Varadero's sentinel hotel guarding its entrance road is an attractive enough place with a lovely palm-fringed pool, integrated colonial-style architecture, and a choice stretch of beach. The food here is good, though points get deducted for the nighttime entertainment – water ballet and magic shows – which are not a patch on the standard Cuban knees-up.

For an ocean-view room you'll pay more, despite the portion of sea visible being tame by peninsula standards.

Hotel Cuatro Palmas RESORT $$$
(Map p216; ☑ 66-70-40; Av 1, btwn Calles 60 & 62; all-incl s/d CUC$106/170; P⊠@≋) One wonders if this former personal residence of

dictator Fulgencio Batista would still appeal to his opulent taste. The first of the big all-inclusive resorts as you head east, Cuatro Palmas has succumbed to tourist kitsch in recent years, though it's still close enough to town for getting around on foot. The beach is also adjacent, though you may need ear muffs.

Villa Cuba
RESORT $$$

(Map p222; ☑ 66-82-80; Av las Américas, Km 2; all-incl 2-/3-/4-/5-/6-bed villas CUC$176/249/314/395/447; P ❄ @ ⛱ ⛹) Imagine a multistory car park crossed with a tacky 1970s holiday camp and you'll get an inkling of the look and ambience at Villa Cuba. With a color scheme that might have been thrown together by a hyperactive five-year-old let loose with some Lego bricks, and dark dead areas under staircases inhabited by dusty plants, this is no Caribbean paradise.

However, for those on a tighter budget there are a multitude of room sizes and prices.

🍴 Eating

You can eat well for under CUC$10 in Varadero in a variety of state restaurants and a new stash of paladares (eight at last count) legalized in 2011. As 95% of the hotels on the eastern end of the peninsula are all-inclusive, you'll find the bulk of the independent eating joints west of Calle 64.

⭐ Paladar Nonna Tina
ITALIAN $

(Map p216; Calle 38, btwn Av 1 & Playa; pizza & pasta CUC$6-10; ⊙11am-11pm) Veteran Cuba visitors will remember an era when the word 'pasta' was a euphemism for 'mush'. But, times have changed and, thanks to new privatization laws that have inspired restaurants such as Nonna Tina (the owner is Italian), the word 'al dente' is no longer an untranslatable foreign term.

You'll find proof in this restaurant's pretty front garden where rabbits munch on carrots while traveling Italio-philes sit down to enjoy thin-crust pizza, pesto linguine and proper cappuccinos.

Kiki's Club
ITALIAN $

(Map p218; cnr Av Kawama & Calle 6; mains CUC$3-6; ⊙noon-10:30pm) Delicious pizzas served with innovative toppings like shrimp are the hallmarks of this place, which sports a terrace and a good cocktail menu: a haven from the overriding blandness of the peninsula's western edge.

La Vicaria
CUBAN $

(Map p216; Av 1, btwn Calles 37 & 38; mains from CUC$4; ⊙noon-10:30pm) Munch with the locals at outside tables under *ranchón*-style canopies: portions are generous, especially if you go for the whopping house special, lobster with chicken and pork (CUC$12.95).

Ranchón Bellamar
CUBAN $

(Map p218; Av 1, btwn Calles 16 & 17; mains CUC$2-5; ⊙10am-10pm) Wedged between the main avenue and the beach, this open-sided thatched *ranchón* is part of the Hotel Sunbeach across the road. With its cheap lunches and maracas-shaking musicians, it's a good bet for an unhurried bite, despite the poor service.

Restaurante el Criollo
CARIBBEAN $

(Map p218; cnr Av 1 & Calle 18; ⊙noon-midnight) This is one of the more enjoyable state-run places serving what its name suggests, typical *comida criolla* for a few convertibles.

Coppelia
ICE CREAM $

(Map p216; Av 1, btwn Calles 44 & 46; ⊙3-11pm) What, a Coppelia with no queues? Set above the subterranean shopping complex in Parque de las 8000 Taquillas, Varadero's ice-cream cathedral is bright, airy and surprisingly uncrowded.

Salsa Suárez
INTERNATIONAL $$

(Map p218; ☑ 61-20-09; Calle 31 No 103, btwn Avs 1 & 3; mains CUC$8-12; ⊙11am-11pm) Possibly the most adventurous and all-encompassing of Varadero's new paladares, Salsa Suárez impresses from the start with its salubrious greenery-covered patio with menu items written artistically on a large blackboard. Food influences are all over the map (tapas, pasta, cheese platters and good old Cuban fare), but it's consistently good, as are the details such as the complimentary bread baskets, and excellent Italian-style coffee.

Restaurante Esquina Cuba
CUBAN $$

(Map p216; cnr Av 1 & Calle 36; ⊙noon-11pm) This place was one-time favorite of Buena Vista Social Club luminary Compay Segundo, and the man obviously had taste. Salivate over the pork special (CUC$13) with lashings of beans, rice and plantain chips under the gaze of the great Cuban ephemera that line the walls – and the resident American car.

Dante
ITALIAN $$

(Map p216; ☑ 66-77-38; Parque Josone; meals CUC$5-10; ⊙noon-10:45pm) Going strong since 1993, Dante takes its name from its entrepreneurial chef who has been rustling up delectable Italian fare to complement the lakeside setting since the place started up. Antipasto starts at CUC$6; Varadero's most impressive wine stash also awaits. Spoil your tastebuds in Cuba while you have the chance. As one of Varadero's best restaurants, it's often full.

La Fondue FRENCH $$
(Map p216; Av 1, cnr Calle 62; mains CUC$10; ⊙noon-midnight) Locals rate this fondue-focused restaurant next to the Mallorca as one of the best in town and it's a welcome change for the palate, too. Beef fillet fondue is the signature dish.

Restaurante Mallorca SPANISH $$
(Map p216; ⊿66-77-46; Av 1, btwn Calles 61 & 62; mains CUC$5-10; ⊙noon-midnight) This is a fine, intimate venue renowned for its paella. It's surprisingly spacious inside, with a well-stocked bar (a good South American wine selection) and generous servings/service.

Barracuda Grill SEAFOOD $$
(Map p216; cnr Av 1 & Calle 58; mains CUC$7; ⊙11am-7pm) In a thatched pavilion overlooking the beach on the grounds of the Barracuda Diving Center, this popular place has understandably tasty fish and shellfish that have satisfied many a post-dive appetite.

Lai-Lai CHINESE $$
(Map p218; cnr Av 1 & Calle 18; meals CUC$6-10; ⊙noon-11pm) An old stalwart set in a two-story mansion on the beach, Lai Lai has traditional Chinese set menus with several courses. If you've been craving some wonton soup, crave no more.

Paladar Casona del Chino Pons CUBAN, CHINESE $$
(Map p218; Av 1 , cnr Calle 27; mains CUC$8-11) Traditional Cuban food with a Chinese influence and above average vegetarian options. Try the fried rice, or sweet and sour chicken while sitting on the wraparound porch of a lovely old wooden Varadero beach house.

Restaurante la Campana CARIBBEAN $$
(Map p216; ⊿66-72-24; Parque Josone; mains CUC$10; ⊙noon-10:30pm) With its rustic stonework, terracotta roof and bell tower, La Campana transports a little bit of the Greek countryside to Parque Josone. It throws some novel takes on Cuban dishes.

El Retiro INTERNATIONAL $$
(Map p216; ⊿66-73-16; ⊙noon-10pm) International cuisine in neoclassical surrounds in Parque Josone.

Varadero 60 INTERNATIONAL $$$
(⊿61-39-86; Calle 60, cnr Av 3; mains CUC$6-17; ⊙noon-midnight) Upping the ante considerably in Varader's new paladar scene is this fine-dining restaurant that exudes an aura of refinement not seen since Benny Moré last cleared his throat and shouted 'dilo!'. There's double meaning in the name – it's on Calle 60 and its theme is 1960s advertisements which adorn the walls of the elegant interior.

Lobster and *solomillo* (steak) are the house specialties and can be combined with some excellent Chilean and Spanish wines.

Restaurante Mesón del Quijote SPANISH $$$
(Map p222; Reparto la Torre; mains CUC$8-15; ⊙noon-midnight) Next to a statue of Cervantes' famous Don who seems to be making off rather keenly toward the all-inclusive resorts, this restaurant is one of the eastern peninsula's only nonresort options. Perched on a grassy knoll above Av las Américas, its Spanish-tinged menu makes a refreshing change from the all-you-can-eat buffet.

Self-Catering
There's a handy grocery store beside **Aparthotel Varazul** (Map p218; Calle 15; ⊙9am-7pm), with others at **Caracol Pelicano** (Map p218; cnr Calle 27 & Av 3; ⊙9am-7:45pm) and **Club Herradura.** (Map p216; Av de la Playa, btwn Calles 35 & 36; ⊙9am-7pm).

Panadería Doña Neli BAKERY $
(Map p216; cnr Av 1 & Calle 43; ⊙24hr) Dependable for bread and pastries. Stock up and head for the beach.

🍷 Drinking & Nightlife

★**The Beatles Bar-Restaurant** BAR
(Map p216; Av 1, cnr Calle 59) A *roquero's* delight has recently sprung up on the edge of Parque Josone honoring the previously banned Beatles in a bar that evokes the swinging spirit of the decidedly un-Cuban 1960s. Meatballs, onion rings and chicken brochettes provide grazing snacks, but the real draw is the live rock 'n' roll that kicks off alfresco at 10pm Monday, Wednesday and Friday.

Count on energetic covers of Led Zep, the Stones, Pink Floyd and you-know-who.

Bar Mirador
BAR

(Map p222; Av las Américas; admission CUC$2) On the top floor of the Mansión Xanadú, Bar Mirador is Varadero's ultimate romantic hangout where happy hour conveniently coincides with sunset cocktails.

Calle 62
BAR

(Map p216; cnr Av 1 & Calle 62; ⊗8am-2am) Set in the transition zone between old and new Varadero, this simple snack bar attracts clientele from both ends. It's good for a cheese sandwich during the day, and the ambience becomes feistier after dark with live music going on until midnight.

Discoteca Havana Club
NIGHTCLUB

(Map p216; cnr Av 3 & Calle 62; admission CUC$5) Near the Centro Comercial Copey. Expect big, boisterous crowds and plenty of male posturing.

Discoteca la Bamba
NIGHTCLUB

(Map p222; guests/nonguests free/CUC$10; ⊗10pm-4am) Varadero's most modern video disco is at Hotel Tuxpán, in eastern Varadero. It plays mostly Latin music and is considered 'hot.'

Palacio de la Rumba
NIGHTCLUB

(Map p222; Av las Américas, Km 2; admission CUC$10; ⊗10pm-3am) Overall, the most banging night out on the peninsula. There's live salsa music at weekends and a good mix of Cubans and tourists. Admission includes your drinks. It's located by the Hotel Bella Costa.

☆ Entertainment

While Varadero's nightlife might look enticing on paper, there's no real entertainment 'scene' as such, and the concept of bar-hopping à la Cancún or Miami Beach is almost nonexistent, unless you're prepared to incorporate some long-distance hiking into your drinking schedule. Most happening spots – the good and, more often than not, the bad – are attached to the hotels.

★ Cabaret Continental
CABARET

(Map p222; Av las Américas; admission incl drink CUC$25; ⊗show 10pm) There's a coolness to the kitsch at the retro Hotel Internacional, which stages a shamelessly over-the-top, Tropicana-style floor show (Tuesday to Sunday), which is, arguably, second only to 'the one' in Havana. Book the dinner at 8pm (booking through your hotel is best), catch the singers and dancers strutting their stuff, and stay after midnight for the tie-loosening disco.

Casa de la Música
LIVE MUSIC

(Map p216; cnr Av de la Playa & Calle 42; admission CUC$10; ⊗10:30pm-3am Wed-Sun) Aping its two popular Havana namesakes, this place has some quality live acts and a definitive Cuban feel. It's in town and attracts a local crowd who pay in pesos.

Club Mambo
LIVE MUSIC

(Map p222; Av las Américas; open bar, admission CUC$10; ⊗10pm-2am Mon-Fri, to 3am Sat & Sun) Cuba's 1950s mambo craze lives on at this quality live music venue – arguably one of Varadero's hippest and best. Situated next to Club Amigo Varadero in the eastern part of town, the CUC$10 entry includes all your drinks. A DJ spins when the band takes a break, but this place is all about live music. There's a pool table if you don't feel like dancing.

Cabaret Cueva del Pirata
CABARET

(Map p222; ☑66-77-51; Autopista Sur; open bar CUC$10; ⊗10pm-3am Mon-Sat) A kilometer east of the Hotel Sol Elite Palmeras, Cabaret Cueva del Pirata presents scantily clad dancers in a Cuban-style floor show with a buccaneer twist (eye patches, swashbuckling moves). This cabaret is inside a natural cave and once the show is over, the disco begins. It's a popular place, attracting a young crowd. Monday's the best night. Book through your hotel.

Centro Cultural Comparsita
CULTURAL CENTER

(Map p216; Calle 60, btwn Avs 2 & 3; admission CUC$1-5; ⊗10pm-3am) An ARTex cultural center on the edge of Varadero town with concerts, shows, dancing, karaoke and plenty of local flavor. Check the current schedule taped on the door.

🔒 Shopping

Caracol shops in the main hotels sell souvenirs, postcards, T-shirts, clothes, alcohol and snack foods. See the new private sector at play in nebulous **Mercado Alegría**, an umbrella term for the private vendors who set up stalls on Av 1 between Calles 42 and 48.

Centro Comercial Hicacos
SHOPPING CENTER

(Map p216; ⊗10am-10pm) Varadero town's modern subterranean mall in Parque de las 8000 Taquillas is small by American standards, but serves the basics including souvenirs, cigars, a spa/gym and an Infotur office.

Casa del Ron
RUM

(Map p216; Av 1, cnr Calle 62) The best selection of rum in Varadero as well as tasting opportunities in a venerable old building with a scale model of Matanzas' Santa Elena distillery to admire as you sup.

Casa de las Américas
BOOKS, MUSIC

(Map p216; cnr Av 1 & Calle 59) A retail outlet of the famous Havana cultural institution, this place sells CDs, books and art.

Casa del Habano
CIGARS

(Map p218; Av de la Playa, btwn Calles 31 & 32; ⊙9am-6pm) The place for cigars: it has top-quality merchandise from humidors to perfume and helpful service. There is another branch (Map p216; ☑66-78-43; cnr Av 1 & Calle 63; ⊙9am-9pm) that serves a wicked cup of coffee in the upstairs cafe.

Galería de Arte Varadero
ART

(Map p216; Av 1, btwn Calles 59 & 60; ⊙9am-7pm) Antique jewelry, museum-quality silver and glass, paintings and other heirlooms from Varadero's bygone bourgeois days are sold here. As most items are of patrimonial importance, everything is already conveniently tagged with export permission.

Plaza América
SHOPPING CENTER

(Map p222; Autopista Sur Km 7; ⊙minimarket 10am-8:30pm) Built in 1997, but already looking dated, Cuba's first bona fide shopping mall is one of Varadero's less inspired architectural creations, though it serves its purpose. Useful outlets include a pharmacy, bank, an Egrem music store, Benetton, restaurants and various souvenir shops.

Taller de Cerámica Artística
ARTS & CRAFTS

(Map p216; Av 1, btwn Calles 59 & 60; ⊙9am-7pm) Next door to Galería de Arte Varadero and Casa de las Américas, you can buy fine artistic pottery that's made on the premises. Most items are in the CUC$200 to CUC$250 range.

Gran Parque de la Artesanía
MARKET

(Map p218; Av 1, btwn Calles 15 & 16) The open-air artisans' market that once stood on the site of the Centro Comercial Hicacos has been reborn further down Av 1.

Librería Hanoi
BOOKS

(Map p216; cnr Av 1 & Calle 44; ⊙9am-9pm) A good selection of books in English, from poetry to politics.

ARTex
SOUVENIRS

(Map p216; Av 1, btwn Calles 46 & 47; ⊙9am-5pm) Showcases CDs, T-shirts, musical instruments and more.

ⓘ Information

DANGERS & ANNOYANCES

Crime-wise, Varadero's dangers are minimal. Aside from getting drunk at the all-inclusive bar and tripping over your bath mat on the way to the toilet, you haven't got too much to worry about. Watch out for mismatched electrical outlets in hotels. In some rooms, a 110V socket might sit right next to a 220V one. They should be labeled, but aren't always.

Out on the beach, a red flag means no swimming allowed due to the undertow or some other danger. A blue jellyfish known as the Portuguese man-of-war can produce a bad reaction if you come in contact with its long tentacles. Wash the stung area with sea water and seek medical help if the pain becomes intense or you have difficulty breathing. They're most common in summer when you'll see them washed up on the beach; tread carefully. Theft of unguarded shoes, sunglasses and towels is routine along this beach.

EMERGENCY

Asistur (☑66-72-77; Av 1 No 4201, btwn Calles 42 & 43; ⊙9am-4:30pm Mon-Fri) Emergency assistance.

INTERNET ACCESS & TELEPHONE

Most hotels have internet access for CUC$6 to CUC$8 an hour. Buy a scratch card from the reception. If you're in a cheaper place, use the public **Etecsa Telepunto**. (cnr Av 1 & Calle 30)

MEDICAL SERVICES

Many large hotels have infirmaries that can provide free basic first aid.

Clínica Internacional Servimed (☑66-77-11; cnr Av 1 & Calle 60; ⊙24hr) Medical or dental consultations (CUC$25 to CUC$70) and hotel calls (CUC$50 to CUC$60). There's also a good pharmacy (open 24 hours) here with items in convertibles.

Farmacia Internacional Marina Chapelín (☑61-85-56; Autopista Sur Km 11, Marina Chapelín; ⊙9am-9pm); Kawama (☑61-44-70; Av Kawama; ⊙9am-9pm); Plaza América (☑66-80-42; Av las Américas Km 6, Plaza América; ⊙9am-9pm)

MONEY

In Varadero, European visitors can pay for hotels and meals in euros. If you change money at your hotel front desk, you'll sacrifice 1% more than at a bank.

Banco de Ahorro Popular (Calle 36, btwn Av 1 & Autopista Sur; ☺8:30am-4pm Mon-Fri) Probably the slowest option.

Banco Financiero Internacional Av 1 (Av 1, cnr Calle 32; ☺9am-7pm Mon-Fri, 9am-5pm Sat & Sun); Plaza América (cnr Av las Américas & Calle 61; ☺9am-noon & 1-6pm Mon-Fri, 9am-6pm Sat & Sun) Traveler's checks and cash advances on Visa and MasterCard.

Cadeca (cnr Av de la Playa & Calle 41; ☺8:30am-6pm Mon-Sat, 8:30am-noon Sun)

POST

Many of the larger hotels have branch post offices.

Post Office (Calle 64, btwn Avs 1 & 2; ☺8am-noon & 1-5pm Mon-Fri, 8am-noon Sat)

Post Office (cnr Av 1 & Calle 36; ☺8am-6pm Mon-Sat)

TOURIST INFORMATION

Infotur (☐66-29-61; cnr Av 1 & Calle 13) Main office is next to Hotel Acuazul, but they have a desk in most large resorts.

TRAVEL AGENCIES

Almost every hotel has a tourism desk where staff will book adventure tours, skydiving, scuba diving, whatever. It's almost always cheaper, however, to go directly to the tour agency.

Cubamar (☐66-88-55; Av 1, btwn Calles 14 & 15) Office on ground floor of Aparthotel Varazul. Arranges trips to Río Canímar.

Cubatur (☐66-72-16; cnr Av 1 & Calle 33; ☺8:30am-6pm) Reserves hotel rooms nationally; organizes bus transfers to Havana hotels and excursions to Península de Zapata and other destinations.

Havanatur (☐66-70-27; Av 3, btwn Calles 33 & 34; ☺8am-6pm)

ⓘ Getting There & Away

AIR

Juan Gualberto Gómez International Airport (☐61-30-16) is 20km from central Varadero toward Matanzas and another 6km off the main highway. Airlines here include Thomas Cook from London and Manchester; Cubana from Buenos Aires and Toronto; Air Berlin from Düsseldorf and four other German cities; Arkefly from Amsterdam; and Air Transat and WestJet from various Canadian cities. The check-in time at Varadero is 90 minutes before flight time.

BUS

Terminal de Ómnibus (cnr Calle 36 & Autopista Sur) has daily air-con **Víazul** (☐61-48-86; ☺7am-noon & 1-7pm) buses to a few destinations.

All four daily Havana buses (CUC$10, three hours) stop at Matanzas (CUC$6, one hour); all bar the second of these also call at Juan Gual-berto Gómez International Airport (CUC$6, 25 minutes). Buses depart from Varadero at 8am, 11:35am, 3:30pm and 6pm.

Two buses run to Trinidad (CUC$20, six hours) via Cienfuegos (CUC$16, 4½ hours) at 8:15am and 2pm. The morning departure also stops at Santa Clara (CUC$11, three hours 20 minutes).

The Santiago bus (CUC$49, 12 hours) leaves nightly at 9:45pm stopping in Cárdenas (CUC$6, 20 minutes), Colón (CUC$6, 1½ hours), Santa Clara (CUC$11, three hours 20 minutes), Sancti Spíritus (CUC$17, five hours), Ciego de Ávila (CUC$19, 6¼ hours), Camagüey (CUC$25), Las Tunas (CUC$33), Holguín (CUC$38) and Bayamo (CUC$41).

If you have the time, you can get to Havana by catching the Víazul bus to Matanzas and taking the Hershey Railway from there.

Aside from the 8:15am and 9:45pm Víazul buses to Cárdenas, you can go on local bus 236, which departs every hour or so from next to a small tunnel marked 'Ómnibus de Cárdenas' outside the main bus station. You can also catch this bus at the corner of Av 1 and Calle 13 (CUC$1). Don't rely on being able to buy tickets for non-Víazul buses from Varadero to destinations in Matanzas province and beyond: the official line is tourists can't take them, and tourists in Varadero are generally recognizable from Cubans. With decent Spanish you could get lucky.

Cubanacán's Conectando runs a handy bus service between hotels in Varadero and hotels in Havana. There's also a daily service between Varadero and Trinidad via Cienfuegos. Prices are similar to Víazul. Book tickets at least a day in advance through Infotur.

CAR

You can hire a car from practically every hotel in town and prices are pretty generic between different makes and models. Once you've factored in fuel and insurance, a standard car will cost you approximately CUC$70 to CUC$80 a day.

Aside from the hotel reps, you can try **Havanautos** (☐61-44-09; cnr Av 1 & Calle 31) or **Cubacar** (☐61-44-10, 66-73-26; cnr Av 1 & Calle 21).

Havanautos (☐25-36-30), **Transtur** (☐25-36-21), **Vía** (☐61-47-83) and Cubacar all have car-rental offices in the airport car park. Expect to pay at least CUC$75 a day for the smallest car (or CUC$50 daily on a two-week basis).

Luxury cars are available at **Rex** (☐66-77-39, 66-75-39). It rents Audi and automatic transmission (rare in Cuba) cars starting from CUC$100 per day.

There's a **Servi-Cupet gas station** (cnr Autopista Sur & Calle 17; ☺24hr) on the Vía Blanca at the entrance to Marina Acua near Hotel

Sunbeach, and one at **Centro Todo En Uno** (Map p216; cnr Calle 54 & Autopista Sur).

If heading to Havana, you'll have to pay the CUC$2 toll at the booth on the Vía Blanca upon leaving.

ℹ Getting Around

TO/FROM THE AIRPORT

Varadero and Matanzas are each about 20km from the spur road to Juan Gualberto Gómez International Airport; it's another 6km from the highway to the airport terminal. A tourist taxi costs CUC$20 to Matanzas and around CUC$25 for the ride from the airport to Varadero. Convince the driver to use the meter and it should work out cheaper. All four Víazul buses bound for Havana call at the airport, leaving at 8am, 11:35am, 3:30pm and 6pm and arriving 25 minutes later. Tickets cost CUC$6.

BUS

Varadero Beach Tour (all-day ticket CUC$5; ⊙ 9:30am-9pm) is a handy open-top double-decker tourist bus with 45 hop on/hop off stops linking all the resorts and shopping malls along the entire length of the peninsula. It passes every half-hour at well-marked stops with route and distance information. You can buy tickets on the bus itself.

There's an additional tour bus to Matanzas and all sights in between.

A gimmicky toy train connects the three large Meliá resorts.

Local buses 47 and 48 run from Calle 64 to Santa Marta, south of Varadero on the Autopista Sur; bus 220 runs from Santa Marta to the far eastern end of the peninsula. There are no fixed schedules. Fares are a giveaway at 20 centavos. You can also utilize bus 236 to and from Cárdenas, which runs the length of the peninsula.

HORSE CART

A state-owned horse and cart around Varadero costs CUC$5 per person for a 45-minute tour or CUC$10 for a full two-hour tour – plenty of time to see the sights.

MOPED & BICYCLE

Mopeds and bikes are an excellent way of getting off the peninsula and discovering a little of the Cuba outside. Rentals are available at most of the all-inclusive resorts, and bikes are usually lent as part of the package. The generic price is CUC$9 per hour and CUC$25 per day, with gas included in hourly rates (though a levy of CUC$6 may be charged on a 24-hour basis, so ask). There's one **Palmares rental post** (cnr Av 1 & Calle 38) in the center of town with mopeds for those not staying at an all-inclusive. This guy might have a couple of rickety bikes with

no gears and 'pedal-backwards' brakes: pay no more than CUC$2 per hour or CUC$15 per day.

TAXI

Metered tourist taxis charge a CUC$1 starting fee plus CUC$1 per kilometer (same tariff day and night). Coco-taxis (*coquitos* or *huevitos* in Spanish) charge less with no starting fee. A taxi to Cárdenas/Havana will be about CUC$20/85 one way. Taxis hang around all the main hotels or you can phone **Cuba Taxi** (☑ 61-05-55) or **Transgaviota** (☑ 61-97-62). The latter uses large cars if you're traveling with big luggage. Tourists are not supposed to use the older Lada taxis. It can be worth haggling.

Cárdenas

POP 109, 552

It's hard to imagine a more jarring juxtaposition. Twenty kilometers east of the bright lights of Varadero lies shabby Cárdenas, home to countless resort-based waiters, front-desk clerks and taxi drivers; but with barely a restaurant, hotel or motorized cab to serve it.

Threadbare after 50 years of austerity, Cárdenas is the Miss Havisham of Cuba: an ageing dowager, once beautiful, but now looking more like a sepia-toned photo from another era. Streets once filled with illustrious buildings have suffered irrevocably since the Revolution, leaving this former sugar port a shadow of its former self.

Cárdenas has nevertheless played an episodic role in Cuban history. In 1850 Venezuelan adventurer Narciso López and a ragtag army of American mercenaries raised the Cuban flag here for the first time in a vain attempt to free the colony from its Spanish colonizers. Other history-making inhabitants followed, including revolutionary student leader José Antonio Echeverría, who was shot during an abortive raid to assassinate President Batista in 1957. This rich past is showcased in three fabulous museums stationed around Parque Echeverría, the city's main plaza, which today constitute the key reason to visit.

Museums aside, the dilapidated facades of Cárdenas can be a shock to travelers coming from Varadero. If you want to see a picture of real Cuban life, it doesn't get more eye-opening; if it's minty mojitos and all-day volleyball you're after, stick to the tourist beaches.

When asking for directions, beware that Cárdenas residents often use the old street

MATANZAS PROVINCE CÁRDENAS

names rather than the new street-naming system (numbers). Double-check if uncertain.

◉ Sights

In among the battered buildings and dingy peso restaurants of central Cárdenas, three excellent museums, all situated on pretty Parque Echeverría, stand out as city highlights.

★ Museo de Batalla de Ideas   MUSEUM
(Av 6, btwn Calles 11 & 12; admission CUC$2, camera CUC$5; ⊙9am-5pm Tue-Sat, 9am-1pm Sun) The newest of Cárdenas' three museums offers a well-designed and organized overview of the history of US-Cuban relations, replete with sophisticated graphics. Inspired by the case of Elián González, a boy from Cardeñas whose mother, stepfather and 11 others drowned attempting to enter the US by boat in 1999, the museum is the solid form of Castro's resulting *batalla de ideas* (battle of ideas) with the US government.

The museum's collection has grown ever since, with the displays' theme naturally centering round the eight months during which Cuba and the US debated the custody of Elián – but it extends also to displays on the quality of the Cuban education system and a courtyard containing busts of anti-imperialists who died for the revolutionary cause. The exhibit that most epitomizes the purpose of the museum, however, is possibly the sculpture of a child in the act of disparagingly throwing away a Superman toy.

Museo Casa Natal de José Antonio Echeverría   MUSEUM
(Av 4 Este No 560; admission incl guide CUC$1; ⊙10am-5pm Tue-Sat, 9am-1pm Sun) This museum has a macabre historical collection including the original garrote used to execute Narciso López by strangulation in 1851. Objects relating to the 19th-century independence wars are downstairs, while the 20th-century Revolution is covered upstairs, reached via a beautiful spiral staircase.

In 1932 José Antonio Echeverría was born here, a student leader slain by Batista's police in 1957 after a botched assassination attempt in Havana's Presidential Palace. There's a statue of him in the eponymous square outside.

Museo Oscar María de Rojas   MUSEUM
(cnr Av 4 & Calle 13; admission CUC$5; ⊙9am-6pm Tue-Sat, 9am-1pm Sun) Cuba's second-oldest museum (after the Museo Bacardí in Santiago) offers more weird artifacts, including a strangulation chair from 1830, a face mask of Napoleon, the tail of Antonio Maceo's horse, Cuba's largest collection of snails and, last but by no means least, some preserved fleas – yes fleas – from 1912.

The museum is set in a lovely colonial building and staffed with knowledgeable official guides.

Catedral de la Inmaculada Concepción   CHURCH
(Av Céspedes, btwn Calles 8 & 9) Parque Colón is the city's other interesting square and here stands the main ecclesiastical building of Cárdenas. Built in 1846, it's noted for its stained glass and purportedly the oldest statue of Christopher Columbus in the western hemisphere.

Dating from 1862, Colón, as he's known in Cuba, stands rather authoritatively with his face fixed in a thoughtful frown and a globe resting at his feet. It's Cárdenas' best photo op.

Flagpole Monument   MONUMENT
(cnr Av Céspedes & Calle 2) No, not just any old flagpole. At the northern end of Av Céspedes, this is a flagpole attached to a monument and commemorates the first raising of the Cuban flag on May 19, 1850.

Arrechabala Rum Factory   FACTORY
(cnr Calle 2 & Av 13) To the northwest of the city center in the industrial zone is where Varadero rum is distilled: the Havana Club rum company was founded here in 1878. The company (and its international partner Bacardi) has recently been entangled in a trademark dispute with the Cuban government and partner Pernod Ricard over the rights to sell Havana Club in the US.

There are no tours officially available.

⌂ Sleeping

Down the road Varadero flaunts more than 50 hotels. Here in humble Cárdenas there are precisely zero now that the once-grand Hotel Dominica (a National Monument next to the cathedral) has closed indefinitely. Fortunately, Cárdenas sports several good (if notoriously hard-to-find) casas particulares.

★ Hostal Ida   CASA PARTICULAR $
(☑52-15-59; Calzada 388, btwn Avs 13 & 15; r CUC$30-35; ⓟ☀) In Hostal Ida – as in most of Cárdenas – the beauty is within. Don't let the tatty street setting put you off. Inside this

plush apartment (with private entrance and garage) you'll find a stunning living room/kitchenette and a decadently furnished bedroom/bathroom that might have floated over from a decent Varadero hotel.

Not surprisingly, owner Lulu once worked at Sandals and his skills extend to an ample CUC$5 breakfast.

Ricardo Domínguez   CASA PARTICULAR $
(☑ 528-94431; cnr Avs 31 & Calle 12; r CUC$35; P ✳) If Ida's is full, make the trek 1.5km northwest of Parque Echeverría to this spick-and-span bungalow with its leafy garden seemingly just plucked from one of Miami's more tasteful suburbs. The price, though, is steep for a casa this far from the center.

✖ Eating

Half the chefs in Varadero probably come from Cárdenas, which adds irony to the city's dire restaurant scene. A couple of new paladares have raised the game slightly.

Slow Cooking D'Alonso   JAPANESE $
(Céspedes No 708; sushi CUC$3) Sit around a small kitchen island with a rum or sake while your Cuban chef cooks up tempura or prepares sushi, and pinch yourself to check that you're still in Cárdenas. There are even chopsticks.

Los Yoa   CUBAN $
(Calzada, cnr Av 13; mains CUC$5-8; ◔6-10pm Wed-Mon) Small local paladar and cafe that has made the most of the new privatization laws and upped the ante in Cárdenas' decidedly iffy culinary scene. Strange pornographic art adorns the walls.

Self-Catering

There are many convertible supermarkets and stores near the cast-iron 19th-century market hall **Plaza Molocoff** (cnr Av 3 Oeste & Calle 12). You can get cheap peso snacks in the market itself and the surrounding area, where merchants peddle everything from fake hair to plastic Buddhas.

Vegetable Market   MARKET $
(Plaza Molocoff; ◔8am-5pm Mon-Sat, 8am-2pm Sun) Inside Plaza Molocoff.

El Dandy   MARKET $
(Av 3, on Plaza Molocoff; ◔9am-5pm Mon-Sat, 9am-noon Sun) Sells drinks and groceries.

✫ Entertainment

Casa de la Cultura   CULTURAL CENTER
(Av Céspedes No 706, btwn Calles 15 & 16) Housed in a beautiful but faded colonial building with stained glass and an interior patio with rockers. Search the handwritten advertising posters for rap *peñas* (performances), theater and literature events.

Cine Cárdenas   CINEMA
(cnr Av Céspedes & Calle 14) Has daily movie screenings.

🛍 Shopping

Librería la Concha de Venus   BOOKS
(Av Céspedes No 551, cnr Calle 12; ◔9am-5pm Mon-Fri, 8am-noon Sat) Books in Spanish.

ⓘ Information

Banco de Crédito y Comercio (cnr Calle 9 & Av 3)

Cadeca (cnr Av 1 Oeste & Calle 12)

Centro Médico Sub Acuática (☑ 52-21-14; Calle 13, channel 16 VHF; per hr CUC$80; ◔8am-4pm Mon-Sat, doctors on-call 24hr) Two kilometers northwest on the road to Varadero at Hospital Julio M Aristegui; has a Soviet recompression chamber dating from 1981.

Etecsa Telepunto (cnr Av Céspedes & Calle 12; ◔8:30am-7:30pm) Telephone and internet services.

Pharmacy (Calle 12 No 60; ◔24hr)

Post Office (cnr Av Céspedes & Calle 8; ◔8am-6pm Mon-Sat)

ⓘ Getting There & Away

The Varadero–Santiago **Víazul** (www.viazul.com) bus stops at the **bus station** (cnr Av Céspedes & Calle 22) once daily in either direction. The eastbound service leaves Varadero at 9:45pm and arrives in Cárdenas at 10:10pm. It then heads east via Colón (CUC$6, one hour), Santa Clara (CUC$11, three hours) and all other stops to Santiago de Cuba (CUC$48, 15½ hours). The Varadero–Trinidad bus leaves Varadero at 8:15am and arrives in Cárdenas at 8:40am before calling at Cienfuegos (CUC$15, 4½ hours) and Trinidad (CUC$19, six hours).

Local buses leave from the bus station to Havana and Santa Clara daily, but they're often full upon reaching Cárdenas. There are also trucks to Jovellanos/Perico, which puts you 12km from Colón and onto possible onward transport to the east. The ticket office is at the rear of the station.

Bus 236 to/from Varadero leaves hourly from the corner of Av 13 Oeste and Calle 13 (50 centavos, but they like to charge tourists CUC$1).

ℹ Getting Around

The main horse-carriage (one peso) route through Cárdenas is northeast on Av Céspedes from the bus station and then northwest on Calle 13 to the hospital, passing the stop of bus 236 (to Varadero) on the way.

The **Servi-Cupet gas station** (cnr Calle 13 & Av 31 Oeste) is opposite an old Spanish fort on the northwest side of town, on the road to Varadero.

San Miguel de los Baños & Around

Nestled away in the interior of Matanzas province amid rolling hills punctuated by vivid splashes of bougainvillea, San Miguel de los Baños is an atmospheric old spa town that once rivaled Havana for elegant opulence. Once, that is. Flourishing briefly as a destination for wealthy folk seeking the soothing medicinal waters that were 'discovered' here in the early 20th century, San Miguel saw a smattering of lavish neoclassical villas shoot up that still line the town's arterial Av de Abril today. But the boom times didn't last. Just prior to the Revolution, pollution from a local sugar mill infiltrated the water supply and the resort quickly faded from prominence. Now, it's a curious mix between an architectural time capsule from a bygone era and something out of a post-apocalyptic John Wyndham novel.

⊙ Sights & Activities

Passing visitors will be shocked at the architectural contrasts here: the smaller houses of the current population juxtaposed with the surreally ostentatious buildings of the glory days, such as the ornate multidomed **Gran**

Hotel y Balneario, on the north side of town, a replica of the Grand Casino at Monte Carlo. Plans to reopen the hotel haven't yet materialized but it's relatively easy to wander the eerie grounds down to the still-standing red-brick Romanesque bath houses. You'll sometimes have to negotiate with a guard at the main entrance; a small tip usually suffices. It's probably best to give bathing a miss, though.

Looming above town are the steep slopes of **Loma de Jacán**, a glowering hill with 448 steps embellished by faded murals of the Stations of the Cross. When you reach the small chapel on top you can drink in the town's best views with the added satisfaction that you are standing at the highest point in the province.

🛏 Sleeping & Eating

Finca Coincidencia　　　CASA PARTICULAR **$**
(☑81-39-23; Carretera Central, btwn Colesio & Jovellanos; r CUC$20; ℗) ⌀ Enhance your taste for bucolic provincial life away from the razzmatazz of the province's north coast at this idyllic farm 14km northeast of San Miguel de los Baños and 6km east of the town of Colesio on the Carretera Central.

You can chill in grounds replete with mango and guava trees, participate in ceramics classes and help out on a farm where 83 types of plants are cultivated.

ℹ Getting There & Away

To get to San Miguel de los Baños, follow Rte 101 from Cárdenas to Colesio where you cross the Carretera Central; the town is situated a further 8km to the southwest of Colesio. A taxi from Cárdenas should cost CUC$20 to CUC$25 – bargain hard. You may be able to catch a ride on a truck/local bus from Cárdenas bus station.

OFF THE BEATEN TRACK

COLÓN

Colón, tucked away in the east of the province 40km east of Jovellanos, makes an interesting journey-breaker on Cuba's Carretera Central. With its striking colonnaded buildings and one of Cuba's prettiest, greenest central plazas, this town is more about ambience than attractions. What you will be seeing in Colón is an example (and there are many across the country) of what Cuba is like for Cubans untouched by the tourism industry and the money it generates.

Stroll up the main thoroughfare Calle Martí to soak up local life on leafy **Parque de la Libertad** (aka Parque de Colón) with its statue of Christopher Columbus among the numerous other busts. Nearby you can blow the cobwebs off the **Iglesia Catholica** (Catholic church), **Escuela de Artes y Oficios** (School of Arts and Works) with its striking colonial revivalist architecture and the optimistically named **Hotel Nuevo Continental** dating from 1937. There is also a museum, an art gallery and an old fort to see.

PENÍNSULA DE ZAPATA

POP 9334

A vast, virtually uninhabited swampy wilderness spanning the entirety of southern Matanzas, the 4520-sq-km Península de Zapata quickens the pulses of wildlife-watchers and divers alike with the country's most important bird species and some of the most magical offshore reef diving secreted in its humid embrace. Most of the peninsula, a protected zone now part of Gran Parque Natural Montemar, was formerly known as Parque Nacional Ciénaga de Zapata: in 2001, it was declared a Unesco Biosphere Reserve.

The sugar-mill town of Australia in the northeast of the peninsula marks the main access point to the park. Near here is one of the region's big tourist money-spinners, the cheesy yet oddly compelling Boca de Guamá, a reconstructed Taíno village.

The road hits the coast at Playa Larga, home to the peninsula's best beaches, at the head of the Bahía de Cochinos where propaganda billboards still laud Cuba's historic victory over the *Yanqui* imperialists in 1961.

Ornithologists and nature lovers will want to veer southwest from here, where the sugarcane plantations fade fast into sticky swamp. This is one of the remotest regions of Cuba, rarely penetrated by tourists. Yet intrepid visitors will reap the benefits: an incredible diversity of birds, as well as endemic reptile and plant species, can be glimpsed in the mangrove-flecked waterways here.

Aside from its reputation as a proverbial banana-skin for US imperialism, the east coast of Bahía de Cochinos also claims some of the best cave diving in the Caribbean and southeast of Playa Larga the dive sites fan out temptingly, accompanied by a couple of less riveting resort hotels.

Accommodations outside of the resorts, however, are thankfully abundant. You can check out excellent options in Central Australia, Playa Larga and Playa Girón.

At last research, the Víazul bus through the peninsula had been reinstated after a brief hiatus. There's also a handy shuttle service between Boca de Guamá and Caleta Buena.

ℹ Information

La Finquita (☑ 91-32-24; Autopista Nacional Km 142; ◷ 9am-5pm Mon-Sat, 8am-noon Sun), a highly useful information center-cum-snack bar run by Cubanacán just by the turn-off toward Playa Larga from the Autopista Nacional, arranges trips into the Península de Zapata and books rooms at the Villa Guamá. The **National Park Office** (☑ 98-72-49; ◷ 8am-4:30pm Mon-Fri, 8am-noon Sat) is at the north entrance to Playa Larga on the road from Boca de Guamá.

Etecsa, the post office and convertible stores are across the Autopista in Jagüey Grande. Insect repellent is absolutely essential on the peninsula and while Cuban repellent is available locally, it's like wasabi on sushi for the ravenous buggers here.

PENINSULA SHUTTLE SERVICE

Complementing the Havana–Cienfuegos–Trinidad Víazul bus which runs through the Zapata peninsula, but has a history of altering (or canceling) its schedule, there is a twice-daily hop on/hop off shuttle bus linking all of the area's key sights. The service starts at Hotel Playa Girón at 9am, heads out to Caleta Buena and then back past Punta Perdiz, Cueva los Peces and Hotel Playa Larga to Boca de Guamá at 10am. The shuttle then leaves Boca de Guamá at 10:30am for the reverse journey. The service is repeated in the afternoon with departure times being 1pm from Hotel Playa Girón and 3:30pm from Boca de Guamá. A ticket for the day costs CUC$3 per person.

Central Australia & Around

No, you haven't just arrived Down Under. About 1.5km south of the Autopista Nacional on the way to Boca de Guamá, is the large disused Central Australia sugar mill, built in 1904.

◉ Sights

Museo de la Comandancia MUSEUM
(admission CUC$1; ◷ 9am-5pm Tue-Sat, 9am-noon Sun) During the 1961 Bay of Pigs invasion, Fidel Castro had his headquarters in the former office of the sugar mill, but today the building is devoted to this revolutionary museum. You can see the desk and phone from where Fidel commanded his forces, along with other associated memorabilia. Outside is the wreck of an invading aircraft shot down by Fidel's troops.

The concrete memorials lining the road to the Bahía de Cochinos mark the spots where defenders were killed in 1961. A more moving testimony to the Bay of Pigs episode is the Museo de Playa Girón.

Finca Fiesta Campesina WILDLIFE RESERVE
(admission CUC$1; ☺9am-6pm) Approximately 400m on your right after the Central Australia exit is a kind of wildlife-park-meets-country fair with labeled examples of Cuba's typical flora and fauna. The highlights of this strangely engaging place are the coffee (some of the best in Cuba and served with a sweet wedge of sugarcane), the bull-riding and the hilarious if slightly infantile games of guinea-pig roulette overseen with much pizzazz by the gentleman at the gate.

It's the only place in Cuba – outside the cockfighting – where you encounter any form of open gambling.

🛏 Sleeping & Eating

There are more casas in Playa Larga (32km) and Playa Girón (48km).

Motel Batey Don Pedro CABIN $
(☑91-28-25; Carretera a Península de Zapata; s/d CUC$26/31; ℗) The best bet for accommodations in the area, this sleepy motel is down a track just south of the turnoff to the Península de Zapata, from Km 142 on the Autopista Nacional at Jagüey Grande. There are 12 rooms in thatched double units with ceiling fans, crackling TVs and patios – and a random frog or two in the bathroom.

The motel is designed to resemble a peasant settlement. For food there is an on-site restaurant serving just-OK food and, a far better option, the Finca Fiesta Campesina at the beginning of the track. English is spoken here and energy-boosting *guarapo* (sugarcane juice) along with some of Zapata's best coffee is served.

Pío Cuá CARIBBEAN $$
(Carretera de Playa Larga Km 8; meals CUC$8-20; ☺11am-5pm) A favorite with Guamá-bound tour buses, this huge place is set up for big groups, but retains fancy decor with lots of stained glass. Shrimp, lobster or chicken meals are pretty good. It's 8km from the Autopista turnoff, heading south from Australia.

❶ Getting There & Away

Víazul buses between Havana and Cienfuegos will stop on the Autopista Nacional 1.5km north of Australia; as this isn't an official stop negotiating a pickup is complicated. Ring the bus stations in Havana or Cienfuegos.

Boca de Guamá

Boca de Guamá may be a tourist creation, but as resorts around here go it's among the more imaginative. Situated about halfway between the Autopista Nacional at Jagüey Grande and the famous Bahía de Cochinos, it takes its name from native Taíno chief Guamá, who made a last stand against the Spanish in 1532 (in Baracoa). The big attraction here is the boat trip through mangrove-lined waterways and across Laguna del Tesoro (Treasure Lake) to a 'recreation' of a Taíno village. Fidel used to holiday here and had a hand in developing the Taíno theme. You'll soon be struggling to draw parallels with pre-Columbian Cuba, however: raucous tour groups and even louder rap music welcome your voyage back in time. Arranged around the dock the boats depart from a cluster of restaurants, expensive snack bars, knickknack shops and a crocodile farm. Palm-dotted grounds here make a pleasant break from the surrounding swampy heat.

◉ Sights

Laguna del Tesoro LAKE
This lake is 5km east of Boca de Guamá via the Canal de la Laguna, accessible only by boat. On the far (east) side of the 92-sq-km body of water is a tourist resort named Villa Guamá, built to resemble a Taíno village, on a dozen small islands.

A sculpture park next to the mock village has 32 life-size figures of Taíno villagers in a variety of idealized poses. The lake is called 'Treasure Lake' due to a legend about some treasure the Taíno supposedly threw into the water just prior to the Spanish conquest (not dissimilar to South American El Dorado legends). The lake is stocked with large-mouth bass, so fishers frequently convene.

Criadero de Cocodrilos CROCODILE FARM
(adult/child incl drink CUC$5/3; ☺9:30am-5pm) 🖋 Inside the Guamá complex near the Villa Guamá departure dock, the Criadero de Cocodrilos farm breeds crocodiles – although the fenced-off lake seems barely more authentic than the Taíno village. Lots of crocs languish about; there are other caged animals here.

It used to be possible to visit the nucleus of this breeding program just across the road from the crocodile farm, run by the Ministerio de Industrias Pesqueras. Two species of crocodiles are raised here: the native *Crocodylus rhombifer* (*cocodrilo* in Spanish) and the *Crocodylus acutus* (*caimán* in Spanish), which is found throughout the tropical Americas. Tourism is not encouraged, however, and security guards will point you back across the road to Boca de Guamás faux farm. On your right as you come from the Autopista, the Criadero de Cocodrilos is a breeding facility, run by the zoo, but try your luck and you could get a guided tour here (in Spanish), taking you through each stage of the breeding program. Prior to the establishment of this program in 1962 (considered the first environmental protection act undertaken by the revolutionary government), these two species of marsh-dwelling crocodiles were almost extinct.

The breeding has been so successful that across the road in the Boca de Guamá complex you can buy stuffed baby crocodiles or dine, legally, on crocodile steak.

If you buy anything made from crocodile leather at Boca de Guamá, be sure to ask for an invoice (for the customs authorities) proving that the material came from a crocodile farm and not wild crocodiles. A less controversial purchase would be one of the attractive ceramic bracelets sold at the nearby **Taller de Cerámica** (⊙9am-6pm Mon-Sat) where you can see five kilns in operation.

🛏 Sleeping & Eating

At the boat dock you'll find **Bar la Rionda** (⊙9:30am-5pm) and **Restaurante la Boca** (set meals CUC$12).

Villa Guamá   CABIN $
(☎91-55-51; s/d CUC$35/38) This place was built in 1963 on the east side of the Laguna del Tesoro, about 8km from Boca de Guamá by boat (cars can be left at the crocodile farm; CUC$1). The 50 thatched *cabañas* (cabins) with bath and TV are on piles over the shallow waters.

The six small islands bearing the units are connected by wooden footbridges to other islands with a bar, *cafetería*, overpriced restaurant and a swimming pool containing chlorinated lake water. Rowboats are available for rent, and the bird-watching at sunrise is reputedly fantastic. You'll need insect repellent if you decide to stay. The ferry transfer is not included in the room price.

🛈 Getting There & Away

The twice-daily Havana–Trinidad Víazul bus runs through the Zapata peninsula; ask the driver if he will leave you at the Boca de Guamá ferry dock. Otherwise, it's your own wheels.

🛈 Getting Around

A passenger ferry (adult/child CUC$12/6, 20 minutes) departs Boca de Guamá for Villa Guamá across Laguna del Tesoro four times a day. Speedboats depart more frequently and whisk you across to the pseudo-Indian village in just 10 minutes any time during the day for CUC$12 per person round-trip (with 40 minutes waiting time at Villa Guamá, two-person minimum). In the morning you can allow yourself more time on the island by going one way by launch and returning by ferry.

You can travel on the hop on/hop off shuttle bus (CUC$3) between Boca de Guamá and Caleta Buena.

Gran Parque Natural Montemar

The largest *ciénaga* (swamp) in the Caribbean, **Ciénaga de Zapata** is one of Cuba's most diverse ecosystems. Crowded into this vast wetland (essentially two swamps divided by a rocky central tract) are 14 different vegetation formations including mangroves, wood, dry wood, cactus, savannah, selva and semideciduous. There are also extensive salt pans. The marshes support more than 190 bird species, 31 types of reptiles, 12 species of mammals, plus countless amphibians, fish and insects (including the insatiable mosquito). There are more than 900 plant species here, some 115 of them endemic. It is also an important habitat for the endangered *manatí* (manatee), the Cuban *cocodrilo* (crocodile; *Crocodylus rhombifer*) and the *manjuarí* (alligator gar; *Atractosteus tristoechus*), Cuba's most primitive fish with an alligator's head but a fishlike body. The almost-extinct dwarf hutia (a kind of wild guinea pig) has the swamp as its only refuge.

The Zapata is the best bird-watching spot in Cuba: the place to come to see *zunzuncitos* (bee hummingbirds; the world's smallest bird), cormorants, cranes, ducks, flamingos, hawks, herons, ibis, owls, parrots, partridges and *tocororos* (Cuba's national bird). There are 18 birds endemic to the region. Numerous migratory birds from North America winter here, making November to April prime bird-watching season. It's also the nation's number-one nexus for catch-and-release sportfishing and fly-fishing, where the *palometa, sábalo* and *robalo,* as well as bonefish, thrive.

Communications in Zapata, unsuitable for agriculture, were almost nonexistent before the Revolution when poverty was the rule. Charcoal makers burn wood from the region's semideciduous forests, and *turba* (peat) dug from the swamps is an important source of fuel. The main industry today is tourism and ecotourists are arriving in increasing numbers. Public transport only runs as far as Playa Larga: to see anything of the *ciénaga* proper you'll need to come here as part of a tour.

✦ Activities

There are four main excursions into the park, with an understandable focus on bird-watching. Itineraries are flexible. Transport is not usually laid on; it's best to arrange beforehand. Cars (including chauffeur-driven jeeps) can be rented from Havanautos (p241) in Playa Girón; bank on between CUC$25 and CUC$40 for car and driver.

Aspiring fishers can arrange **fly-fishing** from canoes or (due to the shallowness of the water) on foot at either Las Salinas or Hatiguanico. Ask at Cubanacán's La Finquita office or just turn up if you have your own gear. Between them the two locations offer Cuba's best angling: Las Salinas has excellent fishing; Hatiguanico is great for Tarpon.

Laguna de las Salinas   BIRD-WATCHING
(per person CUC$10) One of the most popular excursions is to this *laguna* where large numbers of migratory waterfowl can be seen from November to April: we're talking 10,000 pink flamingos at a time, plus 190 other feathered species. The first half of the road to Las Salinas is through the forest, while the second half passes swamps and lagoons. Here, aquatic birds can be observed.

Guides are mandatory to explore the refuge. The 22km visit lasts over four hours but you may be able to negotiate for a longer visit.

Observación de Aves   BIRD-WATCHING
(per person CUC$19) This trip offers an extremely flexible itinerary and the right to roam (with a qualified park ornithologist) around a number of different sites, including the **Reserva de Bermejas**. Among 18 species of endemic bird found here you can

see prized *ferminins, cabreritos* and *gallinuelas de Santo Tomás* – found only on the Península de Zapata.

Río Hatiguanico   BIRD-WATCHING
(per person CUC$19) Switching from land to boat, this excursion takes you on a three-hour 12km river trip through the densely forested northwestern part of the peninsula. You'll have to duck to avoid the branches at some points, while at others the river opens out into a wide delta-like estuary. Birdlife is abundant and you may also see turtles and crocodiles.

You'll need to hire transport to get you the 90km to the start point.

Señor Orestes Martínez Garcías   BIRD-WATCHIING
(☎ 525-39004, 98-75-45; chino.zapata@gmail.com; excursions per person CUC$10-20) Garnering a reputation as the area's most knowledgeable resident bird-watcher, 'El Chino' as he is otherwise known can take you on more personalized, and reportedly highly rewarding ornithological forays into the *ciénaga*. He runs a casa particular in the village Batey Caleton near Playa Larga.

Santo Tomás   OUTDOORS
(per person CUC$10) It's also worth asking about this trip, an excursion that begins 30km west of Playa Larga in the park's only real settlement (Santo Tomás) and proceeds along a tributary of the Hatiguanico – walking or boating, depending on the season. It's another good option for bird-watchers.

ℹ Information

Cubanacán's La Finquita on the Autopista near Central Australia is the park information point, and a good place to book your chosen excursion. The Playa Larga or Girón hotels can also arrange tours, as can Hostal Enrique in the village of Caletón by Playa Larga.

Playa Larga

Continuing south from Boca de Guamá you reach Playa Larga, on the Bahía de Cochinos, after 13km. Larga was one of two beaches invaded by US-backed exiles on April 17, 1961 (although Playa Girón, 35km further south, saw far bigger landings). It's now a diver's paradise. There's a cheapish resort here, a scuba-diving center, and a smattering of casas particulares in the adjacent beachside village of Caletón. With the

Bahía de Cochinos

nearest accommodations for Gran Parque Natural Montemar, it is a good base for environmental excursions around the area.

🛏 Sleeping & Eating

⭐ El Caribeño
CASA PARTICULAR **$**

(📞 98-73-59; fidelscaribe@gmail.com; Al Final de Caletón, Batey Caletón; r CUC$25-30; ❄) A Caribbean beach fantasy awaits you in this fine house whose rustic front terrace is practically diving distance from the sea. The sinuous beach here, backed by crooked palms, is gorgeous and the food (crab and lobster) is fantastically fresh. Friendly owner Fidel Fuentes has just built two new sea-view apartments upstairs.

Hostal Enrique
CASA PARTICULAR **$**

(📞 98-74-25; Caletón; r CUC$20-25; ❄) Five hundred meters down the road to Las Salinas is one of area's better casas with two rooms, both with private bathrooms, a large dining

area (serving large portions of food) and a path from the back garden leading to the often-deserted Caletón beach. Enrique can help arrange diving and bird-watching at distinctly cheaper prices than the hotels hereabouts.

Villa Playa Larga
HOTEL **$**

(📞 98-72-94; s/d low season incl breakfast CUC$34/48; P ❄ ≋) On a small scimitar of white-sand beach by the road, just east of the village of Caletón, this hotel has huge rooms in detached bungalows with bathroom, sitting room, fridge and TV. There are also eight two-bedroom family bungalows. A recent overhaul has spruced the place up slightly, though the restaurant is still pretty forlorn.

ⓘ Getting There & Away

The twice-daily Havana–Trinidad Víazul bus runs through the Zapata peninsula and will stop on request outside Villa Playa Larga.

The hop on/hop off Guamá Bus Tour (CUC$3) links with Playa Girón and Guamá.

ⓘ Getting Around

Taxi, car/moped hire at Playa Girón or the peninsula shuttle service (see box text, p234): your choice.

Playa Girón

The sandy arc of Playa Girón nestles peacefully on the eastern side of the infamous Bahía de Cochinos, 48km south of Boca de Guamá. Notorious as the place where the Cold War almost got hot, the beach is actually named for a French pirate, Gilbert Girón, who met his end here by decapitation in the early 1600s at the hands of embittered locals. In April 1961 it was the scene of another botched raid, the ill-fated, CIA-sponsored invasion that tried to land on these remote sandy beaches in one of modern history's classic David and Goliath struggles. Lest we forget, there are still plenty of propaganda-spouting billboards dotted around rehashing past glories, though these days Girón, with its clear Caribbean waters and precipitous offshore drop-off, is a favorite destination for scuba divers and snorkelers.

Besides some decent private houses, Playa Girón's one and only resort is the modest Villa Playa Girón, a low-key all-inclusive that is perennially popular among the diving fraternity. Long, shady Playa los Cocos,

DIVING & SNORKELING IN THE BAHÍA DE COCHINOS

While the Isla de la Juventud and María la Gorda lead most Cuban divers' wish lists, the Bahía de Cochinos has some equally impressive underwater treats. There's a huge drop-off running 30m to 40m offshore for over 30km from Playa Larga down to Playa Girón, a fantastic natural feature that has created a 300m-high coral-encrusted wall with amazing swim-throughs, caves, gorgonians and marine life. Even better, the proximity of this wall to the coastline means that the region's 30-plus dive sites can be easily accessed without a boat – you just glide out from the shore. Good south coast visibility stretches from 30m to 40m and there is a handful of wrecks scattered around.

Organizationally, Playa Girón is well set up with highly professional instructors bivouacked at five different locations along the coast. Generic dive prices (CUC$25 per immersion, CUC$100 for five or CUC$365 for an open-water course) are some of the cheapest in Cuba. Snorkeling is CUC$5 per hour.

The **International Scuba Center** (☑ 98-41-18), at Villa Playa Girón, is the main diving headquarters. It is complemented by the **Club Octopus International Diving Center** (☑ 98-72-94, 98-72-25), 200m west of Villa Playa Larga.

Eight kilometers southeast of Playa Girón is **Caleta Buena** (☉ 10am-6pm), a lovely sheltered cove perfect for snorkeling and kitted out with another diving office. Black coral ridges protect several sinkholes and underwater caves teeming with the oddly shaped sponges for which the area is renowned: a great opportunity for speleo-scuba diving! Because saltwater meets freshwater the fish here are different to other sites. Admission to the beach is CUC$15 and includes an all-you-can-eat lunch buffet and open bar. Beach chairs and thatched umbrellas are spread along the rocky shoreline. Snorkel gear is CUC$3.

More underwater treasures can be seen at the **Cueva de los Peces** (☉ 9am-6pm), a flooded tectonic fault (or *cenote*), about 70m deep on the inland side of the road, almost exactly midway between Playa Larga and Playa Girón. There are lots of bright, tropical fish, plus you can explore back into the darker, spookier parts of the *cenote* with snorkel or dive gear (bring torches). The beach facing has good snorkeling off a black coral shelf. There's a handy restaurant and an on-site dive outfit.

Just beyond the Cueva is **Punta Perdiz**, another phenomenal snorkeling/scuba-diving spot with the wreck of a US landing craft scuppered during the Bay of Pigs invasion to explore. The shallow water is gemstone-blue here and there's good snorkeling right from the shore. There's a smaller on-site diving concession. It costs CUC$1 to use the thatched umbrellas, beach chairs and showers, and there's another decent restaurant. Nonwater-based activities include volleyball and chances to play the amiable custodians at dominoes. Beware the swarms of mosquitoes and *libélulas* (enormous dragonflies).

MATANZAS PROVINCE PLAYA GIRÓN

where the snorkeling is good, is just a five-minute walk south along the shore. In common with many of Cuba's southern coastal areas, there's often more *diente de perro* (dog's tooth) than soft white sand.

On the main entry road to the hotel there's a pharmacy, a post office and a Caracol shop selling groceries. The settlement of Playa Girón is a tiny one-horse town, so the hotel is the best pit stop if you need any goods or services.

☉ Sights

Museo de Playa Girón   MUSEUM
(admission CUC$2, camera CUC$1; ☉ 8am-5pm) Perhaps unsurprisingly, this museum with its gleaming glass display cases evokes a tangible sense of the history of the famous Cold War episode that unfolded within rifle-firing distance of this spot in 1961. Housed across the street from Villa Playa Girón, it offers two rooms of artifacts from the Bay of Pigs skirmish plus numerous photos with (some) bilingual captions.

The mural of victims and their personal items is harrowing and the tactical genius of the Cuban forces comes through in the graphic depictions of how the battle unfolded. The 15-minute film about the 'first defeat of US imperialism in the Americas' is CUC$1 extra. A British Hawker Sea Fury aircraft used by the Cuban Air Force is parked outside the museum; round the back are other vessels used in the battle.

THE BAY OF PIGS

What the Cubans call Playa Girón, the rest of the world has come to know as the Bay of Pigs 'fiasco,' a disastrous attempt by the Kennedy administration to invade Cuba and overthrow Fidel Castro.

Conceived in 1959 by the Eisenhower administration and headed up by deputy director of the CIA, Richard Bissell, the plan to initiate a program of covert action against the Castro regime was given official sanction on March 17, 1960. There was but one proviso: no US troops were to be used in combat.

The CIA modeled their operation on the 1954 overthrow of the left-leaning government of Jacobo Arbenz in Guatemala. However, by the time President Kennedy was briefed on the proceedings in November 1960, the project had mushroomed into a full-scale invasion backed by a 1400-strong force of CIA-trained Cuban exiles and financed with a military budget of US$13 million.

Activated on April 15, 1961, the invasion was a disaster from start to finish. Intending to wipe out the Cuban Air Force on the ground, US planes painted in Cuban Air Force colors (and flown by Cuban exile pilots) missed most of their intended targets. Castro, who had been forewarned of the plans, had scrambled his air force the previous week. Hence, when the invaders landed at Playa Girón two days later, Cuban sea furies were able to promptly sink two of their supply ships and leave a force of 1400 men stranded on the beach.

To add insult to injury, a countrywide Cuban rebellion that had been much touted by the CIA never materialized. Meanwhile a vacillating Kennedy told Bissell he would not provide the marooned exile soldiers with US air cover.

Abandoned on the beaches, without supplies or military back-up, the invaders were doomed. There were 114 killed in skirmishes and a further 1189 captured. The prisoners were returned to the US a year later in return for US$53 million worth of food and medicine.

The Bay of Pigs failed due to a multitude of factors. First, the CIA had overestimated the depth of Kennedy's personal commitment and had made similarly inaccurate assumptions about the strength of the fragmented anti-Castro movement inside Cuba. Second, Kennedy himself, adamant all along that a low-key landing should be made, had chosen a site on an exposed strip of beach close to the Zapata swamps. Third, no one had given enough credit to the political and military know-how of Fidel Castro or to the extent to which the Cuban Intelligence Service had infiltrated the CIA's supposedly covert operation.

The consequences for the US were far-reaching. 'Socialism or death!' a defiant Castro proclaimed at a funeral service for seven Cuban 'martyrs' on April 16, 1961. The Revolution had swung irrevocably toward the Soviet Union.

🛏 Sleeping & Eating

Aside from Villa Playa Girón, the small settlement of Playa Girón has some decent private houses, with most serving food.

★**Hostal Luis** CASA PARTICULAR **$**
(☑ 99-42-58; r incl breakfast CUC$25-30; P ❄) The first house on the road to Cienfuegos is also the village's premier casa. Instantly recognizable by the blue facade and the two stone lions guarding the gate, youthful Luis and his wife offer four spotless rooms on a large lot with plenty of room for parking. The food is legendary.

KS Abella CASA PARTICULAR **$**
(☑ 98-43-83; r CUC$20-25; ❄) The *señor* is a former chef at Villa Playa Girón now trying out his seafood specialties on his casa guests. The casa is situated on the corner of the main road in the set-back red-and-cream bungalow.

Villa Playa Girón RESORT **$$**
(☑ 98-41-10; all-incl s/d CUC$46/65; P ❄ ☁) On a beach imbued with historical significance lies this rather ordinary hotel. Although billed as an all-inclusive, the Villa Playa Girón with its spartan bungalows and spatially challenged dining room, looks more

like a Cuban campismo. Always busy with divers, the villa is an unpretentious place with clean, basic rooms that are often a long walk from the main block.

The beach is a 50m dash away, though its allure has been spoiled somewhat by the construction of a giant wave-breaking wall. Head south for better sand.

❶ Getting There & Away

The twice-daily Havana–Trinidad Víazul bus runs through the Zapata peninsula and stops outside Villa Playa Girón.

The hop on/hop off Guamá Bus Tour (CUC$3) links with Caleta Buena, Playa Larga and Guamá.

❶ Getting Around

Havanautos (☑ 98-41-23) has a car-rental office at Villa Playa Girón or you can hire a moto for CUC$25 per day.

Servi-Cupet gas stations are located on the Carretera Central at Jovellanos and on Colón at Jagüey Grande, as well as on the Autopista Nacional at Aguada de Pasajeros in Cienfuegos province.

East of Caleta Buena the coastal road toward Cienfuegos is not passable in a normal car; backtrack and take the inland road via Rodas.

Cienfuegos Province

Includes ➡

Best Paladares

➡ Restaurante Villa Lagarto (p252)

➡ Paladar Aché (p252)

➡ El Tranvia (p252)

Best Architectural Icons

➡ Palacio de Valle (p247)

➡ Casa de la Cultura Benjamin Duarte (p246)

➡ Teatro Tomás Terry (p245)

Why Go?

Bienvenue (welcome) to Cienfuegos, Cuba's Gallic heart, which sits in the shadow of the crinkled Sierra del Escambray like a displaced piece of Paris on Cuba's untamed southern coastline. French rather than Spanish colonizers were the pioneers in this region, arriving in 1819 and bringing with them the ideas of the European Enlightenment which they industriously incorporated into their fledgling neoclassical city.

Outside of the city, the coast is surprisingly underdeveloped, a mini-rainbow of emerald greens and iridescent blues, flecked with coves, caves and coral reefs. The province's apex is just inland at El Nicho, arguably the most magical spot in the Topes de Collantes nature park.

Though ostensibly Francophile and white, Cienfuegos' once-muted African 'soul' gained a mouthpiece in the 1940s in Cuba's most versatile musician, Benny Moré. He wasn't the only Afro-Cuban improviser. Nearby, Palmira is famous for its Catholic-Yoruba Santería brotherhoods, which still preserve their powerful slave-era traditions.

When to Go

➡ Cienfuegos' high season doesn't really get going until January and runs through to April, when beach-lovers and divers hit the Caribbean coast.

➡ Party-goers will prefer August and September when, despite the imminent hurricane season, the Cienfuegos carnival and the biannual Benny Moré festival respectively can be enjoyed.

➡ Up at El Nicho in the Sierra del Escambray, travel is tougher in the wet season (August to October) due to difficult road conditions.

History

The first settlers in the Cienfuegos area were Taínos, who called their fledgling principality Cacicazgo de Jagua – a native term for 'beauty'. In 1494 Columbus 'discovered' the Bahía de Cienfuegos (Cuba's third-largest bay, with a surface area of 88 sq km) on his second voyage to the New World, and 14 years later Sebastián de Ocampo stopped by during his circumnavigation of the island. He liked the bay so much he built a house there. The pirates followed: during the 16th and 17th centuries buccaneering raids got so bad the Spanish built a bayside fort, the imposing Castillo de Jagua – one of the most important military structures in Cuba.

CIENFUEGOS

POP 165,113

La ciudad que más me gusta a mí (the city I like the best) singer Benny Moré once said of his home city in the song 'Cienfuegos'. He wasn't the settlement's only cheerleader. Cuba's so-called Perla del Sur (Pearl of the South) has long seduced travelers from around the island with its elegance, enlightened French spirit and feisty Caribbean panache. If Cuba has a Paris, this is most definitely it.

Arranged around the country's most spectacular natural bay, Cienfuegos is a nautical city with an enviable waterside setting. Founded in 1819, it's one of Cuba's newest settlements, but also one of its most architecturally homogeneous, a factor that earned it a Unesco World Heritage Site listing in 2005. Geographically, the city is split into two distinct parts: the colonnaded central zone with its elegant Prado and Parque Martí; and Punta Gorda, a thin knife of land slicing into the bay with a clutch of eclectic early 20th-century palaces, including some of Cuba's prettiest buildings.

While much of Cuba is visibly reeling in the current economic crisis,

Cienfuegos Province Highlights

❶ Stroll amid eclectic 19th-century architecture in gorgeous **Parque José Martí** in the capital (p245).

❷ Chill out in style amid the magnificent rooms, beautiful bars and colonial luxury of **Hotel la Unión** (p250) in Cienfuegos.

❸ Stay in an amazing casa particular in Cienfuegos' classic neighborhood of **Punta Gorda** (p247).

❹ Track the legends of the Santería religion in **Palmira** (p255).

❺ Bask at, or dive off, the beach in **Rancho Luna** (p255)

❻ Spot pink flamingos and pelicans at the little-visited **Laguna Guanaroca** (p257).

❼ Hike to bracing **El Nicho** (p257) and cool down underneath an invigorating waterfall.

Central Cienfuegos

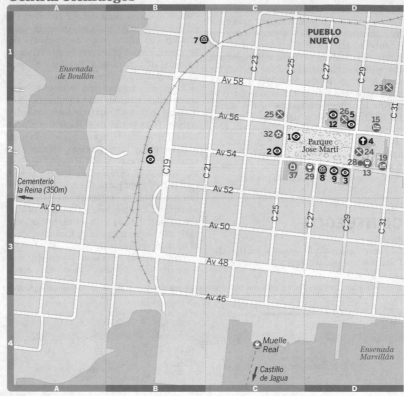

Cienfuegos seems to positively glitter. It's not just Unesco money filtering through. The industry ringing the far side of the Bahía de Cienfuegos – a shipyard, the bastion of Cuba's shrimp-fishing fleet, a thermoelectric plant and a petrochemical hub (currently under construction) – constitutes some of the country's most important. This, together with a pervading sense of tranquility resonating through spruced-up colonial streets refreshingly free of *jineteros* (touts) and a revitalizing seaside vibe make the city as alluring today as Moré found it 60 years ago.

History

Cienfuegos was founded in 1819 by a pioneering French émigré from Louisiana named Don Louis D'Clouet. Sponsoring a scheme to increase the population of whites on the island, D'Clouet invited 40 families from New Orleans and Philadelphia, and Bordeaux in France to establish a fledgling settlement known initially as Fernandina de Jagua. Despite having their initial camp destroyed by a hurricane in 1821, the unperturbed French settlers rebuilt their homes and – suspicious, perhaps, that their first name had brought them bad luck – rechristened the city Cienfuegos after the then governor of Cuba.

With the arrival of the railway in 1850 and the drift west of Cuban sugar growers after the War of Independence (1868–78), Cienfuegos' fortunes blossomed, and local merchants pumped their wealth into a dazzling array of eclectic architecture that harked back to the neoclassicism of their French forefathers.

D-day in Cienfuegos' history came on September 5, 1957 when officers at the local naval base staged a revolt against the Batista dictatorship. The uprising was brutally crushed but it sealed the city's place in revolutionary history.

Modern-day Cienfuegos retains a plusher look than many of its urban counterparts. And with some much-needed Unesco money now arriving, as well as growing industrial clout, the future for the city and its fine array of 19th-century architecture looks bright.

◎ Sights

◎ Parque José Martí

Arco de Triunfo   LANDMARK
(Map p244; Calle 25, btwn Avs 56 & 54) The Arch of Triumph on Cienfuegos' serene central park catapults the plaza into the unique category: there is no other building of its kind in Cuba. Dedicated to Cuban independence, the Francophile monument on the park's western edge ushers you through its gilded gateway toward a marble statue of revolutionary and philosopher José Martí.

Catedral de la Purísima
Concepción Church   CHURCH
(Map p244; Av 56 No 2902; ⊘7am-noon Mon-Fri) Opposite the park, the cathedral dates from 1869 and is distinguished by its wonderful French stained-glass windows. Chinese writing discovered on columns during the ongoing restoration is thought to date from the 1870s. The cathedral is nearly always open; you can also join the faithful for a service (7:30am weekdays, 10am Sundays).

Teatro Tomás Terry   THEATER
(Map p244; ✆51-33-61; Av 56 No 270, btwn Calles 27 & 29; tours CUC$2; ⊘10am-6pm) Sharing French and Italian influences, this theater on the northern side of the *parque* is grand from the outside (look for the gold leafed mosaics on the front facade), but even grander within. Built between 1887 and 1889 to honor Venezuelan industrialist Tomás Terry, the 950-seat auditorium is embellished with

Central Cienfuegos

Carrara marble, hand-carved Cuban hardwoods and whimsical ceiling frescoes.

In 1895 the theater opened with a performance of Verdi's *Aida* and it has witnessed numerous landmarks in Cuban music, as well as performances by the likes of Enrico Caruso and Anna Pavlova.

Colegio San Lorenzo　　NOTABLE BUILDING
(Map p244; Av 56, cnr Calle 29) On the east side of Teatro Café Tomás, this building with its striking colonnaded facade was constructed during the 1920s with funds left by wealthy city patron Nicholas Acea Salvador, whose name also graces one of the city's cemeteries. Admire from the outside only.

**Casa de la Cultura
Benjamin Duarte**　　NOTABLE BUILDING
(Map p244; Calle 25 No 5401; ⊙ 8:30am-midnight) FREE On the western side of Parque Martí, this is the former Palacio de Ferrer (1918), a riveting neoclassical building with Italian marble floors and – most noticeably – a rooftop cupola equipped with a wrought-iron staircase. View-seekers should still be able to clamber up to see spectacular city-wide vistas. Ask just inside the entrance.

Museo Provincial　　MUSEUM
(Map p244; cnr Av 54 & Calle 27; admission CUC$2; ⊙ 10am-6pm Tue-Sat, to noon Sun) The main attraction on the south side of Parque Martí, this museum offers a microcosm of Cienfuegos' history and displays the frilly furnishings of refined 19th-century French-Cuban society, as well as other assorted knickknacks.

Palacio de Gobierno　　NOTABLE BUILDING
(Map p244; Av 54, btwn Calles 27 & 29) Most of Parque Martí's south side is dominated by the grandiose, silvery-grey building where the provincial government (Poder Popular Provincial) holds forth. The Palacio de Gobierno doesn't allow visitors, but you can steal a look at the palatial main staircase through the front door. It's in wonderful condition.

Casa del Fundador　　NOTABLE BUILDING
(Map p244; cnr Calle 29 & Av 54) On the park's southeastern corner stands the city's oldest building, once the residence of city founder

Louis D'Clouet and now a souvenir store. **El Bulevar** (Map p244; Av 54), Cienfuegos' quintessential shopping street, heads east from here to link up with the Paseo del Prado.

West of Parque Martí

A few attractions lie west of Parque José Marti.

Museo Histórico Naval Nacional   MUSEUM
(Map p244; cnr Av 60 & Calle 21; admission CUC$2; ⊙9am-6:30pm Tue-Sat, to 1pm Sun) Across the railway tracks five blocks northwest of the Parque Martí is the eye-catching location of this rose-pink museum, dating from 1933. It's housed in the former headquarters of the Distrito Naval del Sur, and approached by a wide drive flanked with armaments dating from different eras.

It was here in September 1957 that a group of sailors and civilians staged an unsuccessful uprising against the Batista government. The revolt is the central theme of the museum. The ramparts offer great bay views.

Cementerio la Reina   CEMETERY
(cnr Av 50 & Calle 7) The city's oldest cemetery was founded in 1837, and is lined with the graves of Spanish soldiers who died in the Wars of Independence. La Reina is the only cemetery in Cuba where bodies are interred above ground (in the walls) due to the high groundwater levels.

A listed national monument, the cemetery also has a marble statue called *Bella Durmiente*: a tribute to a 24-year-old woman who died in 1907 of a broken heart. It's an evocative place if you're into graveyards, but foreigners aren't generally permitted to enter. Tipping the guard might work. Approach is via Av 50: a long, hot walk or horse-cart ride via the sorry-looking collection of trains passing as the **Museo de Locomotivas** (Map p244; Calle 19).

Paseo del Prado & the Malecón

Stately Paseo del Prado (Calle 37), stretching from the Río el Inglés in the north to Punta Gorda in the south, is the longest street of its kind in Cuba and great to watch *cienfueg-ueños* going about their daily business. The boulevard is a veritable smorgasbord of fine neoclassical buildings and pastel-painted columns.

Malecón   STREET
(Map p248) Keep heading south on the Prado and the street becomes the Malecón as it cuts alongside one of the world's finest natural bays, offering exquisite vistas. Like all sea drives (Havana's being the archetype), this area comes alive in the evening when poets come to muse and couples to canoodle.

Statue of Benny Moré   MONUMENT
(Map p244; cnr Av 54 & Calle 37) Before you hit the Malecón, at the intersection of Av 54 and the Paseo del Prado you can pay your respects to this life-size likeness of the musician with his trademark cane.

Sports Museum   MUSEUM
(Map p244; cnr Calle 37 & Av 48) FREE South of the Moré statue, this little museum is largely devoted to local boxing hero Julio González Valladores, who brought back a gold medal from the 1996 Atlanta Olympics.

Punta Gorda

When the Malecón sea wall runs out, you will know you have landed in Punta Gorda, Cienfuegos' old upper-class neighborhood, characterized by its bright clapboard homes and turreted palaces. Highlighting a 1920s penchant for grandiosity are the cupola-topped **Palacio Azul** (now the Hostal Palacio Azul) and the **Club Cienfuegos**, once an exclusive yacht club and still offering nautical excursions aplenty. Nearby, an inventive **Parque de Esculturas** (Map p248) throws some innovative modern sculpture into the mix.

Palacio de Valle   NOTABLE BUILDING
(Map p248; cnr Calle 37 btwn Avs 0 & 2; ⊙9:30am-11pm) The ultimate in kitsch comes near the end of Calle 37 when, with a sharp intake of breath, you'll stumble upon the *Arabian Nights*-like Palacio de Valle. Built in 1917 by Alcisclo Valle Blanco, a Spaniard from Asturias, the structure resembles an outrageously ornate Moroccan casbah.

Batista planned to convert this colorful riot of tiles, turrets and stucco into a casino, but today it's an (aspiring) upscale restaurant with an inviting terrace bar.

Centro Recreativo la Punta   PARK
(Map p248; ⊙10am-10pm) Lovers come to watch the sunset amid sea-framed greenery at the gazebo on the extreme southern tip of this park. The **bar** is also oddly popular with local police officers.

Punta Gorda

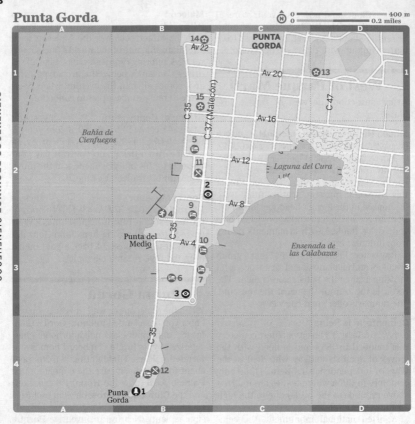

Punta Gorda

◎ East of City Center

Necrópolis Tomás Acea CEMETERY
(Carretera de Rancho Luna Km 2; admission CUC$1;
⊙8am-6pm) One of two national-monument-
listed resting places in Cienfuegos, the Acea
is classed as a 'garden cemetery' and is entered through a huge neoclassical pavilion

CIENFUEGOS' FRENCH-INSPIRED ARCHITECTURE

C'est vrai, the elegant bay-side city of Cienfuegos is Cuba's most Gallic corner. Its innate Frenchness is best exemplified not in its cuisine, where rice and beans still hold sway over *bœuf à la Bourguignonne*, but in its harmonious neoclassical architecture. With its wide, paved streets laid out in an almost perfect grid, Cienfuegos' enlightened 19th-century settlers sought to quash slums, promote hygiene and maximize public space using a system of urban planning later adopted by Baron Haussmann in Paris in the 1850s and '60s. Porches, pillars and columns are the city's most arresting architectural features, with its broad Parisian-style main avenue (El Paseo) which runs north–south for over 3km embellished with neat lines of well-proportioned colonnaded facades painted in an array of pastel colors

Although founded by French émigrés in 1819, most of Cienfuegos' surviving neoclassical buildings date from between 1850 and 1910. By the early 20th century, eclectic features had begun to seep into the architecture. One of the first to break the mold was the Palacio Ferrer (now Casa de la Cultura Benjamin Duarte) in Parque José Martí, built in 1917, whose uncharacteristically decorative cupola started a craze for eye-catching rooftop lookouts.

The flamboyance continued in the 1920s and '30s in the upscale Punta Gorda peninsula, where filthy-rich sugar merchants invested their profits in ever more ostentatious mansions, turning the neighborhood into a mini-Miami. You can track the evolution as you head south on Calle 37 past the regal Palacio Azul and the wedding-cake Club Cienfuegos to the baroque-meets-Moorish Palacio de Valle, possibly Cuba's most riotously eclectic building.

Cienfuegos' city center was declared a World Heritage Site by Unesco in 2005 for being 'an outstanding example of an architectural ensemble representing the new ideas of modernity, hygiene and order in urban planning' in Latin America. Money has since gone into livening up the main square, Parque José Martí, and its environs where various interpretive signboards pinpoint the most important buildings.

(1926) flanked by 64 Doric columns modeled on the Parthenon in Greece. This cemetery contains a monument to the marine martyrs who died during the abortive 1957 Cienfuegos naval uprising. It's 2km east of city center along Av 5 de Septiembre.

🏃 Activities

Marlin Marina Cienfuegos　FISHING, SAILING
(Map p248; ☎ 55-12-41; www.nauticamarlin.com; Calle 35, btwn Avs 6 & 8; ⊙ 11am-8:45pm) Hook up with this 36-berth marina a few blocks north of Hotel Jagua to arrange deep-sea fishing trips. Prices start at CUC$200 for four people for four hours. Multiday trips start at CUC$400/3900 for one night/week (gear and crew included), depending on the boat used.

A classic bay cruise costs CUC$16 for the day or CUC$10 for a two-hour sunset cruise (stopping briefly at Castillo de Jagua). Book through Cubatur or Cubanacán.

Base Náutica Club Cienfuegos　WATER SPORTS
(Map p248; ☎ 52-65-10; Calle 35, btwn Avs 10 & 12; ⊙ 10am-6pm) At this nautical base at the Club Cienfuegos you can organize water sports including kayaking and windsurfing. It also has a tennis court (there is no fence so get used to lots of ball retrieving) and an amusement center with bumper cars and video games. The swimming pool costs CUC$8.

La Bolera　BOWLING
(Map p244; Calle 37, btwn Avs 46 & 48; per hr CUC$1-2; ⊙ 11am-2am) If you're into gimmick-free billiards or bowling, this is your hangout. It also has an ice-cream parlor and occasional live music.

Hotel la Unión Swimming Pool　SWIMMING
(Map p244; Calle 31, cnr Av 54) Even if you're a nonguest, you can use the beautiful Italianate pool at Hotel la Unión for CUC$10.

🎓 Courses

Universidad de Cienfuegos　LANGUAGE
(☎ 52-15-21; www.ucf.edu.cu; Carretera las Rodas Km 4, Cuatro Caminos) Offers Spanish courses ranging from beginner to advanced. The courses last one month and incorporate 64

hours of study (CUC$300). A new course starts each month. Check the website for details.

Tours

Cubanacán
GUIDED TOUR

(Map p244; ☑ 55-16-80; Av 54, btwn Calles 29 & 31) Cubanacán's extremely helpful Cienfuegos office organizes some interesting local tours, including boat trips in the bay (CUC$10), the ever-popular El Nicho excursion (CUC$30), plus other hard-to-reach places such as the Jardín Botánico de Cienfuegos (CUC$10 to CUC$18 depending on group size) and the local cigar factory (CUC$5). You can also organize diving at Rancho Luna and excursions to the Península de Zapata.

Festivals & Events

Local festivals in Cienfuegos include the cultural events marking the foundation of the city on April 22, 1819; the **Carnaval** in August; and the **Benny Moré International Music Festival** in September on odd-numbered years, held in town and in nearby Santa Isabel de las Lajas.

Sleeping

Cienfuegos has some quality private rooms – your best bet for budget accommodation. Those at Punta Gorda are more removed, more atmospheric and generally pricier. There are excellent hotels in Cienfuegos proper and in Punta Gorda.

Central Cienfuegos

★ Bella Perla Marina
CASA PARTICULAR $

(Map p244; ☑ 51-89-91; bellaperlamarina@yahoo.es; Calle 39 No 5818, cnr Av 60; r/ste CUC$25/50; ⓟ ❉ @) In the throes of an ambitious renovation at the time of research, proprietor Waldo has added a stunning rooftop suite to his established two rooms and, in the process, might have invented Cuba's first 'boutique' casa particular. The place has long been popular (the meals get good reviews) for its plant-filled roof terrace, city center location and warm hospitality.

Hostal Colonial Pepe & Isabel
CASA PARTICULAR $

(Map p244; ☑ 51-82-76; hostalcolonialisapepe@gmail.com; Av 52 No 4318, btwn Calles 43 & 45; r CUC$20-25; ❉) Ex-teacher Pepe greets you with a smile as wide as the Bahía de Cienfuegos and has recently upgraded his de-ceptively large colonial house to incorporate five modern rooms set around a narrow upstairs and downstairs terrace. Each room has a queen bed and an extra pull-down single Murphy bed, and two come with additional living room or kitchen space.

Casa las Golondrinas
CASA PARTICULAR $

(Map p244; ☑ 51-57-88; Calle 39, btwn Avs 58 & 60; r CUC$20-25; ❉) Run by a doctor and his wife, this is another gorgeous recently renovated colonial house with two ample rooms.

Casa Prado
CASA PARTICULAR $

(Map p244; ☑ 528-96613; Calle 37 No 4235, btwn Avs 42 & 44; r CUC$20-25; ❉) This has established itself as one of the very best casas in the city center. The two high-ceilinged rooms are replete with period furniture and a twisting staircase leads to a terrace with phenomenal city views. The location is great too: poised on Prado half-way between the city center and the Malecón.

Summon forth all your visions of haughty colonial elegance and you'll arrive prepared.

Casa de la Amistad
CASA PARTICULAR $

(Map p244; ☑ 51-61-43; Av 56 No 2927, btwn Calles 29 & 31; r CUC$20-25; ⓟ ❉) Friendship's the word in this venerable colonial house stuffed full of family heirlooms just off Parque Martí. Legendary food includes the exotic Cola chicken (yes, *pollo* cooked in the 'real thing'). Chatty hosts Armando and Leonor offer two wonderful, well-kept rooms and a lovely roof terrace.

Olga & Eugenio
CASA PARTICULAR $

(Map p244; ☑ 51-77-56; Av 50 No 4109, btwn Calles 41 & 43; r CUC$20-25; ❉) One of the best-value options in Cienfuegos. Two large rooms, clean bathrooms and an attractively tiled roof terrace.

Hotel la Unión
BOUTIQUE HOTEL $$$

(Map p244; ☑ 55-10-20; www.hotellaunion-cuba.com; Calle 31, cnr Av 54; s/d CUC$88/143; ❉ @ ≋) Barcelona, Naples, Paris? There are echoes of all these cities in this plush, colonial-style hotel with its European aspirations and splendid Italianate pool, fit for a Roman emperor. Tucked away in a maze of marble pillars, antique furnishings and two tranquil inner courtyards are 46 well-furnished rooms with balconies either overlooking the street or a mosaic-lined patio.

You'll also find a gym, Jacuzzi and local art gallery. Service is refreshingly efficient:

there's an airy roof terrace that showcases live salsa and a well-regarded restaurant.

Punta Gorda

Villa Lagarto – Maylin & Tony
CASA PARTICULAR $

(Map p248; ☑51-99-66; Calle 35 No 4B, btwn Avs 0 & Litoral; r CUC$35-45; 🅿🌢) Long a leading player in Cuba's casa particular scene, the Lagarto has since morphed into an ambitious paladar, but it still rents out three rooms cocooned on a delightful terrace, all with king-size beds, hammocks and glinting views of the bay. Welcome cocktails greet new guests. If it's full, they'll recommend Casa Los Delfines or Casa Amarilla, both next door.

Vista al Mar
CASA PARTICULAR $

(Map p248; ☑51-83-78; www.vistaalmarcuba.com; Calle 37 No 210, btwn Avs 2 & 4; r CUC$25-30; 🅿🌢) It really is a *vista al mar* (sea view) – in fact, this highly professional casa has even got its own private scoop of beach out back with hammocks.

Villa Nelly
CASA PARTICULAR $

(Map p248; ☑51-15 19; Av 37, btwn Calles 6 & 8; r CUC$20-25; 🌢) Well located, with a self-catering kitchen for guests, a well-stocked bar and an extensive garden.

Hostal Palacio Azul
HOTEL $$$

(Map p248; ☑58-28-28; Calle 37 No 201, btwn Avs 12 & 14; s/d CUC$81/135; 🅿🌢@) A palace posing as a hotel rather than a hotel posing as a palace, the Palacio Azul was one of the first big buildings to grace Punta Gorda on its construction in 1921. Its seven recently renovated rooms are named after flowers and sparkle with plenty of prerevolutionary character.

You'll find an intimate on-site restaurant called El Chelo and an eye-catching rooftop cupola with splendid views.

Perla del Mar
BOUTIQUE HOTEL $$$

(Map p248; ☑55-10-03; Calle 37 btwn Avs 0 & 2; s/d/tr CUC$90/150/210; 🌢@) Opened in September 2012, Perla del Mar takes the 'historical boutique' hotel theme of the nearby Palacio Azul and updates it to the 1950s. The nine rooms have a sleek modernist feel, and two alfresco Jacuzzis are invitingly positioned overlooking the bay. Stairs lead up to a made-for-sunbathing terrace.

Next door the equally boutique-y **Casa Verde** offers eight fin-de-siècle rooms for the same prices.

Hotel Jagua
HOTEL $$$

(Map p248; ☑55-10-03; Calle 37 No 1; s/d CUC$80/130; 🅿🌢@🌢) It's not clear what Batista's brother had in mind when he erected this modern concrete giant on Punta Gorda in the 1950s, though making money was probably the prime motivation. Still, the Jagua is a jolly good hotel – airy and surprisingly plush. Upper rooms (there are seven floors) are best.

Any lack of historical credentials is compensated for by inviting amenities: namely, the fine restaurant, appealing pool, attractive public areas, large bright rooms, in-house cabaret show and beautiful bayside setting.

Eating

Central Cienfuegos

Florida Blanca 18
CUBAN $

(Av 38 No 3720 , btwn Calles 37 & 39; mains from CUC$5; ⊙11:30am-11pm Wed-Mon) Brave new paladar testing the water in the new business climate. There's an inviting interior and excellent prawns.

Teatro Café Tomás
CAFE $

(Map p244; Av 56 No 2703, btwn Calles 27 & 29; ⊙10am-10pm) Cafe, souvenir stall and nightly music venue, this small space wedged between the Teatro Tomás Terry and the neoclassical Colegio San Lorenzo is the most atmospheric place to flop down and observe the morning exercisers in Parque Martí. The flower canopy-covered patio to the side reveals its true personality in the evenings with great live music ranging from *trova* (verse, song) to jazz.

Polineso
SANDWICHES $

(Map p244; Calle 29, btwn Calles 54 & 56) Right under the portals in Parque Jose Martí, this is a salubrious setting for a cold beer or snack.

Restaurant Bouyón 1825
INTERNATIONAL, PARRILLA $$

(Map p244; ☑51-73-76; Calle 25 No 5605; mains CUC$8; ⊙11am-11pm) Handily situated just off the main square, this new paladar specializes in meat cooked *a la parrillada* (on the barbecue). Visiting Argentinians and avowed carnivores will revel in the hearty mixed grill which includes four different meats and is complemented by some robust Chilean reds.

El Tranvia
INTERNATIONAL $$

(Map p244; 52-49-20; Av 52 No 4530 , btwn Calles 45 & 47; mains CUC$10-12; noon-11pm) Eight Cuban cities – including Cienfuegos – once had tram systems. The ambitious new Tranvia has taken this almost forgotten segment of Cienfueguero history and bottled it in a restaurant. The theme extends to the waiters (who dress as station guards), grainy historical photos and vintage bar (which incorporates part of an old carriage).

The food prepared in an open kitchen showcases fajitas and brochettes, but struggles to emulate the decor.

1869 Restaurant
INTERNATIONAL $$

(Map p244; cnr Av 54 & Calle 31; mains CUC$10; breakfast, lunch & dinner) Cienfuegos' most upmarket city-center dining experience can be found in this elegant restaurant in La Unión hotel. Although the food doesn't quite match the lush furnishings, a varied international menu makes a welcome change from rice/beans/pork staples elsewhere.

★Paladar Aché
SEAFOOD, INTERNATIONAL $$

(52-61-73; Av 38, btwn Calles 41 & 43; mains CUC$10-15; noon-10.30pm Mon-Sat) One of only two surviving paladares from the austere 1990s, Aché has taken on the young new opposition and is holding its own. Renovations and extra seating have helped, as has the interesting decor (caged birds, the seven dwarfs re-created as garden gnomes and a wall relief map of Cienfuegos' cultural icons). Local prawns headline the comprehensive menu.

Self-Catering

Mercado Municipal
MARKET $

(Map p244; Calle 31 No 5805, btwn Avs 58 & 60) Groceries in pesos for picnickers and self-caterers.

Doña Neli
BAKERY $

(Map p244; cnr Calle 41 & Av 62; 9am-10:15pm) Provides breakfast goodies (pastries, bread, cakes) in convertibles.

✕ Punta Gorda

Club Cienfuegos
SEAFOOD, INTERNATIONAL $$

(Map p248; 51-28-91; Calle 37, btwn Avs 10 & 12; noon-10:30pm) With a setting as good as this grand old sports-club-cum-restaurant,

it's easy for the food to fall short, which it often does. But there are plenty of options here, with the **Bar Terraza** (Map p248; noon-2:30am) for cocktails and chicken sandwiches; **El Marinero** (Map p248; noon-10pm), a 1st-floor seafood establishment; and **Restaurante Café Cienfuegos** (Map p248; 4pm-10:30pm), a more refined adventurous place on the top floor, where you'll pay CUC$10 for a steak and CUC$6 for a fine paella.

The yacht-club vibe and wraparound dining terraces make for a memorable experience.

Palacio de Valle
SEAFOOD, CARIBBEAN $$

(Map p248; cnr Calle 37 & Av 2; mains CUC$7-12; 10am-10pm) While the food doesn't have as many decorative flourishes as the eclectic architecture, the setting is so unique it would be a shame to miss it. Seafood dominates the menu downstairs; if you aren't enthralled, use the rooftop bar here for a pre-dinner cocktail or post-dinner cigar.

★Restaurante Villa Lagarto
INTERNATIONAL $$$

(Map p248; 51-99-66; Calle 35 No 4B, btwn Av 0 & Litoral; mains CUC$10-15) The truly wondrous bayside setting is emulated by the food and made even more memorable by some of the fastest yet most discreet service you'll see in Cuba. With its excellent prawns, lobster and roast pork, Lagarto is at the vanguard of Cuba's emerging private dining sector and could hold its own in Miami – easily!

Drinking & Nightlife

Bar Terrazas
BAR

(Map p244; 55-10-20; cnr Av 54 & Calle 31) Recreate the dignified days of old with a mojito upstairs at the Hotel la Unión; live music starts at 10pm. Other excellent drinking perches (especially at sunset) can be found at Club Cienfuegos and the upstairs bar of the Palacio de Valle.

Café Ven
COFFEE BAR

(Map p244; Av 56, btwn Calles 33 & 35; 8am-8pm) Strong, thick coffee for trained Cuban palates, or weak lattes for those reared on Starbucks, plus some ultra-sweet cakes.

El Benny
NIGHTCLUB

(Map p244; Av 54 No 2907, btwn Calles 29 & 31; admission per couple CUC$8; 10pm-3am Tue-Sun) It's difficult to say what the Barbarian of Rhythm would have made of this disco-club named in his honor. Bring your dancing shoes, stock up on the rum and Cokes, and come prepared for music that's more techno than mambo.

El Palatino
BAR, SANDWICHES

(Map p244; Av 54 No 2514) Liquid lunches were invented with El Palatino in mind – a dark-wood bar set in one of the city's oldest buildings on the southern side of Parque Martí. Impromptu jazz sets sometimes erupt, but prepare to be hit up for payment at the end of song number three.

☆ Entertainment

★ Patio de ARTex
NIGHTCLUB

(Map p248; cnr Calle 35 & Av 16) A highly recommendable and positively heaving patio in Punta Gorda where you can catch *son* (Cuba's popular music), salsa, *trova* (traditional music) and a touch of Benny Moré

nostalgia live in the evenings as you mingle with true *cienfuegueños*. Do El Benny on Thursday and this on Friday night.

Teatro Tomás Terry
LIVE MUSIC, THEATER

(Map p244; ☑ 51-33-61; Av 56 No 270, btwn Calles 27 & 29; ⊙10pm-late) Best theater in Cuba? The Tomás Terry is certainly a contender. The building is worth a visit in its own right, but you'll really get to appreciate this architectural showpiece if you come for a concert or play; the box office is open 11am to 3pm daily and 90 minutes before show time.

Jardines de Uneac
LIVE MUSIC

(Map p244; Calle 25 No 5413, btwn Avs 54 & 56; admission CUC$2) Uneac's a good bet in any Cuban city for live music in laid-back environs. Here it's quite possibly Cienfuegos' best venue, with an outdoor patio hosting Afro-Cuban *peñas* (musical performances),

---

BENNY MORÉ

No one singer encapsulates the gamut of Cuban music more eloquently than Bartolomé 'Benny' Moré. A great-great-grandson of a king of the Congo, Moré was born in the small village of Santa Isabel de las Lajas in Cienfuegos province in 1919. He gravitated to Havana in 1936 where he earned a precarious living selling damaged fruit on the streets. He then played and sang in the smoky bars and restaurants of Habana Vieja's tough dockside neighborhood, where he made just enough money to get by.

His first big break came in 1943 when his velvety voice and pitch-perfect delivery won him first prize in a local radio singing competition and landed him a regular job as lead vocalist for a Havana-based mariachi band called the Cauto Quartet.

His meteoric rise was confirmed two years later when, while singing at a regular gig in Havana's El Temple bar, he was spotted by Siro Rodríguez of the famed Trío Matamoros, then Cuba's biggest *son*-bolero band. Rodríguez was so impressed that he asked Moré to join the band as lead vocalist for an imminent tour of Mexico. In the late 1940s, Mexico City was a proverbial Hollywood for young Spanish-speaking Cuban performers. Moré was signed up by RCA records and his fame spread rapidly.

Moré returned to Cuba in 1950 a star, and was quickly baptized the Prince of Mambo and the Barbarian of Rhythm. In the ensuing years, he invented a brand new hybrid sound called *batanga* and put together his own 40-piece backing orchestra, the Banda Gigante. With the Banda, Moré toured Venezuela, Jamaica, Mexico and the US, culminating in a performance at the 1957 Oscars ceremony. But the singer's real passion was always Cuba. Legend has it that whenever Benny performed in Havana's Centro Gallego hundreds of people would fill the parks and streets to hear him sing.

With his multitextured voice and signature scale-sliding glissando, Moré's real talent lay in his ability to adapt and seemingly switch genres at will. As comfortable with a tear-jerking bolero as he was with a hip-gyrating rumba, Moré could convey tenderness, exuberance, emotion and soul, all in the space of five tantalizing minutes. Although he couldn't read music, Moré composed many of his most famous numbers, including 'Bonito y sabroso' and the big hit 'Que bueno baila usted.' When he died in 1963, more than 100,000 people attended his funeral. No one in Cuba has yet been able to fill his shoes.

Moré fans can follow his legend in the settlement of **Santa Isabel de las Lajas**, a few kilometers west of Cruces on the Cienfuegos–Santa Clara road, where there's a small **museum**.

trova and top local bands such as the perennially popular Los Novos.

Café Cantante Benny Moré LIVE MUSIC
(Map p244; cnr Av 54 & Calle 37) This is where you might get some suave Benny tunes, especially after hours. A tatty restaurant by day, this place blacks out the blemishes in the evenings when it mixes up mean cocktails and tunes into live traditional music.

Cabaret Guanaroca CABARET
(Map p248; Calle 37 No 1; admission CUC$5; ⊙9:30pm Tue-Fri till late, from 10pm Sat) In Hotel Jagua, the Guanaroca offers a more professional tourist-orientated cabaret extravaganza.

Tropisur NIGHTCLUB, CABARET
(Map p244; cnr Calle 37 & Av 48; admission CUC$1; ⊙Fri-Sun) An open-air venue with a more traditional Cuban vibe is this feisty place on the Prado.

Los Pinitos LIVE MUSIC
(Map p248; cnr Calle 37 & Av 22) A playground for kids during the day, Los Pinitos matures tenfold by nightfall, hosting decent weekend music shows with a Benny Moré bias.

Casa de la Cultura
Benjamin Duarte LIVE MUSIC
(Map p244; Calle 25 No 5403) On Parque Martí in the exquisite Palacio Ferrer, the local culture vultures congregate for various events and expos to match the grandiose setting.

Estadio 5 de Septiembre SPORTS
(Map p248; ☎51-36-44; Av 20, btwn Calles 45 & 55) From October to April, the provincial baseball team – nicknamed Los Elefantes – plays matches here. Its best-ever national series finish was fourth in 1979.

Cine-Teatro Luisa CINEMA
(Map p244; Calle 37 No 5001) The most recently renovated of the city's three cinemas.

Shopping

Cienfuegos' main drag – known officially as Av 54, but colloquially as El Bulevar – is an archetypal Cuban shopping street with not a chain store in sight. The best traffic-free stretch runs from Calle 37 (Paseo del Prado) to Parque Martí, full of shops of all shapes and sizes.

Check out the **Maroya Gallery** (Map p244; Av 54, btwn Calles 25 & 27) for folk art, **Variedades Cienfuegos** (Map p244; cnr Av 54 & Calle 33) for peso paraphernalia or **Casa del**

Habano 'El Embajador' (Map p244; cnr Av 54 & Calle 33) for cigars.

Tienda Terry (Map p244; Av 56 No 270, btwn Calle 27 & 29) in Teatro Tomás Terry is a good bet for books and souvenirs; another well-stocked bookstore is **Librería Dionisio San Román** (Map p244; Av 54 No 3526, cnr Calle 37).

❶ Information

INTERNET ACCESS & TELEPHONE
Etecsa Telepunto (Calle 31 No 5402, btwn Avs 54 & 56; per hr CUC$6; ⊙8:30am-7:30pm)

MEDIA
5 de Septiembre The local newspaper comes out on Fridays.
Radio Ciudad del Mar 1350AM and 98.9FM.

MEDICAL SERVICES
Clínica Internacional (☎55-16-22; Av 10, btwn Calles 37 & 39, Punta Gorda) Excellent newish center catering to foreigners and handling medical (including dental) emergencies. It has a 24-hour pharmacy.
Hotel la Unión (☎55-10-20; Calle 31, cnr Av 54; ⊙24hr) The pharmacy here is aimed at international tourists.

MONEY
Banco de Credito y Comercio (Bandec) (cnr Av 56 & Calle 31) The best exchange rates.
Cadeca (Av 56 No 3316, btwn Calles 33 & 35) Changes cash for convertibles or Cuban pesos.

POST
Post Office (Av 54 No 3514, btwn Calles 35 & 37)

TRAVEL AGENCIES
Cubatur (☎55-12-42; Calle 37 No 5399, btwn Avs 54 & 56) Organizes excursions.
Paradiso (Av 54 No 3301, btwn Calles 33 & 35) Specializes in historical tourism.

❶ Getting There & Away

AIR
Jaime González Airport, 5km northeast of Cienfuegos, receives weekly international flights from Miami and Canada (November to March only). There are no connections to Havana.

BUS
From the **bus station** (☎51-57-20, 51-8114; Calle 49, btwn Avs 56 & 58) there are Víazul buses to Havana three times daily (CUC$20, four hours) at 9:30am, 12:25pm and 5:35pm, and to Trinidad five times a day (CUC$6, one hour 35 minutes) at 12:45pm, 1:30pm, 3:40pm, 5:30pm and 7pm.

There are also two daily buses to Varadero (CUC$17, 4½ hours) at 10:30am and 4:40pm, with the afternoon departure also calling at Santa Clara (CUC$6, 1½ hours). The one Viñales (CUC$32, seven hours 45 minutes) departure of the day is at 9:40am and calls at Havana and Pinar del Río (CUC$31, seven hours). A new Víazul bus leaving daily at 8:20am links Cienfuegos with Santa Clara, Remedios and Morón.

To reach other destinations, you have to connect in Trinidad or Havana. Note that when heading to Trinidad from Cienfuegos, buses originate further west and may be full.

Cienfuegos' bus station is clean and well organized. It also offers cheap and safe luggage storage (CUC$1 per item). A Víazul office on the upper level issues tickets; for local buses to Rancho Luna, Santa Isabel de las Lajas and Palmira for around CUC$1; check the blackboard on the lower level. Tickets must be purchased from the *jefe de turno* (shift manager) downstairs.

TRAIN

The **train station** (☑ 52-54-95; cnr Av 58 & Calle 49; ☉ ticket window 8am-3:30pm Mon-Fri, 8-11:30am Sat) is across from the bus station but, with a traveling time to Havana of 10 hours (versus three by bus), you have to be a serious rail geek to want to enter or exit Cienfuegos by the comically slow *ferrocarril*. For true stoics, train numbers 73 and 74 run to Havana – supposedly daily. You can also reach Santa Clara and Sancti Spíritus..

ⓘ Getting Around

BOAT

A 120-passenger ferry runs to the Castillo de Jagua (CUC$1, 40 minutes) from the **Muelle Real** (cnr Av 46 & Calle 25). Take note – this is a Cuban commuter boat, not a sunset cruise. Check at the port for current schedules. It's supposed to run twice a day in each direction. A smaller ferry (CUC$0.50, 15 minutes) also makes frequent runs between the Castillo and the Hotel Pasacaballo. Last departure from the Castillo is 8pm.

CAR & MOPED

The Servi-Cupet gas station is on Calle 37 at the corner of Av 16 in Punta Gorda. There's another station 5km northeast of Hotel Rancho Luna. **Club Cienfuegos** (☑ 52-65-10; Calle 37, btwn Avs 10 & 12) Hires mopeds for CUC$25 per day. **Cubacar Hotel Rancho Luna** (☑ 54-80-26; Hotel Rancho Luna, Carretera de Rancho Luna Km 16); **Hotel Unión** (☑ 55-16-45; Hotel Union, cnr Av 51 & Calle 31); **Hotel Jagua** (☑ 55-20-14; Calle 37 No 1, Hotel Jagua) Hires cars.

HORSE CARTS

Horse carts and bici-taxis ply Calle 37 charging Cubans one peso a ride and foreigners CUC$1 (Spanish speakers might be able to 'pass' and

PALMIRA

If you're interested in Santería and its affiliated mysteries, stop by at Palmira, 8km north of Cienfuegos, a town famous for its Santería brotherhoods, including the societies of Cristo, San Roque and Santa Barbara. A brief exposé of their raison d'être can be found at the **Museo Municipal de Palmira** (☑ 54-45-33; admission CUC$1; ☉ 10am-6pm Tue-Sat, 10am-1pm Sun) on the main plaza. Cubanacán in Cienfuegos sometimes runs tours here. The main religious festivals are held in early December.

pay a peso). It's a pleasant way to travel between town, Punta Gorda and the cemeteries.

TAXI

There are plenty of cabs in Cienfuegos. Most hang around outside Hotel Jagua and Hotel la Unión, or linger around the bus station. If you have no luck at these spots, phone **Cubacar** (☑ 51-84-54) or **Taxi OK** (☑ 55-11-72). A taxi to the airport from downtown should cost CUC$6.

AROUND CIENFUEGOS

Rancho Luna

Rancho Luna is a diminutive, picturesque beach resort 18km south of Cienfuegos close to the jaws of Bahía de Cienfuegos. It has two midrange, decidedly low-key hotel complexes, but it's also possible to stay in rooms in a privately owned home; about half a dozen casas particulares lie side-by-side on the approach road to Hotel Faro Luna. Protected by a coral reef, the coast has good snorkeling although the beach isn't Varadero standard.

⊙ Sights & Activities

Dive Center   DIVING

(☑ 54-80-87; commercial@marlin.cfg.tur.cu; Carretera Pasacaballos Km 18; dives from CUC$35, open-water certification CUC$365) Besides sunbathing or viewing the *faro* (lighthouse), the main activity here is diving organized through the dive center at Hotel Club Amigo Rancho Luna, which visits 30 sites within a 20-minute boat ride. Caves, profuse marine life and dazzling coral gardens as well as six sunken ships are among the attractions. From November to February harmless whale sharks frequent these waters.

Delfinario   DOLPHIN SHOW

(Carretera Pasacaballos Km 18.5; adult/child CUC$10/6; ☺ 8:30am-4pm Thu-Tue) Cuba's most economical dolphin show is also considered one of its best. There are five resident dolphins, a snack bar and even a dolphin doctor. You can swim with them for CUC$50/33 adult/child.

🛏 Sleeping

Villa Sol   CASA PARTICULAR $

(☑ 52-27-24-48; Carretera Faro Luna; r CUC$20-30; ❉) On the approach road to Hotel Faro Luna, this is the first house on the left. It's in a beautiful spot overlooking the ocean, with bougainvillea in the garden. There are four rooms. If it's full, keep walking; almost every other house in the road rents rooms.

Hotel Pasacaballo   HOTEL $

(☑ 54-80-13; Carretera Pasacaballos Km 22; s/d CUC$34/45; P❉❉) Once popular with Venezuelan medical students, the Pasacaballo is architecturally repulsive but offers

---

LANGUAGE IMMERSION IN CIENFUEGOS

You don't need to a linguistic genius to ascertain that the best way to learn a language is to immerse yourself in its culture – preferably while staying in a paradisiacal beach resort. **Academia Cienfuegos** (www.formationcuba. com) is a Cuban-Canadian conceived Spanish-language program set up with the cooperation of the Cuban cultural agency Paradiso, which mixes 30 hours of language classes with 25 hours of cultural activities over a two-week period. Qualified Cuban teachers, when not in the classroom (which is set enticingly close to Rancho Luna beach in the Hotel Club Amigo Faro Luna), take students on various sojourns to Cienfuegos and its environs incorporating film, poetry, dance, Santería, culture and the natural world. There are five teaching levels and a maximum of 10 students per class. The two-week package costs $750 (without flight). Check the website for upcoming start dates.

---

clean, perfectly decent accommodation at rock-bottom prices in a cracking location. Downstairs by the horse statue you'll find a spacious bar, a restaurant, a pool and pool tables – although given that there's nothing else around for miles, even this array of entertainment may prove insufficient.

The best strip of beach is a 4km hike away.

Hotel Club Amigo Faro
Luna-Rancho Luna   RESORT $$

(☑ 54-80-30; Carretera Pasacaballos Km 18; s/d low season CUC$52/74; P❉@❉) The dark horse of Cuba's south coast, Faro Luna is a refreshingly unpretentious place and one of only two hotels to grace what is possibly Cuba's most un-resort-like resort area. Unlike its neighbor, **Club Amigo Rancho Luna**, the Faro doesn't offer all-inclusive packages, but with a couple of new paladares in the vicinity there are options to eat out.

It is popular with language course groups from Canada. All-inclusive Hotel Rancho Luna next door is home to the local dive school.

🍴 Eating

Restaurante Vista al Mar   CARIBBEAN $$

(Carretera Pasacaballos Km 18; mains CUC$10) At the top of a steep slope not far from the approach road to Hotel Faro Luna, this new paladar looks homespun, but offers some rather unusual and (until recently, unheard of) Cuban menu items, such as venison and whole roast turkey (CUC$30).

ℹ Getting There & Away

Theoretically, there are half a dozen local buses from Cienfuegos daily, but this is Cuba – prepare for waits and chalked-up schedules. The Jagua ferry runs from the dock directly below Hotel Pasacaballo several times throughout the day; more sporadic is the boat from Castillo de Jagua back to Cienfuegos, which was running only twice daily (10am and 3pm) at the time of research. Most reliable is a taxi; a one-way fare to Cienfuegos should cost around CUC$$10 – bargain hard.

An even better way to get here is zipping along from Cienfuegos on a rented moped.

Castillo de Jagua

Predating the city of Cienfuegos by nearly a century, the **Castillo de Nuestra Señora de los Ángeles de Jagua** (admission CUC$3; ☺8am-6pm), to the west of the mouth of

Bahía de Cienfuegos, was designed by José Tantete in 1738 and completed in 1745. Built to keep pirates (and the British) out, it was at the time the third most important fortress in Cuba, after those of Havana and Santiago de Cuba.

Extensive renovation in 2010 gave the castle the makeover it was crying out for. In addition to a cracking view of the bay and a basic museum, the castle also has a reasonably atmospheric restaurant down below, refurbished in 2011.

Passenger ferries from the castle ply the waters to Cienfuegos (CUC$1, 40 minutes) twice daily, leaving Cienfuegos at 8am and 1pm and returning at 10am and 3pm. Another ferry leaves frequently to a landing just below the Hotel Pasacaballo (CUC$0.50, 15 minutes). Cubans pay the equivalent in pesos.

Some distance away on this side of the bay, you might glimpse the infamous **Juragua nuclear power plant**, a planned joint venture between Cuba and the Soviet Union that was conceived in 1976 and incorporated the ominous disused apartment blocks of the adjacent Ciudad Nuclear. Only 288km from Florida Keys, construction met with strong opposition from the US and was abandoned following the collapse of communism. Foreigners can't visit.

Laguna Guanaroca

The representation of the moon on earth according to local Siboney legend, the shimmering **Laguna Guanaroca** (admission incl tour CUC$7; ☺8am-noon) is a mangrove-rimmed saline lake southeast of Cienfuegos. It's second only to Las Salinas on the Zapata Peninsula as a bird magnet, and is the province's only *area protegida* (natural protected area). Trails lead to a viewing platform where flamingos, pelicans and *tocororos* (trogons; Cuba's national bird) are regular visitors. Plant life includes pear, lemon and avocado trees, as well as the *güira*, the fruit used to make maracas. Tours take two to three hours and include a boat trip to the far side of the lake. Arrive early to maximize your chances of seeing a variety of birds.

The reserve entrance (accessible only by hire car or taxi) is 12km from Cienfuegos, off the Rancho Luna road on the cut-through to Pepito Tey. Cubanacán in Cienfuegos runs excursions here for a bargain CUC$10.

Jardín Botánico de Cienfuegos

The 94-hectare **botanic garden** (admission CUC$2.50; ☺8am-5pm), near the Pepito Tey sugar mill, 17km east of Cienfuegos, is one of Cuba's biggest gardens. It houses 2000 species of plants, including 23 types of bamboo, 65 types of fig and 280 different palms (purportedly the greatest variety in one place anywhere in the world). The botanic garden was founded in 1901 by US sugar baron Edwin F Atkins, who initially intended to use it to study different varieties of sugarcane, but instead began planting exotic tropical trees from around the globe.

To reach the gardens you'll need your own wheels. The cheapest method is to go with an organized excursion; Cubanacán in Cienfuegos runs trips for CUC$10. Drivers coming from Cienfuegos should turn right (south) at the junction to Pepito Tey.

El Nicho

While Cienfuegos province's share of the verdant Sierra del Escambray is extensive (and includes the range's highest summit, 1156m Pico de San Juan), access is limited to a small protected area around **El Nicho** (admission CUC$5; ☺8:30am-6:30pm), an outlying segment of the Topes de Collantes Natural Park.

El Nicho is the name of a beautiful waterfall on the Río Hanabanilla, but the area also offers a 1.5km nature trail (Reino de las Aguas), swimming in two natural pools, caves, excellent bird-watching opportunities and a *ranchón*-style (farm-style) restaurant.

The beautiful road to El Nicho via Cumanayagua is legendary for its twists and turns: *tienes mas curvas de la carretera por Cumanayagua* (you have more curves than the road to Cumanayagua) is reportedly a compliment to *chicas* (girls) hereabouts. That said, recent improvements mean the trip from Cienfuegos to El Nicho now takes two hours. The daily truck that serves the small local community leaves at very inconvenient times; hiring a car or a taxi (about CUC$70) is far better. Half-day tours can be organized through the excellent Cubanacán, which also offers an El Nicho trip with onward transportation to Trinidad.

Caribbean Coast

Heading east toward Trinidad in Sancti Spíritus province, postcard views of the Sierra del Escambray loom ever closer until their ruffled foothills almost engulf the coast road, while offshore hidden coral reefs offer excellent diving.

◉ Sights & Activities

Hacienda la Vega HORSEBACK RIDING
(Carretera de Trinidad Km 52; per hr CUC$6) On the main road, approximately 9km east of Villa Guajimico, this bucolic cattle farm is surrounded by fruit trees and has an attached **restaurant** serving the usual Cuban staples (CUC$5 to CUC$10). After the city, it's a good place to relax over a shady lunch.

Unhurried travelers can hire horses and canter down to a nearby beach called Caleta de Castro, where the snorkeling is excellent (bring your own gear).

Villa Guajimico DIVING
(☑ 54-09-46; Carretera de Trinidad Km 42) Unusually for a campismo, Villa Guajimico has its own dive center situated atop an offshore coral ridge. The center serves 16 dive sites, and packages with five immersions go for CUC$125.

🛏 Sleeping & Eating

★ Villa Yaguanabo CABINS $
(☑ 54-00-99, 54-19-05; Carretera de Trinidad Km 55; s/d CUC$22/35; P ❄) Something of an unsung diamond located too close to Trinidad (26km) to delay most of the drive-by traffic, Villa Yaguanabo sits on a sublime stretch of coast at the mouth of the Yaguanabo River.

Using the surprisingly salubrious hotel as a base, you can catch a boat (CUC$2) for a 2km ride upriver to the Valle de Iguanas, where you'll find thermal waters, horseback-riding and a small trail network in the foothills of the verdant Escambray. There's a paladar (Casa Verde) on the main road opposite the hotel offering decent lunch and dinner options.

Villa Guajimico CABINS $
(☑ 54-09-46; Carretera de Trinidad Km 42; r CUC$44-60; P ❄ ✹) This is one of Cubamar's most luxurious campismos. The 51 attractive cabins with their idyllic seaside setting have facilities matching most three-star hotels, acting as a nexus for scuba divers. Also offered are bike hire, car rental, various catamaran or kayaking options and short hiking trails. It's a fully equipped Campertour site too. Cienfuegos–Trinidad buses pass by.

Villa Clara Province

🎵 42 / POP 803,690

Best Beaches

➡ Playa Ensenachos (p277)

➡ Playa Las Salinas (p277)

➡ Playa El Mégano (p277)

➡ Playa Santa María (p276)

Best Local Life

➡ Parque Vidal (p261)

➡ La Marquesina (p268)

➡ La Casa de la Ciudad (p263)

➡ Centro Cultural las Leyendas (p274)

➡ Caibarién (p275)

Why Go?

He wasn't born here, never lived here and died in the distant Bolivian mountains, but Che Guevara is synonymous with Villa Clara, for liberating its capital, Santa Clara, from Batista's corrupt gambling party. Yet, the patchwork of misty tobacco fields and placid lakes wedged between the Sierra del Escambray and Cuba's northern keys offers reasons other than Che to drop by.

The city of Santa Clara is an important junction for cross-country travelers, with a cutting-edge nightlife and some palatial casas particulares, while nearby the Escambray peaks glimmer with adventure possibilities centered on the mirror-like Hanabanilla lake.

Picturesque Remedios is the region's oldest settlement, and its somnolence is annually shattered by a frenzied firework party, Las Parrandas. Northeastward, on Villa Clara's coveted coast, beach life revolves around the archipelago of the Cayerías del Norte, Cuba's fastest-growing resort zone. The presence of an adjacent Unesco Biosphere Reserve has meant development has been relatively sustainable – so far.

When to Go

➡ It's hard to conceive of a better time to take a trip to Villa Clara than December. The 24th, specifically. That's right. Swap a boring Christmas for one of the Caribbean's hottest street parties in Remedios.

➡ Head over to the Cayerías del Norte for the start of the high season, which runs December through March, when the chances of the skies raining on your beach parade are as low as they get.

Villa Clara Province Highlights

1 Trace the legend at Santa Clara's **monument to Ernesto Che Guevara** (p264) and **Monumento a la Toma del Tren Blindado** (p264).

2 Tour Santa Clara's cigar factory, **Fábrica de Tabacos Constantino Pérez Carrodegua** (p263), followed by sublime coffee at **La Veguita** (p263).

3 Plug into the electric nightlife in Santa Clara's **Club Mejunje** (p269).

4 Hike the trails and soak up the solitude of **Embalse Hanabanilla** (p270).

5 People-watch from the plaza's cafes in the colonial pocket of **Remedios** (p272).

6 See the Villa Clara the tourist board forgot to mention

at ramshackle yet heart-warming **Caibarién** (p275).

7 Bask on the balmy beaches of the **Cayo Santa María** (p276).

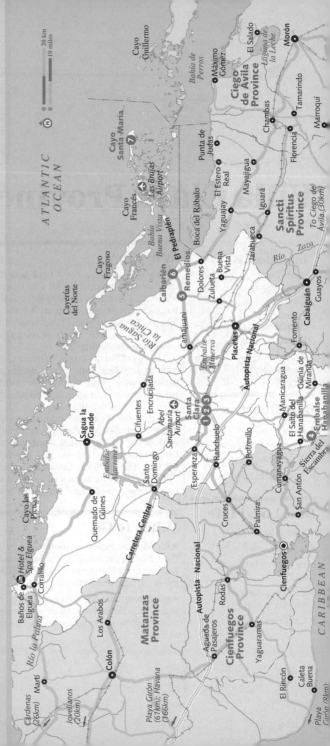

History

The Taíno people were the first known inhabitants of the region, but a re-creation of a settlement at a cheesy hotel outside Santa Clara is their only surviving legacy. Strategically located in the island's geographical center, Villa Clara has historically been a focal point for corsairs, colonizers and revolutionaries vying for material gains. Pirates were a perennial headache in the early colonial years, with the province's first town, Remedios, being moved twice and then abandoned altogether in the late 1600s by a group of families who escaped inland to what is now Santa Clara. Later, the area's demographics were shaken up further by Canary Islanders, who brought their agricultural know-how and distinctive lilting Spanish accents to the tobacco fields of the picturesque Vuelta Arriba region. In December 1958 Ernesto 'Che' Guevara – aided by a motley crew of scruffy *barbudas* (bearded ones) – orchestrated the fall of the city of Santa Clara by derailing an armored train carrying more than 350 government troops and weaponry to the east. The victory rang the death knell for Fulgencio Batista's dictatorship and signaled the triumph of the Cuban Revolution.

SANTA CLARA

POP 239,091

While Varadero courts beach-lovers and Trinidad pulls in history geeks, gritty Santa Clara doesn't stand on ceremony for anyone. Smack bang in the geographic center of Cuba, this is a city of new trends and insatiable creativity, where an edgy youth culture has been testing the boundaries of Cuba's censorship police for almost a decade. Unique Santa Clara offerings include Cuba's only official drag show (in Club Mejunje), and the best *bona fide* rock festival in the country (October's Ciudad Metal). The city's fiery personality has been shaped over time by the presence of the nation's most prestigious university outside Havana, and a long association with Argentinian guerrilla Che Guevara, whose liberating of Santa Clara in December 1958 marked the end of the Batista regime.

History

A good 10,000 miles out in his calculations, Christopher Columbus believed that Cuba-

nacán (or Cubana Khan, an Indian name that meant 'the middle of Cuba'), an Indian village once located near Santa Clara, was the seat of the khans of Mongolia; hence his misguided notion that he was exploring the Asian coast. Santa Clara proper was founded in 1689 by 13 families from Remedios, who were tired of the unwanted attention of passing pirates. The town grew quickly after a fire emptied Remedios in 1692, and in 1867 it became the capital of Las Villas province. A notable industrial center, Santa Clara was famous for its prerevolutionary Coca-Cola factory and its pivotal role in Cuba's island-wide communications network. Today it continues to support a textile mill, a marble quarry and the Constantino Pérez Carrodegua tobacco factory. Santa Clara was the first major city to be liberated from Batista's army in December 1958.

◉ Sights

Santa Clara's sights are liberally distributed to the north, east and west of Parque Vidal. All are within walking distance, with the big Che sight, Conjunto Escultórico Comandante Ernesto Che Guevara, only 2km from the center.

◉ Parque Vidal

Parque Vidal SQUARE

A veritable alfresco theater named for Colonel Leoncio Vidal y Caro, who was killed here on March 23, 1896, Parque Vidal was encircled by twin sidewalks during the colonial era, with a fence separating blacks and whites.

Today all the colors of Cuba's cultural rainbow mix in one of the nation's busiest and most vibrant parks, with old men in *guayabera* shirts gossiping on the shaded benches and young kids getting pulled around in carriages led by goats. Find time to contemplate the statues of local philanthropist Marta Abreu and the emblematic *El Niño de la Bota* (Boy with a Boot), a long-standing city symbol. Since 1902, the municipal orchestra has played rousingly in the park bandstand at 8pm every Thursday and Sunday.

Museo de Artes Decorativas MUSEUM

(Parque Vidal No 27; admission CUC$3; ⊘9am-6pm Mon-Thu, 1-10pm Fri & Sat, 6-10pm Sun) Reserve an hour for this 18th-century mansion turned museum packed with period

Santa Clara

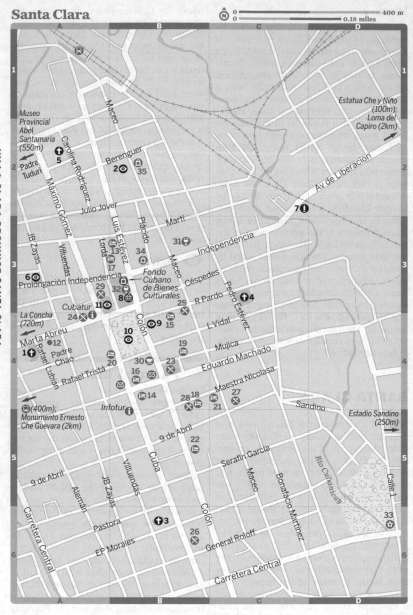

furniture from a whole gamut of styles that seem to ape Cuba's architectural heritage. Look for baroque desks, art nouveau mirrors and art deco furniture. Live chamber music adds to the romanticism in the evenings. Check the noticeboard.

Palacio Provincial　　　CULTURAL BUILDING
(Parque Vidal) On the eastern side of Parque Vidal sits the 1902–12 neoclassical Palacio Provincial, today home to the Martí library and a rare book collection.

Santa Clara

Teatro la Caridad THEATER, HISTORIC BUILDING
(Máximo Gómez, cnr Marta Abreu) Many are deceived by the relatively austere neoclassical facade. But toss CUC$1 to whoever is manning the door and you'll serendipitously discover why the 1885 Teatro La Caridad is one of the three great rural theaters of the colonial era.

The ornate interior is almost identical to the Tomás Terry in Cienfuegos and the Sauto in Matanzas: three tiers, a U-shaped auditorium and decadent marble statues. The rich ceiling fresco by Camilo Zalaya provides the *pièce de résistance*.

◉ North of Parque Vidal

Fábrica de Tabacos Constantino Pérez Carrodegua CIGAR FACTORY
(Maceo No 181 , btwn Julio Jover & Berenguer; admission CUC$4; ⊙ 9-11am & 1-3pm) Santa Clara's tobacco factory, one of Cuba's best, makes a quality range of Montecristos, Partagás and Romeo y Julieta cigars. Tours here are lo-fi compared to those in Havana, and so the experience is a lot more interesting and less rushed. Book tickets through the Cubatur office.

Across the street you'll find **La Veguita** (☎ 20-89-52; Calle Maceo No 176A, btwn Julio Jover & Berenguer; ⊙ 8:30am-5:30pm), the factory's diminutive but comprehensively stocked sales outlet, staffed by a friendly, ultra-professional team of cigar experts. You can buy cheap rum here, and the bar out back brews exquisite coffee.

La Casa de la Ciudad CULTURAL CENTER
(cnr Independencia & JB Zayas; admission CUC$1; ⊙ 8am 5pm) The pulse of the city's progressive cultural life is inside this building northwest of Parque Vidal. If you want to see a side to Santa Clara other than the obligatory Che memorabilia, get chatting to the young artists here. The historic center hosts art expositions (including an original Wifredo Lam sketch), Noches del Danzón and a film museum, as well as impromptu music events.

The real buzz of this place, however, is mingling with the local culture-vultures and finding out what makes this most unprepossessing of Cuban cities tick.

Iglesia de Nuestra Señora del Carmen
CHURCH

(Carolina Rodríguez) The city's oldest church is five blocks north of Parque Vidal. It was built in 1748, with a tower added in 1846. During the War of Independence, it was used as a jail for Cuban patriots. A modern cylindrical monument facing the church commemorates the spot where Santa Clara was founded in 1689 by 13 refugee families from Remedios.

Museo Provincial Abel Santamaría
MUSEUM

(🖃 20-30-41; admission CUC$1; ⊘ 9am-5pm Mon-Fri, to 1pm Sat) Not actually a memorial to Señor Santamaría (Fidel's right-hand man at Moncada – see boxed text p409), but rather a small provincial museum quartered in former military barracks where Batista's troops surrendered to Che Guevara on January 1, 1959. It contains a room on natural history and a room dedicated to Cuban women throughout history.

The museum is on a hilltop at the north end of Esquerra across the Río Bélico. Look for the large cream-colored building behind the horse field.

◉ East of Parque Vidal

Monumento a la Toma del Tren Blindado
MONUMENT

(Boxcar Museum; admission CUC$1; ⊘ 9am-5:30pm Mon-Sat) History was made at the site of this small museum on December 29, 1958, when Ernesto 'Che' Guevara and a band of 18 rifle-wielding revolutionaries barely out of their teens derailed an armored train using a borrowed bulldozer and homemade Molotov cocktails.

SANTA CLARA STREET NAMES

As in most Cuban cities, the streets have two names. The old names are used colloquially by the people who live there. The new ones are printed on street signs.

OLD NAME	NEW NAME
Candelaria	Maestra Nicolasa
Caridad	General Roloff
Nazareno	Serafín García
San Miguel	Calle 9 de Abril
Sindico	Morales

The battle lasted 90 minutes and improbably pulled the rug out from under the Batista dictatorship, ushering in 50 years of Fidel Castro. The museum – east on Independencia, just over the river – marks the spot where the train derailed and ejected its 350 heavily armed government troops. The celebrated bulldozer is mounted on its own plinth at the entrance.

Estatua Che y Niño
MONUMENT

Far more intimate and intricate a monument than its big brother on the other side of town, this statue in front of the Officina de la Provincia (PCC) four blocks east of Tren Blindado shows El Che with a baby (symbolizing the next generation) on his shoulder.

Looking closer you'll see smaller sculptures incorporated into the revolutionary's uniform depicting junctures in his life, including engraved likenesses of the 38 men killed with Guevara in Bolivia concealed within the belt buckle.

Loma del Capiro
LANDMARK

Continuing two blocks further east from the *Estatua Che y Niño*, a road to the right leads to Santa Clara's best lookout, the distinctive Loma del Capiro. The crest is marked by a flag and a series of stakes supporting the metallic but recognizable face of, you've guessed it, Che Guevara.

The hill was a crucial vantage point for his forces during the 1958 liberation of Santa Clara.

Iglesia de Nuestra Señora del Buen Viaje
CHURCH

(cnr Pedro Estévez & R Pardo) East of center is this riotous mix of Gothic, Romanesque and neoclassical architecture.

Iglesia de la Santísima Madre del Buen Pastor
CHURCH

(EP Morales No 4, btwn Cuba & Villuendas) A singular colonial-style church south of the center.

◉ West of Parque Vidal

Conjunto Escultórico Comandante Ernesto Che Guevara
MONUMENT

(Plaza de la Revolución) FREE The end point of many a Che pilgrimage, this monument, mausoleum and museum complex is 2km west of Parque Vidal (via Rafael Tristá on Av de los Desfiles), near the Víazul bus station. Even if you can't stand the Argentine guerrilla for whom many reserve an almost religious reverence, there's poignancy in the vast square that spans both sides of the *carretera*, guarded by a bronze statue of El Che.

The statue was erected in 1987 to mark the 20th anniversary of Guevara's murder in Bolivia, and can be viewed any time. Accessed from the statue's rear, the respectful **mausoleum** (Av de los Desfiles; ⊙9.30am-4pm Tue-Sun) contains 38 stone-carved niches dedicated to the other guerrillas killed in the failed Bolivian revolution. In 1997 the remains of 17 of them, including Guevara, were recovered from a secret mass grave in Bolivia and reburied in this memorial. Fidel Castro lit the eternal flame on October 17, 1997. The adjacent museum houses the details and ephemera of Che's life and death.

The best way to get to the monument is a 30-minute walk, or by hopping on a horse carriage in Calle Marta Abreu outside the cathedral for a couple of pesos.

Catedral de las Santas Hermanas de Santa Clara de Asís CATHEDRAL

(Marta Abreu) Three blocks west of Parque Vidal, Santa Clara's cathedral was constructed amid huge controversy in 1923 after the demolition of the city's original church in Parque Vidal. It contains a fantastic collection of stained-glass windows and a mythical white statue of Mother Mary known (unofficially) as La Virgen de la Charca (Virgin of the Pond).

The statue was discovered in a ditch in the 1980s, having mysteriously disappeared shortly after the cathedral's consecration in 1954. It returned to grace the cathedral in 1995.

 Courses

Santa Clara has Cuba's second-most prestigious university, **Universidad Central Marta Abreu de las Villas** (☐ 28-14-10; www.uclv.edu.cu; Carretera de Camajuaní Km 5.5). Many international students study here, although most arrange everything through universities back home. Non-Cubans have, however, been able to turn up and study Spanish almost impromptu on occasion. Check the website for current details.

You might be able to pick up dancing and percussion lessons at the ever-adaptable **Club Mejunje** (Marta Abreu No 107; ⊙4pm-1am Tue-Sun) if you ask.

 Festivals

Santa Clara's renegade annual offerings include **Miss Trasvesti**, a Miss World–type event with transvestite contestants in March, and October's **Metal Festival**, when headbanging to the country's leading heavy-metal acts happens at various venues across the city.

VILLA CLARA PROVINCE SANTA CLARA

MARTA ABREU

You won't find many places in Cuba without a street dedicated to Marta Abreu, the country's most famed philanthropist, but in her home city of Santa Clara her name and legacy is everywhere, including at the university (Cuba's second-most important). Before Che exploded onto the scene, Abreu had already established herself as the city's best-loved figure, and no wonder: the woman was responsible for the construction of most of Santa Clara's significant buildings, and was an important contributor to the demise of Spanish colonialism in the 1890s. At one time the city was known as the Ciudad de Marta and was renowned for its revelatory social services, instituted by Abreu.

Born into a wealthy family, Abreu soon came to realize the contrasts in living standards between Cuba and comparatively luxurious Europe, and brought about many changes in Santa Clara to help the city rise to greater heights. Her most outstanding contribution remains the Teatro la Caridad, the building of which she oversaw, but the Biblioteca José Martí, Santa Clara's train station, four schools, a weather station, an old people's home and the provincial gas factory also exist because of funds she donated.

It isn't just her public works for which she is remembered, however. A humanitarian who stood for causes small and large, Abreu championed a campaign against homelessness in Santa Clara, funded construction of the power station that gave the city street lighting, and improved sanitation with the creation of public laundry stations. Perhaps most significantly, she raised the vast sum of 240,000 pesos (the equivalent of millions of dollars today) toward the liberation of Cuba from the Spanish in the 1890s.

🛏 Sleeping

★Hostal Florida Center   CASA PARTICULAR **$**
(📞20-81-61; www.hostalfloridacenter.com; Maestra Nicolasa Este No 56, btwn Colón & Maceo; r CUC$20-25; ❋) The Florida gives the Museo de Artes Decorativas a run for its money on the antiques front and could probably steal the limelight from most of Cuba's botanical gardens with its lush central patio stuffed with rare orchids, ferns, birds and a tortoise.

Charismatic owner, Ángel (who speaks English, French and Italian) rents two imaginatively decorated rooms, one a grandiose re-creation of the colonial era, the other a snapshot of early-20th-century art deco. The place is well known as one of Cuba's best casas particulares and consequently gets busy; book ahead.

Authentica Pérgola   CASA PARTICULAR **$**
(📞20-86-86; www.hostalautenticapergola.blogspot.ca; Luis Estévez No 61, btwn Independencia & Martí; r CUC$20-25; ❋) Another casa that makes a lot of people's 'best in Cuba' lists, the Pérgola is set around an Alhambra-esque patio draped in greenery and crowned by a beautiful fountain. Numerous large rooms lead off the patio, and all have private bathrooms. There's a roof terrace and a dining room where fine food is served. The owners are renowned for going well beyond the call of duty.

Hostal Alba   CASA PARTICULAR **$**
(📞29-41-08; Eduardo Machado No 7, btwn Cuba & Colón; r CUC$25-30; ❋) This architectural stunner with lovely antique beds, original tilework and a patio serves amazing breakfasts and is just one block from the main square. The congenial owner Wilfredo is chef at Hostal Florida Center – enough said!

Hostal Familia Sarmiento   CASA PARTICULAR **$**
(📞20-35-10; Lorda No 61, btwn Martí & Independencia; r CUC$20-25; ❋@) Two rooms in a lovely family home just yards from the main square, this casa is safe, convivial and sets high standards. Hostess Geydis is a fantastic cook and prepares huge, delicious breakfasts, while host Carlos is a driver, keen photographer and mine of information on all of Cuba.

Casa de Mercy   CASA PARTICULAR **$**
(📞21-69-41; Eduardo Machado No 4, btwn Cuba & Colón; r CUC$20-25; ❋) There are two rooms with private bathrooms available in this beautiful family house which has two terraces, a dining room, a book exchange and a tempting cocktail menu. English, French and Italian are spoken by the engaging hosts.

Isidoro & Marta   CASA PARTICULAR **$**
(📞20-38-13; Maestra Nicolasa No 74, btwn Colón & Maceo; r CUC$20-25; ❋) This couple's more modern house is kept *muy limpia* (very clean). A long, narrow patio leads to two fine bedrooms sporting Santa Clara's best showers. Breakfast and dinner are served at reasonable rates.

Héctor Martínez   CASA PARTICULAR **$**
(📞21-74-63; R Pardo No 8, btwn Maceo & Parque Vidal; r CUC$20-25; ❋) A quiet haven just off Parque Vidal with a fern-and-flower-filled patio and two huge rooms with two beds (one double) and a writing/domino table.

La Casona Jover   CASA PARTICULAR **$**
(📞20-44-58; Colón No 167, btwn Calle 9 de Abril & Serafín García; r CUC$20-25; ❋) Two large rooms set well back from the road and a small terrace for contemplation.

Hotel Santa Clara Libre   HOTEL **$**
(📞20-75-48; Parque Vidal No 6; s/d CUC$19/30; ❋) Long Santa Clara's default hotel – and its tallest building – this minty-green 168-room eyesore played a key role in the December 1958 battle for the city between Guevara and Batista's government troops (you can still see the bullet holes on the building's facade). Inside, the pokey rooms and tired furnishings are worn, but there are cracking views from the 10th-floor restaurant.

Hotel América   HOTEL **$$**
(Mujica, btwn Colón & Maceo; s/d CUC$60/90; ❋@❄) After years milking the lackluster Santa Clara Libre, the city center has finally got a hotel you'd recommend to your friends rather than your enemies. The 27-room América which opened in April 2012 can't quite claim a 'boutique' moniker, but it's new and keen to please with some interesting details (check out the metal staircase balustrades).

There's an easygoing restaurant and a new outdoor pool.

Villa la Granjita   HOTEL **$$**
(📞21-81-90; Carretera de Maleza Km 21.5; s/d CUC$45/60; P❋@❄) Approximately 3km north of town, La Granjita poses as a native Taíno village and does well with its *bohío*-style (thatched) huts, equipped with all the mod cons, but loses authenticity at

CHE COMANDANTE, AMIGO

Few 20th-century figures have successfully divided public opinion as deeply as Ernesto Guevara de la Serna, better known to his friends (and enemies) as El Che. He has been revered as an enduring symbol of Third World freedom and celebrated as the hero of the Sierra Maestra, and yet Che was also the most wanted man on the CIA hit list. The image of this handsome and often misunderstood Argentine physician-turned-*guerrillero* is still plastered over posters and tourist merchandise across Cuba. But what would the man himself have made of such rampant commercialization?

Born in Rosario, Argentina, in June 1928 to a bourgeois family of Irish-Spanish descent, Guevara was a delicate and sickly child who developed asthma at the age of two. It was an early desire to overcome this debilitating illness that instilled in the young Ernesto a willpower that would dramatically set him apart from other men.

A pugnacious competitor in his youth, Ernesto earned the name 'Fuser' at school for his combative nature on the rugby field. Graduating from the University of Buenos Aires in 1953 with a medical degree, he shunned a conventional medical career in favor of a cross-continental motorcycling odyssey, accompanied by his old friend and colleague Alberto Granado. Their nomadic wanderings – well documented in a series of posthumously published diaries – would open Ernesto's eyes to the grinding poverty and stark political injustices all too common in 1950s Latin America.

By the time Guevara arrived in Guatemala in 1954 on the eve of a US-backed coup against Jacobo Arbenz' leftist government, he was enthusiastically devouring the works of Marx and nurturing a deep-rooted hatred of the US. Deported to Mexico for his pro-Arbenz activities in 1955, Guevara fell in with a group of Cubans that included Moncada veteran Raúl Castro. Impressed by the Argentine's sharp intellect and never-failing political convictions, Raúl – a long-standing Communist Party member himself – decided to introduce Che to his charismatic brother, Fidel.

The meeting between the two men at Maria Antonia's house in Mexico City in June 1955 lasted 10 hours and ultimately changed the course of history. Rarely had two characters needed each other as much as the hot-headed Castro and the calmer, more ideologically polished Che. Both were favored children from large families, and both shunned the quiet life to fight courageously for a revolutionary cause. Similarly, both men had little to gain and much to throw away by abandoning professional careers for what most would have regarded as narrow-minded folly. 'In a revolution one either wins or dies,' wrote Guevara prophetically years later, 'if it is a *real* one.'

In December 1956 Che left for Cuba on the *Granma* yacht, joining the rebels as the group medic. One of only 12 or so of the original 82 rebel soldiers to survive the catastrophic landing at Las Coloradas, he proved himself to be a brave and intrepid fighter who led by example and quickly won the trust of his less reckless Cuban comrades. As a result Castro rewarded him with the rank of Comandante in July 1957, and in December 1958 Che repaid Fidel's faith when he masterminded the battle of Santa Clara, an action that effectively sealed a historic revolutionary victory.

Guevara was granted Cuban citizenship in February 1959 and soon assumed a leading role in Cuba's economic reforms as president of the National Bank and minister of industry. His insatiable work ethic and regular appearance at enthusiastically organized volunteer worker weekends quickly saw him cast as the living embodiment of Cuba's New Man.

But the honeymoon wasn't to last. Disappearing from the Cuban political scene in 1965 amid many rumors and myths, Guevara eventually materialized again in Bolivia in late 1966 at the head of a small band of Cuban *guerrilleros*. After the successful ambush of a Bolivian detachment in March 1967, he issued a call for 'two, three, many Vietnams in the Americas'. Such bold proclamations could only prove his undoing. On October 8, 1967, Guevara was captured by the Bolivian army. Following consultations between the army and military leaders in La Paz and Washington DC, he was shot the next day in front of US advisors. His remains were eventually returned to Cuba in 1997 and reburied in Santa Clara.

nighttime when a cheesy poolside show and blaring disco are more reminiscent of 21st-century Varadero.

Nevertheless, the hotel is better than the usual out-of-town rustic affair, with a good on-site restaurant, a massage therapist and even horseback riding available.

Villa Los Caneyes   HOTEL $$
(☑ 20-45-13; cnr Av de los Eucaliptos & Circunvalación de Santa Clara; s/d CUC$45/60; P ✴ @ 🐾) A mock-indigenous village, Los Caneyes has 95 thatched bungalows (bohios) to La Granjita's 75, though the facilities are a few refurbishments behind its rustic cousin. Built in suitably verdant grounds replete with abundant birdlife, it's 3km from Santa Clara and a favorite with organized coach tours. There's an on-site restaurant and pool.

✖ Eating

Casas particulares and paladares trump the state-run joints.

Several peso cafeterías are near the corner of Independencia Oeste and Zayas, around Cine Cubanacán. Your ever-faithful ice-cream vendor sometimes operates out of a window on Abreu.

El Alba   CUBAN $
(R Pardo, cnr Maceo; ⊘ noon-4pm & 6-9:30pm Tue-Sun) The town's best peso restaurant is a tiny hole-in-the-wall a block east of Parque Vidal. The walls are adorned with imaginative cartoons of Santa Clara life, and comfy sofas ease the wait for a table. The food, when it arrives, comes in copious quantities. Go for the fish if it's available.

Dinos Pizza   CAFETERIA $
(Marta Abreu No 10, btwn Villuendas & Cuba; pizzas CUC$3-6; ⊘ 9am-11pm) Smarter than the average Dinos (which is a small Cuban chain), this Santa Clara branch has computer terminals with internet access (CUC$5 an hour), a pleasant bar, air-conditioning and friendly, helpful staff. It's generally packed with young students and serves OK pizza by Cuban standards.

La Concha   CARIBBEAN, ITALIAN $
(cnr Carretera Central & Danielito; mains CUC$3-8) State-run eatery on the outskirts of town that does a good trade in capturing the coach parties on their way to/from the Che memorial. There are some classy lunchtime bands here. The default lunch is the cheap but passable pizza (from CUC$4).

Restaurante Colonial 1878   INTERNATIONAL $
(Máximo Gómez, btwn Marta Abreu & Independencia; ⊘ noon-2pm & 7-10:30pm) Hold on to the table when you cut your steak here, or you might lose it on the floor. Tough meat aside, 1878 is amiable enough, though the food struggles to live up to the pleasant colonial setting. Pop in for a cocktail or a light lunch.

Coppelia   ICE CREAM $
(cnr Colón & Mujica; ⊘ 10:30am-10pm Tue-Sun) Stock up on peso ice cream at this architecturally hideous, but massive, construction.

Restaurant Florida Center   CUBAN, FUSION $$
(☑ 20-81-61; Maestra Nicolasa No 56, btwn Colón & Maceo; mains CUC$10-12; ⊘ 6-8.30pm) Long known for its food, the town's most famous casa particular has morphed into a refined restaurant presided over by owner Ángel and skilled chef, Wilfredo (owner of nearby Hostal Alba). There are a profusion of dishes and wines served on a lush candlelit patio, though the highlight is the lobster with prawns in a tangy tomato sauce.

Self-Catering

Panadería Doña Neli   BAKERY $
(cnr Maceo Sur & Calle 9 de Abril; ⊘ 7am-6pm) This joyous bakery amid the austere shopfronts on Calle Maceo will have your stomach rumbling with its aromatic fruit cakes, bread and pastries. Arrive early and celebrate breakfast.

Mercado Agropecuario   MARKET $
(Cuba No 269, btwn EP Morales & General Roloff) Small, but centrally located and amply stocked.

🍷 Drinking & Nightlife

La Veguita (p263) serves Santa Clara's best coffee; the peso bars around the corner of Independencia Oeste and Zayas might not look glam, but can rustle up good cocktails. Casas particulares also make for atmospheric evening drinks.

La Marquesina   BAR
(Parque Vidal, btwn Máximo Gómez & Lorda; ⊘ 9am-1am) You can chin-wag with locals of all types in this legendary dive bar under the porches of the equally legendary Caridad theater on the corner of Parque Vidal. The clientele is a potpourri of Santa Clara life – students, bohos, cigar factory workers and the odd off-duty bici-taxi rider.

Rapid-fire Spanish and cold beer from the bottle are de rigueur.

Café Literario
CAFE
(cnr Rafael Tristá & Colón; ⊘9am-9pm) What, a student coffee bar with no laptops? Revisit the pre-Microsoft years with strong espresso, piles of books and plenty of pent-up undergraduate idealism.

Europa
BAR
(cnr Independencia & Luis Estévez; ⊘noon-midnight) Everyone likes to drink at the Europa: that's because it's in prime people-watching territory on the boulevard, and locals and tourists alike feel welcomed on its laid-back street-facing terrace.

El Bar Club Boulevard
NIGHTCLUB
(Independencia No 2, btwn Maceo & Pedro Estévez; admission CUC$2; ⊘10pm-2am Mon-Sat) This much-talked-about cocktail lounge has live bands and dancing, plus the odd humor show. It generally gets swinging about 11pm.

☆ Entertainment

Aside from the places listed here, don't discount the **Biblioteca José Martí** (Colón on Parque Vidal), inside the Palacio Provincial, for refined classical music; **La Casa de la Ciudad** for boleros (love songs) and *trova* (traditional poetic singing); and vibrant **Parque Vidal**, which presents everything from mime artists to full-scale orchestras.

★ Club Mejunje
LIVE MUSIC, NIGHTCLUB
(Marta Abreu No 107; ⊘4pm-1am Tue-Sun; ⊛) Urban graffiti, children's theater, transvestites, old crooners belting out boleros, tourists dancing salsa. You've heard about 'something for everyone', but this is ridiculous. Welcome to Club Mejunje, set in the ruins of an old roofless building given over to sprouting greenery, a local – nay, national – institution, famous for many things, not least Cuba's only official drag show (every Saturday night).

Roll in any day of the week and enjoy an unforgettable 'only in Santa Clara' moment.

Museo de Artes Decorativas
LIVE MUSIC
(Parque Vidal No 27) In the museum's shadowy courtyard there is live music (mostly sit-down concerts) several times weekly, which makes for a relaxing evening. Expect everything from rock to *chachachá*.

Estadio Sandino
SPORT
(Calle 9 de Abril Final) From October to April, you can catch baseball games in this stadium east of the center via Calle 9 de Abril.

Villa Clara, nicknamed Las Naranjas (the Oranges) for their team strip, won a trio of championships from 1993 to 1995 and were losing finalists to their nemesis, Los Industriales (Havana), in 1996, 2003 and 2004.

Historically, they are Cuba's third-biggest baseball team, after the Havana and Santiago heavyweights.

El Bosque
CABARET, NIGHTCLUB
(Cnr Carretera Central & Calle 1; ⊘9pm-1am Wed-Sun) Santa Clara's cabaret hot spot.

Cine Camilo Cienfuegos
CINEMA
(Parque Vidal) This is below Hotel Santa Clara Libre; large-screen English-language films are shown.

🔒 Shopping

Independencia, between Maceo and JB Zayas, is the pedestrian shopping street called the Boulevard by locals. It's littered with all kinds of shops and restaurants and is the bustling hub of city life. An outlet of **ARTex** (Independencia, btwn Luis Estévez & Plácido) sells handicrafts here. And don't forget **La Veguita** for some of the best cigars outside Havana.

ℹ️ Information

INTERNET ACCESS & TELEPHONE
Etecsa Telepunto (Marta Abreu No 55, btwn Máximo Gómez & Villuendas; internet access per hr CUC$6; ⊘8:30am-7pm) Three internet terminals and three phone cabins.

MEDIA
Radio CMHW broadcasts on 840AM and 93.5FM. The *Vanguardia Santa Clara* newspaper is published on Saturday.

MEDICAL SERVICES
Farmacia Internacional (Colón No 106, btwn Maestra Nicolasa & Calle 9 de Abril; ⊘9am-6pm) In the Hotel Santa Clara Libre.

Hospital Arnaldo Milián Castro (🖉27 00 69; btwn Circumvalacion & Av 26 de Julio) Southeast of the city center, just northwest of the intersection with Calle 3. It's the best all-round option for foreigners, often called just Hospital Nuevo.

MONEY
Banco Financiero Internacional (Cuba No 6, cnr Rafael Tristá) Bank.

Cadeca (cnr Rafael Tristá & Cuba; ⊘8:30am-7:30pm Mon-Sat, to 11:30am Sun) On the corner of Parque Vidal.

POST

DHL (Cuba No 7, btwn Rafael Tristá & Eduardo Machado; ☺8am-6pm Mon-Sat, to noon Sun) Postal services.

Post Office (Colón No 10; ☺8am-6pm Mon-Sat, to noon Sun)

TOURIST INFORMATION

Infotur (Cuba No 68, btwn Machado & Maestra Nicolasa; ☺9am-5pm) Handy maps and brochures in multiple languages.

TRAVEL AGENCIES

Cubanacán (☑20-51-89; Colón, cnr Maestra Nicolasa; ☺8am-8pm Mon-Sat)

Cubatur (☑20-89-80; Marta Abreu No 10; ☺9am-6pm) Near Máximo Gómez. Book tobacco factory tours here.

ℹ Getting There & Away

Santa Clara's Abel Santamaría Airport receives weekly flights from Montreal and Toronto, with 99% of passengers getting bussed off to the Cayerías del Norte. There are no flights to Havana. Located in the center of the island, Santa Clara has excellent transport connections heading east or west.

BUS

The **Terminal de Ómnibus Nacionales** (☑20-34-70) is 2.5km out on the Carretera Central toward Matanzas, 500m north of the Che monument.

Tickets for air-conditioned **Víazul** (www.viazul.com) buses are sold at a special ticket window for foreigners at the station entrance.

Three buses leave for Havana (CUC$18, 3¾ hours) at 3:25am, 8:40am and 5:10pm. Buses to Varadero (CUC$11, three hours 20 minutes) leave at 8am, 6pm and 6.15pm.

The Santiago de Cuba (CUC$33) bound bus departs four times daily at 1:15am, 2:10am, 12:05pm and 8.05pm, travelling via Sancti Spíritus (CUC$6, 1¼ hours), Ciego de Ávila (CUC$9, two hours 35 minutes), Camagüey (CUC$15, four hours 25 minutes), Holguín (CUC$26, seven hours 50 minutes) and Bayamo (CUC$26, nine hours 10 minutes).

A new Víazul bus heads north once daily at 9.45am to Remedios (CUC$6, one hour), Caibarién (CUC$6, 1¼ hours), Morón (CUC$13, three hours) and Ciego de Ávila (CUC$16, 3½ hours). An evening bus goes south to Cienfuegos (CUC$6, one hour) and Trinidad (CUC$10, 2½ hours).

The **intermunicipal bus station** (Carretera Central), west of the center via Calle Marta Abreu, has cheap local buses to Remedios, Caibarién and Manicaragua (for Embalse Hanabanilla). Transport could be by bus or truck, it gets overcrowded and isn't 100% reliable.

TRAIN

The **train station** (☑20-28-95) is straight up Luis Estévez from Parque Vidal on the north side of town. The **ticket office** (Luis Estévez Norte No 323) is across the park from the train station.

The comparatively luxurious *Tren Francés* passes through the city every three days, heading for Santiago de Cuba (CUC$41, 12¾ hours) via Camagüey (CUC$19, 4¼ hours). It returns in the other direction for Havana (CUC$21, four hours). Check the schedule well before time.

There's an additional long-distance service to Santiago stopping in Ciego de Ávila, Camagüey and Las Tunas; some trains run on to Guantánamo. In the opposite direction, there are approximately five daily trains to Havana, most of which stop in Matanzas.

Trains to to Cienfuegos and Sancti Spíritus are sporadic (once or twice a week). Trains to Remedios and Caibarién are not currently running. In the fickle world of Cuban trains, information can change weekly and we strongly advise you to double-check all this information at the station a day or two before departing.

ℹ Getting Around

Horse carriages congregate outside the cathedral on Marta Abreu (two pesos per ride). Bici-taxis (from the northwest of the park) cost CUC$1 a ride.

CAR & MOPED

Various agencies in Santa Clara rent wheels.

Cubacar (☑20-20-40; Parque Vidal No 6, Hotel Santa Clara Libre) Rents cars.

Rex (☑22-22-44; Marta Abreu; ☺9am-6pm) Rents luxury cars for around CUC$80 per day. Mopeds are CUC$25 per day.

Servicentro Oro Negro (cnr Carretera Central & Calle 9 de Abril) Just southwest of the center.

TAXI

Private cabs hang around in front of the national bus station and will offer you lifts to Remedios and Caibarién. A state taxi to the same destinations will cost approximately CUC$25 and CUC$30 respectively. To get to Cayo las Brujas, bank on CUC$50/$80 one way/return, including waiting time; drivers generally congregate in Parque Vidal outside Hotel Santa Clara Libre, or you can call **Cubataxi** (☑20-25-55, 20-03-63).

AROUND SANTA CLARA

Embalse Hanabanilla

In Santa Clara, greenery is never far away. Embalse Hanabanilla, Villa Clara's main

OFF THE BEATEN TRACK

THE ESCAMBRAY'S LESSER-KNOWN TRAILS

The Sierra del Escambray is riddled with walking trails. The most accessible and well-publicized routes emanate out of Topes de Collantes in Sancti Spíritus province and are well trodden by tourists based in nearby Trinidad. Far less crowded are the trails that surround Embalse Hanabanilla in Villa Clara province, most of which require a boat transfer from the Hotel Hanabanilla. The hotel has more information on access to trails and walking guides, plus a relief map of the area mounted on a wall in the lobby.

Ruta Natural Por la Rivera A 3.4km trail that follows the contours of the lake, passing coffee plantations and humid foliage replete with butterflies.

Montaña por dentro A 13km hike that connects Embalse Hanabanilla to the El Nicho waterfall on the Cienfuegos side of the Sierra del Escambray.

La Colicambia A 7km adventure culminating in a climb to a mirador with views over the Río Negro valley, the domain of abundant birdlife, including the *tocororo* and *cartacuba*.

Un Reto a Loma Atahalaya A 12km all-encompassing walk that incorporates a climb up the 700m-high Loma Atahalaya with broad views north and south, a waterfall and local campesino house. It finishes at a cave, La Cueva de Brollo.

---

gateway to the Sierra del Escambray, is a 36-sq-km reservoir nestled picturesquely amid traditional farms and broccoli-toned hills. The glittering lake is fjord-like and comes stocked with a famed supply of record-breaking bass. Besides fishers, boaters and nature-lovers are also well catered for, with several excursions and some rewarding lightly trodden hikes available. The area is best accessed by boat from the Hotel Hanabanilla on the reservoir's northwestern shore, some 80km by road south of Santa Clara. Cuba's largest hydroelectric generating station is also headquartered here.

Activities

Whopping 9kg largemouth bass have been caught on the lake, and **fishing trips** can be organized at the hotel: prices start at CUC$50 for four hours for two people with a guide. Boats ferry passengers over to Casa del Campesino, offering coffee, fresh fruit and a taste of bucolic Cuban life. A trail from the hotel heads here too. Another popular **boat trip** is to the Río Negro Restaurant, perched atop a steep stone staircase overlooking the lakeshore, 7km away. You can enjoy *comida criolla* (Creole food) surrounded by nature, and hike up to a **mirador**. Both these boat trips cost CUC$6 per person. Another 2km by boat from Río Negro Restaurant is a tiny quay; disembark for the 1km hike to the **Arroyo Trinitario waterfall**, where you can swim. A couple of other trails lead off from here. You can organize these activities at Hotel Hanabanilla or book a day excursion

(CUC$33 from Santa Clara; CUC$69 from Cayo Santa María).

🛏 Sleeping & Eating

Hotel Hanabanilla   HOTEL $
(☎ 20-84-61; Salto de Hanabanilla; s/d CUC$24/38; P ❄ ☲) Another page from the utilitarian school of Cuban architecture that blemished many a beauty spot in the 1970s, the 125-room Hanabanilla has attempted regular refurbs in the years since, though none have fully eradicated its incongruous ugliness. However, closer inspection reveals well-kept facilities inside, including an à la carte restaurant, a swimming pool, a vista-laden bar and lake-facing rooms with small balconies.

Peaceful during the week but packed with mainly Cuban guests at weekends, it's your only accommodation for miles and the best base for lakeside activities. To get there from Manicaragua, proceed west on route 152 for 13km. Turn left at a junction (the hotel is signposted) and follow the road 10km to the hotel.

ℹ Getting There & Away

The chalked-up bus schedule in Santa Clara advertises daily buses to Manicaragua at 7:40am, 1:30pm and 9:30pm (but check ahead). Theoretically, there are buses from Manicaragua on to Embalse Hanabanilla, but the only practical access is by car, bike or moped. Taxi drivers will energetically offer the trip. Bank on CUC$25 one way in a state cab. Negotiate hard if you want the driver to wait over while you participate in excursions.

Remedios

POP 45,836

A small, tranquil town that goes berserk every Christmas Eve in a cacophonous firework festival known as Las Parrandas, Remedios is one of Cuba's dustier colonial jewels. Some historical sources claim it is Cuba's second-oldest settlement (founded in 1513), although it is officially listed at number eight after Havana. Lack of a Unesco listing or any Trinidad-style marketing means it's left off most standard tourist itineraries, a factor that lends its streets a shabby authenticity. However, with the rapid development of the nearby Cayerias del Norte, Remedios' lazy days could be numbered. The town has recently benefited from a new boutique hotel and harbors some delightful colonial casas particulares.

Sights

Remedios is the only city in Cuba with two churches in its main square, Plaza Martí.

Parroquia de San Juan
Bautista de Remedios   CHURCH

(Camilo Cienfuegos No 20; ⊙9am-noon & 2-5pm Mon-Thu) One of the island's finest ecclesiastical buildings, this church dates from the late 18th century, although a church was founded on this site as early as 1545. The campanile was erected between 1848 and 1858, and its famous gilded high altar and mahogany ceiling are thanks to a restoration project (1944–46) financed by millionaire philanthropist Eutimio Falla Bonet.

The pregnant *Inmaculada Concepción* to the left of the entrance is said to be the only sculpture of its kind (ie expectant) in Cuba. If the front doors are closed, go around to the rear or attend 7:30pm Mass.

Also on Parque Martí is the 18th-century **Iglesia de Nuestra Señora del Buen Viaje**

Remedios

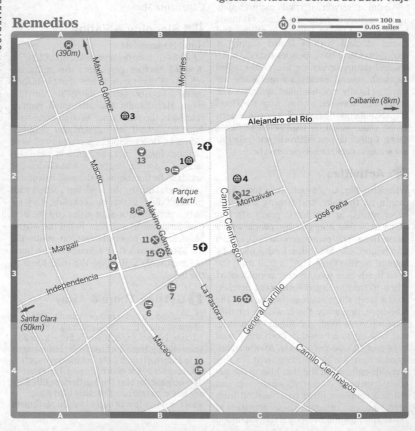

(Alejandro del Río No 66), which is awaiting a long-overdue restoration and is currently closed.

Museo de Música Alejandro García Caturla
MUSEUM

(Parque Martí No 5; admission CUC$1; ◷9am-noon & 1-6pm Mon-Thu, 7-11pm Fri, 2pm-midnight Sat) Between the churches is a museum commemorating García Caturla, a Cuban composer and musician who lived here from 1920 until his murder in 1940. Caturla was a pioneer who integrated Afro-Cuban rhythms into classical music and also served as a lawyer and judge. Look for occasional impromptu concerts.

Museo de las Parrandas Remedianas
MUSEUM

(Máximo Gómez No 71; admission CUC$1; ◷9am-6pm) Visiting this lively museum (and you don't often hear those two words together in provincial Cuba) two blocks off Parque Martí is probably a poor substitute for partying here on December 24, but what the hell? The downstairs photo gallery usually recaps the previous year's *parrandas*, while the upstairs rooms outline the history of this tradition, including scale models of floats and depictions of how the fireworks are made.

Another room is jammed with revelry gear from celebrations past.

Galería del Arte Carlos Enríquez
ART GALLERY

(Parque Martí No 2; ◷9am-noon & 1-5pm) FREE Overlooking the main plaza, this small gallery is named for the gifted painter who hailed from the small Villa Clara town of Zulueta. It displays some interesting local art and stages occasional exhibitions by touring artists.

🛏 Sleeping

★ 'Villa Colonial' – Frank & Arelys
CASA PARTICULAR $

(☑39-62-74; Maceo No 43, cnr Av General Carrillo; r CUC$20-25; ✳@) Frank & Arelys' wonderful colonial house is their pride and joy – and it shows. The three independent rooms have their own entrance, private bathroom, dining area (with stocked fridge), and living room where massive windows give onto the quiet but atmospheric street.

Internet is offered for CUC$3 for 30 minutes, and fine wines and food can be rustled up at short notice.

La Paloma
CASA PARTICULAR $

(☑39-54-90; Parque Martí No 4; r CUC$20-25; P✳) Another grand Remedios casa with tilework and furnishings that would be worth zillions anywhere else, La Paloma dates from 1875 and is right on the main square. The three rooms have massive shower units, art deco beds and doors big enough to ride a horse through.

Hostal San Carlos
CASA PARTICULAR $

(☑39-56-24; José A Peña No 75, btwn Maceo & La Pastora; r CUC$20-25; ✳) Despite some weird design features (you walk through the bathroom to get to the terrace), this friendly casa works hard to emulate the neighboring competition. The two rooms both have roof terrace access.

Hotel Mascotte
BOUTIQUE HOTEL $$

(☑39-53-41; Parque Martí; s/d CUC$55/70; ✳) Take an eloquent colonial Remedios theme and stick it inside a small 'Encanto' hotel (the boutique branch of the Cubanacán chain) and the results are breathtaking. For a dose of comfortable Cuban authenticity, drop by this recently upgraded 10-room gem on the main plaza.

PARRANDAS

Sometime during the 18th century, the priest at Remedios cathedral, Francisco Vigil de Quiñones, had the bright idea of providing local children with cutlery and crockery and getting them to run about the city making noise in a bid to increase mass attendance in the lead-up to Christmas. He could not have imagined what he was starting. Three centuries later and *parrandas*, as these cacophonous rituals became known, have developed into some of the best-known Caribbean street parties. Peculiar to the former Las Villas region of Cuba, *parrandas* take place only in towns in Villa Clara, Ciego de Ávila and Sancti Spíritus provinces, and the biggest party erupts annually in Remedios on December 24.

Festivities kick off at 10pm, with the city's two traditional neighborhoods (El Carmen and El Salvador) grouping together to outdo the other with displays of fireworks and dance, from rumba to polka. The second part of the party is a parade of vast floats, elaborate carnival-like structures only with the fancifully dressed people in the displays standing stock still as the tractor-towed artworks traverse the streets. Further fireworks round off the revelry.

The *parrandas* aren't confined to Remedios. Other towns in former Las Villas province (now Ciego de Ávila, Sancti Spíritus and Villa Clara) stage their own seasonal shenanigans. Though each is different, there are some generic party tricks, such as fireworks, decorative floats and opposing neighborhoods competing for the loudest, brightest and wildest stunts. Camajuani, Caibarién, Mayajigua and Chambas all have (almost) equivalently raucous *parrandas* celebrations.

Hotel Barcelona BOUTIQUE HOTEL **$$**
(José A Peña No 67; s/d CUC$55/70; ❋) The long-awaited sister hotel of the Mascotte offers more of the same colonial eloquence and blends well with the inherent unspoiled feel of Remedios. The finishing flourishes were being added at the time of research.

✗ Eating

El Louvre CAFE **$**
(Máximo Gómez No 122; ☉ 7:30am-midnight) With a gravitational pull on Remedios' scattering of tourists, El Louvre is, so locals proclaim, the oldest bar in the country in continuous service (since 1866) – and who are *you* to argue? Longevity awards aside, the fried-chicken-and-sandwiches menu can't quite match the quaint park-side location. The bar was good enough for Spanish poet Federico García Lorca, who heads the list of famous former patrons.

If you're looking for a room/paladar/taxi, park yourself here and wait for offers.

Portales a la Plaza CUBAN **$**
(Parque Martí, btwn Alejandro del Río & Montaiván) On the opposite side of the plaza to El Louvre, this restaurant is sequestered in a colonial courtyard, which lends atmosphere as you tuck into staples of the pork, banana and rice variety. Pay in pesos.

Restaurante el Curujey CARIBBEAN **$**
(☎ 36-33-05; Carretera Remedios–Caibarién Km 3.5; ☉ 10am-5pm) If you're Cayo-bound from Remedios, this rustic ARTex place 3km out on the Caibarién road is a good bet. It's signposted 'Finca la Cabana' from the highway.

🍷 Drinking

El Güije NIGHTCLUB
(cnr Independencia & Maceo; ☉ 2pm-2am) This is a newish open-air venue; ask about dancing classes during the day.

Bar Juvenil NIGHTCLUB
(Alejandro del Río No 47; ☉ 9pm-1am Sat & Sun) Dancers head here, a courtyard disco near Máximo Gómez (enter via park), with palms, pillars and Moorish tiles. During the day there's table tennis and dominoes; at night it's an alcohol-free party.

☆ Entertainment

Additional cultural activities can be found in **Uneac** (Maceo No 25), and outside in the parks and squares.

Centro Cultural las Leyendas CULTURAL CENTER
(Máximo Gómez, btwn Margalí & Independencia) Next door to El Louvre is an ARTex cultural center with music till 1am Wednesday to Saturday.

Teatro Rubén M Villena THEATER
(Cienfuegos No 30) A block east of the park is an elegant old theater with dance performances, plays and Theater Guiñol for kids. The schedule is posted in the window and tickets are in pesos.

ℹ️ Getting There & Away

The bus station is on the southern side of town at the beginning of the 45km road to Santa Clara. There are half a dozen daily buses to Santa Clara (one hour) and half as many to Caibarién (20 minutes). Fares are negligible. A new daily Víazul bus connects Remedios to Santa Clara (CUC$6), Cienfuegos (CUC$8) and Trinidad (CUC$14) in the south; and Caibarién, Mayajigua, Morón (CUC$7) and Ciego de Ávila (CUC$10) to the east. Southbound the bus leaves at 4.35pm and eastbound at 10.40am.

No trains currently serve Remedios. A state taxi from the bus station to Caibarién will cost roughly CUC$5 one way, and CUC$25 to Santa Clara. A bici-taxi from the bus station to Parque Martí costs two pesos.

Caibarién

POP 37,902

After metropolitan Santa Clara and the colonial splendor of Remedios, this once-busy shipping port on Cuba's Atlantic coast will come as a shock with its crumbling old buildings and decrepit feel. Since the piers slumped into the sea and the provincial sugar mills closed down, Caibarién's economic foundations have been whipped out from under it, and it's never really recovered. Just talking too loudly here seems enough to bring whole houses tumbling down, so fragile do they look.

But the town has a certain charm. Intrepid travelers report that some of their best Cuban experiences come at ultrafriendly Caibarién, which is colorfully framed by its restored *malecón* sea wall and weather-lashed fishing fleet. Nine kilometers east of Remedios and 40km from the alluring Cayerías del Norte, Caibarién is a 'real' corner of Cuba that the authorities forgot to dress up for tourists. The town is famous for its *cangrejo* (crab), the best you'll find in Cuba, while the December *parrandas* are allegedly second only to Remedios in their explosiveness.

The town also makes a cheap base for those keen to catch a glimpse of the pristine *cayos* without shelling out the expensive all-inclusive prices. **Havanatur** (☎ 35-11-71; Av 9,

btwn Calles 8 & 10) can arrange accommodation on Cayo Santa María. There's a **Cadeca** (Calle 10 No 907, btwn Avs 9 & 11) nearby.

👁 Sights

Crab Statue MONUMENT
The entrance to Caibarién is guarded by a giant crustacean designed by Florencio Gelabert Pérez and erected in 1983.

Museo de Agroindustria Azucarero Marcelo Salado MUSEUM
(☎ 36-32-86; admission CUC$3; ⊗ 8am-4pm Mon-Fri) Three kilometers past the crab statue on the Remedios road you'll find one of the nation's best potted histories of slave culture, the sugar industry and pre-diesel locomotives. There's a video of Cuba's sugar industry, models of figures toiling to harvest the product and lots of original machinery, which, while appearing Industrial Revolution-esque to most Western eyes, was imperative in Cuba right up until Castro's clampdown on the industry in the 1990s.

An added bonus is the extensive collection of locomotives (the place is also known as the Museo de Vapor, or Museum of Steam); top billing here goes to Latin America's largest steam engine.

Museo Municipal María Escobar Laredo MUSEUM
(cnr Av 9 & Calle 10) This is the best of the town center attractions and is conveniently placed on the main plaza. It's worth a once-over, if only to marvel at the fact that even humble Caibarién had a heyday.

🛏 Sleeping & Eating

Caibarién is the most economical launchpad for the resort-strewn, casa particular–free zone of the Cayerías del Norte; many indie travelers alight here for this very reason.

Virginia's Pension CASA PARTICULAR $
(☎ 36-33-03; Ciudad Pesquera No 73; r CUC$20-25; 🅿️ ❄️) Among Caibarién's handful of sleeping options, this reputable professional place run by Virginia Rodríguez is the most popular. Food here is delicious and gives you a great chance to sample the obligatory *cangrejo* (crab).

Complejo Brisas del Mar HOTEL $
(☎ 35-16-99; Reparto Mar Azul; s/d CUC$22/29; 🅿️ ❄️ 🏊) Despite the bargain bucket prices, the Brisas on the seafront in Caibarién struggles to pull in economically challenged travelers intent on enjoying some time on

the *cayos*. The rooms have cable TV and are passable if you don't mind a bit of peeling paint, but the service is a little *triste* (sad).

Restaurante La Vicaria   SEAFOOD **$**
(Calle 10 & Av 9; ⊘ 10am-10:30pm) Whooshing in at number one for eating choices (by default) is this establishment on the main square, specializing in fish.

🍷 Drinking & Nightlife

Piste de Baile   NIGHTCLUB
(Calle 4; admission 2 pesos) Surprisingly, Caibarién has a hot, happening disco near the train station. It's known by a generic name (*piste de baile* means dance floor) and jumps with hundreds of young locals on weekends.

❶ Getting There & Away

A new Víazul bus has put Caibarién on the transport network. It passes through town once daily in either direction, heading to Mayajigua and Morón in the east, and Remedios, Santa Clara, Cienfuegos and Trinidad in the south.

Four local buses a day go to Remedios; two carry on to Santa Clara and three go to Yaguajay from Caibarién's old blue-and-white **bus and train station** (Calle 6) on the western side of town. No trains run to Caibarién. The ServiCupet gas station is at the entrance to town from Remedios, behind the crab statue. **Cubacar** (☑ 35-19-60; Av 11, btwn Calles 6 & 8) rents cars at the standard rates and mopeds for CUC$25.

Cayerías del Norte

Cuba's next big tourist project is being hatched on a scattered group of pancake-flat keys situated off the north coast of Villa Clara province. While avoiding some of the erstwhile architectural hideousness of other Cuban resorts, the development here is wide-reaching and rapid, and sits a little awkwardly alongside the Buenavista Unesco Biosphere Reserve, which it abuts. The keys were still a mosquito-infested wilderness until 1998 when the first hotel – Villa las Brujas – went up. Fifteen years later and 5000 hotel rooms support a demographic that is 85% Canadian, with an emphasis on the luxury end of the tourist market. Located on three different keys (Cayo las Brujas, Cayo Ensenachos and Cayo Santa María) linked by an impressive 48km causeway called **El Pedraplén**, the enclave now lists 11 hotels, a *delfinario* (dolphinarium), two

mini-tourist 'towns' and one of Cuba's few nudist beaches.

But the bulldozers haven't finished yet. The Cayerías' ultimate capacity is touted to be 10,000 hotel rooms, ie double its present size. There are also plans for an 18-hole golf course. The Cayerías' longest beach stretches for 13km along the north coast of Cayo Santa María where most of the hotels lie. Though different sections of beach go by different names, it is usually communally known as **Playa Santa María** and is perfect for a relaxed beachcombing stroll.

◎ Sights & Activities

Marina Gaviota   WATER SPORTS
(☑ 35-00-13; Cayo las Brujas) Most water-based activities can be arranged at this marina next to Villa las Brujas. Highlights include a day-long catamaran cruise with snorkeling (CUC$85), a sunset cruise (CUC$57) and deep-sea fishing (CUC$260 for four people). Diving to one of 24 offshore sites is also offered (CUC$65 for two immersions). Most water activities are cancelled if there is a cold weather front.

Acuario-Delfinario
Cayo Santa María   DOLPHIN SHOW
(Cayo Ensenachos; admission CUC$3; ⊘ 9am-11pm) At the entrance to Cayo Ensenachos, the largest *delfinario* (dolphinarium) in Latin America opened in 2011 and is an impressive-looking place set on raised stilts above the shallow water. There are eight resident dolphins, a couple of sea lions and a boat dock. Dolphin shows (CUC$15) kick off daily at 3pm. You can swim with the creatures for CUC$75 and up.

San Pascual   HISTORIC SITE
FREE One of the area's oldest and oddest curiosities is the *San Pascual*, a San Diego tanker built in 1920 that got wrecked in 1933 on the opposite side of nearby Cayo Francés. Later the ship was used to store molasses, and later still it was opened up as a rather surreal hotel-restaurant (now closed).

The journey out to see the ship is included in snorkeling excursions and sunset cruises.

Pueblo la Estrella   SPA, BOWLING
(⊘ 9am-7:30pm) Welcome to a Cuban town full of...Canadians. It's hard to know what to make of this mock colonial village with its imitation Manaca Iznaga tower and phony plaza surrounded by shops, a bowling alley, spa-gymnasium, and restaurants designed

Cayo Santa María Area

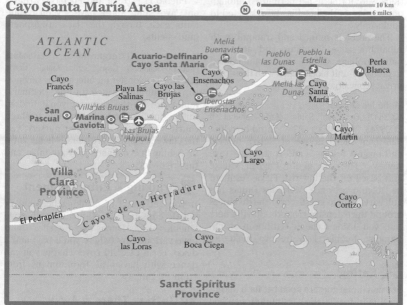

0 — 10 km
0 — 6 miles

ATLANTIC OCEAN

Cayo Francés

Meliá Buenavista

Acuario-Delfinario Cayo Santa María

Pueblo las Dunas

Pueblo la Estrella

Perla Blanca

Cayo Ensenachos

Meliá las Dunas

Cayo Santa María

Playa las Salinas

Cayo las Brujas

Villa las Brujas

San Pascual

Marina Gaviota

Iberostar Ensenachos

Las Brujas Airport

Cayo Martín

Villa Clara Province

Cayo Largo

Cayos de la Herradura

El Pedraplén

Cayo Cortizo

Cayo las Loras

Cayo Boca Ciega

Sancti Spíritus Province

for the resort crowds. Think of it as a curious anomaly that's easier on the eye than your average North American shopping mall.

Opened in 2009, it has recently been followed by another faux town, Pueblo Las Dunas, 2km to the west. Come back in 300 years and see if they're still there.

🛏 Sleeping

There are 11 resorts and a total of nearly 5000 rooms scattered over three islands. To add confusion, the hotels are constantly merging and/or changing ownership (and names). The newest, the luxury Royalton Cayo Santa María, opened in December 2012.

★ **Villa las Brujas** HOTEL, RESORT $$
(☑35-01-99; Cayo las Brujas; all-incl s CUC$76-89, d CUC$86-98; P❋) Sitting atop a small, relatively untamed headland crowned by a statue of a *bruja* (witch), Villa las Brujas has the air of a tropical *Wuthering Heights* when a cold front blows in. It all adds to the unique atmosphere of this comfortable but affordable small resort situated among the mangroves on one of Cuba's prettiest northern keys.

The 24 spacious *cabañas* (cabins) are equipped with coffee machines, cable TV and massive beds, while the Farallón restaurant overlooks a magnificent scoop of Playa las Salinas. The nearest resort to the mainland, Villa las Brujas lies by the marina, 3km from the airport.

Meliá Buenavista RESORT $$$
(☑35-07-00; Punta Madruguilla; r from CUC$408; ❋@≋) Small really is beautiful at the Buenavista (opened December 2010) whose 105 slick new rooms contrast with the 925 at Meliá las Dunas.

Located apart from the other hotels at the western end of the *cayo* with a sunset-facing beach where wine is brought to you by obliging butlers, this is a veritable romantic heaven (kids are banned) where you feel guilty even raising your voice.

Iberostar Ensenachos RESORT $$$
(☑35-03-00; Cayo Ensenachos; all-incl s/d CUC$300/400; P❋@≋≋) A top-end paradise reminiscent of a Maldives private island getaway; this is the only hotel on tiny Cayo Ensenachos and greedily bags two of the best beaches in Cuba (Playa Ensenachos and Playa Mégano). A recent takeover by Iberostar has opened the door to families

(kids were formerly not permitted), though one portion of the hotel is still restricted to adults only.

The decor is refined and tranquil, with Alhambra-esque fountains and attractive natural foliage. Guests are accommodated in pretty 20-unit blocks, each with their own private concierge.

Meliá las Dunas RESORT $$$

(☑ 35-01-00; Cayo Santa María; all-incl d CUC$243; P✷@☲) The mind-boggling 925-room Meliá is one of Cuba's newest and biggest resorts – and it still gets rave reviews. The size of an English village and based on the low-rise Playa Pesquero in Holguín province, Meliá las Dunas has golf carts to help guests cover the distances around the extensive grounds. Staying here puts you inside a classic Caribbean beach-paradise bubble. Feel free to make an escape.

 Eating

For non-hotel guests a good bet for a decent meal is in the Farallón restaurant, perched like a bird's nest overlooking blissful Las Salinas beach. Access is via Villa las Brujas. Lunch with use of beach, bathrooms and parking costs CUC$20.

Pueblo la Estrella and Pueblo las Dunas on Cayo Santa María have several restaurants each, though they lack atmosphere (and clients).

Restaurante 'El Bergantín' SEAFOOD $$$

(Acuario-Delfinario Cayo Santa María; mains CUC$15) The lobster on offer in this Gaviota-run restaurant located in the Delfinario might not be the cheapest you'll find in Cuba, but it's undoubtedly the freshest, courtesy of the on-site lobster nursery; yes, the clawed creatures are literally living within fishing-line distance of your table and they're divine.

🍷 Drinking & Entertainment

If you get bored of drinking beer out of plastic cups in your all-inclusive, the two 'pueblos' – Las Dunas and Estrella – both have various bars (where you'll pay) and a disco. For a CUC$10 cover charge you can dance with bevies of Torontonians from 11pm till 2am.

ℹ️ Getting There & Away

A typical all-inclusive zone, Cayo Santa María was not developed with public transport in mind. **Las Brujas airport** (☑ 35-00-09) has mainly charter flights to Havana. There's a Servicentro gas station opposite. For those not on package

---

MEDICINAL MECCA

Out-of-the-way, out-of-the-ordinary Baños de Elguea, 136km northwest of Santa Clara near the Matanzas provincial border, is a well-established health resort with among the most rejuvenating powers in Latin America (so say regulars). The tradition of coming here to be cleansed of ills dates back to 1860. According to local legend, a slave who had contracted a serious skin disease was banished to what is now known as Baños de Elguea by his master, sugar-mill owner Don Francisco Elguea, so that he wouldn't infect others. Sometime later, the man returned completely cured. He explained that he had relieved his affliction merely by bathing in the region's natural mineral spring. Somewhat surprisingly, his master believed him. A bathhouse was built and the first hotel opened in 1917. Today these sulfur springs and mud are used by medical professionals to treat skin irritations, arthritis and rheumatism. The waters here reach a temperature of 50°C and are rich in bromide, chlorine, radon, sodium and sulfur.

Situated north of Coralillo, **Hotel & Spa Elguea** (☑ 68-62-90; s/d incl breakfast low season CUC$13/20; P✷☲) has 139 rooms with numerous spa treatments, such as mud therapy, hydrotherapy and massages available at the nearby thermal pools. Fancy country spa, this is not – think more Soviet utilitarianism.

The hotel is all but inaccessible by public transport, which gets no further than Coralillo, 9km away. Those seeking cures had better have their own wheels or their best walking legs.

tours with airport pick-ups, access is by rental car or moped, or by hiring a taxi. From Cayo Santa María it is 56km to Caibarién, 65km to Remedios and 110km to Santa Clara. A taxi from Caibarién/Remedios/Santa Clara costs approximately CUC$50/60/80 return, including waiting time, to Villa las Brujas. Cyclists should note that headwinds on the causeway make pedaling problematic. The causeway is accessed from Caibarién and there's a toll booth (CUC$2 each way), where you will need to show your passport or visa.

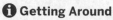 **Getting Around**

Panoramic Bus Tour is a double-decker open-topped shuttle bus that links Villa las Brujas, the Delfinario and all the Cayo Santa María hotels several times daily. Fares are CUC$1.

Sancti Spíritus Province

🎵 41 / POP 466,106

Best Off-the-Beaten-Track

➡ Parque Nacional Caguanes (p306)

➡ La Boca (p301)

➡ Alturas de Banao (p289)

➡ Jobo Rosado Reserve (p306)

Best Waterfalls

➡ El Rocio (p304)

➡ Salto del Caburní (p304)

➡ La Solapa de Genaro (p306)

➡ Cascada Bella (p289)

Why Go?

Sancti Spíritus is the province of good fortune: there's more of everything here, and it's all squeezed into an area half the size of Camagüey or Pinar del Río.

The cities are a perennial highlight. In the east is the understated provincial capital, a soporific mix of weather-beaten buildings and bruised Ladas. South, and within sight of the coast, is ethereal Trinidad, Cuba's time-warped colonial jewel.

Unlike other colonial belles, Trinidad has beaches – nearby Ancón is a stunner, easily the best on Cuba's southern coast – and mountains. Within mirror-glinting distance of the city's colonial core lies the haunting Escambray, which, with a network of decent trails, is Cuba's best hiking area.

The rest of the province hides a surprisingly varied cache of oft-overlooked curiosities, including fishing at Embalse Zaza, a seminal museum to Cuba's guerrilla icon Camilo Cienfuegos in Yaguajay, and the beautiful Bahía de Buenavista.

When to Go

➡ Trinidadians don't wait long after Christmas to rediscover their celebratory style. The Semana de la Cultura Trinitaria (Trinidad Culture Week) takes place during the second week of January and coincides with the city's anniversary.

➡ The quiet month of May is a good time to visit this province, as you can avoid both crowds and bad weather during the off-season.

➡ Stick around until June and you'll witness Trinidad's second big annual shindig, the Fiestas Sanjuaneras, a local Carnaval where rum-fueled horsemen gallop through the streets. Take cover!

Sancti Spíritus Province Highlights

1 Sway to the hypnotic rumba drums in Trinidad's **Palenque de los Congos Reales** (p298).

2 Climb the tower at the Manaca Iznaga for a killer view

of the Unesco-listed **Valle de los Ingenios** (p302).

3 Enjoy a less-visited alternative to Trinidad in the historic city of **Sancti Spíritus** (p282).

4 Explore woodland, waterfalls and war history in the **Jobo Rosado Reserve** (p306).

5 Rent a house in La Boca and stroll the sands of **Playa Ancón** (p301).

6 Hike down to the **Salto del Caburní** (p304) and jump into a frigid natural bathing pool.

7 Commission a boat to take you snorkeling off **Cayo Blanco** (p301).

8 Visit one of half a dozen museums in time-warped **Trinidad** (p288).

CARIBBEAN SEA

To Camagüey (95km)

Ciego de Ávila Province

Villa Clara Province

Cienfuegos Province

20 km
12 miles

SANCTI SPÍRITUS

POP 114,360

Don't underestimate Sancti Spíritus. In any other country this attractive colonial city would be a cultural tour de force. But cocooned inside illustrious Sancti Spíritus province and destined to play second fiddle to Trinidad, it barely gets a look-in. For many visitors therein lies the attraction. Sancti Spíritus is Trinidad without the tourist hassle. You can get served in a restaurant and search for a casa particular (private house that lets out rooms) without an uninvited assemblage of pushy 'guides' telling you that the owner is deceased, on vacation or living in Miami. You can also get comfortable sitting in Parque Serafín Sánchez watching talented kids play stickball while plaintive boleros (romantic love songs) infiltrate streets that never quite earned a Unesco listing.

Founded in 1514 as one of Diego Velázquez' seven original villas, Sancti Spíritus was moved to its present site on the Río Yayabo in 1522. But the relocation didn't stop audacious corsairs, who continued to loot the town until well into the 1660s.

While Trinidad gave the world Playa Ancón, filthy-rich sugar barons and *jineteros* (touts) on bicycles, Sancti Spíritus concocted the dapper *guayabera* (pleated, buttoned) shirt, the *guayaba* (guava) fruit and a rather quaint humpbacked bridge that wouldn't look out of place in Yorkshire, England.

◉ Sights

The main streets north and south of the Av de los Mártires and Calle M Solano axis get an appropriate north/south suffix.

Puente Yayabo   LANDMARK
Looking like something out of an English country village, this quadruple-arched bridge is Sancti Spíritus' signature sight. Built by the Spanish in 1815, it carries traffic across the Río Yayabo and is now a national monument. For the best view (and a mirror-like reflection) hit the outdoor terrace at the Quinta Santa Elena.

The Teatro Principal, alongside the bridge, dates from 1876, and the sun-bleached cobbled streets that lead uphill toward the city center are some of the settlement's oldest. The most sinuous is narrow Calle Llano, where old ladies peddle live chickens door to door, and feisty neighbors gossip noisily in front of their sky-blue or lemon-yellow houses. Also worth a wander are recently rehabilitated Calle Guairo and Calle San Miguel.

Parque Serafín Sánchez   SQUARE
While not Cuba's shadiest or most atmospheric square, pretty Serafín Sánchez is full of understated Sancti Spíritus elegance. Metal chairs laid out inside the pedestrianized central domain are usually commandeered by cigar-smoking grandpas and flirty young couples with their sights set on some ebullient local nightlife.

There's plenty to whet the appetite on the square's south side, where the impressive Casa de la Cultura often exports its music onto the street. Next door the columned Hellenic beauty that today serves as the Biblioteca Provincial Rubén Martínez Villena was built originally in 1929 by the Progress Society.

The magnolia-colored grand dame on the square's northern side is the former La Perla hotel, which lay rotting and unused for years before being turned into a three-level government-run shopping center.

Fundación de la Naturaleza
y El Hombre   MUSEUM
(Cruz Pérez No 1; recommended donation CUC$2; ☉10am-5pm Mon-Fri, to noon Sat) Replicating its equally diminutive namesake in Miramar, Havana, this museum on Parque Maceo chronicles the 17,422km canoe odyssey from the Amazon to the Caribbean in 1987 led by Cuban writer and Renaissance man Antonio Nuñez Jiménez (1923–98). Some 432 explorers made the journey through 20 countries, from Ecuador to the Bahamas, in the twin dugout canoes *Simón Bolívar* and *Hatuey*.

The latter measures over 13m and is the collection's central, prized piece. Beware of sporadic opening hours.

Museo de Arte Colonial   MUSEUM
(Plácido Sur No 74; admission CUC$2; ☉9am-5pm Tue-Sat, 8am-noon Sun) This small museum got a 2012 refurb and displays 19th-century furniture and decorations in an imposing 17th-century building that once belonged to the sugar-rich Iznaga family.

Iglesia Parroquial Mayor
del Espíritu Santo   CHURCH
(Agramonte Oeste No 58; ☉9-11am & 2-5pm Tue-Sat) Overlooking Plaza Honorato is this verging-on-decrepit church. Originally constructed of wood in 1522 and rebuilt in stone in 1680, it's said to be the oldest church in Cuba still standing on its original founda-

tions (although the clock seems to have given out in recent years).

While the interior is crying out for some care and attention, locals are proud of this place. The best time to take a peek is during Sunday morning Mass. A small donation will go a long way.

Plaza Honorato   SQUARE
Formerly known as Plaza de Jesús, this tiny square was where the Spanish authorities once conducted grisly public hangings. Later on, it hosted a produce market, and scruffy peso stalls still line the small connecting lane to the east. The north side of the square is now occupied by a boutique hotel, Hostal del Rijo.

Calle Independencia Sur   STREET
The city's revived shopping street is traffic-free and lined with statues, sculptures and myriad curiosity shops. Check out the opulent **Colonia Española Building**, once a whites only gentlemen's club, now a mini department store. The *agropecuario* (vegetable market) is unusually located right in the city center.

A flea market inhabits Calle Honorato just off Independencia and all around are *vendutas* (small private shops or stalls), illustrating the recent economic relaxation.

Museo de Ciencias Naturales   MUSEUM
(Máximo Gómez Sur No 2; admission CUC$1; ⊙8:30am-5pm Mon-Sat, to noon Sun) Not much of a natural history museum, this colonial house just off Parque Serafín Sánchez has a stuffed crocodile (which will scare the wits out of your kids) and some shiny rock collections.

Museo Provincial   MUSEUM
(Máximo Gómez Norte No 3; admission CUC$1; ⊙9am-6pm Mon-Thu, 9am-6pm & 8-10pm Sat, 8am-noon Sun) This is one of those vaguely comical Cuban museums where guides follow you from room to room as if you're about to make off with the crown jewels. In reality the collection is less distinguished, logging the history of Sancti Spíritus with a dusty stash of ephemera that includes English china, cruel slave artifacts and the inevitable revolutionary M-26/7 paraphernalia.

**Museo Casa Natal de
Serafín Sánchez**   MUSEUM
(Céspedes Norte No 112; admission CUC$0.50; ⊙8am-5pm) Serafín Sánchez was a local patriot who took part in both Wars of In-

dependence and went down fighting in November 1896. The museum cataloguing his heroics was undergoing renovations at the time of research.

**Iglesia de Nuestra Señora
de la Caridad**   CHURCH
(Céspedes Norte No 207) Across from the Fundación de la Naturaleza y El Hombre is this once-handsome building, the city's second church. Its internal arches are a favored nesting spot for Cuban sparrows, who seem unfazed by the church's shocking state of disrepair.

🛏 Sleeping

🛏 In Town

Sancti Spíritus is blessed with two gracious boutique establishments, branded as Encanto hotels, belonging to the Cubanacán chain. Both occupy attractive restored colonial buildings and are blissful nooks to spend a night or two. They are complemented by a handful of pleasant casas particulares.

Hostal Paraíso   CASA PARTICULAR
(✆33-48-58; Máximo Gómez Sur No 11, btwn Honorato & M Solano; r CUC$25; ✷) Hang out amid the hanging plants in these centrally located colonial digs. The house itself dates from 1838, and the original two-bedroom capacity has recently been doubled. The bathrooms are huge and the surrounding greenery is spirit-lifting.

**'Los Richards' –
Ricardo Rodríguez**   CASA PARTICULAR $
(✆32-30-29; Independencia Norte No 28 Altos; r CUC$25; ✷) The small stairway off the main square belies the size of this place. The front room is enormous, dwarfing the two beds, rocking chairs, full bar area and fridge. There's a smaller room out back.

Hostal los Pinos   CASA PARTICULAR $
(✆32-93-14; Carretera Central Norte No 157, btwn Mirto Milián & Coronel Lagón; r CUC$20-25; ✷) Good for travelers in transit, this museum to art deco is on Carretera Central and has a garage, delicious dinners and two comfy rooms.

Estrella González Obregón   CASA PARTICULAR $
(✆32-79-27; Maximo Gomez Norte No 26; r CUC$25) One room with plenty of space and some cooking facilities make this place ideal

Sancti Spíritus

0 200 m
0 0.1 miles

Hostal los Pinos
(400m)

Rafael Río Entero

Silvestre Alonso

3

Parque
Maceo

2

Frank País

Máximo Gómez Norte Sur

Luz Caballero

Tirso Marín

Céspedes Norte

Martí

Adolfo del Castillo

27

5

Maceo

20

Laborní

Estadio José A Huelga
(1.7km)

Cándido Calderón

Juan Gómez

Independencia Norte

18

13   **32**

17

28

9

Parque
Serafín
Sánchez

8

7

16

Av de los Mártires

Plácido

A Rodríguez

Máximo Gómez Norte Sur

Cine
Serafín
Sánchez

Céspedes Sur

Martí

M Solano

25 24

19

15

33

29

21

14

1

26

22

10

Plaza
Honorato

Honorato

San Miguel

Guairo

Plácido Sur

4

Agramonte Oeste

31

Agramonte

Colonia
Española
Building

30

Río Yayabo

Panco Jiménez

6

Av Jesús Menéndez

12

Llano

11

20 de Julio

(50m)

23

Sancti Spíritus

for families. There's a roof terrace with good views of the Escambray Mountains.

★ **Hostal del Rijo** BOUTIQUE HOTEL **$$**
(🕿 32-85-88; Honorato del Castillo No 12; s/d CUC$42/60; ❄@🛜) Even committed casa particular fans will have trouble resisting this meticulously restored 1818 mansion situated on quiet (until the Casa de la Trova opens) Plaza Honorato. Sixteen huge, plush rooms – many with plaza-facing balconies – are equipped with everything a romance-seeking Cuba-phile could wish for, including satellite TV, complimentary shampoos and chunky colonial furnishings.

Downstairs in the elegant courtyard restaurant you'll be served the kind of sumptuous, unhurried breakfast that'll have you lingering until 11am. Oh, what the hell, might as well stay another night.

Hotel Plaza BOUTIQUE HOTEL **$$**
(🕿 32-71-02; Independencia Norte No 1; s/d CUC$38/54; ❄@) The Rijo's sibling, the Plaza is a block north on Parque Serafín Sánchez. Spreading 28 rooms over two stories, the recently refurbished hotel has pulled itself up to boutique standard with fluffy bathrobes, chunky furnishings, a romantic patio bar

and prime viewing windows overlooking the ever-busy square.

It also has a *mirador* (lookout) on the roof and great service throughout. It once lived in the Rijo's shadow, but no longer!

🛏 North of Town

There are two very agreeable hotels along Carretera Central as you head north; either one is a good choice if the city center is full or you're merely passing through.

Villa los Laureles HOTEL **$**
(🕿 32-73-45; Carretera Central Km 383; s/d CUC$23/36; 🅿❄🛜) Not content to rest on them, Los Laureles lines its laurel trees up along a shady entrance drive that beckons visitors into a surprisingly classy Islazul (Cuban hotel chain) out-of-towner. There's no dodgy Soviet architectonics here. In fact, even those with in-the-clouds expectations might fill out a favorable comments card.

Supplementing big, bright rooms with fridges, satellite TV and patio/balcony are an attractive pool, leafy flower-studded gardens and a colorful in-house cabaret (the Tropi), with a nightly show at 9pm.

WORTH A TRIP

EMBALSE ZAZA

Freshwater fishing is not a pastime traditionally associated with Cuba, where visiting fishers tend to sport beards and take to the high seas in pursuit of the Hemingway legend. But, avoiding tourist stereotypes, lake angling is still widely practiced in a handful of constructed reservoirs, including the country's largest, Embalse Zaza, 11km outside Sancti Spíritus.

Created in the early '70s by damming several local rivers, the Zaza covers an area of 113 sq km. Currently, nearly 50% of the reservoir is given over to fishing, with abundant stocks of largemouth bass (weighing up to 8kg) providing rich pickings for anglers. Excursions are run out of the adjacent **Hotel Zaza** (☑ 32-85-12; s/d incl breakfast CUC$11/18; P ✳ @ ✹), an ugly blemish on the landscape even by the cheap and cheerful standards of 1970s Soviet architectonics. Stay in Sancti Spíritus and get a taxi out. A fishing trip costs CUC$30 for four hours. There are also trips to the Río Agabama, on the way to Trinidad, starting at CUC$70.

Villa Rancho Hatuey   HOTEL $
(☑ 32-83-15; Carretera Central Km 384; s/d CUC$26/42; P ✳ @ ✹) Here's the dilemma. Not 1km from Los Laureles' row of gnarly laurel trees lies another veritable Islazul gem, accessible from the southbound lane of Carretera Central. Probably the more peaceful of the two options, Rancho Hatuey spreads 76 rooms in two-story cabins across expansive landscaped grounds set back a good 500m from the road.

While catching some rays around the swimming pool or grabbing a bite in the serviceable on-site restaurant, you might see bus groups from Canada and Communist Party officials from Havana mingling in awkward juxtaposition.

✖ Eating

Never rated highly for its paladares (privately owned restaurants), Sancti Spíritus has acquired a couple of good 'uns in the last couple of years. The state sector is still dominated by a couple of reliable stalwarts.

Quinta Santa Elena   CARIBBEAN $
(San Miguel No 60; dishes CUC$4-8; ☺ 10am-midnight) 'Old clothes' is a name that has never really done justice to Cuba's famous dinner *ropa vieja* (shredded beef). There's certainly nothing old or clothes-like about the dish here, or the equally tasty shrimp in red sauce for that matter.

While the Mesón has the edge on food, the Santa Elena wins the prize for best location, as it's set on a charming riverside patio in front of the city's famous packhorse bridge.

Las Arcadas   CARIBBEAN $
(Independencia Norte No 1) The refined colonial surroundings of the Hotel Plaza add extra flavor to the all-too-familiar *comida criolla* (Creole food).

Cremería el Kikiri   ICE CREAM $
(cnr Independencia Norte & Laborni) What, no Coppelia? Kikiri is Sancti Spíritus' long-standing provincial stand-in and is actually – ahem – better. Alternatively, hang around long enough in Parque Serafín Sánchez and a DIY ice-cream man will turn up with his ice-cream maker that's powered by a washing-machine motor.

Restaurante Hostal del Rijo   INTERNATIONAL $$
(Honorato No 12; mains CUC$5-8) Quiet colonial ambience in the impressive central courtyard of the Rijp or on the lovely terrace. Service is equally good, and there is a notable selection of desserts and coffee.

El 19   INTERNATIONAL $$
(Máximo Gómez 9, btwn Manolo Solano & Honorato del Castillo; mains CUC$8-12; ☺ 6:30am-10pm) While a long way behind the paladar proliferation of Trinidad, Sancti Spíritus has added a couple of strings to its formerly disheveled bow, most notably this central nook where the highlight is sirloin steak.

Mesón de la Plaza   CARIBBEAN, SPANISH $$
(Máximo Gómez Sur No 34; mains CUC$5-8; ☺ noon-2:30pm & 6-10pm) Long a solid option, this state-run restaurant is encased in a 19th-century mansion that once belonged to a Spanish tycoon. You can tuck into classic Spanish staples such as *potaje de garbanzos* (chickpeas with pork) and some chewable

beef while appetizing music drifts in from the Casa de la Trova next door.

Self-Catering

Mercado Agropecuario MARKET $
(cnr Independencia Sur & Honorato) This centrally located *agropecuario* is just off the main shopping boulevard. Stick your head in and see how Cubans shop.

La Época SUPERMARKET $
(Independencia Norte No 50C) Good for groceries and assorted knickknacks.

Drinking & Entertainment

Sancti Spíritus has a wonderful evening ambience: cool, inclusive and unpretentious. You can sample it in any of the following places.

★Uneac LIVE MUSIC
(Unión Nacional de Escritores y Artistas de Cuba, National Union of Cuban Writers & Artists; Independencia Sur No 10) There are friendly nods as you enter, handshakes offered by people you've never met, and a starry-eyed crooner on stage blowing kisses to his girlfriend(s) in the audience. Uneac concerts always feel more like family gatherings than organized cultural events, and Sancti Spíritus' is one of the nicest 'families' you'll meet.

Casa de la Trova Miguel Companioni LIVE MUSIC
(Máximo Gómez Sur No 26) Another of Cuba's famous *trova* (traditional poetic singing) houses, this kicking folk-music venue in a colonial building off Plaza Honorato is on a par with anything in Trinidad. But here the crowds are 90% local and 10% tourist.

Café ARTex NIGHTCLUB
(M Solano; admission CUC$1; ⊙10pm-2am Tue-Sun) On an upper floor on Parque Serafín Sánchez, this place has more of a nightclub feel than the usual ARTex patio. It offers dancing, live music and karaoke nightly and a Sunday matinee at 2pm (admission CUC$3). Thursday is *reggaetón* (Cuban hip-hop) night, and the cafe also hosts comedy.

Good groups to look out for in Sancti Spíritus are the Septeto Espirituanao and the Septeto de Son del Yayabo.

Casa de la Cultura LIVE MUSIC
(☑32-37-72; M Solano No 11) Hosts numerous cultural events that at weekends spill out into the street and render the pavement impassable. It's situated on the southwest corner of Parque Serafín Sánchez.

Casa del Joven Creador LIVE MUSIC
(Céspedes Norte No 118) Instead of hanging around on street corners with their hands in their pockets, Sancti Spíritus' youth head to this happening cultural venue near the Museo Casa Natal de Serafín Sánchez for rock and rap concerts.

Estadio José A Huelga SPORTS
(Circunvalación) From October to April, baseball games are held at this stadium, 1km north of the bus station. The provincial team Los Gallos (the Roosters) last tasted glory in 1979.

Teatro Principal THEATER
(☑232-5755; Av Jesús Menéndez No 102) This landmark architectural icon next to the Puente Yayabo was recently given a comprehensive clean-up. It has weekend matinees (at 10am) with kids' theater.

Cine Conrado Benítez CINEMA
(☑32-53-27; Máximo Gómez Norte No 13) Of the city's two main cinemas, this is your best bet for a decent movie.

Shopping

Anything you might need – from batteries to frying pans – is sold at stalls along the mostly pedestrianised Independencia Sur, which recently benefited from a handsome refurbishment.

Colonia ACCESSORIES
(cnr Independencia Sur & Agramonte; ⊙9am-4pm) Mini department store housed in one of the city's finest colonial buildings.

La Perla SHOPPING CENTER
(Parque Serafín Sánchez; ⊙9am-4pm) Three levels of austerity-busting shopping behind a beautifully restored colonial edifice on Parque Serafín Sánchez.

Galería la Arcada ART, CRAFT
(Independencia Sur No 55) This place has Cuban crafts and paintings worth checking out.

Librería Julio Antonio Mella BOOKS
(Independencia Sur No 29; ⊙8am-5pm Mon-Sat) Erudite travelers can stock up on revolutionary reading material in this store, opposite the post office.

ℹ Information

INTERNET ACCESS & TELEPHONE

Etecsa Telepunto (Independencia Sur No 14; internet access per hr CUC$6; ⊘8:30am-7:30pm) Two rarely busy computer terminals.

MEDIA

Radio Sancti Spíritus CMHT Airing on 1200AM and 97.3FM.

MEDICAL SERVICES

Farmacia Especial (Independencia Norte No 123; ⊘24hr) Pharmacy on Parque Maceo.

Hospital Provincial Camilo Cienfuegos (☐32-40-17; Bartolomé Masó No 128) Five hundred meters north of Plaza de la Revolución.

Policlínico Los Olivos (☐32-63-62; Circunvalación Olivos No 1) Near the bus station. Will treat foreigners in an emergency.

MONEY

Banco Financiero Internacional (Independencia Sur No 2) On Parque Serafín Sánchez.

Cadeca (Independencia Sur No 31) Lose your youth in this line.

POST

Post Office (⊘9am-6pm Mon-Sat) There are two branches: one at Independencia Sur No 8, the other at the Etecsa building, Bartolomé Masó (Bartolomé Masó No 167).

TRAVEL AGENCIES

Cubatur (Máximo Gómez Norte No 7; ⊘9am-5pm Mon-Sat) On Parque Serafín Sánchez.

ℹ Getting There & Away

BUS

The provincial **bus station** (Carretera Central) is 2km east of town. Punctual and air-conditioned **Víazul** (www.viazul.com) buses serve numerous destinations.

Five daily Santiago de Cuba departures (CUC$28, eight hours) also stop in Ciego de Ávila (CUC$6, 1¼ hours), Camagüey (CUC$10, three hours), Las Tunas (CUC$17, five hours and 40 minutes) and Bayamo (CUC$21, seven hours). Five daily Havana (CUC$23, five hours) buses stop at Santa Clara (CUC$6, 1¼ hours). The link to Trinidad (CUC$6, one hour and 20 minutes) leaves at a sleep-reducing 5:30am.

TRAIN

There are two train stations serving Sancti Spíritus. For Havana (eight hours, alternate days) via Santa Clara (two hours), and to Cienfuegos (five hours, once a week), use the main **train station** (Av Jesús Menéndez al final; ⊘ticket window 7am-2pm Mon-Sat), southwest of the Puente Yayabo, an easy 10-minute walk from the city center.

Points east are served out of Guayos, 15km north of Sancti Spíritus, including Holguín (8½ hours), Santiago de Cuba (10¼ hours) and Bayamo (8¼ hours). If you're on the Havana–Santiago de Cuba cross-country express and going to Sancti Spíritus or Trinidad, get off at Guayos.

The ticket office at the Sancti Spíritus train station can sell you tickets for Guayos trains, but you must find your own way to Guayos (CUC$8 to CUC$10 in a taxi, but bargain hard).

TRUCKS & TAXIS

Trucks to Trinidad, Jatibonico and elsewhere depart from the bus station. A state taxi to Trinidad will cost you around CUC$35.

ℹ Getting Around

Horse carts on Carretera Central, opposite the bus station, run to Parque Serafín Sánchez when full (1 peso). Bici-taxis gather at the corner of Laborni and Céspedes Norte. There is a **Cubacar** (☐32-85-33) booth on the northeast corner of Parque Serafín Sánchez; prices for daily car hire start at around CUC$70. The **Servi-Cupet gas station** (Carretera Central) is 1.5km north of Villa los Laureles, on the Carretera Central, toward Santa Clara. Parking in Parque Serafín Sánchez is relatively safe. Ask in hotels Rijo and Plaza, and they will often find a man to stand guard overnight for CUC$1.

SOUTHWEST SANCTI SPÍRITUS PROVINCE

Trinidad

POP 52,896

The first sound in the mornings is the clip-clop of horses' hooves on the cobbled streets followed by the cries of old men selling bread from bicycles *(El pan! El pan!)*. Open your eyes, gaze up at the high wooden louvers of your 200-year-old colonial room, and try to convince yourself you're still living in the 21st century.

Trinidad is one-of-a-kind, a perfectly preserved Spanish colonial settlement where the clocks stopped ticking in 1850 and – apart from the tourists – have yet to restart. Built on huge sugar fortunes amassed in the adjacent Valle de los Ingenios during the early 19th century, the riches of the town's pre-War of Independence heyday are still very much in evidence in illustrious colonial-style

ALTURAS DE BANAO

Still well off the antennae of most guidebooks, which push tourists toward Topes de Collantes, this ecological reserve, situated off the main road between Sancti Spíritus and Trinidad, hides a little-explored stash of mountains, waterfalls, forest and steep limestone cliffs. The reserve's highest peak – part of the Guamuhaya mountain range – is 842m, while its foothills are replete with rivers, abundant plant life, including epiphyte cacti, and the ruins of a handful of pioneering 19th-century farmhouses. The park HQ is at **Jarico**, 3.5km up a beaten track leading off the Sancti Spíritus–Trinidad road. It incorporates a *ranchón* (farm)-style restaurant, visitors center and chalet with eight double rooms (CUC$25). Within shouting distance is the **Cascada Bella** waterfall and a natural swimming pool. From Jarico the 6km **La Sabina trail** leads to an eponymous bio-station, where the recently constructed **La Sabina Chalet** (r CUC$56) offers overnight accommodation and food in four double rooms. Alternatively you can do the hike in a single day with a guide (CUC$3). Entry to the Banao reserve will cost you an extra CUC$3. **Ecotur** (☑ 54-74-19; www.ecoturcuba.co.cu; Antonio Maceo No 461) in Trinidad can organize overnight trips.

mansions bedecked with Italian frescoes, Wedgwood china and French chandeliers.

Declared a World Heritage Site by Unesco in 1988, Trinidad's secrets quickly became public property, and it wasn't long before busloads of visitors started arriving to sample the beauty of Cuba's oldest and most enchanting 'outdoor museum'. Yet tourism has done little to deaden Trinidad's gentle southern sheen. The town retains a quiet, almost soporific air in its rambling cobbled streets replete with leather-faced *guajiros* (country folk), snorting donkeys and melodic, guitar-wielding troubadours.

Ringed by sparkling natural attractions, Trinidad is more than just a potential PhD thesis for history buffs. Twelve kilometers to the south lies platinum-blond Playa Ancón, the south coast's best beach, while looming 18km to the north the purple-hued shadows of the Sierra del Escambray (Escambray Mountains) offer a lush adventure playground.

With its Unesco price tag and a steady stream of overseas visitors, Trinidad, not surprisingly, has an above-average quota of prowling *jineteros*, though mostly they're more annoying than aggressive.

History

In 1514 pioneering conquistador Diego Velázquez de Cuéllar founded La Villa de la Santísima Trinidad on Cuba's south coast, the island's third settlement after Baracoa and Bayamo. Legend has it that erstwhile 'Apostle of the Indians' Fray Bartolomé de las Casas held Trinidad's first Mass under a calabash tree in present-day Plazuela Real del Jigüe. In 1518 Velázquez' former secretary, Hernán Cortés, passed through the town recruiting mercenaries for his all-conquering expedition to Mexico, and the settlement was all but emptied of its original inhabitants. Over the ensuing 60 years it was left to a smattering of the local Taíno people to keep the ailing economy alive through a mixture of farming, cattle-rearing and a little outside trade.

Reduced to a small rural backwater by the 17th century and cut off from the colonial authorities in Havana by dire communications, Trinidad became a haven for pirates and smugglers who conducted a lucrative illegal slave trade with British-controlled Jamaica.

Things began to change in the early 19th century when the town became the capital of the Departamento Central, and hundreds of French refugees fleeing a slave rebellion in Haiti arrived, setting up more than 50 small sugar mills in the nearby Valle de los Ingenios. Sugar soon replaced leather and salted beef as the region's most important product. By the mid-19th century the area around Trinidad was producing a third of Cuba's sugar, generating enough wealth to finance the rich cluster of opulent buildings that characterize the town today.

The boom ended rather abruptly during the Independence Wars, when the surrounding sugar plantations were devastated by fire and fighting. The industry never fully recovered. By the late 19th century the focus of the sugar trade had shifted to

Trinidad

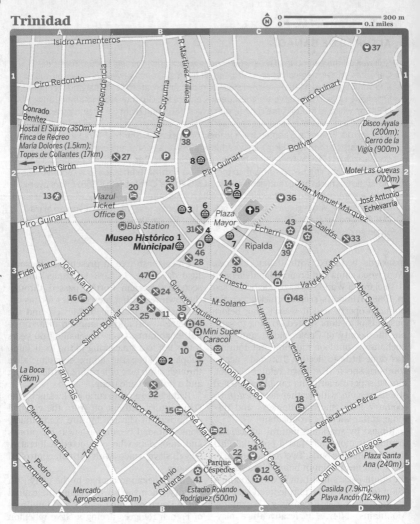

Cienfuegos and Matanzas provinces, and Trinidad slipped into a somnolent and life-threatening economic coma. Trinidad's tourist renaissance began in the 1950s, when President Batista passed a preservation law that recognized the town's historical value. In 1965 the town was declared a national monument, and in 1988 it became a Unesco World Heritage Site.

⊙ Sights

In Trinidad, all roads lead to **Plaza Mayor**, the town's remarkably peaceful main square, located at the heart of the *casco histórico* (old town) and ringed by a quartet of impressive buildings.

★ Museo Histórico Municipal   MUSEUM

(Simón Bolívar No 423; admission CUC$2; ⊙ 9am-5pm Sat-Thu) For Trinidad's showpiece museum look no further than this grandiose structure just off Plaza Mayor, a mansion that belonged to the Borrell family from 1827 to 1830. Later the building passed to a German planter named Kanter, or Cantero, and it's still called Casa Cantero.

Reputedly, Dr Justo Cantero acquired vast sugar estates by poisoning an old slave trader

Trinidad

and marrying his widow, who also suffered an untimely death. Cantero's ill-gotten wealth is well displayed in the stylish neoclassical decoration of the rooms. The view of Trinidad from the top of the tower alone is worth the price of admission. Visit before 11am, when the tour buses start rolling in.

Iglesia Parroquial de la Santísima Trinidad CHURCH
(◎ 11am-12:30pm Mon-Sat) Despite its rather unremarkable outer facade, this church on the northeastern side of Plaza Mayor graces countless Trinidad postcard views. Rebuilt in 1892 on the site of an earlier church destroyed in a storm, the church mixes 20th-century touch-ups with artifacts from as far back as the 18th century, such as the venerated Christ of the True Cross (1713), which occupies the second altar from the front to the left.

Your best chance of seeing it is during Mass at 8pm weekdays, 4pm Saturday, and 9am and 5pm Sunday.

Museo Romántico MUSEUM
(Echerri No 52; admission CUC$2; ◎ 9am-5pm Tue-Sun) Across Calle Simón Bolívar is the glittering Palacio Brunet. The ground floor was built in 1740, and the upstairs was added in 1808. In 1974 the mansion was converted into a museum with 19th-century furnishings, a fine collection of china and various other period pieces. Pushy museum staff may materialize out of the shadows for a tip.

The shop adjacent has a good selection of photos and books in English.

Museo de Arquitectura Trinitaria MUSEUM
(Ripalda No 83; admission CUC$1; ◎ 9am-5pm Sat-Thu) Another public display of wealth sits on the southeastern side of Plaza Mayor in a museum showcasing upper-class domestic architecture of the 18th and 19th centuries.

The museum is housed in buildings that were erected in 1738 and 1785 and joined in 1819. It was once the residence of the wealthy Iznaga family.

Museo de Arqueología Guamuhaya   MUSEUM
(Simón Bolívar No 457; admission CUC$1; ⊙9am-5pm Tue-Sat) On the northwestern side of Plaza Mayor is this odd mix of stuffed animals, native bones and vaguely incongruous 19th-century kitchen furniture. Don't make it your first priority.

Galería de Arte   GALLERY
(cnr Rubén Martínez Villena & Simón Bolívar; ⊙9am-5pm) FREE Admission is completely free at the 19th-century Palacio Ortiz, which today houses an art gallery on the southeastern side of Plaza Mayor. Worth a look for its quality local art, particularly the embroidery, pottery and jewelry. There's also a pleasant courtyard.

Casa Templo de Santería Yemayá   MUSEUM, LANDMARK
(Rubén Martínez Villena No 59, btwn Simón Bolívar & Piro Guinart) No Santería museum can replicate the ethereal spiritual experience of Regla de Ocha (also known as Santería, Cuba's main religion of African origin), though this house has a try with a Santería altar to Yemayá, Goddess of the Sea, laden with myriad offerings of fruit, water and stones.

The house is presided over by *santeros* (priests of the Afro-Cuban religion Santería), who'll emerge from the back patio and surprise you with some well-rehearsed tourist spiel. On the goddess' anniversary (March 19), ceremonies are performed day and night.

Museo Nacional de la Lucha Contra Bandidos   MUSEUM
(Echerri No 59; admission CUC$1; ⊙9am-5pm Tue-Sun) Perhaps the most recognizable building in Trinidad is the dilapidated pastel-yellow bell tower of the former convent of San Francisco de Asís. Since 1986 the building has housed a museum with photos, maps, weapons and other objects relating to the struggle against the various counterrevolutionary bands that took a leaf out of Fidel's book and operated illicitly out of the Sierra del Escambray between 1960 and 1965.

The fuselage of a US U-2 spy plane shot down over Cuba is also on display. You can climb the tower for good views.

Casa de los Mártires de Trinidad   MUSEUM
(Zerquera No 254, btwn Antonio Maceo & José Martí; ⊙9am-5pm) FREE It's easy to miss this small museum dedicated to the 72 Trinidad residents who died in the struggle against Fulgencio Batista (see p464), the campaign against the counterrevolutionaries, and the little-mentioned war in Angola.

Iglesia de Santa Ana   CHURCH
(Plaza Santa Ana, Camilo Cienfuegos) Grass grows around the domed bell tower, and the arched doorways were bricked up long ago, but the shell of this ruined church (1812) defiantly remains. Looming like a time-worn ecclesiastical stencil, it looks ghostly after dark.

Across the eponymous square, which delineates Trinidad's northeastern reaches, is a former Spanish prison (1844) that has been converted into the **Plaza Santa Ana** (Camilo Cienfuegos; ⊙11am-10pm) tourist center. The complex includes an art gallery, handicraft market, ceramics shop, bar and restaurant.

Taller Alfarero   POTTERY
(Andrés Berro No 51, btwn Pepito Tey & Abel Santamaría; ⊙8am-noon & 2-5pm Mon-Fri) FREE Trinidad is known for its pottery. In this large factory, teams of workers make trademark Trinidad ceramics from local clay using a traditional potter's wheel. You can watch them at work and buy the finished product.

🏃 Activities

Ride a bike to one of Cuba's outstanding beaches, work up a sweat on a couple of DIY hikes, or get a different perspective astride a horse.

Playa Ancón   CYCLING
The bicycle ride to Playa Ancón is a great outdoor adventure, and once there you can snorkel, catch some rays or use the swimming pool or Ping-Pong table. The best route by far is via the small seaside village of La Boca (18km one way).

Cerro de la Vigía   HIKING
For views and a workout, walk straight up Calle Simón Bolívar between the Iglesia Parroquial and the Museo Romántico to the destroyed 18th-century **Ermita de Nuestra Señora de la Candelaria de la Popa**, part of a former Spanish military hospital now occupied by a new luxury hotel.

From here it's a 30-minute hike further up the hill to the radio transmitter atop 180m-high Cerro de la Vigía, which delivers

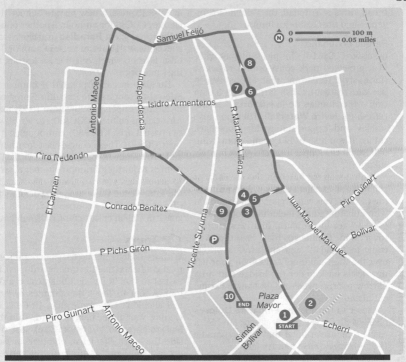

🏃 City Walk
Photographic Walking Tour of Trinidad

START PLAZA MAYOR
END CASA TEMPLO DE SANTERÍA YEMAYA
LENGTH 2KM; 1.5 HOURS

In Trinidad, soft evening sunlight, striking colonial architecture and street scenes that have more in common with the 1850s than the 2010s conspire to create an ideal prowling ground for documentary photographers.

Early evening is a good time to undertake this walk. Start in ① **Plaza Mayor**, the colonial square that features in 1000 postcards. There's always a new way of snapping local life with the ② **Iglesia Parroquial de la Santísima Trinidad** as backdrop.

The classic shot is looking northwest along cobbled Calle Echerri past colonial edifices to the tower of the ③ **Convento de San Francisco de Asís**. Walk a block northwest and try to capture the small sunlit ④ **park** opposite the convent with some human silhouettes. At the end of Echerri, stand back from the ⑤ **T-junction** with Calle Ciro Redondo and wait. More often than not, something inter-

esting will pass at the end of the street – a horse, a 1951 Plymouth, a bicycle.

Turn right on Ciro Redondo then left on Calle Juan Manuel Márquez toward the shabbier, no less photogenic ⑥ **Barrio Los Tres Cruces**. Trinidadian life plays out here as if tourism had never happened. Look out for ladies in curlers, cowboys, kids playing stickball in the ⑦ **plaza**, and old men sitting in doorways. A row of one-story ⑧ **houses** in Calle Juan Manuel Márquez painted a rainbow of colors are luminescent in the slanting light. On Calle Samuel Feijó, horses and riders often congregate with the Sierra del Escambray behind them. More street life waits back on Calle Ciro Redondo. Outside the iconic ⑨ **Taberna Canchánchara** there's nearly always a 1958 Chevy being used as a communal seat. The sight of a *santero* (Santería priest) may delay you momentarily as you pass the ⑩ **Casa Templo de Santería Yemaya** dedicated to the *orisha* (Yoruba god) of the sea. By dusk you're back in Plaza Mayor.

broad vistas of Trinidad, the Valle de los Ingenios and the Caribbean littoral.

Parque el Cubano   HIKING

(admission CUC$6.50) This pleasant spot within a protected park consists of a *ranchón* (farm)-style restaurant that specializes in *pez gato* (catfish), a fish farm and a 3.6km trail – the **Huellas de la História** – to the refreshing **Javira Waterfall**. There are also stables and opportunities for horseback riding. If you hike to El Cubano from Trinidad, you'll clock up a total of approximately 16km.

With a stop for lunch in the *ranchón*, it can make an excellent day trip. Alternatively, for CUC$15 you can organize an excursion with Cubatur (p299), including motor transport. To get to the park, hike west out of town on the Cienfuegos road. Pass the 'Welcome to Trinidad' sign and cross a bridge over the Río Guarabo. A track on your left now leads back under the bridge and up a narrow, poorly paved road for 5km to Parque el Cubano.

Closer to town is the **Finca Ma Dolores** (☑ 99-64-81; Carretera de Cienfuegos Km 1.5), a rustic Cubanacán hotel that hosts sporadic *fiestas campesinas* (country fairs).

Centro Ecuestre Diana   HORSEBACK RIDING

(☑ 99-36-73; www.trinidadphoto.com) 🖋 This unique equestrian center is run out of a *finca* (farm) on the edge of town, but aspiring riders should enquire first with owner Julio at Casa Muñoz (p295) in the *casco histórico*. The *finca* is also a rescue centre for maltreated and ill horses. Julio set up Project Diana a few years ago to promote better equine care and educate local people in humane horse-training techniques.

Various horse-related activities are offered, including nature excursions and riding lessons, but the highlight is the opportunity to see Julio use his horse-whispering techniques to pacify wild, untrained horses. The huge traditional *campesino* (country person) food spread offered at the *finca* has to be tasted to be believed. Prices are between CUC$15 and CUC$30, depending on the activity. Helmets are included for no extra charge.

🎷 Courses

At **Las Ruinas del Teatro Brunet** (Antonio Maceo No 461, btwn Simón Bolívar & Zerquera) you can take drumming lessons (9am to 11am Saturday) and dance lessons (1pm to 4pm Saturday). Dance lessons are also available at Salsa Express, a new private 'school' that charges CUC$5 for an hour. Another option is the travel agent **Paradiso** (paradisotr@sctd.artex.cu; General Lino Pérez No 306, Casa ARTex) in Casa Fischer, which offers salsa lessons for the same price.

Paradiso has incorporated a number of interesting courses into its cultural program, including Cuban architecture (CUC$20), Afro-Cuban culture (CUC$30), *artes plásticas* (visual arts; CUC$30) and popular music (CUC$30). These courses last four hours and are taught by cultural specialists. The courses require a minimum number of six to 10 people, but you can always negotiate. At the same venue there are guitar lessons for CUC$5 an hour and courses in Spanish language or Cuban culture for CUC$8 an hour.

👉 Tours

With its sketchy public transport and steep road gradients (making cycling arduous), it's easiest to visit Topes de Collantes on a day tour. A tour to Topes de Collantes by state taxi shouldn't cost more than CUC$35 including wait time; bargain hard. **Cubatur** (Antonio Maceo No 447; ⊙ 9am-8pm), just outside the *casco histórico*, organizes a variety of hiking and nature trips for between CUC$23 and CUC$43 per person.

Paradiso (www.paradiso.cu; General Lino Pérez No 306, Casa ARTex) offers the best-value day tour to the Valle de los Ingenios (CUC$9 per person), and an artist-studio tour in Trinidad (CUC$10 per person).

Trinidad Travels   HIKING, HORSE RIDING

(☑ 52-82-37-26; www.trinidadtravels.com; Antonio Maceo 613A) One of the best of the new private guides is English- and Italian-speaking Reinier at Trinidad Travels, who leads all kinds of excursions, including hiking in the Sierra del Escambray and horseback riding in the nearby countryside. Salsa and Spanish lessons are also offered.

🎉 Festivals & Events

Semana Santa (Holy Week) is important in Trinidad, and on Good Friday thousands of people form a procession.

🛏 Sleeping

Trinidad has, at a guestimate, 500 casas particulares, meaning competition is hot. Arriving by bus or walking the streets with luggage, you'll be besieged by hustlers working for commissions, or by the casa owners themselves. With so many beautiful homes and hospitable families renting rooms, there's no reason to be rushed. Take your time and shop around.

In Town

★ Casa Muñoz –
Julio & Rosa
CASA PARTICULAR $

(☎ 99-36-73; www.trinidadphoto.com; José Martí No 401 cnr Escobar; d/tr/q CUC$35/40/45; P ❄) Julio is an accomplished published photographer who runs workshops and courses out of his stunning colonial home on documentary photography, religion and life in Cuba's new economic reality (see the website for details). He's also a horse whisperer – his beautiful mare lives out back along with his three dogs and Russian Moskvich.

There are three huge rooms here and a separate duplex apartment (CUC$40 to CUC$60). Delicious food is served on a ground-floor patio or 1st-floor terrace. All the family speak English. Book early – it's insanely popular (licensed US people-to-people groups often come here).

Hostal Yolanda María
CASA PARTICULAR $

(☎ 99-63-81; yoliaye@gmail.com; Piro Guinart No 227; r CUC$25-30) This isn't a casa – it's a palace! There are eight rooms for starters, though only two were being rented at last visit. Dating from the 1700s, the hostal's dazzling interior makes the Museo Romántico look like a jumble sale. There are Italian tiles, French frescoes, a rare Mexican spiral staircase, fabulous terrace views – the list goes on...

Hostal Colina
CASA PARTICULAR $

(☎ 99-23-19; Antonio Maceo No 374, btwn General Lino Pérez & Colón; r CUC$25-35; ❄) Another place that leaves you struggling for superlatives. Although the house dates from the 1830s, it's got a definitive modern touch, giving you the feeling of being in a plush Mexican hacienda. Three pastel-yellow rooms give out onto a patio where you can sit at the plush wooden bar and catch mangoes and avocados as they fall from the trees.

Casa Gil Lemes
CASA PARTICULAR $

(☎ 99-31-42; José Martí No 263, btwn Colón & Zerquera; r CUC$25) More museum-standard digs on Calle Martí, the street that hides 1000 priceless antiques, this casa was one of Trinidad's first and was listed in the first edition of this book in 1997. Cast an eye over

the noble arches in the front room and the religious statues, and save some breath (yes, you'll gasp) for the patio and fountain, a unique array of pots and sea serpents.

Get in early for this one – there's only one room.

Casa Smith
CASA PARTICULAR $

(☎ 99-40-60; www.casasmith.trinidadhostales.com; Callejón Smith No 3, btwn Antonio Maceo & Av Jesús Menéndez; r CUC$20-25; ❄) With three independent rooms off a back patio, this place is clean and relaxing with welcoming hosts. Check out the website for photos and more details.

Casa del Historiador
CASA PARTICULAR $

(☎ 99-36-34; Echerri No 54; r CUC$25-30; ❄) Back in business renting rooms after a brief hiatus, the house of the late City Historian is appropriately historic. Enjoying a perch on the corner of Plaza Mayor, it is one of the town's oldest and most characteristic buildings with two rooms overlooking a sun-dappled rear courtyard.

Hostal El Suizo
CASA PARTICULAR $

(☎ 53-77-28-12; P Pichs Girón No 22; r CUC$25-30; P ❄) Away from the hustle of the center and handily located for a quick entry or exit on the Trinidad–Cienfuegos road, this pink reader-recommended room-terrace with independent entry is run by an expat Swiss *hombre* and his Cuban wife. It is clean, tranquil and known for its adventurous cooking – Thai curry anyone?

Casa Santana
CASA PARTICULAR $

(🖊99-43-72; Antonio Maceo No 425, btwn Zerquera & Colón; r CUC$20-25; 🌢) Another venerable colonial institution on arterial Calle Maceo. It's run by a dentist and his wife, with all the Trinidadian trimmings (huge rooms, weighty antiques, attractive patio).

Motel Las Cuevas
HOTEL $$

(🖊99-61-33; s/d incl breakfast CUC$37/62; P🌢🖿) Perched on a hill above town, Las Cuevas is more hotel than motel, with bus tours providing the main drive-by clientele. While the setting is lush, the rooms – which are arranged in scattered two-storied units – are a little less memorable, as is the breakfast.

Value is added with a swimming pool, well-maintained gardens, panoramic views and the murky Cueva la Maravillosa, accessible down a stairway, where you'll see a huge tree growing out of a cavern (entry CUC$1). The hotel is accessed via a steep road that climbs northeast from the Iglesia de Santa Ana.

Iberostar Grand Hotel
BOUTIQUE HOTEL $$$

(🖊99-60-70; www.iberostar.com; cnr José Martí & General Lino Pérez; s/d/ste CUC$165/220/280; 🌢@🛜) Look out, Habaguanex! One of a handful of Spanish-run Iberostar's Cuban hotels, the five-star Grand oozes luxury the moment you arrive in its fern-filled, tile-embellished lobby. Maintaining 36 classy rooms in a remodeled 19th-century building, the Grand shies away from the standard all-inclusive tourist formula, preferring to press privacy, refinement and an appreciation of history (you are, after all, in Trinidad).

The service is as sleek as the fittings are flash.

Hotel La Ronda
BOUTIQUE HOTEL $$$

(🖊99-61-33; José Martí No 238; s/d CUC$128/170; 🌢@) Re-entering Trinidad's hotel fray after concluding a protracted renovation, the Ronda's second incarnation is a great improvement on its first. A modernist fountain, sharp color accents, old blown-up art nouveau photos and bolero song lyrics inscribed outside every room add interesting, individualistic touches to an impressive colonial whole, easily justifying the 'boutique' label.

🛏 Outside Town

Finca Ma Dolores
HOTEL $$

(🖊99-64-10; Carretera de Cienfuegos Km 1.5; s/d CUC$36/60; P🌢🖿) Trinidad goes rustic with the out-of-town Finca Ma Dolores, 1.5km west on the road to Cienfuegos and Topes de Collantes. It's equipped with hotel-style rooms and cabins – the latter are the better option (try for one with a porch overlooking the Río Guaurabo).

On nights when groups are present, there's a *fiesta campesina* with country-style Cuban folk dancing at 9:30pm (free/CUC$5 for guests/nonguests, including one drink). It also has a swimming pool, a *ranchón* restaurant, and boat and horseback-riding tours. One kilometer west of the Finca Ma Dolores is a **monument to Alberto Delgado**, a teacher murdered by counterrevolutionaries.

✖ Eating

All hail the new privatization laws. In January 2011 there were three private paladares in Trinidad, the same three that had been here for more than a decade. Two years later and there are 54! Suddenly your problem is not finding a paladar, but sifting through the raft of options to find a good one.

Mesón del Regidor
FAST FOOD $

(Simón Bolívar No 424; ⏰10am-10pm) A cafe-cum-restaurant with a friendly ambience and a revolving lineup of local musicians, including the best *trovadores* (traditional singer/songwriters), who'll drop by during the day and serenade you with a song over grilled cheese sandwiches and *café con leche* (coffee with milk). Savor the surprise.

Cafetería las Begonias
CAFE $

(cnr Antonio Maceo & Simón Bolívar; ⏰9am-10pm) This is the daytime nexus for Trinidad's transient backpacker crowd, meaning it's a good source of local information and the best place in town to meet other travelers over sandwiches, espresso and ice cream. It has a bar behind a partition wall, clean-ish toilets in a rear courtyard, and five or six cheap – but always crowded – internet terminals.

Cremería las Begonias
ICE CREAM $

(cnr Antonio Maceo & Simón Bolívar) Just across the street from the eponymous internet cafe is this cafe, which doubles as a Cubatur office and offers the best ice cream in town, as well as coffee and pastries.

Guitarra Mia
CUBAN $$

(☑99-34-52; Jésus Menéndez 19, btwn Camilo Cienfuegos & Lino Pérez; mains CUC$6-8) Drift a few blocks from the old town and the prices magically get cheaper without any measurable drop in the food quality. Music is the theme in this interesting nook that is never short of a group or passing troubadour. From the menu, the *tostones* (plantain pan-fried in oil) stuffed with minced crab linger longest in the memory.

Write your comments on the door (literally) on the way out.

Cubita Restaurant
INTERNATIONAL $$

(Antonio Maceo 471; mains CUC$8-15; ☺11am-midnight) When great food and fine service conspire, it can be a highly pleasurable experience – and one which, until recently, had been hard to find in Trinidad. Fighting hard in a highly competitive field, La Cubita has set a fast pace with its inventive starters, complimentary salads, some wonderfully marinated brochettes and highly discreet service. It's run by Trinidad's famous ceramic-makers.

Sol Ananda
INTERNATIONAL $$

(☑99-82-81; Rubén Martínez Villena 45 cnr Simón Bolívar; mains CUC$8-15; ☺11am-11pm) Fine 18th-century china, grandfather clocks, even an antique bed: Sol Ananda in Trinidad's Plaza Mayor is, on first impressions, more museum than restaurant. Situated in one of the town's oldest houses (dating from 1750) it tackles an ambitious cross-section of global food from traditional Cuban (excellent lamb *ropa vieja*) to South Asian (fish kofta and samosas).

La Ceiba
CUBAN $$

(P Pichs Girón 263; mains CUC$12; ☺noon-11pm) Set in a back patio under the boughs of a giant ceiba tree, this fledgling paladar specializes in chicken in honey and lemon sauce, and serves up Trinidad's favorite cocktail – the *canchánchara* (rum, honey, lemon and water) – in ceramic cups. In good old-fashioned paladar style you must walk right through the middle of the owner's house to reach it.

Restaurante Plaza Mayor
CARIBBEAN $$

(cnr Rubén Martínez Villena & Zerquera; dishes from CUC$4; ☺11am-10pm) The best government-run place courtesy of its on-again/off-again lunchtime buffet, which, for around CUC$10, ought to fill you up until dinnertime.

Restaurante el Jigüe
CARIBBEAN $$

(cnr Rubén Martínez Villena & Piro Guinart; ☺11am-10pm) Stunning setting with less-than-stunning food. Bank on the house specialty, the aptly named *pollo* (chicken) *al Jigüe;* it's baked at least, offering savory flavors distinct from the usual *frito* (fried).

★ Vista Gourmet
CUBAN, INTERNATIONAL $$$

(☑99-67-00; Callejón de Galdos; mains CUC$12-18; ☺noon-midnight) The slickest of the town's newcomer restaurants is perched on a lovely terrace above Trinidad's red-tiled rooftops and run by the charismatic sommelier Bolo. Among many novelties are a table-hopping violinist and a skillful magician who croons Sinatra songs between card tricks.

Equally innovative is the appetizer and dessert buffet spread out invitingly on side tables – both are included in the price of your main dish (which you choose from an à la carte menu). The *lechón asado* (roast pork) and lobster are both recommended. Not surprisingly, the wine list is the best in town.

Self-Catering

Mercado Agropecuario
MARKET $

(cnr Pedro Zerquera & Manuel Fajardo; ☺8am-6pm Mon-Sat, to noon Sun) Trinidad's *agropecuario* (vegetable market) isn't Covent Garden, but you should still be able to get basic fruits and vegetables.

Tienda Universo
SUPERMARKET $

(cnr José Martí & Zerquera) This shop, near Zerquera in the Galería Comercial Universo, is Trinidad's best (and most expensive) grocery store. Head here for yogurt, nuts and those lifesaving biscuits.

🍸 Drinking & Nightlife

Casa de la Música
NIGHTCLUB

FREE One of Trinidad's and Cuba's classic venues, this casa is an alfresco affair that congregates on the sweeping staircase beside the Iglesia Parroquial off Plaza Mayor. A good mix of tourists and locals take in the 10pm salsa show here. Alternatively, full-on salsa concerts are held in the casa's rear courtyard (also accessible from Juan Manuel Márquez; cover CUC$2).

Bar Daiquirí
BAR

(General Lino Pérez No 313; ☺24hr) Presumably Papa Hemingway never dropped by this cozy joint named after the drink he so famously popularized, because the prices are extremely reasonable. Shoehorned into lively Lino Pérez, this is where locals and backpackers warm up on their way to an all-night salsa binge.

Disco Ayala
NIGHTCLUB

(admission CUC$10; ⊙10pm-3am) It might not be the first time you've gone jiving in a cave, but this surreal place up by the Ermita Popa church beats all others for atmosphere. While it's mainly a place to go dancing in the semi-darkness after as many mojitos as you care to sink, this disco also puts on a decent cabaret show.

To get here follow Calle Simón Bolívar from Plaza Mayor up to the Ermita de Nuestra Señora de la Candelaria de la Popa. The disco is 100m further along on your left.

Bodeguita Fando Brothers
BAR, RESTAURANT

(Antonio Maceo 162B cnr Zerquera; ⊙24hr) Functioning both as a paladar and a bar, Fando's is best enjoyed in the early evening, while nursing a beer or cocktail. Unlike other private places, it's open 24 hours.

Taberna la Canchánchara
BAR

(cnr Rubén Martínez Villena & Ciro Redondo) This place is famous for its eponymous house cocktail made from rum, honey, lemon and water. Local musicians regularly drop by for off-the-cuff jam sessions, and it's not unusual for the *canchánchara*-inebriated crowd to break into spontaneous dancing.

☆ Entertainment

Get ready for the best nightlife you'll find outside Havana.

★ Palenque de los Congos Reales
RUMBA

(cnr Echerri & Av Jesús Menéndez; admission free) FREE A must for rumba fans, this open patio on Trinidad's music alley has an eclectic menu incorporating salsa, *son* (Cuban popular music) and *trova*. The highlight, however, is the 10pm rumba drums with soulful African rhythms and energetic fire-eating dancers.

Casa Fischer
CULTURAL CENTER

(General Lino Pérez No 312, btwn José Martí & Francisco Codania; admission CUC$1) This is the local ARTex patio, which cranks up at 10pm with a salsa orchestra (on Tuesday, Wednesday, Thursday, Saturday and Sunday) or a folklore show (Friday). If you're early, kill time at the art gallery (free) and chat to the staff at the on-site Paradiso office about salsa lessons and other courses.

Casa de la Trova
LIVE MUSIC

(Echerri No 29; admission CUC$1; ⊙9pm-2am) Trinidad's spirited casa retains its earthy essence despite the high package-tourist-to-Cuban ratio. Local musicians to look out for here are Semillas del Son, Santa Palabra and the town's best *trovador,* Israel Moreno.

Las Ruinas del Teatro Brunet
LIVE MUSIC

(Antonio Maceo No 461, btwn Simón Bolívar & Zerquera; admission CUC$1) This jazzed-up ruin has an athletic Afro-Cuban show on its pleasant patio at 9:30pm nightly.

Las Ruinas de Sagarte
LIVE MUSIC

(cnr Av Jesús Menéndez & Galdos; admission free; ⊙24hr) FREE Another ruin (Trinidad's full of them) with a good house band and a high-energy, low-pressure dance scene.

Cine Romelio Cornelio
CINEMA

(Parque Céspedes; ⊙8pm Tue-Sun) This cinema, on the southwestern side of Parque Céspedes, shows films nightly.

Estadio Rolando Rodríguez
SPORTS

(Eliope Paz; ⊙Oct-Apr) This stadium, at the southeastern end of Frank País, hosts baseball games.

🛍 Shopping

You can shop until you drop from heat exhaustion in Trinidad, at least at the open-air markets, which are set up all over town. See local painters at work – and buy their paintings, too – at various points along Calles Francisco Toro, Valdés and Muñoz.

Arts & Crafts Market
CRAFT, SOUVENIRS

(Av Jesús Menéndez) This excellent open-air market in front of the Casa de la Trova is the place to buy souvenirs, especially textiles and crochet work. Note: should you see any black coral or turtle-shell items, don't buy them. They're made from endangered species and are forbidden entry into many countries.

Fondo Cubano de Bienes Culturales
CRAFT, SOUVENIRS

(Simón Bolívar No 418; ⊙9am-5pm Mon-Fri, to 3pm Sat & Sun) Just down from Plaza Mayor, this store has a good selection of Cuban handicrafts.

Taller Instrumentos Musicales
MUSICAL INSTRUMENTS

(cnr Av Jesús Menéndez & Valdés Muñoz) Musical instruments are made here and sold in the adjacent shop.

Casa del Habano CIGARS
(cnr Antonio Maceo & Zerquera; ⊙9am-7pm)
Dodge the street hustlers and satisfy your
alcoholic (rum) and tobacco vices here.

Galería La Paulet ART
(Simón Bolívar 411) Interesting selection of
probing, mainly abstract art by local artists.

ℹ Information

INTERNET ACCESS

Café Internet las Begonias (Antonio Maceo
No 473; internet access per half-hr CUC$3;
⊙9am-9pm) On the corner of Simón Bolívar.
Crowded.

Etecsa Telepunto (cnr General Lino Pérez &
Francisco Pettersen; internet access per hr
CUC$6; ⊙8:30am-7:30pm) Telepunto office
with modern, if slow, computer terminals. Less
crowded.

MEDIA

Radio Trinidad Broadcasts over 1200AM.

MEDICAL SERVICES

General Hospital (✉99-32-01; Antonio Maceo
No 6) Southeast of the city center.

Servimed Clínica Internacional Cubanacán
(✉99-62-40; General Lino Pérez No 103 cnr
Anastasio Cárdenas; ⊙24hr) There is an on-
site pharmacy selling products in convertibles.

MONEY

Banco de Crédito y Comercio (José Martí
No 264) Has a new ATM which is supposed to
accept foreign credit cards.

Cadeca (José Martí No 164; ⊙8.30am-8pm
Mon-Sat, 9am-6pm Sun) Between Parque
Céspedes and Camilo Cienfuegos.

POST

Post Office (Antonio Maceo No 418, btwn
Colón & Zerquera)

TRAVEL AGENCIES

Cubatur (Antonio Maceo No 447; ⊙9am-8pm)
Good for general tourist information, plus hotel
bookings, car rentals, excursions etc. State
taxis congregate outside.

Infotur (Camilo Cienfuegos, Plaza Santa Ana)

Ecotur (Antonio Maceo No 461, btwn Simón
Bolívar & Zerquera) Organizes trips to Jobo
Rosado Reserve and Alturas de Banao. Desk in
Las Ruinas del Teatro Brunet.

Paradiso (General Lino Pérez No 306) Cultural
and general tours in English, Spanish and French.

ℹ Getting There & Away

AIR

Alberto Delgado Airport is 1km southwest of
Trinidad, off the road to Casilda. Only Aerotaxi
charters fly here.

BUS

The **bus station** (Piro Guinart No 224) runs
provincial buses to Sancti Spíritus and Cienfuegos, though most foreigners use the more
reliable Víazul service. Tickets are sold at a small
window marked Taquilla Campo near the station
entrance. Check the blackboard for the current
schedule.

The **Víazul ticket office** (⊙8-11:30am &
1-5pm) is further back in the station. This office
is well organized and you can usually book tickets a couple of days in advance.

The Varadero departures can deposit you in
Jagüey Grande (CUC$15, three hours) with stops
on request in Jovellanos, Colesio and Cárdenas.
The Santiago de Cuba departure goes through
Sancti Spíritus (CUC$6, 1½ hours), Ciego de Ávila
(CUC$9, two hours and 40 minutes), Camagüey
(CUC$15, five hours and 20 minutes), Las Tunas
(CUC$22, 7½ hours), Holguín (CUC$26, eight
hours) and Bayamo (CUC$26, 10 hours).

A new once-daily Víazul bus leaving at 7am
does a northern circuit, calling at Cienfuegos,
Santa Clara, Remedios, Caibarién, Mayajigua,
Morón and Ciego de Ávila.

VÍAZUL BUS DEPARTURES FROM TRINIDAD

DESTINATION	COST (CUC$)	DURATION (HR)	DEPARTURE TIMES
Ciego de Ávila	24	6¼	7am
Cienfuegos	6	1½	7:40am, 9am, 10:30am, 3pm, 3:45pm
Havana	25	6⅓	7:40am, 10:30am, 3:45pm
Santa Clara	8	3	3pm
Santiago de Cuba	33	12	8am
Varadero	20	6	9am, 3pm

Trinidad Area

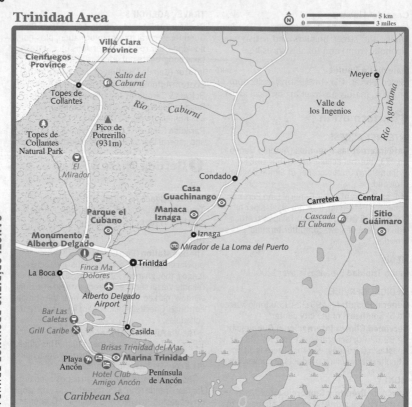

SANCTI SPÍRITUS PROVINCE TRINIDAD

The new Cubanacán **Conectando** bus service has direct daily links with Havana, Varadero and Viñales for similar prices as Víazul. Inquire at **Infotur** (Antonio Maceo No 461).

TRAIN

Train transport out of Trinidad is awful even by Cuban standards. The town hasn't been connected to the main rail network since a hurricane in the early 1990s, meaning the only functioning line runs up the Valle de los Ingenios, stopping in Iznaga (35 minutes) and terminating at Meyer (one hour and 10 minutes). There are supposedly four trains a day, the most reliable leaving Trinidad at 9am and 1pm, but often they don't run; always check ahead at the **terminal** (Lino Pérez final) in a pink house across the train tracks on the western side of the station.

ⓘ Getting Around

BICYCLE

You can usually hire gearless bikes at **Las Ruinas del Teatro Brunet** (Antonio Maceo No 461, btwn Simón Bolívar & Zerquera; per day CUC$3) or you can ask around at your casa particular. These are fine for getting to Playa Ancón, but nowhere near adequate for the steep climbs up to Topes de Collantes.

CAR & TAXI

The rental agencies at the Playa Ancón hotels rent mopeds (CUC$25 per day), or you can try Las Ruinas del Teatro Brunet.

Cubacar (cnr Antonio Maceo & Zerquera) rents cars for approximately CUC$70 per day. It also has an office in Hotel Club Amigo Ancón.

The **Servi-Cupet gas station** (⊙24hr), 500m south of town on the road to Casilda, has an El Rápido snack bar attached. The Oro Negro gas station is at the entrance to Trinidad from Sancti Spíritus, 1km east of Plaza Santa Ana.

Guarded parking is available in certain areas around the *casco histórico*. Ask at your hotel or casa particular, where staff can arrange it.

Trinidad has Havana-style coco-taxis; they cost approximately CUC$5 to Playa Ancón. A car costs from CUC$6 to CUC$8 one way. State-owned taxis tend to congregate outside the Cubatur office on Antonio Maceo. A cab to Sancti Spíritus should cost approximately CUC$35.

HORSE CARTS

Horse carts (costing 2 pesos) leave for Casilda from Paseo Agramonte at the southern end of town.

TRINIDAD TOUR BUS

Trinidad has a handy hop-on/hop-off tourist-oriented **minibus** (all-day ticket CUC$2), similar to Havana's and Viñales', linking its outlying sights. It plies a route from outside the Cubatur office on Antonio Maceo to Finca Ma Dolores, Playa la Boca, Bar las Caletas, and the three Playa Ancón hotels. It runs approximately five times a day in both directions starting at 9am and terminating at 6pm.

Playa Ancón & Around

Playa Ancón, a precious ribbon of white beach on Sancti Spíritus' iridescent Caribbean shoreline, is usually touted – with good reason – to be the finest arc of sand on Cuba's south coast.

While not comparable in all-round quality to the north-coast giants of Varadero, Cayo Coco and Guardalavaca, Ancón has one important trump card: Trinidad, Latin America's sparkling colonial diamond, shimmering just 12km to the north. You can get here in less than 15 minutes by car or in a leisurely 40 minutes on a bike. Alternatively, Ancón has three all-inclusive hotels and a well-equipped marina that runs catamaran trips to a couple of nearby coral keys.

Beach bums who want to be near the water, but don't have the money or inclination to stay at one of the resorts, might consider a homestay in the seaside village of La Boca.

There's no doubting Ancón's beauty, but what gushing tourist brochures fail to mention are the sand fleas: they're famously ferocious at sunrise and sunset. Be warned.

The old fishing port of **Casilda**, 6km due south of Trinidad, is a friendly village with one paved road. On August 17 the **Fiesta de Santa Elena** engulfs little Casilda, with feasting, competitions, horse races and loads of rum. The road from Ancón to Casilda crosses a tidal flat, meaning abundant birdlife is visible in the early morning.

🏃 Activities

From Hotel Club Amigo Ancón, it's 18km to Trinidad via Casilda, or 16km on the much nicer coastal road via La Boca. The hotel pool is also open to nonguests and you can usually nab the Ping-Pong table undetected.

Marina Trinidad FISHING, DIVING
(☑ 99-62-05; www.nauticamarlin.com) This is a few hundred meters north of Hotel Club Amigo Ancón. Eight hours of deep-sea fishing, including transport, gear and guide, costs CUC$400 per boat (maximum four people), or CUC$300 for four hours of troll fishing. Fly-fishing is also possible around the rich mangrove forests of Península de Ancón (CUC$250 for six hours, maximum two people).

Diving with the **Cayo Blanco International Dive Center**, located at the marina, costs CUC$35 per dive and CUC$320 for an open-water course. Cayo Blanco, a reef islet 25km southeast of Playa Ancón, has 22 marked scuba sites where you'll see black coral and bountiful marine life. The marina also runs a seven-hour snorkeling-and-beach tour to **Cayo Blanco** for CUC$45 per person with lunch. There are similar trips to the equally pristine **Cayo Macho**.

Romantic types might want to check out the **sunset cruise** from CUC$20, which has been enthusiastically recommended by readers.

Windward Islands Cruising Company BOAT TOURS
(www.caribbean-adventure.com) This company charters crewed and bareboat monohulls and catamarans out of the Marina Trinidad to the Jardines de la Reina and the Archipiélago de los Canarreos. You can sail with or without guides, on a partial package or an all-inclusive tour. Interested parties should inquire using contact details on the website.

🛏 Sleeping

🛏 La Boca

The small village of La Boca, a few clicks up the coast from Ancón, has about a dozen lovely casas.

'Villa Sonia' – Sonia Santos Barrera CASA PARTICULAR **$**
(☑ 99-29-23; Av del Mar No 11, La Boca; r CUC$25-30; 🅿 ❄) If you need an excuse to stay in La Boca, here it is. A beautiful house with a wraparound porch all to yourself, complete with polished-wood dining area, private kitchen, hammocks, rocking chairs and a thatched gazebo. Situated right opposite the (rocky) beach.

'Villa Río Mar' –
Nestor Manresa   CASA PARTICULAR **$**
(☎99-31-08; San José No 65, La Boca; r without bathroom CUC$20-25; P❄) There are further treats at Río Mar, where this casa's two rooms give out onto a lovely tiled veranda. If it's full, there's more next door.

🛏 Península de Ancón

Ancón's three hotels offer all-inclusive rates.

Hotel Club Amigo Ancón   RESORT **$$**
(☎99-61-23, 99-61-27; Playa Ancón; all-incl s/d CUC$54/86; P❄@🏊) Built during Cuba's 30-year flirtation with Soviet architectonics, the Ancón wouldn't win any beauty contests. Indeed, this steamship-shaped seven-story concrete pile looks more than a little incongruous next to the natural beauty of Ancón beach. But if it's beach proximity you're after, this deal could cut ice.

Some like the hotel's lack of pretension and low prices; others are apt to quote Groucho Marx and say that they'd rather not belong to a club (Amigo) that would have them as a member.

Brisas Trinidad del Mar   RESORT **$$**
(☎99-65-00; Playa Ancón; all-incl s/d CUC$60/100; P❄@🏊) Although it's a kitschy attempt to re-create Trinidad in an all-inclusive resort environment, Brisas wins kudos for rejecting the monolithic architecture of Hotel Club Amigo Ancón in favor of low-rise colonial-style villas. But after barely a decade in operation, the quality of this place has begun to suffer from poor maintenance and decidedly iffy service.

Though the swath of beach is stunning and the massage, sauna, gym and tennis courts are handy for the sports-minded, you might be better off saving a few dollars and opting for Club Amigo.

🍴 Eating & Drinking

Bar las Caletas, at the junction of the road to Casilda, is a local drinking place.

Grill Caribe   CARIBBEAN **$$**
(🕐24hr) Other than the hotel restaurants, there's this place on a quiet beach 2km north of Club Amigo Costasur. It specializes in seafood, such as fish and shrimp or lobster, and charges a pretty price. Strict vegetarians will be disappointed here. It's a great sunset spot.

ℹ Getting There & Away

A shuttle bus run by Transtur links Ancón to Trinidad four times daily (CUC$2). Otherwise, it's a pleasant bike ride or a cheap taxi.

Valle de los Ingenios

Trinidad's immense wealth was garnered not in the town itself, but in a verdant valley 8km to the east. The Valle de los Ingenios (or Valle de San Luis) still contains the ruins of dozens of 19th-century sugar mills, including warehouses, milling machinery, slave quarters, manor houses and a fully functioning steam train. Most of the mills were destroyed during the War of Independence and the Spanish-Cuban-American War, when the focus of sugar-growing in Cuba shifted west to Matanzas. Though some sugar is still grown here, the valley is more famous today for its status as a Unesco World Heritage Site. Backed by the shadowy sentinels of the Sierra del Escambray, the pastoral fields, royal palms and peeling colonial ruins are timelessly beautiful. A horseback-riding tour from Trinidad should take in most (if not all) of the following sites.

◉ Sights

Manaca Iznaga   MUSEUM, LANDMARK
(admission CUC$1; 🐴) The valley's main focal point is 16km northeast of Trinidad. Founded in 1750, the estate was purchased in 1795 by the dastardly Pedro Iznaga, who became one of the wealthiest men in Cuba through the unscrupulous business of slave trafficking. The 44m-high tower next to the hacienda was used to watch the slaves, and the bell in front of the house served to summon them.

Today you can climb to the top of the tower for pretty views, followed by a reasonable lunch (noon to 2:30pm) in the restaurant-bar in Iznaga's former colonial mansion. Don't miss the huge sugar press out back.

Casa Guachinango   LANDMARK
(🕐9am-5pm) Three kilometers beyond the Manaca Iznaga, on the valley's inland road, is an old hacienda built by Don Mariano Borrell toward the end of the 18th century. The building now houses a restaurant. The Río Ay is just below, and the surrounding landscape is truly wonderful. To get to Casa Guachinango, take the paved road to the right, just beyond the second bridge you pass as you come from Manaca Iznaga.

The Meyer train stops right beside the house every morning, and you can walk back to Iznaga from Guachinango along the railway line in less than an hour.

Mirador de la Loma del Puerto VIEWPOINT

Six kilometers east of Trinidad on the road to Sancti Spíritus, this 192m-high lookout provides the best eagle-eye view of the valley with – if you're lucky – a steam train chugging through its midst. There's also a bar.

Sitio Guáimaro LANDMARK

(☻7am-7pm) Seven kilometers east of the Manaca Iznaga turnoff, travel for another 2km south and you'll find the former estate of Don Mariano Borrell, a wealthy early-19th-century sugar merchant. The seven stone arches on the facade lead to frescoed rooms, now a restaurant.

❶ Getting There & Away

There are two train options for getting to and from Valle de los Ingenios – both are equally unreliable. The tourist steam train goes at the speed of Thomas the Tank Engine, but it's a sublime journey when it's running through an impossibly green valley full of munching cows and slender bridges. The train is pulled by the indomitable and classic engine No 52204, built by the Baldwin Locomotive Company of Philadelphia in August 1919. Organized as an excursion (CUC$10), passengers pay for their own lunch separately at the Manaca Iznaga, where they can visit the famous bell tower. Cubatur (p299) in Trinidad will know when the next tourist-train trip is scheduled and if it's working. Tour desks at the Ancón hotels sell the same train tour for CUC$17, including bus transfers to Trinidad.

Horseback riding tours can be arranged at the travel agencies in Trinidad or Playa Ancón. Alternatively, you can contract a horse and guide privately in Trinidad for CUC$15 per six hours.

Topes de Collantes

ELFV //1M

The crenellated, 90km-long Sierra del Escambray is Cuba's second-largest mountain range, and it straddles the borders of three provinces: Sancti Spíritus, Cienfuegos and Villa Clara. Though not particularly high (the loftiest point, Pico de San Juan, measures just 1156m), the mountain slopes are rich in flora and surprisingly isolated. In late 1958 Che Guevara set up camp in these hills on his way to Santa Clara and, less than three years later, CIA-sponsored counter-revolutionary groups operated their own cat-and-mouse guerrilla campaign from the same vantage point.

Though not strictly a national park, Topes is, nonetheless, a heavily protected area. The umbrella park, comprising 200 sq km, overlays four smaller parks – Parque Altiplano, Parque Codina, Parque Guanayara and Parque el Cubano – while a fifth enclave, El Nicho in Cienfuegos province, is also administered by park authority Gaviota.

The park takes its name from its largest settlement, an ugly health resort founded in 1937 by dictator Fulgencio Batista to placate his sick wife, for whom he built a quaint rural cottage. The architecture went downhill thereafter with the construction of an architecturally grotesque tuberculosis sanatorium (now a health 'resort'), begun in the late '30s but not opened until 1954.

Topes de Collantes has two basic hotels open to foreigners, plus excellent guided and unguided hiking. Its junglelike forests harboring vines, lichens, mosses, ferns and eye-catching epiphytes are akin to a giant outdoor biology classroom.

The **Carpeta Central information office** (☻8am-5pm), near the sundial at the entrance to the hotel complexes, is the best place to procure maps, guides and trail info.

◉ Sights

Museo de Arte Cubano Contemporáneo MUSEUM

(admission CUC$3) Believe it or not, Topes de Collantes' monstrous sanatorium once harbored a treasure trove of Cuban art, containing works by Cuban masters such as Tomás Sánchez and Rubén Torres Llorca. Raiding the old collection in 2008 inspired provincial officials to open this infinitely more attractive museum, which displays over 70 works in six *salas* (rooms) spread over three floors. The museum is on the main approach road from Trinidad just before you get to the hotels.

Casa Museo del Café CAFE, MUSEUM

(☻7am-7pm) 🝔 Coffee has been grown in these mountains for over two centuries, and in this small rustic cafe you can fill in the gaps on its boom-bust history while sipping the aromatic local brew (called Cristal Mountain). Just up the road there is the **Jardín de Variedades del Café**, a short stroll around 25 different varieties of coffee plant.

Plaza de las Memorias   MUSEUM

(⊙8am-5pm) **FREE** Topes' token museum is this quaint little display housed in three small wooden abodes just down from the Casa Museo del Café. It tells the history of the settlement and its resident hotels.

🏃 Activities

Topes is the only place in Cuba where you can participate in the burgeoning sport of **canyoning**, but there are limitations and you'd be wise to do your homework first. The up-and-coming scene focuses on four main rivers – the Calburni, Vegas Grandes, Cabagan and Gruta Nengoa – where canyoners travel spectacularly downstream equipped with ropes, wetsuits, helmets and harnesses. The highlight of the trip is a 200m series of vertical cascades over Salto Vegas Grandes. One experienced Canadian outfit offering excursions is **Canyoning Quebec** (www. canyoning-quebec.com), which runs eight-day trips into the Sierra del Escambray.

There are currently no organized tours in-country and no equipment available for hire. At the time of writing there was at least one Gaviota parks guide who was a qualified canyon guide. Ask at the Carpeta Central information office for more up-to-date information.

★Salto del Caburní   HIKING

(entry CUC$6.50) The Blue Riband hike, and the one most easily accessed on foot from the hotels, is to this 62m waterfall that cascades over rocks into cool swimming holes before plunging into a chasm where macho locals dare each other to jump. At the height of the dry season (March to May) you may be disappointed by these falls.

The entry fee is collected at the toll gate to Villa Caburní, just down the hill from the Kurhotel near the Carpeta Central information office (it's a long approach on foot). Allow an hour down and 1½ hours back up for this 5km (round trip) hike. Some slopes are steep and can be slippery after rain.

Sendero los Helechos   HIKING

A 1km trail billed rather ambitiously as an eco-walk, this is basically a shortcut between the Kurhotel and Hotel los Helechos. Look out for snow-white mariposas and multiple species of fern along the route.

Sendero Jardín del Gigante   HIKING

(entry CUC$7) Parque la Represa on the Río Vega Grande, just downhill from La Batata

trail entry, contains 300 species of trees and ferns, including the largest *caoba* (mahogany) tree in Cuba. You can take it all in on this 1km trail.

The small restaurant at the entrance to the garden is in a villa built by Fulgencio Batista's wife, whose love for the area inspired her husband to build the Topes resort.

Sendero la Batata   HIKING

(entry CUC$3) This 6km out-and-back trail to a small cave containing an underground river starts at a parking sign just downhill from Casa Museo del Café. When you reach another highway, go around the right side of the concrete embankment and down the hill. Keep straight or right after this point (avoid trails to the left). Allow an hour each way.

Vegas Grandes   HIKING

(entry CUC$5) The Vegas Grandes trail begins at the apartment blocks known as Reparto el Chorrito on the southern side of Topes de Collantes, near the entrance to the resort as you arrive from Trinidad. Allow a bit less than an hour each way to cover the 2km to the waterfall.

It's possible to continue to the Salto del Caburní, but consider hiring a guide as the paths are poorly signposted.

Hacienda Codina   HIKING

(entry CUC$5) The hacienda is another possible destination. The 3.5km 4WD track begins on a hilltop 2.5km down the road toward Cienfuegos and Manicaragua, 1km before the point at which these roads divide. There's a shorter trail to the hacienda from below Hotel los Helechos that links for part of the way with La Batata, but you'll need a guide to use it.

At the hacienda itself is the 1.2km circular **Sendero de Alfombra Mágica** through orchid and bamboo gardens and past the Cueva del Altar. Also here are mud baths, a restaurant and a scenic viewpoint.

Sendero 'Centinelas del Río Melodioso'   HIKING

(entry CUC$7) The least accessible but by far the most rewarding hike from Topes de Collantes is the 2.5km (5km return) hike in the Parque Guanayara, 15km from the Carpeta Central information office along a series of rough and heavily rutted tracks. For logistical reasons this excursion is best organized with a guide from the Carpeta, or as part of an organized tour from Trinidad with Cubatur (CUC$43 with lunch).

The trail itself begins in cool, moist coffee plantations and descends steeply to **El Rocio** waterfall, where you can strip off and have a bracing shower. Following the course of the Río Melodioso (Melodic River), you pass another inviting waterfall and swimming pool before emerging into the salubrious gardens of the riverside **Casa la Gallega**, a traditional rural hacienda where a light lunch can be organized and camping is sometimes permitted in the lush grounds.

🛏 Sleeping

Hotel los Helechos HOTEL **$**

(☎54-02-31; s/d CUC$27/35; P ❖ ☲) Never 100% at home in its verdant natural surroundings, this clumsy chocolate-box building with its wicker furnishings and holiday-camp-style villas still looks a bit awkward. Not helping matters is the unattractive indoor pool, poky steam baths (if they're working), journeyman restaurant and kitschy local disco (in a natural park).

The saving grace is the restaurant's home-baked bread – surely the best in Cuba.

Villa Caburni CABINS **$**

(☎54-01-80; s/d CUC$23/32; P ❖) This place is a veritable rural gem that offers, in a small park next to the Kurhotel, one- or two-story Swiss-style chalets with kitchenettes and private bathrooms. It is located just behind the Carpeta Central Information Office.

🍴 Eating

Apart from the paladar and restaurant listed here, three other eating options exist on the trails: the **Hacienda Codina**, **Restaurante la Represa** and **Casa la Gallega** (in Parque Guanayara). **El Mirador** (Carretera de Trinidad) is a simple bar with a stunning view halfway up the ascent road from Trinidad.

El Lagarto Verde PALADAR, CUBAN **$$**

(Carretera de Trinidad; meals CUC$10) 🍃 With food so sustainable most of it's collected a few meters from your table, Topes' first paladar (run by the people from Villa Lagarto in Cienfuegos) celebrates its jungly mountain setting. Enjoy fruit shakes from the garden, traditional roast pork and Escambray coffee that is grown, roasted and brewed in the same square kilometer. Magic!

Restaurante Mi Retiro CARIBBEAN **$$**

(Carretera de Trinidad; meals CUC$6-9) Situated 3km back down the road to Trinidad, Restaurante Mi Retiro does fair-to-middling *comida criolla* to the sound of the occasional traveling minstrel.

ℹ Getting There & Away

Without a car, it's very difficult to get here and harder still to get around to the various trailheads. Your best bet is a taxi (CUC$35 return with a two- to three-hour wait), an excursion from Trinidad (CUC$29) or a hire car.

The road between Trinidad and Topes de Collantes is paved, but it's very steep. When wet, it becomes slippery and should be driven with caution. There's also a spectacular 44km road that continues right over the mountains from Topes de Collantes to Manicaragua via Jibacoa (occasionally closed, so check in Trinidad before setting up). It's also possible to drive to/from Cienfuegos via Sierrita on a partly paved, partly gravel road (4WD only).

NORTHERN SANCTI SPÍRITUS PROVINCE

For every 1000 tourists that visit Trinidad, a small handful gets to see the province's narrow northern corridor, which runs between Remedios, in Villa Clara, and Morón, in Ciego de Ávila.

The landscape comprises karstic uplands characterized by caves and covered in semi-deciduous woodland, juxtaposed with a flat, ecologically valuable coastal plain protected in the hard-to-visit (but worth it if you can) Parque Nacional Caguanes.

⊙ Sights & Activities

★**Museo Nacional Camilo Cienfuegos** MUSEUM

(admission CUC$1; ⊙8am-4pm Tue-Sat, 9am-1pm Sun) This excellent museum at Yaguajay, 36km southeast of Caibarién, was opened in 1989 and is eerily reminiscent of the Che Guevara monument in Santa Clara. Camilo fought a crucial battle in this town on the eve of the Revolution's triumph, taking control of a local military barracks (now the Hospital Docente General, opposite the museum).

The museum is directly below a modernist plaza embellished with a 5m-high statue of *El Señor de la Vanguardia* (Man at the Vanguard). It contains an interesting display of Cienfuegos' life intermingled with

OFF THE BEATEN TRACK

JOBO ROSADO RESERVE

This region, protected as an area of 'managed resources', is still little explored by independent travelers, although organized groups are sometimes brought here. Measuring just over 40 sq km, the reserve includes the Sierra de Meneses-Cueto, a range of hills that runs across the north of the province and acts as a kind of buffer zone for the heavily protected Bahía de Buenavista. As in the Sierra Maestra, history is intertwined with the ecology here: General Máximo Gomez battled through these hills during the Spanish-Cuban-American War and in 1958 Camilo Cienfuegos' rebel army (Column No 2) pitched their final command post here. An imaginative monument by sculptor José Delarra marks the spot.

Guided hikes can be organized either through Ecotur or at Villa San José del Lago. Highlights include the 1km **La Solapa de Genaro** hike through tropical savannah to a gorgeous set of waterfalls and swimming holes, and the 800m **Cueva de Valdés** walk through semi-deciduous woodland to a cave. The nexus for the activities is **Rancho Querete**, a biological-station-cum-restaurant near the village of Meneses, just south of Yaguajay, which serves wonderfully simple *comida criolla* (creole food).

facts and mementos from the revolutionary struggle. A replica of the small tank *Dragon I*, converted from a tractor for use in the battle, stands in front of the hospital.

Parque Nacional Caguanes   HIKING, BOAT TOUR
Strict conservation measures mean public access to Parque Nacional Caguanes with its caves, aboriginal remains and flamingos is limited, but not impossible. There is a basic biological station on the coast accessible by a rough road due north of Mayajigua but, rather than just turn up, your best bet is to check details first at the Villa San José del Lago or with Ecotur, which has a handy public office in Trinidad.

The one advertised excursion is **Las Maravillas que Atesora Caguanes** (2½ hours), which incorporates a path to the Humboldt, Ramos and Los Chivos caves and a boat trip around the Cayos de Piedra.

🛏 Sleeping

Villa San José del Lago   HOTEL $
(📞 55-61-08; Antonio Guiteras, Mayajigua; s/d CUC$14/22; ▣ ✳ ☀) This novel spa, once popular with vacationing Americans, is just outside Mayajigua in northern Sancti Spíritus province. The tiny rooms set in a variety of two-story villas nestle beside a small palm-fringed lake (with pedal boats and resident flamingos).

The complex is famous for its thermal waters, which were first used by injured slaves in the 19th century but are now mainly the preserve of holidaying Cubans. The 67 rooms are no-frills, but the setting, wedged between the Sierra de Jatibonico and Parque Nacional Caguanes, is magnificent and makes a good base for some of Cuba's lesser-known excursions. There's a restaurant and snack bar on site.

Chalet Los Álamos   CABINS $
(r from CUC$25) Rustic accommodation (five double rooms) on a learning farm in the Jobo Rosado Reserve that offers the surprising luxuries of electricity, hot water and an on-site restaurant. On the farm you can milk cows, press sugarcane and roast coffee. Book in advance through Ecotur.

ℹ Information

Ecotur (📞 54-74-19; Carretera Yaguajay Km 1.5) The best information portal for the region, just south of Yaguajay on the road to Meneses.

ℹ Getting There & Away

One Víazul bus a day plies the northern route, stopping in Mayajigua. Heading west it calls at Caibarién, Remedios, Santa Clara, Cienfuegos and Trinidad. Going east it calls at Morón and Ciego de Ávila.

Ciego de Ávila Province

🎵 33 / POP 424,400

Best Watersports

➡ Laguna de la Leche (p316)

➡ Jardines de la Reina (p313)

➡ Boat Adventure (p321)

➡ Cayo Media Luna (p321)

Best Places to Stay

➡ Meliá Cayo Coco (p320)

➡ Alojamiento Maité (p315)

➡ Iberostar Daiquirí (p322)

Why Go?

For centuries Ciego de Ávila was little more than an overnight stop on Cuba's arterial east–west highway. Then came Cuba's ambitious post–Special Period tourist project and the resort development of Cayo Coco and Cayo Guillermo (the bright tropical pearls that had once seduced Hemingway) had their drizzling of glorious beaches spruced up and daubed with nearly a dozen exclusive tourist resorts.

Chopped off the western flank of Camagüey province in 1975, Ciego de Ávila has in reality been harboring intriguing secrets for over a century. Various non-Spanish immigrants first arrived here in the 19th century from Haiti, Jamaica, the Dominican Republic and Barbados, bringing with them myriad cultural quirks, exemplified by cricket in Baraguá, voodoo in Venezuela, country dancing in Majagua and explosive fireworks in Chambas.

When to Go

➡ Beach-goers should descend on the *cayos* (keys) between November and March for drier weather that, while cool by Cuban standards, is still pleasantly warm.

➡ Take to the field on August 1 in Baraguá, where people celebrate Slave Emancipation Day with music, dancing and a game of cricket.

➡ Morón's Aquatic Carnival kicks off in September, in the channel leading to the Laguna de Leche.

Ciego de Ávila Province Highlights

1 Eat fresh fish for ridiculously cheap prices at the **Laguna de la Leche** (p316).

2 Dive from a liveaboard into the almost-virgin waters of the secluded **Jardines de la Reina archipelago** (p313).

3 Browse through one of the best municipal museums

in Cuba, **Museo Provincial Simón Reyes** (p309) in Ciego de Ávila.

4 Follow in the wake of Papa Hemingway while deep-sea fishing off **Cayo Guillermo** (p321).

5 Dig your toes in the sand at the beach paradise of **Playa Pilar** (p321).

6 Escape the resorts and immerse yourself in the rustic simplicity of the **Loma de Cunagua** (p317).

7 Marvel at how waste ground got transformed into one of Cuba's most interesting city parks at Ciego de Ávila's **Parque de la Ciudad** (p309).

History

The area now known as Ciego de Ávila province was first prospected in 1513 by Spanish adventurer Pánfilo de Narváez, who set out to explore the expansive forests and plains of the north coast, then presided over by a local Taíno chief called Ornofay. The remnants of a Taíno settlement here, Los Buchillones, constitute the most complete Pre-Columbian remains in the Greater Antilles. Integrating itself into the new Spanish colony of Cuba in the early 1500s, the province got its present name from local merchant Jacomé de Ávila, who was granted an *encomienda* (indigenous workforce) in San Antonio de la Palma in 1538. A small *ciego* (clearing) on Ávila's estate was put aside as a resting place for tired travelers, and it quickly became a burgeoning settlement.

Throughout the 16th and 17th centuries the northern keys provided a valuable refuge for pirates fresh from lucrative raids on cities such as Havana. Two hundred years later a buccaneer of a different kind arrived: American writer Ernest Hemingway, who played his own game of cat and mouse tracking German submarines in the waters off Cayo Guillermo.

During the 19th-century wars of independence, the area was infamous for its 68km-long Morón–Júcaro defensive line, better known to historians as La Trocha. Characterized by its sturdy military installations and manned by a force of up to 20,000 men, the defense system was built up by the ruling Spanish administrators in the 1870s and was designed to stop the marauding Mambís (19th-century rebels) from forging a passage west.

Ciego de Ávila

POP 110,400

Orgullo (pride) surges through Ciego de Ávila in improbably large amounts for a city of such diminutive stature. Hosting one of Cuba's best museums and now its most intriguing urban park, Ciego de Ávila is the most modern of Cuba's provincial capitals, founded in 1840. Growing up originally in the 1860s and '70s as a military town behind the defensive Morón–Júcaro (Trocha) line, it later became an important processing center for the region's lucrative sugarcane and pineapple crops (the pineapple is the local mascot). Ciego's inhabitants refer to their city as 'the city of porches' – a reference to the ornate colonnaded housefronts which characterize the center.

Famous *avileñas* include Cuban pop-art exponent Raúl Martínez and local socialite Ángela Hernández Viuda de Jiménez, a rich widow who helped finance many of the city's early-20th-century neoclassical buildings, including the 500-seat Teatro Principal.

⊙ Sights

Manageable and friendly, Ciego de Ávila engenders a leisurely pace. The city has worked hard to ensure it waylays you, with a new three-block boulevard, appealing parks , and museums which promulgate a relatively low-key history in a nevertheless interesting and relevant way.

★**Museo Provincial Simón Reyes** MUSEUM
(cnr Honorato del Castillo & Máximo Gómez; admission CUC$1; ☉ 8am-10pm Mon-Fri, to 2:30pm Sat & Sun) Quite possibly Cuba's best-presented municipal museum, this mustard-yellow building with a typical *avileña* porch is one convertible well spent. Fascinating exhibits include a scale model of La Trocha, detailed information on Afro-Cuban culture/religion, and explanations on the province's rich collection of traditional festivals.

★**Parque de la Ciudad** PARK
The once-scrubby wasteland between Hotel Ciego de Ávila and the city center on the northwestern edge of town has been transformed into a vast park (featuring an artificial lake – the Lago la Turbina – with boating available, children's playgrounds and good eateries). With its off-beat attractions and amiable understatedness, it's just possibly Cuba's most interesting urban green space.

It's also a good testimony to the wonders that can be worked with scrap: old steam trains have been dusted off in homage to Ciego's transport history; there's impressive *artes plasticos* (modern art) including an elephant statue fashioned from old car parts; and, best among the eating possibilities, an old Aerocaribbean aircraft converted into an intimate restaurant.

Parque Martí SQUARE
All Ciego roads lead to this textbook colonial park laid out in 1877 in honor of King Alfonso XII of Spain, but renamed in the early 20th century for newly martyred Cuban national hero José Martí: expect a 1947 church, the **Iglesia Católico**

Ciego de Ávila

Ciego de Ávila

(Independencia, btwn Marcial Gómez & Honorato del Castillo), a 1911 **Ayuntamiento** (City Hall; no visitors) and a striking theater nearby.

The Iglesia Católico is notably emblazoned with the city's patron saint, San Eugenio de la Palma. One block south, however, grand Teatro Principal more than compensates for the park's lack of illustrious edifices. Built in 1927 with help from local financier Ángela Jiménez, it purportedly has the island's best (theatrical) acoustics.

Museo de Artes Decorativas MUSEUM
(cnr Independencia & Marcial Gómez; admission CUC$1; ☺8am-noon Mon, 9am-5pm Tue-Fri, 1-9pm Sat) This thoughtful collection contains quirky items from a bygone age, such as a working Victrola (Benny Moré serenades

your visit), antique pocket watches and ornate canopy beds with mother-of-pearl inlays. A CUC$1 tip gets you a local guide (in English or Spanish).

Centro Raúl Martínez
Galería de Arte Provincial　　　　GALLERY
(Independencia No 65, btwn Honorato del Castillo & Antonio Maceo; ⊘8am-noon & 1-5pm Mon & Wed, 1-9pm Thu & Fri, 2-10pm Sat, 8am-noon Sun) Duck under the signature Ciego porches along Calle Independencia to reach this gallery where works by Cuba's king of pop art are on permanent display, alongside works by other local artists.

Plano-Mural de Ciego de Ávila　　HISTORIC SITE
(cnr Marcial Gómez & Joaquín de Agüero) A bronze map of the city in the late 19th century here marks the site of its founding on June 26, 1840.

🛏 Sleeping

Ciego's casas (private homestay) act as worthwhile pit stops on the long journey east or west. The city's two hotels could garner a star between them.

★Casa de Maira　　　　CASA PARTICULAR $
(☑22-36-95; Libertad 161; CUC$20-25) It's refreshing to see a *dueña* (proprietress) prioritizing quality over quantity. There's space for two rooms here but instead you have one neat upstairs apartment with a kitchen and two terraces; airport pick-up by request.

Hotel Ciego de Ávila　　　　HOTEL $
(☑22-80-13; Carretera a de Ceballos Km 1.5; s/d CUC$26/42; P❄❄) Where have all the tourists gone? Cayo Coco, probably, leaving this Islazul staple, 2km from the city center and overlooking Parque de la Ciudad, the domain of Cuban sports teams and workers on government-sponsored vacation time. Bog-standard rooms, noisy swimming-pool area and boring breakfasts, but the staff seem friendly.

Casa Hospedaje la Villa　　CASA PARTICULAR $
(☑22-58-54; cnr Chico Valdés & Abraham Delgado; r CUC$15-20; P❄) A bright-pink detached place on the Carretera Central that's easy to find. Tired cyclists and drivers look no further. The two rooms are clean, with the upstairs (balcony included) being best, and there's a carport.

Hotel Santiago-Habana　　　　HOTEL $
(☑22-57-03; cnr Chicho Valdés & Honorato del Castillo; s/d CUC$22/35; ❄) Your one-and-only

town-center option has 76 musty but serviceable rooms that are 1970s motel style, and there's a restaurant and top-floor disco – bring ear plugs.

🍴 Eating

Restaurante el Avión　　　　CUBAN $
(Parque de la Ciudad; CUC$1-5; ⊘noon-10pm) Consider hunting in Parque de la Ciudad for restaurant innovation. El Avión might not offer much out of the ordinary on its menu (although the *ropa vieja* – shredded beef – is great) but you'll be eating in a novel venue: inside an old Aerocaribbean plane. It's just back from the lake near the scrap metal sculptures. Pay in pesos.

Restaurante Don Pepe　　　　CARIBBEAN $
(Independencia No 103, btwn Antonio Maceo & Simón Reyes; mains CUC$1-5; ⊘8-11:45pm Wed-Mon) A bartender named Eladio invented the Coctel Don Pepe here (two shots of orange juice, 1.5 shots of white rum and half a shot of crème de menthe, stirred) back in the day. The restaurant is still serving them, along with good old pork and chicken dishes, in this pleasant colonial building.

Dos Hermanos　　　　CUBAN $
(☑22-31-08; Ciego de Ávila No 55, btwn Honorato del Castillo & Antonio Maceo; mains MN$50-75; ⊘noon-4pm & 6-11pm) Best of the city's new paladares (private restaurants), say locals. Chicken, pork, beef and various seafood dishes: house special is the filling *spaghetti neopolitano*.

Solaris　　　　FUSION $
(Doce Plantas Bldg, cnr Honorato del Castillo & Libertad; mains CUC$1-5; ⊘11am-11pm) City-center joint on 12th floor of the rather ugly Doce Plantas building. It offers excellent city views and has a menu including a special cordon bleu (chicken stuffed with ham and cheese) and its own special Solaris cocktail.

★Don Ávila　　　　CARIBBEAN $$
(Cnr Marcial Gómez & Libertad; CUC$1-5; ⊘11am-11pm) *Numero uno* in Ciego's culinary greatest hits. Plaza-abutting Don Ávila impresses with its regal ambience, on-site cigar outlet, old-gents'-style bar, typically friendly *avileña* service and generous portions of *comida criolla* (creole food).

Self-Catering
Mercado Agropecuario　　　　MARKET $
(Chicho Valdés, btwn Agramonte & Fernando Callejas) This vegetable market is located in a blemished part of town below the overpass.

Supermercado Cruz Verde SUPERMARKET **$**
(cnr Independencia & Marcial Gómez; ☺9am-6pm Mon-Sat, to noon Sun) Sells groceries in one of Ciego's grandest fin de siècle buildings.

 Drinking & Nightlife

La Confronta BAR
(cnr Marcial Gómez & Joaquín Agüero) Amid the well-worn bar stools and Benny Moré paraphernalia you can sample a range of 25 different cocktails. Prices are in Cuban pesos, a tempting (potentially dangerous) proposition for a convertible-loaded traveler. There's also a limited food menu.

La Fontana CAFE
(cnr Independencia & Antonio Maceo; ☺6am-2pm & 3-11pm) Ciego's famous coffee institution has lost its shine since a 2008 renovation failed to evoke the atmosphere of yore. Long queues outside, a fog of cigarette smoke inside.

Piña Colada BAR
(cnr Independencia & Honorato del Castillo; ☺3pm-midnight) You fancied this bar's namesake cocktail in the baking Caribbean sun, right? Uh-uh. You'll shiver as you sip at this icily air-conditioned new place that went for trendy and ended up with sterile. But the cocktails are good.

El Batanga NIGHTCLUB
(Carretera a de Ceballos Km 1.5; admission per couple CUC$3; ☺10pm-2am) Hotel Ciego de Ávila's rowdy disco.

☆ **Entertainment**

For total spontaneity hit the streets on a Saturday night for the wonderful Noches Avileñas, when music and temporary food stands set up in the street around various venues, including the main park.

Cine Carmen CINEMA
(Antonio Maceo No 51, cnr Libertad) Cine Carmen provides big-screen and video offerings dai-

ly. Don't miss the big movie projector spilling film on the Libertad side of the building.

Casa de la Trova Miguel Angel Luna LIVE MUSIC
(Libertad No 130) In the dice-roll of traditional musical entertainment, Ciego's *trova* (song) house scores a magic six with polished Thursday night regional *trovadores* (singers) in a pleasant colonial setting.

Club de los Escritores LIVE MUSIC
(Libertad No 105) There are occasional concerts on the courtyard stage of this graceful colonial building, and a bar decked out in tribal art out back.

Casa de la Cultura CULTURAL CENTER
(Independencia No 76, btwn Antonio Maceo & Honorato del Castillo) All sorts of stuff goes on here, including a Wednesday *danzón* (ballroom dance) club.

Patio de ARTex LIVE MUSIC
(Libertad, btwn Antonio Maceo & Honorato del Castillo; admission MN$5) This trusty alfresco patio has a bit of everything; check the *cartelera* (culture calendar) out front.

Estadio José R Cepero SPORT
(Máximo Gómez) October to April, baseball games take place to the northwest. Ciego's Tigres have experienced a turnaround in fortune of late: 2011 runner up and 2012 champions, following a thrilling, against-the-odds victory over Havana's Los Industriales.

 Shopping

Stroll El Boulevard for typical Cuban fodder. The only place that may have you reaching inside your money belt is ARTex souvenir store **La Época** (Independencia, btwn Antonio Maceo & Honorato del Castillo).

ℹ **Information**

Banco Financiero Internacional (cnr Honorato del Castillo & Joaquín Agüero)

Cadeca (Independencia Oeste No 118, btwn Antonio Maceo & Simón Reyes)

Etecsa Telepunto (Joaquín Agüero No 62; internet per hr CUC$6; ☺8:30am-7pm) Three terminals.

General Hospital (☎22-40-15; Máximo Gómez No 257) Not far from the bus station.

Infotur (☎20-91-09; Doce Plantas Bldg, cnr Honorato del Castillo & Libertad; ☺9am-noon & 1-6pm) Quite possibly Cuba's friendliest, most informative Infotur office. Good info on the city and the Jardines del Rey.

Post Office (cnr Chicho Valdés & Marcial Gómez)

Radio Surco Broadcasting over 1440AM and 98.1FM.

ⓘ Getting There & Away

AIR

Ciego de Ávila's **Máximo Gómez Airport** (AVI; Carretera a Virginia) is 10km northwest of Ceballos, 23km north of Ciego de Ávila and 23km south of Morón.

International flights arrive daily from Canada, Argentina, France, the UK and Italy, and visitors are bussed off to Cayo Coco.

BUS

The **bus station** (Carretera Central), situated about 1.5km east of the center, has daily Víazul services. Five daily Santiago de Cuba (CUC$24, 8½ hours) departures also stop at Camagüey (CUC$6, 1½ hours), Las Tunas (CUC$12, 4½ hours), Holguín (CUC$17, 5¼ hours) and Bayamo (CUC$17, six hours). Four daily Havana (CUC$27, six to seven hours) buses also stop at Sancti Spíritus (CUC$6, 1½ hours) and Santa Clara (CUC$9, 2½ hours). There are also daily buses to Trinidad (CUC$9, 2¾ hours) and Varadero (CUC$19, 6¼ hours). The *circuito norte* Víazul connection now leaves at 2pm daily for Morón (CUC$3, 40 minutes), Caibarién (for Cayo Santa María), Santa Clara, Cienfuegos and Trinidad (CUC$24, 6¼ hours).

TRAIN

The **train station** (22-33-13) is six blocks southwest of the center. Ciego de Ávila is on the main Havana–Santiago railway line. There are nightly trains to Bayamo (CUC$10.50, seven hours), Camagüey (CUC$3.50, 2¼ hours), Guantánamo (CUC$17, 9½ hours), Havana (CUC$15.50, 7½ hours), Holguín (CUC$11, seven hours), Manzanillo (CUC$12, 8½ hours) and Santiago de Cuba (CUC$14, 9¼ hours). Different train numbers run on alternate nights: check the latest timetable before you leave. There are four trains daily to Morón (CUC$1, one hour).

TRUCK

Private passenger trucks leave from the Ferro Ómnibus bus station adjacent to the train station heading in the direction of Morón and Camagüey. Check the blackboards for current details.

ⓘ Getting Around

CAR & MOPED

The **Carretera a Morón gas station** (Carretera de Morón) is just before the bypass road, northeast of the town center. The **Oro Negro gas station** (Carretera Central) is near the bus station.

You can park safely in front of the Hotel Santiago-Habana overnight.

Cubacar (Hotel Ciego de Ávila, Carretera a Ceballos) can help with vehicle rental for around

CIEGO DE ÁVILA PROVINCE CIEGO DE ÁVILA

WORTH A TRIP

JARDINES DE LA REINA

Jardines de la Reina is a 120km-long mangrove-forest and coral-island system situated 80km off the south coast of Ciego de Ávila province and 120km north of the Cayman Islands. The local marine park measures 3800 sq km, with virgin territory left more or less untouched since the time of Columbus. Commercial fishing in the area has been banned, and with a permanent local population of precisely zero inhabitants, visitors must stay on board a two-story, seven-bedroom houseboat called **Hotel Flotante Tortuga**, refurbished in 2008, or venture in from the port of Embarcadero de Júcaro on the mainland aboard the yachts *Halcon* (six-cabin) or *La Reina* (four-cabin). Guests can also use *Caballones* (sleeping six to eight and suited to all kinds of fishing from fly to spin) or the luxury eight-cabin *Avalon Fleet 1*.

The flora consists of palm trees, pines, sea grapes and mangroves, while the fauna – aside from tree rats and iguanas – contains an interesting variety of resident birds, including ospreys, pelicans, spoonbills and egrets. Below the waves the main attraction is sharks (whale and hammerhead), and this, along with the pristine coral and the unequaled clarity of the water, is what draws divers from all over the world.

Getting to the Jardines is not easy – or cheap. The only company currently offering excursions is Italian-run **Avalon** (www.cubanfishingcenters.com). One-week dive packages, which include equipment, six nights of accommodation, guide, park license, 12 dives and transfer from Embarcadero de Júcaro, cost in the vicinity of CUC$1500. Ask for a quote via the website. Another option is to sail with the Windward Islands Cruising Company, departing from Trinidad.

CUC$70 per day. It also rents out mopeds for CUC$24 a day.

TAXI

A taxi ride to the airport will cost around CUC$12; bargain if they're asking more. Book a cab at Hotel Ciego de Ávila or find one in Parque Martí. A one-way ride to Morón is CUC$15; to Cayo Coco it's around CUC$60.

Morón

POP 59,200

Despite its slightly removed position 35km north of Cuba's arterial Carretera Central, Morón remains an important travel nexus (thanks to its railway) and acts as a viable base camp for people not enamored with the resort-heavy Cayo Coco.

Founded in 1543, three centuries before provincial capital Ciego de Ávila, Morón is known island-wide as the Ciudad del Gallo (City of the Cockerel), for a notorious bullying official in the early days who eventually got his comeuppance. Morón has architecture to match its years, with more, better-preserved examples of those Ciego de Ávila columnated house- and shopfronts.

Compact and easygoing, Morón has some excellent casas particulares and offers a surprisingly varied list of things to do in the surrounding countryside.

 Sights

Morón is famous for its emblematic **cockerel**, which stands guard on a roundabout opposite the Hotel Morón on the southern edge of town. It's named after an arrogant ('cocky') and abusive official in the 16th century who got his just desserts at the hands of locals and was driven out of town. The cock crows (electronically) at 6am every morning.

Terminal de Ferrocarriles   NOTABLE BUILDING
(Train Station; Vanhorne, btwn Av de Tarafa & Narciso López) Morón has long been central Cuba's main railway crossroads and exhibits the most elegant railway station outside Havana. Built in 1923, the building's edifice is neocolonial, though inside the busy ticket hall hides a more streamlined art deco look. It's all remarkably well kept. Equally eye-catching is the colorful stained glass skylight.

Museo Caonabo   MUSEUM
(Martí; admission CUC$1; ☺9am-5pm Mon-Sat, 8am-noon Sun) In among the teeming sidewalks and peeling colonnades, this well-laid-out museum of history and archaeology is housed in the city's former bank, an impressive neoclassical building dating from 1919. It's spread over two floors; there is a *mirador* (lookout) on the roof with a good view out over town.

TROCHA DE JÚCARO A MORÓN

Shaped by a volatile history, many of Ciego de Ávila's provincial towns grew up in the mid-19th century around the formidable **Trocha**, a line of fortifications that stretched 68km from Morón in the north to Júcaro in the south, splitting the island in two.

Constructed by the Spanish in the early 1870s using a mixture of black slaves and poorly paid Chinese laborers, the gargantuan Trocha was designed to contain the rebellious armies of the Oriente and stop the seeds of anarchy from spreading west during the First War of Independence.

By the time it was completed in 1872, La Trocha was the most sophisticated military defense system in the colonies, a seemingly unbreakable bastion that included 17 forts, 5000 full-time military guards and a parallel railway line.

Armed to the hilt, it held firm during the First War of Independence, preventing the rebel armies of Antonio Maceo and Máximo Gómez from causing widespread destruction in the richer western provinces of Matanzas and Pinar del Río, where more conservative sugar planters held sway.

Despite renovations that doubled the number of forts and tripled the number of armed guards by 1895, La Trocha proved to be more porous during the Spanish-Cuban-American War, enabling the audacious Maceo to break through and march his army as far west as Pinar del Río.

A handful of old military towers that once acted as lookouts and guardhouses on La Trocha are still scattered throughout the countryside between Ciego de Ávila and Morón, standing as timeworn testaments to a more divisive and violent era.

🛏 Sleeping

Morón's best casas are far superior to its lone 1960s-era hotel.

★ Alojamiento Maité   CASA PARTICULAR $

(☎ 50-41-81; maite68@enet.cu; Luz Caballero No 40B, btwn Libertad & Agramonte; r CUC$20-25; P ✱) Plush facilities and sharp service theme what must be one of Cuba's most professionally run casas particulares. Cast your eye over the wall-mounted TV, starched white sheets (changed daily), complimentary bottles of shampoo, and wine in the fridge, or lounge on the substantial roof terrace with a mojito.

Alojamiento Vista
al Parque   CASA PARTICULAR $

(☎ 50-41-81; yio@moron.cav.sld.cu; Luz Caballero No 49D Altos, btwn Libertad & Agramonte; r CUC$20-25; P ✱ @) There's more of the same comfort and slick service across the street from Maité, in this lovely pale blue house. It has two upstairs rooms and a terrace with views across a well-tended park and is run by Maité's friend Idolka (who speaks some English).

Casa Belky   CASA PARTICULAR $

(☎ 50-57-63; Cristobal Colón No 37; r CUC$20-25) Just one haughty colonial room, but it's a whopper, and with a view onto Parque los Ferrocarriles in possibly the most idyllic location in town. It's just northeast of the train station.

Hotel Morón   HOTEL $

(☎ 50-22-30; Av de Tarafa; s/d CUC$26/42; P ✱ ≋) Morón might be known for its cockerel, but it's the in-house disco that's more likely to keep you awake at this modern-ish, four-story hotel at the southern entrance to town. Package tourists are the main clientele. The pool is a rare highlight; nonguests can ask about day passes. Restaurant on site.

🍴 Eating

Restaurante Maité la Qbana   PALADAR $$

(☎ 50-41-81; Luz Caballero No 40, btwn Libertad & Agramonte; mains around CUC$10; 🖫) Maité is a highly creative cook whose international dishes, prepared with *mucho amor*, will leave you wondering why insipid all-inclusive buffets ever got so popular. Prepare for al dente pasta, fine wine, homemade desserts and paella that has visiting *valencianos* reminiscing about their homeland. It's a good idea to reserve early.

Don Pio Restaurante   CUBAN $$

(Cristobal Colón No 39; CUC$6.50-8.50; ⏰ 10am-10pm) Out you step into the sumptuous back garden of a colonial house – pass the swimming pool and sit down in the *ranchón* (farm)-style, plant-ensconsed, covered patio. Chicken cordon bleu and the like offer diversion from the standard restaurant offerings and there's live piano music at weekends.

Piano Bar   CUBAN $$

(Martí No 386; CUC$12-18; ⏰ noon-11pm) Though you wouldn't guess it from the name, this is one of the best dining options in town outside of the casas. Ticking the main boxes to qualify as 'high end' in provincial Cuba (tablecloths, lack of natural light, icy air-con) you won't find Piano Bar wanting for above-average pork and seafood dishes, or frostily polite service. Live music at weekends.

Self-Catering

On the self-catering front there's the dependable **Doña Neli Dulcería** (Serafín Sánchez No 86, btwn Narciso López & Martí) for bread and pastries and **Supermercado los Balcones** (Martí) for groceries.

🍷 Drinking & Entertainment

The best option is Cabaret Cueva (p317) 6km outside town on the shores of Laguna de la Leche.

Casa de la Cerveza las Fuentes   BAR

(Martí 169) Morón's going overboard to cater to tourists in this ambient-looking new bar. Get the info you need at the on-site Cubatur office first, then start on the beer...

Discoteca Morón   NIGHTCLUB

(Hotel Morón, Av de Tarafa; ⏰ 10pm-late) Young, raucous entertainment-seekers test the patience of sleep-deprived paying guests at the Hotel Morón.

Casa de la Trova Pablo Bernal   LIVE MUSIC

(Libertad No 74, btwn Martí & Narciso López) A good night out in Morón usually decamps at some point to this alfresco music house. Advance bookings are sometimes required, especially for the Wednesday night comedy.

ℹ Information

You'll find internet at **Etecsa** (cnr Martí & Céspedes; ⏰ 8:30am-7:30pm) and there are money-changing facilities at the **Cadeca** (cnr Martí & Gonzalo Arena) in the same street. Information on the Laguna la Redonda and Laguna de la Leche can be procured at **Cubatur** (Martí 169;

9am-5pm), in the same building as Casa de la Cerveza las Fuentes.

ⓘ Getting There & Away

The **bus station** (Martí 12) is on Martí a block back toward the center (north) from the train station. Víazul's latest bus route usefully incorporates Morón in the *circuito norte* (north circuit). Anticlockwise (most relevant), the daily bus leaves Morón at 2:50pm, traverses the north coast to Caibarién, cuts southwest to Santa Clara and Cienfuegos, then heads east to Trinidad (CUC$21, 5½ hours). In the opposite direction, the Ciego de Ávila-bound bus leaves at 12:30pm (CUC$3, 45 minutes). Local buses daily also leave for Ciego de Ávila. From the **train station** (Vanhorne, btwn Av de Tarafa & Narciso López) there are four daily trains to Ciego de Ávila (CUC$1), one to Júcaro and one to Camagüey (CUC$4). The line from Santa Clara to Nuevitas passes through Morón via Chambas.

ⓘ Getting Around

The roads from Morón northwest to Caibarién (112km) and southeast to Nuevitas (168km) are both good. **Cubacar** (Hotel Morón, Av de Tarafa) rents out cars and mopeds, and the **Servi-Cupet gas station** (⊙24hr) is near Hotel Morón.

Around Morón

Just as interesting as Morón itself is the grab bag of attractions to the north.

Laguna de la Leche & Laguna la Redonda

These two large natural lakes lie north of Morón. Redonda is best accessed via the road to Cayo Coco. The 5km entry road for Laguna de la Leche starts just north of Morón's Parque Agramonte. Buses ply the route from the train station.

⊙ Sights & Activities

Laguna de la Leche   LAKE

Laguna de la Leche (Milk Lake), named for its reflective underwater lime deposits, is Cuba's largest natural lake (66 sq km). Its water content is a mixture of fresh and salt water, and anglers flock here to hook the abundant stocks of carp, tarpon, snook and tilapia. Guided fishing trips (CUC$35/70 for four/eight hours) can be arranged from the on-site Flora & Fauna office.

For a little more you can keep your catch and cook it on a mobile barbecue aboard the boat. Explanatory nonfishing boat excursions (CUC$20 for 45 minutes) are also available.

The lake is also the venue for the annual **Morón Aquatic Carnival.** Accessed from the south via a link road from Morón.

Laguna la Redonda   LAKE

(⊙9am-5pm) Anglers, listen up: situated 18km north of Morón, off the Cayo Coco road, the mangroves surrounding this 4-sq-km lake have the island's best square-kilometer density of bass and trout. Four/ eight hours of fishing costs CUC$35/70. Boat trips are available, too, and take in narrow, foliage-covered tributaries – as close to the Amazon as the province comes.

The next world-record largemouth bass will come from Cuba, if fishing here is anything to go by: the lake has already yielded a humongous 9.5kg specimen. Not a fishing fanatic? Rock up at the decent, rustic **bar-restaurant** just for a drink with a lake view. Try the house specialty – a fillet of fish called *calentico* – great with ketchup and Tabasco.

Aguachales de Falla Game Reserve   HUNTING

If you feel the urge, this is where you can take the Hemingway tour to its natural conclusion (Papa loved firing guns at feathered targets). The main attraction of the area for Morón's small-but-dedicated hunting crowd, the reserve contains seven natural lakes and abundant flocks of pigeons, ducks and doves. It's just northwest of Laguna de la Leche.

✗ Eating

★ La Atarraya   SEAFOOD $

(mains CUC$2-7; ⊙noon-6pm) Raised on stilts in a clapboard building just off the southern shoreline of Laguna de la Leche, you'll find one of Cuba's best local fish restaurants. The insanely cheap menu is headlined by *paella valenciana* and *pescado monteroro* (fish fillet with ham and cheese), while the ambience is ebulliently local.

Pescado Frito   SEAFOOD $

(Ranchón la Boca; mains CUC$2-5; ⊙noon-6pm) On Laguna de la Leche's southern shore is this open-air rustic beauty (the sign says 'Ranchón la Boca,' but everyone calls it 'Pescado Frito'). Cross the humpbacked wooden bridge and follow the smell (and crackle) of frying catfish, tilapia and carp.

🍸 Drinking & Entertainment

Cabaret Cueva   CABARET, NIGHTCLUB
(Laguna de la Leche) Locals willingly hitch, walk or carpool to make the 6km trip from Morón to this cabaret in a cave on the southern shores of the Laguna de la Leche.

Loma de Cunagua

Rising like a huge termite mound above the surrounding flatlands, the **Loma de Cunagua** (admission CUC$5; ☺ 9am-4pm), 18km east of Morón, is a protected flora and fauna reserve harboring a *ranchón*-style restaurant, a small network of trails, and excellent birdwatching opportunities. At 364m above sea level, it's the province's highest point, and views over land and ocean are excellent.

Navigate around the reserve via strolls along short bushy trails (in search of tocororos, zunzúns and the like), or by horseback riding. Turn left off the main road at the sign, pay your fee at the gate, and proceed up the steep unpaved road to the summit. A couple of **cabins** (r CUC$30) offer basic overnight accommodation for those in search of some rural tranquility. The Loma is on the Carretera de Bolivia; visits are normally arranged through **Ecotur** (📞 30-81-63; Hotel Sol Coco, Cayo Coco) on Cayo Coco.

Central Patria O Muerte

Cuba's sugar industry is being preserved at this huge rusting ex-sugar mill (c 1914) in the village of Patria, 3km south of Morón.

A 1920 Philadelphia-made Baldwin steam train takes pre-booked tour groups on a 5km jaunt through cane fields to **Rancho Palma** (Carretera a Bolivia Km 7), a bucolic *finca* (farmhouse) with a bar-restaurant where you can sample *guarapo* (pressed cane juice).

The mill and its 263-strong workforce were passed over to the Americans in 1919, and it remained in Yanqui hands until nationalization in 1960. Independent visitors can ask for a tour here, but to get the full train-and-sugarcane treatment you'll need to tag onto a group. Check schedules with Cubatur (p315) in Morón.

Isla Turiguanó

Hold your horses (and cows). You're not in the keys quite yet; Turiguanó isn't a real island. Rather, it is a drained swamp that today plays host to a cattle-breeding ranch, a model revolutionary community and one of Cuba's three pioneering wind farms.

◉ Sights

Ganado Santa Gertrudis   RANCH, RODEO
Santa Gertrudis cattle are bred at this large Isla Turiguanó farm on the main road just before you enter the causeway to Cayo Coco. The adjoining stadium is evidence that in rodeo-land Cuba is right up there with the Calgary Stampede. Cowboys, bulls, horses and lassos are out most weekends around 2pm for exciting 90-minute *espectáculos* (shows).

WORTH A TRIP

LOS BUCHILLONES

Tucked away on the province's northwest coastline, the **Los Buchillones archaeological site** was originally excavated during the 1980s after fishermen began discovering implements such as axe handles and needles in the surrounding swamps.

What became apparent was that Los Buchillones was the location of a sizeable Taíno settlement of between 40 and 50 houses predating European arrival in the region. Everything from *cemíes* (Taíno deities to various Gods of rain, cassava and the like) to canoes and house structures have been subsequently recovered from the excavation site, most of which remains a waterlogged work in progress. The mud at the bottom of the shallow lagoon here was what preserved the artifacts so well and yielded the most significant stash of pre-Columbian relics anywhere in the Greater Antilles.

Many of the artifacts can be seen in either the **Museo Municipal** (Agramonte 80, btwn Calixto García & Martí) in Chambas or Ciego de Ávila's Museo Provincial Simón Reyes (p309). However, anyone with a passing interest in pre-Columbian Cuba should make the trip to the poignant site, complete with a small museum displaying finds, situated halfway between the fishing village of Punta Alegre and Punta San Juan. The once-daily *circuito norte* (north circuit) Víazul bus and a handful of trains pass Chambas, from where Los Buchillones is a 35km drive (public transport is scarce) through Parque Nacional Caguanes.

El Pueblo Holandés VILLAGE

A small community with 49 red-roofed, Dutch-style dwellings, El Pueblo Holandés is on a hill next to the highway, 4km north of Laguna la Redonda. It was built by Celia Sánchez in 1960 as a home for cattle workers. It's an interesting blip on the landscape and worth a short detour.

Florencia

Ringed by gentle hills, the town of Florencia, 40km west of Morón, was named after Florence in Italy by early settlers who claimed that the surrounding countryside reminded them of Tuscany. The town grew up around the Santa Clara–Nuevitas railway in the 1920s. In the early 1990s the Cuban government constructed a hydroelectric dam, the **Liberación de Florencia**, on the Río Chambas and the resulting lake has become a recreational magnet for nature lovers. Activities available here include horseback riding through the Florencia hills, kayaking, aqua-biking, and a boat ride on the lake to a tiny key called La Presa with a restaurant and small zoo. The area's focal point is a ranch called **La Presa de Florencia** (☉9am-5pm) by the side of the lake in Florencia. Get more details at Infotur (p312) in Ciego de Ávila or Cubatur (p315) in Morón. For a place to stay you may get lucky in the lovely **Campismo Boquerón**, 5km west of Florencia, which is normally able to accept foreigners. Enquire at La Presa de Florencia.

Cayo Coco

Situated in the Archipiélago de Sabana-Camagüey, or the Jardines del Rey as travel brochures prefer to call it, Cayo Coco is Cuba's fourth-largest island and the main tourist destination after Varadero. The area north of the Bahía de Perros (Bay of Dogs) was uninhabited before 1992, when the first hotel – the Cojímar – went up on adjoining Cayo Guillermo. The bulldozers haven't stopped buzzing since.

While the beauty of the beaches on these islands is world famous, Cayo Coco pre-1990 was little more than a mosquito-infested mangrove swamp. Early visitors included Diego Velázquez, who named the islands in honour of then King of Spain, Ferdinand II, and later French corsair Jacques de Sores, fresh from successful raids on Havana and Puerto Príncipe. They were followed in 1752 by the island's first landowner, an opportunistic Spaniard named Santiago Abuero Castañeda. Between 1927 and 1955 a community of 600 people scraped a living by producing charcoal for use as domestic fuel

Cayo Coco & Cayo Guillermo

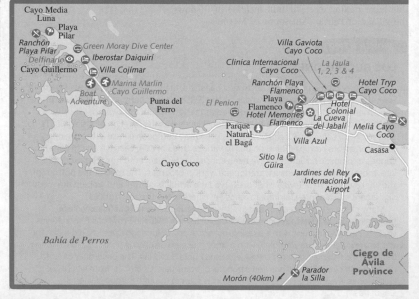

on the island but, with the rise of electrical power after the Revolution, this too died.

Since 1988 Cayo Coco has been connected to the mainland by a 27km causeway slicing across the Bahía de Perros. There are also causeways from Cayo Coco to Cayo Guillermo in the west and to Cayo Romano in the east.

◉ Sights

Parque Natural el Bagá   NATURE RESERVE
(☺ 9:30am-5:30pm) Bagá was a commendable eco project sited on what was Cayo Coco's original airport, a 769-hectare natural park sublimely mixing dense mangroves, lakes, idyllic coastline, trails and an incredible 130 species of bird. It's sublime but, unfortunately, falling into disrepair. The park is no longer staffed by the informative guides that once showed visitors around, although you can meander solo.

Wander about (the guard is more amenable after a tip) and see, alongside the bird species, *jutías* (tree rats), iguanas, crocodiles and flamingos. Cayo Coco hotels may arrange tours here by request. Going independently, you'll miss out on an education in resident wildlife. The jury's out on whether closure is temporary or indefinite.

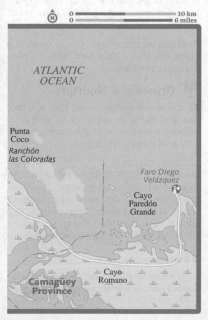

Cayo Paredón Grande   ISLAND

East of Cayo Coco, a road crosses Cayo Romano and turns north to Cayo Paredón Grande and **Faro Diego Velázquez**, a 52m working lighthouse that dates from 1859. This area has a couple of beaches, including much-lauded Playa los Pinos, and is good for fishing.

🏃 Activities

The **Marina Marlin Aguas Tranquilas** (www.nauticamarlin.com), near the Meliá Cayo Coco, offers deep-sea fishing outings (CUC$270 per four hours).

The **Centro Internacional de Buceo Coco Diving** (www.nauticamarlin.com), on the west side of Hotel Tryp Cayo Coco (p320), is accessible via a dirt road to the beach. Scuba diving costs CUC$40, plus CUC$10 for gear. The open-water certification course costs CUC$365; less in low season. The diving area stretches for over 10km mainly to the east, and there are six certified instructors with the capacity for 30 divers per day. **Centro Internacional de Buceo Blue Diving** (www.nauticamarlin.com) in Hotel Meliá Cayo Coco (p320) offers similar services. Dive masters are multilingual, and there are liveaboard options.

☞ Tours

There's no lack of day excursions available from the main hotel information desks, which are usually staffed by Cubatur (p315) or **Cubanacán** representatives. Highlights include Por la Ruta de Hemingway (a journey through the keys mentioned in Hemingway's novel *Islands in the Stream*), a motorboat cruise around Cayo Paredón Grande, a flamingo-spotting tour or a jaunt out to Cayo Mortero via the fabulous snorkelling spot of Grunt Hole for downtime with cold beer and fresh fish. Prices are in the CUC$25 to CUC$30 range.

🛏 Sleeping

Cayo Coco's all-inclusive resorts are policed pretty diligently. Unless you're wearing the 'access all areas' plastic wristband, think twice about sneaking in to use the toilets. Room rates are all-inclusive.

Sitio la Güira   CABINS **$**
(📞 30-12-08; cabaña CUC$25; ❄) 🚗 A simple abode situated on a small farm 8km west of the Servi-Cupet gas station, La Güira rents four pseudo-rustic *bohíos* (thatched huts)

with private bathrooms and – get this – air-con (to dissuade the mosquitoes apparently). There's a *ranchón*-style restaurant and bar on site.

Villa Azul HOTEL **$**
(**🖉**30-12-78; r CUC$32) You're here for the price. This cheapie is a couple of kilometers' walk from the beach, 1500m after the roundabout on the Cayo Guillermo road. Rooms just round the corner from reception and up a couple of floors are best. The standard's not bad, although the odor of tumbleweed is never far away.

★ Meliá Cayo Coco RESORT **$$$**
(**🖉**30-11-80; s/d CUC$335/390; **P**❄**@**☒) This intimate resort on Playa las Coloradas, at the hotel strip's eastern end, is everything you'd expect from Spain's Meliá chain. For a luxury twist try staying in one of the elegant white bungalows perched on stilts in a lagoon. Prices are high, but the Meliá is unashamedly classy and a 'no kids' policy enhances the tranquility.

Hotel Colonial RESORT **$$$**
(**🖉**30-13-11; s/d CUC$125/210; **P**❄**@**☒) The Colonial is a pleasant break from the notoriously appalling design of the usual Cuban all-inclusives: it has Spanish colonial villas with attractively tiled public areas that lend it a somewhat cloistered, refined air.

This was the island's first hotel when it opened in 1993 (ancient history by Cayo Coco standards). It gained notoriety in 1994 when, according to Cuban media, gunmen from right-wing Cuban exile movement Alpha 66 opened fire on the building. Fortunately, no one was hurt.

Hotel Memories Flamenco HOTEL **$$$**
(**🖉**30-41-00; www.memoriesresorts.com; s/d CUC$157/204; **P**❄☒) The latest addition to Cayo Coco's steadily expanding hotel scene, with 624 decent-sized rooms (recently done up, they're pretty clean) in attractive, villa-style, three-floor buildings around two pools (one with a swim-up bar). There's an attractive Asian restaurant, although overall service will leave you wondering which planet those five stars descended from. Staff are on a 'learning curve,' let's say.

Hotel Tryp Cayo Coco RESORT **$$$**
(**🖉**30-13-00; s/d CUC$189/271; **P**❄**@**☒🖬) The family choice. Tryp is a quintessential all-inclusive with a meandering pool, myriad bars and nightly tourist show. Facilities are good, although overzealous poolside 'entertainers' lend the place a holiday-camp feel at times. The 500-plus rooms – in sunny three-story apartment blocks – are big, with balconies and huge beds, although finishes are a little worn, considering room prices.

🍴 Eating

Amid the ubiquitous as-much-as-you-can-eat hotel buffets, there are some rather good independent restaurants – mainly thatched-roof, *ranchón*-style places on or near the beaches.

Restaurant Sitio la Güira CARIBBEAN **$$**
(dishes CUC$2-12; ☉8am-11pm) Set in the old reconstructed charcoal burners' camp, La Güira's food is fresh, plentiful and not too charcoaly. Try the big, fresh sandwiches for CUC$2 or the shrimp plates for CUC$12. Strumming music trios do the rounds.

Parador la Silla CARIBBEAN **$$**
(mains CUC$7-12; ☉9am-5pm) A thatched-roof snack bar halfway along the causeway into Cayo Coco. After a full plate of *comida criolla*, you can climb an adjacent lookout tower and try to spot distant specks of pink (flamingos).

Ranchón Playa Flamenco CARIBBEAN **$$**
(mains CUC$7-12; ☉9am-4pm) Eat exquisite seafood, drink cold beer, swim, snorkel, sunbathe, eat more seafood, drink more beer... you get the picture.

Ranchón las Coloradas CARIBBEAN **$$**
(mains CUC$7-12; ☉9am-4pm) Seafood in a paradisiacal setting.

🍸 Drinking & Nightlife

All the *ranchónes* reviewed have attached bars and the all-inclusive hotels have a full nightly entertainment program (usually only available to hotel guests).

La Cueva del Jabalí NIGHTCLUB
(admission CUC$5; ☉10:30pm-2am Tue-Thu) For those bored with the all-inclusive floor show, this is the only independent entertainment venue, 5km west of the Tryp complex, in a natural cave. The place features a cabaret show and it's free all day to visit the bar.

ℹ Information

Euros are accepted in all the Cayo Coco resorts.
Banco Financiero Internacional At the Servi-Cupet gas station.

Clínica Internacional Cayo Coco ([☎]30-21-58; Av de los Hoteles al final) Provides medical treatment. West of Hotel Colonial, next to Villa Gaviota Cayo Coco.

Infotur (www.infotur.cu) Has a helpful office at the Jardines del Rey airport. There are also desks at most of the main hotels.

❶ Getting There & Around

Cayo Coco's **Aeropuerto Internacional Jardines del Rey** ([☎]30-91-65) is equipped with a 3km runway and can process 1.2 million visitors annually. Weekly flights arrive here from Canada and the UK. There's a daily service to and from Havana (about CUC$90) with Aerocaribbean.

Although getting to Cayo Coco is nigh on impossible without a car or taxi (or bike), getting around has become infinitely easier since the introduction of a **Transtur** ([☎]30-11-75) hop-on/hop-off minibus. The service varies according to season, but expect a minimum service of two buses per day in either direction, with six scheduled for peak times. The bus runs east–west between Meliá Cayo Coco and Playa Pilar, stopping at all Cayo Coco and Cayo Guillermo hotels as well as Parque Natural el Bagá. An all-day pass costs CUC$5.

A taxi to Cayo Coco from Morón will cost about CUC$40; from Ciego de Ávila, closer to CUC$60. You pay a CUC$2 fee to enter the causeway.

You can rent a car or moped at **Cubacar** ([☎]30-12-75) on the second roundabout between the Meliá (p320) and Tryp (p320) complexes. Cubacar also has a desk at all the major hotels. Bicycles are in short supply at Cayo Coco's hotels. Ask around.

Cayo Guillermo

Ah, Cayo Guillermo: haunt of pink flamingos, stunning blond beaches and Cuba's second-most famous Ernesto after Mr Guevara – Señor Hemingway. It was Hemingway who initiated Guillermo's early publicity drive, describing it radiantly in his posthumously published Cuban novel *Islands in the Stream* (1970). Development of the northern *cayos* began in 1988 with the opening of a small floating hotel, and was anchored in 1993 when the first land-based all-inclusive resort on the cayos, Villa Cojímar, received its first guests. Long a prized deep-sea fishing spot, 13-sq-km Guillermo retains a more exotic feel than its larger eastern cousin to which it is connected by a causeway. The mangroves off the south coast are home to pink flamingos and pelicans, and there's a tremendous diversity of tropical fish and crustaceans on the Atlantic reef.

🏃 Activities

Marina Marlin Cayo Guillermo   FISHING
([☎]30-17-37) On the right of the causeway as you arrive from Cayo Coco, this 36-berth marina is one of Cuba's seven certified international entry ports. You can organize deep-sea fishing for mackerel, pike, barracuda, red snapper and marlin here on large boats that troll 5km to 13km offshore. Prices start at CUC$290 per half-day (four persons).

Boat Adventure   BOAT TOUR
This popular activity has its own separate dock on the left-hand side of the causeway

---

PLAYA PILAR
....

Sometimes travel can be anticlimactic; the exalted sight, when you finally get there, doesn't quite live up to the hype. No such letdown applies to **Playa Pilar**, a sublime strip of sand on Cayo Guillermo that's regularly touted as Cuba's, and the Caribbean's, greatest beach. Pilar's claim rests on two lofty pillars. First, there's the diamond-dust white sand, so fine that if you drop a handful, it will blow away rather than hit the ground (so say the locals). Second, there are the rugged 15m-high sand dunes (the largest of their kind in the Caribbean) strafed by rough trails that incite exploration. You can hike along the beach back to Guillermo's nearest hotel, a breathtaking 7km, or pitch north to the *cayo*'s (key's) tip.

The sea at Pilar is warm, shallow and loaded with excellent snorkeling possibilities. One kilometer away across a calm channel lies the shimmering sands of **Cayo Media Luna**, a one-time beach escape of Fulgencio Batista. Regular boats provide passage to the key (CUC$11), or you can partake in a day-long catamaran excursion (CUC$49) including snorkeling and lobster lunch. The hop-on/hop-off bus from Cayo Coco stops at Playa Pilar six times daily in either direction during peak season (two to four times otherwise). There's an excellent bar-restaurant nestled in the dunes.

as you enter Guillermo. For CUC$41 you are treated to a two-hour motorboat trip (with a chance to operate the controls) through the key's natural mangrove channels. Trips leave four times daily starting from 9am.

★**Delfinario**   DOLPHIN SWIM
(🏊 30-15-29; adult/child per session CUC$110/60; ⏱10am-5pm) Cayo Guillermo's new attraction is this center which, like many across Cuba, offers the chance to swim with dolphins. However, this is several notches up on the ecofriendly scale. It advertises itself as an 'interactive' experience (normal interaction time 30 minutes) and it's a well-managed place, with knowledgeable staff who care about the animals' welfare. There's a bar/restaurant on site.

Green Moray Dive Center   DIVING
The dive center is in Hotel Meliá Cayo Guillermo, just north of Iberostar Daiquirí. It charges CUC$45 for one dive with equipment.

🛏 Sleeping & Eating

Guillermo has four hotels at present, lined up on its northern shore; there are plans for two more. As well as the Daiquirí and Cojímar, you'll find the familiar luxury Sol/Meliá combo.

Villa Cojímar   HOTEL **$$**
(🏊 30-17-12; r CUC$85-135; 🅿❄@☷) The oldest hotel on the Sabana-Camagüey archipelago opened back in 1993, and it comprises a rather low-key collection of bungalows in a quiet beachside location. The advertising blurb refers to it as a 'Cuban-style hotel,' but the only Cubans you're likely to meet are the people who make up your room.

★**Iberostar Daiquirí**   HOTEL **$$$**
(🏊 30-16-50; s/d CUC$175/270; 🅿❄@☷) Plenty of shade, a lily pond, and a curtain of water cascading in front of the pool bar add up to make the Daiquirí the pick of the bunch in Guillermo. The 312 rooms are encased in attractive colonial-style apartment blocks, and the thin slice of paradisiacal beach is straight out of the brochure. Extensive gardens are a bonus.

★**Ranchón Playa Pilar**   CARIBBEAN **$$**
(mains CUC$7-12; ⏱9am-4pm) Not staying here? Worry not – Cuba's greatest beach also has an excellent bar and restaurant with fresh lobster and boneless chicken fillets as spectacular as the view.

ℹ Information

Euros are accepted in all the Cayo Guillermo resorts.
Banco Financiero Internacional At Iberostar Daiquirí hotel.

ℹ Getting There & Around

Access information is the same as for Cayo Coco. The twice-daily hop-on, hop-off bus (p321) carries people to and from Cayo Coco, stopping at all four Cayo Guillermo hotels and terminating at Playa Pilar. An all-day ticket costs CUC$5.

Cars can be hired from **Cubacar** (🏊 30-17-43; Villa Cojímar).

Camagüey Province

♩ 32 / POP 780.600

Best Places to Eat

➡ Café Ciudad (p332)

➡ Restaurante 1800 (p332)

➡ El Bucanero (p341)

➡ Restaurante Italiano Santa Teresa (p332)

Best Places to Stay

➡ Gran Hotel (p332)

➡ Casa de Magalis (p337)

➡ Los Vitrales (p330)

➡ Motel la Belén (p336)

Why Go?

Neither Occidente nor Oriente, Camagüey is Cuba's provincial contrarian, a region that likes to go its own way in political and cultural matters – and usually does – much to the chagrin of folks in Havana and Santiago.

Seeds were sown in the colonial era, when Camagüey's preference for cattle ranching over sugarcane meant less reliance on slave labor and more enthusiasm to get rid of a system that bred misery.

Today Cuba's largest province is a mostly pancake-flat pastoral mix of grazing cattle, lazy old sugar mill towns and, in the south, a few low-but-lovely hill ranges. It's flanked by Cuba's two largest archipelagos: the Sabana-Camagüey in the north and the Jardines de la Reina in the south, both underdeveloped and almost virgin in places.

Staunchly Catholic capital Camagüey is, with its alluring architecture and cosmopolitan charm surpassed in Cuba only by Havana, pin-up for the province. It's a fiercely independent city that nurtured revolutionary poet Nicolás Guillén, groundbreaking scientist Carlos J Finlay and an internationally famous ballet company.

When to Go

➡ There's debate about the actual year of Camagüey's founding (the 500th anniversary is being celebrated in 2014 with innumerable parties) – everyone, however, hits the streets in February to celebrate Jornada de la Cultura Camagüeyana (Days of Camagüeyan Culture).

➡ For outdoor enthusiasts, March is prime time for viewing migratory birds on the northern keys.

➡ In Playa Santa Lucía, the amazing underwater shark-feeding show is held when sharks are in the area between June and January.

➡ In September, Camagüey showcases some more of its cultural prowess with the Festival Nacional de Teatro (National Theater Festival).

Camagüey Province Highlights

❶ Retreat into the **Sierra del Chorrillo**, harboring rare birds and petrified forests (p336).

❷ Watch dive instructors fearlessly feed sharks off **Playa Santa Lucía** (p339).

❸ Discover huge flamingo nesting sites on the **Refugio de Fauna Silvestre Río Máximo** (p339).

❹ Say your penance in Camagüey and find Cuba's Catholic soul in a stash of colonial **churches** (p328).

❺ Stop in **Guáimaro**, where Cuba's first constitution was signed (p337).

❻ Go fly-fishing for tarpon and bonefish in the shallow flats off **Cayo Cruz** (p338).

❼ Explore the most sophisticated restaurant scene at one of Camagüey's delectable eateries, like **Restaurante 1800** (p332).

❽ Go shopping for fresh produce with the locals at Camagüey's **Mercado Agropecuario Hatibonico** (p330).

Camagüey

POP 306,400

Welcome to the maze. Camagüey's odd, labyrinthine layout is by-product of two centuries spent fighting off musket-toting pirates like Henry Morgan: tumultuous times led the fledgling settlement to develop a peculiar street pattern designed to confuse pillaging invaders and provide cover for its long-suffering residents (or so legend has it). As a result, Camagüey's sinuous streets and narrow winding alleys are more reminiscent of a Moroccan medina than the geometric grids of Lima or Mexico City.

Sandwiched on Carretera Central halfway between Ciego de Ávila and Las Tunas, the city of *tinajones* (clay pots), as Camagüey is sometimes known, is Cuba's third-largest city, easily the suavest and most sophisticated after Havana, and the bastion of the Catholic Church on the island. Well known for going their own way in times of crisis, the resilient citizens are popularly called '*agramontinos*' by other Cubans, after local First War of Independence hero Ignacio Agramonte, coauthor of the Guáimaro constitution and courageous leader of Cuba's finest cavalry brigade. In 2008 its well-preserved historical center was made Cuba's ninth Unesco World Heritage Site.

Camagüey's warrenlike streets generally inspire travelers, what with their hidden plazas, rearing baroque churches, riveting galleries and congenial bars/restaurants. The flip side is the higher-than-average number of *jineteros* (touts) who can dog you as you stroll. Take to the maze and discover it for yourself.

History

Founded in February 1514 as one of Diego Velázquez' hallowed seven 'villas', Santa María del Puerto Príncipe was originally established on the coast near present-day Nuevitas. Due to a series of rebellions by the local Taíno people, the site of the city was moved twice in the early 16th century, finally taking up its present location in 1528. Its name was changed to Camagüey in 1903, in honor of the camagua tree, which, so runs an indigenous legend, all life is descended from.

Camagüey developed quickly in the 1600s, despite continued attacks by corsairs, with an economy based on sugar production and cattle-rearing. Due to acute water shortages in the area, the townsfolk were forced

CAMAGÜEY STREET NAMES

Asking for directions? To make things even more confusing, locals doggedly stick to using the old names of streets, even though signs and maps carry the new names.

OLD NAME	NEW NAME
Estrada Palma	Agramonte
Francisquito	Quiñones
Pobre	Padre Olallo
Rosario	Enrique Villuendas
San Estéban	Oscar Primelles
San Fernando	Bartolomé Masó
San José	José Ramón Silva
Santa Rita	El Solitario

to make *tinajones* in order to collect rainwater and even today Camagüey is known as the city of *tinajones* – with the pots now serving a strictly ornamental purpose.

Besides swashbuckling independence hero Ignacio Agramonte, Camagüey has produced several personalities of note, including poet and patriot Nicolás Guillén and eminent doctor Carlos J Finlay, the man who was largely responsible for discovering the causes of yellow fever. In 1959 the prosperous citizens quickly fell foul of the Castro revolutionaries when local military commander Huber Matos (Fidel's one-time ally) accused El Líder Máximo of burying the Revolution. He was duly arrested and later thrown in prison for his pains.

Loyally Catholic, Camagüey welcomed Pope John Paul II in 1998, and in 2008 hosted the beatification of Cuba's first saint, 'Father of the Poor' Fray José Olallo, who aided the wounded of both sides in the 1868–78 War of Independence. Raúl Castro attended the ceremony.

◉ Sights

◎ City Centre

★ **Plaza San Juan de Dios** SQUARE
(cnr Hurtado & Paco Recio) Looking more Mexican than Cuban (Mexico was capital of New Spain so the colonial architecture was often superior), Plaza San Juan de Dios is Camagüey's most picturesque and beautifully preserved corner. Its eastern aspect is dominated by the Museo de San Juan de Dios, formerly a hospital. Behind the square's

Camagüey

FLORAT

Hotel Puerto
Principe (160m)

Ignacio Sánchez

15

Train
Station

Joaquín de Agüero

regional
bus station

Av Carlos J Finlay

Parque
Finlay

Airport
Bus 22

LAS
MERCEDES

Quiñones

Santayana

Santa Rosa

San Martín

Esteban Varona

J Ramón Silva

25

23

Heredia

El Solitario

27

P

39
49

47

38

Avellaneda

Padre Olallo

Fidel Céspedes

Calixio
García

Gral Espinosa

San Ramón

Enrique Varona

24

Ramón Guerrero

18

45

46

República

48

Oscar Primelles

Enrique Villuendas

Padre Valencia

Finlay

28

Jaime

Astilleros

Sin Salida

8

42

10

11

Av Agramonte

Plaza de los
Trabajadores

36

30

14

Maceo

32

21

12

50

22

Padre Olallo

Alegría

Iglesia de Santa
Ana (200m)

General Gómez

Avellaneda

Bartolomé Masó

Tío Perico

Príncipe

41

20

5

Plaza
Maceo

Hermanos Agüero

31

Triana

26

Río Hatibonico

Av Tarata

Casa de
Arte Jover

1

29

37

Martí

Parque
Martí

Luaces

Plaza de la
Revolución

17

Parque
Ignacio
Agramonte

Academia

43

Cristo

40

4

7

9
19

Enrique Villuendas

Necropolis de
Camagüey (500m)

44

Río Juan del Toro

Raúl Lamar

Paco Recio

33

Independencia

Cisneros

San Pablo

República

Casino
Campestre

Cornelio Porro

6

Centro Cultural
Caribe (400m);
Restaurante Italiano
Santa Teresa (550m);
Iglesia de la
Caridad (800m)

Hospital

34

35

Hurtado

13

Carretera Central

Plaza San
Juan de Dios

3

Museo
de San Juan
2 de Dios

Plaza San
Juan de Dios

Mercado Agropecuario
Hatibonico (180m)

16

Av de la Libertad

N

0   200 m
0   0.1 miles

Camagüey

CAMAGÜEY PROVINCE CAMAGÜEY

arresting blue, yellow and pink building facades lurk several great restaurants.

★ **Museo de San Juan de Dios** MUSEUM
(admission CUC$1; ⊙9am-5pm Tue-Sat, to 1pm Sun) The Museo de San Juan de Dios is housed in what was once a hospital administered by Father José Olallo, the friar who became Cuba's first saint. It has a front cloister dating from 1728 and a unique triangular rear patio with Moorish touches, built in 1840. Since ceasing to function as a hospital in 1902, the building has served as a teachers college, a refuge during the 1932 cyclone, and the Centro Provincial de Patrimonio directing the restoration of Camagüey's monuments. The museum chronicles Camagüey's history and exhibits some local paintings.

★ **Casa de Arte Jover** GALLERY
(Martí No 154, btwn Independencia & Cisneros) Camagüey is home to two of Cuba's most creative and prodigious contemporary painters, Joel Jover and his wife Ileana Sánchez. Their magnificent home in Plaza Agramonte functions both as a gallery and a piece of art in its own right, with a slew of original art and delightfully kitschy antiques on show.

You're welcome to browse and, if you like high-quality original art, buy a painting. The artists also keep a studio and showroom, the **Estudio-Galería Jover** (Paco

CUBA'S CATHOLIC SOUL

If Cuba has a Catholic soul, it undoubtedly resides in Camagüey, a city of baroque churches and gilded altars, where ecclesial spires rise like minarets above the narrow tangle of streets.

Any exploration of Camagüey's religious history should begin at its most important church, the **Catedral de Nuestra Señora de la Candelaria** (Cisneros No 168), rebuilt in the 19th century on the site of an earlier chapel dating from 1530. The cathedral, which is named for the city's patron saint, was fully restored with funds raised from Pope John Paul II's 1998 visit. While not Camagüey's most eye-catching church, it is noted for its noble Christ statue that sits atop a craning bell tower.

The **Iglesia de Nuestra Señora de la Merced** (Plaza de los Trabajadores), dating from 1748, is arguably Camagüey's most impressive colonial church. Local myth tells of a miraculous figure that floated from the watery depths here in 1601: it's been a place of worship ever since. The active convent in the attached cloister is distinguished by its two-level arched interior, spooky catacombs (where church faithful were buried until 1814) and the dazzling Santo Sepulcro, a solid-silver coffin.

Gleaming after a much-lauded 2007 renovation, **Iglesia de Nuestra Señora de la Soledad** (cnr República & Av Agramonte) is a massive brick structure dating from 1779. Its picturesque cream-and-terracotta tower actually predates the rest of the structure and is an eye-catching landmark on the city skyline. Inside there are ornate baroque frescoes and the hallowed font where Ignacio Agramonte was baptized in 1841.

Baroque becomes Gothic in rectangular Parque Martí, a few blocks east of Parque Ignacio Agramonte, where the triple-spired **Iglesia de Nuestra Corazón de Sagrado Jesús** (cnr República & Luaces) dazzles with its ornate stained glass, ironwork and updated interpretation of Europe's favorite medieval architectural style (a rarity in Cuba).

The **Iglesia de Nuestra Señora del Carmen** (Plaza del Carmen), a twin-towered baroque beauty dating from 1825, is another church that shares digs with a former convent. The Monasterio de las Ursalinas is a sturdy arched colonial building with a pretty, cloistered courtyard that once provided shelter for victims of the furious 1932 hurricane. Today it is the City Historian's offices.

The **Iglesia de San Lazaro** (Cnr Carretera Central Oeste & Calle Cupey) is a beautiful (if diminutive) cream-coloured church dating from 1700, although as interesting is the nearby cloistered hospital constructed nearby a century later by virtuous Franciscan monk Padre Valencia to nurse leprosy victims. It's 2km west of the center.

The **Iglesia de San Cristo del Buen Viaje** (Plaza del Cristo), next door to the necropolis and overlooking a quiet square, is one of the least visited of Camagüey's ecclesial nonet, but it is worth a peek if you're visiting the Necropolis de Camagüey (behind). An original chapel was raised here in 1723, but the current structure is of mainly 19th-century vintage.

Iglesia de la Caridad (cnr Av de la Libertad & Sociedad Patriotica) stands sentinel on the southeastern edge of the city. Constructed originally as a chapel in the 18th century, it got a couple of 20th-century renovations (1930 and 1945) and has a fine silver altar (c 1730) and image of the Virgin de la Caridad del Cobre complete with an embossment of Cuba's national flower, la mariposa (white jasmine).

Finally, there's **Iglesia de Santa Ana** (Plazoleta de Santa Ana), built in 1697 and modified in the 19th century with the help of wealthy hacienda owner Don Miguel Iriarte.

Recio; ⊘ 9am-noon & 3-5pm Mon-Sat) in Plaza San Juan de Dios.

Museo Casa Natal de Ignacio Agramonte
MUSEUM

(Av Agramonte No 459; admission CUC$2; ⊘ 9am-4:45pm Mon-Sat, to 2:30pm Sun) This is the birthplace of independence hero Ignacio Agramonte (1841–73), the cattle rancher who led the Camagüey area's revolt against Spain. The house – an elegant colonial building in its own right – tells the oft-overlooked role of Camagüey and Agramonte in the First War of Independence.

In July 1869 rebel forces under Agramonte bombarded Camagüey, and four years later

Agramonte was killed in action, aged only 32. You can hear Cuban folk singer Silvio Rodríguez' anthem to this hero, a hero who was nicknamed 'El Mayor' (Major), on his album *Días y flores*. The hero's gun is one of his few personal possessions displayed. It's opposite Iglesia de Nuestra Señora de la Merced, on the corner of Independencia.

Parque Ignacio Agramonte   SQUARE
(cnr Martí & Independencia) This dazzling square in the heart of the city lures visitors with rings of marble benches and an equestrian statue (c 1950) of Camagüey's precocious War of Independence hero.

Casa Finlay   MUSEUM
(Cristo, btwn Cisneros & Lugareño; ⊙ 8am-5pm Mon-Fri, to noon Sat) Camagüey's other hero, Dr Carlos J Finlay, was more concerned with saving lives than taking them. This small museum at the site of his birth documents his life and scientific feats, most notably his medical breakthrough in discovering how mosquitoes transmit yellow fever. There's a splendid indoor patio.

Maqueta de la Ciudad   MUSEUM
(cnr Independencia & General Gómez; admission CUC$1; ⊙ 9am-9pm) Cuban cities No 1 (Havana) and No 2 (Santiago) have got them, so why not No 3? Relishing its new Unesco status, Camagüey has built this fine scale model of itself in a pleasant air-conditioned colonial building with a wraparound mezzanine gallery for better viewing. Interesting displays (in Spanish) explain the architecture and urban design.

Galería el Colonial   NOTABLE BUILDING
(cnr Av Agramonte & República; ⊙ 9am-5pm) A shopping complex, Cuban-style, with all its engaging foibles and takes on commerce. It's difficult to say if this pink colonial building, spruced up for the city's 500th anniversary preparations, is more sight or shopaholic satisfier. Certainly you can buy rum or cigars, or sit down for a coffee, but perhaps this is more about the overall experience.

Casa Natal de Nicolás Guillén   CULTURAL CENTER
(Hermanos Agüero No 58; ⊙ 9am-5pm) FREE This modest house gives visitors an insight into Cuba's late national poet and his books, and today doubles as the Instituto Superior de Arte, where local students study music.

⊙ West of the City Centre

Plaza del Carmen   SQUARE
(Hermanos Agüero, btwn Honda & Carmen) Around 600m west of the frenzy of República sits another jaw-droppingly beautiful square, one less-visited than the central plazas. It's backed on the eastern side by the masterful Iglesia de Nuestra Señora del Carmen (p328), one of the prettiest city churches.

Little more than a decade ago Plaza del Carmen was a ruin, but it's now restored to a state better than the original. The cobbled central space has been infused with giant *tinajones*, atmospheric street lamps and unique life-sized sculptures of *camagüeyanos* going about their daily business (reading newspapers and gossiping, mostly).

Martha Jiménez Pérez   GALLERY
(Martí No 282, btwn Carmen & Onda; ⊙ 9am-5pm Mon-Sat) FREE You're in Cuba's ceramics capital so why not gravitate to the studio-gallery of Martha Jiménez Pérez, one of its best living artists, to see everything from pots to paintings being produced and peruse the results? It's on the pedestrian approach to Plaza del Carmen.

Necropolis de Camagüey   CEMETERY
(Plaza del Cristo; ⊙ 7am-6pm) FREE This sea of elaborate, lop-sided, bleached-white Gothic tombs makes up Cuba's most underrated cemetery, secreting the resting place of Camagüey-born independence hero Ignacio Agramonte, among others. It might not quite have the clout of Havana's Cementerio Colón but isn't too far behind in its roll-call of famous incumbents.

Agramonte lies halfway down the second avenue on the left after the entrance (the blue-painted tomb). Harder to find are tombs such as those to Camagüey freedomfighters Tomás Betancourt or Salvador Cisneros Betancourt (once-time President of Cuba); show up for tours which depart from the entrance behind Iglesia de San Cristo de Buen Viaje (early to mid-morning is best).

⊙ North of the City Centre

North of the train station, **Avenida de los Martires** opens up in a kilometer-long symphony of noble colonnaded 19th-century buildings, the most complete such example in Cuba.

Museo Provincial Ignacio Agramonte
MUSEUM

(Av de los Mártires No 2; admission CUC$2; ⊙ 10am-1pm & 2-6pm Tue-Sat, 9am-1pm Sun) Named (like half of Camagüey) after the exalted local War of Independence hero, this cavernous museum, just north of the train station, is in a building that was erected in 1848 as a Spanish cavalry barracks. It now contains some impressive artwork, including much by Camagüey natives like Fidelio Ponce, besides antique furniture and old family heirlooms.

The upstairs art collection features many Camagüey artists: there is both 19th- and early 20th-century art such as the haunting work of *camagüeyano* Fidelio Ponce, and *artes plasticos* (modern art) by nationally renowned figures like Alfredo Sosabravo.

◉ South & East of the City Centre

Casino Campestre
PARK

(Carretera Central) Over the Río Hatibonico from the old town is Cuba's largest urban park, laid out in 1860. There's shaded benches, a baseball stadium, concerts and activities. On a traffic island near the park entrance is a **monument** dedicated to Mariano Barberán and Joaquín Collar, Spaniards who made the first nonstop flight between Spain (Seville) and Cuba (Camagüey) in 1933.

The pair made the crossing in their plane *Cuatro Vientos*, but tragically the plane disappeared when flying to Mexico a week later. Ubiquitous bici-taxis are on hand to pedal you around.

Mercado Agropecuario Hatibonico
MARKET

(Matadero; ⊙ 7am- 6pm) If you visit just one market in Cuba, make sure it's this one. Glued (by mud) beside the murky Río Hatibonico just off the Carretera Central, and characterized by its *pregones* (singsong, often comic, offering of wares) ringing through the stalls, this is a classic example of Cuban-style free enterprise juxtaposed with cheaper but lower-quality government stalls.

The best section to visit is the *herberos* (purveyors of herbs, potions and secret elixirs); also visit the plant nursery where Cubans can buy dwarf mango trees and various ornamental plants. Keep a tight hold on your money belt.

Palacio de los Matrimonios
NOTABLE BUILDING

(cnr Av de la Libertad & Carretera Central) One of several grand buildings on the Av de la Libertad, this Palacio de los Matrimonios, where *camagüeyenos* tie the knot, is one of Cuba's most striking: a mix of colonial and art deco influences. Stroll through shady palm-filled grounds (if they're open) and watch the newlyweds celebrate. One, two, three... ahhh...

🎉 Festivals & Events

The **Jornada de la Cultura Camagüeyana** celebrates the anniversary of the city's founding in February. The annual carnival, known as the **San Juan Camagüeyano**, runs from June 24 to 29 and includes dancers, floats and African roots music. On September 8, there's also a religious festival, the **Nuestra Señora de la Caridad**, to honor the city's – and Cuba's – patron saint.

🛏 Sleeping

'Los Vitrales' – Emma Barreto & Rafael Requejo
CASA PARTICULAR $

(☑ 29-58-66, 52-94-25-22; requejobarreto@gmail.com; Avellaneda No 3, btwn General Gómez & Martí; r CUC$20-25; P ❄) This enormous, painstakingly restored colonial house was once a convent and sports broad arches, high ceilings and dozens of antiques. Three rooms are arranged around a shady patio embellished with over 50 different types of plants and a fantastic tile mural. Owner Rafael is an architect and it shows. The food (vegetarians catered for) is great, too.

Rafael's sister, **Maria Eugenia Requejo** (☑ 25-86-70; Avellameda 3A; CUC$20-25) has an apartment next door.

Dalgis Fernández Hernández
CASA PARTICULAR $

(☑ 28-57-32; Independencía 251 (altos), btwn Hermanos Agüeros & General Gómez) Prize for the largest rooftop terrace: you'll be spending a lot of time sun-basking up top here. Two lovely 2nd-floor rooms and an antique-filled common area are just below.

Hostal de Carmencita
CASA PARTICULAR $

(☑ 29-69-30; Av Agramonte No 259, btwn Padre Olallo & Alegría; r CUC$20-25; P ❄) A well-equipped, self-contained room on the top floor with its own terrace and fridge: the common room below features a computer with internet access exclusively for guest use (gold-dust in Cuba). There's a garage, too

RAFAEL REQUEJO: ARCHITECT & CASA PARTICULAR OWNER, CAMAGÜEY

Why is Camagüey's architecture different from other Cuban cities?

There are various theories, aside from the pirate idea. It could have been Camagüey's former isolation in the center of the island, its opposition to traditional Spanish design laws, its unique location at the confluence of two rivers and close to good cattle-grazing ground, or its plethora of influential churches, each developing separately around their own neighborhoods and plazas.

What are its main architectural features?

Intimate Andalucian-style patios characterized by large *tinajones* (clay pots), pointed *mudéjar* arches, protective wooden and metal window balustrades, *aljibes* (storage wells), stained glass, Greek columns and decorative ceilings.

What are the city's typical buildings?

The Iglesia de Nuestra Señora de la Soledad, the Casa Natal de Ignacio Agramonte and the Casa de la Trova Patricio Ballagas. There are also less obvious buildings, such as the Banco de Crédito y Comercio in Plaza de los Trabajadores and the birthplace of Cuban author Gertrudis Gómez de Avellaneda on Calle Avellaneda No 67.

Where can you find out more about Camagüey's architecture?

Good sources include the City Historian's Office in Plaza del Carmen, or the Centro Provincial de Patrimonio in Plaza San Juan de Dios.

(tight-fitting but nonetheless another rarity in central Camagüey).

Hotel Puerto Principe HOTEL $
(☑ 28-24-69, 28-24-03; Av de los Martires btwn Rotario & Andres Sánchez; s/d CUC$30/48) Next to Museo Provincial Ignacio Agramonte just north of the train station, recently refurbished Puerto Principe has grand aims (the restaurant is ambient, and there's a rooftop bar in the offing) but it's got some way to go to rival the Gran Hotel. That said, the rooms are far larger and quieter than the Colón. A clean, sedate, middle-of-the-road option.

Hotel Colón HOTEL $
(☑ 25-48-78; República No 472, btwn José Ramón Silva & San Martín; s/d incl breakfast CUC$33/48; ✷) A classic long mahogany bar, colorful tile-flanked walls, and a stained-glass portrait of Christopher Columbus over the lobby door give this place a mixed colonial/fin-de-siècle feel, although rooms are mostly tiny. But the Colón is a good base for exploring, and for relaxing in the rear colonial patio; the bar is a favorite of European/Canadian men and their younger Cuban dates.

Yamilet & Edgar CASA PARTICULAR $
(☑ 25-29-91; San Ramón No 209, btwn El Solitario & Heredia; r CUC$20-25) Edgar is a *maletero* (porter) in the Gran Hotel by day, and a casa

owner by night, running this inviting place just northwest of the center with his wife Yamilet. There's one pleasant room with private bath, plus meals and access to a comfortable sitting area.

Hotel Isla de Cuba HOTEL $
(☑ 28-15-14; Oscar Primelles No 453, cnr Ramón Guerrero; s/d/tr incl breakfast CUC$25/40/57; P ✷) An often-overlooked bargain bang in the center of town, the Isla de Cuba is cheap, friendly and keen to please. There's usually space, too: tour groups prefer the Gran or Colón.

Hotel Plaza HOTEL $
(☑ 28-24-13; Van Horne No 1; s/d incl breakfast CUC$30/48; P ✷) No two rooms are alike in this rough-around-the-edges colonial hotel, so peek inside several before deciding. All have sitting areas, TVs and big fridges. Its location opposite the station makes it a logical spot for brutally early train departures (the 5:45am to Santiago, for instance).

Alba Ferraz CASA PARTICULAR $
(☑ 28-30-81; Ramón Guerrero No 106, btwn San Ramón & Oscar Primelles; r CUC$20-25; ✷) Two rooms sharing a bath open onto a rather grand colonial courtyard bedecked with plants. There's a roof terrace and your host,

Alba, can arrange dance and guitar lessons for guests.

Casa los Helechos CASA PARTICULAR $

(✎29-48-68, 52-31-18-97; Republica No 68) Helechos means 'ferns' and there are plenty in the long, thin courtyard of this pleasant colonial house, at the back of which is one sizable room with a private kitchen.

★ **Gran Hotel** HOTEL $$

(✎29-20-93; Maceo No 67, btwn Av Agramonte & General Gómez; s/d incl breakfast CUC$49/78; P❉@☎) This time-warped city center hotel classic dates from 1939. A haughty pre-revolutionary atmosphere stalks the 72 clean rooms reached by a marble staircase or ancient lift replete with cap-doffing attendants. There are bird's-eye citywide views from the 5th-floor restaurant or gorgeous rooftop bar. A piano bar is accessed through the lobby and an elegant renaissance-style swimming pool shimmers out back.

✖ Eating

With restaurants specializing in Italian and Spanish fare, and a couple more offering a Cuban rarity – lamb – Camagüey has ecletic eating establishments.

★ **Café Ciudad** CAFE $

(Plaza Agramonte, cnr Martí & Cisneros; snacks CUC$2-5; ☺10am-10pm) Camagüey has recently made Agramonte-like efforts to carve culinary quality into its historical inheritance. This lovely 'new' colonial plaza-hugging cafe melds grandiosity with great service, emulating anything Havana Vieja has. Try the *jamón serrano* (cured ham) or savour a superb *café con leche* (coffee with milk) under the louvers. The picture occupying one wall shows the exact continuation of the old street.

Restaurante Italiano Santa Teresa ITALIAN $

(✎29-71-08; Av de la Victoria No 12, btwn Padre Carmelo & Freyre; CUC$1.50-5; ☺noon-midnight) A block behind Centro Cultural Caribe, the idyllic, part-covered back patio here is an Italian feast-in-waiting. Divine pizza, great ice cream and more-than-passable espresso in such environs definitely makes this a spot to savor. The wine is admittedly South American but hey, this isn't the time or place to bemoan Cuba's import/export issues.

El Ovejito CARIBBEAN $

(Hermanos Agüero, btwn Honda & Carmen; dishes around CUC$6; ☺noon-10pm) No, the name isn't a joke, El Ovejito does actually serve 'little sheep' (as the name translates). It's situated on sublime Plaza del Carmen with nary a hustler about. This is a state-run place and the menu's more a wish list than a rundown of what's actually available, but there's always cold beer and good coffee.

Café Cubanitas CAFE $

(cnr Independencia & Av Agramonte; meals CUC$1-3; ☺24hr) Another new coffee bar just off Plaza de los Trabajadores, Cubanitas is alfresco and lively, and really does stay open all hours (unlike many Cuban places who state the fact then close early). Most importantly it sells decent snacks and beer. So if you're craving that 3am *ropa vieja* (shredded beef and vegetables in a tomato salsa)...

Cafetería las Ruinas FAST FOOD $

(Plaza Maceo; meals CUC$1-3) A fern-filled colonial patio with a bargain-basement menu of fried chicken and pizza. Order a margarita and strike up a conversation with local street hawkers through the iron railings.

Coppelia ICE CREAM $

(Maceo, btwn Av Agramonte & General Gómez; ice creams under CUC$1) Dark, unspectacular venue for the Camagüey branch of the national ice-cream chain. Get take-out.

★ **Restaurante 1800** INTERNATIONAL $$

(✎28-36-19; Plaza San Juan de Dios; meals CUC$12; ☺10am-midnight) Simply put, the best new restaurant outside Havana. There is not one thing this sensational colonial locale lacks. There is the grandiose front-of-house, plaza-facing part, which, once you've ordered your *camarones enchiladas* (shrimps in feisty tomato salsa) or, perhaps, *ensalada de pulpo* (octopus salad), you realize is merely the trailer to the eating experience.

Included with any meal you order is *gratis* access to a lavish buffet that usually contains European cheeses, meats and crisp salads. Right alongside is the Oriente's most impressive wine cellar and, at the back, there's the barbecue: sit alfresco and load up on succulent grilled meat.

Restaurante la Isabella ITALIAN $$

(cnr Av Agramonte & Independencia; pizzas CUC$5-8; ☺11am-4pm & 6:30-10pm) Camagüey's coolest restaurant was opened during a visit by delegates from Gibara's iconic film festival, Festival Internacional del Cine Pobre, in 2008. Blending Italian food (pizza, lasagna, fettuccine) with a maverick movie-themed decor and director-style seats, the restaurant occupies the site of Camagüey's first ever cinema.

Bodegón Don Cayetano
TAPAS $$

(☑26-19-61; República No 79; tapas CUC$3-5) This is Camagüey's best Spanish-style taverna. Nestled beneath Iglesia de Nuestra Señora de la Soledad, the restaurant has tables spilling into the adjacent alley. Food is primarily Spanish tapas, such as tortilla, chorizo in cider sauce or garbanzos (chickpeas), but the chef's special beefsteak in red wine and mushroom sauce (CUC$7.50) is tempting.

Restaurante Papito Rizo
SEAFOOD $$

(☑28-33-48; Calle D No 13; CUC$8-16; ☉10am-2am) A sensory shock with its bright Disney World-esque color scheme and 'animated' recorded music, Papito Rizo is nevertheless worth visiting for one of Camagüey's most varied, high quality menus (100+ dishes available). Its atmosphere is reminiscent of a *recreo* (countryside restaurant) but seafood specialties and service are top-notch, plus transport out and back (it's way out of center, 2km north of the train station) is offered (CUC$4).

Restaurante de los Tres Reyes
CARIBBEAN $$

(Plaza San Juan de Dios No 18; meals CUC$7; ☉10am-10pm) This handsome colonial digs on Plaza San Juan de Dios sells mainly chicken dishes. Contemplate Camagüey life by one of the giant iron-grilled windows out front or on a plant-bedecked patio behind. Equally romantic **Campana de Toledo** (Plaza San Juan de Dios No 18; ☉10am-10pm) is next door.

Gran Hotel
INTERNATIONAL $$

(Maceo No 67, btwn Av Agramonte & General Gómez; dinner buffet CUC$12) The 5th-floor restaurant here has superb city views and a rather nice buffet; get here early and watch the sun set over the church towers. Way below on street level, cheaper **Gran Hotel Snack Bar** (Maceo No 67, btwn Av Agramonte & General Gómez; ☉9am-11pm) has coffee, sandwiches, chicken and ice cream. The hamburgers (when available) are good and the atmosphere is 1950s retro.

Self-Catering
Mercado Agropecuario Hatibonico
MARKET $

(Matadero; ☉7am-6pm) Recently relocated further along the fetid Río Hatibonico, this is a classic example of a Cuban market where government (lower quality, but cheaper price) and private (vice-versa) produce is sold side by side. Chew on peso sandwiches and fresh *batidos* (fruit shakes, sold in jam jars) and buy fruit and vegetables grown within 500m of where you stand.

There's a good herb section and the market also sells an excellent selection of fruit and vegetables. Watch out for pickpockets.

Panadería Doña Neli
BAKERY

(Maceo; ☉7am-7pm) For bread and delicate cakes, try this particularly well-stocked bakery, opposite the Gran Hotel.

Drinking & Nightlife

Maybe it's the pirate past, but Camagüey has great tavern-style drinking houses.

Bar El Cambio
BAR

(cnr Independencia & Martí; ☉7am-late) The Hunter S Thompson choice. A dive bar with graffiti-splattered walls and interestingly named cocktails, this place consists of one room, four tables and bags of atmosphere.

Taberna Bucanero
BAR

(cnr República & Fidel Céspedes; ☉2-11pm) The buccaneer's choice. Fake pirate figures and Bucanero beer on tap characterize this swashbuckling tavern, which is more reminiscent of an English pub.

La Bigornia
BAR

(República, btwn El Solitario & Oscar Primelles) The young person's choice. This lurid-purple boutique bar-restaurant, with a sports store on its mezzanine level, is where the city's well-dressed (read scantily dressed) 18s to 25s come for date nights and Noche Camagüeyana warm-ups.

Gran Hotel Bar Terraza
BAR

(Maceo No 67, btwn Av Agramonte & General Gómez; ☉1pm-2am) The aesthete's choice. Up top of the Gran Hotel its cocktail maestro will prepare you impeccably concocted mojitos and daiquiris while you gaze at the city's premier vista: all Camagüey is laid out before you. Duck below to the swimming pool for the bizarrely addictive aquatic dance shows, happening several times weekly at 9pm.

☆ Entertainment

Every Saturday night, the raucous **Noche Camagüeyana** spreads up República from La Soledad to the train station, with food and alcohol stalls, music and crowds. Often a rock or *reggaetón* (Cuban hip-hop) concert takes place in the square next to La Soledad.

★ **Teatro Principal** THEATER
(☎29-30-48; Padre Valencia No 64; tickets CUC$5-10; ⊗8:30pm Fri & Sat, 5pm Sun) If a show's on, GO! Second only to Havana in its ballet credentials, the Camagüey Ballet Company, founded in 1971 by Fernando Alonso (ex-husband of number-one Cuban dancing diva Alicia Alonso), is internationally renowned and performances are the talk of the town. Also of interest is the wonderful theater building of 1850 vintage, bedizened with majestic chandeliers and stained glass.

Casa de la Trova Patricio Ballagas LIVE MUSIC
(Cisneros No 171, btwn Martí & Cristo; cover CUC$3; ⊗7pm-1am) An ornate entrance hall gives way to an atmospheric patio where old crooners sing and young couples *chachachá*. One of Cuba's best *trova* (song) houses, where regular tourist traffic doesn't detract from the old-world authenticity. Tuesday's a good night for traditional music.

Centro Cultural Caribe CABARET
(cnr Narciso Montreal & Freyre; tickets CUC$3-6; ⊗10pm-2am, to 4am Fri & Sat) Some say it's the best cabaret outside Havana and, at this price, who's arguing? Book your seat (from the box office on the same day) and pull up a pew for an eyeful of feathers and a few frocks. There's a trousers-and-shirt dress code for men.

Centro de Promoción Cultural Ibero Americano CULTURAL CENTER
(Cisneros, btwn General Gómez & Hermanos Agüero) Check out what's happening at this under-the-tourist-radar cultural center housed in the former Spanish Club, which hosts tango nights and the like.

Sala Teatro José Luis Tasende THEATER
(☎29-21-64; Ramón Guerrero No 51; ⊗8:30pm Sat & Sun) For serious live theater, head to this venue, which has quality Spanish-language performances.

Galería Uneac CULTURAL CENTER
(Cisneros No 159; ⊗5pm & 9pm Sat) **FREE** Folk singing and Afro-Cuban dancing.

Cine Encanto CINEMA
(Av Agramonte) Big-screen showings take place at the city's one reliable movie house.

Estadio Cándido González SPORTS
(Av Tarafa) From October to April, baseball games are held here alongside Casino Campestre. Team Camagüey, known as the Alfareros (the Ceramicists), have an empty trophy

cabinet despite representing Cuba's largest province.

Shopping

Calle Maceo is Camagüey's top shopping street, with a number of souvenir shops, bookstores and department stores and an attractive pedestrian boulevard. At Galería el Colonial (p329) you can check everything from cigars to rum off your to-get list.

Casa de los Santos CRAFT
(Oscar Primelles No 406; ⊗9am-5pm) Interesting primarily as an insight into Camagüey's staunch Catholicism is this small religious outlet (literally a 'hole in the wall') selling homemade statues of the saints.

ARTex Souvenir SOUVENIRS
(República No 381; ⊗9am-5pm) Che T-shirts, mini-*tinajones*, Che key rings, CDs, Che mugs. Get the picture?

Fondo Cubano Bienes Culturales CRAFT
(Av de la Libertad No 112; ⊗8am-6pm Mon-Sat) Sells all kinds of artifacts in a pleasantly nontouristy setting, just north of the train station.

Librería Ateneo BOOKS
(República No 418, btwn El Solitario & San Martín) Large selection of books in Spanish.

Mercado Francisquito MARKET
(Quiñones) Shoes, nuts, bolts, watch parts... join the fray and purchase away.

Information

DANGERS & ANNOYANCES
Camagüey invites more hassle than other cities. Thefts have been reported in its narrow, winding streets, mainly from bag-snatchers who then jump onto a waiting bicycle for a quick getaway. Keep your money belt tied firmly around your waist and don't invite attention. Then there's the *jiniteros* (touts) who will try to squeeze money out of you any which way – maybe 'offering' to take you to the casa you've been searching for (it will transpire to be another one with almost certainly less-desirable facilities). Try to book your accommodation in advance, ideally arranging with the owners to meet you at the bus/train station/airport. And, particularly at these places, be wary of strangers approaching and soliciting 'services'.

INTERNET ACCESS
Etecsa Telepunto (República, btwn San Martín & José Ramón Silva; internet per hr CUC$6) Internet and telephone access.

MEDIA

The local newspaper **Adelante** is published every Saturday. **Radio Cadena Agramonte** broadcasts in the city over frequencies 910AM and 93.5FM; south of the city tune in to 1340AM, and north of the city, 1380AM.

MEDICAL SERVICES

Farmacia Internacional (Av Agramonte No 449, btwn Independencia & República)

Policlínico Integral Rodolfo Ramirez Esquival (☑ 28-14-81; cnr Ignacio Sánchez & Joaquín de Agüero) North of the level crossing from the Hotel Plaza; it will treat foreigners in an emergency.

MONEY

Banco de Crédito y Comercio (cnr Av Agramonte & Cisneros)

Banco Financiero Internacional (Independencia, btwn Hermanos Agüero & Martí)

Cadeca (República No 353, btwn Oscar Primelles & El Solitario)

POST

Post Office (Av Agramonte No 461, btwn Independencia & Cisneros)

TRAVEL AGENCIES

Cubanacán (Maceo No 67, Gran Hotel) The best place for information on Playa Santa Lucía.

Cubatur (Av Agramonte No 421, btwn República & Independencia) Can book hotels in Playa Santa Lucía.

Ecotur (☑ 24-36-93; Oscar Primelles 453) Can arrange excursions to the Hacienda la Belén. In the Hotel Isla de Cuba.

❶ Getting There & Away

AIR

Ignacio Agramonte International Airport (☑ 26-10-10, 26-72-02; Carretera Nuevitas Km 7) is 9km northeast of town on the road to Nuevitas and Playa Santa Lucía.

Air Transat (www.airtransat.com) and **Sunwing** (www.sunwing.ca) fly in the all-inclusive

crowds from Toronto, who are then hastily bussed off to Playa Santa Lucía.

There are three flights weekly to/from Havana with **Aerocaribbean** (cnr Republica & Callejon de Correa).

BUS & TRUCK

The **regional bus station**, near the train station, has trucks to Nuevitas (87km, twice daily) and Santa Cruz del Sur (82km, three daily). You pay in Cuban pesos. Trucks for Playa Santa Lucía (109km, three daily) leave from here as well: ask for *el último* (last in the queue) inside the station and you'll be given a paper with a number; line up at the appropriate door and wait for your number to come up.

Long-distance **Víazul** (www.viazul.com) buses depart **Álvaro Barba Bus Station** (Carretera Central), 3km southeast of the center.

The Santiago de Cuba departure also stops at Las Tunas (CUC$7, two hours), Holguín (CUC$11, 3¼ hours) and Bayamo (CUC$11, 4¼ hours). The Havana bus stops at Ciego de Ávila (CUC$6, 1¾ hours), Sancti Spíritus (CUC$10, four hours), Santa Clara (CUC$15, 4½ hours) and Entronque de Jagüey (CUC$25, 6¼ hours). For Víazul tickets, see the *jefe de turno* (shift manager).

Passenger trucks to nearby towns, including Las Tunas and Ciego de Ávila, also leave from this station. Arriving before 9am will greatly increase your chances of getting on one of these trucks.

Public transport to Playa Santa Lucía is scant unless you're on a prearranged package tour. Expect to pay CUC$70 for a one-way taxi from Camagüey.

TAXI

A taxi to Playa Santa Lucía costs around CUC$70 one way: bargain hard.

TRAIN

The **train station** (cnr Avellaneda & Av Carlos J Finlay) is more conveniently located than the bus station – though its service isn't as convenient. Foreigners buy tickets in convertibles

VÍAZUL BUS DEPARTURES FROM CAMAGÜEY

DESTINATION	COST (CUC$)	DURATION (HR)	DEPARTURE TIMES
Havana	33	9	12:20am, 3:50am, 11:55am, 3:35pm, 10:50pm, 11:50pm
Holguín	11	3	12:40am, 4:40am, 5:55am, 1:25pm, 5:40pm
Santiago de Cuba	18	6	12:40am, 1:55am, 5:55am, 6:45am, 1:25pm, 5:25pm
Trinidad	15	4½	2:20am
Varadero	24	8¼	2:55am

from an unmarked office across the street from the entrance to Hotel Plaza. The *Tren Francés* leaves for Santiago at around 3:19am every third day and for Havana (stopping in Santa Clara) at around 1:47am, also every third day. A first-class ticket is CUC$23. Schedules change frequently: check at the station a couple of days before you intend to travel. Slower *coche motor* (cross-island) trains also serve the Havana–Santiago route, stopping at places such as Matanzas and Ciego de Ávila. Going east there are daily services to Las Tunas, Manzanillo and Bayamo. Heading north there are (theoretically) four daily trains to Nuevitas and four to Morón.

❶ Getting Around

TO/FROM THE AIRPORT

A taxi to the airport should cost around CUC$10 from town, but you can bargain. Or you can hang around for the **local bus (No 22)** from Parque Finlay (opposite the regional bus station) that runs every 30 minutes on weekdays and hourly on weekends.

BICI-TAXIS

Bicycle taxis are found on the square beside La Soledad or in Plaza Maceo. They should cost five pesos, but drivers will probably ask for payment in convertibles.

CAR

Car-rental prices start around CUC$70 a day plus gas, depending on the make of car and hire duration. Companies include **Havanautos** (Carretera Central, Hotel Camagüey, Este Km 4.5).

Guarded parking (CUC$2 for 24 hours) is available for those brave enough to attempt Camagüey's maze in a car. Ask at your hotel or casa particular for details.

There are two **Servi-Cupet gas stations** (Carretera Central; ⊙ 24hr) near Av de la Libertad. Driving in Camagüey's narrow one-way streets is a sport akin to base-jumping. Experts only!

HORSE CARTS

Horse carts shuttle along a fixed route (CUC$1) between the regional bus station and the train station. You may have to change carts at Casino Campestre, near the river.

Florida

POP 56,000

A million metaphoric miles from Miami, the hard-working sugar-mill town of Florida, 46km northwest of Camagüey on the Ciego de Ávila road, is a viable overnighter if you're driving around central Cuba and are too tired to negotiate the labyrinthine streets of Camagüey after dark (a bad idea, whatever your physical or mental state). There's a working rodeo and an Etecsa telephone office.

Two-story **Hotel Florida** (☑ 51-30-11; Carretera Central Km 534; s/d CUC$18/28; P ✳ ❋) is located 2km west of the town center and has 74 adequate rooms. Next door is Cafetería Caney, a thatched restaurant that's better value than the flyblown hotel restaurant.

Passenger trucks run from Florida to Camagüey, where you can connect with Víazul long-distance buses. If you're driving there's a Servi-Cupet gas station in the center of town on Carretera Central.

Sierra del Chorrillo

This protected area 36km southeast of Camagüey contains three low hill ranges: the Sierra del Chorrillo, the Sierra del Najasa and the Guaicanámar (highest point 324m).

Nestled in their grassy uplands is **La Hacienda la Belén** (admission CUC$4), a handsome country ranch run as a nature reserve: contact the Camagüey branch of travel agency Ecotur (p335). As well as boasting many nonindigenous animals, such as zebras, deer, cattle and horses (it breeds among Cuba's best), the park functions as a bird reserve. It's one of the best places in Cuba to view rare species, such as the Cuban parakeet, the giant kingbird and the Antillean palm swift. Another curiosity is a three-million-year-old **petrified forest** of fossilized tree stumps spread over 1 hectare. To find the stumps, drive a few clicks passed the hacienda entrance to the road junction and bear right to reach a dead end at a factory. There's also a far-larger fossilized tree nearby. Treks can be arranged around the reserve by 4WD or on horseback and there are two guided walks. Most popular is Sendero de las Aves (CUC$7, 1.8km), which reveals a cornucopia of birdlife; there's also Sendero Santa Gertrudis (4.5km) covering flora, fauna and a cave.

Countrified but comfortable **Motel la Belén** (☑ 86-43-49; s/d CUC$42/66; ✳ ❋) reclines within the hacienda grounds and boasts a swimming pool, restaurant, TV room and 10 clean, air-conditioned rooms that can accommodate up to 16 people. Glorious landscapes are within stone-chucking distance.

You'll need your own wheels to get to Sierra del Chorrillo. Drive 24km east of Camagüey on Carretera Central, then 30km southeast: the hacienda is just beyond Najasa. Alternatively, negotiate a rate with a taxi in Camagüey.

Guáimaro

POP 29,800

Guáimaro would be just another nameless Cuban town if it wasn't for the famous Guáimaro Assembly of April 1869, which approved the first Cuban constitution and called for emancipation of slaves. The assembly elected Carlos Manuel de Céspedes as president.

◎ Sights

Parque Constitución   PARK

The events of 1869 are commemorated by a large **monument** erected in 1940 in this central park. Around the base of the monument are bronze plaques with likenesses of José Martí, Máximo Gómez, Carlos Manuel de Céspedes, Ignacio Agramonte, Calixto García and Antonio Maceo, the stars of Cuban independence.

The park also contains the mausoleum of Cuba's first – and possibly greatest heroine, Ana Betancourt (1832–1901) from Camagüey, who fought for women's emancipation alongside the abolition of slavery during the First War of Independence.

Museo Histórico   MUSEUM

(Constitución No 85, btwn Libertad & Máximo Gómez; admission CUC$1; ◎ 9am-5pm Mon-Fri) If you're making a pit stop, this museum has a couple of rooms given to art and history.

⊨ Sleeping & Eating

Casa de Magalis   CASA PARTICULAR **$**

(☑ 81-28-91; Olimpo No 5, btwn Benito Morell & Carretera Central; r CUC$20-25) Here's a surprise: it's almost worth the stopover in Guáimaro just to stay at this salmon-pink colonial villa just off the Carretera Central. There's two rooms, one of which has surely Cuba's largest private-rental bathroom, and a terrace to drink in the bucolic views.

There is a Servi-Cupet gas station on your entry into town from Camagüey with an El Rápido snack bar attached.

Nuevitas

POP 46,200

Nuevitas, 87km northeast of Camagüey, is a 27km jaunt north off the Camagüey–Playa Santa Lucía road. It's an amiable industrial town and sugar-exporting port with easy shore access, but not worth a major detour. In 1978 Cuban movie director Manual Oc-

tavio Gómez filmed his revolutionary classic *Una mujer, un hombre, una ciudad* here, giving the city its first, and to date only, brush with fame.

◎ Sights

Museo Histórico Municipal   MUSEUM

(Máximo Gómez No 66; admission CUC$1; ◎ Tue-Sun) The only specific sight in Nuevitas, near Parque del Cañón, is this museum. It has the standard, semi-interesting mix of stuffed animals and sepia-toned photographs; you could also hike up the steps in the town center for sweepings views of the bay and industry in ironic juxtaposition.

Playa Cuatro Vientos   BEACH

Below Hotel Caonaba there's a shaggy **amusement park**, and a bit further along the coast, a local beach from which you can see two of the three small islands, Los Tres Ballenatos, in Bahía de Nuevitas. Another 2km down the coast you'll reach **Santa Rita** at the end of the road – with a pier jutting into the bay.

King Ranch   RANCH

(Carretera de Santa Lucía Km 35; ◎ 10am-10pm) Texans will be flummoxed by such a familiar-sounding name in the wilds of northern Camagüey, but this Wild West apparition is no phony. King Ranch, en route to Playa Santa Lucía, was once an off-shoot of its legendary Texan namesake (the largest ranch in the US). There's a restaurant, a rodeo show and horses for rent.

The ranch was expropriated after the Revolution, kept much the same function, and mostly caters for tour groups from Playa Santa Lucía, but you can turn up unannounced. It's 4km beyond the crossroads where you join the main highway from Camagüey.

⊨ Sleeping & Eating

Hotel Caonaba   HOTEL **$**

(☑ 24-48-03; cnr Martí & Albisa; s/d CUC$27/43; ✳) This friendly, three-story hotel is on a rise overlooking the sea. Arriving from Camagüey, it's at the entrance to town, near a local swimming spot. Rooms have fridges and some have views but don't expect the Ritz. In summer, you can eat at the **restaurant**, 200m along the coast from the amusement park. The hotel also has a terrace bar.

ⓘ Getting There & Away

Nuevitas is the terminus of railway lines from Camagüey via Minas and Santa Clara via Chambas and Morón. The station is near the waterfront on the northern side of town. There *should* be up to four trains a day to Camagüey (CUC$2), and a service on alternate days to Santa Clara, but cancellations are commonplace. Trucks, which are more reliable than buses, leave for Camagüey around 4:30am and 9am.

A **Servi-Cupet gas station** is at the entrance to town. There's a **Transtur** taxi office nearby.

Brasil & Around

A once vibrant, now sleepy, former sugar town situated halfway between Morón and Nuevitas, Brasil is the gateway to the still-virgin Cayo Romano, the archipelago's third-largest island. The area has recently been rediscovered by in-the-know fisherfolk who ply the waters out as far as Cayo Cruz. The flats, lagoons and estuaries off Camagüey's north coast are fly-fishing heaven (bonefish, permit and tarpon concentrated in a designated fishing area of just under 350 sq km that's invariably deserted). The fishing season runs from November to August and no

commercial fishing is allowed. **Ecotur** (☑ 27-49-95 (Havana), 24-36-93 (Camaguey)) runs trips.

For something completely different, you can stay at **Hotel Casona de Romano** (Calle 6, btwn Calles B & C; r from CUC$50; ❋), a beautiful, quasi-stately home, originally built for a local sugar merchant in 1919 and renovated in 2008, with eight rooms, an on-site restaurant and bar. The place caters mainly for fishers in organized groups. Contact Ecotur for more details.

Cayo Sabinal

Cayo Sabinal, 22km to the north of Nuevitas, is virgin territory, a 30km-long coral key with marshes favored by flamingos and iguanas. The land cover is mainly flat and characterized by marshland and lagoons. The fauna consists of tree rats, wild boar and a large variety of butterflies. It's astoundingly beautiful.

◉ Sights & Activities

Fuerte San Hilario   FORT
Cayo Sabinal has quite some history for a wilderness area. Following repeated pirate attacks in the 17th and 18th centuries, the

CAYOS & CAUSEWAYS

In any other country, the necklace of beach-embellished *cayos* (keys) that lies between Cayo Coco and Playa Santa Lucía would have been requisitioned by the biggest, richest hotel chains, but in Cuba, due to a mix of economic austerity and nitpicking government bureaucracy, they remain refreshingly untouched – for now!

Rough causeways and roads were built across Camagüey's *cayos* in the late 1980s in preparation for Cuba's next big tourist project – a plan that, due to Special Period economic meltdown, never got off the ground. Instead, the islands and their unblemished waters have remained the preserve of in-the-know fisherfolk, resolute bird-watchers and those in search of splendid solitude. Running west to east are **Cayo Paredón Grande**, home to checkered lighthouse Faro Diego Velázquez, a sultry beach and bevies of day-trippers from Cayo Coco; **Cayo Romano**, Cuba's third-largest island and a haven for flamingos, mangroves and blood-thirsty mosquitoes; **Cayo Cruz**, a long, sinuous key lying beyond Romano (a causeway links the two) and legendary for its pristine fishing waters (trips are run out of a fishing lodge in the mainland village of Brasil); **Cayo Guajaba**, an untouched roadless wilderness; and **Cayo Sabinal**, which has a rough road and a trio of unblemished beaches, plus an old Spanish fort and lighthouse. Tucked away to the north is 800m-long **Cayo Confites**, where a 21-year-old Fidel Castro hid out in 1947 in preparation for an abortive plot to overthrow the dictatorial regime of Rafael Trujillo in the Dominican Republic (Fidel jumped ship in the Bay of Nipe and swam 15km to shore carrying his weapon!)

You'll need a sturdy car or a bike to penetrate these potholed northern wildernesses. Entry points to Cayo Romano are from Cayo Coco, or Brasil in northwestern Camagüey province. Cayo Cruz is accessed via a causeway from Cayo Romano. Cayo Sabinal is linked to the mainland by a small causeway northwest of Nuevitas. There are police checkpoints, so you'll need your passport.

Spanish built a fort here (1831) to keep marauding corsairs at bay. The fort later became a prison and, in 1875, witnessed the only Carlist uprising (a counterrevolutionary movement in Spain that opposed the reigning monarchy) in Cuba – ever.

Faro Colón   LIGHTHOUSE
(Punta Maternillo) Erected in 1848, Faro Colón is one of the oldest lighthouses still operating on the Cuban archipelago. As a result of various naval battles fought in the area during the colonial era, a couple of Spanish shipwrecks – *Nuestra Señora de Alta Gracia* and the *Pizarro* – rest in shallow waters nearby, providing great fodder for divers.

Playas Bonita & Los Pinos   BEACHES
Of Cayo Sabinal's 30km of beaches, these two compete for top billing. The former has been commandeered for use by daily boat excursions from Playa Santa Lucía and has a rustic *ranchón* (rural restaurant) serving food. Activities on the latter, since the cabins blew away in a hurricane, are more of the do-it-yourself variety (hiking, swimming, philosophizing etc).

❶ Getting There & Away

Choose from private car, taxi or boat. The dirt road to Cayo Sabinal begins 6km south of Nuevitas, off the Camagüey road. You must show your passport at the bridge to the key and pay CUC$5. The 2km causeway linking the key to the mainland was the first one constructed in Cuba and the most environmentally destructive. Playa Santa Lucía tour agencies offer day trips to Cayo Sabinal: by boat from around CUC$69 including transfers and lunch, or by 4WD for CUC$75. Book through hotels.

Playa Santa Lucía

Playa Santa Lucía is an isolated resort 112km northeast of Camagüey, situated on an unbroken 20km-long stretch of pale-yellow beach that competes with Varadero as Cuba's longest. Travelers generally come here to scuba dive on one of the island's best and most accessible coral reefs, lying just a few kilometers offshore. Another highlight is the beach itself – a tropical gem, most of it still deserted – though it collects more seaweed the further you wander from the hotels.

The area around Playa Santa Lucía is flat and featureless, the preserve of flamingos, scrubby bushes and the odd grazing cow. Aside from the microvillage of Santa Lucía

REFUGIO DE FAUNA SILVESTRE RÍO MÁXIMO

Few know about it, and still fewer come here. The wetlands between the Ríos Máximo and Cagüey on the northern coast of Camagüey province are the largest flamingo nesting ground in the world. Add in migratory water fowl, American crocodiles and a healthy population of West Indian manatees and you're talking special, very special. Protected since 1998 as a Refugio de Fauna Silvestre (Wild Fauna Refuge) and, more recently, as a **Ramsar Convention Site**, the Río Máximo delta faces a precarious future due to human and agricultural contamination coupled with occasional droughts. The area is roadless and hard to reach, but trips in can sometimes be organized courtesy of Ecotur (p338).

that serves as lodging for itinerant hotel workers and the ramshackle hamlet of La Boca near the area's best beach (Playa los Cocos) there are no Cuban settlements of note. The swimming, snorkeling and diving are exceptional, however, and the large hotels lay on activities aplenty for those with time and inclination to explore. Packages to Playa Santa Lucía are usually cheaper than those to Cayo Coco (which it predates) though the resorts themselves are less luxuriant and have more of a holiday camp feel. The clientele is primarily Canadian.

⊙ Sights

Playa los Cocos   BEACH
This comma of beach at the end of 20km-long Playa Santa Lucía, 7km from the hotels at the mouth of the Bahía de Nuevitas, is another stunner, with yellow-white sand and iridescent jade water. Sometimes flocks of pink flamingos are visible in Laguna el Real, behind this beach. The great El Bucanero restaurant (p341) is located here.

A horse and carriage from the Santa Lucía hotels to Playa los Cocos is CUC$20 return plus the wait, or you can walk it, jog it, bike it (free gearless-but-adequate bikes are available at all the resorts), or jump in a taxi. This is a fine swimming spot, with views of the Faro Colón (lighthouse) on Cayo Sabinal, but beware of tidal currents further out.

Playa Santa Lucía

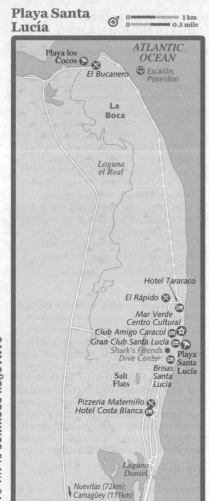

The small Cuban settlement here is known as La Boca. There's a good restaurant (in the pink, smart-looking house) where the fisherman's just-landed catch is cooked up. Sometimes the locals roast a pig on a spit and will invite you across.

🏃 Activities

Playa Santa Lucía is a diving destination extraordinaire that sits alongside what is, purportedly, the world's second-longest coral reef (after Australia's Great Barrier Reef). The 35 scuba sites take in six Poseidon ridges, the Cueva Honda dive site, shipwrecks,

and the abundant marine life, including several types of rays, at the entrance to the Bahía de Nuevitas. A much-promoted highlight is the hand-feeding of 3m-long bull sharks (June to January). The hotels can organize other water activities, including a full-day catamaran cruise along the shoreline (CUC$57 with lunch and snorkeling), a flamingo tour (CUC$59) and deep-sea fishing (CUC$200 for the boat for 3½ hours).

Centro Internacional de Buceo Shark's Friends   DIVING

(www.nauticamarlin.com; Av Tararaco) Shark's Friends is a professional outfit with dive masters speaking English, Italian and German. The center, on the beach between Brisas Santa Lucía and Gran Club Santa Lucía, offers dives (CUC$30 to CUC$40 depending on how many you want), plus night dives (CUC$40) and the famous shark feeds (CUC$65), where cool-as-a-cucumber dive guides chuck food into the mouths of 3m-long bull sharks.

November through January is the best time for the shark-feeding, or dive boats go out every two hours between 9am and 3pm daily (though the last dive is contingent on demand). The open-water course costs CUC$360; a resort course is CUC$60. It also has snorkeling excursions.

🛏 Sleeping

The small hotel strip begins 6km northwest of the roundabout at the entrance to Santa Lucía. The four big ones are Cubanacán resorts whose star ratings and quality decrease as you head northwest. Due to Playa Santa Lucía's size and isolation, it's good to book a room beforehand.

Hotel Tararaco   HOTEL **$**

(✆ 33-63-10; s/d CUC$19/30; ❄) There are no casas particulares in Playa Santa Lucía, so thank Changó for the Tararaco, the strip's oldest hotel (it actually predates the Revolution). Every room has a TV and a little patio, and is within stone-chucking distance of the beach.

Hotel Costa Blanca   HOTEL **$**

(✆ 33-63-73; Av Maternillo No 1; s/d CUC$19/30; ❄) Low-rise Cuban cheapie situated in the microvillage. The ocean is within earshot, but can you make it alive passed the surly glares of the reception staff?

Club Amigo Caracol   RESORT **$$**

(✆ 36-51-58; s/d CUC$86/122; Ⓟ❄@⊠🏊) A newer version of nearby Club Amigo Mayanabo, the Caracol has the edge on its more worn partner and, with its large kids' program, is usually promoted as the beach's family favorite. Ocean-view rooms are fractionally more expensive.

Gran Club Santa Lucía RESORT $$$
(☑33-61-09; s CUC$90-117, d CUC140-156; P❄ @✉♻) Gran Club comes out top on the strip for its 249 colorfully painted rooms (in well-maintained two-story blocks), prettily landscaped grounds and poolside action. **Discoteca la Jungla** is the not-overly-inspiring nightclub that offers an evening music/comedy show with *mucho* audience participation.

Brisas Santa Lucía RESORT $$$
(☑33-63-17; s/d CUC$98/148; P❄@✉♻) This resort has 412 rooms in several three-story buildings. Covering a monstrous 11 hectares, it boasts the strip's top rating of four stars, though with its over-jaunty holiday camp atmosphere (mic-happy pool entertainers and a show where everything is repeated in three languages), it rarely justifies the billing. There is special kids' programming and Shark's Friends dive center is next door.

✖ Eating

Aside from the hotel buffets and the following three gold nuggets, your choices are limited. There's an El Rápido opposite Hotel Tararaco (p340) that serves cheap (for a reason) fast food.

Pizzeria Maternillo PIZZERIA $
(Av Maternillo; ⊙noon-10pm) Why not? Seriously cheap (and tasty) pizza (you pay in pesos; meals average well under CUC$5), the setting's convivial (at least equal to many of the all-inclusive restaurants) and you may just meet a real Cuban. It's right by Hotel Costa Blanca.

★El Bucanero SEAFOOD $$
(Playa los Cocos; meals around CUC$12; ⊙10am-10pm) Located on Playa los Cocos at the Santa Lucía end of the beach, this place is in a different class, serving seafood – lobster and prawns (CUC$12) is the house special – which is enhanced by the setting.

Restaurante Luna Mar SEAFOOD $$
(Playa Santa Lucía; fish dishes CUC$8-12; ⊙10am-10pm) This place, flush up against the beach and wedged between Gran Club Santa Lucía and Club Amigo Caracol, offers exactly the same menu as El Bucanero, but in an easier-to-reach setting.

☆ Entertainment

Outside of the resort entertainment, nothing much happens here.

The **Mar Verde Centro Cultural** (admission CUC$1) has a pleasant patio bar and a cabaret with live music nightly.

🛍 Shopping

The Mar Verde Centro Comercial in between the Gran Club Santa Lucía and Club Amigo Caracol has an ARTex store, a bookstore and a couple of government-run Caracol outlets selling Che Guevara T-shirts and the like.

ℹ Information

The BANDEC (Banco de Crédito y Comercio), where you can change money, is in the Cuban residential area between the Servi-Cupet gas station at the southeastern entrance to Playa Santa Lucía and the hotel strip. Nearby is **Clínica Internacional de Santa Lucía** (☑33-62-03; Ignacio Residencial 14), a well-equipped Cubanacán clinic for emergencies and medical issues. The best pharmacy is in Brisas Santa Lucía. Etecsa, 1.5km further along near the entrance to the hotel zone, has internet access for CUC$6 per hour and international phone capabilities. For tour agencies, Cubanacán, which owns four of the five hotels here, is well represented. There's a good Cubatur office located just outside Gran Club Santa Lucía.

ℹ Getting There & Around

Anything is possible in Cuba, even getting to Playa Santa Lucía without your own transport. The only regular bus heads out from Camagüey every Friday at noon, arriving at Playa Santa Lucía at 1:30pm (it's for workers but they'll normally let you on). A return bus leaves the resorts at 2pm on Sunday and arrives in Camagüey at 3:30pm. This bus is run by Transtur (p517) and costs CUC$18 one way. Reserve one day in advance with Cubatur (p335). Another option for independent travelers is to jump on one of the charter bus links with spare seats. The prices are: Camagüey airport (CUC$20, Thursday) and Holguín airport (CUC$28, Wednesday and Friday). A taxi from Camagüey to Playa Santa Lucía will cost you CUC$70 one way. Alternatively you can get a train to Nuevitas from Morón or Camagüey and taxi it from there.

The Servi-Cupet gas station is at the southeastern end of the strip, near the access road from Camagüey. Another large Servi-Cupet station, with a Servi-Soda snack bar, is just south of Brisas Santa Lucía.

You can rent cars or mopeds (CUC$24 per day, including a tank of gas) at **Cubacar** (Hotel Tararaco) or at any of the other hotels.

Las Tunas Province

♩ 31 / POP 538,000

Best Bucolic Escapes

➡ Monte Cabaniguan (p350)
➡ El Cornito (p346)
➡ Playa La Herradura (p351)

Best Places to Stay

➡ Hotel Cadillac (p347)
➡ Mayra Busto Méndez (p346)
➡ Brisas Covarrubias (p351)
➡ Roberto Lío Montes de Oca (p351)

Why Go?

Las Tunas is the province that's famous for not being famous. Wedged between cosmopolitan Camagüey to the west and the cultural powerhouse of the Oriente to the east, it's usually only experienced by people in transit. Sleepy and unspectacular, its historical legacy rests on the mastery of Victória de Las Tunas, an 1897 War of Independence battle won by Mambí general Calixto García.

Yet Las Tunas' north coast is a largely undiscovered nirvana of colorful coral reefs and deserted eco-beaches that, to date, hosts just one all-inclusive resort. The province's central swath, including the homonymous capital, is cattle-grazing country but this too throws up its surprises: the occasional rodeo or *finca* (farm) with ranchón-style restaurant to contemplate way-off-the-tourist-radar country life.

When to Go

➡ The wettest months are June and October, with over 160mm of average precipitation. July and August are the hottest months of the year.

➡ Las Tunas has many festivals for a small city and the best one is the Jornada Cucalambeana in June.

➡ Festival Internacional de Magia (Magic Festival), held in the provincial capital in November, is another highlight.

➡ The National Sculpture Exhibition, an event befitting the so-called 'City of Sculptures', happens in February.

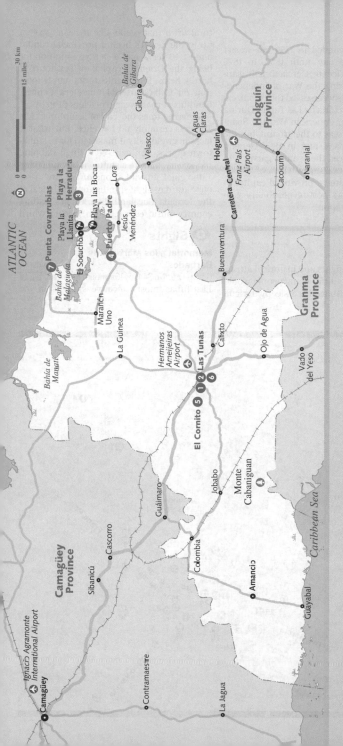

Las Tunas Province Highlights

1 Hunt for the imaginative sculptures embellishing the sleepy cityscape of **Las Tunas** (p344).

2 Check out the dudes with lassos in **Parque 26 de Julio**

(p348), Las Tunas' celebrated twice-annual rodeo.

3 Enjoy the unkempt beaches of **Playa la Herradura**, before resort

developers shatter the tranquility (p351).

4 Linger awhile in friendly, out-on-a-limb seaside town **Puerto Padre** (p350).

5 Roll into El Cornito in June for the **Jornada Cucalambeana** (p346) music festival.

6 Enjoy some slick new provincial accommodation at

Hotel Cadillac (p347) in Las Tunas.

7 Go diving in the largely undiscovered reefs off **Punta Covarrubias** (p351).

History

Las Tunas was founded in 1759 but wasn't given the title of 'city' until 1853. In 1876 Cuban General Vicente García briefly captured the city during the War of Independence, but Spanish successes led the colonizers to rename it La Victoría de Las Tunas. During the Spanish-Cuban-American War the Spanish burned Las Tunas to the ground, but the Mambís fought back, and in 1897 General Calixto García forced the Spanish garrison to surrender in a pivotal Cuban victory.

Las Tunas became a provincial capital in 1976 during Cuba's post-revolutionary geographic reorganization.

Las Tunas

POP 154,000

If it was down to sights and historical attractions alone, it's doubtful many people would bother with Las Tunas. It's a sleepy agricultural town that seems like it hasn't woken up to the fact it's been a provincial capital almost 40 years, and a sleazy reputation for being the Oriente's capital of sex tourism hardly helps. But, thanks to its handy location on Cuba's arterial Carretera Central, handfuls of road-weary travelers drop by.

Referred to as the 'city of sculptures,' Las Tunas is certainly no Florence. But what it lacks in grandiosity it makes up for in small-town quirks. You can see a thigh-slapping rodeo here, admire a statue of a two-headed Taíno chief, go wild at one of the city's riotous Saturday-night shindigs or wax lyrical at the Jornada Cucalambeana, Cuba's leading country-music festival. Go on, give it a whirl!

◎ Sights

Memorial a los Mártires de Barbados MUSEUM
(Lucas Ortíz No 344; ☺ 10am-6pm Mon-Sat) FREE
Las Tunas' most evocative sight is in the

Las Tunas

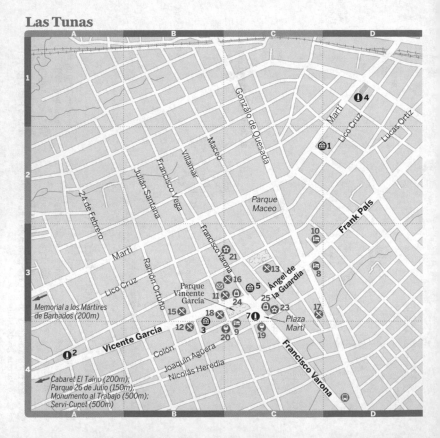

former home of Carlos Leyva González, an Olympic fencer killed in the nation's worst terrorist atrocity: the bombing of Cubana de Aviación Flight 455 in 1976. Individual photos of victims of the attack, which included the entire 24-member Cuban Olympic fencing team, line the museum walls, providing poignant reminders of the fated airplane.

The museum was closed for refurbishment at the time of research.

Museo Provincial General Vicente García
MUSEUM

(cnr Francisco Varona & Ángel de la Guardia; admission CUC$1; ⊘ 9am-5pm Tue-Sat) Housed in the royal-blue town hall with a clock mounted on the front facade, the provincial museum documents local *tunero* history, but was closed for long-term restoration at the time of research.

Sculptures
MONUMENT

Thank goodness for the sculptures in the 'city of sculptures', providing innovative,

much-needed eye candy across Las Tunas' lackluster center. Start the sculpture trail in Plaza Martí, where an inventive bronze **statue** of the 'apostle of Cuban independence' by Rita Longa that doubles as a solar clock was opened in 1995 to commemorate the 100th anniversary of José Martí's death.

Other notables include **La Fuente de Las Antilles**, elaborate interwoven figures symbolising the emergence of the Greater Antilles' indigenous peoples, **Monumento al Trabajo** (cnr Carretera Central & Martí), commemorating Cuban workers, and the pencil-like **Monumento a Alfabetización** (Lucas Ortíz), marking the 1961 act passed in Las Tunas to stamp out illiteracy. You'll have to

---

Las Tunas

get out to Motel el Cornito to see the emblematic Janus-inspired **Cacique Maniabo y Jibacoa**, a two-headed Taíno chief looking in opposite directions.

Back in town the small **Galería Taller Escultura Rita Longa** (cnr Av 2 de Diciembre & Lucas Ortíz) pulls together some fine local work.

Memorial Vicente García   MUSEUM
(Vicente García No 7; admission CUC$1; ⊙ 3-7pm Mon, 11am-7pm Tue-Sat) A colonial-era structure near the eponymous park that commemorates Las Tunas' great War of Independence hero who captured the town from the Spanish in 1876, and torched it 21 years later when the colonizers sought to reclaim it. The limited exhibits include antique weapons and some grainy photos.

Plaza de la Revolución   SQUARE
Las Tunas' revolution square is huge, bombastic and worth a once-over. Check out the huge Lenin-esque **sculpture of Vicente García**, sword raised, and the giant Che billboard.

El Cornito   OUTDOORS
(Carretera Central Km 8; ⊙ 9am-5pm) The grounds around Motel El Cornito (8km outside town) are bamboo woods which offer a welcome, shady diversion from the scorching city bustle. You'll find *ranchón*-style restaurants (favoring the usual booming *reggaetón* music), the site of the old farmhouse of great Las Tunas poet Juan Cristóbal Nápoles Fajardo (aka El Cucalambé) and a reservoir where you can swim.

REMEMBERING OLD FLAMES

Back in the day, Las Tunas was no backwater, but considered key to controlling the entire Oriente. This made it a focal point during the War of Independence, when the city was burned three times. One such burning (1876) was at the hands of city son General Vicente García (you don't have to look far around town to see his legacy in everything from street names to museums) who famously said he would see Las Tunas 'burnt rather than enslaved.' Heated words indeed, and Las Tunas folk don't forget them. Flames, fireworks, torchlight parades and historical re-enactments of García's heroics are a part of the moving Fundación de la Ciudad festival every September 26.

Back toward the main road, there's a zoo, a fun park and a motocross circuit. A taxi here costs CUC$5 to CUC$7 return.

✷✶ Festivals & Events

National Sculpture Exhibition   SCULPTURE
Held every February in this so-called 'city of sculptures.'

Jornada Cucalambeana   MUSIC
Jornada Cucalambeana in June is Cuba's biggest celebration of country music, where local lyricists impress each other with their 10-line *décima* verses. It happens just outside Las Tunas, by Motel El Cornito.

Festival Internacional de Magia   MAGIC
Magic festival held in the provincial capital each November.

🛏 Sleeping

After years in the doldrums, Las Tunas can at last claim at least one decent hotel (the Cadillac). Several private houses rent clean, affordable rooms along Calle Martí and Calle Frank País near the center.

★ **Mayra Busto Méndez**   CASA PARTICULAR $
(☏ 34-42-05; Hirán Durañona No 16, btwn Frank País & Lucas Ortíz; CUC$25) Blink. The sheen coming off the furnishings in this immaculate bungalow might otherwise dazzle you. It's Tardislike inside, too. The size of the room on the left could encompass a couple of most all-inclusive hotel rooms.

Motel el Cornito   CABIN $
(☏ 34-50-15; Carretera Central Km 8; r CUC$20-30) A Cuban-oriented place located in bamboo woods near the site of El Cucalambé's old farm. The Jornada Cucalambeana country music festival takes place here. Some 60 cabins, verging between basic breeze block-style and decent chalets, are scattered through the woods. Phone ahead.

Caballo Blanco – Pepe   CASA PARTICULAR $
(☏ 37-36-58; Frank País No 85 Altos; r CUC$20-25; ❋) This casa has dazzling tiled floors, hotel-standard bathrooms, wall-mounted TVs and operating-room all-round cleanliness (no surprise that Pepe is a doctor). A paladar (privately run restaurant) is also in the offing.

Hotel Las Tunas   HOTEL $
(☏ 34-50-14; Av 2 de Diciembre; s/d CUC$27/43; P ❋ ❋) A last-gasp option: out-of-the-way location, austere rooms, dodgy restaurant

RODEOS

Cattle-herding has a long history in Cuba. Before the Revolution, Cuban cows produced some of the best beef in the Western hemisphere and, although the succulence of the steaks might have suffered since Castro nationalized the ranches, the skill and dexterity of the *vaqueros* (cowboys) has gone from strength to strength.

The cathedral of Cuban rodeo is the Rodeo Nacional in Parque Lenin in Havana – the host, since 1996, of the annual Boyeros Cattleman's Fair. But for a more authentic look at cowboy culture in the island's untrammeled hinterland, head to the prime cattle-rearing provinces of Camagüey and Las Tunas, where the cowboy spirit is particularly strong thanks to famous local son Jorge Barrameda.

Cuban rodeos exhibit all of the standard equestrian attractions with a few quirky Caribbean extras thrown in. Expect myriad horseback-riding events, obnoxious clowns, dexterous *vaqueros* lassoing steers and rugged Benicio del Toro look-a-likes bolting out of rusty paddocks atop ill-tempered 680kg bulls to rapturous cheers from a noisy audience.

The Las Tunas rodeo is reason alone to visit this small city: main events take place twice annually in April and September, in Parque 26 de Julio, but there are various other more impromptu rodeos: ask at the Infotur office.

---

and a wake-you-up-at-2am disco. Room TVs pick up HBO – a small consolation.

★ **Hotel Cadillac** HOTEL $$
(⌨37-27-91; cnr Ángel de la Guardia & Francisco Vega; s/d CUC$45/70; ❄) At last Las Tunas gets a hotel that doesn't give you flashbacks to the Khrushchev and Brezhnev years. Opened in 2009, this rehabilitated, centrally located 1940s beauty is verging on boutique standard with just eight rooms including a lovely corner suite. There are flat-screen TVs, up-to-the-minute bathrooms and a dash of old-fashioned prerevolutionary class. Out front is the Cadillac Snack Bar.

✗ Eating

Las Tunas has two decent government-run restaurants in the city center serving varied *comida criolla* (Creole food); elsewhere menus are fairly scant. The culinary claim to fame around these parts is *caldosa kike y mariana*, a stew of meat and root vegetables with banana: it's even been sung about. Ask around.

★ **El Baturro** CARIBBEAN $
(Av Vicente García, btwn Julián Santana & Ramón Ortuño; ⊙11am-11pm) The walls are covered in scribbled prose – love notes and eulogies to murdered Chilean troubadour Victor Jara – and the plates are stuffed with better-than-average Cuban cooking, including a surprise rabbit dish, making this the best restaurant in Las Tunas.

Cremería las Copas ICE CREAM $
(cnr Francisco Vega & Vicente García; ⊙10am-4pm & 5-11pm) Las Tunas' substitute Coppelia; queue up with your pesos for sundaes or *tres gracias* (three scoops) in flavors such as coconut, and *café con leche* (espresso with milk). Not surprisingly, it's insanely popular. If only they didn't rush you and cram you on tables with strangers, it would be one hugely enjoyable experience.

Restaurante la Bodeguita CARIBBEAN $
(Francisco Varona No 293; ⊙11am-11pm) A Palmares joint, meaning that it's a better bet than the usual peso parlors. You'll get checkered tablecloths here, a limited wine list and what the Cuban government calls 'international cuisine' – read spaghetti and pizza. Try the chicken breast with mushroom sauce for around CUC$5.

La Taberna BARBECUE $
(Parque Maceo, btwn Adolfo Villamar & Maceo; meals CUC$6-10; ⊙noon-2am) Hooray for this spirited barbecue joint on Parque Maceo – whether it's octopus, fish or beef you want grilled, come here. Or for a good cold beer, of course.

Río Chico CUBAN $
(Maceo No 2, btwn Nicolás Heredia & Joaquín Agüera; ⊙10am-11pm) It's too early to tell if this place will be a culinary sensation but, for the moment, let's just say in a city of few eating options, its plant-fringed covered patio makes for good, simple dining on fish/beef/chicken dishes (about CUC$5).

FLIGHT 455

Blink and you'll miss it. The tiny bronze monument beside the Río Hormiguero in unfashionable Las Tunas is Cuba's sole memorial to one of the country's darkest hours.

On October 6, 1976, Cubana de Aviación Flight 455, on its way back to Havana from Guyana, took off after a stopover in Barbados' Seawell airport. Nine minutes after clearing the runway, two bombs went off in the cabin's rear toilet causing the plane to crash into the Atlantic Ocean. All 73 people on board – 57 of whom were Cuban – were killed. The toll included the entire Cuban fencing team fresh from a clean sweep of gold medals at the Central American Championships. At the time, the tragedy of Flight 455 was the worst ever terrorist attack in the Western hemisphere.

Hours after the bombing, two Venezuelan men were arrested in Barbados and a line was quickly traced back to Luis Posada Carriles and Orlando Bosch, two Cuban-born anti-Castro activists with histories as CIA operatives. Arrested in Venezuela in 1977, the men were tried by both civilian and military courts and spent the best part of 10 years in Venezuelan prisons. Bosch was released in 1987 and went to live in the US. Carriles broke out of jail in 1985 in a daring escape in which he dressed up as a priest. A year later he re-emerged in Nicaragua coordinating military supply drops for Contra rebels.

Despite a failed attempt on his life in Guatemala City in 1990, Carriles remained active. In 1997 he was implicated in a series of bombings directed against tourist sites in Havana, and in 2000 he was arrested in Panama City for allegedly attempting to assassinate Fidel Castro. Pardoned in 2004 by outgoing Panamanian president Mireya Moscoso, Carriles sought asylum in the US after the Venezuelan Supreme Court filed an extradition request for him. The US has so far refused to hand him over, claiming that he faces the threat of torture in Venezuela.

As of 2013 Carriles was still living in the US, aged 85. Bosch died in April 2011, aged 84, also in the US. Among some anti-Castro extremists they are hailed as freedom fighters, while to many Cubans they are unrepentant terrorists.

Restaurante 2007 CARIBBEAN $
(Vicente García, btwn Julián Santana & Ramón Ortuño; ⊘ noon-2:45pm & 6-10:45pm) A new-ish attempt at fine dining in Las Tunas (albeit in pesos). The plush interior and suited waiters look promising, but you'll get a friendlier welcome elsewhere.

Self-Catering

To stock up on groceries (or to break bigger bills), try **Supermercado Casa Azul** (cnr Vicente García & Francisco Vega; ⊘ 9am-6pm Mon-Sat, to noon Sun). **Mercado Agropecuario** (Av Camilo Cienfuegos) is a small market not far from the train station.

🍷 Drinking & Nightlife

Casa del Vino Don Juan BAR
(cnr Francisco Varona & Joaquín Agüera; ⊘ 9am-midnight) Wine-tasting in Las Tunas probably sounds about as credible as food rationing in Beverley Hills, yet here it is; and only seven pesos for a shot of Cuba's – er – finest wine, the slightly vinegary Soroa. The Don Juan is a down-to-earth corner bar with large open doors and just a handful of tables. Go just to say you've been there.

Cadillac Snack Bar CAFE
(cnr Ángel de la Guardia & Francisco Vega; ⊘ 9am-11pm) This offshoot of the Hotel Cadillac has tables on a terrace overlooking the Plaza Martí action and serves decent *café con leche*. Join the elderly Italians and their young Cuban escorts, who congregate here daily.

Piano Bar BAR
(cnr Colón & Francisco Vega; ⊘ 9pm-2am) A little more suave than the blazing hotel discos, this place is where you go to hear local Oscar Petersons tinkle on the ivories while you knock back CUC$1 mojitos.

☆ Entertainment

Las Tunas comes alive on Saturday nights when packed streets and fun-seeking locals defy the city's 'boring' image. The main hubs are: Parque Vicente García, where alfresco *son* music competes with modern *reggaetón* (Cuban hip-hop); and Parque 26 de Julio.

★ Parque 26 de Julio FAIRGROUND
(Av Vicente García; ⊘ 9am-6pm Sat & Sun) **FREE** Located in Parque Julio 26 where Vice-

nte García bends into Av 1 de Mayo, it kicks off every weekend with a market, music, food stalls and kids' activities.

Estadio Julio Antonio Mella SPORT
(1ra de Enero) From October to April is baseball season. Las Tunas plays at this stadium near the train station. Los Magos (the Wizards) haven't produced much magic of late and usually compete with the likes of Ciego de Ávila for bottom place in the East League. Other sports happen at the **Sala Polivalente**, an indoor arena near Hotel Las Tunas.

Cabildo San Pedro Lucumí CULTURAL CENTER
(Francisco Varona, btwn Vicente García & Lucas Ortíz; ⊙from 9pm Sun) **FREE** Cultural activities happen at this friendly Afro-Caribbean association, HQ of the Compañía Folklórica Onilé. Sundays there's dancing and drumming.

Teatro Tunas THEATER
(cnr Francisco Varona & Joaquín Agüera) This is a recently revitalized theater that shows quality movies and some of Cuba's best touring entertainment including flamenco, ballet and plays.

Cabaret el Taíno THEATER
(cnr Vicente García & A Cabrera; admission per couple CUC$10; ⊙9pm-2am Tue-Sun) This large thatched venue at the west entrance to town has the standard feathers, salsa and pasties show. Cover charge includes a bottle of rum and cola.

Casa de la Cultura CULTURAL CENTER
(Vicente García No 8) The best place for the traditional stuff with concerts, poetry, dance etc. The action spills out into the street on weekend nights.

🛍 Shopping

The 'city of sculptures' has some interesting local art: check Galería Taller Escultura Rita Longa (p346).

Fondo Cubano de Bienes Culturales ARTS & CRAFTS
(cnr Ángel de la Guardia & Francisco Varona; ⊙9am-noon & 1:30-5pm Mon-Fri, 8:30am-noon Sat) This store sells fine artwork, ceramics and embroidered items opposite the main square.

Biblioteca Provincial José Martí BOOKS
(Vicente García No 4; ⊙Mon-Sat) Books galore.

ℹ Information

Banco Financiero Internacional (cnr Vicente García & 24 de Febrero)

Cadeca (Colón No 41) Money changing.

Cubana (cnr Lucas Ortíz & 24 de Febrero) Travel agent.

Etecsa Telepunto (Francisco Vega, btwn Vicente García & Lucas Ortíz; ⊙8:30am-7pm) Spanking modern air-conditioned haven on the shopping boulevard.

Hospital Che Guevara (☎34-50-12; cnr Avs CJ Finlay & 2 de Diciembre) One kilometer from the highway exit toward Holguín.

Infotur (cnr Ángel de la Guardia & Francisco Varona; ⊙8:15am-4:15pm Mon-Fri & alternate Sat) Travel agent.

Post Office (Vicente García No 6; ⊙8am-8pm)

ℹ Getting There & Away

BUS
The main **bus station** (Francisco Varona) is 1km southeast of the main square. **Víazul** (www.viazul.com) buses have daily departures; tickets are sold by the jefe de turno (shift manager).

There are five daily buses to Havana (CUC$39, 11 hours) leaving at 1:50am, 10am, 1:35pm, 8:50pm and 9:55pm; four to Holguín (CUC$6, 70 minutes) at 2:40am, 6:40am, 8:10am and 3:25pm; one to Varadero (CUC$33, 10½ to 11 hours) at 12:55am; one to Trinidad (CUC$21, 6½ hours) at 12:20am; and five to Santiago (CUC$11, 4¾ hours) at 2:40am, 8:10am, 9am, 3:25pm and 8:05pm.

Most of these buses make stops at Camagüey (CUC$7, 2½ hours), Ciego de Ávila (CUC$13, 4¼ hours), Sancti Spíritus (CUC$17, 5½ to six hours), Santa Clara (CUC$22, seven hours) and Entronque de Jagüey (CUC$26, 9¼ hours). Santiago buses stop at Bayamo (CUC$6, 1¼ hours). To get to Guantánamo or Baracoa, you have to connect through Santiago de Cuba.

TRAIN
The **train station** (Terry Alomá, btwn Lucas Ortíz & Ángel de la Guardia) is near Estadio Julio Antonio Mella on the northeast side of town. See the jefe de turno for tickets. The fast Havana–Santiago Tren Francés doesn't stop in Las Tunas so you're left with slower, less reliable services. Trains to Havana and Santiago (via Camagüey and Santa Clara) leave two days out of three (check ahead). There are daily services to Camagüey and Holguín.

TRUCK
Passenger trucks to other parts of the province, including Puerto Padre, pick up passengers on the main street near the train station, with the last departure before 2pm.

ℹ Getting Around

Taxis hang around outside the bus station, Hotel Las Tunas and the main square. Horse carts run

THE BALCONY OF THE ORIENTE

The Oriente doesn't begin in Shanghai or Hong Kong... in Cuba, anyway, it begins in Las Tunas, a city often referred to as El Balcón del Oriente (The Balcony of the Oriente) for its location on the cusp of two distinctive regions. Prior to 1976 the area east of the settlement was a province in its own right, a large, culturally distinct region that encompassed the present-day provinces of Guantánamo, Santiago de Cuba, Granma and Holguín.

Geographically closer to Haiti than Havana, the Oriente has often preferred to look east rather than west in its bid to cement an alternative Cuban identity, absorbing myriad influences from Hispaniola, Jamaica and elsewhere. It is this soul-searching, in part, which accounts for the region's rich ethnic diversity and penchant for rebellion.

In the historical context, all of Cuba's revolutionary movements have been ignited in the Oriente, inspired by such fiery easterners as Carlos Manuel de Céspedes (from Bayamo), Antonio Maceo (from Santiago) and Fidel Castro (from Birán near Holguín). The region has also been a standard-bearer for the lion's share of Cuba's musical genres, from son and changüí to nueva trova.

Today, Cuba's long-standing east–west rivals continue to trade humorous insults on topics such as language (easterners have a distinctive 'singsong' accent), baseball (Los Industriales versus Santiago is an event akin to Real Madrid versus Barcelona), history (santiagueros have never forgiven habaneros for stealing the mantle of capital city in 1607) and economics (poorer easterners have tended to migrate west for work). While high-and-mighty habaneros will tell you that the rest of Cuba is just a 'green field' and jokingly refer to people from Santiago as palestinos, the proud citizens of the Oriente like to think of themselves as feisty historical liberators and jealous guardians of Cuba's world-famous musical heritage.

---

along Frank País near the baseball stadium to the town center; they cost 10 pesos.

Cubacar (Av 2 de Diciembre) is at Hotel Las Tunas. An **Oro Negro gas station** (cnr Francisco Varona & Lora) is a block west of the bus station. The **Servi-Cupet gas station** (Carretera Central; ☉24hr) is at the exit toward Camagüey.

Monte Cabaniguan

This fauna refuge just south of the municipality of Jobabo on the alluvial plains of the Río Cauto is a vital nesting ground for aquatic birds such as flamingos, the endangered Cuban parakeet and the Cuban treeduck. The area is protected internationally as a Ramsar Wetlands zone. Ecotur runs short aquatic trips here for aspiring twitchers.

Puerto Padre

Languishing in a half-forgotten corner of Cuba's least spectacular province, it's hard to believe that Puerto Padre – or the 'city of mills' as it is locally known – was once the largest sugar port on the planet. But for diehard travelers the wanton abandonment inspires a wistful sense of curiosity. Blessed with a Las Ramblas–style boulevard, a miniature Malecón, and a scrawny statue of Don Quixote standing rather forlornly beneath a weathered windmill that has registered one too many hurricanes, the town is the sort of place where you stop to ask the way at lunchtime and end up, five hours later, tucking into fresh lobster at a bayside eating joint.

◉ Sights

Museo Fernando García Grave de Peralta   MUSEUM
(Yara No 45, btwn Av Libertad & Maceo; admission CUC$1) Lashed by Hurricane Ike, what is effectively the municipal museum contains the usual round of fallen revolutionaries, stuffed animals and antiques. Look out for the antique record players.

Fuerte de la Loma   FORT
(Av Libertad; admission CUC$1; ☉9am-4pm Tue-Sat) This fort, also known as the Salcedo Castle, at the top of the sloping Av Libertad is testimony to Puerto Padre's former strategic importance. There's a small museum with military paraphernalia inside.

🛏 Sleeping & Eating

There are about a dozen casas particulares and little demand.

**★ Roberto Lío
Montes de Oca** CASA PARTICULAR **$**
(☑ 51-57-22; Francisco V Aguilera No 2, btwn Jesús Menéndez & Conrrado Benítez; r CUC$20-25; ❄)
The freshly painted pink facade of this house shines out amid Puerto Padre's ubiquitous dilapidation and acts as a portent for what's inside. The one prettily decorated bedroom smells, looks and is clean. Breakfast and dinner are available from the young hosts for CUC$3 and CUC$5 respectively.

☆ Entertainment

There is a **Casa de la Cultura** (Parque de la Independencia) for nighttime activities or you can just surf the streets in search of friends, conversation or overnight accommodations in a casa particular. The town also has Cuba's newest branch of Uneac (Unión de Escritores y Artistas de Cuba; Union of Cuban Writers and Artists), which puts on shows, dancing and art expos.

❶ Getting There & Away

Puerto Padre is best accessed by truck, leaving from Las Tunas train station, or with your own wheels. A taxi from the provincial capital should cost approximately CUC$30.

Punta Covarrubias

Las Tunas province's only all-inclusive resort is also one of the island's most isolated, situated 41 rutted kilometers northwest of Puerto Padre on a spotless sandy beach at Punta Covarrubias. Sitting aside the blue-green Atlantic, the **Brisas Covarrubias** (☑ 51-55-30; s/d CUC$88/132; P ❄ @ ☀) has 122 comfortable rooms in cabin-blocks (one room is designed for disabled guests). **Scuba diving** at the coral reef 1.5km offshore is the highlight. Packages of two dives per day start at CUC$45 at the Marina Covarrubias. There are 12 dive sites here. Almost all guests arrive on all-inclusive tours and are bused in from Frank País Airport in Holguín, 115km to the southeast. It's very secluded.

Self-sufficient travelers can turn in to the beach at the **mirador** (a tower with fantastic panoramic views), 200m before the hotel, or procure a hotel day-pass for CUC$25.

❶ Getting There & Away

The road from Puerto Padre to Playa Covarrubias is what Cuban taxi drivers call *mas o menos* (more or less) due to regular hotel traffic. West

to Manatí and Playa Santa Lucía is an African-style hole-fest. Drive slowly and carefully!

Playas La Herradura, La Llanita & Las Bocas

Congratulations! You've made it to the end of the road. A captivating alternative to the comforts of Covarrubias can be found at this string of northern beaches hugging the Atlantic coast 30km north of Puerto Padre and 55km from Holguín. There's not much to do here apart from read, relax, ruminate and get lost in the vivid colors of traditional Cuban life.

From Puerto Padre it's 30km around the eastern shore of Bahía de Chaparra to **Playa la Herradura**. The beach is a scoop of golden sand that will one day undoubtedly host an all-inclusive resort. Enjoy it while you can – by yourself. There is a handful of houses legally renting rooms (look for the blue-and-white Arrendador Divisa sign). A long-standing choice is **Villa Papachongo** (☑ Holguín 24-42-41-74; Casa No 137; r CUC$15-20; ❄), right on the beach with a great porch for catching the sunset. Ask around. The place isn't big and everybody knows everybody else.

Continue west on this road for 11km to **Playa la Llanita**. The sand here is softer and whiter than in La Herradura, but the beach lies on an unprotected bend and there's sometimes a vicious chop.

Just 1km beyond, you come to the end of the road at **Playa las Bocas** where there are several more houses for rent along with a small snack store and an open-air bar at the entrance to town. Wedged between the coast and Bahía de Chaparra, you can usually catch a local ferry to El Socucho and continue to Puerto Padre or rent a room in a casa particular.

❶ Getting There & Away

There are trucks that can take you as far as Puerto Padre from Las Tunas, from where you'll have to connect with another ride to the junction at Lora before heading north to the beaches. It's much easier to get up this way from Holguín, changing at the town of Velasco.

Driving is the best shot. The 52km between Las Tunas and Puerto Padre are well-paved; after that it gets decidedly iffy. Taxis will often ask for more payment due to the bad driving conditions.

Holguín Province

24 / POP 1,037,600

Includes ➡

Best Beach Breaks

➡ Cayo Saetía (p376)

➡ Playa Caletones (p365)

➡ Playa Pesquero (p367)

Best Places to Stay

➡ Hotel Ordoño (p366)

➡ Hotel Playa Pesquero (p368)

➡ Villa Don Lino (p367)

Why Go?

'It was absolute poverty but also absolute freedom; out in the open, surrounded by trees, animals, apparitions...'

So said famed dissident-writer Reinaldo Arenas of his childhood in rural Holguín province. Perhaps something in the undeniably entrancing beauty of Holguín's landscapes breeds extremes: Arenas' ideological opposite, Fulgencio Batista, and the ideological opposite of both, one Fidel Castro, were also reared here. The contradictions don't end there. Holguín is where the pine-scented purity of the Sierra del Cristal Mountains is muddied by environmental degradation around Moa's nickel mines, and where the inherent Cuban-ness of Gibara grates with Guardalavaca's tourist swank.

Holguín's beauty was first spied by Christopher Columbus who, by most accounts, docked near Gibara in October 1492 and described the region's broccoli-green forests and shapely coastal hills as the most beautiful land he had ever seen.

These days, you'll spot giant resort enclaves hugging the coast as often as pristine ecosystems. Say *hola* to Guardalavaca, Esmeralda and super-posh Playa Pesquero.

When to Go

➡ In April movie aficionados convene in Gibara for the Festival Internacional del Cine Pobre.

➡ May sees the city of Holguín show its religious spirit during the Romerías de Mayo.

➡ To avoid the peak storm period, arrive when the season ends in mid-November.

➡ You can enjoy the Guardalavaca and Playa Pesquero resorts in prime tourist season from December until early March.

History

Most historians agree that Christopher Columbus first made landfall in Cuba on October 28, 1492, at Cayo Bariay near Playa Blanca, just west of Playa Don Lino (now in Holguín province). The gold-seeking Spaniards were welcomed ashore by *seborucos* and they captured 13 of them to take back to Europe as scientific 'specimens.' Bariay was boycotted in favor of Guantánamo 20 years later when a new colonial capital was set up in Baracoa, and the hilly terrain north of Bayamo was gifted to Captain García Holguín, a Mexican conquistador. The province became an important sugar-growing area at the end of the 19th century when much of the land was bought up and cleared of forest by the US-owned United Fruit Company. Formerly part of the Oriente territory, Holguín became a province in its own right after 1975.

Holguín

POP 277,000

Producer of the nation's four main beers (Cristal, Bucanero, Mayabe and Cacique), Holguín might create a substantial part of Cuba's entertainment industry, but it's intoxicating on its own terms, too. Much like a good Cristal, it refreshes the senses. It welcomes you not with ailing colonial grandeur but with an industrious feistiness: the influence of the US-owned United Fruit Company hereabouts makes parts of the city more resemble a neat North American suburb, while the layout – the high proportion of plazas have landed it the moniker 'ciudad de los parques' (city of parks) and in La Loma de la Cruz it has the best city lookout in all Cuba – makes appreciating Holguín easy.

This is a hard-working and cultural city. Holguín hosts the Ballet Nacional de Cuba, and when you see the well-heeled locals out in action of a Saturday night at one of the classy music venues around town, you'll be hard pushed not to submit to the *holguiñero* spirit and join in.

History

In 1515 Diego Velázquez de Cuéllar, Cuba's first governor, conferred the lands north of Bayamo to Captain García Holguín, one of the island's original colonizers. Setting up a cattle ranch in the province's verdant and fertile hinterland, Holguín and his descendants presided over a burgeoning agricultural settlement that by 1720 had sprouted a small wooden church and more than 450 inhabitants. In 1752 San Isidoro de Holguín (the settlement was renamed after the church) was granted the title of city and by 1790 the population had expanded to 12,000.

Holguín was the setting of much fighting during the two wars of independence when ferocious Mambí warriors laid siege to the heavily fortified Spanish barracks at La Periquera (now the Museo de Historia Provincial). Captured and lost by Julio Grave de Peralta (after whom one of the squares is named), the city was taken for a second time on December 19, 1872, by Cuban general and native son Calixto García, Holguín's posthumous local hero.

With the division of Oriente into five separate provinces in 1976, the city of Holguín became a provincial capital. Besides beer, the key industries are agriculture and nickel. The city has also cultivated an international reputation for drug rehabilitation: Argentine soccer star Diego Maradona came here for rehab in 2000 (it was to be the start of a long-running friendship between the footballer and Fidel Castro). Most recently, Holguín suffered a severe mauling from Hurricane Ike in 2008.

◉ Sights

Holguín is known, somewhat euphemistically, as the 'city of parks' (they're more like squares). Base yourself around the four central squares and you'll see most of what's on offer. No walk is complete without a climb up to La Loma de la Cruz – a little off the grid, but well worth the detour.

★ **Museo de Historia Provincial** MUSEUM
(Map p360; Frexes No 198; admission CUC$1; ⊘8am-4:30pm Tue-Sat, to noon Sun) Now a national monument, the building on the northern side of Parque Calixto García was constructed between 1860 and 1868 and used as a Spanish army barracks during the independence wars. It was nicknamed La Periquera (Parrot Cage) for the red, yellow and green uniforms of the Spanish soldiers who stood guard.

The prize exhibit is an old axe-head carved in the likeness of a man, known as the Hacha de Holguín (Holguín Axe), thought to have been made by indigenous inhabitants in the early 1400s and discovered in 1860. Looking even sharper in its polished glass case is a sword that once belonged to national hero and poet José Martí.

Holguín Province Highlights

1 See Holguín spread out like a map beneath you from the **Loma de la Cruz** (p356).

2 Fork out for some beach time at one of the plush resorts on **Playa Pesquero** (p367).

3 Take a bicycle ride through bucolic villages to the quintessential *holguiñero* town of **Banes** (p372).

4 Marvel at the exotic wildlife at the exclusive island retreat of **Cayo Saetía** (p376).

5 Discover Taíno treasures in one of Cuba's most important archaeological sites at **Museo**

Chorro de Maita (p368) in Guardalavaca.

6 Stay in a hotel-standard casa particular in the relaxed and romantic seaside town of **Gibara** (p364).

7 Peep behind the mask and find out about the Castro family at Fidel's childhood home, **Museo Conjunto Histórico de Birán** (p374).

8 Splash out on a trip to the **Salto del Guayabo** (p374) from its spectacularly perched overlook.

Parque Peralta   SQUARE

(Parque de las Flores; Map p360) This square is named for General Julio Grave de Peralta (1834–72), who led an uprising against Spain in Holguín in October 1868. His marble statue (1916) faces the imposing Catedral de San Isidoro. On the western side of the park is the Mural de Origen, which depicts the development of Holguín and of Cuba from indigenous times to the end of slavery.

★Catedral de San Isidoro   CATHEDRAL

(Map p360; Manduley) Dazzling white and characterized by its twin domed towers, the Catedral de San Isidoro dates from 1720 and was one of the town's original constructions. Added piecemeal over the years, the towers are of 20th-century vintage and in 1979 it became a cathedral. A hyper-realistic statue of Pope Jean Paul II stands to the right of the main doors.

★La Loma de la Cruz   LANDMARK

At the northern end of Maceo you'll find a stairway built in 1950, with 465 steps ascending a 275m-high hill with panoramic views, a restaurant and a 24-hour bar. A cross was raised here in 1790 in hope of relieving a drought, and every May 3 during Romerías de Mayo devotees climb to the summit where a special Mass is held.

It's a 20-minute walk from town or you can flag a bici-taxi to the foot of the hill for around 10 Cuban pesos. This walk is best tackled early in the morning when the light is pristine and the heat not too debilitating.

Parque Calixto García   SQUARE

(Map p360) This wide, expansive park is more about atmosphere than architecture. It was laid out in 1719 as the original Plaza de Armas and served for many years as the town's meeting point and marketplace. The centerpiece today is a 1912 statue of General Calixto García, around which congregate a

Holguín

multifarious mixture of old sages, baseball naysayers and teenagers on the prowl.

In the southwestern corner of Parque Calixto García is the **Centro de Arte** (Map p360; Maceo No 180; ⏱9am-4pm Mon-Sat) **FREE**, a bright gallery that shares space with **Biblioteca Alex Urquiola** (Map p360; Maceo No 178), named after a local revolutionary and housing Holguín's biggest book collection.

Parque Céspedes   SQUARE
(Parque San José; Map p360) Holguín's youngest park is also its shadiest. Named for 'Father of the Motherland' Carlos Manuel de Céspedes – his statue stands center-stage next to a monument honoring the heroes of the War of Independence – the cobbled central square is dominated by the **Iglesia de San José** (Map p360; Manduley No 116).

The church, with its distinctive dome and bell tower (1842), was once used by the In-

dependistas as a lookout tower. Locals still refer to the park by its old name, San José.

Casa Natal de Calixto García   MUSEUM
(Map p360; Miró No 147; admission CUC$1; ⏱9am-5pm Tue-Sat) To learn more about the militaristic deeds of Holguín's local hero, head to this house situated two blocks east of the namesake park. The hugely underestimated García – who stole the cities of Las Tunas, Holguín and Bayamo from Spanish control between 1896 and 1898 – was born here in 1839.

This small collection gives a reasonable overview of his life: military maps, old uniforms and even a spoon he ate with on the campaign trail in 1885.

Musco de Historia Natural   MUSEUM
(Map p360; Maceo No 129, btwn Parques Calixto García & Peralta; admission CUC$1; ⏱9am-10pm Tue-Sat) You'll find more stuffed animals here than in a New York toy store – everything from the world's smallest frog to the world's smallest hummingbird. There's a big collection of the unique yellow polymita seashells found on Cuba's far-east coastline.

Plaza de la Marqueta   SQUARE
Long earmarked for a major renovation, hopelessly ruined Plaza de la Marqueta is a plaza of possibilities that remain unfulfilled. Laid out in 1848 and rebuilt in 1918,

Holguín

⊙ **Sights**
1 Plaza de la Revolución..........................F1
   Tomb of Calixto García ....(see 1)

🛏 **Sleeping**
2 Don Santiago.....................................C4
3 Hotel Pernik.......................................F2
4 'La Palma' – Enrique R Interián
   Salermo A1
5 Villa Janeth B3
6 Villa Liba..A1

✴ **Eating**
7 Agropecuario......................................C4
8 Agropecuario......................................E3
9 El Ciruelo...A3
10 Peso Stalls...E3
11 Restaurante 1910...............................B3
   Taberna Pancho...........................(see 3)

☺ **Entertainment**
   Disco Havana Club......................(see 3)
12 Estadio General Calixto García..........E2

the square is dominated by an impressive covered marketplace supposedly undergoing a transformation into a top-notch concert hall (after a decade of rumors, however, the work has yet to start).

Running along the north and south sides of the plaza are myriad shops that are meant to provide quality shopping but, to date, number only a couple of music and cigar outlets.

Parque Don Quixote PARK

(cnrs Aguilera, Av Los Alamos & Av VI Lenin) Miguel de Cervantes fans, get excited: in this park near the Víazul bus station is surely Cuba's biggest statue of the Don, in full tilt against the windmills, while Sancho Panza looks on, somewhat embarrassed.

Plaza de la Revolución SQUARE

(Map p356) Holguín is a city most *fiel* (faithful), and its bombastic revolutionary plaza, east of the center, is a huge monument to the heroes of Cuban independence, bearing quotations from José Martí and Fidel Castro.

Massive rallies are held here every May 1 (Labor Day). The **tomb of Calixto García** (Map p356), containing his ashes, is also here, is a smaller monument to García's mother.

Fábrica de Órganos ORGAN FACTORY

(Carretera de Gibara No 301; ⊗8am-4pm Mon-Fri) This is the only mechanical music-organ factory in Cuba. This small factory produces about six organs a year, as well as guitars and other instruments.

A good organ costs between the equivalent of US$10,000 and US$25,000. Eight professional organ groups exist in Holguín (including the Familia Cuayo, based at the factory): if you're lucky, you can hear one playing on Parque Céspedes on Thursday afternoon or Sunday morning.

Mirador de Mayabe LOOKOUT

The Mirador de Mayabe is a motel-cum-restaurant high on a hill 10km from Holguín city. It gained fame for a beer-drinking donkey named Pancho, who hung out near the bar in the 1980s. The original Pancho died in 1992 and they're now onto Pancho IV who also drinks beer. Traditional country shows occur here most weeks.

A bus runs to Holguín from the bottom of the hill, 1.5km from the motel, three times a day.

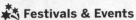 ## Festivals & Events

Romerías de Mayo RELIGIOUS

Romerías de Mayo is Holguín's big annual pilgrimage, held on May 3: devotees climb Loma de la Cruz for a special mass.

Carnaval STREET CARNIVAL

Holguín's annual shindig happens in the third week of August with outdoor concerts and copious amounts of dancing, roast pork and potent potables.

🛌 Sleeping

There's a dearth of midrange and top-end options in the centre.

'La Palma' – Enrique R
Interián Salermo CASA PARTICULAR $

(Map p356; ☑42-46-83; Maceo No 52A, btwn Calles 16 & 18, El Llano; r CUC$25; ❄) Enrique's detached neocolonial house dates from 1945 and is situated in the shadow of the Loma de la Cruz. The slightly removed location is worth the minor inconvenience. Enrique is a fantastic host and his spacious house has a pleasant garden – with table tennis!

Furthermore, his son is a talented painter and sculptor and you can check out the terracotta bust of Che Guevara in the living room next to an unusual 3m-long canvas copy of Da Vinci's *The Last Supper* (with St John as a woman).

Motel el Bosque HOTEL $

(☑48-11-40; Av Jorge Dimitrov; s/d incl breakfast CUC$30/45; ꟼ❄❄) One kilometer beyond Hotel Pernik (p359) and at least one notch up on the quality ratings, the 69 solar-powered duplex bungalows here are set among extensive green grounds. There's a relaxing bar beside the swimming pool (nonguests can use it for a small fee) and the late-night music decibels aren't as ear-shattering as its noisy neighbor (the Pernik).

Villa Liba CASA PARTICULAR $

(Map p356; ☑42-38-23; Maceo No 46, cnr Calle 18; r CUC$20-25; ❄) The *alma* (soul) of a place is most important, right? At Jorge's smart, sizable bungalow, looking like something out of a 1950s North American suburb, *alma* fairly bubbles over. Jorge is a modern-day Pablo Neruda with whimsical anecdotes aplenty on Holguín life, while his wife is an accomplished masseuse and Reiki specialist (treatments CUC$15) and his daughter gives violin recitals over dinner.

Hotel Pernik
HOTEL $

(Map p356; ✆48-10-11; cnr Avs Jorge Dimitrov & XX Aniversario; s/d incl breakfast CUC$30/45; P✷@⛱) The nearest decent hotel to the city center is another dose of Soviet-inspired '70s nostalgia. It has attempted to counter its dour reputation in recent years by letting local artists decorate the rooms in their colorful art. The breakfast buffet is plentiful and there's an information office, Cadeca and internet cafe; however, the hotel suffers from the usual foibles of interminable renovations and blaring late-night music.

Villa Janeth
CASA PARTICULAR $

(Map p356; ✆42-93-31; Cables No 105; r CUC$20-25; ✷) Janeth has a very clean, very spacious house with two upstairs rooms far above the average Holguín standard. Follow the passageway back and you'll get to a self-contained kitchen and terrace. There's another amenable house a few doors down on the corner with Manduley if these guys are full.

Don Santiago
CASA PARTICULAR $

(Map p356; ✆42-61-46; Narciso López No 258 Altos; r CUC$25; ✷) A 2nd-floor apartment with bags of holguiñero atmosphere: there's one comfortable room here, and your hosts will happily gas all night with you about architecture, traveling and the like.

Maricela García Martínez
CASA PARTICULAR $

(Map p360; ✆47-10-49; Miró No 110, btwn Martí & Luz Caballero; r CUC$20-25) You don't get much more central than this. The downstairs bedroom is a little on the dark side, but it has an en-suite bath, while the upstairs room is a mini-apartment, of sorts. Plus you're a block from the central parks.

Villa Mirador de Mayabe
HOTEL $

(✆42-54-98; Alturas de Mayabe; bungalows CUC$50; P✷⛱) This motel, high up on the Loma de Mayabe, 10km southeast of Holguín, has 24 rooms tucked into lush grounds. The views, taking in vast mango plantations, are especially good from the pool.

✗ Eating

The 2011 relaxing of restrictions on paladares (privately owned eateries) benefited Holguín more than most cities: there are now some great new options.

El Ciruelo
CHINESE $

(Map p356; ✆52-91-84-14; Victoria No 108 Altos, btwn Aguilera & Frexes; mains CUC$2-4; ⊙5-11pm) You're in Cuba's Oriente, not the Orient, and thus this could be the best Chinese restaurant around. It's small but beautifully decorated (bonsai trees, bamboo chairs), with an open upper terrace overlooking a wild garden, and a Chinese- and seafood-based menu. The chop suey and seafood platter are two standout choices.

Taberna Pancho
CARIBBEAN $

(Map p356; Av Jorge Dimitrov; mains CUC$2-4; ⊙noon-10pm) This central bar, inspired by the Mirador de Mayabe's famous beer-drinking donkey, has echoes of a Spanish taberna, done up in dark wood. The menu includes actual chorizo (unusual in Cuba), and draft Mayabe beer comes in proper frosted glasses. Nothing on the menu is more than CUC$3.

Cafetería Cristal
FAST FOOD $

(Map p360; Edificio Pico de Cristal, cnr Manduley & Martí; meals CUC$1-3; ⊙24hr) Nothing wrong with this plaza-fronting joint, which is typical of such joints across Latin America: reliable, affordable chicken meals dished up by formal waiters whose elegance prepares you for cuisine far superior to what you end up getting. The air-con does its best to replicate a frigid day in Vancouver; perch on the outside terrace with the surprisingly great house coffee and soak up Holguín life.

Cremería Guamá
ICE CREAM $

(Map p360; cnr Luz Caballero & Manduley; ⊙10am-10:45pm) A Coppelia in all but name. Lose an hour underneath the striped red-and-white awning overlooking pedestrianized Calle Manduley and enjoy peso ice cream alfresco.

★ Restaurante 1910
RESTAURANT $$

(Map p356; ✆42-39-94; www.1910restaurantebar.com; Mártires No 143, btwn Aricochea & Cables; meals CUC$8-11; ⊙noon-midnight) Holguín has too many restaurants named after dates but 1910 is red-letter day as far as innovative food goes in this city. Neither the eating area (a colonial house hung with chandeliers) nor the courteous service can be faulted, and that's before you've started on the specialty steak (CUC$11) with dried spaghetti latticework (delicious).

Wash it down with any one of a fine selection of South American wines (poured into specially embossed 1910 wineglasses) and enjoy. This is attention to detail you rarely get eating out in Cuba.

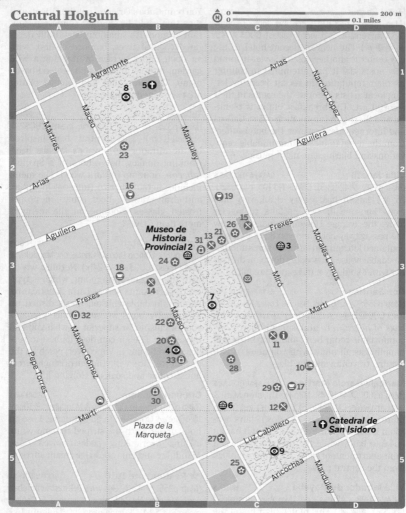

N 0 ———————— 200 m
  0 ———————— 0.1 miles

HOLGUÍN PROVINCE HOLGUÍN

Museo de Historia Provincial 2

Plaza de la Marqueta

Catedral de San Isidoro

Salón 1720 CARIBBEAN **$$**
(Map p360; Frexes No 190 cnr Miró; mains CUC$6-8; 12:30-10:30pm) This is a painstakingly restored wedding-cake mansion where you can tuck into paella (CUC$6) or chicken stuffed with vegetables and cheese (CUC$8); there are even complimentary crackers offered. In the same colonial-style complex you can find a cigar shop, bar, boutique, car rental and a terrace with nighttime music. Check out the wall plaques that give interesting insights into Holguín's history.

Ranchón Los Almendros PARRILLA **$$**
(42-96-52; José A Cardet No 68, btwn Calles 12 & 14; meals CUC$10; 10am-11pm) So clean and professionally run is the kitchen here that they've decided to make it open, so the aromas of the copious portions of grilled meat infiltrate every corner of this *ranchón* (rural restaurant) in the city.

Self-Catering

There is an **agropecuario** (vegetable market; Map p356) off Calle 19, the continuation of Morales Lemus near the train station, and another **agropecuario** (Map p356) on Calle 3

Central Holguín

◎ Top Sights
1 Catedral de San Isidoro D5
2 Museo de Historia Provincial B3

◎ Sights
Biblioteca Alex Urquiola............... (see 20)
3 Casa Natal de Calixto García................. C3
4 Centro de Arte.................................. B4
5 Iglesia de San José B1
6 Museo de Historia Natural.................... C4
7 Parque Calixto García............................ C3
8 Parque Céspedes.................................... B1
9 Parque Peralta C5

🛏 Sleeping
10 Maricela García Martínez...................... D4

🍴 Eating
11 Cafetería Cristal.................................... C4
12 Cremería Guamá.................................... C4
13 La Epoca... C3
14 La Luz de Yara.. B3
15 Salón 1720 .... C3

🍷 Drinking & Nightlife
Bar Terraza................................... (see 15)
16 La Caverna.. B2

17 La Tienda el Encanto............................. C4
18 Las 3 Lucías.. B3
19 Taberna Mayabe..................................... C2

🎭 Entertainment
20 Biblioteca Alex
Urquiola B4
21 Casa de la Música C3
22 Casa de la Trova B4
23 Casa Iberoamericana............................. B2
24 Cine Martí B3
25 Cominado Deportivo
Henry García
Suárez.. C5
Disco Cristal.................................. (see 11)
26 Jazz Club C3
27 Salón Benny Moré C5
28 Teatro Comandante
Eddy Suñol C4
29 Uneac.. C4

🛍 Shopping
30 El Jigue... B4
31 Fondo de Bienes
Culturales B3
32 Librería Villena Botev............................ A4
33 Pentagrama B4

in Dagoberto Sanfield. There are plenty of **peso stalls** (Map p356) beside the baseball stadium.

La Luz de Yara SUPERMARKET $
(Map p360; cnr Frexes & Maceo; ⊙ 8:30am-7pm Mon-Sat, to noon Sun) Relatively well-stocked Cuban department store and supermarket with a bakery section on Parque Calixto García.

La Epoca SUPERMARKET $
(Map p360; Frexes No 194; ⊙ 8:30am-7pm Mon-Sat, 9:30am-2pm Sun) Another supermarket option on Parque Calixto García.

🍷 Drinking & Nightlife

Stand down all other claimants: Holguín brews the best beer in Cuba. The large Fábrica de Cerveza on the outskirts of the city produces the nation's two most popular beers, Cristal and Bucanero, as well as local favorites Mayabe and Cacique. The local bars aren't too flash, but you can cobble together a decent pub crawl here. In no specific order, hit on some of the following.

Taberna Mayabe BAR
(Map p360; Manduley, btwn Aguilera & Frexes; ⊙ 3-6pm & 8pm-midnight Tue-Sun) Not the famous

mirador (viewpoint) but Pancho the beer-drinking donkey would have a field day on pedestrian-only Manduley, where wooden tables and ceramic mugs equal a hearty pub atmosphere. The eponymous local brew is served.

Las 3 Lucías CAFE
(Map p360; cnr Mártires & Frexes; ⊙ 3pm-1am) *Lucía* was a 1968 classic Cuban film about the lives of three women, each named Lucía, in different periods: the War of Independence, the 1930s and the 1960s. Such is the premise for this fancy bar, decorated in Cuban film memorabilia and evoking a classy atmosphere of yesteryear (save for the big wall-mounted TV). The cocktails are good, the coffee's alright and the atmosphere is pretty unique.

Bar Terraza BAR
(Map p360; Frexes, btwn Manduley & Miró; ⊙ 9pm-2am) Perched above Salón 1720, this is the poshest spot to sip a mojito with views over Parque Calixto García and regular musical interludes.

La Tienda el Encanto CAFE
(Map p360; Manduley s/n btwn Martí & Luz Caballero; ⊙ 9am-6pm) Holguín's best coffee; and on the 2nd floor of a department store, too.

La Caverna
BAR, LIVE MUSIC

(Map p360; cnr Aguilera & Maceo; ☺4pm-2am) Not a cave, but a bar named in honor of The Beatles, whose songs are reproduced by local bands such as Los Beltas and Retorno. Graffiti adorns walls decorated with familiar Fab Four album covers.

Casa de la Música
NIGHTCLUB

(Map p360; cnr Frexes & Manduley; ☺Tue-Sun) There's a young, trendy vibe at this place on Parque Calixto García. If you can't dance, stay static sinking beers on the adjacent Terraza Bucanero (entry via Calle Manduley).

Disco Cristal
NIGHTCLUB

(Map p360; 3rd fl, Edificio Pico de Cristal, Manduley No 199; admission CUC$2; ☺9pm-2am Tue-Thu) A nexus for Holguín's dexterous dancers (most of whom are young, cool and determined to have a good time), this place is insanely popular at weekends when you'll find lots of inspiration for the salsa/rap/*reggaetón* (Cuban hip-hop) repertoire.

Cabaret Nuevo Nocturno
NIGHTCLUB

(admission CUC$8; ☺10pm-2am) This is a Tropicana-style cabaret club beyond the Servi-Cupet gas station 3km out on the road to Las Tunas.

Disco Havana Club
NIGHTCLUB

(Map p356; Hotel Pernik, cnr Avs Jorge Dimitrov & XX Aniversario; guest/nonguest CUC$2/4; ☺10pm-2am Tue-Sun) Holguín's premier disco. If you're staying at the hotel, the music will visit you – in your room – like it or not, until 1am.

☆ Entertainment

★ Uneac
CULTURAL CENTER

(Unión Nacional de Escritores y Artistas de Cuba; National Union of Cuban Writers and Artists; Map p360; Manduley, btwn Luz Caballero & Martí) If you only visit one Uneac in Cuba – there are 14 in total, at least one per province – make it this one. Situated in a lovingly restored house on car-free Calle Manduley, this friendly establishment offers literary evenings with famous authors, music nights, patio theater (including Lorca) and cultural reviews.

There's an intermittent bar on a gorgeous central patio, and regular art exhibitions: invariably the city's best.

Teatro Comandante Eddy Suñol
THEATER

(Map p360; Martí No 111) Holguín's premier theater is an art deco treat from 1939 on Parque Calixto García. It hosts both the Teatro Lírico Rodrigo Prats and the Ballet Nacional de Cuba and is renowned both nationally and internationally for its operettas, dance performances and Spanish musicals. Check here for details of performances by the famous children's theater Alas Buenas and the Orquesta Sinfónica de Holguín (Holguín Symphony Orchestra).

Salón Benny Moré
LIVE MUSIC

(Map p360; cnr Luz Caballero & Maceo; ☺show 10:30pm) Holguín's impressive new outdoor music venue is the best place to round off a bar crawl with some live music and dancing.

Biblioteca Alex Urquiola
THEATER

(Map p360; Maceo No 180) Culture vultures steam the creases out of their evening dresses to come here to see live theater, and performances by the Orquesta Sinfónica de Holguín.

Casa de la Trova
LIVE MUSIC

(Map p360; Maceo No 174; ☺Tue-Sun) Old guys in Panama hats croon under the rafters, musicians in *guayaberas* (pleated, buttoned shirts) blast on trumpets, and elderly couples in their Sunday best map out a perfect *danzón* (traditional Cuban ballroom dance colored with African influences). So timeless, so Holguín.

Casa Iberoamericana
CULTURAL CENTER

(Map p360; www.casadeiberoamerica.cult.cu; Arias No 161) Situated on quieter Parque Céspedes, this paint-peeled place frequently hosts *peñas* (musical performances) and cultural activities.

Jazz Club
JAZZ

(Map p360; cnr Frexes & Manduley; ☺8pm-3am) The jazz jams get moving around 8pm and continue weaving magic until 11pm. Then there's piped music until 3am. There's a sporadically functioning daytime cafe downstairs.

Cine Martí
CINEMA

(Map p360; Frexes No 204; tickets MN$1-2) The best of a quintet of city-center cinemas; head here for big-screen movies. It's on Parque Calixto García.

Estadio General Calixto García
SPORT

(Map p356; off Av de los Libertadores; admission CUC$1-2) Mosey on down to this stadium to see Holguín's baseball team, former giant-killers the *perros* (dogs) who snatched the national championship from under the noses of the 'big two' in 2002. The stadium also houses a small but interesting **sport museum**.

**Cominado Deportivo
Henry García Suárez**   SPORT
(Map p360; Maceo; admission MN$1; ☉ boxing matches 8pm Wed, 2pm Sat) You can catch boxing matches at this spit-and-sawdust gym on the western side of Parque Peralta, where three Olympic medalists have trained. You can also pluck up the courage to ask about some (noncontact) training sessions. They're very friendly.

🛍 Shopping

Fondo de Bienes Culturales   ARTS & CRAFTS
(Map p360; Frexes No 196; ☉ 10am-3pm Mon-Fri, 9am-noon Sat) This shop on Parque Calixto García has one of the best selections of Cuban handicrafts.

Pentagrama   MUSIC
(Map p360; cnr Maceo & Martí; ☉ 9am-9pm) Official outlet of the Cuban state record company Egrem, selling a wide-ranging stash of CDs.

Librería Villena Botev   BOOKS
(Map p360; cnr Frexes & Máximo Gómez; ☉ 9am-5pm) Some good magazines here, including cultural Cuban monthly *Temas* along with a popular 'book of the week' nomination.

El Jigue   BOOKS, SOUVENIRS
(Map p360; cnr Martí & Mártires; ☉ 9am-5pm) Bookstore and souvenir outlet adjacent to Plaza de la Maqueta.

ℹ Information

The local newspaper *Ahora* is published on Saturday. Radio Ángulo CMKO can be heard on 1110AM and 97.9FM.

Etecsa Telepunto (☉ 8:30am-7:30pm) There are only telephones at the Parque Calixto García (cnr Martí & Maceo, Parque Calixto García) branch, while Calle Martí (Calle Martí, btwn Mártires & Máximo Gómez; internet per hr CUC$6) has three usually busy computer terminals.

Post Office (Manduley No 183; ☉ 10am-noon & 1-6pm Mon-Fri) There's a DHL office at this branch, on Parque Calixto García; you'll find another post office at Parque Céspedes (Maceo No 114; ☉ 8am-6pm Mon-Sat).

Banco de Crédito y Comercio (Arias) Bank on Parque Céspedes with ATM.

Banco Financiero Internacional (Manduley No 167, btwn Frexes & Aguilera)

Cadeca (Manduley No 205, btwn Martí & Luz Caballero) Money changing.

Cubatur (Edificio Pico de Cristal, cnr Manduley & Martí) Travel agent bivouacked inside the Cafetería Cristal.

Farmacia Turno Especial (Maceo No 170; ☉ 8am-10pm Mon-Sat) Pharmacy on Parque Calixto García.

Hospital Lenin (☎ 42-53-02; Av VI Lenin) Will treat foreigners in an emergency.

Infotur (1st fl, Edificio Pico de Cristal, cnr Manduley & Martí) Tourist information.

ℹ Getting There & Away

AIR

There are up to 16 international flights a week into Holguín's well-organized **Frank País Airport** (HOG; ☎ 42-52-71), 13km south of the city, including from Amsterdam, Düsseldorf, London, Montreal and Toronto. Almost all arrivals get bussed directly off to Guardalavaca and see little of Holguín city.

Domestic destinations are served by **Cubana** (Edificio Pico de Cristal, cnr Manduley & Martí), which flies daily to Havana (about CUC$100 one way, 1¼ hours).

BUS

The **Interprovincial Bus Station** (cnr Carretera Central & Independencia), west of the center near Hospital Lenin, has air-conditioned **Víazul** (www.viazul.com) buses leaving daily.

The Havana bus (CUC$44, 12 hours, four times daily) stops in Las Tunas, Camagüey, Ciego de Ávila, Sancti Spíritus and Santa Clara. The Santiago bus (CUC$11, 3½ hours, thrice daily) also stops in Bayamo. There are also daily buses to Trinidad (CUC$26, 7¾ hours) and Varadero (CUC$38, 11¼ hours).

CAR

Colectivos (shared cars) run to Gibara (CUC$4) and Puerto Padre in Las Tunas province from Av Cajigal. To **Guardalavaca** (CUC$5) they leave from Av XX Aniversario near Terminal Dagoberto Sanfield Guillén.

TRAIN

The **train station** (Calle V Pita) is on the southern side of town. Foreigners must purchase tickets in convertibles at the special **Ladis ticket office** (☉ 7:30am-3pm). The ticket office is marked 'U/B Ferrocuba Provincial Holguín' on the corner of Manduley, opposite the train station.

For any of the following, you will have to change trains at the Santiago–Havana mainline junction in Cacocum, 17km south of Holguín. Theoretically, there's one daily morning train to Las Tunas (CUC$3, two hours), an 8am train every three days to Guantánamo, three daily trains to Santiago de Cuba (CUC$5, 3½ hours), and two daily trains (10:19pm and 5:28am) to Havana (CUC$26, 15 hours). The latter train stops in Camagüey (CUC$6.50), Ciego de Ávila (CUC$10.50), Santa Clara (CUC$15.50) and Matanzas (CUC$22.50).

The only service that operates with any regularity is the train to Havana. The service to Santiago de Cuba is rather irregular. Research beforehand.

TRUCK

The **Terminal Dagoberto Sanfield Guillén** (Av de los Libertadores), opposite Estadio General Calixto García, has at least two daily trucks to Banes and Moa.

ℹ Getting Around

TO/FROM THE AIRPORT

The public bus to the airport leaves daily around 2pm from the **airport bus stop** (General Rodríguez No 84) on Parque Martí near the train station. A tourist taxi to the airport costs from CUC$15 to CUC$20. It's also possible to spend your last night in Bayamo and then catch a taxi (CUC$20 to CUC$25) to Holguín airport.

BICI-TAXI

Holguín's bici-taxis are ubiquitous. They charge MN$5 for a short trip, MN$10 for a long one.

CAR

You can rent or return a car at **Cubacar**, with branches at **Hotel Pernik** (Av Jorge Dimitrov, Hotel Pernik), **Aeropuerto Frank País** (⌨ 46-84-14; Aeropuerto Frank País) and **Cafetería Cristal** (cnr Manduley & Martí).

A **Servi-Cupet gas station** (Carretera Central; ⌚ 24hr) is 3km out of town toward Las Tunas; another station is just outside town on the road to Gibara. An **Oro Negro gas station** (Carretera Central) is on the southern edge of town. The road to Gibara is north on Av Cajígal; also take this road and fork left after 5km to reach Playa la Herradura.

TAXI

A **Cubataxi** (Máximo Gómez No 302, cnr Martí) to Guardalavaca (54km) costs around CUC$35. To Gibara one way should cost no more than CUC$20.

Gibara

POP 36,000

Matched only by Baracoa for its wild coastal setting, Gibara is one of those special places where geography, meteorology and culture have conspired to create something tempestuous and unique. Though your first impres-

sion might not be open-mouthed incredulity (Hurricane Ike almost wiped the town off the map in 2008), suspend your judgment; Gibara casts a more subtle spell.

Columbus first arrived in the area in 1492 and called it Río de Mares (River of Seas) for the Ríos Cacoyugüin and Yabazón that drain into the Bahía de Gibara. The current name comes from *jiba,* the indigenous word for a bush that still grows along the shore.

Refounded in 1817, Gibara prospered in the 19th century as the sugar industry expanded and the trade rolled in. To protect the settlement from pirates, barracks and a 2km wall were constructed around the town in the early 1800s, making Gibara Cuba's second walled city (after Havana). The once sparkling-white facades earned Gibara its nickname, La Villa Blanca.

Holguín's outlet to the sea was once an important sugar-export town that was linked to the provincial capital via a railway. With the construction of the Carretera Central in the 1920s, Gibara lost its mercantile importance, and after the last train service was axed in 1958 the town fell into a sleepy slumber from which it has yet to awaken.

Situated 33km from Holguín via a scenic road that undulates through friendly, eye-catching villages, Gibara is a small, intimate place characterized by pretty plazas, crumbling Spanish ruins and a postcard view of the saddle-shaped Silla de Gibara that so captivated Columbus, while just outside town beckon some of the Oriente's wildest, most wondrous beaches.

Each year in April Gibara hosts the Festival Internacional de Cine Pobre (International Low-Budget Film Festival) which draws films and filmmakers from all over the world.

◉ Sights

Having swept up after the devastation of Hurricane Ike in 2008, Gibara has regained some of its color and vibe. Though the specific sights are few, rather like Baracoa, this is more a town to stroll the streets and absorb the local flavor.

Spanish Forts   FORTS

At the top of Calle Cabada is **El Cuartelón**, a crumbling-brick Spanish fort with graceful arches that provides stunning town and bay views. Continue on this street for 200m to Restaurante el Mirador (p366) for an even better vantage point. You'll see remnants of the old fortresses here and at the **Fuerte**

POOR MAN'S FILM FESTIVAL

There's no red carpet, no paparazzi and no Brangelina, but what the **Festival Internacional de Cine Pobre** (International Low-Budget Film Festival) lacks in glitz it makes up for in raw, undiscovered talent. Then there's the setting – ethereal Gibara, Cuba's crumbling Villa Blanca, a perfect antidote to the opulence of Hollywood and Cannes.

Inaugurated in 2003, the Cine Pobre was the brainchild of late Cuban director Humberto Solás, who fell in love with this quintessential fisherman's town after shooting his seminal movie *Lucía* here in 1968.

Open to independent filmmakers of limited means, the festival takes place in April and, despite limited advertising, attracts up to US$100,000 in prize money. Lasting for seven days, proceedings kick off with a gala in the Cine Jiba followed by film showings, art expositions and nightly music concerts. The competition is friendly but hotly contested, with prizes used to reward and recognize an eclectic cache of digital movie guerrillas drawn from countries as varied as Iran and the US.

Fernando VII, on the point beyond Parque de las Madres, a block over from Parque Calixto García. There's also a sentinel tower at the entrance to the town, coming in from Holguín.

Parque Calixto García   SQUARE
The centerpiece of this park lined with weird *robles africanos* – African oaks with large penis-shaped pods – is **Iglesia de San Fulgencio** (1850). The Statue of Liberty in front commemorates the Spanish-Cuban-American War. On the western side of the square, in a beautiful colonial palace (more interesting than the stuffed stuff it collects), is the **Museo de Historia Natural** (Luz Caballero No 23; admission CUC$1; ⊙ 8am-noon & 1-5pm Mon-Sat). Through barred windows you can watch women rolling cheroots in the **cigar factory** across the square.

Museo de Historia Municipal   MUSEUM
(CUC$1) Two museums share the colonial mansion (1872) at Independencia No 19: this history museum downstairs, and the **Museo de Artes Decorativas** upstairs. Both were closed indefinitely for repair at the time of writing. Across the street is **Galería Cosme Proenza** (Independencia No 32), with wall-to-wall works by one of Cuba's foremost painters.

Caverna de Panaderos   CAVES
This complex cave system with 19 galleries and a lengthy underground trail is close to town at the top end of Calle Independencia. There are no official tourist facilities, but you can look inside with a local guide and some torches. Ask in your casa particular for current details.

Beaches
There are a couple of decent beaches within striking distance of Gibara.

Playa los Bajos   BEACH
Los Bajos, to the east of Gibara, is accessible by a local *lancha* (ferry; CUC$1 each way) that leaves at least twice daily from the fishing pier on La Enramada, the waterfront road leading out of town. These boats cross the Bahía de Gibara to **Playa los Bajos**, from where it's 3km east to Playa Blanca. Both beaches are sandy, with swimming.

Should the ferry be out of action, Los Bajos is a rough 30km drive via Floro Pérez and Fray Benito.

Playa Caletones   BEACH
You'll need some sort of transport (bike, taxi, rental car) to get to this lovely little beach, 17km west of Gibara. The apostrophe-shaped stretch of white sand and azure sea here is a favorite of Holguín vacationers. The town is ramshackle, with no services except rustic **Restaurante La Esparanza** on the beachfront road, serving up some of Cuba's most delectable fresh seafood on an upstairs terrace overlooking the water.

Ask here about freshwater *pozas* (pools) where you can go swimming. DIY divers can part with CUC$10 to be guided to some caves 5km further along, which purportedly contain some of Cuba's best cave diving. You'll need your own equipment. The cave system goes back some 3000m, with water depth about 15m.

🛏 Sleeping
Gibara has some of the province's best options for bedding down.

★ Hotel Ordoño
HOTEL $$

(☑84-44-48; J Peralta, cnr Donato Mármol & Independencia; s/d/ste CUC$65/82/112; ❋) Opened in January 2013, this 27-room revamped colonial wonder is one of Cuba's best hotels and, yep, pinch yourself, you really are in the backwater of Gibara. The service is as bright as the decor is tasteful (check the 3rd-floor individually decorated ceilings, painted with flocks of birds and the like). Still, rooms have mod-cons such as flat-screen TVs picking up international channels.

Grab a bite in the downstairs restaurant or sun yourself on the lovely two-floor roof terrace with spectacular views across Gibara.

Hostal los Hermanos
CASA PARTICULAR $

(☑84-45-42; Céspedes No 13, btwn Luz Caballero & J Peralta; r CUC$20-25; ❋) Bedizened with colonial splendor, you can relax here, in one of four big bedrooms, with a salubrious patio and fountain, signature Gibara stained glass and delicious meals, all located a block and a half from Parque Calixto García. The house also doubles up as a paladar for nonguests.

Hostal El Patio
CASA PARTICULAR $

(☑84-42-69; J Mora No 19, btwn Cuba & J Agüero; r CUC$20-25) Tucked away behind this high-walled patio is Gibara's cosiest digs: a lovely part-covered patio leading to two rooms (the back one is best). Mealtimes are magical in this little getaway and the coffee, served pretty much all the time, is great.

Hostal Sol y Mar
CASA PARTICULAR $

(☑52-40-21-64; J Peralta No 59; r CUC$20-25) In a blue-and-yellow house right on the waterfront is this house that seems just-landed from somewhere in Canada's Maritime provinces. At the time of writing there was one simple room with plans for a second underway, but the young host, who can speak French, English, Dutch and German, will make your stay a pleasant one. There's a self-catering kitchen.

Villa Caney
CASA PARTICULAR $$

(☑84-45-52; Sartorio No 36, btwn J Peralta & Luz Caballero; r CUC$20-25; ❋) There's more stunning Gibara beauty here, captured in a sturdy stone colonial house that withstood the category 4 force of Hurricane Ike. Two rooms off an impressive courtyard are large and have private baths.

Eating

Slowly, at the speed of a Cadillac on a pot-holed track, things are modernizing. Some enterprising casas particulares operate as paladares, bolstering possibilities.

La Cueva
PARRILLA $

(Calle 2da, cnr Carretera a Playa Caletones; dishes CUC$4; ⊙noon-midnight) Finally, Gibara's eating scene starts to get imaginative with this place, which grows its own herbs to garnish those grills and even has a small farm. There's a *ranchón*-style part and a more formal restaurant area above. It's at the northern end to town.

Restaurante Las Terrazas
SEAFOOD $

(☑84-44-61; Calixto García No 40 cnr Céspedes; CUC$6-8; ⊙noon-11pm) This is where to head for fresh fish: cooked in the traditional style of the *pesadores gibareños* (fishermen of Gibara).

Restaurante el Mirador
FAST FOOD $

(⊙24hr) Perched high above town near El Cuartelón, this place has a view to die for but not much in the way of good food.

☆ Entertainment

For theater and dance, it's the historic **Casino Español** (1889). **Patio Colonial**, wedged between the Museo de Historia Natural and Casino Español, is an atmospheric outdoor cafetería that hosts regular musical performances.

Cine Jiba
CINEMA

(Parque Calixto García) Cuba's improbable poor man's film festival hosts most of its cutting-edge movies in this small but quirky cinema covered with colorful art-house movie posters. If you're going to go to the cinema anywhere in Cuba, it should be in Gibara – it's a local rite of passage.

Centro Cultural Batería Fernando VII
CULTURAL CENTER

(Plaza del Fuerte) The diminutive Spanish fort hovering above the choppy ocean is today an atmospheric cultural center run by ARTex that puts on weekend shows and serves food and drink from a sinuous bar-restaurant.

Casa de Cultura
CULTURAL CENTER

(Parque Colón) You might catch a salsa night here, or gain an appreciation of the poetry of Nicolas Guillén in the pleasant inner courtyard.

ℹ Information

Most services line Calle Independencia.
Bandec (cnr Independencia & J Peralta) Also changes traveler's checks.
Post Office (Independencia No 15) There are few public phones here.

ℹ Getting There & Away

There are no Víazul buses to Gibara. Travelers can tackle the route with Cuban transport on a truck or shared *colectivo* (collective taxis; CUC$4) from Holguín. The **bus station** is 1km out on the road to Holguín. There are two daily buses in each direction. A regular taxi (to Holguín) should cost CUC$20.

For drivers heading toward Guardalavaca, the link road from the junction at Floro Pérez is hell at first, but improves just outside Rafael Freyre. There's an **Oro Negro gas station** at the entrance to town.

Playa Pesquero & Around

Of Holguín's three northern resort areas, Playa Pesquero (Fishermen's Beach) is the most high-end. There are four tourist colossi here, including the five-star Hotel Playa Pesquero (p368), and the strip has a luxury Caribbean sheen missing elsewhere on the island. Not surprisingly, the adjacent beach is sublime, with golden sand, shallow, warm water and great opportunities for snorkeling. The resorts and beaches are accessible off the main Holguín–Guardalavaca road via a spur road just before the Cuatro Palmas junction.

◉ Sights & Activities

Both of the sights below as well as Las Guanas at Playa Esmeralda are part of the **Parque Natural Cristóbal Colón**.

**Parque Nacional
Monumento Bariay**   HISTORIC SITE
(admission CUC$8; ⊙ 9am-5pm) Ten kilometers west of Playa Pesquero and 3km west of Villa Don Lino is **Playa Blanca**; Columbus is thought to have landed somewhere near here in 1492, and this great meeting of two cultures is commemorated in a varied mix of sights, the centerpiece of which is an impressive Hellenic-style monument designed by Holguín artist Caridad Ramos for the 500th anniversary of the landing in 1992.

Other points of interest include an **information center**, the remains of a 19th-century **Spanish fort**, three reconstructed Taíno Indian huts and an **archaeological museum**. It makes a pleasant afternoon's sojourn.

★**Bioparque Rocazul**   NATURE RESERVE
(⊙ 9am-5pm) Located just off the link road that joins Playa Turquesa with the other Pesquero resorts, this protected bio-park offers the usual hand-holding array of outdoor activities under the supervision of a nonnegotiable government guide. It's a commendable environmental effort in a major resort area, but the limitations on your right to roam can be a little stifling (and costly).

Leisurely walking excursions go for CUC$8/10/12 for one/two/three hours. You can go horseback riding for CUC$16 an hour or fishing for CUC$29. All-inclusive packages cost CUC$40. The park is extensive with hills, trails, ocean access and the **Casa de Compay Kike**, a working farm where you can sample Cuban food and coffee. There's a friendly bar at the entrance to the park where you can weigh up the financial pros and cons.

🛏 Sleeping

Campismo Silla de Gibara   CABINS $
(☑ 42-15-86; s/d CUC$14/22; ❄) This rustic campismo (camping installation) sits on sloping ground beneath Gibara's signature saddle-shaped hill. Reached via a rough road between Floro Pérez and Rafael Freyre, it's 35km southeast of Gibara itself and 1.5km off the main road. There are 42 rooms sleeping two, four or six people, but come for the views, not the comfort.

There's also a cave you can hike to, 1.5km up the hill, and horses for rent. It's best to make reservations with Cubamar (p129) in Havana rather than just turn up.

★**Villa Don Lino**   CABINS $$
(☑ 43-03-08; s/d from CUC$49/78; ❄) The cheap alternative to Playa Pesquero's 'big four,' Don Lino's 36 single-story *cabañas* (cabins) are planted right on its own diminutive white beach, and make for a romantic retreat. There's a small pool, nighttime entertainment and an element of Cuban-ness missing in the bigger resorts. Villa Don Lino is 8.5km north of Rafael Freyre along a spur road.

Casa de Compay Kike   CABINS $$
(☑ 43-33-10, ext 115; s/d CUC$49/84) 🍽 A rustic *finca* (farm) in the Parque Rocazul where you can sidle up to nature in one of two cab-

ins and pretend you're a million miles from All-Inclusive Land.

★ Hotel Playa Pesquero RESORT $$$

(☑43-35-30; s/d CUC$175/280; P❄✳@☀❋)
Once Cuba's biggest hotel, Playa Pesquero had its mantle stolen in 2007 by the precocious Sirenis la Salina in Varadero, but who cares? With 933 rooms, the Pesquero is no slouch and no ugly duckling either. Beautifully landscaped grounds over 30 hectares include Italianate fountains, fancy shops, seven restaurants, spa, floodlit tennis courts, and acres of swimming pool space.

And then there's the beach...in a word, beautiful. Opened in 2003 by Fidel Castro, the loquacious leader's speech is reprinted on a wall in the reception area. Fortunately, it was one of his shorter efforts.

Occidental
Grand Playa Turquesa RESORT $$$

(☑43-35-40; s/d CUC$150/200; P❄@☀)
Slightly apart from the other resorts on its own clean scoop of beach (known confusingly as Playa Yuraguanal), Turquesa writes the word 'privacy' into its four stars. Otherwise you're looking at all the usual high-end, all-inclusive givens – meaning most punters are happy to never leave the complex.

Hotel Playa Costa Verde RESORT $$$

(☑43-35-20; s/d/tr CUC$150/230/327; P❄@☀❋) Stuck somewhere between elegance and simplicity, the Costa Verde feels a bit faux – not that top-notch facilities are lacking. There's a Japanese restaurant, a gym, colorful gardens and a lagoon you cross to get to the beach. Good diving trips are run out of the confusingly named Blau Costa Verde next door.

Guardalavaca

Guardalavaca is a string of megaresorts draped along a succession of idyllic beaches 54km northeast of Holguín. But glimmering in the background, the landscape of rough green fields and haystack-shaped hills remind you that rural Cuba is never far away.

In the days before towel-covered sunloungers and poolside bingo, Columbus described this stretch of coast as the most beautiful place he had ever laid eyes on. Few modern-day visitors would disagree. Love it or hate it, Guardalavaca's enduring popularity has its raison d'être: enviable tropical beaches, verdant green hills and sheltered turquoise coral reefs that teem with aquatic action. More spread out than Varadero and less isolated than Cayo Coco, for many discerning travelers Guardalavaca gets the R and R balance just right – relaxation and realism.

In the early 20th century this region was an important cattle-rearing area and the site of a small rural village (Guardalavaca means, quite literally, 'guard the cow'). The tourism boom moved into first gear in the late 1970s when local *holguiñero* Fidel Castro inaugurated Guardalavaca's first resort – the sprawling Atlántico – by going for a quick dip in the hotel pool. The local economy hasn't looked back since.

The resort area is split into three separate enclaves: Playa Pesquero, Playa Esmeralda and, 7km to the east, Guardalavaca proper, the original hotel strip that is already starting to peel around the edges. Guardalavaca has long allowed beach access to Cubans, meaning it is less snooty and flecked with a dash of local color.

⦿ Sights

Museo Chorro de Maita MUSEUM

(admission CUC$2; ⊙9am-5pm Tue-Sat, to 1pm Sun) ⊘ This archaeological-site-based museum protects the remains of an excavated Indian village and cemetery, including the well-preserved remains of 62 human skeletons and the bones of a barkless dog. The village dates from the early 16th century and is one of nearly 100 archaeological sites in the area. New evidence suggests indigenous peoples were living here many decades after Columbus' arrival.

Across from the museum is a reconstructed Aldea Taína (Taíno village; admission CUC$5; ❋) that features life-sized models of native dwellings and figures in a replicated indigenous village. Shows of native dance rituals are staged here and there's also a restaurant.

Parque Natural Bahía
de Naranjo NATURE RESERVE

(☑43-00-06; packages from CUC$40) The Parque Natural Bahía de Naranjo, 4km southwest of Playa Esmeralda and about 8km from the main Guardalavaca strip, is an island complex designed to keep the resort crowds entertained. An aquarium (⊙9am-9pm; ❋) is on a tiny island in the bay and your entry fee includes a zippy boat tour of the islands included in the complex, and a sea lion and dolphin show (noon daily).

Guardalavaca

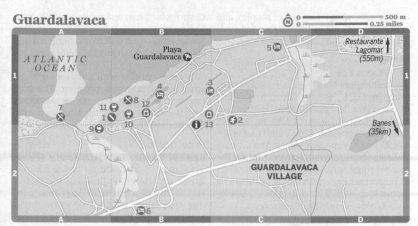

There are various packages starting at around CUC$40, depending on what you want to do – yacht trips, seafaris etc – so check around before you embark. For an extra CUC$50 or so you can swim with the dolphins for 20 minutes. All of Guardalavaca's (and Playa Esmeralda's) hotel tour desks sell aquarium excursions. Boats to the aquarium leave from the Marina Bahía de Naranjo.

🏃 Activities

You can arrange horseback riding at the **horseback-riding center** opposite Club Amigo Atlántico, starting at CUC$8 per hour. You can rent **mopeds** at all the hotels for up to CUC$30 per day. Most all-inclusive resorts include bicycle use, but the bikes are fairly basic (no gears). The road between Guardalavaca and Playa Esmeralda, and on to Playa Pesquero, is flat and quiet and makes an excellent day excursion. For a bit more sweat you can make it to Banes and back (66km round trip).

Diving

Guardalavaca has some excellent diving (better than Varadero and up there with Cayo Coco). The reef is 200m out and there are 32 dive sites, most of which are accessed by boat. Highlights include caves, wrecks, walls and La Corona, a giant coral formation said to resemble a crown. Guardalavaca beach's one dive center, **Eagle Ray Marlin Dive Center** (Cubanacán Náutica; ☏ 43-01-85), is on the beach behind **Disco Club la Roca** (admission CUC$1; ☉1-5pm & 9:30pm-3am). There's another outlet in Playa Esmeralda

(ask at the hotels) that serves the same reefs. All outfits offer generic prices and facilities. There are open-water certification courses for CUC$365, and dives for CUC$45, with discounts for multiple dives.

Boat Trips

Many other water-based excursions leave from the **Marina Gaviota Puerto de Vita** (☏ 43-04-75) and can be booked through the hotels. There's the ubiquitous sunset cruise possibilities (CUC$65 to CUC$129), deep-sea fishing (CUC$270 for up to six people), and occasional catamaran trips across Bahía de Vita with snorkeling and open bar.

Hiking

Las Guanas Eco-Archaeological Trail
NATURE RESERVE

(admission CUC$3; ⊙ 8am-4:30pm) At the end of the Playa Esmeralda road is this self-guided hike, which at CUC$3 for 1km of trail, is quite possibly Cuba's (and one of the world's) most expensive walks. You'd better walk slowly to get your money's worth! The marked route (with several more kilometers of bushwhacking on fire trails leading to a picturesque bluff with a lighthouse) apparently boasts 14 endemic plant species.

Eco-Parque Cristóbal Colón
NATURE RESERVE

Cheaper than Las Guanas, but pretty barren post-Hurricane Ike, this area is reachable via a track off the hotel access road. There's a small animal 'zoo' here and a rustic *finca* restaurant called **Conuco de Mongo Viña** where you can grab a bite.

👉 Tours

The **Cubanacán** travel desk in the lobby of the Club Amigo Atlántico – Guardalavaca offers an interesting 'beer tour' of Holguín city, leaving at 6:30pm every Sunday (CUC$20).

🛏 Sleeping

Guardalavaca now offers private rooms, so you are not obliged to shell out for the all-inclusives if you don't want to. There are dozens of apartments to rent in Guardalavaca village opposite the entrance to the all-inclusive zone.

Guardalavaca

Villa Bely
CASA PARTICULAR $

(📞 52-61-41-92; villabely@gmail.com; r CUC$30) The top-floor apartment at this rose-pink house is bigger and better than your average hotel room, coming with a kitchen-diner and a sumptuous sleeping area raised on a dais. There's a second room below. It's just opposite the last highway exit from the all-inclusive zone.

Club Amigo Atlántico – Guardalavaca
RESORT $$

(📞 43-01-21; s/d CUC$81/122; P ❄ @ 🐾 🏄) This hard-to-fathom resort is a fusion of the former Guardalavaca and Atlántico hotels, the latter of which is the resort's oldest, completed in 1976 and christened by Fidel Castro, who went for a quick dip in the pool. The architecture in this small 'village' (there are an astounding 600 rooms here) is a bog-standard mishmash of villas, bungalows and standard rooms.

It's ever-popular with families for its extensive kids' activities program. The hotel has two locations. The rooms associated with the former Hotel Guardalavaca are further from the beach but also less noisy.

Hotel Brisas
RESORT $$$

(📞 43-02-18; s/d CUC$154/228; P ❄ @ 🐾 🏄) This uber-resort made up of the Villa las Brisas and Hotel las Brisas at the eastern end of the beach is a package-tour paradise that stirs memories of 1970s British holiday camps. Bonuses are the huge comfortable rooms, floodlit tennis courts and general lack of pretension. The kitsch is never far from the surface, but it's both quieter and more upmarket than Club Amigo's offerings.

Playa Esmeralda

Two megaresorts line this superior stretch of beach, located 6km to the west of Guardalavaca and accessed by a spur just east of the Cayo Naranjo boat launch. Esmeralda occupies the middle ground between Guardalavaca's economy and Playa Pesquero's opulence.

⭐ Paradisus Río de Oro
RESORT $$$

(📞 43-00-90; s/d CUC$455/510; P ❄ @ 🐾) Elegant and environmentally conscious (a tough combination), this 292-room resort has five star written all over it, and is often touted as the best resort in Cuba. There's massage available in a cliffside hut, a Japanese restaurant floating on a koi pond, and garden villas with private pools. Paradise is the word. It's adults only.

Sol Río Luna Mares Resort
RESORT $$$

(📞 43-00-30; s/d CUC$117/168; P ❄ @ 🐾 🏄) This two-in-one hotel is an amalgamation of the former Sol Club Río de Luna and the Meliá Río de Mares. Rooms are large and come with a few extras (such as coffee machines), but the main advantages for luxury seekers over Guardalavaca is the superior food (Mexican and Italian restaurants) and the better beach (beach toys are included in the price).

Rooms are also available in cabins at **Villa Cayo Naranjo**. Enquire at the hotel desks for details.

✕ Eating

There are a handful of options outside of the all-inclusive resorts, mainly in Guardalavaca itself.

Vicaria Guardalavaca FAST FOOD **$**
(meals about CUC$5; ⊘9am-9:45pm) You'll feel like an outcast eating at this place beside Centro Comercial Guardalavaca, while everyone else tucks into the all-you-can-eat buffets a couple of hundred meters away. Nevertheless, pizzas are big and service is quick and amiable. A good meal for two won't break CUC$10.

Restaurante Lagomar PALADAR **$**
(meals CUC$3-5; ⊘noon-midnight) You can get some esoteric magic in Guardalavaca! Head east to the end of the dual carriageway, then turn left and then right on a track down through the Guardalavaca neighborhood of El Cayuelo, at the end of which the Lagomar serves up classic Cuban dishes in its atmospheric little restaurant. The odd all-inclusive-guest-in-the-know stops by. El Cayuelo is earmarked for more hotel development: enjoy it while you can.

El Ancla SEAFOOD **$$**
(seafood mains around CUC$10; ⊘9am-10:30pm) Somehow El Ancla, which is situated on a rocky promontory of land at the far western end of Guardalavaca beach, didn't get blown away by Hurricane Ike and has survived to serve its excellent lobster in front of magnificent sea views.

Cayo Naranjo SEAFOOD **$$**
(Cayo Naranjo) On Gaviota's theme park of a *cayo* (key), this will be your only lunch option. Fortunately it's pretty good, with a signature plate of Marinera Especial pushing the fish theme.

🍺 Drinking & Entertainment

Los Amigos BAR
(⊘9am-9pm) At the epicenter of Guardalavaca's liveliest strip of beach (accessed via the flea market just west of Club Amigo Atlántico), Los Amigos is a bog-standard beach shack with beer, music and enough ingredients to muster up a sand-free, fish and rice lunch.

La Rueda BAR
(⊘7am-11pm) A Palmares bar (next to the Boulevard) that provides a welcome haven from the resorts. Small snacks and ice cream are also available.

🛍 Shopping

Boulevard SOUVENIRS
This touristy handicraft market caters to resort clients from the surrounding area. It's art, crafts, postcards and cheap clothing – there's nothing much outside the knick-knack box.

Centro Comerical los Flamboyanes SHOPPING CENTER
Guardalavaca's small shopping mall has a limited cache of stores, including a handy Casa del Habano which has all the smoke you need and then some.

ℹ Information

Euros are accepted in all the Guardalavaca, Playa Esmeralda and Pesquero resorts. Additionally, all the big hotels have money-changing facilities. The Clinica Internacional 24-hour pharmacy was closed following hurricane damage at the time of writing, but the major hotels here all have drugstores.

Asistur (✆43-01-48; Centro Comercial Guardalavaca; ⊘8:30am-5pm Mon-Fri, to noon Sat) Traveler emergency assistance.

Banco Financiero Internacional (Centro Comercial Guardalavaca) In the shopping complex just west of Club Amigo Atlántico – Guardalavaca.

Canadian Consulate (✆43-03-20; Suite 1, Club Amigo Atlántico – Guardalavaca)

Cubatur (⊘8am-4pm) Travel agent just behind the Centro Comercial los Flamboyanes.

Ecotur (Centro Comercial Guardalavaca) Runs nature-themed trips to places such as Cayo Saetía, Baracoa and Gran Piedra.

ℹ Getting There & Away

Club Amigo Atlántico – Guardalavaca can sometimes arrange transfers to Holguín for CUC$10; ask around. A taxi from Guardalavaca to Holguín will cost a heftier CUC$35 one way for the car. For radio taxis, call **Cubataxi** (✆43-01-39) or **Transgaviota** (✆43-49-66). Colectivos (shared taxis) run from Guardalavaca village to Holguín for CUC$5.

Marina Gaviota Puerto de Vita (✆43-04-45) is an international entry port for yachts and boats and has 38 berths. There's a hardware store, restaurant, electricity and customs authorities on site.

ℹ Getting Around

A hop-on/hop-off double-decker bus in Guardalavaca links the three beach areas and the Aldea Taína. The red-and-blue bus is operated by Transtur. Theoretically it runs three times a day in either direction, but check at your hotel to see if there are any glitches. Drop-offs include Parque Rocazul, Playa Pesquero, Playa Costa Verde, Playa Esmeralda hotels, Club Amigo Atlántico – Guardalavaca and the Aldea Taína. Tickets cost CUC$5 for an all-day pass.

Coches de caballo (horse carriages) run between Playas Esmeralda and Guardalavaca, or you can rent a moped (CUC$24 per day) or bicycle (free if you're staying at an all-inclusive) at all of the resort hotels. All the rental agencies have offices in Guardalavaca and can also rent out mopeds.

For car rental, try **Cubacar** (Club Amigo Atlántico – Guardalavaca). A **Servi-Cupet gas station** (⊘ 24hr) is situated between Guardalavaca and Playa Esmeralda.

Banes

POP 44,500

The former sugar town of Banes, situated just north of the Bahía de Banes, is the site of one of Cuba's most notable ironies. Cuban president Fulgencio Batista was born here in 1901. Then, 47 years later, in the local clapboard church of Nuestra Señora de la Caridad, another fiery leader-in-waiting, Fidel Castro, tied the knot with the blushing Birta Díaz Balart. A generous Batista gave them a US$500 gift for their honeymoon.

Founded in 1887, this effervescent company town was a virtual fiefdom of the US-run United Fruit Company until the 1950s and many of the old American company houses still remain. These days in the sun-streaked streets and squares you're more likely to encounter cigar-smoking cronies slamming dominoes, and moms carrying meter-long loaves of bread; in short, everything Cuban that is missing from the all-inclusive resorts.

In September 2008 Banes was pummeled by Hurricane Ike but, true to Cuba's survivalist spirit, the town recovered remarkably quickly.

⊙ Sights & Activities

If you're coming from the resorts, Banes' biggest attraction will probably be enjoying the street life provided by a stroll through town. Don't miss the fine old company houses that once provided homes for the fat cats of United Fruit. If you're fit and adventurous, getting here by bicycle is a rare treat, taking you through undulating bucolic terrain.

Iglesia de Nuestra Señora de la Caridad   CHURCH

On October 12, 1948, Fidel Castro Ruz and Birta Díaz Balart were married in this unusual art deco church on Parque Martí in the center of Banes. After their divorce in 1954, Birta remarried and moved to Spain. Through their only child, Fidelito, Fidel has several grandchildren.

Museo Indocubano Bani   MUSEUM

(General Marrero No 305; admission CUC$1; ⊘ 9am-5pm Tue-Sat, 8am-noon Sun) This museum's small but rich collection of indigenous artifacts is one of the best on the island. Don't miss the tiny golden fertility idol unearthed near Banes (one of only 20 gold artifacts ever found in Cuba). For an additional CUC$1 staff will take you on a tour of interesting sites in Banes.

Steam Locomotive 964   TRAIN

(Calle Tráfico, El Panchito) Railway enthusiasts shouldn't miss this old steamer built at the HK Porter Locomotive Works in Pittsburgh, Pennsylvania, in 1888, now on display 400m east of the bus station.

Playa de Morales   BEACH

One day in the not-too-distant future (after its been Cancun-ized), we'll all wax nostalgic about this precious strip of sand situated 13km east of Banes along the paved continuation of Tráfico. For the time being enjoy this fishing village while you can, whiling away an afternoon dining with locals and watching the men mend their nets. A few kilometers to the north is the even quieter **Playa Puerto Rico**.

🛏 Sleeping

There are no hotels in the town proper, but Banes has some superfriendly private renters.

Villa Lao   CASA PARTICULAR $

(☏ 80-30-49; Bayamo No 78, btwn José M Heredia & Augusto Blanco; r CUC$20-25) Shimmeringly clean, professionally run house with two rooms; grab the upstairs one with its kitchen and plant-laden terrace, if possible. It's got the front porch rocker thing going on, too, overlooking the central park.

Casa 'Las Delicias'   CASA PARTICULAR $

(☏ 80-29-05; Augusto Blanca No 1107, btwn Bruno Merino & Bayamo; r CUC$20-25; ❀) One spick-and-span room, a private entrance, friendly owners and decent food in the downstairs

BRUISED FRUIT

United Fruit is a name riddled with historical contradictions. On one hand, the company gave the world the Big Mike, the first mass-produced imported banana; on the other, it developed a reputation for meddling covertly in the internal affairs of successive Latin American 'banana republics' – including Cuba.

Formed back in 1899 when Minor C Keith's Costa Rica–based banana-growing company merged with Andrew Preston's Boston fruit import business, United Fruit quickly morphed into a huge global monolith that went on to become one of the world's first multinational corporations.

In the early 1900s, the company invested in 36 hectares of sugar plantations in eastern Cuba, where they constructed 544km of railroad and two large sugar mills – the Boston and the Preston – in what is now Holguín province. One of the company's early laborers was Ángel Castro (father of Fidel), who helped clear land for the company's burgeoning plantations before setting up on his own in Birán in 1915. Encased in an expansive new rural estate, Castro Senior began hiring out labor to United Fruit for a tidy profit and quickly became a wealthy man.

Holguín was soon the darling scion of United Fruit in Cuba, with provincial towns such as Banes and Mayarí sporting prosperous Americanized enclaves that owed both their existence and wealth to the omnipresent US-owned conglomerate. But dissatisfaction among Cubans was quietly growing.

Like many nationalistically minded leftists, Fidel Castro was incensed with the clandestine role United Fruit played in the 1954 overthrow of Jacobo Arbenz' socialist government in Guatemala and, spurred on by other radicals such as Che Guevara, was determined to make amends.

The payback began during the revolutionary war when Fidel's rebel army famously burned the fields of his late father's Birán estate in a portentous taste of things to come.

On taking power in 1959, Castro nationalized all United Fruit land and property in Cuba and sent its owners back to the US. Unable to gain financial compensation from the Cuban government, the company attempted to get even two years later by lending two ships from its Great White Fleet (the largest private navy in the world) to Cuban mercenaries taking part in the abortive Bay of Pigs landings. But the invasion was unsuccessful.

United Fruit's demise was exacerbated in 1975 when CEO Eli Black committed suicide by jumping from the 44th floor of New York's PanAm building, after it was alleged he had bribed the Honduran president US$1.2 million to pull out of a banana cartel hostile to United Fruit's interests.

The company rebranded in 1984 and was reincarnated as Chiquita Brands. Meanwhile, in Cuba, the legacy of United Fruit can still be seen in the peeling colonial houses of Banes and – more ironically – at the former Castro farm in Birán.

---

paladar; what more could you ask from tranquil Banes?

Casa CASA PARTICULAR $
(80-22-04; Calle H No 15266, btwn Veguitas & Francisco Franco) This classic colonial abode stands guard at the entrance to the town center and has one huge room (those ceilings must be 7m high) with private bath and fridge.

✖ Eating

DIYers can find groceries in a couple of supermarkets – **La Epoca** and **Isla de Cuba** on the main nexus of General Marrero.

Restaurant el Latino CARIBBEAN $$
(General Marrero No 710; meals around CUC$5; ☺11am-11pm) A top Banes choice is this Palmares place with all the usual Creole dishes delivered with a little extra flair and charm. Service is good, and the accompanying musicians are unusually talented and discreet.

☆ Entertainment

Cafe Cantante LIVE MUSIC
(General Marrero No 320) This gregarious, music-filled patio is the top spot in Banes, with honking municipal band rehearsals, discos, *son* (Cuba's basic form of popular music) septets and zen-inducing jazz jams.

Casa de Cultura
CULTURAL CENTER

(General Marrero No 320) FREE This venue, housed in the former Casino Español (1926), has a regular Sunday *trova* (traditional poetic song) matinee at 3pm and Saturday *peña del rap* (rap music session) at 9pm.

ℹ️ Information

Banes is one of those towns with no street signs and locals who don't know street names, so prepare to get lost.

ℹ️ Getting There & Away

From the **bus station** (cnr Tráfico & Los Ángeles), one morning bus goes to Holguín (72km) daily (supposedly). An afternoon bus connects with the train to Havana. Trucks leave Banes for Holguín more frequently. A taxi from Guardalavaca (33km) will cost around CUC$20 one way, or you can tackle it with a moped (easy) or bicycle (not so easy) in a fantastic DIY day trip.

Birán

Fidel Castro Ruz was born on August 13, 1926, at the **Finca las Manacas** (Casa de Fidel) near the village of Birán, south of Cueto. The farm, which was bought by Fidel's father Ángel in 1915, is huge, and includes its own workers village (a cluster of small thatched huts for the mainly Haitian laborers), a cockfighting ring, a post office, a store and a telegraph. The several large yellow wooden houses that can be glimpsed through the cedar trees are where the Castro family lived.

Museo Conjunto Histórico de Birán
MUSEUM

(admission/camera/video CUC$10/20/40; ⊙ 9am-noon & 1:30-4pm Tue-Sat, to noon Sun) Finca las Manacas opened as a museum in 2002 under this unassuming name, supposedly to downplay any Castro 'personality cult' (the modesty extends to the signage, which is nonexistent). This gaggle of orange-colored buildings on an expanse of lush grounds constitutes a *pueblito* (small town) and makes for a fascinating excursion, featuring Castro's schoolhouse and family home and everything from a post office to a butcher's.

Around the various houses here you can see more than 100 photos, assorted clothes, Fidel's childhood bed and his father's 1918 Ford motorcar. Perhaps most interesting is the schoolhouse (Fidel sat in the middle of the front row, apparently), with pictures of young Fidel and Raúl and Fidel's birth certificate, made out in the name of Fidel Casano Castro Ruz. A cemetery contains the graves of Fidel and Raúl's father, Ángel. The site illustrates, if nothing else, the extent of the inheritance that this hot-headed ex-lawyer gave up when he lived in the Sierra Maestra for two years surviving on a diet of crushed crabs and raw horse meat.

Sierra del Cristal

Cuba's own 'Little Switzerland' is a rugged amalgam of the Sierra del Cristal and the Altiplanicie de Nipe that contains two important national parks. **Parque Nacional Sierra Cristal**, Cuba's oldest, was founded in 1930 and harbors 1213m Pico de Cristal, which is the province's highest summit. Of more interest to travelers is the 5300-hectare **Parque Nacional la Mensura**, 30km south of Mayarí, which protects the island's highest waterfall, yields copious Caribbean pines and hosts a mountain research center run by the Academia de Ciencias de Cuba (Cuban Academy of Sciences). Notable for its cool alpine microclimate and for hosting 100 or more species of endemic plants, La Mensura offers hiking and horseback riding and accommodation in a Gaviota-run eco-lodge.

The song you've certainly heard more than any other in Cuba since your plane touched down – the Buena Vista Social Club hit 'Chan Chan' – refers in its opening lines to the towns of Macarné, Cueto and Mayarí; these towns flank the Sierra del Cristal and the road between them is often dubbed **Ruta de Chan Chan** (Chan Chan Route), frequently traversed by aficionados of lead singer Compay Segundo and co.

◉ Sights & Activities

Most activities can be organized at Villa Pinares del Mayarí or via excursions from Guardalavaca's hotels (CUC$78 by 4WD or CUC$110 by helicopter).

Salto del Guayabo
WATERFALL

At just over 100m in height, Guayabo (15km from the Villa Pinares de Mayarí) is considered the highest waterfall in Cuba. There's a spectacular overlook, and the guided 1.2km hike to its base through fecund tropical forest costs CUC$5 and includes swimming in a natural pool.

WILL HISTORY ABSOLVE HIM?

Has the world misunderstood Fidel Castro? Is this rugged survivor of the Cold War and the catastrophic economic meltdown that followed just a Machiavellian dictator responsible for driving an immovable wedge into US–Cuban relations? Or is he the de facto leader of an unofficial Third World alliance pioneering the fight for equal rights and social justice on the world stage? To get closer to the personality that lies behind the public mask we must (as every good Freudian knows) delve into his childhood.

Born near the village of Birán in Holguín province on August 13, 1926, the illegitimate product of a relationship between Spanish-born landowner Ángel Castro and his cook and housemaid Lina Ruz (they later married), Fidel grew up as a favored child in a large and relatively wealthy family of sugar farmers. Educated at a Jesuit school and sent away to study in the city of Santiago at the age of seven, the young Castro was an exceptional student whose prodigious talents included a photographic memory and an extraordinary aptitude for sport. Indeed, legend has it that at the age of 21, Fidel – by then a skilled left-arm pitcher – was offered a professional baseball contract with the Washington Senators.

At the age of 13 Fidel staged his first insurrection, a strike organized among his father's sugarcane workers against their exploitative boss, a gesture that did little to endear him to the fraternal fold.

One year later the still-teenage Castro penned a letter to US President FD Roosevelt congratulating him on his re-election and asking the American leader for a US$10 bill 'because I have not seen a US$10 bill and I would like to have one of them.' Rather ominously for future US–Cuban relations, the request was politely turned down.

Undeterred, Fidel marched on. Upon completion of his high school certificate in 1945, his teacher and mentor Father Francisco Barbeito predicted sagely that his bullish star pupil would 'fill with brilliant pages the book of his life.' With the benefit of hindsight, he wasn't far wrong. Armed with tremendous personal charisma, a wrought-iron will and a natural ability to pontificate interminably for hours on end, Fidel made tracks for Havana University where his forthright and unyielding personality quickly ensured he excelled at everything he did.

Training ostensibly as a lawyer, Castro spent the next three years embroiled in political activity amid an academic forum that was riddled with gang violence and petty corruption. 'My impetuosity, my desire to excel, fed and inspired the character of my struggle,' he recalled candidly years later.

Blessed with more lives than a cat, Castro has survived a failed putsch, 15 months in prison, exile in Mexico, a two-year guerrilla war in the mountains and a reported 617 attempts on his life. His sense of optimism in the face of defeat is nothing short of astounding. With his rebel army reduced to a ragged band of 12 men after the Granma landing, he astonished his beleaguered colleagues with a fiery victory speech. 'We will win this war,' he trumpeted confidently. 'We are just beginning the fight!'

As an international personality who has outlasted 11 American presidents, the 21st-century incarnation of Fidel Castro that emerged following the Special Period was no less enigmatic than the revolutionary leader of yore. Fostering his own peculiar brand of Caribbean socialism with an unflinching desire to 'defend the Revolution at all costs,' the ever-changing ideology that Castro so famously preached is perhaps best summarized by biographer Volker Skierka as 'a pragmatic mixture of a little Marx, Engels and Lenin, slightly more of Che Guevara, a lot of José Martí, and a great deal indeed of Fidel Castro.'

Castro stepped out of public life in July 2006 after a serious bout of diverticulitis and handed the reins of power to his younger brother Raúl. Despite penning regular articles for national newspaper *Granma* and making the odd jarring public statement on world affairs, he looks destined to see out his final years like a Caribbean Napoleon wistfully pondering his historical legacy from his lonely island prison. Whether history will absolve him is still anybody's guess.

Sendero la Sabina   TRAIL
More flora can be observed on the Sendero la Sabina, a short interpretive trail at the Centro Investigaciones para la Montaña (1km from the hotel), which exhibits the vegetation of eight different ecosystems, a 150-year-old tree – the 'Ocuje Colorado' – and some rare orchids.

Hacienda la Mensura   FARM
Eight kilometers from Villa Pinares del Mayari is this breeding center for exotic animals such as antelope and *guapeti*. Horseback riding can be arranged here.

Farallones de Seboruco   CAVES
Speleologists may want to ask about trips to these ghostly caves, designated a national monument, which contain aboriginal cave paintings.

Sleeping

Villa Pinares del Mayarí   HOTEL $
(52-14-12; s/d CUC$30/40; P ❄ ❄)
One in a duo of classic Gaviota Holguín hideaways – Villa Cayo Saetía (p376) is the other Pinares del Mayarí stands at 600m elevation between the Altiplanicie de Nipe and Sierra del Cristal, 30km south of Mayarí on a rough dirt road. Part chalet resort, part mountain retreat, this isolated rural gem is situated in one of Cuba's largest pine forests, and the two- and three-bedroom cabins, with hot showers and comfortable beds, make it seem almost alpine-esque. There's also a large restaurant, bar, sports court, gym, and a small natural lake (El Cupey) 300m away which is great for an early morning dip.

Getting There & Away
The only way to get to Villa Pinares del Mayarí and Parque Nacional la Mensura outside an organized tour is via car, taxi or bicycle (if you're adventurous and it's not a Cuban one). The access road is rough and in a poor state of repair, but it's passable in a hire car if driven with care. If arriving from Santiago the best route is via the small settlement of Mella.

Cayo Saetía

East of Mayarí the road becomes increasingly potholed and the surroundings, while never losing their dusty rural charm, progressively more remote. The culmination of this rustic drive is lovely Cayo Saetía, a small, flat wooded island in the Bahía de Nipe that's connected to the mainland by a small bridge. During the 1970s and '80s this was a favored hunting ground for communist apparatchiks who enjoyed spraying lead into the local wildlife. Fortunately those days are now gone. Indeed, ironic as it may sound, Cayo Saetía is now a protected wildlife park with 19 species of exotic animals, including camels, zebras, antelopes, ostriches and deer. Bisected by grassy meadows and adorned by hidden coves and beaches, it's the closet Cuba gets to an African wildlife reserve. Well worth a visit.

Sleeping

Campismo Río Cabonico   CABINS $
(59-41-18; r per person from CUC$5) This place is at Pueblo Nuevo, 9km east of Levisa and 73km west of Moa, about 900m south of the main road. The 23 cabins with baths and fans on a low terrace beside the Río Cabonico (decent swimming) have four or six beds. It may accept foreigners, if there's space; check ahead or contact Cubamar (p129) in Havana.

Villa Cayo Saetía   CABINS $$
(42-53-20; d CUC$60-70, ste CUC$85-100; ❄) This wonderfully rustic but comfortable resort on a 42-sq-km island at the entrance to the Bahía de Nipe is small, remote and more upmarket than the price suggests. The 12 rooms are split into rustic and standard *cabañas* with a minimal price differential. You'll feel as if you're 1000 miles from anywhere.

The in-house restaurant, La Güira – decked out Hemingway-style with hunting trophies mounted on the wall like gory art – serves exotic meats such as antelope.

Getting There & Around
There are three ways to explore Cayo Saetía, aside from the obvious two-legged sorties from the villa itself. A one-hour 4WD safari costs CUC$9, while there are also excursions by horse and boat. Though isolated you can secure passage on a twice-weekly Gaviota helicopter from Guardalavaca (CUC$124, Saturday and Monday) or a bus-boat combo from the town of Antilles. If arriving by car, the control post is 15km off the main road. Then it's another 8km along a rough, unpaved road to the resort. A hire car will make it – with care.

Granma Province

📖 23 / POP 836,400

Best Hikes

➡ Comandancia de la Plata (p388)

➡ El Salto (p396)

➡ Pico Turquino (p390)

➡ Sendero Arqueológico Natural el Guafe (p395)

Best Revolutionary Sites

➡ Alegria del Pio (p394)

➡ Comandancia de la Plata (p388)

➡ Casa Natal de Carlos Manuel de Céspedes (p380)

➡ Museo las Colorados (p394)

Why Go?

Few parts of the world get named after yachts, which helps explain why in Granma (christened for the boat in which Fidel Castro and his bedraggled revolutionaries clambered ashore to kickstart the overthrowing of the Batista regime in earnest in 1956) Cuba's *viva la Revolución* spirit burns most fiercely. This land is where José Martí died and where Granma native Carlos Manuel de Céspedes freed his slaves and formally declared Cuban independence for the first time in 1868.

The alluringly isolated countryside helped the Revolutionary cause. Road-scarce Granma is one of Cuba's remotest regions with lofty tropical mountains dense enough to have harbored a fugitive Fidel Castro for over two years in the 1950s.

Isolation has bred a special brand of Cuban identity. Granma's settlements are esoteric places enlivened with weekly street parties (outdoor barbecues, archaic hand-operated street organs), and provincial capital Bayamo is among the most tranquil and cleanest places in the archipelago.

When to Go

➡ Pockets of Granma have a balmy climate and during January and February Marea del Portillo is the warmest place in Cuba.

➡ Bayamo's biggest celebration is also in January (the Incendio de Bayamo, on the 12th).

➡ In the far-wetter Sierra Maestra mountains, March and April are the driest times for hiking, with bearable nighttime temperatures.

➡ December 2 is the anniversary of the Granma landing and it is celebrated with a ceremony at Los Coloradas.

Granma Province Highlights

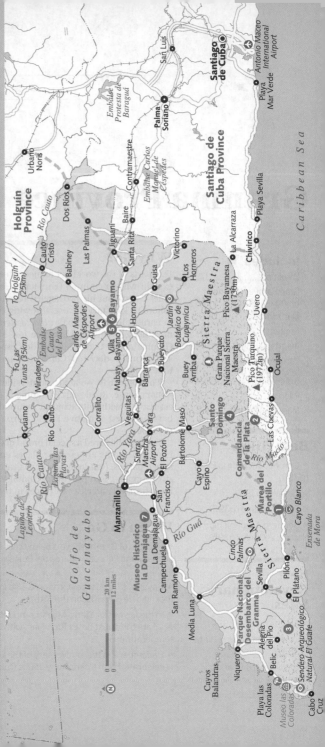

1 Enjoy one of Cuba's balmiest microclimates in **Marea del Portillo** (p396).

2 Trek to Fidel's wartime headquarters at **Comandancia de la Plata** (p388) in Gran Parque Nacional Sierra Maestra.

3 Investigate marine terraces and archaeological remains in **Parque Nacional Desembarco del Granma** (p394).

4 Get a dose of mountain air and customs in **Santo Domingo** (p389).

5 Immerse yourself in the unique Bayamo party spirit with pork roast, street organs,

a chess game, or a fiesta like **Fiesta de la Cubania** (p385).

6 Relax by the river with the *bayameses* (people from Bayamo) in **Parque Chapuzón** (p382).

7 Visit the site of Cuba's first cry of independence in **Museo Histórico la Demajagua** (p392).

History

Stone petroglyphs and remnants of Taíno pottery unearthed in Parque Nacional Desembarco del Granma suggest the existence of native cultures in the Granma region long before the Spanish arrived.

Columbus, during his second voyage, was the first European to explore the area, taking shelter from a storm in the Golfo de Guacanayabo. All other early development schemes came to nothing and by the 17th century Granma's untamed coast had become the preserve of pirates and corsairs.

Granma's real nemesis didn't come until October 10, 1868, when sugar-plantation owner Carlos Manuel de Céspedes called for the abolition of slavery from his Demajagua sugar mill near Manzanillo, freed his own slaves by example and incited the First War of Independence.

Drama unfolded again in 1895 when the founder of the Cuban Revolutionary Party, José Martí, was killed in Dos Ríos just a month and a half after landing with Máximo Gómez off the coast of Guantánamo to ignite the Spanish-Cuban-American War.

Then on December 2, 1956, Fidel Castro and 81 rebel soldiers disembarked from the yacht *Granma* off the province's coast at Playa las Coloradas (ironically, the boat that literally launched the Revolution – and later gave the province its present name – was purchased from an American, who had named it in honor of his grandmother). Routed by Batista's troops shortly after landing in a sugarcane field at Alegría del Pío, 12 or so survivors managed to escape into the Sierra Maestra, establishing headquarters at Comandancia de la Plata.

From there they coordinated the armed struggle, broadcasting their progress and consolidating their support among sympathizers nationwide. After two years of harsh conditions and unprecedented beard growth, the forces of the M-26-7 (July 26 Movement) triumphed in 1959.

Bayamo

POP 166,200

Predating both Havana and Santiago, and cast for time immemorial as the city that kick-started Cuban independence, Bayamo has every right to feel self-important. Yet somehow it doesn't. The city's affectionate name-tag, *ciudad de los coches* (*coches* means horsecarts) is a far more telling appraisal of its ambience: an easygoing, slow-paced, trapped-in-time place that is less about industrial drive and more about, well, horses. Cuba's balmiest provincial capital resounds to the clip-clop of hooves, and an estimated 40% of the population utilize the four-legged friends each day for getting about.

That's not to say that *bayameses* aren't aware of their history. '*Como España quemó a Sagunto, así Cuba quemó a Bayamo*,' ('As the Spanish burnt Sagunto, the Cubans burnt Bayamo') wrote José Martí in the 1890s, highlighting the sacrificial role that Bayamo has played in Cuba's convoluted historical development. But while the self-inflicted 1869 fire might have destroyed many of the city's classic colonial buildings (don't worry – there are still plenty left to see here), it did nothing to undermine its underlying spirit or its long-standing traditions.

Today, Bayamo is known for its cerebral chess players (Céspedes was the Kasparov of his day) and Saturday night street parties, often to the theme tune of antiquated street organs (imported via Manzanillo). All three are on show at the weekly Fiesta de la Cubanía, one of the island's most authentic street shows – *bayamés* to its core.

History

Founded in November 1513 as the second of Diego Velázquez de Cuéllar's seven original villas (after Baracoa) in Cuba, Bayamo's early history was marked by Indian uprisings and bristling native unrest. But with the indigenous Taíno decimated by deadly European diseases such as smallpox, the short-lived insurgency soon came to an end. By the end of the 16th century Bayamo had grown rich and was established as the most important cattle-ranching and sugarcane-growing center in the region. Frequented by pirates, the town filled its coffers further in the 17th and 18th centuries via a clandestine smuggling ring that was run out of the nearby port of Manzanillo. Bayamo's new class of merchants and landowners lavishly invested their money in fine houses and expensive overseas education for their offspring.

One such protégé was local lawyer-turned-revolutionary Carlos Manuel de Céspedes, who, defying the traditional colonial will, led an army against his hometown in 1868 in an attempt to wrest control from the conservative Spanish authorities. But

Bayamo

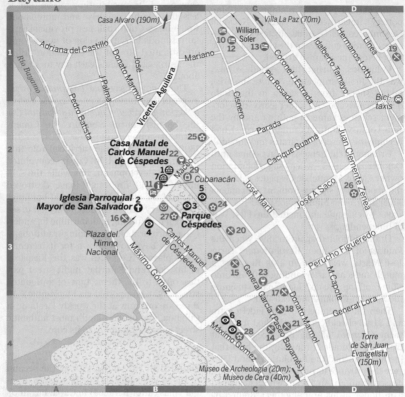

the liberation proved short-lived. After the defeat of an ill-prepared rebel army by 3000 regular Spanish troops near the Río Cauto on January 12, 1869, the townspeople – sensing an imminent Spanish reoccupation – set their town on fire rather than see it fall into enemy hands.

Bayamo was also the birthplace of Perucho Figueredo, who was the composer of the Cuban national anthem, which begins, rather patriotically, with the words *Al combate corred, bayameses* (Run to battle, people of Bayamo).

In 2006, Fidel Castro gave his last (to date) large-scale public oration in Bayamo's Plaza de la Patria. He was there to give his annual commemorative 'Triumphs of the Revolution' speech, but he was taken ill shortly thereafter and within days he had handed power over to his younger brother Raúl.

⊙ Sights

★ Casa Natal de Carlos Manuel de Céspedes   MUSEUM

(Maceo No 57; admission CUC$1; ⊙ 9am-5pm Tue-Fri, 9am-2pm & 8-10pm Sat, 10am-1:30pm Sun) Birthplace of the 'father of the motherland,' this museum is where Céspedes was born (April 18, 1819) and spent his first 12 years. Céspedes memorabilia inside is complemented by a collection of period furniture. It's notable architecturally as Bayamo's only remaining two-story colonial house: one of the few buildings to survive the 1869 fire.

★ Parque Céspedes   SQUARE

(Plaza de la Revolución) One of Cuba's leafiest and friendliest squares, and the birthplace of the man himself, Bayamo's central meeting point is officially known as Plaza de la Revolución. Despite its easygoing airs and secondary role as the city's best outdoor music venue (orchestras regularly play here),

the square is loaded with historical significance.

In 1868 Céspedes proclaimed Cuba's independence in front of the columned **Ayuntamiento** (City Hall). The square is surrounded by a smorgasbord of grand monuments and beautified further by big, shady trees. Facing each other in the center are a bronze statue of Carlos Manuel de Céspedes (hero of the First War of Independence) and a marble bust of Perucho Figueredo, with the words of the Cuban national anthem, which Figueredo scribed, carved upon it.

★**Iglesia Parroquial
Mayor de San Salvador** CHURCH
There's been a church on this site since 1514. The current edifice dates from 1740, but got devastated in the 1869 fire, so much of what you see results from building work in 1919. One original section surviving the fire is the

Capilla de la Dolorosa (donations accepted; ⊗9am-noon & 3-5pm Mon-Fri, 9am-noon Sat) with its gilded wooden altar.

A highlight of the main church is the central arch, which exhibits a mural depicting the blessing of the Cuban flag in front of the revolutionary army on October 20, 1868. Outside, Plaza del Himno Nacional is where the Cuban national anthem, 'La Bayamesa,' was sung for the first time in 1868.

Museo Provincial
MUSEUM

(Maceo No 55; admission CUC$1) Directly next door to Céspedes' ex-home, the provincial museum completes Bayamo's historical trajectory with a yellowing city document dating from 1567 and a rare photo of Bayamo immediately after the fire.

Paseo Bayamés
NEIGHBORHOOD

(Calle General García) Bayamo's main shopping street (officially known as Calle General García) was pedestrianized in the 1990s and reconfigured with funky artwork. Here you'll find wax museum Museo de Cera (p383) and, next door, **Museo de Arqueología** (admission CUC$1). There are plans to extend the Paseo a few blocks further south.

Casa de Estrada Palma
CULTURAL CENTER

(Céspedes No 158) Tomás Estrada Palma, Cuba's first postindependence president, was born here in 1835. One-time friend of José Martí, Estrada Palma was disgraced post-Revolution for his perceived complicity with the US over the Platt Amendment. His birth house is now the seat of Uneac (Unión Nacional de Escritores y Artistas de Cuba; National Union of Cuban Writers and Artists).

You'll find little about the famous former occupant inside, but the courtyard contains a palm (dating from 1837) that would (we assume) have come into contact with Palma.

Ventana de Luz Vázquez
LANDMARK

(Céspedes, btwn Figueredo & Luz Vázquez) A forerunner of the national anthem, co-written by Céspedes (and, confusingly, also called 'La Bayamesa') was first sung from here on March 27, 1851. A memorial plaque has been emblazoned onto the wall next to the wood-barred colonial window.

Torre de San Juan Evangelista
LANDMARK

(cnr José Martí & Amado Estévez) A church dating from Bayamo's earliest years stood at this busy intersection until it was destroyed in the great fire of 1869. Later, the church's tower served as the entrance to the first cemetery in Cuba, which closed in 1919. The cemetery was demolished in 1940 but the tower survived.

A **monument** to local poet José Joaquín Palma (1844–1911) stands in the park diagonally across the street from the tower, and beside the tower is a bronze **statue of Francisco Vicente Aguilera** (1821–77), who led the independence struggle in Bayamo.

Plaza de la Patria
PLAZA

(Av Felino Figueredo) This is where Fidel Castro gave his final public speech in July 2006 before being taken ill and stepping down as president. The monument to Cuban greats here features Manuel de Céspedes, Antonio Maceo, Máximo Gómez, Perucho Figueredo and, subtly placed left of center, Fidel: it is currently the only monument he appears on in Cuba. It's six blocks northeast of the bus station.

Museo Ñico López
MUSEUM

(Abihail González; ⊙8am-noon & 2-5:30pm Tue-Sat, 9am-noon Sun) **FREE** This museum is in the former officers' club of the Carlos Manuel de Céspedes military barracks, 1km southeast of Parque Céspedes. On July 26, 1953, this garrison was attacked by 25 revolutionaries led by Ñico López in tandem with the assault on Moncada Barracks in Santiago de Cuba, in order to prevent reinforcements from being sent.

López escaped to Guatemala, and was the first Cuban to befriend Ernesto 'Che' Guevara, but was killed shortly after the *Granma* landed in 1956.

Fabrica de los Coches
FACTORY

(Prolongacion General García No 530; admission CUC$1 donation; ⊙7am-3pm) It's worth the jaunt from the center to observe the goings-on at Cuba's only handcrafted *coche* (horse cart) production line. Most horse carts you'll see in Cuba are metal, but these are fashioned in wood and take far longer (up to three months per cart) to produce.

You'll see horse carts in various stages of completion, meet the workers and be able to buy Bayamo's best souvenir: miniature model horse carts with incredible attention to detail. The big ones cost about 8000 pesos (CUC$325) and don't fit quite so well into a suitcase.

Parque Chapuzón
PARK

(Av Amado Éstevez; ⊞) An oasis of greenery beckons not a kilometer from Bayamo's center, where the Río Bayamo has carved a lush belt through the urban grid. Locals come to this blissful spot to relax, water their horses, have a family barbecue or swim (as can you, if you like). Footpaths and gazebo-shaped stalls that sell food and drink embellish the banks, but they never detract from the all-pervading atmosphere of tranquility.

⚡ Activities

Cubans love chess, and nowhere more so than in Bayamo. Check out the streetside chess aficionados who set up on Saturday nights during the Fiesta de la Cubanía. The **Academia de Ajedrez** (José A Saco No 63, btwn General García & Céspedes) is the place to go to improve your pawn-king-four technique.

Forty-five-minute **horse-and-cart tours** can be arranged at the **Cubanacán desk** (Hotel Telegrafo, Maceo No 53) for CUC$4 per person.

🧭 Tours

There are now good private guided tours operating in Bayamo: for the city and for further afield (Gran Parque Nacional Sierra Maestra).

Julio César Aguilera Vila   GUIDED TOUR
(✆ 42-25-53; per 1½ hr CUC$5) Julio speaks English, German, French and Dutch, and offers informed tours around Bayamo's many historic sights.

Anley Rosales Benitez   GUIDED TOUR
(✆ 52-92-22-09; www.bayamotravelagent.com; Carretera Central No 478) Anley specialises in trips to the Sierra Maestra, which can be difficult to access without your own transport. The highlight tour takes in the Revolutionary sites of the 1956–58 years when the rebels were holed up hereabouts, like the village where Fidel famously played baseball with locals (per two people CUC$40).

These guys also arrange everything from transport to the Alto del Naranjo trailhead (for the Comandancia de la Plata/Pico Turquino hikes; CUC$40) or Bayamo airport pick-up. All-inclusive Comandancia de la Plata excursions are CUC$115 for two people.

🎊 Festivals

Big annual events include **Incendio de Bayamo**, on January 12, remembering the city's 1869 burning with live music and theatrical and performances in Parque Céspedes and culminating in fireworks launched from nearby buildings.

🛏 Sleeping

Casa de la Amistad   CASA PARTICULAR $
(✆ 42-57-69; gabytellez2003@yahoo.es; Pío Rosado No 60, btwn Ramíriez & N López; r CUC$25; ⓟ ❄ @) Gabriel and Rosa let out most of the upper floor of their pastel-shaded house as a separate apartment with its own entrance, kitchen, sitting area, bedroom and bathroom. They are fine hosts who speak excellent English, and there's even an internet connection.

Villa La Paz   CASA PARTICULAR $
(✆ 42-39-49; Coronel J Estrada No 32, btwn William Soler & Av Milanés; r CUC$20-25) There's nothing antiquated about this house, boasting mod cons such as broadband internet and downstairs guest room with flat-screen TV. The Russian-Cuban English-speaking hosts are good fun, too. Try scoring the upstairs room: it looks right onto the expansive wraparound terrace.

BAYAMO ART

Bayamo wasn't just the nation's leader in regime changing, it's also at the forefront of Cuba's *artes plasticos* (modern art) movement. On Paseo Bayamés you'll see the evidence working wonders. Halfway along is Cuba's only wax museum, **Museo de Cera** (✆ 42-65-25; General García No 261; admission CUC$1; ⊙ 9am-noon & 1-5pm Mon-Fri, 2-9pm Sat, 9am-noon Sun), with convincing likenesses of Cuban personalities Polo Montañez, Benny Moré, local hero Carlos Puebla and the like. But with the **Escuela de Artes Plasticos** (School of Modern Art; General Gacía btwn General Lora & Bartholomé Masó) at center stage on this pedestrian street, as well as the artists' collective **Pequeña Dimension** (General García cnr Manuel de Socorro) – both places where you can go and watch top artisans creating their works – it's unsurprising the entire boulevard has become a vivid wash of wacky murals and lampposts posing as trees and paint tubes. And three blocks behind the bus station, it's wood carving that steals the show, with the trees of an entire former avenue having been whittled into fanciful shapes. Some of Bayamo's artists happily invite you into their homes to show you their work: try the house of **Raylven Friman Ramírez** (✆ 42-66-86; General García 451), whose abstract paintings take worlds you thought you recognized, then dismantle and reassemble them in kaleidoscopic colour.

Casa Alvaro CASA PARTICULAR $
(☎ 42-48-61; Av Vincente Aguilera No 240; r CUC$20-25) Three sizable, modern rooms here, and breakfasts among Bayamo's best, with divine *bocadillos* (toasted ham and cheese sandwiches) and Spanish tortillas, on a terrace that exudes tranquility despite the busy location.

Villa Pupi & Villa América CASA PARTICULAR $
(☎ 42-30-29; yuri21504@gmail.com; Coronel J Estrada No 76-78; r CUC$20-25) Three rooms in this family-run enterprise (two upstairs in América, one next door and downstairs in Pupi). All three have use of Villa Pupi's vast roof terrace, where you can dine on superb local cooking.

Juan Valdés CASA PARTICULAR $
(☎ 42-33-24; Pío Rosado No 64, btwn Ramírez & N López; r CUC$20-25; P ✴) Two doors down from Casa de la Amistad, Juan rents out one room, but it's effectively an apartment on the upper floor with its own bedroom, bathroom, kitchen, sitting area and balcony overlooking rambling Pío Rosado.

Ana Martí Vázquez CASA PARTICULAR $
(☎ 42-53-23; Céspedes No 4; r CUC$25; P) As close as you can get to Parque Céspedes without actually being in it, Ana's rooms score highly for size, cleanliness and decent food. The front room is accessed by stairs so steep they almost constitute a ladder. The long, thin, brighter back room has a double and single bed plus windows that open onto a light-filled inner courtyard.

Villa Bayamo HOTEL $
(☎ 42-31-02; s/d/cabin CUC$15/24/32; P ✴ ⚏) Out-of-town option (it's 3km southwest of the center on the road to Manzanillo) with a definitive rural feel and a rather pleasant swimming pool overlooking fields at the back. Well-appointed rooms and a reasonable restaurant.

Hotel Sierra Maestra HOTEL $
(☎ 42-79-70; Carretera Central; s/d CUC$19/30; P ✴ ⚏) With a ring of the Soviet '70s about it, the Sierra Maestra hardly merits its three stars, although rooms have had some much-needed attention in the last three years, and public areas are handsome enough. Three kilometers from the town center, it's OK for an overnighter.

★**Hotel Royalton** HOTEL $$
(☎ 42-22-90; Maceo No 53; s/d CUC$44/70; ✴) The Royalton is Bayamo's best hotel. The 33 rooms have been upgraded to boutique standard with power showers and flat-screen TVs; there's also a roof terrace. Downstairs an attractive bar complements the reception area with seats spilling out onto a sidewalk terrace overlooking leafy Parque Céspedes. The on-site **Plaza restaurant** is a good eating option.

🍴 Eating

There's some unique street food in Bayamo, sold from the stores along Calle Saco and in Parque Céspedes. Otherwise you're dealing with mainly local restaurants with prices in Cuban pesos. Aside from the places reviewed here, you'll find decent *comida criolla* (Creole food) in the Royalton's atmospheric Restaurante Plaza.

★**Restaurante San Salvado de Bayamo** CARIBBEAN $
(Maceo 107; CUC$2-10; ⊙ noon-11pm) This splendid colonial place is new, but already a candidate for Bayamo's best restaurant. Get serenaded by violinists as you taste food that, thanks to the knowedgeable owner, plumbs way deeper than the obvious and taps into indigenous/bucaneer influences on regional cuisine. Try tortilla with cassava and local cheese, for example. Oh, and those shrimps come with a very special garlic sauce...

La Sevillana SPANISH $
(☎ 42-14-95; General García, btwn General Lora & Perucho Figueredo; mains CUC$3-10; ⊙ noon-2pm & 6-10:30pm) Come see Cuban chefs attempt Spanish cuisine – paella and *garbanzos* (chickpeas). This is a new kind of peso restaurant, with a dress code (no shorts), a doorman in a suit, and a reservations policy. Press your trousers, brush up on your Spanish, but don't expect *sevillano* creativity.

La Cosa Nostra ITALIAN $
(cnr Marmol & Perucho Figueredo; mains CUC$2-5; ⊙ noon-11pm) The mob's coming! Make a virtual leap to an elegant 1920s Chicago where the dishes pack a punch and come with names like Pizza Don Corleone. The portions of lasagna are a force to be reckoned with. Downsides are the overly icy air-conditioning and the sometimes inattentive service, but we are in Cuba and you wanted Italian, right?

Restaurante Vegetariano VEGETARIAN $
(General García No 173; ⊙ 7-9am, noon-2:30pm & 6-9pm; ☎) Manage your expectations before you check out this peso place. This is Cuba where *vegetarianismo* is still in its infancy.

Don't expect nut roast, but you should be able to order something other than the ubiquitous omelet.

Cuadro Gastronómica de
Luz Vázquez
FAST FOOD $

(off General García, btwn Figueredo & General Lora; dishes from MN$10) Along this short lane are parked at least a dozen clean-looking food carts selling *bayamés* street snacks in Cuban pesos. Bank on hot dogs, croquettes, ice cream, sardines and empanadas.

★ La Bodega
CARIBBEAN $$

(Plaza del Himno Nacional No 34; mains CUC$5-15, cover after 9pm CUC$3; ☺11am-1am) The front opens onto Bayamo's main square; the rear terrace overlooks Río Bayamo and is fringed by a bucolic backdrop that will leave you wondering if you've been transported to an isolated country villa. Try the beef and taste the coffee, or relax on the open terrace before the traveling troubadours arrive at 9pm.

Self-Catering
El Siglo
BAKERY $

(cnr General García & Saco; ☺9am-8pm) Fresh warm cakes sold in pesos.

Mercado Agropecuario
MARKET $

(Línea) The vegetable market is in front of the train station. There are many peso food stalls along here also.

Mercado Cabalgata
SUPERMARKET $

(General García No 65; ☺9am-9pm Mon-Sat, to noon Sun) This store on the main pedestrian street sells basic groceries.

🍷 Drinking

Bar la Esquina
BAR

(cnr Donato Marmol & Maceo; ☺11am-1am) International cocktails are served in this tiny corner bar replete with plenty of local atmosphere.

La Taberna
BAR

(General García, btwn Saco & Figueredo; ☺10am-10pm) This busy new local place on the main shopping street has beer on tap in proper pint glasses and a constant buzz of conversation. Pay in Cuban pesos.

Cafe Serrano
CAFE

(cnr Carretera Central & Av Amado Estevez; ☺24hr) Do you like really good coffee? Do you like it cheap? Come here and pay in pesos for caffeinated delights like the *coctele de cafe* (coffee cocktail) with mint and cream.

Piano Bar
BAR

(cnr General García & Bartholomé Masó; ☺2pm-2am) Ice-cold air-con, starched tablecloths, stern waiters, good live music from piano recitals to *trovadores* (folk singers) and crooners of *musica romantica*. So plush it's sometimes invite-only.

☆ Entertainment

The two main hotels – the Royalton (p384) and the Sierra Maestra (p384) – have decent bars; the latter also has a loud but popular disco.

Cine Céspedes
CINEMA

(admission CUC$2) This cinema is on the western side of Parque Céspedes, by the post office. It offers everything from Gutiérrez Alea to the latest Hollywood blockbuster.

Teatro Bayamo
THEATER

(☏42-51-06; Reparto Jesús Menéndez) Six blocks northeast of the bus station, opposite Plaza de la Patria, lies one of the Oriente's most impressive theaters, converted into its current function only in 2007, and constructed originally in 1982. The *vitrales* (stained glass windows) in the lobby are sensational. Performances are usually Wednesday, Saturday or Sunday.

Centro Cultural Los Beatles
LIVE MUSIC

(Zenea, btwn Figueredo & Saco; admission MN$10; ☺6am-midnight) Just as the West fell for the exoticism of the Buena Vista Social Club, the Cubans fell for the downright brilliance of the Fab Four. This quirky place hosts Beatles tribute bands (in Spanish) every weekend. Unmissable!

Uneac
CULTURAL CENTER

(Céspedes No 158; ☺4pm) **FREE** You can catch heartfelt boleros on the flowery patio

---

FIESTA DE LA CUBANÍA

Bayamo's quintessential nighttime attraction is an ebullient and unique street party, the likes of which you'll find nowhere else in Cuba. Set up willy-nilly along **Calle Saco**, it includes the locally famous pipe organs, whole roast pig, an eye-watering oyster drink called *ostiones* and – incongruously in the middle of it all – rows of tables laid out diligently with chess sets. Dancing is, of course, de rigueur. The action kicks off at 8pm-ish on Saturday.

here in the former home of disgraced first president Tomás Estrada Palma, the man invariably blamed for handing Guantánamo to the *Yanquis*.

Cabaret Bayamo
CABARET

(Carretera Central Km 2; ☉9pm Fri-Sun) Bayamo's glittery nightclub/cabaret opposite the Hotel Sierra Maestra draws out the locals on weekends in their equally glittery attire.

Casa de la
Trova la Bayamesa
TRADITIONAL MUSIC

(cnr Maceo & Martí; admission CUC$1; ☉9pm Tue-Sun) One of Cuba's best *trova* houses, in a lovely colonial building on Maceo. Pictures on the wall display the famous '70s afro of Bayamo-born *trova* king Pablo Milanés.

Casa de la Cultura
CULTURAL CENTER

(General García No 15) Wide-ranging cultural events, including art expos, on the east side of Parque Céspedes.

Estadio Mártires de Barbados
SPORTS

(Av Granma) From October to April there are baseball games at this stadium, found approximately 2km east of the center.

🛍 Shopping

Paseo Bayamés is the main pedestrian shopping street but, with few tourists, stores are mainly aimed at Cubans.

ARTex
SOUVENIRS

(General García No 7) The usual mix of Che Guevara T-shirts and bogus Santería dolls in Parque Céspedes.

ℹ Information

Bayamo is the biggest city in Cuba without ATMs.

Banco de Crédito y Comercio (cnr General García & Saco) Bank.

Banco Financiero Internacional (Carretera Central Km 1) In a big white building near the bus terminal.

Cadeca (Saco No 101) Money changing.

Campismo Popular (☎42-24-25; General García No 112) Make bookings for La Sierrita and Las Colorados campismos (camping installations) here.

Cubanacán (Hotel Telegrafo, Maceo No 53) Arranges hikes to Pico Turquino (two days per person CUC$68, transport included) and Parque Nacional Desembarco del Granma (CUC$45 per person, transport included), among other places.

Ecotur (☎48-70-06, ext 639; Hotel Sierra Maestra) Travel agency; also good for booking excursions to Gran Parque Nacional Sierra Maestra.

Etecsa Telepunto (General García, btwn Saco & Figueredo; internet access per hr CUC$6; ☉8:30am-7pm) Three internet terminals; rarely busy.

Farmacia Internacional (☎42-95-96; General García, btwn Figueredo & Lora; ☉8am-noon & 1-5pm Mon-Fri, 8am-noon Sat & Sun) Pharmacy.

Hospital Carlos Manuel de Céspedes (☎42-50-12; Carretera Central Km 1) Hospital.

Infotur (☎42-34-68; Plaza del Himno Nacional cnr Joaquín Palma; ☉8am-noon & 1-4pm) One of those really courteous, helpful information offices: often a rare breed in Cuba.

Post Office (cnr Maceo & Parque Céspedes; ☉8am-8pm Mon-Sat)

ℹ Getting There & Away

AIR

Bayamo's **Carlos Manuel de Céspedes Airport** (airport code BYM) is about 4km northeast of town, on the road to Holguín. Cubana (Martí No 52) flies to Bayamo from Havana twice a week (about CUC$100, two hours). There are no international flights to or from Bayamo.

BUS & TRUCK

The **provincial bus station** (cnr Carretera Central & Av Jesús Rabí) has **Víazul** (www.viazul. com) buses to several destinations.

There are three buses a day to Havana (CUC$44, 13½ hours), one to Varadero at 10:20pm (CUC$41, 12½ hours), one to Trinidad at 9:45pm (CUC$26, nine hours), and five to Santiago (CUC$7, two hours). Buses heading west also stop at Holguín, Las Tunas, Camagüey, Ciego de Ávila, Sancti Spíritus, and Santa Clara.

Passenger trucks leave from an adjacent terminal for Santiago de Cuba, Holguín, Manzanillo, Pilón and Niquero. You can truck it to Bartolomé Masó, which is as close as you can get on public transport to the Sierra Maestra trailhead. Trucks leave when full and you pay as you board.

The **intermunicipal bus station** (cnr Saco & Línea), opposite the train station, receives mostly local buses of little use to travelers, although trucks to Guisa leave from here.

TAXIS

State taxis can be procured for hard-to-reach destinations such as Manzanillo (CUC$30), Pilón (CUC$75) and Niquero (CUC$80). Prices are estimates and will depend on the current price of petrol. Nonetheless, at the time of writing it was cheaper to reach all these places by taxi than by hired car.

TRAIN

The **train station** (cnr Saco & Línea) is 1km east of the center. There are three local trains a day to Manzanillo (via Yara). Other daily trains serve Santiago and Camagüey. The long-distance Havana–Manzanillo train passes through Bayamo every third day (CUC$25).

❶ Getting Around

Cubataxi (☑ 42-43-13) can supply a taxi to Bayamo airport for CUC$5, or to Aeropuerto Frank País in Holguín for CUC$35.

A taxi to Villa Santo Domingo (setting-off point for the Alto del Naranjo trailhead for Sierra Maestra hikes) or Comandancia de la Plata will cost approximately CUC$35 one way. There's a taxi stand in the south of town near Museo Ñico López.

Cubacar (Carretera Central) rents out cars at the Hotel Sierra Maestra.

The **Servi-Cupet gas station** (Carretera Central) is between Hotel Sierra Maestra and the bus terminal as you arrive from Santiago de Cuba.

The main horse-cart route (MN$1) runs between the train station and the hospital, via the bus station. **Bici-taxis** (a few pesos a ride) are also useful for getting around town. There's a stand near the train station.

Around Bayamo

Most are lured toward the so-close-you-can-almost-touch-them mountains, but Bayamo's hinterland hides some less obvious haunts.

AND THEN THERE WERE THREE...

It seemed like an ignominious defeat. Three days after landing in a crippled leisure yacht on Cuba's southeastern coast, Castro's expeditionary force of 82 soldiers had been decimated by Batista's superior army. Some of the rebels had fled, others had been captured and killed. Escaping from the ambush, Castro found himself cowering in a sugarcane field along with two ragged companions; his 'bodyguard,' Universo Sánchez, and diminutive Havana doctor, Faustino Pérez. 'There was a moment when I was commander-in-chief of myself and two others,' said the man who would one day go on to overthrow the Cuban government, thwart a US-sponsored invasion, incite a nuclear standoff and become one of the most enduring political figures of the 20th century.

Hunted by ground troops and bombed from the air by military planes, the trio lay trapped in the cane field for four days and three nights. The hapless Pérez had inadvertently discarded his weapon; Sánchez, meanwhile, had lost his shoes. Wracked by fatigue and plagued by hunger, Fidel continued to do what he always did best. He whispered incessantly to his beleaguered colleagues – about the Revolution, about the philosophies of José Martí. Buoyantly he pontificated about how 'all the glory of the world would fit inside a grain of maize.' Sánchez, not unwisely, concluded that his delirious leader had gone crazy and that their grisly fate was sealed – it was just a matter of time.

At night, Fidel – determined not to be caught alive – slept with his rifle cocked against his throat, the safety catch released. One squeeze of the finger and it would have been over. No Cuban Revolution, no Bay of Pigs, no Cuban Missile Crisis.

Fatefully, the moment didn't arrive. With the army concluding that the rebels had been wiped out, the search was called off. Choosing their moment, Fidel and his two companions crept stealthily northeast toward the safety of the Sierra Maestra, sucking on stalks of sugarcane for nutrition.

It was a desperate fight for survival. For a further eight days the rebel army remained a bedraggled trio as the fugitive soldiers dodged army patrols, crawled through sewers and drank their own urine. It wasn't until December 13 that they met up with Guillermo García, a *campesino* (country person) sympathetic to the rebel cause, and a corner was turned.

On December 15 at a safe meeting house, Fidel's brother, Raúl, materialized out of the jungle with three men and four weapons. Castro was ecstatic. Three days later a third exhausted band of eight soldiers – including Che Guevara and Camilo Cienfuegos – turned up, swelling the rebel army to an abject 15.

'We can win this war,' proclaimed an ebullient Fidel to his small band of not-so-merry men. 'We have just begun the fight.'

◉ Sights & Activities

Jardín Botánico de Cupaynicu   GARDEN
(Carretera de Guisa Km 10; admission with/without guide CUC$2/1) For a floral appreciation of Bayamo's evergreen hinterland, head to this botanic garden about 16km outside the city off the Guisa road. It's on very few itineraries, so you can have the serene, serendipitous 104 hectares more or less to yourself. There are 74 types of palms, scores of cacti, blooming orchids and sections for endangered and medicinal plants.

The guided tour (Spanish only) gains you access to greenhouses, notable for the showy ornamentals. To get here, take the road to Santiago de Cuba for 6km and turn left at the signposted junction for Guisa. After 10km you'll see the botanic garden sign on the right. Trucks in this direction leave from the intermunicipal bus station in front of the train station.

Laguna de Leonero   LAKE
This algae-filled natural lake in the Cauto River delta, 40km northwest of Bayamo, is loaded with memorable fly-fishing possibilities. Black bass are the prized catch here: fishing season is November to March. Ecotur (p386) runs yacht excursions from CUC$250 for a maximum of six people. For more details contact its office in Bayamo's Hotel Sierra Maestra.

Dos Ríos Obelisk   MONUMENT
At Dos Ríos, 52km northeast of Bayamo, almost in Holguín, a white obelisk overlooking the Río Cauto marks the spot where José Martí was shot and killed on May 19, 1895. Go 22km northeast of Jiguaní on the road to San Germán and take the unmarked road to the right after crossing the Cauto.

Gran Parque Nacional Sierra Maestra

Comprising a sublime mountainscape of broccoli-green peaks and humid cloud forest, and home to honest, hardworking *campesinos* (country folk), the Gran Parque Nacional Sierra Maestra is an alluring natural sanctuary that still echoes with the gunshots of Castro's guerrilla campaign of the late 1950s. Situated 40km south of Yara, up a very steep 24km concrete road from Bartolomé Masó, this precipitous, little-trammeled region contains the country's highest peak, Pico Turquino (just over the border in Santiago de Cuba province), unlimited birdlife and flora, and the rebels' one-time wartime headquarters, Comandancia de la Plata.

History

History resonates throughout these mountains, the bulk of it linked indelibly to the guerrilla war that raged throughout this region between December 1956 and December 1958. For the first year of the conflict Fidel and his growing band of supporters remained on the move, never staying in one place for more than a few days. It was only in mid-1958 that the rebels established a permanent base on a ridge in the shadow of Pico Turquino. This headquarters became known as La Plata and it was from here that Castro drafted many of the early revolutionary laws while he orchestrated the military strikes that finally brought about the ultimate demise of the Batista government.

◉ Sights & Activities

The Santiago de Cuba chapter has more information on the Pico Turquino hike (p434), which is equally doable, and a 13km, four-hour hike from Alto del Naranjo.

★**Comandancia de la Plata**   LANDMARK
Topping a crenellated mountain ridge amid thick cloud forest, this pioneering camp was established by Fidel Castro in 1958 after a year on the run in the Sierra Maestra. Well camouflaged and remote, the rebel HQ was chosen for its inaccessibility and it served its purpose very well – Batista's soldiers never found it.

Today it remains much as it was left in the '50s, with 16 simple wooden buildings providing an evocative reminder of one of the most successful guerrilla campaigns in history. It's easy to appreciate the site's strategic location. The main site, culminating in the Casa de Fidel (Fidel's House) is approached via an open space, then a climb through thick trees.

Highlights include the small museum, near the beginning of the complex, the masterfully designed Casa de Fidel with its seven concealed escape routes in case the Revolution's leaders got discovered, and the steep climb up Radio Rebelde to the radio-communications buildings where the rebel's early broadcasts were aired. The hospital buildings, a wake-up call to the brutality of guerilla medical care, lie far below along

Gran Parque Nacional Sierra Maestra

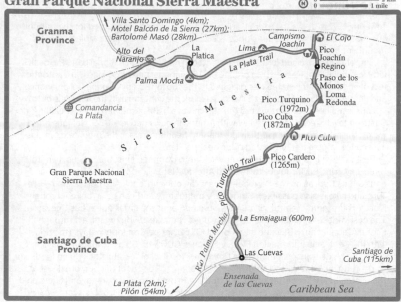

a separate path (positioned here so the injured wouldn't give away the camp location in their agony).

Comandancia de la Plata is controlled by the Centro de Información de Flora y Fauna in Santo Domingo. Aspiring guerrilla-watchers must first hire a guide at the park headquarters, then get transport (or walk) 5km up to Alto del Naranjo, and then proceed on foot along a muddy track for the final 4km. These days you're looking at a price of CUC$20, plus CUC$5 if you want to use a camera (photos of the site were banned until 2009). For further information, contact Ecotur (p386) in Bayamo.

★ **Santo Domingo** VILLAGE
(museum admission CUC$1; ⊗ museum hrs vary) This tiny village nestles in a deep green valley beside the gushing Río Yara. Communally it provides a wonderful slice of peaceful Cuban *campesino* life that has carried on pretty much unchanged since Fidel and Che prowled these shadowy mountains in the 1950s. If you decide to stick around, you can get a taste of rural socialism at the local school and medical clinic, or ask at Villa Santo Domingo about the tiny village **museum**. Locals have also been known to offer horseback riding, pedicure treatments, hikes to natural swimming pools

and some classic old first-hand tales from the annals of revolutionary history.

The park closes at 4pm but rangers won't let you pass after mid-morning, so set off early to maximize your visit.

Alto del Naranjo LANDMARK
All trips into the park begin at the end of the near-vertical, corrugated-concrete access road at Alto del Naranjo (after Villa Santo Domingo the road gains 750 vertical meters in just 5km). To get here it's an arduous two-hour walk, or zippy ride in a 4WD. There's a wondrous view of the plains of Granma from this 950m-high lookout, otherwise it's a launching pad for La Plata (3km) and Pico Turquino (13km).

🛏 Sleeping & Eating

★ **Villa Santo Domingo** HOTEL $
(☎ 56-55-68, 56-58-34; s CUC$28-44, d CUC$45-70; ✳) This villa, 24km south of Bartolomé Masó, flanks the gateway to Gran Parque Nacional Sierra Maestra. There are 40 cabins (20 cheaper concrete ones and 20 newer ones in smart wooden buildings) next to the Río Yara. The setting, among cascading mountains and *campesino* huts, is idyllic. It's the best jumping-off point for Comandancia de la Plata and Pico Turquino.

PICO TURQUINO

Towering 1972m above the azure Caribbean, Pico Turquino – so named for the turquoise hue that colors its steep upper slopes – is Cuba's highest and most regularly climbed mountain.

Carpeted in lush cloud forest and protected in a 140-sq-km national park, the peak's lofty summit is embellished by a bronze bust of national hero José Martí. In a patriotic test of endurance, the statue was dragged to the top in 1953 by a young Celia Sánchez and her father, Manuel Sánchez Silveira, to mark the centennial of the apostle's birth.

Four years later, Sánchez visited the summit again, this time with a rifle-wielding Fidel Castro in tow to record an interview with American news network CBS. Not long afterwards, the rebel army pitched their permanent headquarters in the mountain's imposing shadow, atop a tree-protected ridge near La Plata.

Best tackled as a through trek from the Santo Domingo side, the rugged, two- to three-day grind up Turquino starts from Alto del Naranjo above Santo Domingo and ends at Las Cuevas on the Caribbean coast (an out-and-back Alto del Naranjo–Pico Turquino hike is also possible). Guides are mandatory and can be arranged through Flora y Fauna employees at Villa Santo Domingo or at the small hut at Las Cuevas. The cost varies, depending on how many days you take. If you organize it through Ecotur/Cubanacán in Bayamo, bank on CUC$68 per person for two days (the price with the Centro de Información Flora y Fauna is CUC$45/65 per two/three days but doesn't include transportation from Bayamo). You'll also need to stock up on food, warm clothing, candles and some kind of sleeping roll or sheet (dinner/breakfast at the overnight shelters is included, but nothing in between). Even in August it gets cold at the shelters, so be prepared. Water is available along the trail, but is scarce: carry reserves.

The trail through the mountains from Alto del Naranjo passes the village of La Platica (water), Palma Mocha (campsite), Lima (campsite), Campismo Joachín (shelter and water), El Cojo (shelter), Pico Joachín, Paso de los Monos, Loma Redonda, Pico Turquino (1972m), Pico Cuba (1872m; with shelter and water at 1650m), Pico Cardero (1265m) and La Esmajagua (600m; with basic refreshments) before dropping down to Las Cuevas on the coast. The first two days are spent on the 13km section to Pico Turquino (normally overnighting at the Campismo Joachín and/or Pico Cuba shelters), where a prearranged guide takes over and leads you down to Las Cuevas. As with all guide services, tips are in order. Prearranging the second leg from Pico Cuba to Las Cuevas is straightforward and handled by park staff.

These hikes are well coordinated and the guides are efficient. The sanest way to begin is by overnighting at Villa Santo Domingo and setting out in the morning (you should enter the park gate by 10am). Transport from Las Cuevas along the coast is sparse with one scheduled truck on alternate days. Arrange onward transport from Las Cuevas in advance. Approaching from Santo Domingo, you will not (officially) be able to do the Comandancia de la Plata and Pico Turquino hikes the same day, but must stay overnight in the village and then begin the Pico Turquino hike the following day.

You can also test your lungs by going for a challenging early morning hike up a painfully steep road to Alto del Naranjo (5km; 750m of ascent). Other attractions include horseback riding, river swimming and traditional music in the villa's restaurant. Fidel stayed here on various occasions (in hut 6) and Raúl dropped by in 2001 after scaling Pico Turquino at the ripe old age of 70. Breakfast is included.

Casa Sierra Maestra　CASA PARTICULAR **$**
(Santo Domingo; r CUC$20-25) Across the river from the park entrance (just up from the stepping stones) this rustic place has four perfectly decent rooms (two in separate cabins) and an atmospheric *ranchón* (farm)-style bar-restaurant. Chickens cluck, and rural bliss descends. Reservations are difficult as there are no phone lines, so contact Anley Rosales Benitez (p383) in Bayamo.

Motel Balcón de la Sierra HOTEL $
(☑59-51-80; s/d CUC$22/30; P ❄ ☎) One kilometer south of Bartolomé Masó and 16km north of Santo Domingo, this is nestled in the mountain foothills but a little distant for easy access to the park. A swimming pool and restaurant are perched on a small hill with killer mountain views, while 20 air-conditioned cabins are scattered below. Lovely natural ambience juxtaposed with the usual basic-but-functional Islazul furnishings

ℹ Information

Aspiring visitors should check the current situation before arriving in the national park. Tropical storms and/or government bureaucracy have been known to put the place temporarily out of action.

The best source of information is Cubamar (p129) in Havana, or you can go straight to the horse's mouth by directly contacting Villa Santo Domingo (p389). These guys can put you in touch with the Centro de Información de Flora y Fauna next door. Additional information can be gleaned at the Ecotur office (p386) in Bayamo.

ℹ Getting There & Around

There's no public transport from Bartolomé Masó to Alto del Naranjo (and trucks to Bartolomé Masó from Bayamo are infrequent and uncomfortable). A taxi from Bayamo to Villa Santo Domingo should cost from CUC$35 one way. Ensure it can take you all the way; the last 7km before Villa Santo Domingo is extremely steep but passable in a normal car. Returning, the hotel should be able to arrange onward transport for you to Bartolomé Masó, Bayamo or Manzanillo.

A 4WD vehicle with good brakes is necessary to drive the last 5km from Santo Domingo to Alto del Naranjo; it's the steepest road in Cuba with 45% gradients near the top. Powerful 4WDs pass regularly, usually for adventurous tour groups, and you may be able to find a space on board for approximately CUC$5 (ask at Villa Santo Domingo). Alternatively, it's a tough but rewarding 5km hike.

Manzanillo

POP 105,800

Bayside Manzanillo might not be pretty but, like most low-key Granma towns, it has an infectious feel. Hang out in the semi-ruined central park with its old-fashioned street organs and distinctive neo-Moorish architecture and you'll quickly make a friend or three. With bare-bones transport links and

only one grim state-run hotel, few travelers make it here. As a result, Manzanillo is a good place to get off the standard guidebook trail and see how Cubans have learned to live with 50 years of austerity.

Founded in 1784 as a small fishing port, Manzanillo's early history was dominated by smugglers and pirates trading in contraband goods. The subterfuge continued into the late 1950s, when the city's proximity to the Sierra Maestra made it an important supply center for arms and men heading up to Castro's revolutionaries in their secret mountaintop headquarters.

Manzanillo is famous for its hand-operated street organs, which were first imported into Cuba from France in the early 20th century (and are still widely in use). The city's musical legacy was solidified further in 1972 when it hosted a government-sponsored *nueva trova* (philosophical folk music) festival that culminated in a solidarity march to Playa las Coloradas.

◉ Sights

Manzanillo is well known for its striking architecture, a psychedelic mélange of wooden beach shacks, Andalusian-style townhouses and intricate neo-Moorish facades. Check out the old **City Bank of NY building** (cnr Merchán & Dr Codina), dating from 1913, or the ramshackle wooden abodes around Perucho Figueredo, between Merchán and JM Gómez.

Parque Céspedes PARK
Manzanillo's central square is notable for its priceless **glorieta** (gazebo, bandstand), an imitation of the Patio de los Leones in Spain's Alhambra, where Moorish mosaics, a scalloped cupola and arabesque columns set off a theme that's replicated elsewhere. Nearby, a permanent **statue of Carlos Puebla,** Manzanillo's famous homegrown troubadour, sits contemplatively on a bench.

On the eastern side of Parque Céspedes, Manzanillo's **Museo Histórico Municipal** (Martí No 226; ◷8am-noon & 2-6pm Tue-Fri, 8am-noon & 6-10pm Sat & Sun) FREE gives the usual local history lesson with a revolutionary twist while the **Iglesia la Purisma Concepción** is a neoclassical beauty from 1805, with an impressive gilded altarpiece.

Celia Sánchez Monument MONUMENT
About eight blocks southwest of the park lies Manzanillo's most evocative sight. Built in 1990, this terracotta tiled staircase embel-

WORTH A TRIP

MEDIA LUNA

One of a handful of small towns punctuating the swaying sugar fields between Manzanillo and Cabo Cruz, Media Luna (population 15,493) is worth a pit stop on the basis of its Celia Sánchez connections. The Revolution's 'first lady' was born here in 1920 in a small clapboard house that is now the **Celia Sánchez Museum** (Paúl Podio No 111; admission CUC$1; ◷ 9am-5pm Mon-Sat).

If you have time, take a stroll around this quintessential Cuban sugar town dominated by a tall soot-stained mill (now disused) and characteristic clapboard houses decorated with gingerbread embellishments. There is also a lovely **glorieta**, almost as outlandish as Manzanillo's. The main park is the place to get a take on the local street theater while supping on quick-melting ice cream.

A signposted road from Media Luna leads 28km to **Cinco Palmas** where a monument marks the spot where Castro's depleted rebel army regrouped after the debacle of the *Granma* landing in December 1956.

lished with colorful ceramic murals runs up Calle Caridad between Martí and Luz Caballero. The birds and flowers on the reliefs represent Sánchez, lynchpin of the M-26-7 (July 26 Movement) and longtime aid to Castro, whose visage appears on the central mural near the top of the stairs. It's a moving memorial with excellent views out over the city and bay.

★ **Museo Histórico la Demajagua** MUSEUM
(admission CUC$1; ◷ 8am-6pm Mon-Fri, 8am-noon Sun) It started with a cry. Ten kilometers south of Manzanillo is the moving sight of the sugar estate of Carlos Manuel de Céspedes, whose *Grito de Yara* and subsequent freeing of his slaves on October 10, 1868, marked the opening of Cuba's independence wars. There's a small museum and the Demajagua bell that Céspedes tolled to announce Cuba's (then unofficial) independence.

In 1947 an as yet unknown Fidel Castro 'kidnapped' the bell and took it to Havana in a publicity stunt to protest against the corrupt Cuban government. Also awaiting at La Demajagua are the remains of Céspedes' *ingenio* (sugar mill), and a poignant monument (with a quote from Castro). To get here, travel south 10km from the Servi-Cupet gas station in Manzanillo, in the direction of Media Luna, and then another 2.5km off the main road, toward the sea.

Criadero de Cocodrilos CROCODILE FARM
(admission CUC$5; ◷ 7am-6pm Mon-Fri, 7-11am Sat) The nearby Río Cauto delta is home to a growing number of wild crocodiles, so it's no surprise to encounter one of Cuba's half dozen or so crocodile farms here.

There are close of 1000 crocs at this breeding farm, although they're all of the less-endangered 'American' variety. The farm is 5km south of Manzanillo on the road to Media Luna.

🛏 Sleeping & Eating

Manzanillo – thank heavens – has a smattering of private rooms, as there's not much happening on the hotel scene. The city's renowned for its fish, including the delicious liseta, but overall restaurant choices are dire: if in doubt eat at your casa particular, or drop in on the weekend Sábado en la Calle when the locals cook up traditional whole roast pig.

★ **Adrián & Tonia** CASA PARTICULAR $
(🖃 57-30-28; Mártires de Vietnam No 49; r CUC$20-25; 🅿 ❄) This attractive casa would stand out in any city, let alone Manzanillo. The position, on the terracotta staircase to the Celia Sánchez monument, obviously helps. But Adrián and Tonia have gone beyond the call of duty with a vista-laden terrace, plunge pool and dinner provided in a paladar next door.

Casa Peña de Juan Manuel CASA PARTICULAR $
(🖃 57-26-28; Maceo No 189 cnr Loma; r CUC$20-25) The public areas resemble a refined museum and the one ample room and quiet plant-filled terrace don't disappoint.

Hotel Guacanayabo HOTEL $
(🖃 57-40-12; Circunvalación Camilo Cienfuegos; s/d CUC$25/40; ❄ ☀) The austere Islazul-run Guacanayabo resembles a tropical reincarnation of a Gulag camp. Stay if you must.

Complejo Costa Azul PARRILLA **$**
(☺food noon-9:30pm daily, cabaret 8pm-midnight Tue-Sun) Down by the bay is this grillhouse and cabaret thrown into one. It's highly likely neither amenity will blow your mind but, nevertheless, the eating and entertainment are nigh-on as good as it gets here. Pay in pesos.

Cafetería la Fuente ICE-CREAM PARLOR **$**
(cnr Avs Jesús Menéndez & Masó; ☺8am-midnight) The Cubans are as stalwart about their ice cream as the British are about their tea. Come what may, the scooper's always in the tub. Join the line here to sweeten up your views of surrounding Parque Céspedes.

Drinking & Entertainment

Manzanillo's best 'gig' takes place on Saturday evenings in the famed **Sábado en la Calle**, a riot of piping organs, roasted pigs, throat-burning rum and, of course, dancing locals. Don't miss it!

Bodegón Pinilla BAR
(Martí 212; ☺9am-8pm Mon-Thu, to 2am Fri and Sat) A new two-level place on the peatonal (pedestrianized section) and a good bet for a beer.

Teatro Manzanillo THEATER
(Villuendas, btwn Maceo & Saco; admission MN$5; ☺shows 8pm Fri-Sun) Touring companies such as the Ballet de Camagüey and Danza Contemporánea de Cuba perform at this lovingly restored venue. Built in 1856 and restored in 1926 and again in 2002, this 430-seat beauty is packed with oil paintings, stained glass and original detail.

Casa de la Trova TRADITIONAL MUSIC
(Merchán No 213; admission MN$1) In the spiritual home of *nueva trova*, a renovation of the local *trova* house was long overdue. Pay a visit to this hallowed and freshly painted musical shrine where Carlos Puebla once plucked his strings.

Uneac CULTURAL CENTER
(cnr Merchán & Concession) **FREE** For traditional music you can head for this dependable option, which has Saturday and Sunday night *peñas* (musical performances) and painting expos.

❶ Information

Banco de Crédito y Comercio (cnr Merchán & Saco)

Cadeca (Martí No 188) Two blocks from the main square. With few places accepting convertibles here, you'll need some Cuban pesos.

Post Office (cnr Martí & Codina) One block from Parque Céspedes.

Etecsa (cnr Martí & Codina; ☺8:30am-7pm) Internet terminals.

❶ Getting There & Away

AIR

Manzanillo's **Sierra Maestra Airport** (airport code MZO) is on the road to Cayo Espino, 8km south of the Servi-Cupet gas station in Manzanillo. **Sunwing** (www.sunwing.ca) flies directly from Toronto and Montreal in winter and transfers people directly to the Marea del Portillo hotels.

A taxi between the airport and the center of town should cost approximately CUC$6.

BUS & TRUCK

The **bus station** (Av Rosales) is 2km northeast of the city center. There are no Víazul services. This narrows your options down to *guaguas* (local Cuban buses) or trucks (no reliable schedules, and long queues). Services run several times a day to Yara and Bayamo in the east and Pilón and Niquero in the south. For the latter destinations you can also board at the crossroads near the Servi-Cupet gas station and the hospital, which is also where you'll find the *amarillos* (transport officials).

CAR

Cubacar (⌨ 57-77-36) has an office at the Hotel Guacanayabo. There's a sturdy road running through Corralito up into Holguín, making this the quickest exit from Manzanillo toward points north and east.

TRAIN

All services from the train station on the north side of town are via Yara and Bayamo. All are painfully slow. Every third day there's a link to Havana.

❶ Getting Around

Horse carts (MN$1) to the bus station leave from Dr Codina between Plácido and Luz Caballero. Horse carts along the Malecón to the shipyard leave from the bottom of Saco.

Niquero

POP 21,600

Niquero, a small fishing port and sugar town located in the isolated southwest corner of Granma, is dominated by the Roberto Ramírez Delgado sugar mill, which was built in 1905 and nationalized in 1960. It is one of the few mills in the area still in operation after the closedowns of 2002.

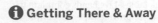

Like many Granma settlements, Niquero is characterized by its distinctive clapboard houses and has a lively **Noche de Cubanilla**, when the streets are closed off and dining is at sidewalk tables. Live bands complete with organ grinders provide the entertainment.

Ostensibly, there isn't much to do in Niquero, but you can explore the **park**, where there's a **cinema**, and visit the town's small **museum**. Look out for a **monument** commemorating the oft-forgotten victims of the *Granma* landing, who were hunted down and killed by Batista's troops in December 1956.

Niquero makes a good base from which to make a visit to the Parque Nacional Desembarco del Granma (p394). There are two Servi-Cupet petrol stations, a bank, a nightclub and plenty of spontaneous streetside action.

🛏 Sleeping

Hotel Niquero　　　　　　　　　　HOTEL **$**
(📞59-23-68; Esquina Martí; s/d CUC$18/28; 🅿❄) Here's a surprise, and a far-from-unpleasant one. Nestled in Niquero's center, this low-key, out-on-a-limb hotel situated opposite the local sugar factory actually has substantially sized, amenable rooms with little balconies overlooking the street. The affordable on-site restaurant can rustle up a reasonable beef steak with sauce. Better hunker down because it's the only accommodation in town.

Alegria del Pio

Pause for a moment. You're on hallowed revolutionary ground. Accessed via 28km of potholed purgatory from a turn-off in Niquero, this is the spot where Castro's shipwrecked rebels were intercepted by Batista's army in 1956 and forced to split up and flee. A monument went up in 2009 to mark the event and from the end of the road there are a couple of little-used trails which can be undertaken independently or with a guide; enquire with Ecotur (p386) in Bayamo or at the Parque Nacional Desembarco del Granma.

Morlotte-Fustete is a 2km trail that traverses the spectacular marine terraces (sometimes using wooden ladders) and takes in the **Cueva del Fustete**, a 5km-long cavern replete with stalagmites and stalactites, and the **Hoyo de Morlotte**, a 77m deep dolina caused by water corrosion. **El Samuel** is a 1.3km trail to the **Cueva Espelunca**, another cave thought to have been used by indigenous peoples for religious ceremonies.

Alegria del Pio is also the official finish point for the 30km hike from Las Coloradas that replicates the path of the shipwrecked rebels in December 1956, although now the trail does run right on up into the Sierra Maestra. As there are no facilities here you'll need to bring all your own food and water.

Parque Nacional Desembarco del Granma

Mixing unique environmental diversity with heavy historical significance, the **Parque Nacional Desembarco del Granma** (admission CUC$5) consists of 275 sq km of teeming forests, peculiar karst topography and uplifted marine terraces. It is also a spiritual shrine to the Cuban Revolution – the spot where Castro's stricken leisure yacht *Granma* limped ashore in December 1956.

Named a Unesco World Heritage Site in 1999, the park protects some of the most pristine coastal cliffs in the Americas. Of the 512 plant species identified thus far, about 60% are endemic and a dozen of them are found only here. The fauna is equally rich, with 25 species of mollusk, seven species of amphibian, 44 types of reptile, 110 species of bird and 13 types of mammal.

In El Guafe, archaeologists have uncovered the second-most important community of ancient agriculturists and ceramic-makers discovered in Cuba. Approximately 1000 years old, the artifacts discovered include altars, carved stones and earthen vessels along with six idols guarding a water goddess inside a ceremonial cave. As far as archaeologists are concerned, it's probably just the tip of the iceberg.

◎ Sights

Museo las Colorados　　　　　　MUSEUM
(admission CUC$5; ⊙8am-6pm) A large monument just beyond the park gate marks the *Granma's* landing spot. A small museum outlines the routes taken by Castro, Guevara and the others into the Sierra Maestra, and there's a full-scale replica of the *Granma* which – if you're lucky – a machete-wielding guard will let you climb inside to wonder how 82 men ever made it.

The entry ticket includes a visit to the simple reconstructed hut of the first *campesino* (a poor charcoal-burner) to help Fidel after the landing. An enthusiastic guide will also accompany you along a 1.3km path through dense mangroves to the ocean and the spot where the *Granma* ran aground, 70m offshore.

Sendero Arqueológico Natural el Guafe
TRAIL

(admission CUC$3) About eight kilometers southwest of Las Coloradas is this well-signposted 2km-long trail, the park's headline nature/archaeological hike. An underground river here has created 20 large caverns, one of which contains the famous Ídolo del Agua, carved from stalagmites by pre-Columbian Indians; there's also a 500-year-old cactus, butterflies, 170 different species of birds (including the tiny colibrí), and multiple orchids.

You should allow two hours for the stroll in order to take in everything. A park guide can guide you through the more interesting features for an extra CUC$2. There are hundreds of flies here. Bring repellent.

The park is flecked with other trails, the best of which is the 30km trek to Alegria del Pio replicating the journey of the 82 rebels who landed here in 1956. Due to its length and lack of suitable signage, this rarely tackled trail is best done with a guide (the trail actually runs on a further 70km into the Sierra Maestra, if you're feeling energetic. Inquire at Ecotur (p386) in Bayamo beforehand. You'll need to arrange for transport to meet you at Alegria del Pio.

Comunidad Cabo Cruz
VILLAGE

Three kilometers beyond the El Guafe trailhead is a tiny fishing community with skiffs bobbing offshore and sinewy men gutting their catch on the golden beach. The 33m-tall Vargas lighthouse here (erected 1871) now belongs to the Cuban military. In its shadow lies Restaurante el Cabo, source of the cheapest fresh seafood you'll find anywhere.

There's good swimming and shore snorkeling east of the lighthouse; bring your own gear as there are no facilities.

Sleeping & Eating

Campismo las Coloradas
CAMPISMO $

(Carretera de Niquero Km 17; s/d CUC$8/12; ✳) A Category 3 campismo with 28 duplex cabins standing on 500m of murky beach, 5km southwest of Belic, just outside the park. All cabins have air-con and baths and there's a restaurant, a games hall and water-

sport rental on site. You can book through Cubamar (☑78-33-25-24, 78-33-25-23; www.cubamarviajes.cu; Calle 3, btwn Calle 12 & Malecón, Vedado; ◷8:30am-5pm Mon-Sat) in Havana.

★ Restaurante el Cabo
SEAFOOD $

(◷7am-9pm Tue-Sun) The cheapest seafood in Cuba comes straight out of the Caribbean behind this restaurant that lies in the shadow of the Vargas lighthouse. Expect fresh fillets of snapper and swordfish, and prices in Cuban pesos that top out at the equivalent of CUC$2 a meal.

Ranchón las Colorados
CARIBBEAN $$

(meals CUC$1-3; ◷noon-7pm) A traditional thatched-roof restaurant selling fairly basic *comida criolla* just before the park gates, this place does the business if you're hungry after a long drive.

ℹ Getting There & Away

Ten kilometers southwest of Media Luna the road divides, with Pilón 30km to the southeast and Niquero 10km to the southwest. Belic is 16km southwest of Niquero. It's another 6km from Belic to the national park entry gate.

If you don't have your own transport, getting here is tough. Irregular buses go as far as the Campismo las Coloradas daily and there are equally infrequent trucks from Belic. As a last resort, you can try the *amarillos* in Niquero. The closest gas stations are in Niquero.

Pilón

POP 12,700

Pilón is a small, isolated settlement wedged between the Marea del Portillo resorts and the Parque Nacional Desembarco del Granma. It is the last coastal town of any note before Chivirico over 150km to the east. Since its sugar mill shut down nearly a decade ago, Pilón has lost much of its raison d'être, though the people still eke out a living despite almost nonexistent transport links and a merciless bludgeoning from Hurricane Dennis in 2005. The Casa Museo Celia Sánchez Manduley (admission CUC$1; ◷9am-5pm Mon-Sat), a museum in honour of the Revolution's 'First Lady' who briefly lived at this address in Pilón, was closed for refurbishment at the time of research. Pilón does boast a weekly street party – similar to those in Manzanillo and Bayamo – with whole roast pig, shots of rum and plenty of live music. This is the Sábado de Rumba (◷8pm Sat), and is your best chance of seeing the popular Cuban dance called the *pilón* (named after the town), which imitates the rhythms of pounding sugar.

The hotels at Marea del Portillo run a weekly Saturday evening transfer bus to Pilón for CUC$5 return. Getting here otherwise will involve a car, long-distance bike or winging it with the *amarillos*. The Servi-Cupet gas station is by the highway at the entrance to Pilón and sells snacks and drinks. Drivers should be sure to fill up here; the next gas station is in Santiago de Cuba, nearly 200km away.

Marea del Portillo

There's something infectious about Marea del Portillo, a tiny south-coast village bordered by two low-key all-inclusive resorts. Wedged into a narrow strip of dry land between the glistening Caribbean and the cascading Sierra Maestra, it occupies a spot of great natural beauty – and great history.

The problem for independent travelers is getting here. There is no regular public transport, which means that you may, for the first time, have to go local and travel with the *amarillos*. Another issue for beach lovers is the sand, which is of a light gray color and may disappoint those more attuned to the brilliant whites of Cayo Coco.

The resorts themselves are affordable and well-maintained places but they are isolated; the nearest town of any size is lackluster Manzanillo, 100km to the north. Real rustic Cuba, however, is a gunshot outside the hotel gates.

🏃 Activities

There's plenty to do here, despite the area's apparent isolation. Both hotels operate horseback riding for CUC$5 per hour (usually to El Salto) or a horse-and-carriage sojourn along the deserted coast road for CUC$4. A 4WD tour to Las Yaguas waterfall is CUC$49 and trips to Parque Nacional Desembarco del Granma start at about the same price. Trips can be booked at Cubanacán desks in either hotel.

Centro Internacional
de Buceo Marea de Portillo   DIVING, FISHING

Adjacent to Hotel Marea del Portillo, this Cubanacán-run dive center offers scuba diving for a giveaway CUC$30/59 per one/two immersions. A more exciting dive to the

Cristóbal Colón wreck (sunk in the 1898 Spanish-Cuban-American War) costs CUC$70 for two immersions. Deep-sea fishing starts at CUC$200 for a boat (four anglers) plus crew and gear.

Other water excursions include a seafari (with snorkeling) for CUC$35, a sunset cruise for CUC$15 and a trip to uninhabited Cayo Blanco for CUC$25.

El Salto   HIKING

This wondrous 20km out-and-back hike starts right outside the hotel complex. Turn right onto the coast road and then, after approximately 400m, hang left onto an unpaved track just before a bridge. The track winds through some fields, joins a road and traverses a dusty, scattered settlement. On the far side of the village a dam rises above you. Rather than take the paved road up the embankment to the left, branch right and, after 200m, pick up a clear path that rises steeply up above the dam and into view of the lake behind. This beautiful path tracks alongside the lake before crossing one of its river feeds on a wooden bridge. Go straight on and uphill here and, when the path forks on the crest, bear right. Heading down into a verdant tranquil valley, pass at a **casa de campesino** (the friendly owners keep bees and will give you honey, coffee, and a geographical reorientation), cross the river (Río Cilantro) and then follow it upstream to **El Salto** where there's a small waterfall, a shady thatched shelter and an inviting swimming hole.

Salto de Guayabito   HIKING

Starting in the village of **Mata Dos** about 20km east of Marea, this hike is normally done as part of an organized trip from the hotels. Groups – who often embark on horseback – follow the Río Motas 7km upstream to an enchanting waterfall surrounded by rocky cliffs, ferns, cacti and orchids.

🛏 Sleeping

★ Hotel Marea del Portillo   HOTEL $$

(📞 59-70-08; s/d CUC$64/92/113; 🅿 ❄ @ 🐾) It's not Cayo Coco, but it barely seems to matter here. In fact, Marea's all-round functionalism and lack of big-resort pretension seem to work well in this traditional corner of Cuba. The 74 rooms are perfectly adequate, the food buffet does a good job, and the dark sandy arc of beach is within baseball-pitching distance of your balcony/patio.

Servicing older Canadians and some Cuban families means there is a mix of people here; plus plenty of interesting excursions to some of the island's lesser heralded sights.

Hotel Farallón del Caribe HOTEL **$$$**
(☎59-70-82, 59-71-83; s/d CUC$95/120; P✳@≋) Perched on a low hill with the Caribbean on one side and the Sierra Maestra on the other, the Farallón is Marea's bigger, richer sibling. Three-star all-inclusive facilities are complemented by five-star surroundings and truly magical views. Exciting excursions can be organized into Parque Nacional Desembarco del Granma, or you can simply sit by the pool/beach doing absolutely nothing.

The resort is popular with package-tour Canadians bussed in from Manzanillo.

Villa Turística Punta Piedra HOTEL **$**
(☎59-70-62, 59-44-21; s/d CUC$28/40; P✳≋) On the main road 5km west of Marea del Portillo and 11km east of Pilón, this small low-key resort, comprising 13 rooms in two single-story blocks, makes an interesting alternative to the larger hotels. There's a restaurant, and an intermittent disco located on a secluded stretch of sandy beach. Staff will be delighted (if absolutely gobsmacked) with your custom!

ⓘ Getting There & Away

The journey east to Santiago is one of Cuba's most spectacular, but, since Hurricane Sandy, only passable in a 4WD. If you hike it to Las Cuevas, you can pick up public transport there (even that's sporadic). There aren't even any *amarillos* here. The occasional Cuban buses do run via Pilón to Bayamo; ask around. **Cubacar** (☎59-70-05; ☎) has a desk at Hotel Marea del Portillo.

ⓘ Getting Around

The hotels rent out scooters for approximately CUC$24 a day. Cars are available from Cubacar, or you can join in an excursion with Cubanacán at the hotels. The route to El Salto can be covered on foot.

Santiago de Cuba Province

⤴ 22 / POP 1,048,000

Best Bars

➡ Casa de las Tradiciones (p421)

➡ Casa de la Música (p420)

➡ Club Nautico (p420)

➡ Bar Sindo Garay (p420)

Best Places to Stay

➡ Hostal San Basilio (p417)

➡ Hotel Horizontes el Saltón (p432)

➡ Casa Colonial 'Maruchi' (p415)

➡ Brisas Sierra Mar (p433)

➡ Hostal Las Terrazas (p415)

Why Go?

Stuck out in Cuba's mountainous 'Oriente' region and long a hotbed of rebellion and sedition, Santiago's cultural influences have often come from the east, imported via Haiti, Jamaica, Barbados and Africa. For this reason the province is often cited as being Cuba's most 'Caribbean' enclave, with a raucous West Indian–style carnival and a cache of *folklórico* dance groups that owe as much to French-Haitian culture as they do to Spanish.

As the focus of Spain's new colony in the 16th and early 17th centuries, Santiago de Cuba enjoyed a brief spell as Cuba's capital until it was usurped by Havana in 1607. The subsequent slower pace of development has some distinct advantages. Drive 20km or so along the coast in either direction from the provincial capital and you're on a different planet, a land full of rugged coves, crashing surf, historical coffee plantations and hills replete with riotous endemism.

When to Go

➡ July is the key month in Santiago de Cuba's cultural calendar, when the city is *caliente* (hot) in more ways than one. The month begins with the vibrant Festival del Caribe and ends with the justifiably famous Carnaval.

➡ More music is on offer in March at the Festival Internacional de Trova, when the city rediscovers its musical roots.

➡ The period between these two events (March through June) is renowned for its high water clarity, ensuring excellent diving conditions off the south coast.

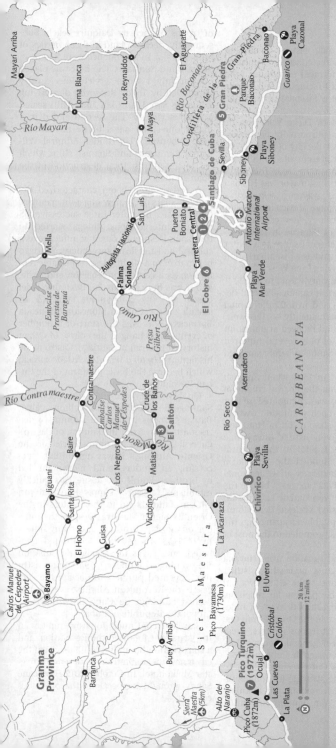

Santiago de Cuba Province Highlights

1 Stroll around the illustrious incumbents of Santiago de Cuba's **Cementerio Santa Ifigenia** (p412).

2 Visit the **Cuartel Moncada** (p408) in Santiago de Cuba and evaluate the audacity (or folly) of Castro's 1953 insurrection.

3 Make an eco-escape to luscious mountain getaway **El Saltón** (p432).

4 Explore Cuba's Afro-Cuban dance genres at a **folklórico show** in Santiago de Cuba.

5 Trace the history of Cuba's French-inspired coffee culture at **Cafetal la Isabelica** (p426) in Gran Piedra.

6 Undertake a pilgrimage to **El Cobre** (p431) to visit the shrine of Cuba's patron saint, La Virgen de la Caridad.

7 Stand atop Cuba's highest mountain, **Pico Turquino** (p434), next to the bust of José Martí, and admire the view.

8 Dive to the wreck of Spanish warship **Cristóbal Colón** (p433) off the wild coast near Chivirico.

History

Illuminated by a rich cast of revolutionary heroes and characterized by a cultural legacy that has infiltrated everything from music and language to sculpture and art, the history of Santiago is inseparable from the history of Cuba itself.

Founded in 1514 by Diego Velázquez de Cuéllar (his bones purportedly lie underneath the cathedral), the city of Santiago de Cuba moved to its present site, on a sharp horseshoe of harbor in the lee of the Sierra Maestra, in 1522. Its first mayor was Hernán Cortés – Velázquez' wayward secretary – who departed to explore Mexico in 1518.

Installed as the colony's new capital, after the abandonment of Baracoa in 1515, Santiago enjoyed a brief renaissance as a center for copper-mining, and as a disembarkation point for slaves arriving from West Africa via Hispaniola. But the glory wasn't to last.

In 1556 the Spanish captains-general departed for Havana and in 1607 the capital was transferred permanently to the west. Raided by pirates and reduced at one point to a small village of only several hundred people, embattled Santiago barely survived the ignominy.

The tide turned in 1655 when Spanish settlers arrived from the nearby colony of Jamaica; this influx was augmented further in the 1790s as French plantation owners on the run from a slave revolt in Haiti settled in the city's Tivolí district. Always one step ahead of the capital in the cultural sphere, Santiago founded the Seminario de San Basilio Magno as an educational establishment in 1722 (six years before the founding of the Universidad de La Habana) and in 1804 wrested ecclesiastical dominance from the capital by ensuring that the city's top cleric was promoted to the post of archbishop.

Individuality and isolation from Havana soon gave Santiago a noticeably distinct cultural heritage and went a long way in fuelling its insatiable passion for rebellion. Much of the fighting in both Wars of Independence took place in the Oriente, and one of the era's most illustrious fighters, great *mulato* (mixed-race) general Antonio Maceo, was born in Santiago de Cuba in 1845.

In 1898, just as Cuba seemed about to triumph in its long struggle for independence, the US intervened in the Spanish-Cuban-American War, landing a flotilla of troops on nearby Daiquirí beach. Subsequently, decisive land and sea battles of both Wars of Independence were fought in and around Santiago. The first was played out on July 1 when a victorious cavalry charge led by Teddy Roosevelt on outlying Loma de San Juan (San Juan Hill) sealed a famous victory. The second ended in a highly one-sided naval battle in Santiago harbor between US (under Admiral William T Sampson) and Spanish ships which led to the almost total destruction of the Spanish fleet.

A construction boom characterized the first few years of the new, quasi-independent Cuban state, but after three successive US military interventions, things started to turn sour. Despite its ongoing influence as a cultural and musical powerhouse, Santiago began to earn a slightly less respectable reputation as a center for rebellion and strife, and it was here on July 26, 1953, that Fidel Castro and his companions launched an assault on the Cuartel Moncada (Moncada Barracks). This was the start of a number of events that changed the course of Cuban history. At his trial in Santiago, Castro made his famous *History Will Absolve Me* speech, which became the basic platform of the Cuban Revolution.

On November 30, 1956, the people of Santiago de Cuba rose in rebellion against Batista's troops in a futile attempt to distract attention from the landing of Castro's guerrillas on the western shores of the Oriente. Although it was not initially successful, an underground movement led by brothers Frank and Josué País quickly established a secret supply line that ran vital armaments up to the fighters in the Oriente's Sierra Maestra. Despite the murder of the País brothers and many others in 1957–58, the struggle continued unabated, and it was in Santiago de Cuba, on the evening of January 1, 1959, that Castro first appeared publicly to declare the success of the Revolution. All these events have earned Santiago de Cuba the title 'Hero City of the Republic of Cuba.'

Santiago continued to grow rapidly in the years that followed the Revolution, and a construction boom in the 1990s gifted the city a new theater, a train station and a five-star Meliá hotel. In October 2012 Hurricane Sandy wrought havoc along the province's coast.

Santiago de Cuba

POP 444,800

You can take Santiago de Cuba in one of two ways: a hot, aggravating city full of hustlers and hassle that'll have you gagging to get on the first bus back to Havana; or a glittering cultural capital that has played an instrumental part in the evolution of Cuban literature, music, architecture, politics and ethnology. Yes, Santiago divides opinions among Cubans and foreigners almost as much as one of its most famous former scholars, Fidel Castro. Some love it, others hate it; few are indifferent.

Enlivened by a cosmopolitan mix of Afro-Caribbean culture and situated closer to Haiti and the Dominican Republic than to Havana, Santiago's influences tend to come as much from the east as from the west, a factor that has been crucial in shaping the city's distinct identity. Nowhere else in Cuba will you find such an inexorably addictive colorful combination of people or such a resounding sense of historical destiny. Diego Velázquez de Cuéllar made the city his second capital, Fidel Castro used it to launch his embryonic nationalist Revolution, Don Facundo Bacardí based his first-ever rum factory here, and just about every Cuban music genre from salsa to *son* (Cuba's popular music) first emanated from somewhere in these dusty, rhythmic and sensuous streets.

Setting-wise, Santiago could rival any of the world's great urban centers. Caught dramatically between the indomitable Sierra Maestra and the azure Caribbean, the city's *casco histórico* (historical center) retains a time-worn and slightly neglected air that's vaguely reminiscent of Salvador in Brazil, or the seedier parts of New Orleans.

Santiago is also hot, in more ways than one. While the temperature rises into the 30s out on the street, *jineteros* (touts) go about their business in the shadows with a level of ferocity unmatched elsewhere in Cuba. Then there's the pollution, particularly bad in the central district, where cacophonous motorcycles swarm up and down narrow streets better designed for horses or pedestrians. Travelers should beware. While never particularly unsafe, everything in Santiago feels a little madder, more frenetic and a tad more desperate, and visitors should be prepared to adjust their pace accordingly.

☉ Sights

⊙ Casco Histórico

Parque Céspedes PARK

(Map p406) If there's an archetype for romantic Cuban street life, Parque Céspedes is it. A throbbing kaleidoscope of walking, talking, hustling, flirting, guitar-strumming humanity, this most ebullient of city squares, with the bronze bust of **Carlos Manuel de Céspedes**, the man who kick-started Cuban independence in 1868, at its heart, is a sight to behold any time of day or night.

Old ladies gossip on shady park benches, a guy in a panama hat drags his dilapidated double bass over toward the Casa de la Trova, and sultry señoritas in skin-tight lycra flutter their eyelashes at the male tourists on the terrace of the Hotel Casa Granda. Parque Céspedes is also, aside from a jarring modernist bank on its west side, a treasure trove of colonial architecture.

The **Casa de la Cultura Miguel Matamoros** (Map p406; General Lacret 651), on the square's eastern aspect, is the former San Carlos Club, a social center for wealthy *santiagüeros* until the Revolution. Next door, British novelist Graham Greene once sought literary inspiration in the terrace-bar of the Hotel Casa Granda (1914). The neoclassical **Ayuntamiento** (City Hall; Map p406; cnr Gen-

Santiago de Cuba

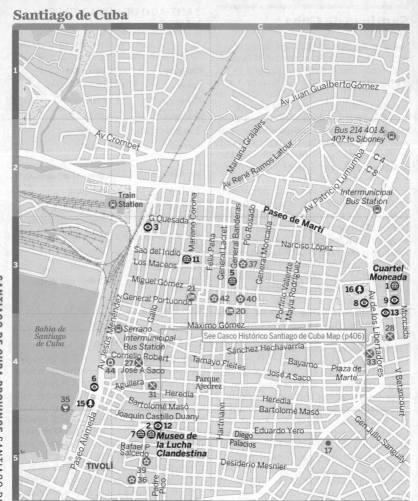

eral Lacret & Aguilera), on the northern side of the square, was erected in the 1950s using a design from 1783 and was once the site of Hernán Cortés' mayoral office. Fidel Castro appeared on the balcony of the present building on the night of January 2, 1959, trumpeting the Revolution's triumph.

★ **Casa de Diego Velázquez** MUSEUM
(Map p406; Felix Peña No 602) The oldest house still standing in Cuba, this arresting early colonial abode dating from 1522 was the official residence of the island's first governor. Restored in the late 1960s, the Andalusian-

style facade with fine, wooden lattice windows was inaugurated in 1970 as the **Museo de Ambiente Histórico Cubano** (Map p406; admission CUC$2; ⏰9am-1pm & 2-4:45pm Mon-Thu, 2-4:45pm Fri, 9am-9pm Sat & Sun).

The ground floor was originally a trading house and gold foundry, while the upstairs was where Velázquez lived. Today, rooms display period furnishings and decoration from the 16th to 19th centuries. Check the two-way screens, where you could look out without being observed: a Turkish influence (Turkey had an increasing influence on European style at this time). Visitors are also

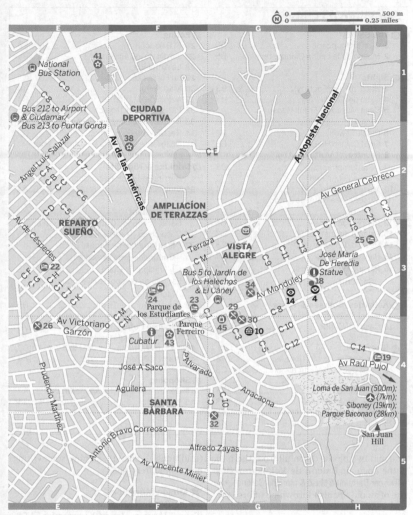

taken through an adjacent 19th-century neoclassical house.

★ Catedral de Nuestra Señora de la Asunción
CHURCH

(Map p406; ⊙ Mass 6:30pm Mon & Wed-Fri, 5pm Sat, 9am & 6:30pm Sun) Santiago's most important church is stunning both inside and out. There has been a cathedral on this site since the city's inception in the 1520s, though a series of pirate raids, earthquakes and dodgy architects put paid to at least three previous incarnations. The present cathedral, characterized by its two neoclassical towers,

was completed in 1922; the remains of first colonial governor, Diego Velázquez, are still buried underneath.

Meticulously restored, the cathedral's interior is a magnificent mélange of intricate ceiling frescoes, hand-carved choir stalls and an altar honoring the venerated Virgen de la Caridad. The adjacent **Museo Arquidiocesano** (Map p406; ⊙ 9am-5pm Mon-Fri, to 2pm Sat, to noon Sun) is rather a disappointment by comparison, housing a dullish collection of furniture, liturgical objects and paintings including the *Ecce homo*, believed to be Cuba's oldest painting. Behind the cathe-

Santiago de Cuba

dral and two blocks downhill from the park is the open-air **Balcón de Velázquez** (Map p406; cnr Bartolomé Masó & Mariano Corona), the site of an old Spanish fort which offers ethereal views over the terracotta-tiled roofs of the Tivolí neighborhood toward the harbor.

Calle Heredia STREET
The music never stops on Calle Heredia, Santiago's most sensuous street and also one of its oldest. The melodies start in the paint-peeled Casa del Estudiante (p421), where *danzón* (ballroom dance)-strutting pensioners mix with svelte rap artists barely out of their teens. One door up is Cuba's original Casa de la Trova (p421), a beautiful balconied townhouse redolent of New Orleans' French quarter.

Casa de la Trova is dedicated to pioneering Cuban *trovador* José 'Pepe' Sánchez (1856–1928), and first opened as a *trova*

(traditional poetic singing/songwriting) house in March 1968.

★**Museo Municipal**
Emilio Bacardí Moreau MUSEUM
(Bacardí Museum; Map p406; admission CUC$2; ⊙1-5pm Mon, 9am-5pm Tue-Fri, to 1pm Sat) Narrow Pío Rosado links Calle Heredia to Calle Aguilera and the fabulous Grecian facade of the Bacardí Museum. Founded in 1899 by rum magnate, war hero and city mayor Emilio Bacardí y Moreau (the palatial building was built to spec), the museum is one of Cuba's oldest and most eclectic, with some absorbing artifacts amassed from Bacardí's travels.

These include an extensive weapons' collection, paintings from the Spanish costumbrismo (19th-century artistic movement that predated Romanticism) school and the only Egyptian mummy on the island.

Casa Natal de José María de Heredia
MUSEUM

(Map p406; Heredia No 260; admission CUC$1; ⊗9am-6pm Tue-Sat, to 9pm Sun) A small museum illustrating the life of one of Cuba's greatest Romantic poets (1803–39) and the man after whom the street is named, José María de Heredia. Heredia's most notable work, 'Ode to Niagara', is inscribed outside, and attempts to parallel the beauty of Canada's Niagara Falls with his personal feelings of loss about his homeland. Like many Cuban independence advocates, Heredia was forced into exile, dying in Mexico in 1839.

Museo del Carnaval
MUSEUM

(Map p406; Heredia No 303; admission CUC$1; ⊗9am-5pm Tue-Sat, 2-10pm Sun) A colorful museum displaying the history of Santiago's Carnaval tradition, the oldest and biggest between Río and Mardi Gras. Drop in to see floats, effigies and the occasional *folklórico* dance show on the patio.

Maqueta de la Ciudad
MUSEUM

(Map p406; Mariano Corona No 704; admission CUC$1) Aping Havana's two impressive scale models of the city, Santiago has come up with its own incredibly detailed 'Maqueta.' Interesting historical and architectural information is displayed on illustrated wall panels and you can climb up to a mezzanine gallery for a true vulture's-eye city view. For more views, gravitate to the cafe-terrace at the back.

★ Museo del Ron
MUSEUM

(Map p406; Bartolomé Masó No 358; admission CUC$2; ⊗9am-5pm Mon-Sat) While not as impressive as its Havana equivalent, this museum is also refreshingly devoid of the Havana Club sales bias. It offers an insightful outline of the history of Cuban rum (old machinery, examples of bottlings throughout the last century) along with a potent shot of the hard stuff (*añejo*).

Encased in a handsome townhouse, it has a bar below so hidden away it's reminiscent of a speakeasy, but with a knowledgeable bartender on hand to serve you up their 'recommendations.'

Plaza de Dolores
SQUARE

(Map p406; cnr Aguilera & Porfirio Valiente) East of Parque Céspedes is the pleasant and shady Plaza de Dolores, a former marketplace now dominated by the 18th-century **Iglesia de Nuestra Señora de los Dolores** (Map p406; cnr Aguilera & Porfirio Valiente). After a fire in the 1970s, the church was rebuilt as a concert hall (Sala de Conciertos Dolores). Many restaurants and cafes flank this square. It's also Santiago's most popular gay cruising spot.

Plaza de Marte
SQUARE

(Map p406) Guarding the entrance to the *casco histórico,* motorcycle-infested Plaza de Marte was formerly a macabre 19th-century Spanish parade ground, where prisoners were executed publicly for revolutionary activities. Today, the plaza is Santiago de Cuba's *esquina caliente* (hot corner), where local baseball fans plot the imminent downfall of Havana's Industriales. The tall column with a red cap perched on top symbolizes liberty.

Memorial de Vilma Espín Guillois
MUSEUM

(Map p406; Sánchez Hechavarría No 473; admission CUC$1) This erstwhile home of Cuba's former 'first lady,' Vilma Espín, the wife of Raúl Castro and instrumental force in the success of the Cuban Revolution, opened in 2010, three years after her death. This house, where she lived from 1939 to 1959, is packed with lucid snippets of her life.

The daughter of a lawyer to the Bacardí clan, Vilma was first radicalized after a meeting with Frank País in Santiago in 1956. Joining the rebels in the mountains, she went on to found the influential Federation of Cuban Women in 1960.

Iglesia de Nuestra Señora del Carmen
CHURCH

(Map p406; Félix Peña No 505) You can dig deeper into Santiago's ecclesiastical history in this tumbledown construction, a hall church dating from the 1700s that is the final resting place of Christmas-carol composer Esteban Salas (1725–1803), one-time choir master of Santiago de Cuba's cathedral.

Museo Tomás Romay
MUSEUM

(Map p406; cnr José A Saco & Monseñor Barnada; admission CUC$1; ⊗8:30am-5:30pm Tue-Fri, 9am-2pm Sat) A block west of Plaza de Marte is this natural-science museum collecting natural history and archaeology artifacts, with some modern art thrown in.

Iglesia de San Francisco
CHURCH

(Map p406; Juan Bautista Sagarra No 121) This three-nave church is another understated

Casco Histórico Santiago de Cuba

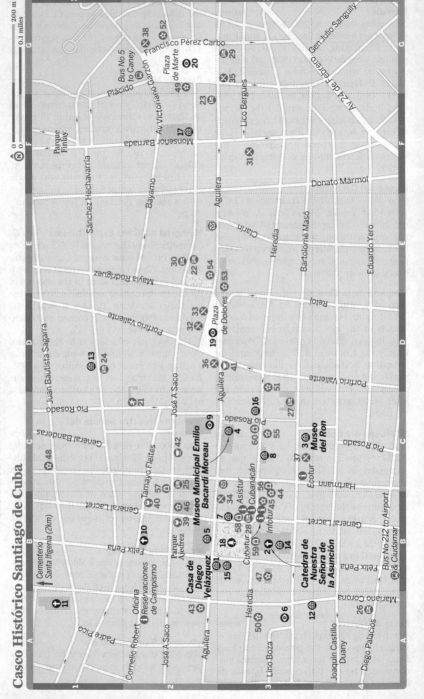

Casco Histórico Santiago de Cuba

18th-century ecclesiastical gem situated three blocks north of Parque Céspedes.

Gobierno Provincial   NOTABLE BUILDING
(Poder Popular; Map p406; cnr Pío Rosado & Aguilera) Situated opposite the Bacardí Museum, the equally Hellenic provincial government seat is another building from Cuba's 20th-century neoclassical revival. No public entry is permitted.

◎ South of the Casco Histórico

Tivolí   NEIGHBORHOOD
Santiago's old French quarter was first settled by colonists from Haiti in the late 18th and early 19th centuries. Set on a south-facing hillside overlooking the shimmering harbor, its red-tiled roofs and hidden patios are a tranquil haven these days, with old men pushing around dominoes, and

ebullient kids playing stickball amid pink splashes of bougainvillea.

The century-old **Padre Pico steps** (Map p402; cnr Padre Pico & Diego Palacios), cut into the steepest part of Calle Padre Pico, stand at the neighborhood's gateway.

⭐**Museo de la Lucha Clandestina** MUSEUM (Map p402; General Jesús Rabí No 1; admission CUC$1; ⊙9am-5pm Tue-Sun) This gorgeous yellow colonial-style building now houses a museum detailing the underground struggle against Batista in the 1950s. It's a fascinating, if macabre, story enhanced by far-reaching views from the balcony. Across the street is the **house** (Map p402; General Jesús Rabí No 6) where Fidel Castro lived from 1931 to 1933, while he was a student in Santiago de Cuba. The house is not open for visits.

The museum was a former police station attacked by M-26-7 activists on November 30, 1956, to divert attention from the arrival of the tardy yacht *Granma*, carrying Fidel Castro and 81 others. It's up the slope from the western end of Diego Palacios.

Parque Alameda PARK (Map p402; Av Jesús Menéndez) Below the Tivoli quarter, this narrow park embellishes a little-visited dockside promenade that opened in 1840 and was redesigned in 1893. At the north end you'll see the old **clock tower** (Map p402), *aduana* (customs house) and cigar factory. A curious mix of smart architecture and port-side sketchiness, its fresh(er) sea air makes it good for a stroll.

◉ North of Casco Histórico

North of the historic center, Santiago de Cuba turns residential.

⭐**Cuartel Moncada** MUSEUM (Moncada Barracks; Map p402; Av Moncada; museum admission CUC$2; ⊙museum 9am-5pm Mon-Sat, to 1pm Sun) Santiago's famous Moncada Barracks, a grand crenallated building completed in 1938, is now synonymous with one of history's greatest failed putsches. Moncada earned immortality on July 26, 1953, when more than 100 revolutionaries, led by then little-known Fidel Castro, stormed Batista's troops at what was then Cuba's second-most important military garrison.

After the Revolution, the barracks, like all others in Cuba, was converted into a school called Ciudad Escolar 26 de Julio, and in 1967 a **museum** (Map p402) was installed near gate 3, where the main attack took place. As Batista's soldiers had cemented over the original bullet holes from the attack, the Castro government remade them (this time without guns) years later as a poignant reminder. The museum (one of Cuba's best) contains a scale model of the barracks plus interesting and sometimes grisly artifacts, diagrams and models of the attack, its planning and its aftermath. Most moving, perhaps, are the photographs of the 61 fallen at the end.

The first barracks on this site was constructed by the Spanish in 1859, and actually takes its name after Guillermón Moncada, a War of Independence fighter who was held prisoner here in 1874.

Museo-Casa Natal de Antonio Maceo MUSEUM (Map p402; Los Maceos No 207; admission CUC$1; ⊙9am-5pm Mon-Sat) This important museum is where the *mulato* general and hero of both Wars of Independence was born, on June 14, 1845, and it exhibits highlights of Maceo's life with photos, letters and a tattered flag that was flown in battle. Known as the Bronze Titan in Cuba for his bravery in battle, Maceo was the definitive 'man of action.'

In his 1878 Protest of Baraguá, he rejected any compromise with the colonial authorities and went into exile rather than sell out to the Spanish. Landing at Playa Duaba in 1895, he marched his army as far west as Pinar del Río before being killed in action in 1896.

Casa Museo de Frank y Josué País MUSEUM (Map p402; General Banderas No 226; admission CUC$1; ⊙9am-5pm Mon-Sat) Integral to the success of the Revolution, the young País brothers organized the underground section of the M-26-7 in Santiago de Cuba until Frank's murder by the police on July 30, 1957. The exhibits in this home-turned-museum tell the story. It's located about five blocks southeast of Museo-Casa Natal de Antonio Maceo.

Plaza de la Revolución SQUARE (museum admission free; ⊙museum 8am-4pm Mon-Sat) As with all Cuban cities, Santiago has its bombastic Revolution square. This one's placed strategically at the junction of two sweeping avenues and anchored by an eye-catching statue of dedicated city hero (and native son) Antonio Maceo (or the modernist rendition of). Underneath the giant mound/plinth a small **museum**

MONCADA – THE 26TH OF JULY MOVEMENT

Glorious call to arms or poorly enacted putsch – the 1953 attack on Santiago's Moncada Barracks, while big on bravado, came to within a hair's breadth of destroying Castro's nascent revolutionary movement before the ink was even dry on the manifesto.

With his political ambitions decimated by Batista's 1952 coup, Castro – who had been due to represent the Orthodox Party in the canceled elections – quickly decided to pursue a more direct path to power by swapping the ballot box for a rifle.

Handpicking and training 116 men and two women from Havana and its environs, the combative Fidel, along with his trusty lieutenant, Abel Santamaría, began to put together a plan so secret that even his younger brother Raúl was initially kept in the dark.

The aim was to storm the Cuartel Moncada, a sprawling military barracks in Santiago (in Cuba's seditious Oriente region) with a shabby history as a Spanish prison. Rather than make an immediate grab for power, Castro's more savvy plan was to capture enough ammunition to escape up into the Sierra Maestra from where he and Santamaría planned to spearhead a wider popular uprising against Batista's malignant Mafia-backed government.

Castro chose Moncada because it was the second-biggest army barracks in the country, yet distant enough from Havana to ensure it was poorly defended. With equal sagacity, the date was set for July 26, the day after Santiago's annual carnival when police and soldiers would be tired and hungover from the boisterous revelries.

But as the day of attack dawned, things quickly started to go wrong. The plan's underlying secrecy didn't help. Meeting in a quiet rural farmhouse near the village of Siboney, many recruits arrived with no idea that they were expected to fire guns at armed soldiers and they nervously baulked. Secondly, with all but one of the Moncadistas drawn from the Havana region (the only native *santiagüero* was an 18-year-old local fixer named Renato Guitart), few were familiar with Santiago's complex street layout and after setting out at 5am in convoy from the Siboney farm, at least two cars became temporarily lost.

The attack, when it finally began, lasted approximately 10 minutes from start to finish and was little short of a debacle. Splitting into three groups, a small contingent led by Raúl Castro took the adjacent Palacio de Justicia, another headed up by Abel Santamaría stormed a nearby military hospital, while the largest group led by Fidel attempted to enter the barracks itself.

Though the first two groups were initially successful, Fidel's convoy, poorly disguised in stolen military uniforms, was spotted by an outlying guard patrol and only one of the cars made it into the compound before the alarm was raised.

In the ensuing chaos, five rebels were killed in an exchange of gunfire before Castro, seeing the attack was futile, beat a disorganized retreat. Raúl's group also managed to escape, but the group in the hospital (including Abel Santamaría) were captured and later tortured and executed.

Fidel escaped into the surrounding mountains and was captured a few days later; but, due to public revulsion surrounding the other brutal executions, his life was spared and the path of history radically altered.

Had it not been for the Revolution's ultimate success, this shambolic attempt at an insurrection would have gone down in history as a military nonevent. But viewed through the prism of the 1959 Revolution, it has been depicted as the first glorious shot on the road to power.

It also provided Fidel with the political pulpit he so badly needed. 'History will absolve me,' he trumpeted confidently at his subsequent trial. Within six years it effectively had.

documents his life. Other notable buildings bordering the square include modern Teatro Heredia and the National Bus Station.

Bacardí Rum Factory   LANDMARK
(Fábrica de Ron; Map p402; Av Jesús Menéndez, opposite train station) While it's not as swanky as its modern Bahamas HQ, the original Bacardí factory, which opened in 1868, oozes history.

Spanish-born founder Don Facundo dreamt up the world-famous Bacardí bat symbol after finding a colony of the winged mammals living in the factory's rafters. The Cuban government continues to make traditional rum here – the signature Ron Caney brand as well as Ron Santiago and Ron Varadero.

The Bacardí family, however, fled the island post-Revolution. In total, the factory knocks out nine million liters of rum a year, 70% of which is exported. There are currently no factory tours, but the **Barrita de Ron Havana Club** (Map p402; Av Jesús Menéndez No 703; ⊘9am-6pm), a tourist bar attached to the factory, offers rum sales and tastings. A great billboard opposite the station announces Santiago's modern battle cry: *Rebelde ayer, hospitalaria hoy, heroica siempre* (Rebellious yesterday, hospitable today, heroic always).

Parque Histórico Abel Santamaría PARK
(Map p402; cnr General Portuondo & Av de los Libertadores) This is the site of the former Saturnino Lora Civil Hospital, stormed by Abel Santamaría and 60 others on that fateful July day. On October 16, 1953, Fidel Castro was tried in the Escuela de Enfermeras for leading the Moncada attack. It was here that he made his famous *History Will Absolve Me* speech.

The park contains a giant Cubist **fountain** (Map p402) engraved with the countenances of Abel Santamaría and José Martí. It gushes out a veritable Niagara Falls of water.

Palacio de Justicia LANDMARK
(Map p402; cnr Av de los Libertadores & General Portuondo) On the opposite side of the street to the park, this court building was taken by fighters led by Raúl Castro during the Moncada attack. They were supposed to provide cover fire to Fidel's group from the rooftop but were never needed. Many of them came back two months later to be tried and sentenced in the court.

⊙ Vista Alegre

In any other city, Vista Alegre would be a leafy upper-middle-class neighborhood (indeed, it once was); but in revolutionary Cuba the dappled avenues and whimsical early-20th-century architecture are the domain of clinics, cultural centers, government offices, state-run restaurants and a handful of esoteric points of interest.

City Walk
A Walk Through History

START PARQUE ALAMEDA
END CUARTEL MONCADA
LENGTH 2KM; THREE TO FOUR HOURS

Against a backdrop of spinach-green mountains and a steely blue bay, a walking tour of Santiago's *casco histórico* (old town) is an obligatory rite of passage for first-time visitors keen to uncover the steamy tropical sensations that make this city tick.

Start beside the bay with your sights set uphill. Parque Alameda inhabits the rundown thoroughfare facing Santiago's not-so-busy port. Most of the excitement lies east in a hilly neighborhood colonized by French-Haitians in the early 1800s and baptized ❶ **El Tivolí** (p407). Tivolí is one of Santiago's most picturesque quarters, where red-roofed houses and steep streets retain a time-warped atmosphere. The neighborhood's only real 'sight' is the ❷ **Museo de la Lucha Clandestina** (p408), reached by following Calle Diego Palacios uphill from the port. From the museum take the famous ❸ **Padre Pico steps** (p408) – a terracotta staircase built into the hillside – downhill to Calle Bartolomé Masó where a right turn will take you to the breeze-lapped ❹ **Balcón de Velázquez** (p404), site of an ancient fort. This stupendous view was once contemplated by early Spanish colonists looking out for pirates.

Head east next, avoiding the angry roar of the motorbikes, until you resurface in ❺ **Parque Céspedes** (p401). The ❻ **Casa de Diego Velázquez** (p402), with its Moorish fringes and intricate wooden arcades, is believed to be the oldest house in Cuba and anchors the square on its west side. Contrasting impressively on the south is the mighty, mustard facade of the ❼ **Catedral de Nuestra Señora de la Asunción** (p403). This building has been ransacked, burned, rocked by earthquakes and rebuilt, then remodeled and restored and ransacked again. Statues of Christopher Columbus and Fray Bartolomé de las Casas flank the entrance in ironic juxtaposition.

If you're tired already, step out onto the lazy terrace bar at **8 Hotel Casa Granda** (p417) on the southeastern corner of the park, for mojitos or Montecristo cigars, or both. Graham Greene came here in the 1950s on a clandestine mission to interview Fidel Castro. The interview never came off, but he managed instead to smuggle a suitcase of clothes up to the rebels in the mountains.

Follow the music as you exit and plunge into the paint-peeled romance of Calle Heredia, Santiago's – and one of Cuba's – most atmospheric streets, which rocks like New Orleans at the height of the jazz era. Its centerpiece is the infamous **9 Casa de la Trova** (p421).

Heading upstream on Heredia you'll pass street stalls, cigar peddlers, a guy dragging a double bass, and countless motorbikes. That yellowish house on the right with the poem emblazoned on the wall is **10 Casa Natal de José María de Heredia** (p405), birthplace of one of Cuba's greatest poets. You might find a living scribe in **11 Uneac** (p422), the famous national writers' union a few doors down. Check out the *cartelera* (culture calendar) advertising the week's offerings. Plenty more legends are offered up in print in **12 Librería la Escalera** (p423), a roguish bookstore

across the street where busking musicians often crowd the stairway. Cross the street next (mind that motorbike) and stick your nose into the **13 Museo del Carnaval** (p405).

Divert along Pío Rosado one block to Aguilera where you'll be confronted by the sturdy Grecian columns of the **14 Museo Municipal Emilio Bacardí Moreau** (p404). Narrow Aguilera winds uphill to the shady **15 Plaza de Dolores** (p405), which remains amazingly tranquil, considering the ongoing motorcycle mania. There are benches to relax on underneath the trees while you weigh up if you've got enough energy to keep going or abort into one of the nearby bars or restaurants.

Stalwarts should continue east to **16 Plaza de Marte** (p405), the third of the *casco histórico's* pivotal squares and far more manic than the other two.

The walk ends in what is perhaps Santiago's most politically significant site, the art-deco **17 Cuartel Moncada** (p408), a one-time military barracks where the first shots of Cuba's Castro-led Revolution were fired in 1953. Today it is a school, but a preserved section at the rear where the skirmishes between the soldiers and rebels took place is now one of Cuba's most interesting museums.

Loma de San Juan MONUMENT

(San Juan Hill) Future American president Teddy Roosevelt forged his reputation here when, flanked by the immortal rough-riders, he supposedly led a fearless cavalry charge against the Spanish to seal a famous US victory. Protected on pleasantly manicured grounds adjacent to the modern-day Motel San Juan, Loma de San Juan marks the spot of the Spanish-Cuban-American War's only land battle (on July 1, 1898).

In reality, it is doubtful Roosevelt even mounted his horse in Santiago, while the purportedly clueless Spanish garrison – outnumbered 10 to one – managed to hold off more than 6000 American troops for 24 hours. Cannons, trenches and numerous US monuments, including a bronze rough rider, enhance the classy gardening, while the only acknowledgement of a Cuban presence is the rather understated monument to the unknown Mambí soldier.

Casa del Caribe CULTURAL BUILDING

(Map p402; Calle 13 No 154; ⊘9am-5pm Mon-Fri) **FREE** Founded in 1982 to study Caribbean life, this cultural institution organizes the Festival del Caribe and the Fiesta del Fuego every July and also hosts various concert nights. Interested parties can organize percussion courses here or studies in Afro-Cuban culture.

Museo de la Imagen MUSEUM

(Map p402; Calle 8 No 106; admission CUC$1; ⊘9am-5pm Mon-Sat) A short but fascinating journey through the history of Cuban photography from Kodak to Korda, with little CIA spy cameras and lots of old and contemporary photos. The museum also guards a library of rare films and documentaries.

Palacio de Pioneros LANDMARK

(Map p402; cnr Av Manduley & Calle 11) This eclectic mansion (built between 1906 and 1910) was once the largest and most opulent in Santiago. Since 1974 it has been a developmental center for kids. In the garden is an old MiG fighter plane on which the younger (*pioneros*) pioneers play. The traffic circle at the corner of Av Manduley and Calle 13 contains an impressive marble **statue** (cnr Av Manduley & Calle 13) of poet José María de Heredia.

◉ Around Santiago de Cuba

Cementerio Santa Ifigenia CEMETERY

(Av Crombet; admission CUC$1; ⊘8am-6pm) Nestled peacefully on the city's western extrem-ity, the Cementerio Santa Ifigenia is second only to Havana's Necrópolis Cristóbal Colón in its importance and grandiosity. Created in 1868 to accommodate the victims of the War of Independence and a simultaneous yellow-fever outbreak, the Santa Ifigenia includes many great historical figures among its 8000-plus tombs, notably the mausoleum of José Martí.

Names to look out for include Tomás Estrada Palma (1835–1908), Cuba's now disgraced first president; Emilio Bacardí y Moreau (1844–1922) of the famous rum dynasty; María Grajales, the widow of independence hero Antonio Maceo; Mariana Grajales, Maceo's mother; 11 of the 31 generals of the independence struggles; the Spanish soldiers who died in the battles of San Juan Hill and Caney; the 'martyrs' of the 1953 Moncada Barracks attack; M-26-7 activists Frank and Josué País; father of Cuban independence, Carlos Manuel de Céspedes (1819–74); and international celebrity-cum-popular-musical-rake, Compay Segundo (1907–2003) of Buena Vista Social Club fame.

The highlight of the cemetery, for most, is the quasi-religious mausoleum to national hero José Martí (1853–95). Erected in 1951 during the Batista era, the imposing hexagonal structure is positioned so that Martí's wooden casket (draped solemnly in a Cuban flag) receives daily shafts of sunlight. This is in response to a comment Martí made in one of his poems that he would like to die not as a traitor in darkness, but with his visage facing the sun. A round-the-clock guard of the mausoleum is changed, amid much pomp and ceremony, every 30 minutes.

Horse carts go along Av Jesús Menéndez, from Parque Alameda to Cementerio Santa Ifigenia (1 peso); otherwise it's a good leg-stretching walk.

★Castillo de San Pedro de la Roca del Morro FORT, MUSEUM

(El Morro; admission CUC$4; ⊘8am-7:30pm; 🅿) A Unesco World Heritage Site since 1997, the San Pedro fort sits impregnably atop a 60m-high promontory at the entrance to Santiago harbor, 10km southwest of the city. The stupendous views from the upper terrace take in the wild western ribbon of Santiago's coastline backed by the velvety Sierra Maestra.

The fort was designed in 1587 by famous Italian military engineer Giovanni Bautista Antonelli (who also designed La Punta and El Morro forts in Havana) to protect Santiago from pillaging pirates who had success-

Greater Santiago de Cuba

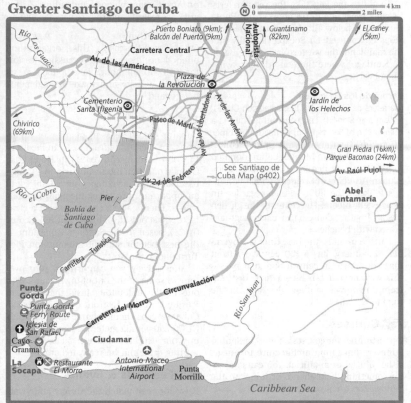

fully sacked the city in 1554. Due to financial constraints, the building work didn't start until 1633 (17 years after Antonelli's death) and it carried on sporadically for the next 60 years. In the interim British privateer Henry Morgan sacked and partially destroyed it. Finally finished in the early 1700s, El Morro's massive batteries, bastions, magazines and walls got little opportunity to serve their true purpose. With the era of piracy in decline, the fort was converted into a prison in the 1800s and it stayed that way – bar a brief interlude during the 1898 Spanish-Cuban-American War – until Cuban architect Francisco Prat Puig mustered up a restoration plan in the late 1960s.

Today, the fort hosts the swashbuckling Museo de Piratería, with another room given over to the US-Spanish naval battle that took place in the bay in 1898.

To get to El Morro from the city center you can take bus 212 to Ciudamar and cover the final 20 minutes on foot. Alternatively, a round-trip taxi ride from Parque Céspedes with wait should cost no more than CUC$15.

Cayo Granma
ISLAND

A small, populated key near the jaws of the bay, Cayo Granma is a little fantasy island of red-roofed wooden houses – many of them on stilts above the water – that guard a traditional fishing community. You can hike up to the small whitewashed **Iglesia de San Rafael** at the key's highest point, or walk around the whole island in 15 minutes.

The best thing about this place, however, is just hanging out and soaking up a bit of the real Cuba. The only official eating establishment is the seafood-biased Restaurante el Cayo, although the just-refurbished blue-and-white clapboard Palmares restaurant, jutting out over the water on the *cayo's* (key's) far side, should expand options. Sadly, Cayo Granma took a beating in Hurricane Sandy and several buildings lie in ruins.

To get to the key, take the regular ferry (leaving every one to 1½ hours) from Punta Gorda just below El Morro fort. The boat stops en route at La Socapa (actually still the mainland; the western jaw of the Bahía de Santiago) where there are decent swimming beaches.

Jardín de los Helechos
GARDEN

(Carretera de El Caney No 129; admission CUC$1; ☺9am-5pm Mon-Fri) The peaceful garden is a lush haven of 350 types of ferns and 90 types of orchids. It's the erstwhile private collection of *santiagüero* Manuel Caluff, donated in 1984 to the Academia de Ciencias de Cuba (Cuban Academy of Science), which continues to keep the 3000-sq-meter garden in psychedelic bloom. The center of the garden has an inviting dense copse-cum-sanctuary dotted with benches.

For the orchids, the best time is November to January. Bus 5 (20 centavos) from Plaza de Marte in central Santiago passes this way, or you can hire a taxi. It's 2km from downtown Santiago de Cuba on the road to El Caney.

Courses

Opportunities for courses abound in Santiago; everything from architecture to music, either official or unofficial. You can sign up for something beforehand, or jump on the bandwagon when you arrive.

UniversiTUR
LANGUAGE

(☑64-31-86; www.uo.edu.cu; Universidad de Oriente, cnr Calle L & Ampliación de Terrazas) Arranges Spanish courses. Monthly rates for 60-hour courses (three hours a day, five days a week) start at CUC$250.

Ballet Folklórico Cutumba
MUSIC, DANCE

(Map p402; Teatro Galaxia, cnr Avs 24 de Febrero & Valeriano Hierrezuelo) Santiago's *folklórico* groups are highly inclusive and can organize dance and percussion lessons either in groups or individually. Start with the Cutumba who often perform at Hotel las Américas. Also helpful is Conjunto Folklórico de Oriente.

Casa del Caribe
MUSIC, DANCE

(Map p402; ☑64-22-85; Calle 13 No 154) The portal of all things Santería (Afro-Cuban religion) organizes dance lessons in conga, *son* and salsa; it's CUC$5 per hour. Resident staff member Juan Eduardo Castillo can also organize lessons in percussion. Real aficionados can inquire about in-depth courses on Afro-Cuban religions and culture. These guys are experts and they're very flexible.

Cuban Rhythm
MUSIC, DANCE

(www.cubanrhythm.com) This organization offers dance lessons and percussion lessons for CUC$10 an hour. Take a look at its excellent website and make arrangements beforehand.

Tours

Cubatur (p424) sells all manner of excursions, for everything from La Gran Piedra to El Cobre. Cubanacán (p424) in Hotel Casa Granda offers an interesting trip to a Cuban baseball game including a signed shirt and an opportunity to meet the players afterwards. There's also a chance to visit a cigar factory just outside of town (CUC$5). Ecotur (p424), based in the Santiago Aquarium, is the best bet for summit attempts on Pico Turquino to the west.

Alternatively, you can arrange your own tour to some of the out-of-town sights with one of the ubiquitous taxis that park in Parque Céspedes in front of the cathedral. Cubataxi cabs should charge approximately CUC$0.50 per kilometer for longer trips. Tot up your expected mileage, factor in some waiting time, and get ready to bargain.

Festivals & Events

Few cities can match the variety and vivacity of Santiago de Cuba's annual festivals.

The summer season begins with the **Fiesta de San Juan** (June 24), celebrated with processions and conga dancing by cultural associations called *focos culturales*. This is followed by the 'big two': the **Festival del Caribe, Fiesta del Fuego** (Festival of Caribbean Culture, Fire Celebration) in early July followed by Santiago de Cuba's **Carnaval**, held in the last week of July.

Other celebrations include the following.

Boleros de Oro
MUSIC

Arrive in mid- to late June for this crooner's extravaganza that is replicated in various cities throughout the country.

Festival Internacional Matamoros Son
MUSIC

A tribute to one of Santiago de Cuba's musical greats (Miguel Matamoros), this kicks off in late October with dances, lectures, concerts and workshops. Main venues include the Casa de la Trova and the Teatro Heredia.

CARNAVAL CRAZINESS: A VERY VIVID HISTORY

OK, Santiago is pretty crazy at any time. But come Carnaval in July the city's hotchpotch of peoples and influences (we're talking Spanish, French-Haitian, Jamaican and African, plus music from *son* – Cuba's popular music – to rumba to Santería) come together in one of the Caribbean's most frenzied street parties. Sure, it's no Río, and Trinidad & Tobago's carnival is bigger too, but Carnaval de Santiago de Cuba is less on the tourist radar and that added authenticity might just give it the edge over those more-famed celebrations.

The carnival's origins here make it particularly interesting: unlike most Latin American carnivals, this did not develop around a Lent-based celebration of deep religious significance. In Santiago, Carnaval became an amalgam of several separate days of fun and diversion (*mamarrachos*, which fell around the time of saints days such as San Juan on June 24 or Santa Ana on July 26, but lacked any further religious significance). Their primary purpose was instead to give laborers downtime after the January to May period of sugarcane harvesting; at one time, they were even dubbed '*festivales de las clases bajas*' (festivals of the lower classes). Spanish authorities tolerated the festivities as a means of distracting the poor from other more serious forms of rebellion (and quickly Carnaval became synonymous with debauchery and scandal). In a delicious modern-day touch of irony, Carnaval now culminates in the Día de la Rebeldía Nacional (July 26), held in honour of Cuba's most famous rebellion (albeit failed): the assault on the Moncada Barracks.

Santiago's carnivals were probably at their zenith some time in the 19th century, although folk back then knew them only as the aforementioned *mamarrachos*: a byword for parties in which more or less anything could happen. Horse races, large-scale bonfires, food fights, copious alcohol consumption, *cantos de pullas* (mocking, satirical songs) and what the Spanish authorities thought of as overly sensual dancing.

Now Santiago's carnival isn't *quite* so *loco* (crazy) but it hasn't waned much. The horse races and throwing of food, drink and the like at other festival-goers are gone, but alcohol and music remain key elements. A distinguishing theme are the *comparasas* (parades) which were satirical or even anti-establishment in origin. *Comparasas* subdivide again into the *congas* (traditionally simpler, but feistier performances by poorer people in large groups with somewhat manic percussion accompaniment) and more-elaborate *paseos* (usually horse-drawn parades, more lavish in scale and similar to European-style carnival floats). Av Victoriano Garzón is the hub of parade action. There's a specially brewed Carnaval beer (Cerveza de Termo), numerous food stands with the likes of roast suckling pig, innumerable colourful costumes, dances and musical performances (even by Cuba's excessive standards) and...and you should go, because this is one festival in which words cannot do justice. Santiago's Museo del Carnaval (p405) is a good first port of call to whet your taste buds.

Festival Internacional de Coros   MUSIC
The international choir festival in late November brings in some strong international singing groups for some cultural cross-fertilization and spirit-lifting music.

🛏 Sleeping

Hostal Las Terrazas   CASA PARTICULAR $
(Map p406; ☎ 62-05-22; martingisel78@yahoo.es; Diego Palacios No 177, btwn Padre Pico & Mariano Corona; r CUC$20-25; P ❄) The young hosts run a surgically clean house three blocks from Parque Céspedes. There are two large rooms, but the reason to stay is in the name: the *terrazas* (terraces). The top-level leaf-draped terrace has some of the city's finest views, and in the evening becomes a convergence point for travelers.

English-speaking Gisel and Martin have already amassed 12 years of exprience in the hospitality trade and are true professionals. They can also make a really good coffee. Guarded parking is nearby.

Casa Colonial 'Maruchi'   CASA PARTICULAR $
(Map p402; ☎ 62-07-67; maruchib@yahoo.es; Hartmann No 357, btwn General Portuondo & Máximo Gómez; r CUC$25; ❄) Maruchi is quintessential Santiago and is the best advert the city could give. For a start it's a hive of all things Santería. You'll meet all types here: *santeros* (priests of Santería), backpackers

and foreign students studying for PhDs on the Regla de Ocha. The food's legendary and the fecund courtyard equally sublime.

A third upstairs guest room has just been completed to complement the two courtyard-facing beauties with bare-brick walls below.

Hotel Libertad HOTEL $
(Map p406; ☎62-77-10; Aguilera No 658; s/d CUC$26/42; ❄ @) Cheap Cuban hotel chain Islazul breaks out of its ugly Soviet-themed concrete block obsession and goes colonial in this venerable sky-blue beauty on Plaza de Marte. Eighteen clean (if sometimes dark) high-ceilinged rooms and a pleasant streetside restaurant are a bonus. The belting (until 1am) rooftop disco isn't.

Nelson Aguilar Ferreiro & Deysi Ruíz Chaveco CASA PARTICULAR $
(Map p406; ☎65-63-72; José A Saco No 513; r CUC$20-25) Slap-bang in the center but with a quieter more suburban feel, this is one of Santiago's better casas. It has a secluded plant-filled patio from which lead two spick-

---

CITY OF HEROES

When it comes to heroic icons Santiago de Cuba shows little modesty. Indeed, the city is known nationally by the moniker 'City of Heroes.' Here's a rundown of four of them – one a poet, one a warrior, one an underground resistance fighter and one a rum baron-turned-patriot.

Antonio Maceo

Known as the 'Bronze Titan' for his wartime heroics, Maceo was a *mulato* (mixed-race) general during the slave era who led from the front in both Independence Wars and was revered as one of the few Mambís (Cuban rebels) who never sold out to the Spanish. The definitive 'man of action' to José Martí's intellectual 'man of ideas,' Maceo was injured 22 times on the battlefield until his luck ran out in a skirmish outside Havana in December 1896. You can see him re-created in bronze in Plaza de la Revolución (p408), or visit his birth-house and museum (p408) in the city center.

Frank País

Dead by the age of 22, Frank País had a short life that left a long legacy. In the mid-'50s he began forming revolutionary cells in Santiago in resistance to the Batista regime, and his role in organizing and coordinating the urban underground was vital in cementing supply routes from the city up to Fidel Castro's rebels in the mountains. País was murdered by Batista's police in July 1957, but he had already created the bedrock for Castro's future success. Today, he is honored all over Cuba in streets, squares, monuments and even an airport (Holguín). You can visit his birth-house (p408) in Calle General Banderas.

Emilio Bacardí

Today, the relationship between Bacardí and the Cuban government is famously fraught but back in the 1890s, under the auspices of Bacardí-clan scion, Emilio, it was far less caustic. Emilio led a dual life as the head of a lucrative rum dynasty, and as a plotting *independista*, unbending in his opposition to the Spanish during the Spanish-Cuban-American War. He was imprisoned more than once for his 'transgressions' but returned heroically to Santiago in 1898 where he became the city's first mayor and a beacon of tolerance and sanity in the fledgling nation. He was also responsible for founding Cuba's first museum.

José María Heredia y Heredia

A man of words rather than action, Heredia expressed his revolutionary thoughts through poetry instead of politics. But such nuanced observations were still enough to provoke the ire of the heavy-handed Spanish authorities and, in 1823, he was arrested on a trumped-up conspiracy charge and banished from Cuba for life. Most of his later work was written from exile and is heavy with nostalgia for the homeland he missed. Heredia's birth-house in the street that bears his name is now a museum (p405) with the words of his poem 'Ode to Niagara' emblazoned on the wall outside.

and-span double rooms. The dinner menu is huge, with nearly 100 items.

Casa Lola
CASA PARTICULAR $

(Map p402; ✐65-41-20; Mariano Corona No 309, btwn General Portuondo & Miguel Gómez; r CUC$20-25) With a large back garden crowned by a gazebo, you'll hardly be needing plaza chill-out time (there's your own central square, right outside your room). The room itself is attractively done up, with a large balcony overlooking the street.

Aichel & Corrado
CASA PARTICULAR $

(Map p406; ✐62-27-47; José A Saco No 516, btwn Mayía Rodríguez & Donato Mármol; r CUC$20-25; ❆) A thick-in-the-action house on José A Saco (Enramadas) with two rooms perched on a terrace high above the street. The one at the front is the spiffiest.

Casa Nenita
CASA PARTICULAR $

(Map p406; ✐65-41-10; Sánchez Hechavarría No 4/2, btwn Pío Rosado & Porfirio Valiente; r CUC$20-25) Santiago throws up another *palacio* (palace) of colonial splendor that gives away little from its street appearance. Dating from 1850, Nenita's house has soaring ceilings, original floor tiles and a truly amazing back patio.

Casa Marcos
CASA PARTICULAR $

(Map p402; ✐66-36-76; Calle G No 109 Altos; apt CUC$25) Watch for your reflection in the floor of this well-scrubbed apartment near Cuartel Moncada. A porch with rockers, a well-appointed kitchen-living area and a bedroom at the rear: great, especially if you're staying that little bit longer.

Caridad Leyna Martínez
CASA PARTICULAR $

(Map p402; ✐64-29-55; Calle 14 No 352, Reparto Vista Alegre; r CUC$20-25) This tranquil place out in once-posh Vista Alegre has two rooms with large fridges and en-suite bathrooms not far from the Loma de San Juan.

Hotel Balcón del Caribe
HOTEL $

(✐69-10-11, 69-15-06; Carretera del Morro Km 7.5; s/d incl breakfast CUC$24/38; ❆❆) The tremendous setting next to El Morro castle is counter-balanced by the usual humdrum Islazul hotel-chain foibles: flowery curtains, ancient mattresses and furnishings salvaged from a 1970s garage sale. But there's a pool and the view is stunning. Get a room inside the complex, not a grottier external cabin. It's located 10km from the city center; you'll need your own wheels if you're staying.

Arelis González
CASA PARTICULAR $

(Map p406; ✐65-29-88; Aguilera No 615; r CUC$20-25) This striking blue classical facade on Aguilera is just off Plaza de Marte. It's a noisy street, but the house has a nice ambience. There are two OK rooms and a gorgeous roof terrace now opened as a paladar. The gnarly vines on level two are used to make grape juice.

Gran Hotel Escuela
HOTEL $

(Map p406; ✐65-30-20; José A Saco No 310; s/d CUC$23/35; ❆) In the retro-fest that is Calle José A Saco, this old four-story establishment has huge rough-edged rooms that fairly dwarf the single beds and wall-mounted small-screen TVs: bargain-basement, sure – but at these prices you're almost undercutting the casas particulares.

Villa Gaviota
HOTEL $

(Map p402; ✐64-13-70; Av Manduley No 502, btwn Calles 19 & 21, Vista Alegre; s/d CUC$29/40; ❆❆❆) Sitting pretty in an oasis of calm in Santiago's salubrious Vista Alegre district, Villa Gaviota has been upgraded from the tacky holiday camp of yore to embrace a sharper, edgier look. Features include a swimming pool, restaurant, three bars, billiards room and laundry.

★ Hostal San Basilio
HOTEL $$

(Map p406; ✐65-17-02; Bartolomé Masó No 403, btwn Pío Rosado & Porfirio Valiente; s/d CUC$65/90; ❆) Lovely eight-room San Basilio (named for the original name of the street in which it lies) is cozy, comfortable and refreshingly contemporary – with a romantic colonial setting. Rooms come with clever little frills such as DVD players, umbrellas, bathroom scales and mini bottles of rum, and the communal patio drips with ferns. A small restaurant serves breakfast and lunch.

Hotel Versalles
HOTEL $$

(✐69-10-16; Alturas de Versalles; s/d incl breakfast CUC$43/62; ❆❆❆) Not to be confused with the namesake rumba district of Matanzas, or the resplendent home of Louis XIV, this modest hotel is on the outskirts of town off the road to El Morro. A recent upgrade has injected some style into its inviting pool and its comfortable rooms with small terraces.

Hotel Casa Granda
HOTEL $$

(Map p406; ✐65-30-24; Heredia No 201; s/d CUC$78/112; ☺ Roof Garden Bar 11am-1am; ❆) This elegant hotel (1914), artfully described by Graham Greene in his book *Our Man in*

Havana, has 58 rooms and a classic red-and-white-striped front awning. Greene used to stay here in the late 1950s when he enjoyed relaxing on the streetside terrace, while his famous pen captured the nocturnal essence of the city as it wafted up from the bustling square below. Half a century later, the atmosphere is little different.

Aside from Che Guevara posters and some seriously erratic service on reception, not much has changed. The hotel's 5th-floor Roof Garden Bar is well worth the CUC$2 minimum consumption charge, and the terrace just above Parque Céspedes is an obligatory photo stop for foreign tourists on the lookout for bird's-eye city views. There's music here most nights and an occasional buffet on the roof.

Hotel las Américas   HOTEL $$
(Map p402; ☎64-20-11; cnr Avs de las Américas & General Cebreco; s/d CUC$44/70; P❄@☀) A lower-quality option opposite the Meliá. The 70 rooms offer the usual Islazul interiors though the general facilities – restaurant, 24-hour cafetería, small pool, nightly entertainment and car rental – are comprehensive for the price.

Meliá Santiago de Cuba   HOTEL $$$
(Map p402; ☎68-70-70; cnr Av de las Américas & Calle M; s/d CUC$120/160; P❄@☀☎) A blue-mirrored monster (or marvel, depending on your taste) dreamt up by respected Cuban architect José A Choy in the early '90s, the Meliá is Santiago's only 'international' hotel. There are real bathtubs (in every room), three pools, four restaurants, various shopping facilities and a fancy bar on the 15th floor. The downsides are its out-of-center location and lack of genuine Cuban charm.

✖ Eating

How is it possible? More than one million inhabitants and a medley of culture to intimidate most similarly sized cities around the globe, but a restaurant scene that's so lean it's laughable. The outlook is generally mediocre, with the odd get-out-of-jail card. Paladares haven't blossomed like they have in other Cuban cities, either.

In the heart of the *casco histórico*, Calle José A Saco is now designated traffic-free daily until at least 9pm. It offers all manner of mobile food units selling *comida ligera* (light food).

Jardín de los Enramadas   ICE CREAM $
(Map p402; cnr José A Saco & Gallo; ⊙9:45am-11:45pm) Occupying a block just down from the *casco histórico* en route to the port, this garden is devoted to ornamental plants and great ice cream (which comes with marshmallows and biscuits). Service is exemplary.

Bendita Farándula   PALADAR $
(Map p406; Monseñor Barranda s/n, btwn Aguilera & Heredia; mains CUC$3-8; ⊙noon-11pm) Of the city's scant half-decent paladares, try this one. You would probably never wander in here unbidden, but with an ambience somehow reminiscent of a bistro in a provincial French town, this cozy two-floored place with guests' musings on the walls does Santiago's only *pescado con leche de coco* (fish with coconut sauce; a Barracoan speciality) and a really nice *bistek de cerdo con jamon y queso* (pork steak with ham and cheese).

Restaurante España   SEAFOOD $
(Map p402; Victoriano Garzón; mains CUC$3-7; ⊙noon-10pm) Get ready for the Arctic blast of air-con and readjust your Cuban food preconceptions before you walk into España. It specializes in seafood cooked with panache and – on occasion – fresh herbs. Try the lobster or tangy prawns, but bypass the Cuban wine, which is almost undrinkable.

La Arboleda   ICE CREAM $
(Map p402; cnr Avs de los Libertadores & Victoriano Garzón; ice creams under CUC$1; ⊙10am-11:40pm Tue-Sun) Santiago's ice-cream cathedral is a little out of the center, not that this lessens the queue length. Yell out *¿Quién es último?* (who is last?) and take your place on the Av de los Libertadores side of the parlor. Milkshakes are sometimes sold from the outside window.

La Fortaleza   CUBAN $
(Map p402; cnr Av Manduley & Calle 3; mains CUC$2-5; ⊙noon-11:30pm) What a shame. A conducive setting amid Vista Alegre's mansions, a spacious, inviting shady patio and above-average food (pay in pesos) made infinitely more palatable by the lunchtime live music, but? A big fat zero for the quality of service.

Santiago 1900   CARIBBEAN $
(Map p406; Bartolomé Masó No 354; mains MN$50-150; ⊙noon-midnight) In the former Bacardí residence you can dine on the standard chicken, fish or pork for Cuban pesos in a plush dining room that recently recovered

its fin de siècle colonial airs. Beware the draconian dress code. No shorts or T-shirts.

Pan.com
FAST FOOD $

(Map p406; Aguilera, btwn General Lacret & Hartmann; snacks CUC$3; ⊘11am-11pm) Havana's refreshingly efficient fast(ish)-food chain has a smaller less-efficient Santiago branch. The menu is ostensibly long; the actual availability is another ballgame. Hamburgers are usually a safe bet.

La Perla del Dragón
CHINESE $

(Map p406; Aguilera, btwn Porfirio Valiente & Mayía Rodríguez; mains around CUC$5; ⊘11am-11pm) So-so Chinese restaurant with a nice setting on Plaza de Dolores.

★ Madrileño
INTERNATIONAL $$

(Map p402; ☑ 64-41-38; mains CUC$6-15; ⊘noon-11pm) Just because it wasn't particularly hard to cruise in at number one spot in Santiago's restaurant scene doesn't mean you shouldn't respectfully doff your *sombrero* (hat) to Madrileño's classy climb to culinary heights. This sumptuous colonial abode in Vista Alegre has dining from front terrace to back patio (the house is big and constitutes a substantial eating space).

You could go for dependable Italian fare, succulent smoked steaks or seafood; whatever you choose will be a memorable evening (the best time to visit, although it's open for lunch). No harm in booking early: it's popular.

Paladar Salón Tropical
PALADAR $$

(Map p402; ☑ 64-11-61; Luis Fernández Marcané No 310, Reparto Santa Bárbara; mains CUC$10; ⊘5pm-midnight Mon-Sat, noon-midnight Sun) The city's best paladar is a few blocks south of Hotel las Américas on a pleasant rooftop terrace with fairy lights and city views. The food is plentiful and tasty with a varying menu of succulent smoked meat served with the likes of *congrí* (rice flecked with black beans) or delicious *yuca con mojo* (starchy root vegetables with garlic lime sauce). Reservations are a good idea.

Hotel Casa Granda
CAFE $$

(Map p406; Heredia No 201, Casa Granda; snacks CUC$2-6; ⊘9am-midnight) Positioned like a whitewashed theater box overlooking the colorful cabaret of Parque Céspedes, the Casa Granda's Parisian-style terrace cafe has to be one of the best people-watching locations in Cuba. Food-wise you're talking snacks (burgers, hot dogs, sandwiches etc),

and service-wise you're talking impassive, verging on the grumpy – but with this setting, who cares?

Restaurante el Morro
CARIBBEAN $$

(Castillo del Morro; lunch CUC$12; ⊘noon-9pm) The spectacular cliff-side, castle-hugging location does help. Years of dealing with big tour groups has made the staff jaded, and the eating experience, crammed amid the busloads of European/North American 50-somethings, isn't Cuba's most authentic, but the food is good and the setting sublime. The restaurant was good enough for Paul McCartney, who once ate here during a whistle-stop 2000 visit.

According to the waiters, the world's most famous vegetarian made do with an omelet. For meat-eaters, the complete *comida criolla* (Creole food) lunch (CUC$12) is a better bet, a filling spread that includes soup, roast pork, a small dessert and one drink. Take bus 212 to Ciudamar and walk the last 20 minutes, or take a taxi.

Ristorante Italiano la Fontana
ITALIAN $$

(Map p402; cnr Av de las Américas & Calle M, Meliá Santiago de Cuba; ⊘11am-11pm) Pizza *deliciosa* (from CUC$5) and lasagna *formidable* (CUC$8), ravioli and garlic bread (CUC$1); *mamma mía,* this has to be the number-one option for breaking away from all that chicken and pork!

Restaurante Matamoros
CARIBBEAN $$

(Map p406; cnr Aguilera & Porfirio Valiente; mains CUC$5-10) Some interesting wall art, a couple of bolero-singing *muchachas* (girls) and a decent menu (if you're happy with chicken and pork) have breathed new life into this once-dingy joint on Plaza Dolores that celebrates the life and career of Cuba's greatest *son* exponents, the Trio Matamoros.

La Teresina
CARIBBEAN $$

(Map p406; Aguilera, btwn Porfirio Valiente & Mayía Rodríguez; mains CUC$5-12; ⊘11am-11pm) One in a triumvirate of inviting-looking restaurants along the north side of Plaza de Dolores, La Teresina doesn't quite live up to its splendid colonial setting. But the terrace is shady, the beers affordable and the food – a familiar mix of spaghetti, pizza and chicken – enough to take the edge off a hungry appetite.

El Barracón
CARIBBEAN $$$

(Map p402; ☑ 66-18-77; Av Victoriano Garzón; mains CUC$15-28; ⊘noon-midnight) El Barracón opened its doors amid much publicity in

August 2008 to reignite the roots of Afro-Cuban culture and cuisine. The fanfare was justified. The restaurant's interior, a mix of atmospheric Santería shrine and *cimarrón* (runaway slave), is intriguing, and the creative food is even better. Try the delicious *tostones* (fried plantain patties) filled with chorizo and cheese, or opt for the lamb special.

Restaurante Zunzún CARIBBEAN $$$
(Map p402; Av Manduley No 159; CUC$8-28; ⊙noon-10pm Mon-Sat, to 3pm Sun) Dine in bygone bourgeois style in this mansion-turned-restaurant. Zunzún, in the once upscale Vista Alegre neighborhood, has always been one of Santiago's best restaurants. Exotic dishes include chicken curry, paella or a formidable cheese plate and cognac. Expect professional, attentive service and entertaining troubadours. The Madrileño and El Barracón match it for quality these days though, and do so for less money.

Self-Catering

Supermercado Plaza
de Marte SUPERMARKET $
(Map p406; Av Victoriano Garzón; ⊙9am-6pm Mon-Sat, to noon Sun) One of the better-stocked supermarkets in town, with a great ice-cream selection and cheap bottled water. It's in the northeastern corner of Plaza de Marte.

Panadería Doña Neli BAKERY $
(Map p406; cnr Aguilera & Gen Serafin Sánchez; ⊙7:30am-8pm) Hard-currency bakery on Plaza de Marte vending divine-smelling bread and cakes, with a scowl.

Municipal Market MARKET $
(Map p402; cnr Aguilera & Padre Pico) The main market, two blocks west of Parque Céspedes, has a poor selection considering the size of the city.

Drinking & Nightlife

For drinks with a view, the roof terrace of Hotel Casa Granda (p419) is recommended, as is (in daytime) the surprise back terrace of Maqueta de la Ciudad (p405). The Museo del Ron (p405) has a divey but decent bar down below (also daytime only).

★**Bar Sindo Garay** BAR
(Map p406; cnr Tamayo Fleites & General Lacret; ⊙11am-11pm) A museum (to one of Cuba's most famous *trova* musicians, Sindo Garay, most renowned for his composition *Perla*

marina) as much as a bar, this is a smart, new, usually packed place with two levels, serving great cocktails on recently pedestrianized Tamayo Fuentes.

Café Ven CAFE
(Map p406; José A Saco, btwn Hartmann & Pío Rosado; ⊙9am-9pm) Valuable new cafe tucked into busy Saco (Enramadas) with lung-enriching air-con, interesting coffee *cafetal* (plantation) paraphernalia and life-saving sandwiches, cakes and devilishly good espresso or mocha.

Café la Isabelica CAFE
(Map p406; cnr Aguilera & Porfirio Valiente; ⊙9am-9pm) Smokier, darker cantina-type cafe with the prices in pesos.

Casa de la Música BAR, NIGHTCLUB
(Map p406; Mariano Corona No 564; admission CUC$3-10; ⊙10pm-4am) Similar to the venues in Havana, this Casa de la Música features a mix of live salsa and taped disco and is usually a cracking night out.

Club Nautico BAR
(Map p402; off Paseo Alameda; ⊙noon-midnight) Enlivening Paseo Alameda with its lively *ranchón* (farm)-style bar suspended over the water, with a great view over the bay, this is an airy locale to escape the sizzling Santiago heat. It does cheap food, too, including lobster and other seafood. Pay in pesos or CUC.

Bar la Fontana di Trevi BAR
(Map p406; General Lacret; ⊙noon-2am) For a peso beer or rum, the bar of this central place is alright: the restaurant next door looks inviting but isn't.

☆ Entertainment

'Spoilt for choice' would be an understatement in Santiago. For what's happening, look for the bi-weekly *Cartelera Cultural*. The reception desk at Hotel Casa Granda usually has copies. Every Saturday night Calle José A Saco becomes a happening place called **Noche Santiagüera**, where street food, music and crowds make an all-night outdoor party. Calle Heredia, meanwhile, is Santiago's Bourbon Street, a musical cacophony of stabbing trumpets, multilayered bongos and lilting guitars. For the more secretive corners, prowl the streets with your ears open and let the sounds lure you in.

★ **Casa de las Tradiciones** LIVE MUSIC
(Map p402; General J Rabí No 154; admission CUC$1; ⊘ from 8:30pm) The most discovered 'undiscovered' spot in Santiago nevertheless still retains its smoke-filled, foot-stomping, front-room feel. Hidden in the gentile Tivolí district, this is the venue where some of Santiago de Cuba's most exciting ensembles, singers and soloists take turns improvising. Friday nights are reserved for straight-up, classic *trova*, à la Ñico Saquito and the like. There's a gritty bar, and some colourful art work.

Casa de la Trova LIVE MUSIC
(Map p406; Heredia No 208) Santiago's shrine to the power of traditional music is still going strong four decades on, continuing to attract big names such as Buena Vista Social Club singer Eliades Ochoa. Warming up on the ground floor in the late afternoon, the action slowly gravitates upstairs where, come 10pm, everything gets a shade more *caliente* (hot).

Tropicana Santiago CABARET
(entry from CUC$35; ⊘ from 10pm Wed-Sun) Anything Havana can do, Santiago can do better – or at least cheaper. Styled on the Tropicana original, this 'feathers and baubles' Las Vegas–style floor show is heavily hyped by all the city's tour agencies who offer it for CUC$35 plus transport (Havana's show is twice the price, but in no way twice as good).

It's located out of town, 3km north of the Hotel las Américas, so a taxi or rental car is the only independent transport option, making the tour-agency deals a good bet. The Saturday night show is superior.

Casa del Estudiante LIVE MUSIC
(Map p406; ☎ 62-78-04; Heredia No 204; admission CUC$1; ⊘ from 9pm Wed, Fri & Sat, 1pm Sun) Grab a seat (or stand in the street) and settle down for whatever this spontaneous place can throw at you: orchestral *danzón*, folkloric rumba, lovelorn *trovadores* (traditional singers) or rhythmic *regguetón* (Cuban hip-hop).

FOLKLÓRICO DANCE GROUPS

Santiago de Cuba is home to more than a dozen *folklórico* (Afro-Cuban dance) groups, which exist to teach and perform traditional Afro-Cuban *bailes* (dances) and pass on their traditions to future generations. Most of the groups date from the early 1960s and all enjoy strong patronage from the Cuban government.

A good place to find out about upcoming *folklórico* events is at the **Departamento de Focos Culturales de la Dirección Municipal de Cuba** (Map p402; ☎ 65-69-82; Los Maceos No 501, btwn General Bandera & Pío Rosado), which acts as a kind of HQ for the various *cabildos* (Afro-Cuban brotherhoods) and dance groups, most of which are bivouacked nearby. Another good nexus is the Casa del Caribe (p412) in Vista Alegre.

Also worth seeking out are the **Conjunto Folklórico de Oriente** (Map p406; Hartmann No 407) and the **Foco Cultural Tumba Francesa** (Map p402; Pio Rosado No 268), a colorful group of French-Haitian drumming masters who can be seen in their rehearsal rooms on Tuesdays and Thursdays at 9pm.

Ballet Folklórico Cutumba (Map p402; Teatro Galaxia, cnr Avs 24 de Febrero & Valeriano Hierrezuelo; admission CUC$2) This internationally known Afro-Cuban-Franco-Haitian *folklórico* dance group was founded in 1960 and currently appears at Teatro Galaxia (while its home base, the Teatro Oriente, is being renovated). You can see the group practice between 9am and 1pm Tuesday to Friday or attend an electrifying *café teatro* at 10pm every Saturday.

The 55-strong troupe performs such dances as the *tumba francesa, columbia, gagá, guaguancó, tajona* and *conga oriental*. It's one of the finest programs of its kind in Cuba and has toured the world from New York to New Zealand.

Foco Cultural el Tivolí (Map p402; Desiderio Mesnier No 208; ⊘ 8pm Mon-Fri) Carnaval practice for the Sarabanda Mayombe happens weekly at this Tivolí *foco* (a show that takes place in Tivolí). Saturdays at 5pm it performs a *mágica religiosa* program of *orishas* (Afro-Cuban religious deities), *bembé* (Afro-Cuban drumming ritual) and *palo monte* (Bantu-derived Afro-Cuban religion) at nearby Casa de las Tradiciones.

Patio ARTex LIVE MUSIC
(Map p406; Heredia No 304; ☺11am-11pm) **FREE**
Art lines the walls of this shop-and-club combo that hosts live music both day and night in a quaint inner courtyard; a good bet if the Casa de la Trova is full, or too frenetic.

Patio los Dos Abuelos LIVE MUSIC
(Map p406; Francisco Pérez Carbo No 5; admission CUC$2; ☺9:30pm-2am Mon-Sat) The old-timers' label (*abuelos* means grandparents) carries a certain amount of truth. This relaxed live-music house is a bastion for traditional *son* sung the old-fashioned way. The musicians are seasoned pros and most of the patrons are perfect ladies and gentlemen.

Iris Jazz Club JAZZ
(Map p406; General Serafin Sanchez, btwn José A Saco & Bayamo; CUC$3; ☺8pm-midnight Mon-Sat) Great new venue. Sit on the upper balcony surrounded by pictures of the puffing jazz greats and watch some surprisingly youthful and incredibly intuitive exponents of Santiago's small but significant jazz scene.

Teatro José María Heredia THEATER
(Map p402; ☑64-31-90; cnr Avs de las Américas & de los Desfiles; ☺box office 9am-noon & 1-4:30pm) Santiago's huge, modern theater and convention center went up during the city refurbishment in the early 1990s. Rock and folk concerts often take place in the 2459-seat Sala Principal, while the 120-seat Café Cantante Niagara hosts more esoteric events. Ask about performances by the Compañía Teatro Danza del Caribe.

Casa de la Cultura Miguel Matamoros LIVE MUSIC
(Map p406; General Lacret, btwn Aguilera & Heredia; admission CUC$1) This cultural stalwart in historic digs on Parque Céspedes hosts many crowded musical events, including rumba and *son;* check the *cartelera* (calendar) posted at the door. It also presents some good art expos.

Santiago Café CABARET
(Map p402; cnr Av de las Américas & Calle M; admission CUC$5; ☺10pm-2am) This is the Hotel Meliá Santiago de Cuba's slightly less spectacular version of the Tropicana. Cabarets take place on Saturdays with a disco afterwards. It's on the hotel's 1st floor. Head up to the 15th floor for the exciting Bello Bar.

Teatro Martí THEATER
(Map p402; Félix Peña No 313; ♿) Children's shows are staged at 5pm on Saturday and Sunday at this theater near General Portuondo, opposite the Iglesia de Santo Tomás.

Sala de Conciertos Dolores LIVE MUSIC
(Map p406; cnr Aguilera & Mayía Rodríguez; ☺from 8:30pm) You can catch the Sinfónica del Oriente at this former church on Plaza de Dolores, plus the impressive children's choir (at 5pm). The *cartelera* is posted outside.

Orfeón Santiago LIVE MUSIC
(Map p406; Heredia No 68) This classical choir sometimes allows visitors to attend its practice sessions from 9am to 11:30am Monday to Friday.

Subway Club LIVE MUSIC
(Map p406; cnr Aguilera & Mayía Rodriguez; CUC$5; ☺8pm-1am or 2am) Stylish new venue with interesting solo acts singing their hearts out to great piano music come nightfall. Good fun.

Cine Rialto CINEMA
(Map p406; Félix Peña No 654) This cinema, next to the cathedral, is one of Santiago de Cuba's favorites, showing large-screen films and video.

Cine Cuba CINEMA
(Map p406; cnr José A Saco & General Lacret) Recipient of a recent refurbishment, this place is the best in town with an inviting lobby and a decent array of movies.

Uneac CULTURAL CENTER
(Unión Nacional de Escritores y Artistas de Cuba, Union of Cuban Writers & Artists; Map p406; Heredia No 266) First stop for art fiends seeking intellectual solace in talks, workshops, encounters and performances – in a gorgeous colonial courtyard.

Sport

Estadio de Béisbol Guillermón Moncada STADIUM
(Map p402; Av de las Américas) This stadium is on the northeastern side of town. During the baseball season, from October to April, there are games at 7:30pm Tuesday, Wednesday, Thursday and Saturday, and 1:30pm Sunday (1 peso). The Avispas (Wasps) are the main rivals of Havana's Industriales with National Series victories in 2005, 2007, 2008 and 2010. Cubanacán runs trips to Avispa games with a visit to the dressing room afterwards to meet the players.

Gimnasio Cultura Física GYM
(Map p406; Pio Rosado No 455, btwn Saco & Hechavarría; ☺6am-6:45pm Mon-Fri, 8am-4pm Sat, 8am-

noon Sun) For a wicked workout drop into this gym with its well-pummeled punching bags, rusty old weights and cold showers.

Wamby Bolera
BOWLING
(Map p402; cnr Victoriano Garzón & Calle 7) Anyone for indoor bowling? Stick CUC$0.25 in one of the two machines and roll the balls. There's an on-site cafe.

Shopping

Innovative creativity is inscribed into the louvers in colonial Santiago, and a brief sortie around the *casco histórico* will reveal exciting snippets of eye-catching art. Decent craft stalls are set up in Calle Heredia most days.

ARTex
SOUVENIRS
From mouse pads to Che trinkets, the **General Lacret** (Map p406; General Lacret, btwn Aguilera & Heredia) branch below Hotel Casa Granda collects any type of Cuban souvenir imaginable. The **Heredia** (Map p406; Heredia No 208, Patio ARTex; ⊙11am-7pm Tue-Sun) branch at the Casa de la Trova focuses more on music, with a respectable selection of CDs and cassettes.

Discoteca Egrem
MUSIC
(Map p406; José A Saco No 309; ⊙9am-6pm Mon-Sat, to 2pm Sun) The definitive Cuban specialist music store; this retail outlet of Egrem Studios has a good selection of local musicians.

La Maison
CLOTHING
(Map p402; Av Manduley No 52; ⊙10am-6pm Mon-Sat) The Santiago version of the famous Havana fashion house, located in an appropriately grand Vista Alegre *maison* (house).

Galería de Arte de Oriente
ARTS & CRAFTS
(Map p406; General Lacret No 656) Probably the best gallery in Santiago de Cuba, the art here is consistently good.

Centro de Negocios Alameda
SHOPPING CENTER
(Map p402; cnr Av Jesus Menéndez & José A Saco; ⊙8:30am-4:30pm) The port's latest regeneration project is opening this shopping center in a colonial building: internet, a pharmacy, the immigration office and a Cubanacán desk, besides shops.

Librería Internacional
BOOKS
(Map p406; ☑68-71-47; Heredia, btwn General Lacret & Félix Peña) On the southern side of Parque Céspedes. Decent selection of political titles in English; sells postcards and stamps.

Librería la Escalera
BOOKS
(Map p406; Heredia No 265; ⊙10am-11pm) A veritable museum of old and rare books stacked ceiling high. Sombrero-clad *trovadores* often sit on the stairway and strum.

Information

DANGERS & ANNOYANCES
Santiago is well known, even among Cubans, for its overzealous *jineteros* (hustlers), all working their particular angle – be it cigars, paladares, *chicas* (girls) or unofficial 'tours'. Sometimes it can seem impossible to shake off the money-with-legs feeling, but a firm 'no' coupled with a little light humor ought to keep the worst of the touts at bay.

Santiago's traffic is second only to Havana's in its environmental fallout. Making things worse for pedestrians is the plethora of noisy motorcyclists weaving for position along the city's sinuous 1950s streets. Narrow or nonexistent sidewalks throw further obstacles into an already hazardous brew.

EMERGENCY
Asistur (☑68-61-28; www.asistur.cu; Heredia No 201) Situated under the Casa Granda Hotel, this office specializes in offering assistance to foreigners, mainly in the insurance and financial fields.

Police (☑116; cnr Mariano Corona & Sánchez Hechavarría)

INTERNET ACCESS & TELEPHONE
Etecsa Multiservicios (cnr Heredia & Félix Peña; internet access per hr CUC$6; ⊙8:30am-7:30pm) Three internet terminals in a small office on Plaza Céspedes.

Etecsa Telepunto (cnr Hartmann & Tamayo Fleites; internet access per hr CUC$6; ⊙8:30am-7:30pm)

MEDIA
Radio Mambí CMKW At 1240AM and 93.7FM.
Radio Revolución CMKC Broadcasting over 840AM and 101.4FM.
Radio Siboney CMDV Available at 1180AM and 95.1FM.
Sierra Maestra Local paper published Saturday.

MEDICAL SERVICES
Clínica Internacional Cubanacán Servimed (☑64-25-89; cnr Av Raúl Pujol & Calle 10, Vista Alegre; ⊙24hr) Capable staff speak some English. A dentist is also present.

Farmacia Clínica Internacional (☑64-25-89; cnr Av Raúl Pujol & Calle 10; ⊙24hr) Best pharmacy in town, selling products in convertibles.

Farmacia Internacional (☑68-70-70; Meliá Santiago de Cuba, cnr Av de las Américas &

Calle M; ☺8am-6pm) In the lobby of the Meliá Santiago de Cuba, it sells products in convertibles.

MONEY

Banco de Crédito y Comercio (Felix Peña No 614) Housed in the jarring modern building in Plaza Céspedes.

Banco Financiero Internacional (cnr Av de las Américas & Calle I)

Bandec (cnr Felix Peña & Aguilera) Another branch at José A Saco (cnr José A Saco & Mariano Corona).

Cadeca Branches at Hotel las Américas (cnr Avs de las Américas & General Cebreco); Aguilera (Aguilera No 508) and Meliá Santiago de Cuba (cnr Av de las Américas & Calle M)

POST

DHL (Aguilera No 310)

Post Office You can find a post office on Aguilera (Aguilera No 519) and Calle 9 (Calle 9, Ampliación de Terrazas), near Av General Cebreco; telephones are here, too.

TOURIST INFORMATION

Cubanacán (Heredia No 201) This very helpful desk is in the Hotel Casa Granda.

Cubatur (Av Victoriano Garzón No 364 , cnr Calle 4) Another branch at Heredia (Heredia No 701; ☺8am-8pm).

Ecotur (☑68-72-79; General Lacret No 701 cnr Heredia, cnr Hartmann) In the same building as Infotur.

Infotur (☑66-94-01; General Lacret No 701 cnr Heredia) Helpful location; less so the staff. There's also a branch in Antonio Maceo International Airport.

Oficina Reservaciones de Campismo (Cornelio Robert No 163; ☺8:30am-noon & 1-4:30pm Mon-Fri, 8am-1pm Sat) For information on the Caletón Blanco and La Mula campismos (camping installations).

ℹ Getting There & Away

AIR

Antonio Maceo International Airport (airport code SCU) is 7km south of Santiago de Cuba,

off the Carretera del Morro. International flights arrive from Paris-Orly, Madrid, Toronto and Montreal on **Cubana** (cnr José A Saco & General Lacret). Toronto and Montreal are also served by **Sunwing** (www.sunwing.ca) and **Canjet** (www.canjet.com) and **AeroCaribbean** (General Lacret, btwn Bartolomé Masó & Heredia) flies weekly between here and Port Au Prince, Haiti and twice weekly to Santo Domingo. **American Eagle** (www.aa.com) runs regular charters to and from Miami serving the Cuban-American community.

Internally, Cubana flies nonstop from Havana to Santiago de Cuba two or three times a day (about CUC$110 one way, 1½ hours). There are also services to Holguín.

BUS

The **National Bus Station** (cnr Av de los Libertadores & Calle 9), opposite the Heredia monument, is 3km northeast of Parque Céspedes. **Víazul** (www.viazul.cu) buses leave from the same station.

The Havana bus stops at Bayamo (CUC$7, two hours), Holguín (CUC$11, 3½ to 4 hours), Las Tunas (CUC$11, five hours), Camagüey (CUC$18, 7½ hours), Ciego de Ávila (CUC$24, 9½ hours), Sancti Spíritus (CUC$28, 10 to 10½ hours) and Santa Clara (CUC$33, 11 to 12 hours). The Trinidad bus can drop you at Bayamo, Las Tunas, Camagüey, Ciego de Ávila and Sancti Spíritus. The Baracoa bus stops in Guantánamo.

TRAIN

The modern French-style **train station** (cnr Av Jesús Menéndez & Martí) is situated near the rum factory northwest of the center. The *Tren Francés* leaves at 8:17pm every third day for Havana (CUC$50, 16 hours), stopping at Camagüey (CUC$11) and Santa Clara (CUC$20) en route.

Another slower *coche motor* (cross-island) train (CUC$30) also plies the route to Havana every third day when a *Tren Francés* isn't running, additionally stopping at Las Tunas, Ciego de Ávila, Guayos and Matanzas.

Cuban train schedules are fickle, so you should always verify beforehand what train leaves when, and get your ticket as soon as possible thereafter.

VÍAZUL BUS DEPARTURES FROM SANTIAGO DE CUBA

DESTINATION	COST (CUC$)	DURATION (HR)	DEPARTURE
Baracoa	15	4¾	7:45am
Havana	51	13-14½	8am, 3:15pm, 6:45pm, 10pm
Trinidad	33	12	7:30pm
Varadero	49	15	8pm

TRUCK

Intermittent passenger trucks leave **Serrano Intermunicipal Bus Station** (cnr Av Jesús Menéndez & Sánchez Hechavarría) near the train station to Guantánamo and Bayamo throughout the day. Prices are a few pesos and early morning is the best time to board. For these destinations, don't fuss with the ticket window; just find the truck parked out front going your way. Trucks for Caletón Blanco and Chivirico also leave from here.

The **Intermunicipal Bus Station** (Terminal Cuatro, cnr Av de los Libertadores & Calle 4), 2km northeast of Parque Céspedes, has two buses a day to El Cobre. Two daily buses also leave for Baconao from here.

❶ Getting Around

TO/FROM THE AIRPORT

A taxi to or from the airport should cost CUC$10, but drivers will often try to charge you more. Haggle hard before you get in. You can also get to the airport on bus 212, which leaves from Av de los Libertadores opposite the Hospital de Maternidad. Bus 213 also goes to the airport from the same stop, but visits Punta Gorda first. Both buses stop just beyond the west end of the airport parking lot to the left of the entrances.

TO/FROM THE TRAIN/BUS STATIONS

To get into town from the train station, catch a southbound horse cart (1 peso) to the clock tower at the north end of Parque Alameda, from which Aguilera (to the left) climbs straight up to Parque Céspedes. Horse carts between the National Bus Station (they'll shout 'Alameda') and train station (1 peso) run along Av Juan Gualberto Gómez and Av Jesús Menéndez. A taxi to the Víazul bus station costs CUC$4.

BUS & TRUCK

Useful city buses include bus 212 to the airport and Ciudamar, bus 213 to Punta Gorda (both of these buses start from Av de los Libertadores, opposite Hospital de Maternidad, and head south on Felix Peña in the *casco histórico*), and bus 214 or 407 to Siboney (from near Av de los Libertadores No 425). Bus 5 to El Caney stops on the northwestern corner of Plaza de Marte and at General Cebreco and Calle 3 in Vista Alegre. These buses (20 centavos) run every hour or so; more frequent trucks (1 peso) serve the same routes.

Trucks to El Cobre and points north leave from Av de las Américas near Calle M. On trucks and buses you should be aware of pickpockets and wear your backpack in front.

CAR & MOPED

Santiago de Cuba suffers from a chronic shortage of rental cars (especially in peak season) and you might find there are none available; however, the locals have an indefatigable Cuban ability to *conseguir* (manage or get) and *resolver* (resolve or work out).

The airport offices usually have better availability than those in town. If you're completely stuck, you can usually rent one at the Hotel Guantánamo, two hours to the east.

Cubacar (Hotel las Américas; cnr Avs de las Américas & General Cebreco; ⊙ 8am-10pm) rents out mopeds for CUC$24 per day. There is also an office at Antonio Maceo International Airport.

Guarded parking is available in Parque Céspedes, directly below the Hotel Casa Granda. Official attendants, complete with small badges, charge CUC$1 a day and CUC$1 a night.

The **Servi-Cupet gas station** (cnr Avs de los Libertadores & de Céspedes) is open 24 hours. There's an Oro Negro gas station on the Carretera del Morro (cnr Av 24 de Febrero & Carretera del Morro) and another Oro Negro on the Carretera Central (Carretera Central) at the northern entrance to Santiago de Cuba.

TAXI

There's a Turistaxi stand in front of Meliá Santiago de Cuba. Taxis also wait on Parque Céspedes near the cathedral and hiss at you expectantly as you pass. Always insist the driver uses the *taxímetro* (meter) or hammer out a price beforehand. To the airport, it will be between CUC$5 and CUC$7 depending on the state of the car.

Bici-taxis charge about 5 pesos per person per ride.

Siboney

Playa Siboney is Santiago's Playas del Este, an exuberant seaside town 19km east that's more rustic village than deluxe resort. Guarded by precipitous cliffs and dotted with a mixture of craning palms and weather-beaten clapboard houses, the setting here is laid-back and charming, with a beach scene that mixes fun-seeking Cuban families and young, nubile *santiagüeras* with their older, balder foreign partners.

In terms of quality, Siboney's small crescent of grayish sand is none too inspiring. But Siboney compensates for this in price (cheap), location (it's on the doorstep of Parque Baconao) and all-embracing Cuban atmosphere. There are a few legal casas particulares here and a decent sit-down restaurant on a hill overlooking the beach. For those craving a break from hustler-heavy, sweltering Santiago, it makes a good little hideaway.

◉ Sights

Granjita Siboney MUSEUM
(admission CUC$1; ⊙ 9am-5pm) Had the Revolution been unsuccessful, this red-and-white farmhouse, 2km inland from Playa Siboney on the road to Santiago de Cuba, would be the forgotten site of a rather futile putsch. As it is, it's another shrine to the glorious episode that is Moncada. It was from this place, at 5:15am on July 26, 1953, that 26 cars under the command of Fidel Castro left to attack the military barracks in Santiago de Cuba.

The house retains many original details, including the dainty room used by two *compañeras* (female revolutionaries) who saw action, Haydee Santamaría and Melba Hernández. There are also photos, weapons and personal effects related to Moncada. Note the well beside the building, where weapons were hidden before the attack.

Overlooking the stony shoreline nearby is an American war memorial dated 1907, recalling the US landing here on June 24, 1898.

🛏 Sleeping & Eating

Post-hurricane, the number of casas particulares in this small seaside settlement have decreased. Cheap peso food stalls hog the beachfront.

Ovidio González Salgado CASA PARTICULAR $
(☎ 39-93-40; Av Serrano; r CUC$20-25) A reader-recommended place with two rooms above the local pharmacy, serving great meals.

Anselmo Rondoú Benítez CASA PARTICULAR $
(☎ 39-92-36; Calle Ovelisco No 13; r CUC$25) Smart, recently done-up place with one room right by the western end of the beach.

Sitio del Compay CARIBBEAN $
(Av Serrano s/n; mains CUC$5-10; ⊙ noon-midnight) Take note, dear diner, you're in the former house of musical sage turned international icon Francisco Repilado, the man responsible for writing the immortal song 'Chan Chan,' which you've probably already heard a dozen times since your plane landed.

Born in a small shack by this site in 1907, Compay Segundo, as he was more commonly known, shot to superstardom aged 90 as the guitarist/winking joker in Ry Cooder's Buena Vista Social Club. Sitio del Compay (formerly Restaurante La Rueda) is Siboney's only real dining option and would have kept old Francisco happy with its no-frills *comida criolla*, friendly service and good beach views.

ℹ Getting There & Away

Bus 214 runs from Santiago de Cuba to Siboney from near Av de los Libertadores 425, opposite Empresa Universal, with a second stop at Av de Céspedes 110. It leaves about once hourly between 4am and 8:45am (hit-and-miss thereafter), and bus 407 carries on to Juraguá three times a day. Passenger trucks also shuttle between Santiago de Cuba and Siboney.

A taxi to Playa Siboney will cost CUC$20 to CUC$25, depending on whether it's state or private.

La Gran Piedra

Crowned by a 63,000-ton boulder that perches like a grounded asteroid high above the Caribbean, the Cordillera de la Gran Piedra forms part of Cuba's greenest and most biodiverse mountain range. Not only do the mountains have a refreshingly cool microclimate, they also exhibit a unique historical heritage based on the legacy of some 60 or more coffee plantations set up by French farmers in the latter 18th century. On the run from a bloody slave rebellion in Haiti in 1791, enterprising Gallic immigrants overcame arduous living conditions and terrain to turn Cuba into the world's number-one coffee producer in the early 19th century. Their craft and ingenuity have been preserved in a Unesco World Heritage Site that is centered on the Cafetal la Isabelica. The area is also included in the Baconao Unesco Biosphere Reserve, instituted in 1987.

◉ Sights

The steep 12km road up the mountain range becomes increasingly beautiful as the foliage closes in and the valley opens up below. Mango trees are ubiquitous here.

La Gran Piedra MOUNTAIN
(admission CUC$1) You don't need to be Tenzing Norgay to climb the 459 stone steps to the summit of La Gran Piedra at 1234m. The huge rock on top measures 51m in length and 25m in height and weighs...a lot. On a clear day there are excellent views out across the Caribbean and on a dark night you are supposedly able to see the lights of Jamaica.

Cafetal la Isabelica MUSEUM
(admission CUC$2; ⊙ 8am-4pm) The hub of the Unesco World Heritage Site bestowed in 2000 on an area called the First Coffee Plantations in the Southeast of Cuba. It's a 2km hike beyond La Gran Piedra on a rough road

to the impressive two-story stone mansion, with its three large coffee-drying platforms. The platforms were built in the early 19th century by French émigrés from Haiti, and were once one of more than 60 in the area.

There's a workshop and artifacts, and you can stroll around the pine-covered plantation grounds at will. It's worth using a guide (for a tip) to show you round as there are no explanatory notices.

🏃 Activities

You can visit the ruins of many of the 100-plus coffee plantations on foot. Trails lead out from Cafetal la Isabelica, but there are no signs. Inquire at la Isabelica about the possibility of hiring a local farmer to show you around for a prearranged fee.

🛏 Sleeping & Eating

Villa la Gran Piedra   HOTEL **$**
(📞 65-12-05; s/d CUC$15/24; 🅿 ❄) Villa la Gran Piedra, Cuba's highest hotel at 1225m, had its cabins destroyed in the 2012 hurricane so now it's more a restaurant-with-rooms, right by the entrance to the La Gran Piedra view-point. The restaurant is good enough, the rooms are plain, and various short hiking trips are available.

ℹ Getting There & Away

A steep, winding paved road climbs 1.2 vertical kilometers from the junction with the coast road near Siboney (on the 214 bus route) through *muchos* potholes. A taxi from Santiago de Cuba costs approximately CUC$50 to CUC$65 (bargain hard) for the round trip. Sturdy Cubans and the odd ambitious foreigner hike up 12km from the bus stop at the road junction in Las Guásimas.

Parque Baconao

Parque Baconao, covering 800 sq km between Santiago de Cuba and the Río Baconao, is as wondrous as it is weird. A Unesco Biosphere Reserve that is also home to an outdoor car museum and a rather odd collection of 240 life-sized dinosaur sculptures, it looks like an historically displaced Jurassic Park, yet in reality acts as an important haven for a whole ecosystem of flora and fauna.

CAFETALES

Cubans have always been enthusiastic coffee drinkers. But, while the shade-loving national coffee crop thrives in the cool tree-covered glades of the Sierra del Escambray and Sierra Maestra, it's not indigenous to the island.

Coffee was first introduced to Cuba in 1748 from the neighboring colony of Santo Domingo, yet it wasn't until the arrival of French planters from Haiti in the early 1800s that the crop was grown commercially.

On the run from Toussaint Louverture's slave revolution, the displaced French found solace in the mountains of Pinar del Río and the Sierra Maestra, where they switched from sugarcane production to the more profitable and durable coffee plant.

Constructed in 1801 in what is now the Sierra del Rosario Reserve in Artemisa province, Cafetal Buenavista was the first major coffee plantation in the New World. Not long afterward, planters living in the heavily forested hills around La Gran Piedra began constructing a network of more than 60 *cafetales* (coffee farms) using pioneering agricultural techniques to overcome the difficult terrain. Their stoic efforts paid off and, by the second decade of the 19th century, Cuba's nascent coffee industry was thriving.

Buoyed by high world coffee prices and aided by sophisticated new growing techniques, the coffee boom lasted from 1800 to about 1820, when the crop consumed more land than sugarcane. At its peak there were more than 2000 *cafetales* in Cuba, concentrated primarily in the Sierra del Rosario region and the Sierra Maestra to the east of Santiago de Cuba.

Production began to slump in the 1840s with competition from vigorous new economies (most notably Brazil) and a string of devastating hurricanes. The industry took another hit during the War of Independence, though the crop survived and is still harvested today on a smaller scale using mainly traditional methods.

The legacy of Cuba's pioneering coffee industry is best seen in the Archaeological Landscape of the First Coffee Plantations in the Southeast of Cuba, a Unesco World Heritage Site dedicated in 2000 in the foothills of the Sierra Maestra close to La Gran Piedra.

La Gran Piedra & Parque Baconao

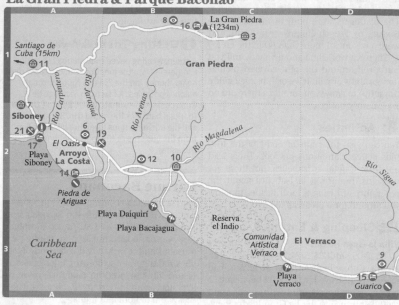

La Gran Piedra & Parque Baconao

Not surprisingly, the Unesco tag wasn't earned for a museum full of old cars (or for a field full of concrete dinosaurs, for that matter). According to biological experts, Baconao boasts more than 1800 endemic species of flora and numerous types of endangered bats and spiders. Encased in a shallow chasm with the imposing Sierra Maestra on one side and the placid Caribbean on the other, the biodiversity of the area (which includes everything from craning royal palms to prickly cliffside cacti) is nothing short of remarkable.

The beaches are smaller here than those on the northern coast but there's fishing, and some 70 scuba-diving sites nearby, including the *Guarico*, a small steel wreck just south of Playa Sigua. Baconao is also famous for its crabs. From mid-March to early May

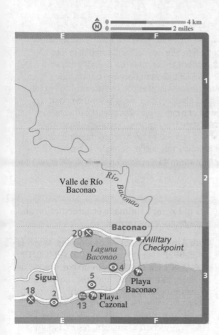

from a nearby prison. The **Museo de Historia Natural** (admission CUC$1; ⏰8am-4pm Tue-Sun) is also here, but something of an anticlimax after the surrealism of the prehistoric beasts.

Museo Nacional de Transporte Terrestre
MUSEUM

(admission CUC$1; ⏰8am-5pm) 'What's the point?', you might well ask when you stumble upon this alfresco museum 2km east of Valle de la Prehistoria. It's all very impressive that they've nabbed Benny Moré's 1958 Cadillac, the Chevrolet Raúl Castro got lost in on the way to the Moncada Barracks and Cuban singer Rosita Fornés' lovely Ford T-Bird.

But in Cuba, where '50s car relics are as common as cheap cigars, it's the equivalent of a Toyota Yaris museum in Kyoto.

Playa Daiquirí
BEACH

The main US landings during the Spanish-Cuban-American War took place on June 24, 1898 at this beach, 2km down a side road from the Museo Nacional de Transporte Terrestre. They might have named a cocktail after it, but the area is now a holiday camp for military personnel and entry is prohibited.

Comunidad Artística Verraco
GALLERY

(⏰9am-6pm) Ten kilometers past the Playa Daiquirí turn-off lies another village of painters, ceramicists and sculptors who maintain open studios (turn-off unsigned). Here you can visit the artists and buy original works of art. All it lacks is a good organic cafe.

Exposición Mesoamericana
PARK

(admission CUC$1) Every Cuban resort area seems to have an attraction replicating indigenous scenes. Here it's the Exposición Mesoamericana, just east of Club Amigo Carisol – Los Corales. Indigenous cave art from Central and South America is arranged in caves along the coastal cliffs.

Laguna Baconao
LAKE

At the Laguna Baconao, 2km northeast of Los Corales, you'll find a restaurant, rowboats for hire (CUC$2 per person; CUC$10 minimum) and several short lakeside hikes, plus a forlorn-looking zoo with crocodiles and the like. The lake supposedly contains resident wild dolphins. The **Sendero al Cimarron** (admission CUC$2) guided trail skirts 2km of the western shoreline, revealing some of the wildlife of this 80% salt, 20% freshwater lake.

tens of thousands of large land crabs congregate along the coast beyond Playa Verraco.

⊙ Sights

In addition to the following sights, there are several hurricane-damaged beaches, of which the best is probably **Playa Cazonal**, by Club Amigo Carisol-Los Corales.

Fiesta Guajira
RANCH

(admission CUC$5; ⏰9am & 2pm Wed & Sun) Situated in El Oasis artists' community, opposite the turn-off to the old Club Bucanero, this Ecotur-run *finca* (farm) formerly ran rodeos with *vaqueros* (Cuban cowboys) but post-hurricane is focused round a rustic restaurant, and a cockpit.

Valle de la Prehistoria
AMUSEMENT PARK

(admission CUC$1; ⏰8am-6pm) One of the oddest in a plethora of odd attractions is this Cuban Jurassic Park, cast in stone, that serendipitously materializes beside the meandering coastal road. Here giant brontosauruses mix with concrete cavemen and women, seemingly oblivious to the fact that 57 million years separated the two species' colonization of planet Earth.

You can take in the full 11 hectares of this surreal kitsch park with its 200 lifesized concrete dinosaurs built by inmates

HURRICANE SANDY

Eastern Cuba is no stranger to hurricanes, but when Hurricane Sandy struck in late October 2012 it caused particularly severe detriment to Siboney, La Gran Piedra and Parque Baconao (not to mention an estimated US$2 billion of damage nationwide). Once-lovely beaches like those at Siboney suffered devastatation. The dive center-hotel of Club Bucanero was levelled and the damage is clear further away from the coast, too, with the hillsides below La Gran Piedra depleted of many trees. Local authorities are working hard to make repairs, with plans to renovate the Aquario Baconao already nigh-on complete, but bear in mind this area might not look quite like the brochure pictures for a while. The curious (or the nihilists) might feel compelled to consider tripping out to the Club Bucanero site just to witness what the power of Caribbean wind and water is capable of.

A road from the hamlet of Baconao follows the lake's north shore to the decent Restaurante Casa de Rolando.

From **Playa Baconao** at the eastern corner of the lake, the paved road continues 3.5km up beautiful **Valle de Río Baconao** before turning into a dirt track. Soldiers at a checkpoint at the village turn back people trying to use the direct coastal road to Guantánamo because it passes alongside the US Naval Base. To continue east, you must backtrack 50km to Santiago de Cuba and take the inland road.

🏃 Activities

Horseback riding is available at Finca la Porvenir and Laguna Baconao.

Centro Internacional de Buceo Carisol los Corales DIVING
(www.nauticamarlin.com; Club Amgio Carisol – Los Corales) Situated in the hotel of the same name 45km east of Santiago, this center nevertheless picks up divers at the other hotels around about daily. Scuba diving costs CUC$30/59 per one/two dives with gear, and two boats can take up to 20 people to any of the 24 local dive sites. The open-water certification course is CUC$365. There are shipwrecks close to shore here and you can feed black groupers by hand.

The water off this bit of coast is some of Cuba's warmest (25°C to 28°C); best visibility is between February and June.

🛌 Sleeping

Rosa & Enrique CASA PARTICULAR $
(☑ 58-22-75-29; Carretera Baconao Km 17.5, Comunidad Artística Verracao; r CUC$25) If you can bag this room (it's often full with visiting artisans) it's one of the best about. You'll reside in the house of two ceramicists: expect lots of loving handmade ornamentation and a gorgeous leafy terrace.

Club Amigo Carisol – Los Corales RESORT $$
(☑ 35-61-21; all-incl s/d/tr CUC$91/130/178; P ❄ @ 🏊) There's the swim-up bar, umbrellas in the piña coladas, and the government-sponsored band knocking out *Guantanamera* as you tuck into your lukewarm buffet dinner. You must be back in all-inclusive land. This two-piece Cubanacán resort is situated 44km east of Santiago on the coast's best section of beach (although it's been damaged by successive hurricanes).

Bonuses are a tennis court, a disco, multiple day trips on offer and bright, spacious clean rooms. Nonguests can purchase a day pass for CUC$15 including lunch.

Hotel Costa Morena HOTEL $$
(☑ 35-61-35; s/d CUC$44/70; P ❄ 🏊) This place is at Sigua, 44km southeast of Santiago de Cuba. It has attractive architecture and a large terrace right on the cliffs, but no direct beach access. There is nevertheless good sea swimming, with protection afforded by a reef. A shuttle will bus you to the beach at Club Amigo Carisol – Los Corales.

🍴 Eating

If you're stuck you can try the restaurant at Club Amigo Carisol – Los Corales or the restaurant at **Aquario Baconao** (Carretera Bacanao, btwn Costa Morena & Club Amigo Carisol – Los Corales; admission CUC$7; ⊙ 9am-5pm).

Finca el Porvenir CARIBBEAN $$
(Carretera de Baconao Km 18; ⊙ 9am-5pm) Situated on the left of the main Carretera about 4km east of El Oasis, this Palmares-run *finca* knocks out no-frills *comida criolla* with a great swimming pool and horseback riding available on site. The only obstacle

to chillaxing is the blaring poolside music: sound familiar?

Restaurante Casa de Rolando SEAFOOD $$
(Carretera Baconao Km 53; ⊗10:30am-5pm) This scenic joint on the north shore of Laguna Baconao serves mostly seafood.

Fiesta Guajira CARIBBEAN $$
(Carretera Baconao, El Oasis; ⊗9am-5pm) Once a rodeo, now mainly just a restaurant.

ⓘ Getting There & Away

Most people access Baconao's spread-out sights by private car, taxi or as part of an organized trip from Santiago de Cuba. Cubataxi usually charges approximately CUC$0.50 per kilometer out this way or you can hire a moped from **Cubacar** (Club Bucanero) for CUC$24 per day.

Bus 415 from the municipal bus terminal in Santiago's Av de la Libertad plies this route three times a day, but the bus timetables are not set in stone. Check ahead.

When planning your visit, remember the coastal road from Baconao to Guantánamo is closed to nonresidents.

ⓘ Getting Around

Cubacar in Club Amigo Carisol – Los Corales has cars and mopeds.

The **Servi-Cupet gas station** (Complejo la Punta; ⊗24hr) is 28km southeast of Santiago de Cuba.

El Cobre

The **Basílica de Nuestra Señora del Cobre**, high on a hill 20km northwest of Santiago de Cuba on the old road to Bayamo, is Cuba's most sacred pilgrimage site and shrine of the nation's patron saint: La Virgen de la Caridad (Our Lady of Charity), or Cachita, as she is also known. In Santería, the Virgin is syncretized with the beautiful *orisha* Ochún (Yoruba goddess of love and dancing and a religious icon to almost all Cuban women). Ochún is represented by the color yellow, mirrors, honey, peacock feathers and the number five. In the minds of many worshippers, devotion to the two religious figures is intertwined.

Legend dictates that the Virgin figurine was first discovered at sea, floating on a board in the Bay of Nipe in 1612 by three fishermen called the 'three Juans', who were caught up in a violent storm. With their lives in danger they pulled the figurine from the water and found the words 'I am the Virgin of Charity' inscribed upon the board. As the storm subsided and their lives were spared, they assumed a miracle had been granted, and from this a legend was born.

The copper mine at El Cobre has been active since pre-Columbian times and was once the oldest European-operated mine in the Western hemisphere (by 1530 the Spanish had a mine here). However, it was shut in 2000. Many young villagers, who previously worked in the mine, now work over tourists hereabouts, offering to 'give' you shiny but worthless chalcopyrite stones from the mine. You'll find a firm but polite '*No, gracias!*' usually does the trick. The road to the basilica is lined with sellers of elaborate flower wreaths, intended as offerings to La Virgen, and hawkers of miniature 'Cachitas'.

FAMOUS GIFTS TO CACHITA

Many have offered gifts and keepsakes to the Virgin of El Cobre – some of them famous. The most celebrated donor was Ernest Hemingway, who elected to leave the 23-karat gold medal he won for the Nobel Prize for Literature in 1954 to the 'Cuban people.' Rather than hand it over to the Batista regime, Hemingway donated the medal to the Catholic Church, who subsequently placed it in the *sanctuario*. The medal was stolen temporarily in the 1980s but, despite being retrieved a few days later, it has since been kept locked away from public view.

In 1957 Lina Ruz left a small guerilla figurine at the feet of the Virgin to pray for the safety of her two sons, Fidel and Raúl Castro, who were then fighting in the Sierra Maestra. Fate – or was it the spirit of El Cobre? – shone brightly. Both sons are now into their 80s and still going!

More recently, dissident Cuban blogger Yoani Sánchez visited the Virgin and left her Ortega and Gasset journalistic award in the sanctuary where, in her own words, 'the long arm of censor does not enter.'

⊙ Sights

**Basílica de Nuestra
Señora del Cobre**   CHURCH
(⊙6am-6pm) Stunning as it materializes above the village of El Cobre, Cuba's most revered religious site shimmers against the verdant hills behind. Apart from during Mass (8am except on Wednesday, with additional Sunday services at 10am and 4:30pm), La Virgen lives in a small chapel above the visitors center on the side of the basilica. To see her, take the stairs on either side of the entry door. For such a powerful entity, she's amazingly diminutive, some 40cm from crown to the hem of her golden robe. Check out the fine Cuban coat of arms in the center; it's an amazing work of embroidery. During Mass, Nuestra Señora de la Caridad faces the congregation from atop the altar inside the basilica.

The 'room of miracles' downstairs in the visitors center contains thousands of offerings giving thanks for favors bestowed by the virgin. Clumps of hair, a TV, a thesis, a tangle of stethoscopes, a raft inner-tube sculpture (suggesting they made it across the Florida Straits safely) and floor-to-ceiling clusters of teeny metal body parts crowd the room.

Follow the signs through the town of El Cobre to the **Monumento al Cimarrón**. A 10-minute hike up a stone staircase brings you to this anthropomorphic sculpture commemorating the 17th-century copper-mine slave revolt. It's now the location of one of Cuba's most important Santería gatherings in July, Ceremonia a las Cimarrones (part of the Fiesta del Caribe). Views are superb from up here; walk to the far side of the sculpture for a vista of copper-colored cliffs hanging over the aqua-green reservoir.

🛏 Sleeping & Eating

Hospedaría el Cobre   HOSTEL **$**
(☑34-62-46; s/d CUC$25/40) This large building behind the basilica has 15 basic rooms with one, two or three beds, all with bath. Meals are served punctually at 7am, 11am and 6pm, and there's a large, pleasant sitting room. The nuns here are very hospitable. House rules include no drinking and no unmarried couples. A convertible donation to the sanctuary is appreciated. Foreigners should reserve up to 15 days in advance.

There are several peso stalls in town where you can get *batidos* (fruit shakes), pizza and smoked-pork sandwiches.

ℹ Getting There & Away

Bus 2 goes to El Cobre twice a day from the **Intermunicipal Bus Station** (cnr Av de los Libertadores & Calle 4) in Santiago de Cuba. Trucks are more frequent on this route.

A Cubataxi from Santiago de Cuba costs around CUC$25 for a round trip.

If you're driving toward Santiago de Cuba from the west, you can join the Autopista Nacional near Palma Soriano, but unless you're in a hurry, it's better to continue on the Carretera Central via El Cobre, which winds through picturesque hilly countryside.

El Saltón

Basking in its well-earned eco-credentials, El Saltón is a tranquil mountain escape in the Tercer Frente municipality, where hills that once echoed with the sound of crackling rifle fire now reverberate to the twitter of tropical birds. Secluded and hard to reach (that's the point), it consists of a lodge, a hilltop *mirador* (viewpoint) and a 30m cascading waterfall with an adjacent natural pool ideal for swimming. Eco-guides can offer horseback riding or hiking to thermal baths or into the nearby cocoa plantations at Delicias del Saltón. Alternatively, you can just wander off on your own through myriad mountain villages with alluring names like Filé and Cruce de los Baños.

🛏 Sleeping

Hotel Horizontes el Saltón   HOTEL **$$**
(☑56-64-95; Carretera Puerto Rico a Filé; s/d with breakfast CUC$40/60; P🅿❄) 🖉 The 22-room lodge is spread over three separate blocks that nestle like hidden tree houses amid thick foliage. Spirit-lifting extras include a sauna, hot tub, massage facilities, and the hotel's defining feature, a refreshing natural waterfall and pool. The hotel has an OK restaurant-bar with a popular pool table, adjacent to a gushing mountain river. All this compensates for the rooms themselves (which are nothing special).

ℹ Getting There & Away

To get to El Saltón continue west from El Cobre to Cruce de los Baños, 4km east of Filé village. El Saltón is 3km south of Filé. With some tough negotiating in Santiago de Cuba, a sturdy taxi will take you here for CUC$40. Money well spent.

Chivirico & Around

POP 5800

Chivirico, 75km southwest of Santiago de Cuba and 106km east of Marea del Portillo, is the only town of any significance on the enticing south-coast highway, itself a rollercoaster of plummeting mountains, crinkled bays and crashing surf that makes up one of Cuba's loveliest road trips. Transport links are relatively good up until Chivirico but, heading west, they quickly deteriorate.

Chivirico itself has little to offer, although there is a challenging trek that begins at Calentura, 4km to the west. It crosses the Sierra Maestra to Los Horneros (20km), from where truck transport to Guisa is usually available. Whether skittish local authorities will let you loose in the area is another matter. Don't just turn up – ask around at somewhere like Cubatur in Santiago or the Brisas Sierra Mar hotel before heading out.

🛏 Sleeping

Campismo Caletón Blanco CABINS $
(☑ 62-57-97; Caletón Blanco Km 30, Guamá; s/d CUC$15/25; 🅿 ❄) One of two handy campismos situated along this route (the other is La Mula), this is one of Cubamar's top campismos, the closest to Santiago (30km) and the newest. Twenty-two bungalows sleep two to four people. There's also a restaurant, snack bar, bike rental and facilities for campervans. Make your reservations with Cubamar's Havana office before arrival.

Brisas Sierra Mar RESORT $$
(☑ 32-91-10; all-incl s/d CUC$70/100; 🅿 ❄ @ 🌊 ⛱) This isolated but inviting place is at Playa Sevilla, 63km west of Santiago de Cuba and a two-hour drive from the airport. The big, pyramid-shaped hotel is built into a terraced hillside and has a novel elevator to take you down to a brown-sand beach famous for its sand fleas. A remarkable coral wall great for snorkeling is just 50m offshore (dolphins sometimes frequent these waters, too).

Horseback riding is available here, there's a **Marlin Dive Center** on the premises, and there are plenty of special kids' programs (kids under 13 stay free). The hotel gets a lot of repeat visits. Nonguests can buy a CUC$35 day pass that includes lunch, drinks and sport until 5pm. If you're doing the south coast by bike, it's a nice indulgence.

ℹ Getting There & Away

Trucks run to Chivirico throughout the day from the Serrano Intermunicipal Bus Station opposite the train station in Santiago de Cuba. There are also three buses a day.

Theoretically, one daily truck trundles along to Campismo la Mula and the Pico Turquino trailhead but, since Hurricane Sandy, transport on to Marea del Portillo is almost unheard of (the road is nigh-on impassable).

El Uvero

A major turning point in the revolutionary war took place in this nondescript settlement 23km west of Chivirico, on May 28, 1957, when Castro's rebel army – still numbering less than 50 – audaciously took out a government position guarded by 53 of Batista's soldiers. By the main road are two red trucks taken by the rebels and nearby a double row of royal palms leads to a large **monument** commemorating the brief but incisive battle. It's a poignant, little-visited spot.

Pico Turquino Area

Near the border of Granma and Santiago de Cuba provinces is the pinprick settlement of Las Cuevas, embarkation point for quick ascents of Cuba's highest mountain.

◉ Sights

Museo de la Plata MUSEUM
(admission CUC$1; ⊙ Tue-Sat) Five kilometers west of Las Cuevas (which is 40km west of El Uvero) is this small museum at La Plata, just below the highway. The first successful skirmish of the Cuban Revolution happened here on January 17, 1957. Museum exhibits include the piece of paper signed by the 15 *Granma* survivors who met up at Cinco Palmas in late 1956.

Marea del Portillo is 46km to the west. Don't confuse this La Plata with Comandancia La Plata, Fidel Castro's Sierra Maestra Revolutionary headquarters.

🏃 Activities

Cristóbal Colón DIVING
The well-preserved wreck of Spanish cruiser *Cristóbal Colón* lies where it sank in 1898, about 15m down and only 30m offshore near La Mula. This is Cuba's greatest wreck dive; a genuine remnant of the Spanish-Cuban-American War. Dive centers from Sierra Mar

CYCLING FROM SANTIAGO DE CUBA TO PICO TURQUINO

The 125km coastal road connecting Santiago de Cuba and Pico Turquino is arguably Cuba's most scenic cycle, enhanced by the fact that local traffic is minimal. However, while the majority of the road is paved, certain stretches are gravelly or damaged so tackling it with a sturdy pair of wheels is advisable. At the time of writing there were no good bike shops in Santiago so your best bet is to bring a bike from home. If you don't have that luxury you should be able to borrow a bike in Santiago (or even find someone willing to build a bike from scratch in exchange for a handshake and a can of Bucanero). As with most things in Cuba: where there's a will, there's a way.

Day one takes you out of Santiago along the coast to Chivirico. Cycling in Cuba's cities is never a peaceful experience and Santiago is no exception. Expect *reggaetón* (Cuban hip-hop) beats, choking exhaust pipes and carefree pedestrians blocking your way as you negotiate the uphill Paseo de Martí road out of the city. Keep faith that this will all be forgotten by the time you reach Playa Mar Verde (after 17km), the first of many pebbly beaches punctuating this coastal route.

The 55km ride from here to Chivirico is a pleasure; you'll likely see more stray pigs than cars, and scurrying crabs outnumber humans. Some stretches suffer from nasty potholes but the tailwind is generous. The old Motel Guama, some 4km east of Chivirico, is now closed, although the casas particulares in town, despite being Cuban-only, are particularly adept at turning a blind eye to foreigners' non-Cuban-ness! Brisas Sierra Mar at Playa Sevilla is another accommodation possibility. For food hereabouts, the most unique option is the restaurant on Cayo Damas Island: paddleboats operate on request just a kilometer west of the motel. Take the opportunity to stock up on bottled water and Brinky biscuits in Chivirico as there are few other vendors from here on.

You're in for a treat on day two. A few manageable uphill climbs are rewarded with the kind of long, winding downhill runs that cyclists fantasize about, though you'll struggle to resist stopping to photograph the impressive views that unfold with the craggy Sierra Maestra mountains crashing abruptly into the azure Caribbean.

Some 50km later, after passing over a dramatically cracked bridge and around a disintegrated tunnel, you'll roll up at Pico Turquino HQ: the end of this route but by no means the end of the road. From here some will trek to Cuba's highest summit. Others will keep going along the coast to Pilón, Manzanillo and beyond. Whatever you choose to do, the southern coastal road is an unforgettable cycle and, at least for now, it's yours.

By Greg Dickinson

and Club Amigo Carisol – Los Corales (in Parque Baconao) come here. No scuba gear is available, but you can see the wreck with a mask and snorkel.

Hiking

You can hike up the Río Turquino to Las Posas de los Morones, which has a few nice swimming pools (allow four hours round trip). You must wade across the river at least three times unless it's dry.

Pico Turquino   HIKING
The **Pico Turquino** (shelter 2 days & 1 night CUC$30) hike is often tackled from Las Cuevas on the remote coast road 130km west of Santiago de Cuba (along with the other trailhead, Santo Domingo in Granma Province). If summiting the mountain is your main aim, this is probably the quick-est, easiest route. If you want to immerse yourself in the area's history and hike to Comandancia la Plata, set out from Santo Domingo. Both options can be linked in a spectacularly thorough trek with Ecotur (p424) – onward transport is better from the Santo Domingo side.

The hike from Las Cuevas can be organized at relatively short notice at the trailhead. A good option is to book through Ecotur in Santiago de Cuba.

➜ Camps & Shelters
The trail from Las Cuevas begins on the south-coast highway, 7km west of Ocujal and 51km east of Marea del Portillo. This trek also passes Cuba's second-highest peak, Pico Cuba (1872m). Allow at least six hours to go up and four hours to come down, more if it has been raining, as the trail floods and

becomes a mud slick in parts. Be sure you're on the trail by 6:30am at latest to do the out-and-back day hike. You can sleep at Campismo la Mula, 12km east; self-sufficient hikers can also pitch camp or take the basic beds at Las Cuevas visitors center. The CUC$15 per person fee (camera CUC$5 extra) that you pay at the visitors center/trailhead includes a compulsory Cuban guide. You can stay overnight at the shelter on Pico Cuba (an additional CUC$30) if you don't want to descend the same day. Alternatively, you can do the entire Las Cuevas–Santo Domingo (with transport from Alto del Naranjo) two-day hike by arranging to be met by a new team of guides at Pico Turquino, including a side trip to Castro's former headquarters at Comandancia la Plata, for CUC$65.

➡ The Route

This hike is grueling: you're gaining almost 2km in elevation across only 9.6km of trail. But shade and peek-a-boo views provide plenty of respite. Fill up on water before setting out. The well-marked route leads from Las Cuevas to La Esmajagua (600m; 3km; there's water here), Pico Cardero (1265m; quickly followed by a series of nearly vertical steps called Saca la Lengua, literally 'flops your tongue out'), Pico Cuba (1872m; 2km; water and shelter here) and Pico Turquino (1972m; 1.7km). When the fog parts and you catch your breath, you'll behold a bronze bust of José Martí standing on the summit of Cuba's highest mountain. You can overnight at the rudimentary Pico Cuba shelter on the ascent or descent. There's a basic kitchen, wood-fired stove and plank beds (no mattresses) or, if those are taken, floor space.

➡ What to Bring

Trekkers should bring sufficient food, warm clothing, a sleeping bag and a poncho –

precipitation is common up here (some 2200mm annually), from a soft drizzle to pelting hail. Except for water, you'll have to carry everything you'll need, including extra food to share if you can carry it and a little something for the *compañeros* (comrades) who take 15-day shifts up on Pico Cuba.

Ask ahead if you would like an English-speaking guide (there are several, but most are based on the Santo Domingo side). Also ask about food provision at Pico Cuba. Drinks are available for purchase at the Las Cuevas trailhead. Tipping the guides is mandatory – CUC$3 to CUC$5 is sufficient. For competitive types, the (unofficial) summit record by a guide is two hours and 45 minutes. So if you're feeling energetic...

🛏 Sleeping

Campismo la Mula   CABINS $
(Carretera Granma Km 120; s/d CUC$7/10) On a remote pebble beach, 12km east of the Pico Turquino trailhead, La Mula has 50 small cabins popular with holidaying Cubans, hikers destined for Turquino and the odd hitchhiking south-coast adventurer. It's pretty much the only option on this isolated stretch of coast. Check with Cubamar or the Oficina Reservaciones de Campismo in Santiago de Cuba before turning up.

If it's full, you may be able to pitch a tent. There's also a rustic cafe and restaurant on site.

ℹ Getting There & Away

Private trucks and the odd rickety bus connect La Mula to Chivirico, but they are sporadic; don't bank on more than one per day. A taxi from Santiago should cost CUC$50 to CUC$60. Traffic is almost nonexistent in this neck of the woods.

Guantánamo Province

🗾 21 / POP 511,100

Best Places to Eat

➡ Restaurante 1870 (p441)

➡ Bar-Restaurante La Terraza (p450)

➡ La Rosa Nautica (p450)

➡ Rancho Toa (p452)

Best Wildlife Excursions

➡ El Yunque (p453)

➡ Parque Nacional Alejandro de Humboldt (p453)

➡ Río Toa (p452)

➡ Boca de Yumurí (p445)

Why Go?

To many people, Guantánamo conjures up pictures of nameless prisoners in orange jumpsuits. But Cuba's wettest, driest, hottest, oldest and most mountainous province isn't just an anachronistic US Naval Base. Cuba in the modern sense started here in 1511, when Diego Velázquez and his band of colonizers landed uninvited on the rain-lashed eastern coastline. Today it lives on in Baracoa, the city Velázquez founded, one of the country's most isolated settlements and beautifully unique as a consequence.

The province's rugged transport artery is La Farola, one of the seven engineering marvels of modern Cuba, a weaving roller coaster that travels from the dry cacti-littered southern coast up into the humid Cuchillas Toa mountains. Overlaid by the fecund Parque Nacional Alejandro de Humboldt, this heavily protected zone is one of the last, and most biologically diverse, swaths of virgin rainforest left in the Caribbean.

When to Go

➡ Baracoa's biggest festival, the Semana de la Cultura (p448) Baracoesa, is in late March/early April.

➡ The city of Guantánamo gets animated in mid-December for the Festival Nacional de Changüí.

➡ Avoid the worst of Baracoa's heavy storms by staying away in September and October. Guantánamo's climate varies hugely, but it's dependent more on geography than season.

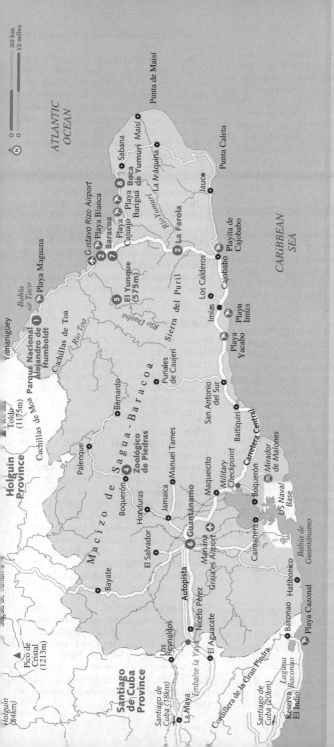

Guantánamo Province Highlights

1 Find the world's smallest frog in **Parque Nacional Alejandro de Humboldt**, the the Caribbean's most diverse national park. (p453).

2 Sample the culinary smorgasbord of exotic **Baracoa** (p445).

3 Cycle **La Farola**, the lighthouse road from Cajobabo to Baracoa (p452).

4 Get an eye-full of the stony statues at the **Zoológico de Piedras** (p445).

5 Hike through the tropical jungle up to Baracoa's mysterious flat-topped mountain, **El Yunque** (p453).

6 Uncover the mysteries of *changüí* music in the city of **Guantánamo** (p442).

7 Imagine Taíno life pre-Columbus at Baracoa's **Museo Arqueológico 'La Cueva del Paraíso'** (p446).

8 Jump on board a local boat upstream from the **Boca de Yumurí** through the jaws of a mysterious river gorge (p445).

History

Long before the arrival of the Spanish, the Taíno populated the mountains and forests around Guantánamo, forging a living as fishermen, hunters and small-scale farmers. Columbus first arrived in the region in November 1492, a month or so after his initial landfall near Gibara, and planted a small wooden cross in a beautiful bay he ceremoniously christened Porto Santo – after an idyllic island off Portugal where he had enjoyed his honeymoon. The Spanish returned again in 1511 under the auspices of Columbus' son Diego in a flotilla of four ships and 400 men that included the island's first governor, Diego Velázquez de Cuéllar. Building a makeshift fort constructed from wood, the conquistadors consecrated the island's first colonial settlement, Villa de Nuestra Señora de la Asunción de Baracoa, and watched helplessly as the town was subjected to repeated attacks from hostile local Indians led by a rebellious *cacique* (chief) known as Hatuey.

Declining in importance after the capital moved to Santiago in 1515, the Guantánamo region became Cuba's Siberia – a mountainous and barely penetrable rural backwater where prisoners were exiled and old traditions survived. In the late 18th century the area was recolonized by French immigrants from Haiti who tamed the difficult terrain in order to cultivate coffee, cotton and sugarcane on the backs of African slaves. Following the Spanish-Cuban-American War, a new power took up residence in Guantánamo Bay – the all-powerful Americans, intent on protecting their economic interests in the strategically important Panama Canal region. Despite repeated bouts of mudslinging in the years since, the not-so-welcome *Yanquis,* as they are popularly known, have repeatedly refused to budge.

Guantánamo

POP 216,700

Every traveler knows journey-breakers can provide those magic ingredients that make a trip memorable, and so Guantánamo must reconcile itself to being a journey-breaker with big potential for serendipity. This might seem strange, given its spot as an internationally hot political topic due to the nearby US naval base (see p440), which often leaves those who stop off more-or-less utterly unprepared for what to expect in the city itself.

Visually remarkable Guantánamo is not, and this accounts for its low profile on the tourist 'circuit.' But its nightlife is truly formidable, and the city has even spawned its own unique brand of traditional *son* (Cuba's popular music) known as *son-changüí.* The feisty *guantanameros* have also produced 11 Olympic gold medalists, blasted a man into orbit (Cuban cosmonaut Arnaldo Méndez)... then there's the small matter of *that* song – 'Guantanamera' (if you've made it this far, you'll have already heard it 25 times).

'Discovered' by Columbus in 1494, a settlement wasn't built here until 1819, when French plantation owners evicted from Haiti founded the town of Santa Catalina del Saltadero del Guaso. In 1843 the burgeoning city changed its name to Guantánamo and in 1903 the bullish US Navy took up residence in the bay next door. Sparks have been flying ever since.

◉ Sights

Ostensibly unexciting, Guantánamo's geometric city grid has a certain rhythm. Tree-lined Av Camilo Cienfuegos a few blocks south of Bartolomé Masó, with its morning exercisers, bizarre sculptures and central Ramblas-style walkway, is the best place to get into the groove.

Palacio Salcines   NOTABLE BUILDING
(cnr Pedro A Pérez & Prado) Local architect Leticio Salcines (1888–1973) left a number of impressive works around Guantánamo including his personal residence built in 1916, a lavish monument said to be the building most representative of the city. The *palacio* (palace) is now a **museum** of colorful frescoes, Japanese porcelain and the like, but is currently closed for indefinite restoration.

On the palace's turret is **La Fama**, a sculpture designed by Italian artist Americo Chine that serves as the symbol of Guantánamo, her trumpet announcing good and evil.

Plaza Mariana Grajales   SQUARE
The huge, bombastic **Monument to the Heroes**, glorifying the Brigada Fronteriza 'that defends the forward trench of socialism on this continent,' dominates Plaza Mariana Grajales, 1km northwest of the train station and opposite Hotel Guantánamo. It's one of the more impressive 'Revolution squares' on the island.

Guantánamo

Guantánamo

◎ Sights

1	Biblioteca Policarpo Pineda Rustán	C4
2	Museo Municipal	A3
3	Palacio Salcines	B3
4	Parque Martí	B3
5	Parroquia de Santa Catalina de Riccis	B3

🛏 Sleeping

| 6 | Hotel Martlí | B3 |
| 7 | Lissett Foster Lara | B2 |

✗ Eating

8	Bar-Restaurante Olimpia	B3
9	Plaza del Mercado Agro Industrial	C3
10	Restaurante 1870	B3

☕ Drinking & Nightlife

11	Casa de las Promociones Musicales 'La Guantanamera'	B4
12	Club Nevada	B4
13	La Ruina	B4

✪ Entertainment

14	Casa de Changüí	D2
15	Casa de la Cultura	B3
16	Casa de la Trova (Parque Martí)	B3
17	Cine Huambo	B3
18	Tumba Francesa Pompadour	D2

Museo Municipal   MUSEUM
(cnr José Martí & Prado; admission CUC$1;
⊙ 2-6pm Mon, 8am-noon & 3-7pm Tue-Sat) This
esoteric museum contains some interest-ing US Naval Base ephemera including prerevolutionary day passes and some revealing photos.

Parque Martí SQUARE

Anchored by the 1863 **Parroquia de Santa Catalina de Riccis** has benefited from a substantial facelift in recent years: a lick of paint, information boards and a clutch of interesting new shops, restaurants and entertainment nooks, strung along vibrant boulevards. Sitting timelessly amid the ac-tion is a seated **statue** of 'El Maestro' from whom the square takes its name.

Biblioteca Policarpo Pineda Rustán LIBRARY (cnr Los Maceos & Emilio Giro) Another Salcines creation was this beautiful provincial library which was once the city hall (1934–51). Trials of Fulgencio Batista's thugs were held here

GITMO – A SHORT HISTORY

Procured via the infamous Platt Amendment in 1903 in the aftermath of the Spanish-American War, the US' initial reason for annexing Guantánamo Bay (or Gitmo, as generations of homesick US marines have unsentimentally dubbed it) was primarily to protect the eastern approach to the strategically important Panama Canal.

In 1934 an upgrade of the original treaty reaffirmed the lease terms and agreed to honor them indefinitely unless both governments accorded otherwise. It also set an annual rent of approximately US$4000, a sum that the US continues to cough up, but which the Cubans won't bank on the grounds that the occupation is illegal (Castro alleg-edly stored the checks in the top drawer of his office desk).

Until 1958, when motorized traffic was officially cut off between Guantánamo and the outside world, hundreds of Cubans used to travel daily into the base for work, and there were still a handful of workers making the commute up until the turn of the 21st century. Expanded post-WWII, the oldest US military base on foreign soil has gone through many metamorphoses in the last 50 years, from tense Cold War battleground to the most virulent surviving political anachronism in the Western hemisphere.

Castro was quick to demand the unconditional return of Guantánamo to Cuban sov-ereignty in 1959 but, locked in a Cold War deadlock with the Soviet Union and fearing the Cuban leader's imminent flight to Moscow, the US steadfastly refused. As relations between the countries deteriorated, Cuba cut off water and electricity to the base while the Americans surrounded it with the biggest minefield in the Western hemisphere (the mines were removed in 1996).

The more recent history of the facility has been equally notorious. In January 1992, 11,000 Haitian migrants were temporarily held here, and in August 1994 the base was used to house 32,000 Cubans picked up by the US Coast Guard while trying to reach Florida. In May 1995 the Cuban and US governments signed an agreement allowing these refugees to enter the US but, since then, illegal Cuban immigrants picked up by the US Coast Guard at sea have been returned to Cuba under the 'wet foot, dry foot' policy.

Since 2002 the US has held more than 750 prisoners with suspected Al-Qaeda or Taliban links at Camp Delta in Guantánamo Bay without pressing criminal charges. De-nied legal counsel and family contact while facing rigorous interrogations, the detainees mounted hunger strikes and at least four are known to have committed suicide. Follow-ing calls from Amnesty International and the UN in 2004 to close down the base and reports from the Red Cross that certain aspects of the camp regime were tantamount to torture, the US released 420 prisoners and charged just three of them. As of early 2013, the US government intended to repatriate some of the remaining 165 or so prison-ers to other countries for rehab or release, and transfer the rest to prisons in the US.

In January 2009 President Barack Obama promised to shut down Guantánamo's detention camps and thus end what he termed 'a sad chapter in US history'. However, due to bipartisan opposition in Congress, Obama failed to meet his one-year deadline on this issue. The force-feeding of some 100 inmates on hunger strike in May 2013 was widely condemned by the international community, putting pressure on the president to take steps to close the camp. Obama has restated his intention to do this, but, many months into his second term, it remained unclear how and when the closure would be completed.

in 1959, and a number were killed when they snatched a rifle and tried to escape.

✨ Festivals & Events

Festival Nacional de Changüí   MUSIC
Mid-December celebration of *changüí*.

Noches Guantanameras   STREET PARTY
(⊘8pm Sat) Saturday nights are reserved for this local coming together, when Calle Pedro A Pérez is closed to traffic and stalls are set up in the street: come and enjoy whole roast pig, belting music and copious amounts of rum.

🛏 Sleeping

★Villa La Lupe   HOTEL $
(☑38-26-12; Carretera de El Salvador Km 3.5; s/d CUC$24/38; P ❄ ➰) Located 5km north of the city on the road to El Salvador, Villa La Lupe – named after a song by Moncada and *Granma* survivor Juan Almeida – is Guantánamo's best lodging. Attractive, spacious cabins are arranged around a clean central swimming pool, and the adjacent restaurant, which serves the usual staples of pork and rice, overlooks a leafy river.

Lissett Foster Lara   CASA PARTICULAR $
(☑32-59-70; Pedro A Pérez No 761, btwn Prado & Jesús del Sol; r CUC$20-25; ❄) Like many *guantanameras,* Lissett speaks perfect English and her house is polished, comfortable and decked out with the kind of plush fittings that wouldn't look amiss in a North American suburb. There are three rooms, including a delightful one on the substantial roof terrace.

Hotel Guantánamo   HOTEL $
(☑38-10-15; Calle 13 Norte, btwn Ahogados & 2 de Octubre; s/d CUC$25/40; P ❄ ➰) A lick of paint and some newly planted flowers in the garden, and hey presto: Hotel Guantánamo's back in business after a couple of years serving as a convalescent home for Operación Milagros. The generic rooms are clean, the pool has water in it, and there's a good reception bar-cafe mixing up tempting mojitos and serving coffee. It's 1km northwest of the train station.

Hotel Martlí   HOTEL $$
(☑32-95-00; cnr Aguilera & Calixto García; s/d CUC$35/56) A welcome addition overlooking Parque Martí in a revamped colonial building with, by Guantánamo standards, what could be described as sumptuous rooms.

Entertainment-wise, there's the rooftop terrace restaurant with deafening music and the street-level bar circled by *jineteras* (female touts).

🍴 Eating

At weekends Parque Martí is a smorgasbord of mobile food stalls selling cheap fried *comida ligera* (light food).

★Restaurante 1870   CUBAN $
(Flor Crombet; meals CUC$2-5; ⊘noon-11pm) Before this place opened opposite Parque Martí, you would be forgiven for thinking Guantánamo never had a colonial heyday. But here we go. The sweeping marble staircase takes you up to the plushly ornamented balcony-bar from where you can gaze down on the main eating area: beef, chicken, pork...the works.

Restaurante Girasoles   CARIBBEAN $
(cnr Calle 15 Norte & Ahogados; meals CUC$1-5; ⊘noon-9.30pm) A nude statue, not a *girasol* (sunflower), marks the entrance to what is, by process of elimination, one of Guantánamo's best restaurants. Behind the Hotel Guantánamo, Girasoles serves up (albeit at a snail's pace) chicken and fish, occasionally in interesting sauces. The terrace is popular for an afternoon drink.

Bar-Restaurante Olimpia   BURGERS $
(cnr Calixto García & Aguilera; ⊘9am-midnight) A celebration of Guantánamo's remarkable Olympic Games records, this bar-restaurant displays framed baseball shirts, boxing vests and athletics memorabilia. Inside there's a small open patio and a mezzanine bar where you can enjoy beers, relatively substantial burgers, and the usual Cuban suspects: all with a vista of adjacent Parque Martí.

Self-Catering

Plaza del Mercado Agro Industrial MARKET $
(cnr Los Maceos & Aguilera; ⊘7am-7pm Mon-Sat, to 2pm Sun) The town's public vegetable market is a red-domed Leticio Salcines creation and is rather striking (inside and out).

🍷 Drinking & Nightlife

Two newly pedestrianized streets – Aguilera and Flor Crombet – leading a block east of Parque Martí are embellished by lively bars where preened *guantanameros* like to flaunt their fake designer clothing.

La Ruina   BAR
(cnr Calixto García & Emilio Giro; ⊘10am-1am)
This shell of a ruined colonial building has
9m ceilings; there are plenty of benches to
prop you up against after you've downed yet
another beer and there's a popular karaoke
scene for those with reality-TV ambitions.
The bar menu's good for a snack lunch.

**Casa de las Promociones
Musicales 'La Guantanamera'**   NIGHTCLUB
(Calixto García, btwn Flor Crombet & Emilio Giro)
Another well-maintained concert-orientated
venue, with Thursday rap *peñas* (performances) and Sunday *trova* (traditional poetic
singing) matinees. This casa is perhaps the
town's most revered music house.

Club Nevada   NIGHTCLUB
(Pedro A Pérez No 1008 Altos cnr Bartolomé Masó;
admission CUC$1) Probably the best city disco;
it's a rooftop rave-up, as the best of them
often are.

☆ Entertainment

Guantánamo has its own distinctive musical culture, the subgenre of *son* known as
changüí (see below). You can get a taste at
some of the following venues.

Casa de Changüí   LIVE MUSIC
(Serafín Sánchez No 710, btwn N López & Jesús del
Sol) As primary pulpit for Guantánamo's
indigenous music, this is *the* place to experience *changüí* and a shrine to its main
exponent, local *timbalero* (percussionist)
Elio Revé.

★ Tumba Francesa Pompadour   LIVE MUSIC
(Serafín Sánchez No 715) This peculiarly
Guantánamo nightspot situated four
blocks east of the train station specializes
in a unique form of Haitian-style dancing.
Programs include *mi tumba baile* (*tumba*
dance), *encuentro tradicional* (traditional
get-together) and *peña campesina* (country
music).

Casa de la Trova (Parque Martí)   LIVE MUSIC
(cnr Pedro Pérez & Flor Crombet; admission CUC$1)
The only Cuban city with two *trova* houses,
Guantánamo offers options galore. This one
is the more traditional haunt with *viejos*
(old men) in Panama hats casting aside their
arthritis to dance athletically.

Casa de la Trova (ARTex)   LIVE MUSIC
(Máximo Gómez No 1062; admission CUC$1;
⊘8pm-1am Tue-Sun) Housed in a royal-blue
building on a quiet street, Casa de la Trova

CHANGÜÍ

Before you write off Guantánamo as a glorified bus stop between Santiago and Baracoa,
lend an ear to the syncopated strains of *changüí*, the city's native music genre that
predates *son* (Cuba's popular music) and is widely considered to be the first authentic
melding of African drums and Spanish guitars in a Caribbean setting.

Changüí's origins are sketchy and complex. Its roots lie in the fusion of two antiquated musical rites known as *nengon* and *kiribá*, both concocted in the mountains
of the Oriente during the late 19th century. The former was the staple of black sugar
workers living in the vicinity of Guantánamo City; the latter was a product of the Baracoa region where it had absorbed myriad French slave and indigenous Taíno influences.
Both *nengon* and *kiribá* were highly percussive sounds that used simple instrumenta-
tion (sometimes a tree stump was hit to keep rhythm). But, as the music became more
complex, incorporating guitars and melodies, it split into two new genres. Pure *nengon*
played in Santiago de Cuba province developed into *son,* while *nengon* mixed with *kiribá*
in Guantánamo province evolved into what is today called *changüí*.

Definitive *changüí* music is nearly always played by a four-piece band consisting of
bongos, *tres* (guitar), *güiro* and *marimbula* overlaid by a vocalist. Rhythmically, it is
more syncopated and layered than *son,* lacking the distinctive *son clave* (beat), which
instead is provided by the *tres*. In the early 20th century when *son* was 'dressed up' and
taken to Havana, where it metamorphosed into salsa, *changüí* stayed close to home,
finding its most famous exponent in local *guantanamero* Elio Revé, whose Orquestra
Revé nurtured the likes of jazz giant Chucho Valdés and salsa-songo-king Juan Formell
(of Los Van Van). As a result *changüí* is considered to be a much purer musical style
than *son* that has remained true to its Oriente roots.

Mk 2 is openly referred to as 'the place.' It offers the local blend of traditional sounds with a *son-changüi* bias.

Casa de la Cultura CULTURAL CENTER
(Pedro A Pérez; admission free) This venue holds classical concerts and Afro-Cuban dance performances.

Cine Huambo CINEMA
(Parque Martí) Revamped cinema in the heart of the Parque Martí action.

Estadio Van Troi SPORTS
Baseball games are played from October to April at this stadium in Reparto San Justo, 1.5km south of the Servi-Cupet gas station. Despite a strong sporting tradition, Guantánamo team – nicknamed Los Indios – are perennial underachievers who seldom make the play-offs.

❶ Information

Banco de Crédito y Comercio (Calixto García, btwn Emilio Giro & Bartolomé Masó) Two branches on this block.

Cadeca (cnr Calixto García & Prado) Money changing.

Clínica Internacional (Flor Crombet No 305, btwn Calixto García & Los Maceos; ⊘9am-5pm) On the northeast corner of Parque Martí.

Etecsa Telepunto (cnr Aguilera & Los Maceos; internet access per hr CUC$6; ⊘8:30am-7:30pm) Four computers plus hardly any tourists equals no queues.

Havanatur (Aguilera, btwn Calixto García & Los Maceos; ⊘8am-noon & 1:30-4:30pm Mon-Fri, 8:30-11:30am Sat) Travel agency.

Hospital Agostinho Neto (☎35-54-50; Carretera de El Salvador Km 1; ⊘24hr) At the western end of Plaza Mariana Grajales near Hotel Guantánamo. It will help foreigners in emergencies.

Oficina de Monumentos y Sitios Históricos (Los Maceos, btwn Emilio Giro & Flor Crombet) For a fuller exposé of Guantánamo's interesting architectural heritage you could ask here about a map of city walking trails.

Post Office (Pedro A Pérez; ⊘8am-1pm & 2-6pm Mon-Sat) On the western side of Parque Martí. There's also a DHL office here.

Radio Trinchera Antimperialista CMKS Trumpets the word over 1070AM.

Venceremos & Lomería Two local newspapers published on Saturday.

❶ Getting There & Away

AIR

Cubana (Calixto García No 817) flies five times a week (CUC$124 one way, 2½ hours) from Havana to Mariana Grajales Airport (also known as Los Canos Airport). There are no international flights.

BUS

The rather inconveniently placed Terminal de Ómnibus (bus station) is 5km west of the center on the old road to Santiago (a continuation of Av Camilo Cienfuegos). A taxi from the Hotel Guantánamo should cost CUC$3 to CUC$4.

There are daily **Víazul** (www.viazul.com) buses to Baracoa (CUC$10, three hours, 9:35am) and Santiago de Cuba (CUC$6, 1¾ hours, 5:30pm).

CAR

The Autopista Nacional to Santiago de Cuba ends near Embalse la Yaya, 25km west of Guantánamo, where the road joins the Carretera Central (work to extend this road continues). To drive to Guantánamo from Santiago de Cuba, follow the Autopista Nacional north about 12km to the top of the grade, then take the first turn to the right. Signposts are sporadic and vague, so take a good map and keep alert.

TRAIN

The **train station** (Pedro A Pérez), several blocks north of Parque Martí, has one departure for Havana (CUC$32, 19 hours, 8:50am) every third day via Camagüey, Ciego de Ávila, Santa Clara and Matanzas. Purchase tickets in the morning of the day the train departs at the office on Pedro A Pérez.

TRUCK

Trucks to Santiago de Cuba and Baracoa leave from the Terminal de Ómnibus and allow you to disembark in the smaller towns in between.

Trucks for Moa park on the road to El Salvador north of town near the entrance to the Autopista.

❶ Getting Around

Havanautos (Cupet Guantánamo) is by the Servi-Cupet gas station on the way out of town toward Baracoa.

The **Oro Negro gas station** (cnr Los Maceos & Jesús del Sol) is another option to fill up on gas before the 150km trek east to Baracoa.

Taxis hang out around Parque Martí. Bus 48 (20 centavos) runs between the center and the Hotel Guantánamo every 40 minutes or so. There are also plenty of bici-taxis.

ZOOLÓGICO DE PIEDRAS

A surreal spectacle even by Cuban standards, the **Zoológico de Piedras** (admission CUC$1; ☺9am-6pm Mon-Sat) is an animal sculpture park set amid thick foliage in the grounds of a mountain coffee farm, 20km northeast of Guantánamo. Carved quite literally out of the existing rock by sculptor Angel Iñigo Blanco starting in the late 1970s, the sculptures now number more than 300 and range from hippos to giant serpents. To get here you'll need your own wheels or a taxi. Head east out of town and fork left toward Jamaica and Honduras. The 'zoo' is in the settlement of Boquerón.

Around Guantánamo US Naval Base

Mirador de Malones

Traditionally, it has been possible to enjoy a distant view of the base from the isolated Mirador de Malones on a 320m-high hill just to the east. Visits here are currently suspended. Check the current status beforehand at Hotel Guantánamo or one of the Gaviota-run hotels in Baracoa.

Should you get lucky, the entrance to the *mirador* (lookout) is at a Cuban military checkpoint on the main Baracoa highway, 27km southeast of Guantánamo.

Caimanera

Contrary to popular belief, Caimanera (not Guantánamo) is the nearest Cuban town to the US Naval Base. Situated on the west shore of Guantánamo Bay just north of the US military checkpoint, this fishing settlement of 10,000 people (many of them first- or second-generation Jamaicans) was a boomtown before the revolution when local workers were employed in the naval station. According to old-timers, the most popular profession was prostitution. Since 1959 Caimanera has struggled economically. A sole hotel acted as a lookout spot for curious 'Bay-watchers' before the era of Bush Jnr and Camp Delta. It reopened for preorganized visits in 2009.

To the west of Caimanera the dry cacti-covered hills are characterized by *moni-tongos* (rocky, wind-eroded plateaus). The region has a high level of endemism and is protected as a fauna reserve. There are trails here, but you'll need to be on an organized trip to access them.

🛏 Sleeping

Hotel Caimanera　　　　　　　HOTEL **$**
(☎49-94-14; s/d incl breakfast from CUC$16/25, 2-person bungalow CUC$32; [P][❄][⊠]) This oddly attractive (considering its position) hotel is on a hilltop at Caimanera, near the perimeter of the US Naval Base, 21km south of Guantánamo. It has peculiar rules which permit only groups of seven or more on prearranged tours with an official Cuban guide to stay and enjoy the lookout. Ask at the Havanatur office in Guantánamo about joining a trip.

ℹ Getting There & Away

Caimanera is the eastern terminus of the Cuban railway network (which doesn't extend to Baracoa). There are supposedly four trains a day to Guantánamo City.

South Coast

The long, dry coastal road from Guantánamo to the island's eastern extremity, Punta de Maisí, is Cuba's spectacular semi-desert region, where cacti nestle on rocky ocean terraces and prickly aloe vera poke out from the scrub. Several little stone beaches between Playa Yacabo and Cajobabo make refreshing pit stops for those with time to linger, while the diverse roadside scenery – punctuated at intervals by rugged purple mountains and impossibly verdant riverside oases – impresses throughout.

⊙ Sights

Playita de Cajobabo　　　　　　BEACH
At the far end of this usually deserted beach, just before the main road bends inland, there is a **monument** commemorating José Martí's 1895 landing here to launch the Second War of Independence. A colorful billboard depicts the bobbing rowboat making for shore with Martí sitting calmly inside, dressed rather improbably in trademark dinner suit, not a hair out of place.

It's a good **snorkeling** spot, flanked by dramatic cliffs. The famous La Farola (the lighthouse road; see boxed text, p452) starts here. Cyclists, take a deep breath...

🛌 Sleeping

Campismo Yacabo   CABINS **$**
(s/d CUC$7.50/11) This place, by the highway 10km west of Imías, has 18 well-maintained cabins overlooking the sea near the mouth of the river, and sometimes accepts foreigners (check ahead). The cabins sleep four to six people and make a great budget beach getaway.

Punta de Maisí

From Cajobabo, the coastal road continues 51km northeast to La Máquina. As far as Jauco, the road is good; thereafter it's less so. Coming from Baracoa to La Máquina (55km), it's a good road as far as Sabana, then rough in places from Sabana to La Máquina. Either way, La Máquina is the starting point of the very rough 13km track down to Punta de Maisí: best covered in a 4WD.

This is Cuba's easternmost point and there's a **lighthouse** (1862) and a small fine white-sand beach. You can see Haiti 70km away on a clear day.

At the time of writing the Maisí area was designated a military zone and not open to travelers.

Boca de Yumurí & Around

Five kilometers south of Baracoa a road branches left off La Farola and travels 28km along the coast to **Boca de Yumurí** at the mouth of Río Yumurí. Near the bridge over the river is the **Túnel de los Alemanes** (German Tunnel), an amazing natural arch of trees and foliage. Though lovely, the dark-sand beach here has become *the* day trip from Baracoa. Hustlers hard-sell fried fish meals, while other people peddle colorful land snails called *polymitas*. These snails have become rare as a result of being harvested wholesale for tourists, so refuse all offers. From the end of the beach a boat taxi (CUC$2) heads upstream to where the steep river banks narrow into a haunting natural gorge.

Boca de Yumurí makes a superb bike jaunt from Baracoa (56km round trip): hot, but smooth and flat with great views and many potential stopovers (try **Playa Bariguá** at Km 25). You can arrange bikes in Baracoa – ask at your casa particular. Taxis

will also take you here from Baracoa, or you can organize an excursion with Cubatur (CUC$22).

Between Boca de Yumurí and Baracoa there are some beautiful beaches. Heading west, first up is **Playa Cajuajo**, a little-visited sandy expanse accessible via a 5km trail from the Río Mata through biologically diverse woodland. Ecotur in Baracoa runs trips here. There's also delightful little **Playa Mangalito**, where the beach-abutting restaurant will prepare you fresh octopus and a coconut to drink.

Baracoa

POP 40,800

Take a pinch of Tolkien, a dash of Gabriel García Márquez, mix in a large cup of 1960s psychedelia and temper with a tranquilizing dose of Cold War–era socialism. Leave to stand for 400 years in a geographically isolated tropical wilderness with little or no contact with the outside world. The end product: Baracoa – Cuba's weirdest, wildest and most unique settlement, which materializes like a surreal apparition after the long dry plod along Guantánamo's southern coast.

Cut off by land and sea for nearly half a millennium, Cuba's oldest city is, for most visitors, one of its most interesting. Founded in 1511 by Diego Velázquez de Cuéllar, Baracoa is a visceral place of fickle weather and haunting legends. Semi-abandoned in the mid-16th century, the town became a Cuban Siberia where rebellious revolutionaries were sent as prisoners. In the early 19th century French planters crossed the 70km-wide Windward Passage from Haiti and began farming the local staples of coconut, cocoa and coffee in the mountains; this is when the economic wheels finally began to turn.

Baracoa developed in relative isolation from the rest of Cuba until the opening of La Farola (p452) in 1964, a factor that has strongly influenced its singular culture. Today its premier attractions include trekking up mysterious El Yunque, (the region's signature flat-topped mountain), or indulging in some inspired local cooking using ingredients and flavors found nowhere else in Cuba.

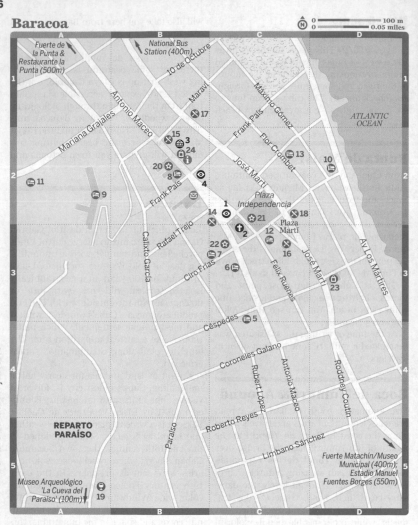

Baracoa

GUANTÁNAMO PROVINCE BARACOA

⊙ Sights & Activities

⊙ In Town

★ Museo Arqueológico 'La Cueva del Paraíso' MUSEUM

(Moncada; admission CUC$3; ⊙ 8am-5pm) Baracoa's most impressive museum is exhibited in a series of caves (Las Cuevas del Paraíso) that were once Taíno burial chambers. Among nearly 2000 authentic Taíno pieces are unearthed skeletons, ceramics, 3000-year-old petroglyphs and a replica of the *Ídolo de Tabaco* – a sculpture found

in Maisí in 1903 and considered to be one of the most important Taíno finds in the Caribbean.

One of the staff will enthusiastically show you around. The museum is 800m southeast of Hotel El Castillo.

Fuerte Matachín FORT

(cnr José Martí & Malecón; admission CUC$1; ⊙ 8am-noon & 2-6pm) Baracoa is protected by a trio of muscular Spanish forts. This one, built in 1802 at the southern entrance to town, now houses the **Museo Municipal**. The beautiful building showcases an engaging

Baracoa

chronology of Cuba's oldest settlement including *polymita* snail shells, the story of Che Guevara and the chocolate factory, and the particular strand of music Baracoa gave birth to: *kiribá,* a forefather of *son.*

There are also exhibits relating to Magdalena Menasse (née Rovieskuya, 'La Rusa') after whom Alejo Carpentier based his famous book *La Consagración de la Primavera* (The Rite of Spring).

Catedral de Nuestra Señora de la Asunción
CHURCH
(Antonio Maceo No 152) A topic Baracoans lament about pretty frequently is the renovation of their main church. There's been a building on this site since the 16th century, but this is the least notable version: refurbished in 2011 and (despite looking attractive enough) keeping few features true to its previous incarnation, dating from 1833.

Its most famous artifact is the priceless **Cruz de la Parra**, a wooden cross said to have been erected by Columbus near Baracoa in 1492. Carbon dating has authenticated the age of the cross (it dates from the late 1400s), but has indicated it was originally made out of indigenous Cuban wood, thus disproving the legend that Columbus brought the cross from Europe.

Facing the cathedral is the **Bust of Hatuey**, a rebellious Indian *cacique* who was burned at the stake near Baracoa in 1512 after refusing to convert to Catholicism. Also on triangular Plaza Independencia (this being Baracoa, they couldn't have a square plaza) is the neoclassical **Poder Popular**

(Antonio Maceo No 137), a municipal government building which you can admire from the outside.

Museo del Cacao
MUSEUM
(Antonio Maceo, btwn Maraví & Frank País; ⊙7am-11pm) **FREE** It's as much slightly overpriced cafe as it is museum, but with a heads-up on the history of cacao hereabouts, plus guys out the back concocting chocolates, it's a damned good prequel to sitting down for a piping-hot cup of the sweet stuff, Baracoa-style.

El Castillo de Seboruco
FORT
Baracoa's highest fort was begun by the Spanish in 1739 and finished by the Americans in 1900; it is now Hotel El Castillo. There's an excellent view of El Yunque's flat top over the shimmering swimming pool. A steep stairway at the southwestern end of Calle Frank País climbs directly up.

Fuerte de la Punta
FORT
Another Spanish fort that has watched over the harbor entrance at the northwestern end of town since 1803. Pumelled by Hurricane Ike in 2008, it's now a rather pleasant restaurant.

⊙ Southeast of Town

Parque Natural Majayara
PARK
(per person CUC$3-5) ⦿ Southeast of town in the Parque Natural Majayara are a couple of magical **hikes**, plus **swimming** and an archaeological trail in the grounds of a lush family farm. It's all a very low-key, laid-back

GUANTÁNAMO PROVINCE BARACOA

diversion. Passing the Fuerte Matachín, hike southeast past the baseball stadium and along the dark-sand beach for 20 minutes to the Río Miel, where eager volunteers can row you across for CUC$1.

On the other side, bear left following a track up through a cluster of rustic houses to another junction. A guard-post here is sometimes staffed by an official who will collect CUC$2. Turn left again and continue along the vehicle track until the houses clear and you see a fainter single-track path leading off left to Playa Blanca, an idyllic spot for a picnic.

Staying straight on the track, you'll come to a trio of wooden homesteads. The third of these houses belongs to the Fuentes family. Do not continue alone past this point as you are entering a military zone. For a donation, Señor Fuentes will lead you on a hike to his family finca (farm) where you can stop for coffee and tropical fruit. Further on he'll show you the Cueva de Aguas, a cave with a sparkling, freshwater swimming hole inside. Tracking back up the hillside you'll come to an archaeological trail with more caves and marvelous ocean views.

◉ Northwest of Town

Follow the aroma of chocolate on the road out of town toward Moa.

Playa Duaba   BEACH
Heading north on the Moa road, take the Hotel Porto Santo/airport turnoff and continue for 2km past the airport runway to a black-sand beach at the river mouth where Antonio Maceo, Flor Crombet and others landed in 1895 to start the Second War of Independence. There's a memorial monument here and close-up views of El Yunque, though the beach itself isn't sunbathing territory.

Fábrica de Chocolate   FACTORY
The delicious sweet smells filling the air in this neck of the woods are concocted in the famous chocolate factory, 1km past the airport turnoff, opened not by Willy Wonka but by Che Guevara in 1963. It's not currently accepting visits (or golden tickets!).

Fábrica de Cucuruchu   FACTORY
Undoubtedly the only factory in the world that makes *cucurucho,* Baracoa's sweetest treat, wrapped in an environmentally friendly palm frond (see the boxed text p450). You can usually buy it on site.

◯ Tours

Organized tours are a good way to view Baracoa's hard-to-reach outlying sights, and the Cubatur and Ecotur offices on Plaza Independencia can book excursions including El Yunque (CUC$20), Parque Nacional Alejandro de Humboldt (CUC$22 to CUC$25), Río Toa (CUC$18 to CUC$20) and Boca de Yumurí (CUC$22).

José Ángel Delfino Pérez   GUIDED TOUR
(☑ 64-13-67) José arranges innovative, professional tours: the best head out toward Boca de Yumurí, taking in cacao plantations, chocolate tastings and isolated beaches (CUC$25), or encompass Punta de Maisí and lunch in the house of a *pescador* (fisherman) for CUC$57. The larger the group, the lower the per person rate. José does trips to Río Toa and Parque Nacional Alejandro de Humboldt, too. You can also contact him via the casa particular of Nilson Abad Guilaré.

✵ Festivals & Events

Semana de la Cultura Baracoesa   FESTIVAL
(◔ late Mar/early Apr) Locals hit the streets to celebrate the 1895 landing of Antonio Maceo.

🛏 Sleeping

★ Nilson Abad Guilaré   CASA PARTICULAR $
(☑ 64-31-23; abadcub@gmail.com; Flor Crombet No 143, btwn Ciro Frías & Pelayo Cuervo; r CUC$25; ✳) Nilson's a real gent who keeps one of the cleanest houses in Cuba. This fantastic self-contained apartment has a huge bathroom, kitchen access and roof terrace with sea views. The fish dinners with coconut sauce in Nilson's Bar-Restaurante La Terraza are to die for.

Isabel Castro Vilato   CASA PARTICULAR $
(☑ 64-22-67; Mariana Granjales No 35; r CUC$25) Down behind Hotel El Castillo, this green clapboard-and-stone house secretes two massive rooms and a beautiful terrace that would, were it public, be Baracoa's premier plaza.

Hostal la Habanera   HOTEL $
(☑ 64-52-73; Antonio Maceo No 126; s/d CUC$35/40; ✳) Atmospheric and inviting in a way only Baracoa can muster, La Habanera sits in a restored pastel-pink colonial mansion. The four front bedrooms share a street-facing balcony replete with tiled floor and rocking chairs: perfect for imbibing that quintessential Baracoa ambience

(street hawkers, hip-gyrating music, seafood a-frying in the restaurants). The downstairs lobby boasts a bar, a restaurant and an interesting selection of local books.

Hostal 1511 HOTEL $
(☑ 64-57-00; Ciro Frías, btwn Rubert López & Maceo; s/d CUC$35/40) The year 1511 is Baracoa's foundation date, and this new place is a landmark too for offering dead-central accommodations with abundant colonial vibe. The model ship in reception sets the tone for an overtly nautical decor (blues, whites) that works best in the more-charming upstairs rooms.

La Casona CASA PARTICULAR $
(☑ 64-21-33; Félix Ruenes No 1 Altos; r CUC$20-25) Rarely is a city's most central casa among its best, but the young hosts here have achieved that honor with this place: one 2nd-floor room, another on the way and a knockout terrace. And it's all spotless.

Casa Colonial Lucy CASA PARTICULAR $
(☑ 64-35-48; astralsol36@gmail.com; Céspedes No 29, btwn Rubert López & Antonio Maceo; r CUC$20; ❄) A perennial favorite, Casa Lucy – which dates from 1840 – has a lovely local character with patios, porches and flowering begonias. There are two rooms as well as terraces here on different levels and the atmosphere is quiet and secluded. Lucy's son can speak four languages and offers salsa lessons and massage.

Casa Colonial Ykira Mahiquez CASA PARTICULAR $
(☑ 64-38-81; Antonio Maceo No 168A, btwn Ciro Frías & Céspedes; r CUC$20; ❄) Welcoming and hospitable, Ykira is Baracoa's hostess with the mostess and serves a mean dinner made with homegrown herbs. Her cozy house is one block from the cathedral, with a full terrace and *mirador* with sea views.

Hotel la Rusa HOTEL $
(☑ 64-30-11; Máximo Gómez No 161; s/d CUC$25/30; ❄) Russian émigré Magdalena Rovieskuya (aka 'La Rusa') once posted aid to Castro's rebels up in the Sierra Maestra and first came to Baracoa in the 1930s. She built a 12-room hotel and became a local celebrity, receiving esteemed guests such as Errol Flynn, Che Guevara and Fidel Castro. After her death in 1978, La Rusa became a more modest government-run joint right on the seafront.

Casa Elexey & Dorkis CASA PARTICULAR $
(☑ 64-34-51; Flor Crombet No 58 Altos; r CUC$20-25; ❄) Upstairs at Elexey and Dorkis' place you'll find two clean nicely furnished rooms flooded with natural light. There's an *azulejo*-studded terrace with Atlantic views – ideal for a couple of days of lazy relaxation.

★ Hotel El Castillo HOTEL $$
(☑ 64-51-65; Loma del Paraíso; s/d CUC$44/60; ❄ ❄) You could recline like a colonial-era conquistador in this historic place housed in the hilltop Castillo de Seboruco, except that conquistadors didn't have access to swimming pools, satellite TV or a room maid who folds towels into ships, swans and the like. This fine Gaviota-run hotel has just added 28 rooms in a new cleverly integrated block, an addition that adds kudos to the jaw-dropping El Yunque views.

Hotel Porto Santo HOTEL $$
(☑ 64-51-06; Carretera del Aeropuerto; s/d CUC$44/60; P ❄ ❄) On the bay where Columbus, allegedly, planted his first cross is this peaceful, well-integrated low-rise hotel. Situated 4km from the town center and 200m from the airport, there are 36 more-than-adequate rooms all within earshot of the sea. A steep stairway leads down to a tiny, wave-lashed beach.

✗ Eating

After the dull monotony of just about everywhere else, eating in Baracoa is a full-on sensory experience. Cooking here is creative, tasty and – above all – different. To experience the real deal, eat in your casa particular.

Cafetería el Parque FAST FOOD $
(Antonio Maceo No 142; ⊙ 24hr) The favored meeting place of just about everyone in town, you're bound to end up here at this open terrace at some point, tucking into spaghetti and pizza or downing beers as you watch the world go by.

Casa del Chocolate CAFE $
(Antonio Maceo No 123; ⊙ 7:20am-11pm) It's enough to make even Willy Wonka wonder. You're sitting next to a chocolate factory but, more often than not, there's none to be had in this bizarre little casa just off the main square. On a good day it sells chocolate ice cream and the hot stuff in mugs.

BARACOAN CUISINE

Unlike countries such as Italy and France, Cuba doesn't really have a *regional* cuisine, at least not until you arrive in Baracoa where everything, including the food, is different. Home to the country's most fickle weather, Baracoa has used its wet microclimate and geographic isolation to jazz up notoriously unambitious Cuban cuisine with spices, sugar, exotic fruits and coconuts. Fish anchors most menus yet even the seafood can pull some surprises. Count on tasting freshwater prawns the size of mini-lobsters or tiny tadpole-like *teti* fish drawn from the Río Toa between July to January during a waning moon.

The biggest taste explosion is a locally concocted coconut sauce known as *lechita* – a mixture of coconut milk, tomato sauce, garlic and a medley of spices best served over prawns, *aguja* (swordfish) or dorado. Other main course accompaniments include *bacán,* raw green plantain melded with crabmeat and wrapped in a banana leaf; or *frangollo,* a similar concoction where the ground bananas are mixed with sugar.

Sweets are another Baracoa tour de force thanks largely to the ubiquity of the cocoa plant and the presence of the famous Che Guevara chocolate factory. Baracoan chocolate is sold all over the island, although the Museo del Cacao (p447) is an obvious sampling point. You're likely to get it for breakfast in your casa particular, stirred into a local hot-chocolate drink known as *chorote.* Baracoa's most unique culinary invention is undoubtedly *cucurucho,* a delicate mix of dried coconut, sugar, honey, papaya, guayaba, mandarin and nuts (no concoction is ever quite alike) that is wrapped in an ecologically friendly palm frond. There's a *cucurucho* factory on the coast road to Moa just past the chocolate factory but, by popular consensus, the best stuff is sold by the *campesinos* (country people) on La Farola coming into town from Guantánamo.

★ La Rosa Nautica   CARIBBEAN $$

(1 de Abril No 185 Altos; meals CUC$4-16; ⊘noon-midnight) Out on the airport road, this nautically themed 2nd-floor restaurant is now Baracoa's upmarket option, particularly if you can nab the cozy private eating area up above the main deck. Some of the city's best waiters preside over proceedings, and you could go for chicken, pizza or pasta besides the stand-out seafood options.

Restaurante la Punta   CARIBBEAN $$

(Fuerte de la Punta; ⊘10am-11pm) Cooled by Atlantic breezes, the Gaviota-run La Punta aims to impress with well-prepared, garnished food in the lovely historical surrounds of the La Punta fort. Go on a Saturday night when there's accompanying music.

★ Bar-Restaurante La Terraza   PALADAR $$

(Flor Crombet No 143, btwn Ciro Frías & Pelayo Cuervo; meals CUC$6-8; ⊘noon-3pm & 6:30-11pm) Up above his house on a spectaular two-level terrace decorated in quirky Afro-Caribbean style, Nilson Abad Guilaré serves some of the best food around, particularly if you like *pescado con leche de coco* (fish fillet with coconut sauce).

Paladar el Colonial   PALADAR $$

(José Martí No 123; mains CUC$10; ⊘lunch & dinner) The town's oldest paladar (privately owned restaurant) has been knocking out good food for years with an exotic Baracoan twist. Still run out of a handsome wooden clapboard house on Calle José Martí, the menu has become a bit more limited in recent times (less octopus and more chicken), though you still get the down-to-earth service and the delicious coconut sauce.

Self-Catering

Tienda la Primada   SUPERMARKET $

(Plaza Martí, cnr Ciro Frías; ⊘8:30am-4:30pm Mon-Sat, to noon Sun) Get in line for the good selection of groceries here.

Dulcerito la Criolla   BAKERY $

(José Martí No 178) This place sells bread, pastries and – when it feels like it – the famous Baracoan chocolate.

🍷 Drinking & Entertainment

★ El Ranchón   NIGHTCLUB

(admission CUC$1; ⊘from 9pm) Atop a long flight of stairs at the western end of Coroneles Galano, El Ranchón mixes an exhilarating hilltop setting with taped disco and salsa music and legions of resident *jineteras* (women who attach themselves to male foreigners). Maybe that's why it's so insanely popular. Watch your step on the way down – it's a scary 146-step drunken tumble.

★Casa de la Trova Victorino
Rodríguez   TRADITIONAL MUSIC
(Antonio Maceo No 149A) Cuba's smallest, zaniest, wildest and most atmospheric *casa de la trova* (*trova* house) rocks nightly to the voodoo-like rhythms of *changüí-son*. Order a mojito in a jam jar, sit back and enjoy the show.

Casa de la Cultura   CULTURAL CENTER
(Antonio Maceo No 124, btwn Frank País & Maraví) This venue does a wide variety of shows including some good rumba incorporating the textbook Cuban styles of *guaguancó*, *yambú* and *columbia* (subgenres of rumba). Go prepared for *mucho* audience participation. There's a good *spectaculo* (show) on the terrace, La Terraza, every Saturday at 11pm: expect rumba, Benny Moré, and the local hairdresser singing Omara Portuondo.

Cine-Teatro Encanto   CINEMA
(Antonio Maceo No 148) The town's only cinema is in front of the cathedral. It looks disused but you'll probably find it's open.

Estadio Manuel Fuentes Borges   SPORTS
From October to April, baseball games are held at this stadium situated, literally, on the beach. It's possibly the only ground in Cuba where players come into bat with the taste of fresh sea spray on their lips. It's just southeast of the Museo Municipal.

🛍 Shopping

Good art is easy to find in Baracoa and, like most things in this whimsical seaside town, it has its own distinctive flavor.

ARTex   SOUVENIRS
(José Martí, btwn Céspedes & Coroneles Galano) For the usual tourist fare check out this place.

Taller la Musa   ART
(Antonio Maceo No 124) Call by this place for typically imaginative Baracoan art. There's another studio in the Casa de la Cultura opposite.

ℹ Information

Banco de Crédito y Comercio (Antonio Maceo No 99; ⊙8am-2:30pm Mon-Fri)

Banco Popular de Ahorro (José Martí No 166; ⊙8-11:30am & 2-4:30pm Mon-Fri) Cashes traveler's checks.
Cadeca (José Martí No 241) Money exchange.
Clínica Internacional (☑64-10-37; cnr José Martí & Roberto Reyes; ⊙24hr) A newish place that treats foreigners; there's also a hospital 2km out of town on the road to Guantánamo.
Cubatur (Antonio Maceo No 181; ⊙8am-noon & 2-5pm Mon-Fri) Helpful office that organizes tours to El Yunque and Parque Nacional Alejandro de Humboldt.
Ecotur (☑64-36-65; Coronel Cardoso No 24; ⊙9am-5pm) Organizes more specialized nature tours to the Duaba, Toa and Yumurí rivers.
Etecsa Telepunto (cnr Antonio Maceo & Rafael Trejo; internet access per hr CUC$6; ⊙8:30am-7:30pm) Internet and international calls.
Infotur (Antonio Maceo, btwn Frank País & Maraví; ⊙8:30am-5:30pm) Very helpful.
Post Office (Antonio Maceo No 136; ⊙8am-8pm)
Radio CMDX 'La Voz del Toa' Broadcasts over 650AM.

ℹ Getting There & Away

The closest train station is in Guantánamo, 150km southwest.

AIR

Gustavo Rizo Airport (airport code BCA) is 4km northwest of the town, just behind the Hotel Porto Santo. The four weekly flights from Havana to Baracoa are with Aerocaribbean and Aerogaviota (CUC$125 to CUC$165 one way, Tuesday, Thursday, Friday and Sunday). Book via the Oficina de Reservaciones (☑64-53-74; Martí No 181).

The planes (and occasionally buses) out of Baracoa can be fully booked, so don't come here on a tight schedule without outbound reservations.

BUS

The National Bus Station (cnr Av Los Mártires & José Martí) has Víazul (www.viazul.com) buses to Guantánamo (CUC$10, three hours), continuing to Santiago de Cuba (CUC$15, five hours) daily at 2:15pm. Bus tickets can be reserved in advance through Cubatur for a CUC$5 commission, or you can usually stick your name on the list a day or so beforehand. Trucks to Moa (departures from 6am) also leave from here along the very bumpy road northwest.

Transtur has implemented a Saturday service from the main hotels via Moa to Holguín (CUC$30). Ask at Hotels El Castillo, La Habanera or Porto Santo.

LA FAROLA

Separated from the rest of the island by the velvety peaks of the Cuchillas del Toa, the only way in or out of Baracoa before the 1960s was by sea. However, 450 years of solitude finally came to an end in 1964 with the opening of La Farola (the lighthouse road), a present from Fidel Castro to Baracoa's loyal revolutionaries who had supported him during the war in the mountains.

Fifty-five kilometers in length, La Farola traverses the steep-sided Sierra del Puril before snaking its way precipitously down through a landscape of gray granite cliffs and pine-scented cloud forest, and falling with eerie suddenness upon the lush tropical paradise of the Atlantic coastline.

Giant ferns sprout from lichen-covered rocks; small wooden *campesino* (country) huts cling to sharp bends; and local hawkers appear, seemingly out of nowhere, holding up bananas, oranges and a sweet-tasting, local delicacy wrapped in a palm frond and known as *cucuruchu*.

Construction of La Farola actually began during the Batista era, but the project was indefinitely shelved when it ran into problems with engineering and funds (workers weren't paid). Reignited after the Revolution, the ambitious highway ultimately took 500 workers more than four years to build and consumed 300kg of concrete per square meter.

Today, La Farola remains the only fully paved route into Baracoa and is responsible for 75% of the town's supplies. Listed as one of the seven civil engineering wonders of modern Cuba (and the only one outside Havana), it crosses from the island's driest zone to its wettest and deposits travelers in what, for many, is its most magical and serendipitous destination.

ⓘ Getting Around

The best way to get to and from the airport is by taxi (CUC$5) or bici-taxi (CUC$2), if you're traveling light.

There's a helpful **Havanautos** (☎ 64-53-44) car-rental office at the airport. **Cubacar** (☎ 64-51-55) is at Hotel Porto Santo. The **Servi-Cupet gas station** (José Martí; ⊘24hr) is at the entrance to town and also 4km from the center, on the road to Guantánamo. If you're driving to Havana, note that the northern route through Moa and Holguín is fastest but the road disintegrates rapidly after Playa Maguana. Most locals prefer the La Farola route.

Bici-taxis around Baracoa should charge five pesos a ride, but they often ask 10 to 15 pesos from foreigners.

Most casas particulares will be able to procure you a bicycle for CUC$3 per day. The ultimate bike ride is the 20km ramble down to Playa Maguana, one of the most scenic roads in Cuba. Lazy daisies can rent mopeds for CUC$24 either at Cafetería el Parque or Hotel El Castillo.

Northwest of Baracoa

The rutted road heading out of town toward Moa is a green paradise flecked with palm groves, rustic farmsteads and serendipitous glimpses of the ocean.

◉ Sights & Activities

Finca Duaba
FARM

(⊘8am-7pm) 🅿 FREE Five kilometers out of Baracoa on the road to Moa and then 1km inland, Finca Duaba offers a fleeting taste of the Baracoan countryside. It's a verdant farm surrounded with profuse tropical plants and embellished with a short *cacao* (cocoa) **trail** that explains the history and characteristics of the plant. There's also a good *ranchón*-style restaurant and the opportunity to swim in the Río Duaba. A bici-taxi can drop you at the road junction.

Río Toa
RIVER

Ten kilometers northwest of Baracoa is the third-longest river on the north coast of Cuba and the country's most voluminous. The Toa is also an important bird and plant habitat. Cocoa trees and the ubiquitous coconut palms are grown in the Valle de Toa. A vast hydroelectric project on the Río Toa was abandoned after a persuasive campaign led by the Fundación de la Naturaleza y El Hombre convinced authorities it would do irreparable ecological damage; engineering and economic reasons also played a part.

The **Rancho Toa** is a Palmares restaurant reached via a right-hand turnoff just before the Toa bridge. You can organize boat or kayak trips here for CUC$5 to CUC$10 and watch acrobatic Baracoans scale *cocotero* (coconut palm). A traditional Cuban feast of whole roast pig is available if you can rustle up enough people (eight, usually).

Most of this region lies within the **Cuchillas del Toa Unesco Biosphere Reserve**, an area of 2083 sq km that incorporates the Alejandro de Humboldt World Heritage Site. This region contains Cuba's largest rainforest, with trees exhibiting many precious woods, and has a high number of endemic species.

El Yunque MOUNTAIN

Baracoa's rite of passage is the 8km (up and down) hike to the top of this moody, mysterious mountain. At 575m, El Yunque (the Anvil) isn't Kilimanjaro, but the views from the summit, and the flora and birdlife along the way, are stupendous. Cubatur offers this tour almost daily (CUC$18 per person, minimum two people). The fee covers admission, guide, transport and a sandwich. The hike is hot (bring up to 2L of water) and usually muddy. It starts from the campismo (camping installation) 3km past Finca Duaba (4km from the Baracoa–Moa road). Bank on seeing *tocororo* (Cuba's national bird), *zunzún* (the world's smallest bird), butterflies and *polymitas*.

If you're not up to bagging the peak itself, ask about the 7km **Sendero Juncal-Rencontra** that bisects fruit plantations and rainforest between the Duaba and Toa rivers. Ecotur in Baracoa has details.

Playa Maguana BEACH

Not quite the tranquil getaway it once was, Maguana is still nonetheless magical, a relatively undone Caribbean beach with a rustic food shack that is populated primarily by fun-seeking Cubans who roll up in their vintage American cars and haul their prized music boxes out of the boot. Aside from the fenced-off Villa Maguana and a couple of basic food concessions, there's no infrastructure here – all part of the attraction. Watch your valuables!

🛏 Sleeping & Eating

★ **Villa Maguana** HOTEL $$

(☑64-53-72; Carretera a Moa Km 20; s/d CUC$66/83; ᴾ❄) Knocking the socks off any Cuban all-inclusive resort is this delightful place 22km north of Baracoa, consisting of four rustic wooden villas housing 16 rooms in total. Environmental foresight sees it cling precariously to Maguana's famously dreamy setting above a bite-sized scoop of sand guarded by two rocky promontories. There's a restaurant and some less rustic luxuries in the rooms such as satellite TV, fridge and air-con.

Campismo el Yunque CABINS $

(☑64-52-62; r CUC$10) Simple Cuban-style campismo offering very basic cabins at the end of the Finca Duaba road, 9km outside of town. The El Yunque hike starts here.

Playa Maguana Snack Bar CARIBBEAN $

(☉9am-5pm) Right on the beach; this open-sided snack bar is good for cheese sandwiches, beer and rum.

Parque Nacional Alejandro de Humboldt

'Unmatched in the Caribbean' is a phrase often used to describe this most dramatic and diverse of Cuban national parks, named after German naturalist-explorer Alexander von Humboldt who first came here in 1801. The accolade is largely true. Designated a Unesco World Heritage Site in 2001, Humboldt's steep pine-clad mountains and creeping morning mists protect an unmatched ecosystem that is, according to Unesco, 'one of the most biologically diverse tropical island sites on earth.'

Perched above the Bahía de Taco, 40km northwest of Baracoa, lies 600-odd sq km of pristine forest and 2641 hectares of lagoon and mangroves. With 1000 flowering plant species and 145 types of fern, it is far and away the most diverse plant habitat in the entire Caribbean. Due to the toxic nature of the underlying rocks in the area, plants have been forced to adapt in order to survive. As a result, endemism here is high – 70% of the plants found here are endemic, as are nearly all 20 species of amphibians, 45% of the reptiles and many of the birds. Endangered bird species protected here include Cuban Amazon parrots, hook-billed kites and ivory-billed woodpeckers.

🏃 Activities

The park contains a small **visitors center** (Carretera a Moa) where you pay the CUC$10 park entrance fee. It's staffed with biologists and has a network of trails leading to waterfalls, a *mirador* and a massive karst system with caves around the Farallones de Moa. Four trails are currently open to the public, taking in only a tiny segment of the park's 594 sq km. Typically, you can't just wander around on your own. The available hikes are: **Balcón de Iberia**, at 7km the park's most challenging loop which bisects both agricultural land and pristine rainforest and includes a swim in a natural pool near the Salto de Agua Maya waterfall; **El Recreo**, a 2km stroll around the bay; and the **Bahía de Taco circuit**, which incorporates a boat trip (with a manatee-friendly motor developed by scientists here) through the mangroves and the idyllic horseshoe-shaped bay, plus a 2km hike. A new **hike** encompasses an eight-hour reconnoiter deeper into the forest, featuring bird and orchid observation. Each option is accompanied by a highly professional guide (if you're showing up independently get to the visitor center before 10am to secure one). Prices range from CUC$5 to CUC$10, depending on the hike, but most people organize an excursion through Cubatur in Baracoa which includes transport and a pit stop on Playa Maguana on the way back (CUC$24).

⊙ Getting There & Away

The park visitors center is approximately halfway between Baracoa and Moa. You can arrange a tour through an agency in Baracoa or get here independently. The gorgeously scenic road is a collection of holes but passable in a hire car if driven with care. This road continues into Holguín province, improving just before Moa.

Understand
Cuba

Cuba Today

Change. The word echoes like a mantra around Cuba. You hear it in the barber shop and at the taxi rank, in the paladar (privately owned restaurant) kitchen and on the beach, in the fresh-produce market and among the omnipresent gaggle of bici-taxi riders that congregate in the plaza.

Best on Film

Che: The Argentine (Steven Soderbergh; 2008) First part of the classic biopic focuses on Che's Cuban years.
Before Night Falls (Julian Schnabel; 2000) The life and struggles of Cuban writer Reinaldo Arenas.
Fresa y Chocolate (Tomás Gutiérrez Alea; 1993) Marries the improbable themes of homosexuality and communism.
El Ojo del Canario (Fernando Pérez; 2010) Pérez' atmospheric biopic of José Martí picked up numerous Latin film awards.

Best in Print

Our Man in Havana (Graham Greene; 1958) Greene pokes fun at both the British Secret Service and Batista's corrupt regime.
Cuba and the Night (Pico Iyer; 1996) Perhaps the most evocative book about Cuba ever written by a foreigner.
Dirty Havana Trilogy (Pedro Juan Gutiérrez; 2002) Dirty, itchy study of life and sex in Havana during the Special Period.
Che Guevara: A Revolutionary Life (Jon Lee Anderson; 1997) Anderson's meticulous research led to the unearthing of Che's remains in Bolivia.

As Raúl Castro's leadership comes into maturity there is a shaky optimism in the air, a cautious belief that the government might actually be doing something to kick-start the economy and improve the livelihoods of its people.

Raúl's Reforms

The modifications began tentatively in 2008 when newly inaugurated president Raúl Castro passed reforms that permitted Cubans access to tourist hotels, and allowed them to purchase mobile phones and myriad electronic goods; rights taken for granted in most democratic countries, but long out of reach to the average Cuban.

It was followed in January 2011 by the biggest economic and ideological shake-up since the country waved *adiós* to Batista. Intended to 'defend, maintain and continue perfecting socialism' by borrowing from capitalism, and to take the sting out of the worst global recession in living memory, the radical new laws aimed to lay off half a million government workers and stimulate the private sector by granting business licenses to 178 state-recognized professions – everything from hairdressers to disposable lighter refillers.

While people's mouths were still agape, the government went one step further in October 2011, legalizing car sales and allowing Cubans to buy and sell their homes for the first time in half a century. Perhaps the boldest move so far was a decree announced in late 2012 that allows Cubans to travel freely abroad for the first time since 1961.

How Far Will He Go?

By 2013 Cuba had witnessed its most dramatic economic shift in decades, with nearly 400,000 people working in the private sector, 250,000 more than in 2010. But it was still far from anything like Western-style capitalism. Some businesses are little more than tables full of old junk, others have just legalized what they were doing illegally for years. Then there are the nit-picking regulations – standard practice in Cuba – coupled with the perennial fear that the economic relaxation might be ephemeral, a solution to the worldwide recession. Yet, despite reams of red tape and a healthy suspicion of a government that has a habit of giving with one hand while taking away with the other, many Cubans remain sanguine. Some have even gone as far as to say that the charisma-challenged Raúl has achieved more in five years than his stubborn brother did in the previous 50. The big question is: how much farther is he prepared to go?

Meanwhile....90 Miles to the North

Meanwhile, on the other side of the Straits of Florida, the Obama administration has signaled its own aperture. Using his powers of presidential decree, the US's 44th president has eased restrictions on Cuban Americans traveling to Cuba and sanctioned more licensed people-to-people trips for curious Americans keen to indulge in organized (and legal) 'cultural exchange.' Nonetheless, the 50-year-old trade embargo remains the 'elephant in the room,' a divisive anachronism stoked by regular squabbles, the latest being the imprisonment of US citizen Alan Gross in March 2011, a development contractor accused by the Cubans of importing satellite equipment for domestic dissidents.

In the US, demographics may be the game-changer that finally brings some sense to the argument. Both now in their 80s, the Castro brothers have outlived most of their exiled enemies. Slowly, public opinion among Cubans in Florida is shifting toward a more moderate stance.

Unleashing the Future

With octogenarian Raúl announcing he will not govern beyond 2018, Cuba's future might yet find a more moderate path. For over half a century, the country's fate has been dictated by political extremes – aging revolutionaries on one hand and bitter exiles on the other. Stuck in the middle are 11 million Cuban people, many of them talented, determined and hungry for change. There's the hardworking casa particular owner dreaming of opening a hotel, the enterprising chef dabbling in fusion cuisine, the nostalgic exile eyeing a small Cuban-based business start-up. From Punto de Maisí to Cabo de San Antonio, Cuba is witnessing the reawakening of its creative energy. It's as if a crossbow that has been wound back for 50 years has suddenly been let go. You ain't seen nothing yet.

POPULATION: **11.07 MILLION**

PERCENTAGE OVER 65 YEARS: **12%**

LIFE EXPECTANCY: **77.8 YEARS**

INFANT MORTALITY: **4.83 PER 1000**

DOCTOR/PATIENT RATIO: **1:156**

LITERACY RATE: **99.8%**

if Cuba were 100 people

65 would be white
25 would be mixed
10 would be black

belief systems
(% of population)

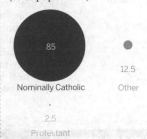

85
Nominally Catholic

12.5
Other

2.5
Protestant

population per sq km

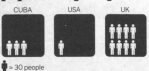

CUBA   USA   UK

≈ 30 people

History

Embellished by extraordinary feats of revolutionary derring-do, and plagued routinely by the meddling armies of foreign invaders, Cuba has achieved a historical importance far greater than its size would suggest. The underlying and – until the 1960s – ongoing historical themes have been external interference and internal strife, and the results of both have often been bloody.

Best Historical Sites

Museo de la Revolución (p94), Havana

Cuartel Moncada (p408), Santiago de Cuba

Comandancia de la Plata (p388), Granma

Fortaleza de San Carlos de la Cabaña (p87), Havana

A Turbulent Historical Trajectory

Since the arrival of Columbus in 1492, Cuba has witnessed a turbulent historical trajectory that has included genocide, slavery, two bitter independence wars, a period of corrupt and violent quasi-independence, and, finally, a populist revolution that, despite early promise, hit a metaphoric pause button. The fallout has led to the emigration of almost one-fifth of the Cuban population, mostly to the US.

For the sake of simplicity, the country's historical eras can be divided into three broad categories: pre-colonial, colonial and post-colonial. Before 1492 Cuba was inhabited by a trio of migratory civilizations that originated in the Orinoco Basin of South America before island-hopping north. Their cultures have been only partially evaluated to date, primarily because they left very little behind in the way of documentary evidence.

Cuba's colonial period was dominated by the Spanish and the divisive issue of slavery, which lasted from the 1520s until abolition in 1886. Slavery left deep wounds on Cuba's collective psyche, but its existence and final quashing was integral to the evolution of the country's highly distinctive culture, music, dance and religion. Understand this and you're halfway to understanding the complexities of the contemporary nation.

Post-colonial Cuba has had two distinctive sub-eras, the second of which can be further subdivided in two. The period from the defeat of Spain in 1898 to the Castro coup of 1959 is usually seen as an age of quasi-independence with a strong American influence. It was also a time

TIMELINE

BC 2000
The Guanahatabeys, Cuba's earliest known Stone Age civilization, is known to be living in the caves along the coast of present-day Pinar del Río province.

AD 1100
Taíno people start arriving in Cuba after leapfrogging their way across the islands of the Lesser Antilles from the Orinoco Basin in present-day Venezuela.

1492
Christopher Columbus lands in Cuba in modern-day Holguín province. He sails for a month along the coast, as far as Baracoa, planting religious crosses and meeting with the indigenous Taínos.

characterized by violence, corruption and frequent insurrection on the part of opposition groups intent on toppling the government.

The post-1959 Castro era breaks conveniently into two stages: the age of Soviet domination from 1961 to 1991, and the historical trajectory from the Special Period till the present day, when Cuba, despite its devastating economic difficulties, became a truly independent power for the first time.

Pre-Colonial Cuba

The first known civilization in Cuba was that of the Guanahatabeys, a primitive Stone Age people who lived in caves and eked out a meager existence as hunter-gatherers. At some point over a 2000-year period, the Guanahatabeys were gradually pushed west into what is now Pinar del Río province, displaced by the arrival of another pre-ceramic culture known as the Siboneys. The Siboneys were a slightly more developed group of fishermen and small-scale farmers who settled down comparatively peacefully on the archipelago's sheltered southern coast. By the second millennium AD, they were also gradually displaced by the more sophisticated Taíno, who liked to use Siboneys as domestic servants.

The Taínos first started arriving in Cuba around 1100 AD in a series of waves, concluding a migration process that had begun on mainland South America several centuries earlier. Related to the Greater Antilles Arawaks, the new peace-loving natives were escaping the barbarism of the cannibalistic Caribs who had colonized the Lesser Antibes, pushing the Taínos northwest into Puerto Rico, Hispaniola and Cuba.

Taíno culture was more developed and sophisticated than that of its predecessors; the adults practiced a form of cranial transformation by flattening the soft skulls of their young children, and groups lived together in villages characterized by their thatched *bohios* (rustic huts) and *bateys* (communal 'plazas').

The Taínos were skillful farmers, weavers, ceramicists and boat-builders, and their complex society exhibited an organized system of participatory government that was overseen by a series of local *caciques* (chiefs). Sixty percent of the crops still grown in Cuba today were pioneered by Taíno farmers, who even planted cotton for use in hammocks, fishing nets and bags. They were also the first of the world's pre-Columbian cultures to nurture the delicate tobacco plant into a form that could easily be processed for smoking.

Columbus described the Taíno with terms such as 'gentle,' 'sweet,' 'always laughing' and 'without knowledge of what is evil,' which makes the genocide that came later even harder to comprehend. Estimates vary wildly as to how many indigenous people populated Cuba pre-Columbus, though 100,000 is a good consensus figure. Within 30 years 90% of the Taínos had been wiped out.

Independence War Heroes

Carlos Manuel de Céspedes (1819–74)

Máximo Gómez (1836–1905)

Calixto García (1839–98)

Ignacio Agramonte (1841–73)

Antonio Maceo (1845–96)

1508	1511	1522	1555
Spanish navigator Sebastián de Ocampo circumnavigates Cuba, establishing that it's an island and disproving Columbus' long-held idea that it might be a peninsula of the Asian continent.	Diego Velázquez lands at Baracoa with 400 colonizers, including Hernán Cortés (the future colonizer of Mexico). The new arrivals construct a fort and quickly make enemies of the local Taínos.	The first slaves arrive in Cuba from Africa, ushering in an era that was to last for 350 years and have a profound effect on the development of Cuban culture.	The age of piracy is inaugurated. French buccaneer Jaques de Sores attacks Havana and burns it to the ground. In response, the Spanish start building a huge network of forts.

Colonial Cuba
Columbus & Colonization

When Columbus neared Cuba on October 27, 1492, he described it as 'the most beautiful land human eyes had ever seen,' naming it 'Juana' in honor of a Spanish heiress. But deluded in his search for the kingdom of the Great Khan, and finding little gold in Cuba's lush and heavily forested interior, Columbus quickly abandoned the territory in favor of Hispaniola (modern-day Haiti and the Dominican Republic).

'DISCOVERERS' OF CUBA

Cuba wasn't discovered by Europeans; people had lived on the archipelago for millennia before 1492. Nonetheless, Cubans popularly like to claim that their country has had three nominal 'discoverers.' The role of the first, Christopher Columbus, is well documented, but the contributions of the second and third deserve more explanation.

Alexander von Humboldt (1769–1859)

Arriving in Cuba in 1800, German naturalist and geographer Humboldt was one of the first outsiders to recognize Cuba's special cultural, ecological and historical heritage. For him, the archipelago belonged neither to North nor South America, but to an independent domain of its own. Its uniqueness was embedded in its ecology. Humboldt was amazed by Cuba's striking endemism and vast array of unique species, describing it as a kind of Caribbean Galapagos where conflicting natural processes appeared to exist in contradiction. He also noted marked differences between Cuba and the other countries in South America. Though colonially backward, Cuba was, nonetheless, highly metropolitan; it had a strong national identity but still relied heavily on its Spanish overlords; and, while ostensibly civilized, it maintained a highly uncivilized slave system (which ultimately lingered longer than any other country in Latin America, bar Brazil). Above all, Humboldt concluded, Cuba was fascinatingly complex.

Fernando Ortíz (1881–1969)

Ortíz was an anthropologist and Renaissance man from Havana who, building on Humboldt's themes, concentrated his studies on the archipelago's unique cultural synthesis made up of a mix of African slaves, colonizing Spaniards, French exiles, immigrant Chinese and watered-down remnants of pre-Columbian Taíno culture. Ortíz called what had happened in Cuba 'transculturation,' the melding of old imported cultures into a new one that was unique and original in its own right. His specialty was black culture (he invented the term 'afrocuban') and his studies in this area led to a far better understanding and appreciation of African art, music, religion and language in Cuban culture. In 1955 Ortíz was nominated for the Nobel Peace Prize for his vast anthropological work and his 'love for culture and humankind.'

1607	1741	1762	1791
Havana is declared capital of Cuba and becomes the annual congregation point for Spain's Caribbean treasure fleet, loaded up with silver from Peru and gold from Mexico.	A British Navy contingent under the command of Admiral Edward Vernon briefly captures Guantánamo Bay during the War of Jenkin's Ear, but is sent packing after a yellow fever epidemic.	Spain joins France in the Seven Years' War, provoking the British to attack and take Havana. They occupy Cuba for 11 months before exchanging it for Florida in 1763.	A bloody slave rebellion in Haiti causes thousands of white French planters to flee west to Cuba, where they set up the earliest coffee plantations in the New World.

The colonization of Cuba didn't begin until nearly 20 years later in 1511, when Diego Velázquez de Cuéllar led a flotilla of four ships and 400 men from Hispaniola to conquer the island for the Spanish Crown. Docking near present-day Baracoa, the conquistadors promptly set about establishing seven *villas* (towns) on the main island – Havana, Trinidad, Baracoa, Bayamo, Camagüey, Santiago de Cuba and Sancti Spíritus – in a bid to bring their new colony under strong central rule. Watching nervously from the safety of their *bohíos* (thatched huts), a scattered population of Taínos looked on with a mixture of fascination and fear.

Despite Velázquez's attempts to protect the local Indians from the gross excesses of the Spanish swordsmen, things quickly got out of hand and the invaders soon found that they had a full-scale rebellion on their hands. Leader of the embittered and short-lived insurgency was the feisty Hatuey, an influential Taíno *cacique* and archetype of the Cuban resistance. Hatuey was eventually captured and burned at the stake, Inquisition-style, for daring to challenge the iron fist of Spanish rule.

With the resistance decapitated, the Spaniards set about emptying Cuba of its relatively meager gold and mineral reserves, using the beleaguered natives as forced labor. Slavery was nominally banned under a papal edict, but the Spanish forged a legal loophole by introducing a ruthless *encomienda* system, whereby thousands of natives were rounded up and forced to work for Spanish landowners on the pretext that they were receiving free 'lessons' in Christianity. The brutal system lasted 20 years before the 'Apostle of the Indians,' Fray Bartolomé de Las Casas, appealed to the Spanish Crown for more humane treatment, and in 1542 the *encomiendas* were abolished for the indigenous people. For the unfortunate Taínos, the call came too late. Those who had not already been worked to death in the gold mines quickly succumbed to fatal European diseases such as smallpox, and by 1550 only about 5000 scattered survivors remained.

PUEBLOS INDIOS

In the 17th century the Spanish herded the remaining indigenous population into towns known as *pueblos indios*. Old and New World cultures cross-fertilized, allowing Indian practices and words to seep into everyday Cuban life.

The Independence Wars

With its brutal slave system established, the Spanish ruled their largest Caribbean colony with an iron fist for the next 200 years despite a brief occupation by the British in 1792 (see p85). Cuba's creole landowners worried about a repetition of Haiti's brutal 1791 slave rebellion, held back when the rest of Latin America took up arms against the Spanish in the 1810s and 1820s. As a result, the nation's independence wars came more than half a century after the rest of Latin America had broken away from Spain. But when they arrived, they were no less impassioned – or bloody.

The First Independence War

Fed up with Spain's reactionary policies and enviously eyeing Lincoln's new American dream to the north, *criollo* (Spaniards born in the Americas)

1808	1850	1868	1878
Pre-empting the Monroe Doctrine, US president Thomas Jefferson proclaims Cuba 'the most interesting addition which could be made to our system of states,' thus beginning a 200-year US fixation.	Venezuelan filibuster Narciso López raises the Cuban flag for the first time in Cárdenas during an abortive attempt to 'liberate' the colony from Spain.	Céspedes frees his slaves in Manzanillo and proclaims the *Grito de Yara*, Cuba's first independence cry and the beginning of a 10-year war against the Spanish.	The Pact of El Zanjón ends the First War of Independence. Cuban general Antonio Maceo issues the Protest of Baraguá and resumes hostilities the following year before disappearing into exile.

landowners around Bayamo began plotting rebellion in the late 1860s. The spark was auspiciously lit on October 10, 1868, when Carlos Manuel de Céspedes, a budding poet, lawyer and sugar-plantation owner, launched an uprising from his Demajagua sugar mill near Manzanillo in the Oriente. Calling for the abolition of slavery and freeing his own slaves in an act of solidarity, Céspedes proclaimed the famous *Grito de Yara*, a cry of liberty for an independent Cuba, encouraging other disillusioned separatists to join him. For the colonial administrators in Havana, such an audacious bid to wrest control was an act tantamount to treason. The furious Spanish reacted accordingly.

Fortunately for the loosely organized rebels, the cagey Céspedes had done his military homework. Within weeks of the historic *Grito de Yara*, the diminutive lawyer-turned-general had raised an army of more than 1500 men and marched defiantly on Bayamo, taking the city in a matter of days. But initial successes soon turned to lengthy deadlock. A tactical decision not to invade western Cuba, along with an alliance between *peninsulares* (Spaniards born in Spain but living in Cuba) and the Spanish, soon put Céspedes on the back foot. Temporary help arrived in the shape of *mulato* (mixed-race) general Antonio Maceo, a tough and uncompromising Santiagüero, nicknamed the 'Bronze Titan' for his ability to defy death on countless occasions, and the equally formidable Dominican Máximo Gómez. But despite economic disruption and the periodic destruction of the sugar crop, the rebels lacked a dynamic political leader capable of uniting them behind a singular ideological cause.

With the loss of Céspedes in battle in 1874, the war dragged on for another four years, reducing the Cuban economy to tatters and leaving an astronomical 200,000 Cubans and 80,000 Spanish dead. Finally, in February 1878 a lackluster pact was signed at El Zanjón between the uncompromising Spanish and the exhausted separatists, a rambling and largely worthless agreement that solved nothing and acceded little to the rebel cause. Maceo, disgusted and disillusioned, made his feelings known in the antidotal 'Protest of Baraguá,' but after an abortive attempt to restart the war in 1879, both he and Gómez disappeared into a prolonged exile.

The Second Independence War

Cometh the hour, cometh the man. José Martí – poet, patriot, visionary and intellectual – had grown rapidly into a patriotic figure of Bolívarian proportions in the years following his ignominious exile in 1871, not just in Cuba but in the whole of Latin America. After his arrest at the age of 16 during the First War of Independence for a minor indiscretion, Martí had spent 20 years formulating his revolutionary ideas abroad in places as diverse as Guatemala, Mexico and the US. Although impressed by American business savvy and industriousness, he was equally repelled by

Che Guevara – whose father's family name was Guevara Lynch – can trace his Celtic roots back to a Patrick Lynch, who was born in Galway in Ireland in 1715, and who emigrated to Buenos Aires via Bilbao in 1749.

1886	1892	1895
After more than 350 years of exploitation and cross-Atlantic transportation, Cuba becomes the second-last country in the Americas to abolish slavery.	From exile in the US, José Martí galvanizes popular support and forms the Cuban Revolutionary Party, starting to lay the groundwork for the resumption of hostilities against Spain.	José Martí and Antonio Maceo arrive in Cuba to ignite the Second Independence War. Martí is killed at Dos Ríos in May and is quickly elevated to a martyr.

BRENT WINEBRENNER / GETTY IMAGES ©

➜ José Martí statue

the country's all-consuming materialism and was determined to present a workable Cuban alternative.

Dedicating himself passionately to the cause of the resistance, Martí wrote, spoke, petitioned and organized tirelessly for independence for well over a decade and by 1892 had enough momentum to coax Maceo and Gómez out of exile under the umbrella of the Partido Revolucionario Cubano (PRC; Cuban Revolutionary Party). At last, Cuba had found its Bolívar.

Predicting that the time was right for another revolution, Martí and his compatriots set sail for Cuba in April 1895, landing near Baracoa two months after PRC-sponsored insurrections had tied down Spanish forces in Havana. Raising an army of 40,000 men, the rebels promptly regrouped and headed west, engaging the Spanish for the first time on May 19 in a place called Dos Ríos. It was on this bullet-strafed and strangely anonymous battlefield that Martí, conspicuous on his white horse and dressed in his trademark black dinner suit, was shot and killed as he charged suicidally toward the Spanish lines. Had he lived he would certainly have become Cuba's first president; instead, he became a hero and a martyr whose life and legacy would inspire generations of Cubans in years to come.

Conscious of mistakes made during the First War of Independence, Gómez and Maceo stormed west with a scorched-earth policy that left everything from the Oriente to Matanzas in flames. Early victories quickly led to a sustained offensive and, by January 1896, Maceo had broken through to Pinar del Río, while Gómez was tying down Spanish forces near Havana. The Spaniards responded with an equally ruthless general named Valeriano Weyler, who built countrywide north–south fortifications to restrict the rebels' movements. In order to break the underground resistance, *guajiros* (country people) were forced into camps in a process called *reconcentración,* and anyone supporting the rebellion became liable for execution. The brutal tactics started to show results, and on December 7, 1896, the Mambís (the name for the 19th-century rebels fighting Spain) suffered a major military blow when Antonio Maceo was killed south of Havana trying to break out to the east.

Enter the Americans

By this time Cuba was a mess: thousands were dead, the country was in flames, and William Randolph Hearst and the US tabloid press were leading a hysterical war campaign characterized by sensationalized, often inaccurate reports about Spanish atrocities.

Preparing perhaps for the worst, US battleship *Maine* was sent to Havana in January 1898, on the pretext of 'protecting US citizens.' Its touted task never saw fruition. On February 15, 1898, the *Maine* exploded out of

José Martí Sites

Museo-Casa Natal de José Natal, Havana

Memorial a José Martí (p99), Havana

Cemeterio Santa Ifigenia (p412), Santiago de Cuba

Dos Ríos (p388), Granma

In the 1880s there were over 100,000 Chinese people living in Cuba, mainly as cheap labor on sugar plantations in and around the Havana region.

1896	1898	1902	1920
After sustaining more than 20 injuries in a four-decade military career, Antonio Maceo meets his end at Cacahual, Havana, where he is killed in an ambush.	Following the loss of the battleship USS *Maine*, the US declares war on Spain and defeats its forces near Santiago. A four-year US occupation begins.	Cuba gains nominal independence from the US and elects Tomás Estrada Palma as its president. US troops are called back three times within the first 15 years of the republic.	Sharp increases in world sugar prices after WWI spearhead the so-called 'Dance of the Millions' in Cuba. Huge fortunes are made overnight. A heavy economic crash quickly follows.

the blue in Havana Harbor, killing 266 US sailors. The Spanish claimed it was an accident, the Americans blamed the Spanish, and some Cubans accused the US, saying it provided a convenient pretext for intervention. Despite several investigations conducted over the following years, the real cause of the explosion may remain one of history's great mysteries, as the hulk of the ship was scuttled in deep waters in 1911.

After the *Maine* debacle, the US scrambled to take control. They offered Spain US$300 million for Cuba and, when this deal was rejected, demanded a full withdrawal of the Spanish from the island. The long-awaited US-Spanish showdown that had been simmering imperceptibly beneath the surface for decades had finally resulted in war.

The only important land battle of the conflict was on July 1, when the US Army attacked Spanish positions on San Juan Hill just east of Santiago de Cuba. Despite vastly inferior numbers and limited, antiquated weaponry, the under-siege Spanish held out bravely for over 24 hours before future US President Theodore Roosevelt broke the deadlock by leading a celebrated cavalry charge of the Rough Riders up San Juan Hill. It was the beginning of the end for the Spaniards, and an unconditional surrender was offered to the Americans on July 17, 1898.

Post-Colonial Cuba
Independence or Dependence?
On May 20, 1902, Cuba became an independent republic – or did it? Despite three years of blood, sweat and sacrifice during the Spanish-Cuban-American War, no Cuban representatives were invited to the historic peace treaty held in Paris in 1898 that had promised Cuban independence *with conditions*. The conditions were contained in the infamous Platt Amendment, a sly addition to the US 1901 Army Appropriations Bill that gave the US the right to intervene militarily in Cuba whenever it saw fit. The US also used its significant leverage to secure itself a naval base in Guantánamo Bay in order to protect its strategic interests in the Panama Canal region. Despite some opposition in the US and a great deal more in Cuba, the Platt Amendment was passed by Congress and was written into Cuba's 1902 constitution. For Cuban patriots, the USA had merely replaced Spain as the new colonizer and enemy. The repercussions have been causing bitter feuds for over a century and still continue today.

The Batista Era
Fulgencio Batista, a *holguinero* (person from Holguín) of mixed race from the town of Banes, was a wily and shrewd negotiator who presided over Cuba's best and worst attempts to establish an embryonic democracy in the 1940s and '50s. After an army officers' coup in 1933, he had

A 1976 book entitled *How the Battleship Maine Was Destroyed* concluded that the explosion of the *Maine* in Havana Harbor in 1898 was caused by the spontaneous combustion of coal in the ship's bunker.

1925	1933	1940	1952
Gerardo Machado is elected president and institutes a massive program of public works, but his eight-year reign turns increasingly despotic as his declining popularity leads to resentful unrest.	The 1933 revolution is sparked by an Army Officers' Coup that deposes the Machado dictatorship and installs Fulgencio Batista in power.	Cuba adopts the '1940 Constitution', considered one of the most progressive documents of its era, guaranteeing rights to employment, property, minimum wage, education and social security.	Batista stages a bloodless military coup, canceling the upcoming Cuban elections in which an ambitious young lawyer named Fidel Castro was due to stand.

taken power almost by default, gradually worming his way into the power vacuum it left amid the corrupt factions of a dying government. From 1934 onwards Batista served as the army's chief of staff and, in 1940 in a relatively free and fair election, he was duly elected president. Given an official mandate, Batista began to enact a wide variety of social reforms and set about drafting Cuba's most liberal and democratic constitution to date. But neither the liberal honeymoon nor Batista's good humor were to last. Stepping down after the 1944 election, the former army sergeant handed power over to the politically inept President Ramón Grau San Martín, and corruption and inefficiency soon reigned like never before.

The Revolutionary Spark is Lit

Aware of his underlying popularity and sensing an easy opportunity to line his pockets with one last big paycheck, Batista cut a deal with the American Mafia, promising to give them carte blanche in Cuba in return for a cut of their gambling profits, and positioned himself for a comeback. On March 10, 1952, three months before scheduled elections that he looked like losing, Batista staged a military coup. Wildly condemned by opposition politicians inside Cuba, but recognized by the US government two weeks later, Batista quickly let it be known, when he suspended various constitutional guarantees including the right to strike, that his second incarnation wouldn't be as enlightened as his first.

After Batista's coup, a revolutionary circle formed in Havana around the charismatic figure of Fidel Castro, a lawyer by profession and a gifted orator who had been due to stand in the canceled 1952 elections. Supported by his younger brother Raúl and aided intellectually by his trusty lieutenant Abel Santamaría (later tortured to death by Batista's thugs), Castro saw no alternative to the use of force in ridding Cuba of its detestable dictator. Low on numbers but determined to make a political statement, Castro led 119 rebels in an attack on the strategically important Moncada army barracks in Santiago de Cuba on July 26, 1953. The audacious and poorly planned assault failed dramatically when the rebels' driver (who was from Havana) took the wrong turning in Santiago's badly signposted streets and the alarm was raised.

Fooled, flailing and hopelessly outnumbered, 64 of the Moncada conspirators were rounded up by Batista's army and brutally tortured and executed. Castro and a handful of others managed to escape into the nearby mountains, where they were found a few days later by a sympathetic army lieutenant named Sarría, who had been given instructions to kill them. 'Don't shoot, you can't kill ideas!' Sarría is alleged to have shouted on finding Castro and his exhausted colleagues. By taking Castro to jail instead of doing away with him, Sarría ruined his military career, but saved Fidel's life. (One of Fidel's first acts after the Revolution

---

In December 1946 the Mafia convened the biggest ever get-together of North American mobsters in Havana's Hotel Nacional, under the pretence that they were going to see a Frank Sinatra concert.

Cuba's First Three Presidents

Tomás Estrada Palma (1902–06)

José Miguel Gómez (1906–13)

Mario García Menocal (1913–21)

1953	1956	1958	1959
Castro leads a band of rebels in a disastrous attack on the Moncada army barracks in Santiago. He uses his subsequent trial as a platform to expound his political plans.	The *Granma* yacht lands in eastern Cuba with Castro and 81 rebels aboard. Decimated by the Cuban Army, only about a dozen survive to regroup in the Sierra Maestra.	Che Guevara masterminds an attack against an armored train in Santa Clara, a military victory that finally forces Batista to concede power. The rebels march triumphantly on Havana.	Castro is welcomed ecstatically in Havana. The new government passes the historic First Agrarian Reform Act. Camilo Cienfuegos' plane goes missing over the Cuban coast off Camagüey.

triumphed was to release Sarría from prison and give him a commission in the revolutionary army.) Castro's capture soon became national news, and he was put on trial in the full glare of the media spotlight. Fidel defended himself in court, writing an eloquent and masterfully executed speech that he later transcribed into a comprehensive political manifesto entitled *History Will Absolve Me*. Basking in his newfound legitimacy and backed by a growing sense of dissatisfaction with the old regime in the country at large, Castro was sentenced to 15 years' imprisonment on Isla de Pinos (a former name for Isla de la Juventud). Cuba was well on the way to gaining a new national hero.

In February 1955 Batista won the presidency in what were widely considered to be fraudulent elections and, in an attempt to curry favor with growing internal opposition, agreed to an amnesty for all political prisoners, including Castro. Believing that Batista's real intention was to assassinate him once out of jail, Castro fled to Mexico, leaving Baptist schoolteacher Frank País in charge of a fledgling underground resistance campaign that the vengeful Moncada veterans had christened the 26th of July Movement (M-26-7).

The Revolution

In Mexico City, Castro and his compatriots plotted and planned afresh, drawing in key new figures such as Camilo Cienfuegos and Argentine doctor Ernesto 'Che' Guevara, both of whom added strength and panache to the nascent army of disaffected rebel soldiers. On the run from the Mexican police and determined to arrive in Cuba in time for an uprising that Frank País had planned for late November 1956 in Santiago de Cuba, Castro and 81 companions set sail for the island on November 25 in an old and overcrowded leisure yacht named *Granma*. After seven dire days at sea they arrived at Playa Las Coloradas near Niquero in the Oriente on December 2 (two days late). Following a catastrophic landing – 'It wasn't a disembarkation; it was a shipwreck,' a wry Guevara later commented – they were spotted and routed by Batista's soldiers in a sugarcane field at Alegría de Pío three days later.

Of the 82 rebel soldiers who had left Mexico, little more than a dozen managed to escape. Splitting into three tiny groups, the survivors wandered around hopelessly for days half-starved, wounded and assuming that the rest of their compatriots had been killed in the initial skirmish. 'At one point I was Commander in Chief of myself and two other people,' Fidel commented sagely years later. However, with the help of the local peasantry, the dozen or so hapless soldiers finally managed to reassemble two weeks later in Cinco Palmas, a clearing in the shadows of the Sierra Maestra, where a half-delirious Fidel gave a rousing and premature

---

1000 LAWS

Castro's government passed over 1000 laws in its first year (1959), including rent and electricity cost reductions, the abolition of racial discrimination and the First Agrarian Reform Act.

In 1991 Castro declared a five-year *período especial* (Special Period) austerity program that sent living standards plummeting.

1961	1962	1967
Cuban mercenaries with US backing stage an unsuccessful invasion at the Bay of Pigs. The US declares a full trade embargo. Cuba embarks on a highly successful literacy campaign.	The discovery of medium-range nuclear missiles in Cuba, installed by the Soviet Union, brings the world to the brink of nuclear war in the so-called Cuban Missile Crisis.	Che Guevara is hunted down and executed in Bolivia in front of CIA observers after a 10-month abortive guerrilla war in the mountains.

→ Che Guevara memorial

HUMAN RIGHTS

'Human rights' in Cuba has long been the revolution's Achilles heel. To speak out against the government in this tightly controlled, politically paranoid society is a serious and heavily punishable crime that – if it doesn't first land you in jail – is likely to lead to job stagnation, petty harassment and social ostracism.

The Castro era got off to a bad start in January 1959 when the revolutionary government – under the auspices of Che Guevara – rounded up Batista's top henchmen and summarily executed them inside Havana's La Cabaña fort with barely a lawyer in sight. Within a matter of months the Cuban press had been silenced and worried onlookers in the US were vociferously calling 'foul.'

In the years since, Cuba has scored badly on most global human rights indices with the world's two most respected human rights bodies, Amnesty International and Human Rights Watch, regularly berating the government for its refusal to respect the rights of assembly, association and expression, and other basic civil liberties.

Cuba's international image took another hit during 2003's 'Black Spring' when the government rounded up 75 dissidents, who they claimed were agents of the US, and handed them all lengthy jail terms. After an international outcry, all of the dissidents were eventually released, the last in 2011. Notwithstanding, harassment and intimidation of dissidents, including peaceful protesters such as the 'Ladies in White,' continues.

Cuba's supporters often justify the alleged human rights violations with tit-for-tat arguments. When the Americans complain of Cuban jail conditions and purported use of torture, they reply 'Guantánamo.' When the US questions the case of imprisoned American development contractor Alan Gross, they point to the 'Cuban Five' (five Cubans imprisoned in the US on similarly flimsy spying charges).

There have been improvements in recent years. Gay persecution, once rife at all levels of Cuban society, is largely a thing of the past. Religious persecution is similarly rare. Freedom of expression and the press, however, remain frustratingly stifled, although, in the internet age, some high-profile bloggers, most notably Yoani Sánchez, have managed to reach an international audience.

HISTORY POST-COLONIAL CUBA

victory speech. 'We will win this war,' he proclaimed confidently. 'We are just beginning the fight!'

The comeback began on January 17, 1957, when the guerrillas scored an important victory by sacking a small army outpost on the south coast in Granma province called La Plata. This was followed in February by a devastating propaganda coup when Fidel persuaded *New York Times* journalist Herbert Matthews to come up into the Sierra Maestra to interview him. The resulting article made Castro internationally famous and gained him much sympathy among liberal Americans. Suffice to say, by this point he wasn't the only anti-Batista agitator. On March 13, 1957,

1968	1970	1980	1988
The Cuban government nationalizes 58,000 small businesses in a sweeping socialist reform package. Everything falls under strict government control.	Castro attempts to achieve a 10-million-ton sugar harvest. The plan fails and Cuba begins to wean itself off its unhealthy dependence on its mono-crop.	Following an incident at the Peruvian embassy, Castro opens the Cuban port of Mariel. Within six months 125,000 have fled the island for the US in the so-called Mariel Boatlift.	Cuban forces play a crucial role in the Battle of Cuito Cuanavale in Angola, a serious defeat for the white South African army and its system of apartheid.

university students led by José Antonio Echeverría attacked the Presidential Palace in Havana in an unsuccessful attempt to assassinate Batista. Thirty-two of the 35 attackers were shot dead as they fled, and reprisals were meted out on the streets of Havana with a new vengeance. Cuba was rapidly disintegrating into a police state run by military-trained thugs.

Elsewhere passions were running equally high. In September 1957 naval officers in the normally tranquil city of Cienfuegos staged an armed revolt and set about distributing weapons among the disaffected populace. After some bitter door-to-door fighting, the insurrection was brutally crushed and the ringleaders rounded up and killed, but for the revolutionaries the point had been made. Batista's days were numbered.

Back in the Sierra Maestra, Fidel's rebels overwhelmed 53 Batista soldiers at an army post in El Uvero in May and captured more badly needed supplies. The movement seemed to be gaining momentum and ,despite losing Frank País to a government assassination squad in Santiago de Cuba in July, support and sympathy around the country was starting to mushroom. By the beginning of 1958 Castro had established a fixed headquarters at La Plata (not to be confused with the La Plata in

THE SPECIAL PERIOD

Following the demise of the Soviet Union in 1991, the Cuban economy – reliant since the 1960s on Soviet subsides – went into freefall. Almost overnight half of the country's industrial factories closed, the transport sector ground to a halt, and the national economy shrunk by as much as 60%.

Determined to defend the revolution at all costs, Fidel Castro stubbornly battened down the hatches and announced that Cuba was entering a 'Special Period in a Time of Peace' *(período especial)*, a package of extreme austerity measures that reinforced widespread rationing and made acute shortages an integral part of everyday life. It was an unprecedented turnaround that quickly resonated throughout all levels of society. Suddenly Cubans, who had been relatively well-off a year or so earlier, faced a massive battle just to survive.

The stories of how ordinary Cubans got through the darkest days of the Special Period are as remarkable as they are shocking. In three fearsome years the average Cuban lost over a third of their body weight and saw meat pretty much eradicated from their diet. In the social forum, the Special Period invented a whole new culture of conservation and innovation, and elements of this communal belt-tightening still characterize the Cuban way of life today.

The worst years of the Special Period were 1991–94, though the recovery was slow with proper progress only possible after Cuba forged closer ties with Venezuela (and its oil) in the early 2000s.

1991	1993	2002	2003
The Soviet Union collapses and Cuba heads toward its worst economic collapse of modern times, entering what Castro calls a 'Special Period in a Time of Peace.'	Attempting to revive itself from its economic coma, Cuba legalizes the US dollar, opens up the country to tourism and allows limited forms of private enterprise.	Half of Cuba's sugar refineries are closed, signaling the end of a three-century-long addiction to the boom-bust mono-crop. Laid-off sugar workers continue to draw salaries and are offered free education.	The Bush administration tightens the noose for US citizens traveling to Cuba. Many political dissidents are arrested by Cuban authorities in an island-wide crackdown.

Granma province) in a cloud forest high up in the Sierra Maestra, and was broadcasting propaganda messages from Radio Rebelde (710AM and 96.7FM) all across Cuba. The tide was starting to turn.

Sensing his popularity waning, Batista sent an army of 10,000 men into the Sierra Maestra in May 1958, on a mission known as Plan FF (*Fin de Fidel* or End of Fidel). The intention was to liquidate Castro and his merry band of loyal guerrillas who had now burgeoned into a solid fighting force of 300 men. The offensive became something of a turning point as the rebels – with the help of the local *campesinos* (country people) – gradually halted the onslaught of Batista's young and ill-disciplined conscript army. With the Americans increasingly embarrassed by the no-holds-barred terror tactics of their one-time Cuban ally, Castro sensed an opportunity to turn defense into offense and signed the groundbreaking Caracas Pact with eight leading opposition groups calling on the US to stop all aid to Batista. Che Guevara and Camilo Cienfuegos were promptly dispatched to the Escambray Mountains to open up new fronts in the west, and by December, with Cienfuegos holding down troops in Yaguajay (the garrison finally surrendered after an 11-day siege) and Guevara closing in on Santa Clara, the end was in sight. It was left to Che Guevara to seal the final victory, employing classic guerrilla tactics to derail an armored train in Santa Clara and split the country's battered communications system in two. By New Year's Eve 1958, the game was up: a sense of jubilation filled the country, and Che and Camilo were on their way to Havana unopposed.

In the small hours of January 1, 1959, Batista fled by private plane to the Dominican Republic. Meanwhile, materializing in Santiago de Cuba the same day, Fidel made a rousing victory speech from the town hall in Parque Céspedes before jumping into a 4WD and traveling across the breadth of the country to Havana in a Caesar-like cavalcade. The triumph of the Revolution was seemingly complete.

Cuba's history since the revolution has been a David and Goliath tale of confrontation, rhetoric, Cold War stand-offs and an omnipresent US trade embargo that has featured 11 US presidents and two infamous Cuban leaders – both called Castro. For the first 30 years, Cuba allied itself with the Soviet Union as the US used various retaliatory tactics (all unsuccessful) to bring Fidel Castro to heel, including a botched invasion, 600-plus assassination attempts and one of the longest economic blockades in modern history. When the Soviet bloc fell in 1989–91, Cuba stood alone behind an increasingly defiant and stubborn leader, surviving, against all odds, through a decade of severe economic austerity known as the Special Period. GDP fell by more than half, luxuries went out the window, and a wartime spirit of rationing and sacrifice took hold among a populace that, ironically, had prised itself free from foreign (neo)colonial influences for the first time in its history.

The 'wet foot dry foot' law (Cuban Adjustment Act) signed by Bill Clinton in 1995 means that only Cubans who make it onto US soil can apply for citizenship. Those picked up at sea are sent home.

Of the 12 or so men that survived the disastrous *Granma* landing in December 1956, only three were still alive in 2013: Fidel Castro, Raúl Castro and Ramiro Valdés.

2006	2009	2011	2013
Castro is taken ill just before his 80th birthday with diverticulitis disease and steps down from the day-to-day running of the country. He is replaced by his brother Raúl.	The inauguration of Barack Obama signifies a long-awaited thaw in Cuban-US relations. In an early act of rapprochement, Obama loosens restrictions for Cuban-Americans, returning to the island to visit relatives.	Raúl Castro signals economic movement by announcing that the government plans to cut half a million jobs from the state sector and open up private enterprise to over 175 licensed businesses.	Raúl Castro's government continues its political aperture allowing Cubans to travel abroad unrestricted for the first time in 51 years, although lack of funds remain a barrier for many.

The Cuban Way of Life

Slipping through the outskirts of a provincial Cuban city on a tour bus, the country, on first impression, can seem austere, poor, and devoid of color. But what you see in this perennially contradictory archipelago isn't always what you get. Cuba requires patience, clandestine sleuthing, and plenty of scratching beneath the surface. Decipher the local way of life – warts and all – and you will quickly uncover its irrepressible musical energy, a non-stop dance that carries on in spite of everything.

Habana Vieja is one of the most crowded quarters in Latin America with over 70,000 people living in an area of just 4.5 sq km.

A Recipe for Being Cuban

Take a dose of WWII rationing, and a pinch of Soviet-era austerity, add in the family values of South America, the educational virtues of the US, and the loquaciousness of the Irish. Mix with the tropical pace of Jamaica and innate musicality of pastoral Africa before dispersing liberally around the sultry streets of Havana, Santiago de Cuba, Camagüey and Pinar del Río.

Life in Cuba is an open and interactive brew. Spend time in a local home and you'll quickly start to piece together an archetype. There's the pot of coffee brewing on the stove, and the rusty Chinese bike leant languidly against the wall of the front room, the faded photo of José Martí above the TV, and the statue of the venerated Virgin of El Cobre lurking in the shadows. Aside from the house-owner and their mother, brother, sister and niece, every Cuban home has a seemingly endless queue of 'visitors' traipsing through. A shirtless neighbor who's come over to borrow a wrench, the local busybody from the CDR (Committee for the Defense of the Revolution), a priest popping by for a glass of rum *sin hielo* (no ice); plus the cousin, the second cousin, the long-lost friend, the third cousin twice removed...you get the picture. Then there are the sounds: a cock crowing, a saxophonist practicing his scales, dogs barking, car engines exploding, a salsa beat far off, and those all-too-familiar shouts from the street. *Dime, hermano! Que pasa, mi amor? Ah, mi vida – no es fácil!*

Yes. *No es fácil* – it ain't easy. Life in Cuba is anything but easy but, defying all logic, it's perennially colorful and rarely dull.

Cuba has 70,000 qualified doctors. The whole of Africa has only 50,000.

Lifestyle

Survivors by nature and necessity, Cubans have long displayed an almost inexhaustible ability to bend the rules and 'work things out' when it matters. The two most overused verbs in the national phrasebook are *conseguir* (to get, manage) and *resolver* (to resolve, work out), and Cubans are experts at doing both. Their intuitive ability to bend the rules and make something out of nothing is borne out of economic necessity. In a small nation bucking modern sociopolitical realities, where monthly salaries top out at around the equivalent of US$25, survival can often mean getting innovative as a means of supplementing personal income. Cruise the crumbling streets of Centro Habana and you'll see people *conseguir*-ing and *resolver*-ing wherever you go. There's the casa particular owner offering guided tours using his car as a taxi, or the lady selling lobsters in defiance of government regulations. Other schemes may be ill-gotten or garnered through trickery, such as the *compañero* (comrade) who pockets the odd blemished cigar from the day job to sell to unsuspecting Canadians. Old Cuba hands know one of the most popular ways to make extra cash is working with (or over) tourists.

In Cuba, hard currency (ie convertible pesos) rules, primarily because it is the only way of procuring the modest luxuries that make living in this austere socialist republic more comfortable. Paradoxically, the post-1993 double economy has reinvigorated the class system the Revolution worked so hard to neutralize, and it's no longer rare to see Cubans with access to convertibles touting designer clothing while others hassle tourists mercilessly for bars of soap. This stark re-emergence of 'haves' and 'have-nots' is among the most ticklish issues facing Cuba today.

READ ALL ABOUT IT – THE BLOGGING REVOLUTION

With a literacy rate of 99.8% and a longstanding love of books, it is not surprising that Cuba is producing a growing number of eloquent bloggers, despite the difficulties in gaining internet access. Here are a few of the higher profile sites representing views right across the political spectrum.

Generación Y (Yoani Sánchez; www.desdecuba.com/generaciony) Sánchez is Cuba's most famous blogger (and dissident) and her gritty blog 'Generación Y' has been testing the mettle of Cuba's censorship police since April 2007. An unapologetic critic of the Cuban government, she has attracted a huge international audience (US President Barack Obama once replied to one of her posts) and won numerous awards, including the Ortega & Gasset prize for digital journalism. In 2013, Sánchez was granted a visa under Cuba's new travel laws and took off on a highly publicized world tour.

El Yuma (Ted Henken; www.elyuma.blogspot.com) Longstanding Cuba commentator, and Chair of Black and Hispanic Studies at Baruch College, New York, Henken has studied and written extensively about the Cuban blogosphere. His regularly updated blog has some excellent links to other sites.

Havana Times (www.havanatimes.org) A website and 'blog cooperative' started by American writer Circles Robinson in 2008 that positions itself as anti-Castro and anti-embargo.

Paquito El de Cuba (Francisco Rodriguez; http://paquitoeldecuba.wordpress.com; Spanish only) Cuban journalist Francisco Rodriguez is gay, communist, HIV-positive and a proud father. He is also the writer of a fascinating blog.

Along the Malecon (Tracy Eaton; www.alongthemalecon.blogspot.com) Former bureau chief for the *Dallas Morning News* in Havana (2000–05), Eaton is still a regular in-depth reporter in Cuba.

Yasmin Portales (http://yasminsilvia.blogspot.ca; Spanish only) Yasmin, who describes herself as a Marxist-feminist, is a strong voice in the Rainbow Project, an initiative for LGBT rights.

Babalú Blog (www.babalublog.com) Based in Miami and unyieldingly pro-US embargo, this blog is edited by Alberto de la Cruz. Carlos Eire, professor of History and Religious Studies at Yale University and author of the celebrated memoir *Waiting for Snow in Havana*, is a contributor.

La Joven Cuba (http://lajovencuba.wordpress.com; Spanish only) Blog set up and maintained by three professors from Matanzas University who style themselves as followers of Antonio Guíteras, a socialist Cuban politician from the 1930s.

Other social traits that have emerged since the Revolution are more altruistic and less divisive. In Cuba sharing is second nature and helping out your *compañero* with a lift, a square meal or a few convertibles when they're in trouble is considered a national duty. Check the way that strangers interact in queues or at transport intersections and notice how in Cuban houses neighbors share everything from tools to food to babysitting time without a second thought.

Cubans are informal. The *tú* form of Spanish address is much more common that the formal *usted*, and people greet each other with a variety of friendly addresses. Don't be surprised if a complete stranger calls you *mi amor* (my love) or *mi vida* (my life), and expect casa particular owners to regularly open the front door shirtless (men), or with their hair in rollers (women). To confuse matters further, Cuban Spanish is rich in colloquialisms, irony, sarcasm and swear words.

In June 2008 the Cuban government legalized sex-change operations and agreed to provide them free to qualifying parties.

The Home Front

While Cuban homes sport the basics (fridges, cookers, microwaves), they still lack the expensive trappings of 21st century consumerism. Car ownership is approximately 38 per 1000, compared to 800 per 1000 in the US; few households sport tumble dryers (spot the flailing lines of drying clothes); and that impressive breakfast laid out by your casa particular owner at 8am probably took three hours of searching and queuing to procure (there are no convenient one-stop supermarkets in Cuba). Not that this dents home pride: gathered ornaments and mementos, however old and kitschy, are displayed with love and kept ruthlessly clean. Nonetheless, to most outsiders, the local lifestyle seems old-fashioned and austere. What makes Cuba different from somewhere like Mexico City or Philadelphia though, is the government's heavy subsidies of every facet of life, meaning there are few mortgages, no health-care bills, no

CDRS

Loyal neighborhood watch groups or undercover snooping agencies – the function of Cuba's grassroots Committees for the Defense of the Revolution (CDRs) is not always obvious, especially to visiting outsiders. Created in September 1960 to weed out supposed 'informers' during a time of heavy political paranoia, these ubiquitous local political committees quickly became the 'eyes and ears of the revolution' tasked with being ultra-vigilant in an era of heightened counter-revolutionary activity.

Love them or hate them, the organizations have endured. Walk through any Cuba settlement today and you'll see the tell-tale white signs on every street corner denoting the local CDR block name and number, along with its generic slogan, *En cada barrio, revolución!* (In every neighborhood, revolution!). Though not technically compulsory, membership is considered a 'wise' career move and imperative if you want to avoid reams of bureaucratic hassle and countless pairs of prying eyes. Not surprisingly, 95% of eligible Cubans belong to a CDR, and countrywide the organization has 130,000 branches.

Famous for their micromanagement methods, CDRs have long been one of the government's prime tools in quashing dissent and maintaining a compliant population. Control is administered through elected local officials who keep a constant eye out for so-called 'suspicious' activity in the neighborhood – anything from contact with a foreigner to a family's spending habits – and files are kept on everyone. But, at the community level, the committees engage in other less meddlesome tasks. CDRs organize street festivals, lead vaccination campaigns, explain government policy, and encourage people to contribute to blood banks. They have also been instrumental in Cuba's successful hurricane evacuations, and play a big role in keeping the crime rate low. For the government's opponents, however, the snooping mentality is hard to swallow, and Cuban dissident Elizardo Sánchez once labeled CDRs a 'systematic and mass violation of human rights.'

college fees and fewer taxes. Expensive nights out cost next to nothing in Cuba where tickets for the theater, the cinema, the ballpark or a music concert are state-subsidized and considered a right of the people.

The Winds of Change

The changes brought about by Raúl Castro's economic reforms have ushered both excitement and trepidation into Cuban households. After over a generation of living in a tightly controlled socialist economy with an overly paternalistic state apparatus infiltrating every aspect of daily life, Cubans opting to jump bravely into the private sector have had to wave goodbye to some comforting assurances. Although most people have welcomed the opportunity to finally open up long dreamt about business ventures, failure rates are high in a country whose two-tier economy still makes it difficult to advertise, arrange credit and get access online.

As always, the Cubans have faced up to the new challenges with their customary grit and creativity. Restaurant quality has skyrocketed since 2011, casa particular owners are planning mini-hotels, and talented artists, photographers, linguists and travel guides, stifled for decades by petty bureaucracy, have finally started to reap the fruits of their labor. Life is slowly changing, and this time it appears to be for the better.

Sport

Considered a right of the masses, professional sport was abolished by the government after the Revolution. Performance-wise it was the best thing the new administration could have done. Since 1959 Cuba's Olympic medal haul has rocketed into the stratosphere. The crowning moment came in 1992 when Cuba – a country of 11 million people languishing low on the world's rich list – brought home 14 gold medals and ended fifth on the overall medals table. It's a testament to Cuba's high sporting standards that their 11th-place finish in Athens in 2004 was considered something of a national failure.

Characteristically, the sporting obsession starts at the top. Fidel Castro was once renowned for his baseball-hitting prowess, but what is lesser known was his personal commitment to the establishment of a widely accessible national sporting curriculum at all levels. In 1961 the National Institute of Sport, Physical Education and Recreation (INDER) founded a system of sport for the masses that eradicated discrimination and integrated children from a young age. By offering paid leisure-time to workers and dropping entrance fees to major sports events, the organization caused participation in popular sports to multiply tenfold by the 1970s, and the knock-on effect to performance was tangible.

Cuban *pelota* (baseball) is legendary and the country is riveted during the October–March regular season, turning rabid for the playoffs in April. You'll see passions running high in the main square of provincial capitals, where fans debate minute details of the game with lots of finger-wagging in what is known as a *peña deportiva* (fan club) or *esquina caliente* (hot corner).

Cuba is also a giant in amateur boxing, as indicated by champions Teófilo Stevenson, who brought home Olympic gold in 1972, 1976 and 1980, and Félix Savón, another triple medal winner, most recently in 2000. Every sizable town has an arena called *sala polivalente,* where big boxing events take place, while training and smaller matches happen at gyms, many of which train Olympic athletes.

Havana city Historian Eusebio Leal Spengler was born in the city in 1942. He has a degree in history and archaeological sciences, and a masters in Latin American, Caribbean and Cuban studies.

Cuba high-jumper Javier Sotomayor has held the world record (2.45m) for the event since 1993, and has recorded 17 of the 24 highest jumps ever.

Elements of French culture imported via Haiti in the 1790s are still visible in Cuba today, particularly in the French-founded settlements of Guantánamo and Cienfuegos.

WILLY CHIRINO – YA VIENE LLEGANDO

Longstanding Florida resident and poetic mouthpiece of the patriotic exile community in the US, Willy Chirino is an icon to many Cubans on both sides of the Straits of Florida for his poignant but joyously danceable songs of loss, hope and living *fuera de su idioma* (outside your language).

Born in Consolación del Sur in Pinar del Río province in 1949, Chirino went to the US as a teenager in 1961 during the infamous Operation Pedro Pan, when middle-class Cuban families sent their children abroad amid fears that the Castro government was going to abduct and indoctrinate them.

His concerts in the US are well known for their passion-invoking sing-alongs, and there is barely a dry eye in the house when he breaks into his magnum opus '(Nuestra dia) Ya Viene Llegando' (Our Day is Coming), about the traumatic experience of being packed off alone to a foreign land. The song perfectly encapsulates the intangible elements of being Cuban, irrespective of class, politics or country of residence, with references to hummingbirds, José Martí, the *danzón* (ballroom dancing) and Benny Moré.

Chirino was banned from performing in Cuba for several decades but, as part of Raúl Castro's recent political defrosting, the ban on Chirino and various other Cuban exile musicians was quietly lifted in August 2012. The prospect of the singer – now in his 60s – playing in Havana's Plaza de la Revolución is no longer a distant pipe dream. *Ya Viene Llegando* – and sooner than you think!

Multiculturalism

A convergence of three different races and numerous nationalities, Cuba is a multicultural society that, despite difficult challenges, has been relatively successful in forging racial equality.

The annihilation of the indigenous Taíno by the Spanish and the brutality of the slave system left a bloody mark in the early years of colonization, but the situation had improved significantly by the second half of the 20th century. The Revolution guarantees racial freedom by law, though black Cubans are still far more likely to be stopped by the police for questioning, and over 90% of Cuban exiles in the US are of white descent. Black people are also under-represented in politics; of the victorious rebel army officers that took control of the government in 1959 only a handful (Juan Almeida being the most obvious example) were black or mixed race.

According to the most recent census, Cuba's racial breakdown is 24% *mulato* (mixed race), 65% white, 10% black and 1% Chinese. Aside from the obvious Spanish legacy, many of the so-called 'white' population are the descendants of French immigrants who arrived on the island in various waves during the early part of the 19th century. Indeed, the cities of Guantánamo, Cienfuegos and Santiago de Cuba were all either pioneered or heavily influenced by French *émigrés*, and much of Cuba's coffee and sugar industries owe their development to French entrepreneurship.

The black population is also an eclectic mix. Numerous Haitians and Jamaicans came to Cuba to work in the sugar fields in the 1920s and they brought many of their customs and traditions with them. Their descendants can be found in Guantánamo and Santiago in the Oriente or places such as Venezuela in Ciego de Ávila province, where Haitian voodoo rituals are still practiced.

Religion

Religion is among the most misunderstood and complex aspects of Cuban culture. Before the Revolution, 85% of Cubans were nominal Roman

Catholics, though only 10% attended church regularly. Protestants made up most of the remaining church-going public, though a smattering of Jews and Muslims have always practiced in Cuba and still do. When the Revolution triumphed, 140 Catholic priests were expelled for reactionary political activities and another 400 left voluntarily, while the majority of Protestants, who represented society's poorer sector, had less to lose and stayed.

When the government declared itself Marxist-Leninist and therefore atheist, life for *creyentes* (literally 'believers') took on new difficulties. Though church services were never banned and freedom of religion never revoked, Christians were sent to Unidades Militares de Ayuda a la Producción (UMAPs; Military Production Aid Units), where it was hoped hard labor might reform their religious ways; homosexuals and vagrants were also sent to the fields to work. This was a short-lived experiment, however. More trying for believers were the hard-line Soviet days of the '70s and '80s, when they were prohibited from joining the Communist Party and few, if any, believers held political posts. Certain university careers, notably in the humanities, were off-limits as well.

Things have changed dramatically since then, particularly in 1992 when the constitution was revised, removing all references to the Cuban state as Marxist-Leninist and recapturing the laical nature of the government. This led to an aperture in civil and political spheres of society for religious adherents, and to other reforms (eg believers are now eligible for party membership). Since Cuban Catholicism gained the papal seal of approval with Pope John Paul II's visit in 1998, church attendance has surged and was rewarded further with the arrival of his successor Pope Benedict XVI in 2012. It's worth noting that church services have a strong youth presence. There are currently 400,000 Catholics regularly attending Mass and 300,000 Protestants from 54 denominations. Other denominations such as the Seventh Day Adventists and Pentecostals are rapidly growing in popularity.

Santería

Of all Cuba's cultural mysteries (and there are many), Santería is the most complex, cloaking an inherent 'African-ness' and leading you down an unmapped road that is at once foggy and fascinating.

A syncretistic religion that hides African roots beneath a symbolic Catholic veneer, Santería is a product of the slave era, but remains deeply embedded in contemporary Cuban culture where it has had a major impact on the evolution of the country's music, dance and rituals. Today, over three million Cubans identify as believers, including numerous writers, artists and politicians.

Santería's misrepresentations start with its name; the word is a historical misnomer first coined by Spanish colonizers to describe the 'saint worship' practiced by 19th-century African slaves. A more accurate moniker is Regla de Ocha (way of the *orishas*), or Lucumí, named for the original adherents who hailed from the Yoruba ethno-linguistic group in southwestern Nigeria, a prime looting ground for brutal slave-traders.

Fully initiated adherents of Santería (called *santeros*) believe in one God known as Oludomare, the creator of the universe and the source of Ashe (all life forces on earth). Rather than interact with the world directly, Oludomare communicates through a pantheon of *orishas*, various imperfect deities similar to Catholic saints or Greek gods, who are blessed with different natural (water, weather, metals) and human (love, intellect, virility) qualities. *Orishas* have their own feast days, demand their own food offerings, and are given numbers and colors to represent their personalities.

THE CUBAN WAY OF LIFE RELIGION

CASTRO

Longevity runs in the Castro family. Fidel's older brother Ramón, aged 89, is still alive. His older sister Angela died, aged 88, in 2012.

Main Cuban Crops

Bananas

Citrus fruit

Coffee

Mangos

Pineapples

Rice

Sugarcane

Tobacco

Unlike Christianity or Islam, Santería has no equivalent to the Bible or Koran. Instead, religious rites are transmitted orally and, over time, have evolved to fit the realities of modern Cuba. Another departure from popular world religions is the abiding focus on 'life on earth' as opposed to the afterlife, although Santería adherents believe strongly in the powers of dead ancestors, known as *egun*, whose spirits are invoked during initiation ceremonies.

Santería's syncretism with Catholicism occurred surreptitiously during the colonial era when African animist traditions were banned. In order to hide their faith from the Spanish authorities, African slaves secretly twinned their *orishas* with Catholic saints. Thus, Changó the male *orisha* of thunder and lightning was hidden somewhat bizarrely behind the feminine form of Santa Bárbara, while Elegguá, the *orisha* of travel and roads, became St Anthony de Padua. In this way an erstwhile slave praying before a statue of Santa Bárbara was clandestinely offering his/her respects to Changó, while Afro-Cubans ostensibly celebrating the feast day of Our Lady of Regla (September 7) were, in reality, honoring Yemayá. This syncretization, though no longer strictly necessary, is still followed today.

Literature & the Arts

Leave your preconceptions about 'art in a totalitarian state' at home. The breadth of Cuban cinema, painting and literature could put many far more politically libertarian nations to shame. The Cubans seem to have a habit of taking almost any artistic genre and reinventing it for the better. You'll pick up first-class flamenco, ballet, classical music and Shakespearean theater here, not to mention Lorca plays, alternative cinema and illuminating deconstructions of Gabriel García Márquez novels.

Literary Cuba

Spend an evening conversing with the Cubans and you'll quickly realize that they *love* to talk. This loquaciousness extends to books. Maybe it's something they put in the rum, but since time immemorial, writers in this highly literate Caribbean archipelago have barely paused for breath, telling and retelling their stories with passionate zeal and, in the process, producing some of most groundbreaking and influential literature in Latin America.

Contemporary writer Leonardo Padura Fuentes is well known for his quartet of Havana-based detective novels, *Los cuatro estaciones* (Four Seasons).

The Classicists

Any literary journey should begin in Havana in the 1830s. Cuban literature found its earliest voice in *Cecilia valdés*, a novel by Cirilo Villaverde (1812–94), published in 1882 but set 50 years earlier in a Havana divided by class, slavery and prejudice. It's widely considered to be the greatest Cuban novel of the 19th century.

Preceding Villaverde, in publication if not historical setting, was romantic poet and novelist Gertrudis Gómez Avellaneda. Born to a rich Camagüeyan family of privileged Spanish gentry in 1814, Avellaneda was a rare female writer in a rigidly masculine domain. Eleven years before *Uncle Tom's Cabin* woke up America to the same themes, her novel *Sab,* published in 1841, tackled the prickly issues of race and slavery. It was banned in Cuba until 1914 due to its abolitionist rhetoric. What contemporary critics chose not to see was Avellaneda's subtle feminism, which depicted marriage as just another form of slavery.

Further east, neoclassical poet and native *santiagüero*, José María Heredia y Heredia, lived and wrote mainly from exile in Mexico, after being banished for allegedly conspiring against the Spanish authorities. His poetry, including the seminal *Himno del desterrado*, is tinged with a nostalgic romanticism for his homeland. He died like so many 19th-century poets – young, unfulfilled and in exile.

Graham Greene originally set his comic take on British espionage in Soviet-occupied Tallinn, Estonia. But a chance visit to Havana changed his mind. The novel ultimately became *Our Man in Havana.*

The Experimentalists

Cuban literature grew up in the early 1900s. Inspired by a mixture of José Martí's modernism and new surrealistic influences wafting over from Europe, the first half of the 20th century was an age of experimentation for Cuban writers. The era's literary legacy rests on three giant pillars: Alejo Carpentier, a baroque wordsmith who invented the much-copied style of *lo real maravilloso* (magic realism); Guillermo Cabrera Infante,

MARTÍ – A CATEGORY OF HIS OWN

Rarely does an author step out of normal categorization and stand alone, but José Julián Martí Pérez was no ordinary human being. A pioneering philosopher, revolutionary and modernist writer, Martí broadened the political debate in Cuba beyond slavery (which was abolished in 1886) to issues such as independence and – above all – freedom. His instantly quotable prose remains a rare unifying force among Cubans around the world, whatever their political affiliations, and he is similarly revered by Spanish speakers globally for his internationalism, which has put him on a par with Simón Bolívar.

Martí's writing covered a huge range of genres: essays, novels, poetry, political commentaries, letters and even a hugely popular children's magazine called *La edad de oro* (Golden Age). He was an accomplished master of aphorisms, and his powerful one-liners still crop up in everyday Cuban speech. His two most famous works, published in 1891, are the political essay *Nuestra América* (Our America) and his collected poems, *Versos sencillos* (Simple Verses), both of which laid bare his hopes and dreams for Cuba and Latin America.

a Joycean master of colloquial language who pushed the parameters of Spanish to barely comprehensible boundaries; and José Lezama Lima, a gay poet of Proustian ambition, whose weighty novels were rich in layers, themes and anecdotes. None were easy to read, but all broke new ground inspiring erudite writers far beyond Cuban shores (Márquez and Rushdie among them). Swiss-born Carpentier's magnum opus was *El siglo de las luces* (Explosion in a Cathedral), which explores the impact of the French Revolution in Cuba through a veiled love story. Many consider it to be the finest novel ever written by a Cuban author. Infante, from Gibara, rewrote the rules of language in *Tres tristes tigres* (Three Trapped Tigers), a complex study of street life in pre-Castro Havana. Lezama Lima, meanwhile, took an anecdotal approach to novel writing in *Paradiso* (Paradise), a multilayered, widely interpreted evocation of Havana in the 1950s with homoerotic undertones.

Grasping at the coattails of this verbose trio was Miguel Barnet, an anthropologist from Havana, whose *Biografía de un cimarrón* (Biography of a Runaway Slave), published in 1963, gathered testimonies from 103-year-old former slave Esteban Montejo and crafted them into a fascinating written documentary of the brutal slave system nearly 80 years after its demise.

Heberto Padilla (1932–2000) was a Cuban poet whose dissident writings in the 1960s led to his imprisonment, inspiring the 'Padilla Affair'.

Enter Guillén

Born in Camagüey in 1902, *mulato* (mixed race) poet Nicolás Guillén was far more than just a writer: he was a passionate and lifelong champion of Afro-Cuban rights. Rocked by the assassination of his father in his youth, and inspired by the drum-influenced music of former black slaves, Guillén set about articulating the hopes and fears of dispossessed black laborers with the rhythmic Afro-Cuban verses that would ultimately become his trademark. Famous poems in a prolific career included the evocative *Tengo* (I Have) and the patriotic *Che comandante, amigo* (Commander Che, Friend).

Working in self-imposed exile during the Batista era, Guillén returned to Cuba after the Revolution whereupon he was given the task of formulating a new cultural policy and setting up the Writer's Union called Uneac (Unión de Escritores y Artistas de Cuba).

Best Uneac Cultural Venues

Huron Azul (p121), Havana

Holguín (p362)

Sancti Spíritus (p287)

Santiago de Cuba (p422)

Cienfuegos (p253)

Puerto Padre (p351)

The Dirty Realists

In the 1990s and 2000s, baby boomers that had come of age in the era of censorship and Soviet domination began to respond to radically different influences in their writing. Some fled the country, others remained; all tested the boundaries of artistic expression in a system weighed down by censorship and creative asphyxiation.

Stepping out from the shadow of Lezama Lima was Reinaldo Arenas, a gay writer from Holguín province, who, like Guillermo Cabrera Infante, fell out with the Revolution in the late '60s and was imprisoned for his efforts. Arenas finally escaped to the US in 1980 during the Mariel boatlift. He went on to write his hyperbolic memoir, *Antes que anochezca* (Before Night Falls), about his imprisonment and homosexuality. Published in the US in 1993, it met with huge critical acclaim.

The so-called 'dirty realist' authors of the late '90s and early 2000s took a more subtle approach to challenging contemporary mores. Pedro Juan Gutiérrez earned his moniker 'tropical Bukowski' for the *Dirty Havana Trilogy*, a sexy, sultry study of Centro Habana during the Special Period. The trilogy held up a mirror to the desperate economic situation but steered clear of direct political polemics. Zoé Valdés, born the year Castro took power, has been more direct in her criticism of the regime, particularly since leaving Cuba for Paris in 1995. Her most readily available novels (translated into English) are *I Gave You All I Had* and *Dear First Love*.

Postmodern Italian writer Italo Calvino was actually born in the Havana suburb of Santiago de Las Vegas in 1923. His family returned to San Remo, Italy, in 1925, when he was just two years old.

LITERATURE & THE ARTS CINEMA

Cinema

Cuban cinema has always been closer to the European art-house tradition than to the formulaic movies of Hollywood, especially since the Revolution, when cultural life veered away from American influences. Few notable movies were made until 1959, when the new government formed the Instituto Cubano del Arte e Industria Cinematográficos (Icaic), headed up by longtime film sage and former Havana University student Alfredo Guevara, who held the position on and off until 2000. The 1960s were Icaic's *Década de oro* (golden decade) when, behind an artistic veneer, successive directors were able to test the boundaries of state-imposed censorship and, in some cases, gain greater creative license. Innovative movies of this era poked fun at bureaucracy, made pertinent comments on economic matters, questioned the role of intellectualism in a socialist state and, later on, tackled previously taboo gay issues. The giants behind the camera were Humberto Solás, Tomás Gutiérrez Alea and Juan Carlos Tabío, who, working under Guevara's guidance, put cutting-edge Cuban cinema on the international map.

Cuba's first notable post-revolutionary movie, the joint Cuban-Soviet *Soy Cuba* (I am Cuba; 1964) was directed by a Russian, Mikhail Kalatozov, who dramatized the events leading up to the 1959 Revolution in four interconnecting stories. Largely forgotten by the early '70s, the movie was resurrected in the mid-1990s by American director Martin Scorsese, who, upon seeing the film for the first time, was astounded by its cinematography, atmospheric camera work and, above all, technically amazing tracking shots. The film gets a rare 100% rating on the 'Rotten Tomatoes' website and has been described by one American film critic as 'a unique, insane, exhilarating spectacle.'

CASAS DE LA CULTURA

Every provincial town in Cuba, no matter how small, has a Casa de la Cultura that acts as a nexus for the country's bubbling cultural life. Casas de la Cultura stage everything from traditional salsa music to innovative comedy nights, with upcoming events penned onto a *cartelera* (calendar) outside. On top of this, countless other theaters, organizations and institutions bring highbrow art to the masses completely free – yes, *free* – of charge.

MARTÍ

Serving his apprenticeship in the 1960s, Cuba's most celebrated director, Tomás Gutiérrez Alea, cut his teeth directing art-house movies such as *La muerte de un burócrata* (Death of a Bureaucrat; 1966), a satire on excessive socialist bureaucratization; and *Memorias de subdesarrollo* (Memories of Underdevelopment; 1968), the story of a Cuban intellectual too idealistic for Miami, yet too decadent for the austere life of Havana. Teaming up with fellow director Juan Carlos Tabío in 1993, Gutiérrez went on to make another movie classic, the Oscar-nominated *Fresa y chocolate* (Strawberry and Chocolate) – the tale of Diego, a skeptical homosexual who falls in love with a heterosexual communist militant. It remains Cuba's cinematic pinnacle. Humberto Solás, a master of *cine pobre* (low-budget) movies, first made his mark in 1968 with the seminal *Lucía*. It explored the lives of three Cuban women at key moments in the country's history: 1895, 1932 and the early 1960s. Solás made his late-career masterpiece, *Barrio Cuba,* in 2005. It's the tale of a family torn apart by the historical upheavals of the Revolution.

Since the death of Gutiérrez Alea in 1996 and Solás in 2008, Cuban cinema has passed the baton to a new and equally talented stash of movie guerrillas. Their uncrowned king is Fernando Pérez, who leapt onto the scene in 1994 with the Special Period classic *Madagascar,* focusing on an inter-generational struggle between a mother and daughter. Pérez's peak to date is 2003's *Suite Habana*, a moody documentary about a day in the life of 13 real people in the capital that uses zero dialogue. Pérez's closest 'rival' is Juan Carlos Cremata, whose 2005 road movie *Viva Cuba*, a study of class and ideology as seen through the eyes of two children, garnered much international praise.

Havana's growing influence in the film culture of the American hemisphere is highlighted each year in the Festival Internacional del Nuevo Cine Latinoamericano held every December in Havana. Described as the ultimate word in Latin American cinema, this annual get-together of critics, sages and filmmakers has been fundamental in showcasing recent Cuban classics to the world.

Painting & Sculpture

Thought-provoking and visceral, modern Cuban art combines lurid Afro-Latin American colors with the harsh reality of the 52-year-old Revolution. For foreign art lovers visiting Cuba it's a unique and intoxicating brew. Forced into a corner by the constrictions of the culture-redefining Cuban Revolution, modern artists have invariably found that, by co-opting (as opposed to confronting) the socialist regime, opportunities for academic training and artistic encouragement are almost unlimited. Encased in such a volatile, creative climate, abstract art in Cuba – well established in its own right before the Revolution – has flourished.

The first flowering of Cuban art took place in the 1920s when painters belonging to the so-called *Vanguardia* movement relocated temporarily to Paris to learn the ropes from the avant-garde European school then dominated by the likes of Pablo Picasso. One of the Vanguardia's earliest exponents was Victor Manuel García (1897–1969), the genius behind one of Cuba's most famous paintings, *La gitana tropical* (Tropical Gypsy; 1929), a portrait of an archetypal Cuban woman with her luminous gaze staring into the middle distance. The canvas, displayed in Havana's Museo Nacional de Bellas Artes, is often referred to as the Latin Mona Lisa. Victor Manuel's contemporary, Amelia Peláez (1896–1968), was another Francophile who studied in Paris, where she melded avant-gardism with more primitive Cuban themes. Though Peláez worked with many different materials, her most celebrated work was in murals, including the 670-sq-meter tile mural on the side of the Hotel Habana Libre.

In 2010, Cuban film director Fernando Pérez brought the early life of José Martí to the screen in a film called *El ojo del canario* (Eye of the Canary).

Top Contemporary Artists

José Villa

Joel Jover

Flora Fong

José Rodríguez Fúster

Tomás Sánchez

WIFREDO LAM

In the international context, art in Cuba is dominated by the prolific figure of Wifredo Lam (1902–82), painter, sculptor and ceramicist of mixed Chinese, African and Spanish ancestry. Born in Sagua La Grande, Villa Clara province, in 1902, Lam studied art and law in Havana before departing for Madrid in 1923 to pursue his artistic ambitions in the fertile fields of post-WWI Europe. Displaced by the Spanish Civil War in 1937, he gravitated toward France, where he became friends with Pablo Picasso and swapped ideas with pioneering surrealist André Breton. Having absorbed various cubist and surrealist influences, Lam returned to Cuba in 1941, where he produced his own seminal masterpiece, *La Jungla* (Jungle), considered by critics to be one of the developing world's most representative paintings.

After the high-water mark of Wifredo Lam, Cuban art was organized around a group of abstract painters known as the *Grupo de los once* (Group of Eleven). One of its leaders was Raúl Martínez from Ciego de Ávila, a pioneer of pop art, poster art and revolutionary iconography. His famous portrait studies have featured personalities such as Camilo Cienfuegos, José Martí and Che Guevara, while his film posters (including for the Humberto Solás movie *Lucía*) have become classics of 1960s pop art.

Art has enjoyed strong government patronage since the Revolution (albeit within the confines of strict censorship), exemplified with the opening of the Instituto Superior de Arte in the outlying Havana neighborhood of Cubanacán in 1976.

Music & Dance

Juxtapose two ancient cultures from two very different continents (Africa and Europe). Relocate them to a slave society in a far-off tropical land. Give them some drums, a maraca and a couple of improvised guitars. See what happens.

The *danzón* was originally an instrumental piece. Words were added in the late 1920s and the new form became known as the *danzónete*.

Into the Mix

Rich, vibrant, layered and soulful, Cuban music has long acted as a standard-bearer for the sounds and rhythms emanating out of Latin America. This is the land where salsa has its roots, where elegant white dances adopted edgy black rhythms, and where the African drum first fell in love with the Spanish guitar. From the down-at-heel docks of Matanzas to the bucolic villages of the Sierra Maestra, the amorous musical fusion went on to fuel everything from *son*, rumba, mambo, *chachachá, charanga, changüí, danzón* and more.

Aside from the obvious Spanish and African roots, Cuban music has drawn upon a number of other influences. Mixed into an already exotic melting pot are genres from France, the US, Haiti and Jamaica. Conversely, Cuban music has also played a key role in developing various melodic styles and movements in other parts of the world. In Spain they called this process *ida y vuelta* (return trip) and it is most clearly evident in a style of flamenco called *guajira*. Elsewhere the 'Cuban effect' can be traced back to forms as diverse as New Orleans jazz, New York salsa and West African Afrobeat.

Described by aficionados as 'a vertical representation of a horizontal act,' Cuban dancing is famous for its libidinous rhythms and sensuous close-ups. Inheriting a love for dancing from birth and able to replicate perfect salsa steps by the age of two or three, most Cubans are natural performers who approach dance with a complete lack of self-consciousness – a notion that can leave visitors from Europe or North America feeling as if they've got two left feet.

Danzón Days

In the mid-19th century Cuba's first hybrid musical genre, the *habanera*, a traditional European-style dance with a syncopated drumbeat, had risen to the fore. It lasted until the 1870s when the Cubans, always hungry for innovation, began to adapt it, injecting *habanera* rhythms with ever more complex African influences and ultimately creating what became known as the *danzón*.

The invention of the *danzón* is usually credited to innovative Matanzas band leader Miguel Failde, who first showcased it with his catchy dance composition *Las Alturas de Simpson* in Matanzas in 1879. Elegant and purely instrumental in its early days, the *danzón* was slower in pace than the *habanera,* and its intricate dance patterns required dancers to circulate in couples rather than groups, a development that scandalized polite society at the time. From the 1880s onward, the genre exploded, expanding its peculiar syncopated rhythm, and adding such improbable extras as conga drums and vocalists. By the early

20th century the *danzón* had evolved from a stately ballroom dance played by an *orchestra típica* into a more jazzed-up free-for-all that was also known alternatively as *charanga, danzonete* or *danzón-chá*. Not surprisingly, it became Cuba's national dance, though since it was primarily a bastion of moneyed white society, it was never considered a true hybrid.

Africa Calling

While drumming in the North American colonies was ostensibly prohibited, Cuban slaves were able to preserve and pass on many of their musical traditions via influential Santería *cabildos* – religious brotherhoods that re-enacted ancient African percussive music on simple *batá* drums or *chequeré* rattles. Performed at annual festivals or on special Catholic saints' days, this rhythmic yet highly textured dance music was offered up as a form of religious worship to the *orishas* (deities).

Over time the ritualistic drumming of Santería evolved into a more complex genre known as rumba. Rumba was first concocted in the docks of Havana and Matanzas during the 1890s when ex-slaves, exposed to a revolving series of outside influences, began to knock out soulful rhythms on old packing cases in imitation of various African religious rites. As the drumming patterns grew more complex, vocals were added, dances emerged and, before long, the music had grown into a collective form of social expression for all black Cubans.

Spreading in popularity throughout the 1920s and '30s, rumba gradually spawned three different but interrelated dance formats: *guaguancó*, an overtly sexual dance; *yambú*, a slow dance; and *columbia*, a fast, aggressive dance often involving fire torches and machetes. The latter originated as a devil dance of the Náñigo rite, and today it's performed only by solo men.

Pitched into Cuba's cultural melting pot, these rootsy yet highly addictive musical variants slowly gained acceptance among a new audience of middle-class whites, and by the 1940s the music had fused with *son* (Cuba's popular music) in a new subgenre called *son montuno*, which, in turn, provided the building blocks for salsa.

Indeed, so influential was Cuban rumba by the end of WWII that it was transposed back to Africa with experimental Congolese artists such as Sam Mangwana and Franco Luambo (of OK Jazz fame), using ebullient Cuban influences to pioneer *soukous*, their own variation on the rumba theme.

Raw, expressive and exciting to watch, Cuban rumba is a spontaneous and often informal affair performed by groups of up to a dozen musicians. Conga drums, claves, *palitos* (sticks), *marugas* (iron shakers) and *cajones* (packing cases) lay out the interlocking rhythms, while the vocals

Types of Cuban Dance

....
Chachachá
....
Guaguancó
....
Mambo
....
Danzón
....
Columbia
....
Yambú

BEST PLACES FOR MÚSICA CUBANA

→ **Son** Casa de la Trova (p421), Santiago de Cuba

→ **Nueva Trova** Casa de la Trova (p298), Trinidad

→ **Salsa/Timba** Casa de la Música (p140), Centro Habana

→ **Reggaetón** Noche Camagüeyana (p333), Camagüey

→ **Rumba** Callejón de Hamel (p121), Havana

→ **Jazz** Jazz Club La Zorra y El Cuervo (p121), Havana

→ **Classical** Basílica Menor de San Francisco de Asís (p121), Havana

CHARANGAS

alternate between a wildly improvising lead singer and an answering *coro* (chorus).

Rising Son

Cuba's two most celebrated 19th-century sounds, rumba and *danzón*, came from the west – specifically the cities of Havana and Matanzas. But as the genres remained largely compartmentalized between separate black and white societies, neither can be considered true hybrids. The country's first real musical fusion came from the next great sound revolution, *son*.

Son first emerged from the mountains of Cuba's Oriente region in the second half of the 19th century, though the earliest known testimonies go back as far as 1570. It was one of two genres to arise at around the same time (the other was *changüí*), both of which blended the melodies and lyricism of Spanish folk music with the drum patterns of recently freed African slaves. *Son's* precursor was *nengon*, an invention of black sugar-plantation workers who had evolved their percussive religious chants into a form of music and song. The leap that took place from *nengon* to *son* is unclear and poorly documented, but at some point in the 1880s or '90s the *guajiros* (country folk) in the mountains of present-day Santiago de Cuba and Guantánamo provinces began blending *nengon* drums with the Cuban *tres* (guitar with three sets of double strings) while over the top a singer improvised words from a traditional 10-line Spanish poem known as a *décima*.

In its pure form, *son* was played by a sextet consisting of guitar, *tres*, double bass, bongo and two singers who played maracas and claves (sticks that tap out the beat). Coming down from the mountains and into the cities, the genre's earliest exponents were the legendary Trio Oriental, who stabilized the sextet format in 1912 when they were reborn as the Sexteto Habanero. Another early *sonero* was singer Miguel Matamoros, whose self-penned *son* classics such as 'Son de la Loma' and 'Lágrimas Negras' are de rigueur among Cuba's ubiquitous musical entertainers, even today.

In the early 1910s *son* arrived in Havana, where it adopted its distinctive rumba clave (rhythmic pattern), which later went on to form the basis of salsa. Within a decade it had become Cuba's signature music, gaining wide acceptance among white society and destroying the myth that black music was vulgar, unsophisticated and subversive.

By the 1930s the sextet had become a septet with the addition of a trumpet, and exciting new musicians such as blind *tres* player Arsenio Rodríguez – a songwriter who Harry Belafonte once called the 'father of salsa' – were paving the way for mambo and *chachachá*.

Barbarians of Rhythm

In the 1940s and '50s the *son* bands grew from seven pieces to eight and beyond, until they became big bands boasting full horn and percussion sections that played rumba, *chachachá* and mambo. The reigning mambo king was Benny Moré, who with his sumptuous voice and rocking 40-piece all-black band was known as El Bárbaro del Ritmo (The Barbarian of Rhythm).

Mambo grew out of *charanga* music, which itself was a derivative of *danzón*. Bolder, brassier and altogether more exciting than its two earlier incarnations, the music was characterized by exuberant trumpet riffs, belting saxophones and regular enthusiastic interjections by the singer (usually in the form of the word *dilo!* or 'say it!'). The style's origins are mired in controversy. Some argue that it was invented by native *habanero* (person from Havana) Orestes López after he penned a new rhythmically

Charangas were Cuban musical ensembles that showcased popular *danzón*-influenced pieces.

dextrous number called 'Mambo' in 1938. Others give the credit to Matanzas band leader Pérez Prado, who was the first musician to market his songs under the increasingly lucrative mambo umbrella in the early '40s. Whatever the case, mambo had soon spawned the world's first universal dance craze, and from New York to Buenos Aires people couldn't get enough of its infectious rhythms.

A variation on the mambo theme, the *chachachá*, was first showcased by Havana-based composer and violinist Enrique Jorrín in 1951 while playing with the Orquesta América. Originally known as 'mambo-rumba,' the music was intended to promote a more basic kind of Cuban dance that less-coordinated North Americans would be able to master, but it was quickly mambo-ized by overenthusiastic dance competitors, who kept adding complicated new steps.

Salsa & Its Off-Shoots

Salsa is an umbrella term used to describe a variety of musical genres that emerged out of the fertile Latin New York scene in the 1960s and '70s, when jazz, *son* and rumba blended to create a new, brassier sound. While not strictly a product of Cubans living in Cuba, salsa's roots and key influences are descended directly from *son montuno* and owe an enormous debt to innovators such as Pérez Prado, Benny Moré and Miguel Matamoros.

The self-styled Queen of Salsa was Grammy-winning singer and performer Celia Cruz. Born in Havana in 1925, Cruz served the bulk of her musical apprenticeship in Cuba before leaving for self-imposed exile in the US in 1960. But due to her longstanding opposition to the Castro regime, Cruz' records and music have remained largely unknown on the island despite her enduring legacy elsewhere. Far more influential on their home turf are the legendary salsa outfit Los Van Van, a band formed by Juan Formell in 1969 and one that still performs regularly at venues across Cuba. With Formell at the helm as the group's great improviser, poet, lyricist and social commentator, Los Van Van are one of the few contemporary Cuban groups to have created their own unique musical genre – that of songo-salsa. The band also won top honors in 2000 when they memorably took home a Grammy for their classic album *Llego Van Van*.

Modern salsa mixed and merged further in the '80s and '90s, allying itself with new cutting-edge musical genres such as hip-hop, *reggaetón* (Cuban hip-hop) and rap, before coming up with some hot new alternatives, most notably *timba* and songo-salsa.

Timba is, in many ways, Cuba's own experimental and fiery take on traditional salsa. Mixing New York sounds with Latin jazz, *nueva trova* (philosophical folk and guitar music), American funk, disco, hip-hop and even some classical influences, the music is more flexible and aggressive than standard salsa, incorporating greater elements of the island's potent Afro-Cuban culture. Many *timba* bands such as Bambaleo and La Charanga Habanera use funk riffs and rely on less-conventional Cuban instruments such as synthesizers and kick drums. Others – such as NG La Banda, formed in 1988 – have infused their music with a more jazzy dynamic.

Traditional jazz, considered the music of the enemy in the Revolution's most dogmatic days, has always seeped into Cuban sounds. Jesús 'Chucho' Valdés' band Irakere, formed in 1973, broke the Cuban music scene wide open with its heavy Afro-Cuban drumming laced with jazz and *son*, and the Cuban capital boasts a number of decent jazz clubs. Other musicians associated with the Cuban jazz set include pianist Gonzalo Rubalcaba, Isaac Delgado and Adalberto Álvarez y Su Son.

Filin' is a term derived from the English word 'feeling.' It was a style of music showcased by jazz crooners in the 1940s and '50s. In Cuba *filin'* grew out of bolero and *trova*.

The Trovadores

The original *trovadores* were like wandering medieval minstrels, itinerant songsmiths who plied their musical trade across the Oriente region in the early 20th century, moving from village to village and city to city with the carefree spirit of gypsies. Equipped with simple acoustic guitars and armed with a seemingly limitless repertoire of soft, lilting rural ballads, early Cuban *trovadores* included Sindo Garay, Nico Saquito and Joseíto Fernández, the man responsible for composing the overplayed Cuban *trova* classic *Guantanamera*.

As the style developed into the 1960s, new advocates such as Carlos Puebla from Bayamo gave the genre a grittier and more political edge, penning classic songs such as 'Hasta Siempre Comandante,' his romantic if slightly sycophantic ode to Che Guevara.

Traditional *trova* is still popular in Cuba today, though its mantle has been challenged since the '60s and '70s by its more philosophical modern offshoot, *nueva trova*.

Sindo Garay was one of Cuba's original *trovadores*. Born in Santiago de Cuba, he lived until the age of 99 and claimed to have shaken hands with both José Martí and Fidel Castro.

Rap, Reggaetón & Beyond

The contemporary Cuban music scene is an interesting mix of enduring traditions, modern sounds, old hands and new blood. With low production costs, solid urban themes and lots of US-inspired crossover styles, hip-hop and rap are taking the younger generation by storm.

NUEVA TROVA – THE SOUNDTRACK OF A REVOLUTION

The 1960s were heady days for radical new forms of musical expression. In the US Dylan released *Highway 61 Revisited,* in Britain the Beatles concocted *Sgt Pepper* while, in the Spanish-speaking world, musical activists such as Chilean Víctor Jara and Catalan Joan Manuel Serrat were turning their politically charged poems into passionate protest songs.

Determined to develop their own revolutionary music apart from the capitalist West, the innovative Cubans – under the stewardship of Haydee Santamaría, director at the influential Casa de las Américas – came up with *nueva trova*.

A caustic mix of probing philosophical lyrics and folksy melodic tunes, *nueva trova* was a direct descendent of pure *trova*, a bohemian form of guitar music that had originated in the Oriente in the late 19th century. Post-1959, *trova* became increasingly politicized and was taken up by more sophisticated artists such as Manzanillo-born Carlos Puebla, who provided an important bridge between old and new styles with his politically tinged ode to Che Guevara, 'Hasta Siempre Comandante' (1965).

Nueva trova came of age in February 1968 at the Primer Encuentro de la Canción Protesta, a concert organized at the Casa de las Américas in Havana and headlined by such rising stars as Silvio Rodríguez and Pablo Milanés. In a cultural context, it was Cuba's mini-Woodstock, an event that resounded forcefully among leftists worldwide as a revolutionary alternative to American rock 'n' roll.

In December 1972 the nascent *nueva trova* movement gained official sanction from the Cuban government during a music festival held in the city of Manzanillo to commemorate the 16th anniversary of the *Granma* landing.

Highly influential throughout the Spanish-speaking world during the '60s and '70s, *nueva trova* has often played an important role as an inspirational source of protest music for the impoverished and downtrodden populations of Latin America, many of whom looked to Cuba for spiritual leadership in an era of corrupt dictatorships and US cultural hegemony. This solidarity was reciprocated by the likes of Rodríguez, who penned numerous internationally lauded classics such as 'Canción Urgente para Nicaragua' (in support of the Sandinistas), 'La Maza' and 'Canción para mi Soldado' (a song about the Angolan War).

Born in the ugly concrete housing projects of Alamar, Havana, Cuban hip-hop, rather like its US counterpart, has gritty and impoverished roots.

First beamed across the nation in the early 1980s when American rap was picked up on homemade rooftop antennae from Miami-based radio stations, the new music quickly gained ground among a young urban black population who were culturally redefining themselves during the inquietude of the Special Period. By the '90s groups such as Public Enemy and NWA were de rigueur on the streets of Alamar and by 1995 there was enough hip-hop to throw a festival.

Tempered by Latin influences and censored by the parameters of strict revolutionary thought, Cuban hip-hop – or *reggaetón* as locals prefer to call it – has shied away from US stereotypes, instead taking on a progressive flavor all its own. Instrumentally the music uses *batá* drums, congas and electric bass, while lyrically the songs tackle important national issues such as sex tourism and the difficulties of the stagnant Cuban economy.

Despite being viewed early on as subversive and anti-revolutionary, Cuban hip-hop has gained unlikely support from inside the Cuban government, whose art-conscious legislators consider the music to have played a constructive social role in shaping the future of Cuban youth. Fidel Castro has gone one step further, describing hip-hop as 'the vanguard of the Revolution' and – allegedly – trying his hand at rapping at a Havana baseball game.

Today there are upwards of 800 hip-hop groups in Cuba, and the Cuban Rap Festival is well into its second decade. The event even has a sponsor, the fledgling Cuban Rap Agency, a government body formed in 2002 to give official sanction to the country's burgeoning alternative music scene. Groups to look out for include Obsession, 100% Original, Freehole Negro (co-fronted by a woman) and Anónimo Consejo, while the best venues are usually the most spontaneous ones.

It's hard to categorize Interactivo, a collaboration of young, talented musicians led by pianist Robertico Carcassés. Part funk, jazz and rock, and very 'in the groove,' this band jams to the rafters – a guaranteed good time. Interactivo's bassist is Yusa, a young black woman whose eponymous debut album made it clear she's one of the most innovative musicians on the Cuban scene today. Other difficult-to-categorize modern innovators include X Alfonso, an ex-student of the Conservatorio Amadeo Roldán; and dynamic *nueva trova*-rock duo Buena Fe, whose guitar-based riffs and eloquent lyrics push the boundaries of art and expression within the confines of the Cuban Revolution.

Son Revisited

In the late 1990s US guitar virtuoso Ry Cooder famously breathed new life into Cuban *son* music with his remarkable *Buena Vista Social Club* album and its accompanying movie directed by Wim Wenders. Linking together half a dozen or so long-retired musical sages from the 1940s and '50s, including 90-year-old Compay Segundo (writer of Cuba's second-most played song, 'Chan Chan'), dulcet singer Ibrahim Ferrer and pianist Rúben González (ranked by Cooder as the greatest piano player he had ever heard), the unprepossessing American producer sat back in the studio and let his ragged clutch of old-age pensioners work their erstwhile magic.

The album sold five million copies worldwide, won a Grammy and launched a world tour that included gigs in Amsterdam and New York. It also led to a noticeable increase in Cuban tourism, and the songs from

---

MUSIC & DANCE SON REVISITED

Best Casas de la Trova

Baracoa

Santiago de Cuba

Trinidad

Camagüey

Sancti Spíritus

COUNTRY GIRL

'Guajira Guantanamera' means 'country girl from Guantánamo.' Written by *trovador* Joseito Fernández, most of the original lyrics have been replaced with words from José Martí's *Versos sencillos*.

ROCK 'N' ROLL REBELS

Cuban rockers have always been – by necessity – a more rebellious breed than their non-Cuban counterparts, risking not just a ticking off from their parents but government condemnation, social ostracism and even imprisonment in the pursuit of their art. In the 1960s and '70s rock culture was forced underground after the music was effectively banned by a Cuban leadership who considered it decadent, counter-revolutionary and an undesirable product of the capitalist West. The situation thawed a little in the 1980s, particularly after the fall of the hard-line ideologies in Eastern Europe. In 1988, a brave group of Cuban *roqueros* opened the soon-to-be legendary Patio de Maria in Havana, and the music had a venue. A year later it gained a festival, too, the Ciudad Metal in Santa Clara which was quickly reincarnated as Cuba's edgiest and most alternative city.

By the '90s even Fidel Castro was cottoning on to the talents of John Lennon, late singer/songwriter of the once-banned Beatles with whom he shared a penchant for utopian politics and beards. On the 20th anniversary of Lennon's death in 2000, Castro unveiled a statue of the bespectacled ex-Beatle in a park in Vedado, Havana and declared him a 'revolutionary.'

Never on the standard rock tour circuit, Cuba welcomed its first foreign rock band in 2001 when Welsh punks The Manic Street Preachers played in front of 5000 fans in Miramar's Karl Marx Theater (each paying 25 cents for the privilege). A 74-year-old Fidel Castro was in the audience to enjoy tracks such as 'Baby Elian' and 'When Robeson Sings' (in which he is name-checked). It was loud, he declared, but 'not as loud as war.'

Since the Patio de Maria closed in 2004, the nexus for *roqueros* in Havana has been the corner of Calle 23 and Av G in Vedado. This rather nebulous gathering spot was complemented in 2011 by the opening of the officially sanctioned Submarino Amarillo (Yellow Submarine) bar in Parque Lennon, Vedado.

Cuban rock bands to listen out for include Zeus, Hypnosis, Rice and Beans and – most controversial by far – the punk rock outfit Porno para Ricardo headed up by Gorki Águilar, a vociferous critic of the Cuban government.

the album – 'Chan Chan,' 'Cuarto de Tula,' 'Dos Gardenias' et al – have since become staples for musical groups performing in tourist areas. Unruffled by the acclaim, most Cubans are happy to sit back and listen to the more modern sounds of *timba*, *reggaetón* and songo-salsa.

Landscape & Wildlife

Measuring 1250km from east to west and between 31km and 193km from north to south, Cuba is the Caribbean's largest island with a total land area of 110,860 sq km. Shaped like one of its signature crocodiles and situated just south of the Tropic of Cancer, the country is actually an archipelago made up of 4195 smaller islets and coral reefs. Its unique set of ecosystems have been fascinating and perplexing scientists and naturalists ever since Alexander von Humboldt frst mapped them in the early 1800s.

The Cuban Landscape

Formed by a volatile mixture of volcanic activity, plate tectonics and erosion, the landscape of Cuba is a lush and varied concoction of caves, mountains, plains and *mogotes* (strange flat-topped hills). The highest point, Pico Turquino (1972m), is situated in the east among the lofty triangular peaks of the Sierra Maestra. Further west, in the no less majestic Sierra del Escambray, ruffled hilltops and gushing waterfalls straddle the borders of Cienfuegos, Villa Clara and Sancti Spíritus provinces. Rising like purple shadows in the far west, the 175km-long Cordillera de Guanguanico is a more diminutive range that includes the protected Sierra del Rosario Biosphere Reserve and the distinctive pincushion hills of the Valle de Viñales.

Lapped by the warm turquoise waters of the Caribbean Sea in the south, and the foamy white chop of the Atlantic Ocean in the north, Cuba's 5746km of coastline shelters more than 300 natural beaches and features one of the largest tracts of coral reef in the world. Home to approximately 900 reported species of fish and more than 410 varieties of sponge and coral, the country's unspoiled coastline is a marine wonderland and a major reason why Cuba has become renowned as a diving destination extraordinaire.

The 7200m-deep Cayman Trench between Cuba and Jamaica forms the boundary of the North American and Caribbean plates. Tectonic movements have tilted the island over time, creating uplifted limestone cliffs along parts of the north coast and low mangrove swamps on the south. Over millions of years Cuba's limestone bedrock has been eroded by underground rivers, creating interesting geological features including the 'haystack' hills of Viñales and more than 20,000 caves countrywide.

As a sprawling archipelago, Cuba contains thousands of islands and keys (most uninhabited) in four major offshore groups: the Archipiélago de los Colorados, off northern Pinar del Río; the Archipiélago de Sabana-Camagüey (or Jardines del Rey), off northern Villa Clara and Ciego de Ávila; the Archipiélago de los Jardines de la Reina, off southern Ciego de Ávila; and the Archipiélago de los Canarreos, around Isla de la Juventud. Most visitors will experience one or more of these island idylls, as the majority of resorts, scuba diving and virgin beaches are found in these regions.

Being a narrow island, never measuring more than 200km north to south, Cuba's capacity for large lakes and rivers is severely limited

Cuba's Isla Grande (main island) is the 17th-largest island in the world by area: slightly smaller than Newfoundland, but marginally bigger than Iceland.

Cuba's Highest Mountains

Pico Turquino
1972m, Santiago de Cuba province

Pico Cuba
1872m, Santiago de Cuba province

Pico Bayamesa
1730m, Granma province

(preventing hydroelectricity). Cuba's longest river, the 343km-long Río Cauto that flows from the Sierra Maestra in a rough loop north of Bayamo, is only navigable by small boats for 110km. To compensate, 632 *embalses* (reservoirs) or *presas* (dams), covering an area of more than 500 sq km altogether, have been created for irrigation and water supply; these supplement the almost unlimited groundwater held in Cuba's limestone bedrock.

Lying in the Caribbean's main hurricane region, Cuba has been hit by some blinders in recent years, including three devastating storms in 2008 – its worst year for more than a century.

Cuba's Longest River

Name *Río Cauto*

Length *343km*

Navigable length *110km*

Basin area *8928 sq km*

Source *Sierra Maestra Mountains*

Mouth *Caribbean Sea*

Protected Areas

Cuba protects its land in multiple ways: at a local level it has set up fauna reserves, bio-parks and areas of managed resources; at a national level it sponsors national parks and natural parks; and international protection is provided in the form of Unesco Biosphere Reserves, Unesco World Heritage Sites and Ramsar Convention Sites. The most ecologically important and vulnerable zones (such as the Ciénaga de Zapata and the rainforest around Baracoa) are protected at more than one level. For example, Parque Nacional Alejandro de Humboldt is a national park, a Unesco World Heritage Site *and* part of the Cuchillos de Toa Unesco Biosphere Reserve. Lower down the pecking order, the smaller parks suffer from less- watertight restrictions and can be more open to rule-bending.

Unesco & Ramsar Sites

The highest level of environmental protection in Cuba is provided by Unesco, which has created six biosphere reserves over the last 25 years. Biosphere reserves are areas of high biodiversity that rigorously promote conservation and sustainable practices. After a decade and a half of successful reforestation the Sierra del Rosario became Cuba's first Unesco Biosphere Reserve in 1985. It was followed by Cuchillos del Toa (1987),

CUBA'S PROTECTED AREAS

AREA NAME	YEAR DESIGNATED	OUTSTANDING FEATURES
Unesco Biosphere Reserves		
Sierra del Rosario	1985	eco practices
Cuchillos del Toa	1987	primary rainforest
Península de Guanahacabibes	1987	turtle nesting site
Baconao	1987	coffee culture
Ciénaga de Zapata	2000	largest wetlands in Caribbean
Buenavista	2000	karst formations
Ramsar Convention Sites		
Ciénaga de Zapata	2001	largest wetlands in Caribbean
Buenavista	2002	karst formations
Ciénaga de Lanier	2002	unusual mosaic of ecosystems
Humedal del Norte de Ciego de Ávila	2002	unique coastal lakes
Humedal Delta del Cauto	2002	large population of aquatic birds
Humedal Río Máximo-Cagüey	2002	significant flamingo nesting site
'Natural' Unesco World Heritage Sites		
Parque Nacional Desembarco del Granma	1999	pristine marine terraces
Parque Nacional Alejandro de Humboldt	2001	high endemism

Protected Areas

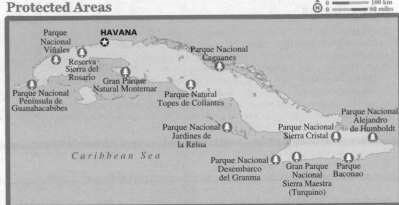

Península de Guanahacabibes (1987), Baconao (1987), Ciénaga de Zapata (2000) and the Bahía de Buenavista (2000). Additionally, two of Cuba's nine Unesco World Heritage Sites are considered 'natural' sites, ie nominated primarily for their ecological attributes. They are: Parque Nacional Desembarco del Granma (1999), hailed for its uplifted marine terraces, and Parque Nacional Alejandro de Humboldt (2001), well known for its extraordinary endemism. Complementing the Unesco sites are half a dozen Ramsar Convention Sites that were earmarked in 2001–02 to conserve Cuba's vulnerable wetlands. The Ramsar Convention gives added protection to the Ciénaga de Zapata and Bahía de Buenavista, and also throws a lifeline to previously unprotected regions such as the Lanier Swamp on the Isla de la Juventud (prime crocodile territory), the expansive Río Cauto delta in Granma and Las Tunas, and the vital flamingo nesting sites on the north coasts of Camagüey and Ciego de Ávila provinces.

National Parks

The definition of a national park is fluid in Cuba (some are often referred to as natural parks or flora reserves) and there's no umbrella organization as in Canada or the USA. A handful of the 14 listed parks – most notably Ciénaga de Zapata – now lie within Unesco Biosphere Reserves or Ramsar Convention Sites, meaning their conservation policies are better monitored. The country's first national park was Sierra del Cristal, established in 1930 (home to Cuba's largest pine forest), though it was 50 years before the authorities created another, Gran Parque Nacional Sierra Maestra (also known as Turquino), which safeguards Cuba's highest mountain. Other important parks include Viñales, with its *mogotes*, caves and tobacco plantations; Caguanes, an amalgam of *cayos* (keys) and caves surrounded by the Bahía de Buenavista; and Gran Piedra, near Santiago de Cuba, which is overlaid by the Baconao Unesco Biosphere Reserve. Two important offshore national parks off the south coast are the Jardines de la Reina, an archipelago and legendary diving haven off the coast of Ciego de Ávila province; and the rarely visited Cayos de San Felipe off the coast of Pinar del Río province.

Parque Nacional Alejandro de Humboldt is named for German naturalist Alexander von Humboldt (1769–1859) who visited the island between 1801 and 1804.

Other Reserves

On top of its national parks and Unesco sites, Cuba protects land in flora and fauna reserves, eco-reserves and areas of managed resources. Examples include the Sierra del Chorrillo in Camagüey and the Reserva

NATURAL SPAS

Cuban spas look more like utilitarian hospitals than candlelit pampering houses – not that this detracts from their powers of recuperation. The nation's most popular spas are fed by thermal, mineral-rich water sources and are connected to economical Islazul hotels. They offer a mixture of baths, gymnasiums and assorted therapies.

The nation's oldest spa is at San Diego de los Baños in Pinar del Río province where the thermal waters were purportedly discovered by a sick slave in 1632. The perennially dilapidated *balneario* (spa), which opened in 1951, has swimming pools (32–38°C), mud therapy, massage, and on-site medical staff. It is used to treat many ailments, most notably rheumatism.

Cuba's hottest thermal waters – a bubbling 45–50°C – are at the isolated Hotel Elguea in Villa Clara province. The sulfurous on-site spa facility offers similar treatments to San Diego de los Baños. Beware the odor of rotten eggs.

A more physically attractive spa is located at San José del Lago in Sancti Spíritus province where a hotel and assorted outdoor pools are shaded by palm trees. A small lake with boats and resident flamingos add to the ambience. The waters here are high in bicarbonate and calcium and are apparently good for treating psoriasis.

Ecológica Varahicacos in Varadero. Some smaller reserves, such as Jobo Rosado in northern Sancti Spíritus province, act as buffer zones to larger parks such as the Bahía de Buenavista Unesco Biosphere Reserve.

Although Cuba's interconnecting network of protected areas is often confusing (many parks have two interchangeable names) – and sometimes overlapping – the sentiment's the same: environmental stewardship with a solid governmental backing.

Wildlife

While it isn't exactly the Serengeti, Cuba has an unusual share of indigenous fauna, and serious animal-watchers won't be disappointed. Birds are probably the biggest draw and Cuba is home to more than 350 different varieties, two dozen of them endemic. Head to the mangroves of Ciénaga de Zapata near the Bahía de Cochinos (Bay of Pigs) or to the Península de Guanahacabibes in Pinar del Río for the best sightings of the blink-and-you'll-miss-it *zunzuncito* (bee hummingbird), the world's smallest bird and, at 6.5cm, not much longer than a toothpick. These areas are also home to the *tocororo* (Cuban trogon), Cuba's national bird, which sports the red, white and blue colors of the Cuban flag. Other popular bird species include *cartacubas* (a type of bird indigenous to Cuba), herons, spoonbills, parakeets and rarely seen Cuban pygmy owls.

Flamingos are abundant in Cuba's northern keys where they have established the largest nesting ground in the western hemisphere in the Río Máximo delta in Camagüey province, with numbers in the tens of thousands.

Land mammals have been hunted almost to extinction with the largest indigenous survivor the friendly *jutía* (tree rat), a 4kg edible rodent that scavenges on isolated keys living in relative harmony with armies of inquisitive iguanas. The vast majority of Cuba's other 38 species of mammal are from the bat family.

Cuba harbors a species of frog so small and elusive that it wasn't discovered until 1996 in what is now Parque Nacional Alejandro de Humboldt near Baracoa. Still lacking a common name, the endemic amphibian is known as *Eleutherodactylus iberia*; it measures less than 1cm in length, and has a range of only 100 sq km.

Other odd species include the *mariposa de cristal* (Cuban clear-winged butterfly), one of only two clear-winged butterflies in the world;

Endemic Fauna

Cuban crocodile

Bee hummingbird

Tocororo (bird)

Jutía (tree rat)

Cuban gar (fish)

Eleutherodactylus iberia (frog)

Cuban boa (snake)

Cuban red bat

the rare *manjuarí* (Cuban alligator gar), an ancient fish considered a living fossil; and the *polymita*, a unique land snail distinguished by its festive yellow, red and brown bands.

Reptiles are well represented in Cuba. Aside from iguanas and lizards, there are 15 species of snake, none of them poisonous. Cuba's largest snake is the *majá*, a constrictor related to the anaconda that grows up to 4m in length; it's nocturnal and doesn't usually mess with humans. The endemic Cuban crocodile *(Crocodylus rhombifer)* is relatively small but agile on land and in water. Its 68 sharp teeth are specially adapted for crushing turtle shells. Crocs have suffered from major habitat loss in the last century though greater protection since the 1990s has seen numbers increase. Cuba has established a number of successful *criaderos* (crocodile) breeding farms, the largest of which is at Guama near the Bay of Pigs. Living in tandem with the Cuban croc is the larger American crocodile *(Cacutus)* found in the Zapata Swamps and in various marshy territories on Cuba's southern coast.

Cuba's marine life makes up for what the island lacks in land fauna. The manatee, the world's only herbivorous aquatic mammal, is found in the Bahía de Taco and the Península de Zapata, and whale sharks frequent the María la Gorda area at Cuba's eastern tip from August to November. Four turtle species (leatherback, loggerhead, green and hawksbill) are found in Cuban waters and they nest annually in isolated keys or on the protected western beaches of the Península de Guanahacabibes.

Endangered Species

Due to habitat loss and persistent hunting by humans, many of Cuba's animals and birds are listed as endangered species. These include the critically endangered Cuban crocodile, which has the smallest habitat range of any crocodile, existing only in 300 sq km of the Ciénega de Zapata (Zapata Swamp) and in the Lanier Swamp on Isla de la Juventud. Protected since 1996, wild numbers now hover at around 6000. Other vulnerable species include the *jutía,* which was hunted mercilessly during the Special Period, when hungry Cubans tracked them for their meat (they still do – in fact, it is considered something of a delicacy); the tree boa, a native snake that lives in rapidly diminishing woodland areas; and the elusive *carpintero real* (ivory-billed woodpecker), spotted after a 40-year gap in the Parque Nacional Alejandro de Humboldt near Baracoa in the late 1980s, but not seen since.

BIRD-WATCHING

Cuba offers a bird-watching bonanza year-round and no serious ornithologist should enter the country without their binoculars close at hand. Your experience will be enhanced by the level of expertise shown by many of Cuba's naturalists and guides in the key bird-watching zones. Areas with specialist bird watching trails or trips include the Cueva las Perlas trail in Parque Nacional Península de Guanahacabibes, the Maravillas de Viñales trail in Parque Nacional Viñales, the Sendero la Serafina in the Reserva Sierra del Rosario, the Observación de Aves tour in Gran Parque Natural Montemar, Parque Natural el Bagá on Cayo Coco, and the Sendero de las Aves in Hacienda la Belén in Camagüey province.

Must-sees include the *tocororo* (Cuban trogon), the *zunzuncito* (bee hummingbird), the Cuban tody, the Cuban parakeet, the Antillean palm swift, the *cartacuba* (an indigenous Cuban bird) and, of course, the flamingo – preferably in a flock. Good spots for some DIY bird-watching are on Cayo Romano and adjacent Cayo Sabinal, although you'll need a car to get here. Specialists and ivory-billed-woodpecker seekers will enjoy Parque Nacional Alejandro de Humboldt.

TOCORORO

In the forested mountains of rural Cuba, there are few birds as striking or emblematic as the *tocororo*.

Endemic to the island, the *tocororo* – or Cuban trogon, to give it its scientific name – is a medium-sized black-and-white bird with a bright red belly and a bluish-green patch between the wings. Other distinctive features include a sharp serrated bill and a sweeping concave tail.

Easy to spot if you know where to look, the bird is widely distributed throughout Cuba in heavily forested areas, especially near rivers and streams. The unusual name is derived from its distinctive call which sounds out: *to-co-ro-ro*.

Long venerated for its striking plumage, the *tocororo* was chosen as Cuba's national bird due to its coloring (which replicates the red, white and blue of the Cuban flag) and its apparent resistance to captivity. Nationalistically minded Cubans will tell you that *tocororos* are instinctively libertarian, and if you cage one, it will quickly die.

The seriously endangered West Indian manatee, while protected from illegal hunting, continues to suffer from a variety of human threats, most notably from contact with boat propellers, suffocation by fishing nets and poisoning from residues pumped into rivers from sugar factories.

Cuba has an ambiguous attitude toward the hunting of turtles. Hawksbill turtles are protected under the law, though a clause allows for up to 500 of them to be captured per year in certain areas (Camagüey and Isla de la Juventud). Travelers will occasionally encounter *tortuga* (turtle) on the menu in places such as Baracoa. You are advised not to partake as these turtles may have been caught illegally.

Plants

Cuba is synonymous with the palm tree; through songs, symbols, landscapes and legends the two are inextricably linked. The national tree is the *palma real* (royal palm), and it's central to the country's coat of arms. It's believed there are 20 million royal palms in Cuba and locals will tell you that wherever you stand on the island, you'll always be within sight of one. Standing single file by the roadside or clumped on a hill, these majestic trees reach up to 40m in height and are easily identified by their lithe trunk and green stalk at the top. There are also *cocotero* (coconut palm); *palma barrigona* (big-belly palm) with its characteristic bulge; and the extremely rare *palma corcho* (cork palm). The latter is a link with the Cretaceous period (between 65 and 135 million years ago) and is cherished as a living fossil. You can see examples of it on the grounds of the Museo de Ciencias Naturales Sandalio de Noda and La Ermita, both in Pinar del Río province. All told, there are 90 palm-tree types in Cuba.

Other important trees include mangroves, in particular the spiderlike mangroves that protect the Cuban shoreline from erosion and provide an important habitat for small fish and birds. Mangroves account for 26% of Cuban forests and cover almost 5% of the island's coast; Cuba ranks ninth in the world in terms of mangrove density, and the most extensive swamps are situated in the Ciénaga de Zapata.

The largest native pine forests grow on Isla de la Juventud (the former Isle of Pines), in western Pinar del Río, in eastern Holguín (or more specifically the Sierra Cristal) and in central Guantánamo. These forests are especially susceptible to fire damage, and pine reforestation has been a particular headache for the island's environmentalists.

Rainforests exist at higher altitudes – between approximately 500m and 1500m – in the Sierra del Escambray, Sierra Maestra and Macizo de Sagua-Baracoa mountains. Original rainforest species include ebony and

MANATEES

The Caribbean manatee can grow 4.5m long and weigh up to 600kg. They can consume up to 50kg of plant life a day.

mahogany, but today most reforestation is in eucalyptus, which is grace-ful and fragrant, but invasive.

Dotted liberally across the island, ferns, cacti and orchids contribute hundreds of species, many endemic, to Cuba's cornucopia of plant life. For the best concentrations check out the botanical gardens in Santiago de Cuba for ferns and cacti and Pinar del Río for orchids. Most orchids bloom from November to January, and one of the best places to see them is in the Reserva Sierra del Rosario. The national flower is the graceful *mariposa* (butterfly jasmine); you'll know it by its white floppy petals and strong perfume.

Medicinal plants are widespread in Cuba due largely to a chronic shortage of prescription medicines (banned under the US embargo). Pharmacies are well stocked with effective tinctures such as aloe (for cough and congestion) and a bee by-product called *propólio*, used for everything from stomach amoebas to respiratory infections. On the home front, every Cuban patio has a pot of *oregano de la tierra* (Cuban oregano) growing and if you start getting a cold you'll be whipped up a wonder elixir made from the fat, flat leaves mixed with lime juice, honey and hot water.

> It is estimated that Cuba harbors between 6500 and 7000 different species of plant, almost half of which are endemic.

Environmental Issues

Most of Cuba's environmental threats are of human origin and relate either to pollution or habitat loss, often through deforestation. Efforts to conserve the archipelago's diverse ecology were almost nonexistent until 1978, when Cuba established the National Committee for the Protection and Conservation of Natural Resources and the Environment (Comarna). Attempting to reverse 400 years of deforestation and habitat destruction, the body set about designating green belts and initiating ambitious reforestation campaigns. The conservation policies are directed by Comarna, which acts as a coordinating body, overseeing 15 ministries and ensuring that current national and international environmental legislation is being carried out efficiently. This includes adherence to the important international treaties that govern Cuba's six Unesco Biosphere Reserves and nine Unesco World Heritage Sites.

Cuba's greatest environmental problems are aggravated by an econ-omy struggling to survive. As the country pins its hopes on tourism to save the financial day, a contradictory environmental policy has evolved. Therein lies the dilemma: how can a developing nation provide for its people *and* maintain high (or at least minimal) ecological standards?

> **Cayos with a Hotel Infrastructure**
>
> Largo del Sur
>
> Santa María
>
> Las Brujas
>
> Coco
>
> Guillermo
>
> Levisa
>
> Ensenachos
>
> Saetía

ECO-RESORTS

Cuba's flagship eco-hotel is **La Moka** (☎57-86-00; Las Terrazas; s/d CUC$80/110; P☀☎) in the small eco-village of Las Terrazas in the Sierra del Rosario. The hotel, built in 1994 in a Unesco Biosphere Reserve, follows sustainable principles and is famous for the large tree growing through the roof of its lobby. Other genuine environmental hotels are Hotel Horizontes El Saltón (p432) in the Sierra Maestra foothills near Santiago de Cuba and Villa Pinares del Mayarí (p376), run by Gaviota in the hilly pine forests of Holguín province.

Cuban travel agency Ecotur (p46) sponsors a growing stash of rural accommodation located in Cuba's protected areas. Most of these rustic chalets and cabins have electricity, hot water, shared or private bathrooms and *ranchón* (rural farm)-style restaurants. Some also act as farms, environmental learning centers, or bio-stations.

Highlights include the Guabina equestrian center near Pinar del Río, the Jarico and La Sabina chalets in the Alturas de Banao in Sancti Spíritus province and Finca La Esperanza near Baracoa.

Deforestation

It is estimated that at the time of Columbus' arrival, 95% of Cuba was virgin forest. By 1959, thanks to unregulated land-clearing for sugarcane and citrus plantations, this area had been reduced to 16%. Large-scale tree-planting and the organization of significant tracts of land into protected parks has seen this figure creep back up to 24% (making it the leader in Latin America), but there is still a lot of work to be done. Las Terrazas in Pinar del Río province provided a blueprint for reforestation efforts in the late 1960s, when it saved hectares of denuded woodland from ecological disaster. More recent efforts have focused on safeguarding the Caribbean's last virgin rainforest in Parque Nacional Alejandro de Humboldt and adding protective forest fringes to wetlands in the Río Cauto delta.

Causeways

An early blip in Cuba's economy-versus-ecology struggle was the 2km-long stone *pedraplén* (causeway) constructed to link offshore Cayo Sabinal with mainland Camagüey in the late 1980s. This massive project, which involved piling boulders in the sea and laying a road on top (without any bridges), interrupted water currents and caused irreparable damage to bird and marine habitats. And to what end; no resorts, as yet, inhabit deserted Cayo Sabinel. Other longer causeways were later built connecting Jardines del Rey to Ciego de Ávila (27km long) and Cayo Santa María to Villa Clara (a 48km-long monster). This time more eco-friendly bridges have enabled a healthier water flow, though the full extent of the ecological damage won't be known for another decade at least.

Wildlife & Habitat Loss

Maintaining healthy animal habitats is crucial in Cuba, a country with high levels of endemism and hence a higher threat of species extinction. The problem is exacerbated by the narrow range of endemic animals, such as the Cuban crocodile that lives almost exclusively in the Ciénaga de Zapata, or the equally rare *Eleutherodactylus iberia* (the world's smallest frog). The latter has a range of just 100 sq km and exists only in the Parque Nacional Alejandro de Humboldt, whose formation in 2001 undoubtedly saved it from extinction. Other areas under threat include the giant flamingo nesting sites on the Sabana-Camagüey archipelago, and Moa, where contaminated water runoff has played havoc with the coastal mangrove ecosystems favored by manatees.

Building new roads and airports, and the frenzied construction of giant resorts on virgin beaches, exacerbate the clash between human activity and environmental protection. The grossly shrunken extent of the Reserva Ecológica Varahicacos in Varadero due to encroaching resorts is one example. Cayo Coco – part of an important Ramsar-listed wetland that sits adjacent to a fast-developing hotel strip – is another.

Overfishing (including turtles and lobster for tourist consumption), agricultural runoff, industrial pollution and inadequate sewage treatment have contributed to the decay of coral reefs. Diseases such as yellow band, black band and nuisance algae have begun to appear. The rounding up of wild dolphins as entertainers in *delfinarios* (dolphinariums) has also rankled many activists (performing dolphins are supposed to be bred in captivity).

Pollution

As soon as you arrive in Havana or Santiago de Cuba, the air pollution hits you like a sharp slap on the face. Airborne particles, old trucks belching black smoke and by-products from burning garbage are just some of

COFFEE

Approximately 2% of Cuba's arable land is given over to coffee production and the industry supports a workforce of 265,000.

THE WORLD'S MOST SUSTAINABLE COUNTRY?

With its antiquated infrastructure and fume-belching city traffic, Cuba might not seem like a font of innovative environmentalism. But in 2006, in an environmental report entitled *The Living Planet*, the World Wild Fund for Nature (WWF) named Castro's struggling island nation as the only country in the world with sustainable development.

The WWF based its study on two key criteria: a human welfare index (life expectancy, literacy and GDP) and the ecological footprint (the amount of land needed to fulfill a person's food and energy needs). Most countries failed to meet their sustainability requirements either because their ecological footprint was too high (the mega-consuming West), or their human welfare index was too low (the poverty-stricken countries of Africa and Asia). Cuba, with its excellent health and education indices and low rates of consumption, proved to be the only exception.

It would be naive to suggest that Cuba achieved its sustainability record through foresight alone. On the contrary, the Cubans are largely ecologists by necessity. The country's sustainability credentials were first laid out in the Special Period when, shorn of Soviet subsidies and marginalized from the world economy by a US trade embargo, rationing and recycling measures were necessary to survive.

To their credit, the Cubans haven't wavered since. Despite a car-ownership ratio of 38 per 1000 (the US is closer to 800 per 1000) and an almost total absence of chemical fertilizers, the country refused to take the easy route toward greater prosperity post–Special Period and, instead, quickly fell in with the new global environmental zeitgeist. Visit a Cuban casa particular these days and you'll find that dinner is made in a pressure cooker, all the light bulbs are LEDs and the old inefficient 1950s fridge has, more often than not, been replaced by a more eco-friendly (and quieter) model.

the culprits. Cement factories, sugar refineries and other heavy industries have also made their (dirty) mark. The nickel mines engulfing Moa serve as stark examples of industrial concerns taking precedence: this is some of the prettiest landscape in Cuba, turned into a barren wasteland of lunar proportions. Unfortunately there are no easy solutions; nickel is one of Cuba's largest exports, a raw material the economy couldn't do without. And while old American cars in Havana might paint a romantic picture to tourists, they're hardly fuel efficient or clean. Then there's the public transport – even Fidel has gone on the record to lament the adverse health effects of Cuba's filthy buses.

Environmental Successes

On the bright side of the environmental equation is the enthusiasm the Cuban government has shown for reforestation and protecting natural areas – especially since the mid-1980s – along with its willingness to confront mistakes from the past. Havana Harbor, once Latin America's most polluted, has been undergoing a massive cleanup, as has the Río Almendares, which cuts through the heart of the city. Both programs are beginning to show positive results. Sulfur emissions from oil wells near Varadero have been reduced, and environmental regulations for developments are now enforced by the Ministry of Science, Technology and the Environment. Fishing regulations, as local fishers will tell you, have become increasingly strict. Striking the balance between Cuba's immediate needs and the future of its environment is one of the Revolution's increasingly pressing challenges.

Las Terrazas is the nation's most obvious eco-success, though there have been others. Visitors to Cayo Coco can check out Parque El Bagá, a former airport that is now an ecopark, while on the Isla de la Juventud, Cuban crocodiles have been successfully reintroduced into the wild in the expansive Lanier Swamp.

The US & Cuba

Despite its location 90 miles off the shores of Florida, Cuba remains, in the eyes of most Americans, one of the last great travel mysteries. Since 1963, when the US government instituted a de facto Cuban travel ban, visits to the country by US nationals have been problematic, although under the auspices of the Obama administration the relationship has undergone a partial defrosting.

Freeze & Thaw

In 2010 the general assembly of the UN voted against the continuance of the US embargo on Cuba by 187 votes to three.

Whether the thaw is permanent remains to be seen. Traditionally, sporadic rapprochements between the Cuban and US governments have been limited and ephemeral. President Jimmy Carter loosened the regulations for licensed travel to Cuba for religious, educational and cultural groups in the late 1970s but, following the Mariel Boatlift and the accession of Ronald Reagan in 1980–81, the doors quickly shut. The Clinton administration attempted a second relaxation in 1995 and by the early 2000s an estimated 150,000 licensed US travelers were visiting Cuba annually (along with another 50,000 illegal 'tourists'). However, following Castro's crackdown on Cuban dissidents in 2003's 'Black Spring' and the ensuing diplomatic finger-wagging, the George W Bush administration closed the doors to all but the most determined American travelers.

In April 2009 the Obama administration widened the goalposts when it allowed Cuban-Americans to visit their families in Cuba as often as they liked (under Bush II they had been restricted to one visit every three years). Using his powers of presidential decree, Obama also permitted Cuban-Americans to send unlimited remittances to relatives across the water, providing a vital source of revenue for Cubans attempting to start businesses under Raúl Castro's new privatization laws.

But, before ordinary Americans start ironing the creases out of their *guayaberas* (shirts) and getting ready to reacquaint themselves with mambo dancing, Guantanameras and *real* cigars, it is important to do some pre-trip homework. To travel legally to Cuba, all US citizens must first have a valid license. The **US Department of the Treasury** (www. treasury.gov/resource-center/sanctions/Programs/pages/cuba.aspx) currently issues two types – 'general' licenses (good for contracted journalists, government officials and Cubans visiting families) which don't require prior approval; and 'specific' licenses (catering largely to academic institutions, religious organizations, freelance journalists and people engaged in humanitarian work) which require prior approval. 'Specific' licenses – the type which most non-Cuban-Americans need – must be applied for in writing and are dealt with on a case-by-case basis. Check the Treasury website to see if you qualify.

Crime & Punishment

Technically, Americans aren't banned from physically traveling to Cuba; rather, they are banned from making 'travel-related transactions' in the country, a ruling which pretty much amounts to the same thing.

PUTTING PRESSURE ON THE EMBARGO

Recent surveys in the US suggest that a majority of Americans are opposed to the US embargo and its associated travel ban. A 2012 Angus Reid poll concluded that 62% of Americans would restore diplomatic ties with Cuba, 57% favor ending the travel ban, and 51% want to end the trade embargo. The travel ban is also opposed by leading dissidents in Cuba. In June 2010, 74 dissidents (including blogger Yoani Sánchez and representatives of the human rights group the 'Ladies in White') signed a letter to the US Congress supporting a bill to end travel restrictions for Americans. The UN General Assembly passes annual resolutions against the US embargo, usually by a margin of 182 to four, with the US, Israel, Palau and the Marshall Islands voting against.

The measure was brought into force by President Kennedy in 1963 by invoking the 1917 Trading with the Enemy Act. In theory, breaking this law can land you a $55,000 fine or up to 10 years in jail, though prosecutions are rare – and have become rarer since Obama succeeded George W Bush. As a result, many thousands of Americans circumnavigate the law every year by flying to Cuba out of third countries such as Mexico, Canada and the Bahamas. Cuban customs officials never stamp foreign passports.

There is only one statue of an American president in Cuba – that of Abraham Lincoln, which furnishes the Parque de la Fraternidad in Centro Habana.

Licensed Travel Agencies

In January 2011 the license bureaucracy became a lot easier with the re-introduction of government-sanctioned people-to-people trips (cultural trips with licensed providers) that were discontinued by the George W Bush administration in 2003. The people-to-people program reflects efforts by the US government to engage US citizens in 'purposeful travel' to Cuba by bringing them into contact with ordinary Cubans in the hope of bolstering trust and mutual understanding between the two countries. On these trips, authorized agents handle the license paperwork, leaving participants with fewer legal worries and more downtime to enjoy organized excursions in a similar way to other vacationers. The US Treasury department has issued licenses to approximately 140 registered people-to-people travel companies since 2011, including travel pioneers **Insight Cuba** (www.insightcuba.com), who first ran excursions to the country during the Clinton era, along with **Moto Discovery** (www.motodiscovery.com), **Friendly Planet** (www.friendlyplanet.com), **Grand Circle Foundation** (www.grandcirclefoundation.org) and **Geographic Expeditions** (www.geoex.com).

Another result of the Obama administration's initiative has been the introduction of more charter flights serving Cuba from the US. Prior to January 2011 only three US airports (NYC, LA and Miami) ran regular Cuba charters but, in the years since, five new airports (including Chicago and Atlanta) have added authorized flights for licensed travelers.

To minimize disruption in a country which has no formal diplomatic relations with the US, various specialist organizations have grown up to smooth the way for first-time Cuba travelers seeking guidance and advice. One of the oldest and most trusted is Marazul (p515), a travel agency founded in 1979 that helps both individuals and groups with license inquiries, flight bookings, hotel reservations, and in-country transportation.

One of the most complicated issues for US travelers in Cuba is money. US–issued credit and debit cards are not accepted by Cuban banks and changing US dollars incurs a 10% commission. Consequently, it is advisable to change sufficient cash funds into Canadian dollars or euros prior to your visit and store your money in a money belt and/or hotel

US Presidents who tried to buy Cuba from Spain

1808 –
Thomas Jefferson – undisclosed sum

1848 –
James Polk – $100 million

1854 –
Franklin Pierce – $130 million

1898 –
William McKinley – $300 million

safe-deposit box when in-country. Furthermore, licensed travelers are restricted to a State Department spending allowance currently set at between $125 and $144 per day depending on where you are in Cuba. See http://aoprals.state.gov/web920/per_diem.asp for updates.

For most visitors the hassle of reaching Cuba is well worth it. Castro's time capsule promises to be like nowhere else you've ever visited. Even better, most Americans are surprised to find that ordinary Cubans bear them no animosity. You will be welcomed with open arms – and by some of the best music on the planet.

Survival Guide

Directory A–Z

Accommodations

Cuban accommodations run the gamut from CUC$10 beach cabins to five-star resorts. Solo travelers are penalized price-wise, paying 75% of the price of a double room.

Budget

In this price range, casas particulares are almost always better value than a hotel. Only the most deluxe casas particulares in Havana will be over CUC$50, and in these places you're assured quality amenities and attention. In cheaper casas particulares (CUC$15 to CUC$20), you may have to share a bathroom and will have a fan instead of air-con. In the rock-bottom places (campismos, mostly), you'll be lucky if there are sheets and running water, though there are usually private bathrooms. If you're staying in a place intended for Cubans, you'll compromise materially, but the memories are guaranteed to be platinum.

Midrange

The midrange category is a lottery, with some boutique colonial hotels and some awful places with spooky Soviet-like architecture and atmosphere. In midrange hotels you can expect air-con, private hot-water bathroom, clean linens, satellite TV, a restaurant and a swimming pool, although the architecture is often uninspiring and the food not exactly gourmet.

Top End

The most comfortable top-end hotels are usually partly foreign-owned and maintain international standards (although service can sometimes be a bit lax). Rooms have everything that a midrange hotel has, plus big, quality beds and linens, a minibar, international phone service, and perhaps a terrace or view. Havana has some real gems.

Price Differentials

Factors influencing rates are time of year, location and hotel chain. Low season is generally mid-September to early December and February to May (except for Easter

week). Christmas and New Year is what's called extreme high season, when rates are 25% more than high-season rates. Bargaining is sometimes possible in casas particulares – though as far as foreigners go, it's not really the done thing. The casa owners in any given area pay generic taxes, and the prices you will be quoted reflect this. You'll find very few casas in Cuba that aren't priced between CUC$15 and CUC$50, unless you're up for a long stay. Prearranging Cuban accommodation has become easier now that more Cubans (unofficially) have access to the internet.

Types of Accommodations

CAMPISMOS

Campismos are where Cubans go on vacation (an estimated one million use them annually). Hardly camping, most of these installations are simple concrete cabins with bunk beds, foam mattresses and cold showers. There are over 80 of them sprinkled around the country in rural areas. Campismos are ranked either *nacional* or *internacional*. The former are (technically) only for Cubans, while the latter host both Cubans and foreigners and are more upscale, with air-con and/or linens. There are currently a dozen international campismos in Cuba ranging from the hotel-standard Aguas Claras (Pinar del Río) to the more basic Puerto Rico Libre (Holguín).

For advance bookings, contact the excellent **Cubamar** (☑833-2523, 833-2524; www.cubamarviajes.cu; Calle 3, btwn Calle 12 & Malecón, Vedado; ◷8:30am-5pm Mon-Sat) in Havana for reservations. Cabin accommodation in international campismos costs from CUC$10 to CUC$60 per bed.

CASAS PARTICULARES

Private rooms are the best option for independent travelers in Cuba and a great way of meeting the locals on their home turf. Furthermore, staying in these venerable, family-orientated establishments will give you a far more open and less censored view of the country, and your understanding and appreciation of Cuba will grow far richer as a result. Casa owners also often make excellent tour guides.

You'll know houses renting rooms by the blue insignia on the door marked 'Arrendador Divisa.' There are thousands of casas particulares all over Cuba – well over 3000 in Havana alone and more than 500 in Trinidad. From penthouses to historical homes, all manner of rooms are available from CUC$15 to CUC$50. Although some houses will treat you like a business paycheck, the vast majority of casa owners are warm, open and impeccable hosts.

Government regulation has eased since 2011, and renters can now let out multiple rooms if they have space. Owners pay a monthly tax per room depending on location (plus extra for off-street parking) to post a sign advertising their rooms and to serve meals. These taxes must be paid whether or not the rooms are rented. Owners must keep a register of all guests and report each new arrival within 24 hours. For these reasons, you will find it hard to bargain for rooms. You will also be requested to produce your passport (not a photocopy). Penalties are high for infractions. Regular government inspections ensure that conditions inside casas remain clean, safe and secure. Most proprietors offer breakfast and dinner for an extra rate. Hot showers are a prerequisite. In general, rooms these days provide at least two beds (one is usually a double), fridge, air-con, fan and private bathroom. Bonuses could include a terrace or patio, private entrance, TV, security box, kitchenette and parking space.

BOOKINGS & FURTHER INFORMATION

Due to the plethora of casas particulares in Cuba, it has been impossible to include even a fraction of the total. The ones chosen are a combination of reader recommendations and local research. If one casa is full,

they'll almost always be able to recommend to you someone else down the road.

The following websites list a large number of casas across the country and allow online booking.

Cubacasas (www.cubacasas.net) The best online source for casa particular information and booking; up to date, accurate and with colorful links to hundreds of private rooms across the island (in English and French).

Casa Particular Organization (www.casaparticularcuba.org) Reader-recommended website for pre-booking private rooms.

HOTELS

All tourist hotels and resorts are at least 51% owned by the Cuban government and are administered by one of five main organizations. Islazul is the cheapest and most popular with Cubans (who pay in Cuban pesos). Although the facilities can be variable at these establishments and the architecture a tad Sovietesque, Islazul hotels are invariably clean, cheap, friendly and, above all, Cuban. They're also more likely to be situated in the island's smaller provincial towns. One downside is the blaring on-site discos that often keep guests awake until the small hours. Cubanacán is a step up and offers a nice mix of budget and midrange options in both

HOTEL WEBSITES

Ninety-five percent of Cuba's hotels are run by one of the following companies. For more information see their websites.

➡ **Cubanacán** (www.cubanacan.com)

➡ **Gaviota** (www.gaviota-grupo.com)

➡ **Gran Caribe** (www.grancaribe.cu)

➡ **Habaguanex** (www.habaguanexhotels.com)

➡ **Islazul** (www.islazul.cu)

➡ **Sol Meliá** (www.solmeliacuba.com)

cities and resort areas. The company has recently developed a new clutch of affordable boutique-style hotels (the Encanto brand) in attractive city centers such as Sancti Spíritus, Baracoa, Remedios and Santiago. Gaviota manages higher-end resorts including glittering 933-room Playa Pesquero, though the chain also has a smattering of cheaper 'villas' in places such as Santiago and Cayo Coco. Gran Caribe does midrange to top-end hotels, including many of the all-inclusive resorts in Havana and Varadero. Lastly, Habaguanex is based solely in Havana and manages most of the fastidiously restored historic hotels in Habana Vieja. The profits from these ventures go toward restoring Habana Vieja, which is a Unesco World Heritage Site. Except for Islazul properties, tourist hotels are for guests paying in convertible pesos only. Since May 2008 Cubans have been allowed to stay in any tourist hotels, although financially most of them are still out of reach.

At the top end of the hotel chain you'll often find foreign chains such as Sol Meliá and Iberostar running hotels in tandem with Cubanacán, Gaviota or Gran Caribe – mainly in the resort areas. The standards and service at these types of places are not unlike resorts in Mexico and the rest of the Caribbean.

Customs Regulations

Cuban customs regulations are complicated. For the full scoop see www.aduana.co.cu.

Items You Are Allowed to Bring In

Travelers are allowed to bring in personal belongings (including photography equipment, binoculars, a musical instrument, tape recorder, radio, personal computer, tent, fishing rod, bicycle, canoe and other sporting gear), and up to 10kg of medicines.

Items that do not fit into the categories mentioned above are subject to a 100% customs duty to a maximum of CUC$1000.

Prohibited Items

Items prohibited from entry into Cuba include narcotics, explosives, pornography, electrical appliances broadly defined, light motor vehicles, car engines and products of animal origin. Canned, processed and dried food are no problem, nor are pets.

Items You Are Allowed to Take Out

You are allowed to export 50 boxed cigars duty-free (or 23 singles), US$5000 (or equivalent) in cash and only CUC$200.

Exporting undocumented art and items of cultural patrimony is restricted and involves fees. Normally, when you buy art you will be given an official 'seal' at point of sale. Check this before you buy. If you don't get one, you'll need to obtain one from the **Registro Nacional de Bienes Culturales** (Calle 17 No 1009, btwn Calles 10 & 12, Vedado, Havana; ⊙9am-noon Mon-Fri). Bring the objects here for inspection, fill in a form, pay a fee of between CUC$10 and CUC$30, which covers from one to five pieces of artwork, and return 24 hours later for the certificate.

Climate

Havana

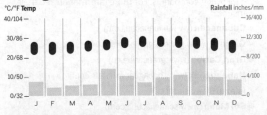

Sancti Spíritus

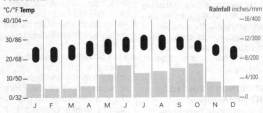

Santiago De Cuba

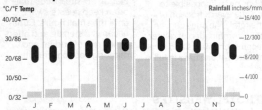

Electricity

110V/220V/60Hz

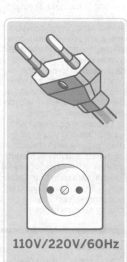

110V/220V/60Hz

Embassies & Consulates

All embassies are in Havana, and most are open from 8am to noon on weekdays. Australia is represented in the Canadian Embassy. New Zealand is represented in

the UK Embassy. The US is represented by a 'US Interests Section.' Canada has additional consulates in Varadero and Guardalavaca. Most embassies are open from 8am to noon on weekdays.

Australia See Canada.

New Zealand See UK.

Austrian Embassy (☑7-204-2825; Av 5A No 6617 cnr Calle 70, Miramar)

Canadian Embassy (☑7-204-2516; Calle 30 No 518, Playa) Also represents Australia.

Danish Consulate (☑7-33-81-28; 4th fl, Paseo de Martí No 20, Centro Habana)

French Embassy (☑7-204-2308; Calle 14 No 312, btwn Avs 3 & 5, Miramar)

German Embassy (☑7-833-2539; Calle 13 No 652, Vedado)

Italian Embassy (☑7-204-5615; Av 5 No 402, Miramar)

Japanese Embassy (☑7-204-3508; Miramar Trade Center, cnr Av 3 & Calle 80, Playa)

Mexican Embassy (☑7-204-7722; Calle 12 No 518, Miramar)

Netherlands Embassy (☑7-204-2511; Calle 8 No 307, btwn Avs 3 & 5, Miramar)

Spanish Embassy (☑7-866-8029; Cárcel No 51, Habana Vieja)

Swedish Embassy (☑7-204-2831; Calle 34 No 510, Miramar)

Swiss Consulate (☑7-204-2611; Av 5 No 2005, btwn Avs 20 & 22, Miramar)

UK Embassy (☑7-214-2200; Calle 34 No 702, Miramar) Also represents New Zealand.

US Interests Section (☑7-833-3026; Calzada, US Interests Section, btwn Calles L & M, Vedado)

Food

For legions of gastronomes, Cuban cuisine was, for a long time, something of an international joke. From

FOOD PRICES

It will be a very rare meal in Cuba that costs over CUC$25. Restaurant listings use the following price brackets for meals.

Budget ($) less than CUC$7

Midrange ($$) CUC$7 – CUC$15

Top End ($$$) more than CUC$15

the empty-shelved ration shops of Centro Habana to the depressing ubiquity of soggy ham-and-cheese sandwiches, which seemed to serve as the country's only viable lunch option, it was a question of less feast, more famine. But while celebrity chefs might remain scarce in many of Cuba's uninspiring government-run restaurants, the opening up of the private sector in 2011 has ushered in a full-on culinary revolution.

Staples & Specialties

Popularly known as *comida criolla* (Creole food), Cuban meals are characterized by *congrí* (rice flecked with black beans), meat (primarily pork, closely followed by chicken and beef), fried plantains (green bananas), salad (limited to seasonal ingredients) and root vegetables, usually *yuca* (cassava) and *calabaza* (pumpkinlike squash).

Pescado (fish) is also readily available. Though you'll come across dorado, *aguja* (swordfish), and occasionally octopus and crab in some of the specialist seafood places, you're more likely to see *pargo* (red snapper), lobster or prawns.

Cubans are also aficionados of ice cream and the nuances of different flavors are heatedly debated. Coppelia ice cream is legendary, but ridiculously cheap tubs of other brands (440g for CUC$1) can be procured almost everywhere, and even the machine-dispensed peso stuff ain't half bad.

Drinks

Cuba's rum cocktails are world famous. There's the minty mojito, the shaved ice daiquirí and the sugary Cuba Libre (rum and Coke) to name but three. Havana Club is Cuba's most celebrated ron (rum), with Silver Dry (the cheapest) and three-year-old Carta Blanca used for mixed drinks, while five-year-old Carta de Oro and seven-year-old Añejo are best enjoyed in a highball. Cuba's finest rum is Matusalem Añejo Superior, brewed in Santiago de Cuba since 1872. Other top brands include Varadero, Caribbean Club and Caney (made at the old Bacardí factory in Santiago de Cuba, though the name Bacardí is anathema as the exiled family decided to sue the Cuban government under US embargo laws). Most Cubans drink their rum straight up and, on more informal occasions, straight from the bottle.

Top beer brands include Mayabe, Hatuey and the big two: Cristal and Bucanero. Imported beers include Lagarto, Bavaria and Heineken.

Where to Eat & Drink
GOVERNMENT-RUN RESTAURANTS

Government-run restaurants operate in either pesos or convertibles. Peso restaurants are nearly always grim and are notorious for handing you a nine-page menu (in Spanish), when the only thing available is fried chicken. There are, however, a few newer exceptions to this rule, most notably in Santiago de Cuba. Peso restaurants will normally accept payment in CUC$, though sometimes at an inferior exchange rate to the standard 25 to one.

Restaurants that sell food in convertibles are generally more reliable, but this isn't

capitalism: just because you're paying more doesn't necessarily mean better service. Food is often limp and unappetizing, and discourse with bored waiters can be worthy of a Monty Python sketch. There are a few highlights. The Palmares group runs a wide variety of excellent restaurants countrywide from bog-standard beach shacks to the New York Times–lauded El Aljibe in Miramar, Havana. The government-run company Habaguanex operates some of the best restaurants in Cuba in Havana, and Gaviota has recently tarted up some old staples. Employees of state-run restaurants will not earn more than CUC$20 a month (the average Cuban salary), so tips are highly appreciated.

PALADARES

Paladares are small family-run restaurants that are permitted to operate privately provided they pay a monthly tax to the government. First established in 1995 during the economic chaos of the Special Period, paladares owe much of their success to the sharp increase in tourist traffic on the island, coupled with the bold experimentation of local chefs who, despite a paucity of decent ingredients, have heroically managed to keep the age-old traditions of Cuban cooking alive. Paladar meals can cost anything between CUC$8 and CUC$30.

Vegetarians

In a land of rationing and food shortages, strict vegetarians (ie no lard, no meat bullion, no fish) will have a hard time. Cubans don't really understand vegetarianism, and when they do (or when they say they do), it can be summarized rather adroitly with one key word: omelet – or, at a stretch, scrambled eggs. Cooks in casas particulares, who may already have had experience cooking meatless dishes for

other travelers, are usually much better at accommodating vegetarians; just ask.

Gay & Lesbian Travelers

While Cuba can't be called a queer destination (yet), it's more tolerant than many other Latin American countries. The 1994 hit movie Fresa y Chocolate (Strawberry and Chocolate) sparked a national dialogue about homosexuality, and Cuba is pretty tolerant, all things considered. People from more accepting societies may find this tolerance too 'don't ask, don't tell' or tokenistic (everybody has a gay friend/relative/coworker, whom they'll mention when the topic arises), but what the hell, you have to start somewhere and Cuba is moving in the right direction.

Lesbianism is less tolerated and seldom discussed and you'll see very little open displays of gay pride between female lovers. There are occasional fiestas para chicas (not necessarily all-girl parties but close); ask around at the Cine Yara in Havana's gay cruising zone.

Cubans are physical with each other and you'll see men hugging, women holding hands and lots of friendly caressing. This type of casual touching shouldn't be a problem, but take care when that hug among friends turns overtly sensual in public.

Health

From a medical point of view, Cuba is generally safe as long as you're reasonably careful about what you eat and drink. The most common travel-related diseases, such as dysentery and hepatitis, are acquired by the consumption of contaminated food and water. Mosquito-borne illnesses are not a significant concern on most of the islands within the Cuban archipelago.

Prevention is the key to staying healthy while traveling around Cuba. Travelers who receive the recommended vaccines and follow commonsense precautions usually come away with nothing more than a little diarrhea.

Insurance

Since May 2010 Cuba has made it obligatory for all foreign visitors to show proof of their medical insurance when entering the country.

Should you end up in hospital, call **Asistur** (866-4499, emergency 866 8527; www.asistur.cu; Paseo de Martí No 208, Centro Habana; 8:30am-5:30pm Mon-Fri, 8am-2pm Sat) for help with insurance matters and medical assistance. The company has regional offices in Havana, Varadero, Cienfuegos, Cayo Coco, Camagüey, Guardalavaca and Santiago de Cuba.

Outpatient treatment at international clinics is reasonably priced, but emergency and prolonged hospitalization gets expensive (the free medical system for Cubans should only be used when there is no other option).

Should you have to purchase medical insurance on arrival, you will pay between CUC$2.50 and CUC$3 per day for coverage of up to CUC$25,000 in medical expenses (for illness) and CUC$10,000 for repatriation of a sick person.

Health Care for Foreigners in Cuba

The Cuban government has established a for-profit health system for foreigners called **Servimed** (7-24-01-41; www.servimedcuba.com), which is entirely separate from the free, not-for-profit system that takes care of Cuban citizens. There are more than 40 Servimed health centers across the island, offering primary care as well

as a variety of specialty and high-tech services. If you're staying in a hotel, the usual way to access the system is to ask the manager for a physician referral. Servimed centers accept walk-ins. While Cuban hospitals provide some free emergency treatment for foreigners, this should only be used when there is no other option. Remember that in Cuba medical resources are scarce and the local populace should be given priority in free health-care facilities.

Almost all doctors and hospitals expect payment in cash, regardless of whether you have travel health insurance or not. If you develop a life-threatening medical problem, you'll probably want to be evacuated to a country with state-of-the-art medical care. Since this may cost tens of thousands of dollars, be sure you have insurance to cover this before you depart.

There are special pharmacies for foreigners also run by the Servimed system, but all Cuban pharmacies are notoriously short on supplies, including pharmaceuticals. Be sure to bring along adequate quantities of all medications you might need, both prescription and over the counter. Also, be sure to bring along a fully stocked medical kit. Pharmacies marked *turno permanente* or *pilotos* are open 24 hours.

Water

Tap water in Cuba is not reliably safe to drink. Bottled water called Ciego Montero is available almost everywhere and rarely costs more than CUC$1.

Internet Access

With state-run telecommunications company Etecsa re-establishing its monopoly as service provider, internet access is available all over the country in Etecsa's spanking new *telepuntos*.

You'll find one of these swish, air-conditioned sales offices in almost every provincial town, and it is your best point of call for fast and reliable internet access. The drill is to buy a one-hour user card (CUC$6) with scratch-off *usuario* (code) and *contraseña* (password) and help yourself to an available computer. These cards are interchangeable in any *telepunto* across the country, so you don't have to use up your whole hour in one go.

The downside of the Etecsa monopoly is that there are few, if any, independent internet cafes outside the *telepuntos*. As a general rule, most three- to five-star hotels (and all resort hotels) will have their own internet cafes, although the fees here are often higher (sometimes as much as CUC$12 per hour).

As internet access for Cubans is restricted (they're only allowed internet under supervision, eg in educational programs or if their job deems it necessary), you may be asked to show your passport when using a *telepunto* (although if you look obviously foreign, they won't bother). On the plus side, the Etecsa places are open long hours and are seldom crowded.

Wi-fi is slowly catching on in Cuba's four- and five-star hotels. When it is available, it usually costs CUC$8 an hour and is rather slow.

Language Courses

Cuba's rich cultural tradition and the abundance of highly talented, trained professionals make it a great place to study Spanish. Technological and linguistic glitches, plus general unresponsiveness, make it hard to set up courses before arriving, but you can arrange everything once you get here. In Cuba, things are always better done face to face.

The largest organization offering study visits for foreigners is **UniversiTUR SA** (☎7-261-4939, 7-55-57-77; agencia@universitur.get.tur.cu; Calle 30 No 768-1, btwn Calle 41 & Av Kohly, Nuevo Vedado, Havana). UniversiTUR arranges regular study and working holidays at any of Cuba's universities and at many other higher education or research institutes. Its most popular programs are intensive courses in Spanish language and Cuban culture, run at La Universidad de La Habana. UniversiTUR has 17 branch offices at various universities throughout Cuba, all of which provide the same services, though prices vary.

Students heading to Cuba should bring a good bilingual dictionary and a basic 'learn Spanish' textbook, as such books are scarce or expensive in Cuba. You might sign up for a two-week course at a university to get your feet wet and then jump into private classes once you've made some contacts.

Legal Matters

Cuban police are everywhere and they're usually very friendly – more likely to ask you for a date than a bribe. Corruption is a serious offense in Cuba, and typically no one wants to get mixed up in it. Getting caught out without identification is never good; carry some around just in case (a driver's license, a copy of your passport or a student ID card should be sufficient).

Drugs are prohibited in Cuba, though you may still get offered marijuana and cocaine on the streets of Havana. Penalties for buying, selling, holding or taking drugs are serious, and Cuba is making a concerted effort to treat demand and curtail supply; it is only the foolish traveler who partakes while on a Cuban vacation.

Maps

Signage is awful in Cuba, so a good map is essential for drivers and cyclists alike. The comprehensive *Guía de Carreteras*, published in Italy, includes the best maps available in Cuba. It usually comes free when you hire a car, though some travelers have been asked to pay between CUC$5 and CUC$10. It has a complete index, a detailed Havana map and useful information in English, Spanish, Italian and French. Handier is the all-purpose *Automapa Nacional*, available at hotel shops and car-rental offices.

The best map published outside Cuba is the Freytag & Berndt 1:1.25 million *Cuba* map. The island map is good, and it has indexed town plans of Havana, Playas del Este, Varadero, Cienfuegos, Camagüey and Santiago de Cuba.

For good basic maps, pick up one of the provincial *Guías* available in Infotur offices.

Money

This is a tricky part of any Cuban trip, as the double economy takes some getting used to. Two currencies circulate in Cuba: convertible pesos (CUC$) and Cuban pesos (referred to as *moneda nacional*, abbreviated MN). Most things tourists pay for are in convertibles (eg accommodation, rental cars, bus tickets, museum admission and internet access). At the time of writing, Cuban pesos were selling at 25 to one convertible, and while there are many things you can't buy with *moneda nacional*, using them on certain occasions means you'll see a bigger slice of authentic Cuba. The prices listed are in convertibles unless otherwise stated.

Making everything a little more confusing, euros are also accepted at the Varadero, Guardalavaca, Cayo Largo del Sur, Cayo Coco and Cayo Guillermo resorts, but once you leave the resort grounds, you'll still need convertibles.

The best currencies to bring to Cuba are euros, Canadian dollars or pounds sterling. The worst is US dollars, for which you will be penalized with a 10% fee (on top of the normal commission) when you buy convertibles (CUC$). Since 2011 the Cuban convertible has been pegged 1:1 to the US dollar, meaning its rate will fluctuate depending on the strength/weakness of the US dollar. At the time of writing, traveler's checks issued by US banks could be exchanged at branches of Banco Financiero Internacional, but credit cards issued by US banks could not be used at all. Note that Australian dollars are not accepted anywhere in Cuba.

Cadeca branches in every city and town sell Cuban pesos. You won't need more than CUC$10 worth of pesos a week. There is almost always a branch at the local *agropecuario* (vegetable market). If you get caught without Cuban pesos and are drooling for that ice-cream cone, you can always use convertibles; in street transactions such as these, CUC$1 is equal to 25 pesos and you'll receive change in pesos. There is no black market in Cuba, only hustlers trying to fleece you with money-changing scams.

ATMs & Credit Cards

When the banks are open, the machines are working and the phone lines are live, credit cards are an option – as long as the cards are not issued by US banks. When weighing up whether to use a credit card or cash, bear in mind that the charges levied by Cuban banks are similar for both (around 3%). However, your home bank may charge additional fees for ATM/credit card transactions. Ideally, it is best to arrive in the Cuba with a stash of cash and a credit card to use as back-up.

Almost all private business in Cuba (ie casas particulares and paladares) is conducted in cash.

Cash advances can be drawn from credit cards, but the commission is the same. Check with your home bank before you leave, as many banks won't authorize large withdrawals in foreign countries unless you notify them of your travel plans first.

ATMs, which are becoming more common, are good for non-American credit cards. They are the equivalent to obtaining a cash advance over the counter. Non-US Mastercards don't currently work in Cuban ATMs though they can be used inside banks to withdraw money over the counter. Visa should work in both.

Some, but not all, debit cards work in Cuba. Check with both your home bank and the local Cuban bank before using them. It is safer to use them inside banking hours in case your card gets 'eaten'.

Cash

Cuba is a cash economy and credit cards don't have the importance or ubiquity that they do elsewhere in the western hemisphere. Although carrying just cash is far riskier than the usual cash/credit-card/traveler's-check mix, it's infinitely more convenient. As long as you use a concealed money belt and keep the cash on you or in your hotel's safety deposit box at all times, you should be OK.

It's better to ask for CUC\$20/10/5/3/1 bills when you're changing money, as many smaller Cuban businesses (taxis, restaurants etc) can't change anything bigger (ie CUC\$50 or CUC\$100 bills) and the words *no hay cambio* (no change) resonate everywhere. If desperate, you can always break big bills at hotels.

Denominations & Lingo

One of the most confusing parts of a double economy is terminology. Cuban pesos are called *moneda nacional* (abbreviated MN) or *pesos Cubanos* or simply pesos, while convertible pesos are called *pesos convertibles* (abbreviated CUC), or simply pesos (again!). More recently people have been referring to them as *cucs*. Sometimes you'll be negotiating in pesos (Cubanos) and your counterpart will be negotiating in pesos (convertibles). It doesn't help that the notes look similar as well. Worse, the symbol for both convertibles and Cuban pesos is \$. You can imagine the potential scams just working these combinations.

The Cuban peso comes in notes of one, five, 10, 20, 50 and 100 pesos; and coins of one (rare), five and 20 centavos, and one and three pesos. The five-centavo coin is called a *medio*; the 20-centavo coin is a *peseta*. Centavos are also called *kilos*.

The convertible peso comes in multicolored notes of one, three, five, 10, 20, 50 and 100 pesos, and coins of five, 10, 25 and 50 centavos, and one peso.

Post

Letters and postcards sent to Europe and the US take about a month to arrive. While *sellos* (stamps) are sold in Cuban pesos and convertibles, correspondence bearing the latter has a better chance of arriving. Postcards cost CUC\$0.65 to all countries. Letters cost CUC\$0.65 to the Americas, CUC\$0.75 to Europe and CUC\$0.85 to all other countries. Prepaid postcards, including international postage, are available at most hotel shops and post offices and are the surest bet for successful delivery. For important mail, you're better off using DHL, which is located in all the major cities; it costs CUC\$55 for a 900g letter pack to Australia, or CUC\$50 to Europe.

Public Holidays

Officially Cuba has nine public holidays. Other important national days to look out for include January 28 (anniversary of the birth of José Martí); April 19 (Bay of Pigs victory); October 8 (anniversary of the death of Che Guevara); October 28 (anniversary of the death of Camilo Cienfuegos); and December 7 (anniversary of the death of Antonio Maceo).

January 1 Triunfo de la Revolución (Liberation Day)

January 2 Día de la Victoria (Victory of the Armed Forces)

May 1 Día de los Trabajadores (International Worker's Day)

July 25 Commemoration of Moncada Attack

July 26 Día de la Rebeldía Nacional – Commemoration of Moncada Attack

July 27 Commemoration of Moncada Attack

October 10 Día de la Indepedencia (Independence Day)

December 25 Navidad (Christmas Day)

December 31 New Year's Eve

Safe Travel

Cuba is generally safer than most countries, and violent attacks are extremely rare. Petty theft (eg rifled luggage in hotel rooms or unattended shoes disappearing from the beach) is common, but preventative measures work wonders. Pickpocketing is preventable: wear your bag in front of you on crowded buses and at busy markets, and only take what money you'll need when you head out at night.

Begging is more widespread and is exacerbated by tourists who hand out money, soap, pens, chewing gum and other things to people on the street. If you truly want to do something to help, pharmacies and hospitals will accept medicine donations, schools happily take pens, paper, crayons etc, and libraries will gratefully accept books. Alternatively pass stuff on to your casa particular owner or leave it at a local church. Hustlers are called *jineteros/jineteras* (male/female touts), and can be a real nuisance.

Telephone

The Cuban phone system is still undergoing upgrades, so beware of phone-number changes. Normally a recorded message will inform you of recent upgrades. Most of the country's Etecsa *telepuntos* have now been completely refurbished, which means there will be a spick-and-span (as well as air-conditioned) phone and internet office in almost every provincial town.

Cell phone usage has become much more widespread in Cuba in the past few years.

Cell Phones

Cuba's cell-phone company is called **Cubacel** (www.cubacel.com). You can use your own GSM or TDMA type phones in Cuba, though you'll have to pay an activation fee (approximately CUC$30). Cubacel has numerous offices around the country (including at the Havana airport) where you can do this. After this you're looking at between CUC$0.30 to CUC$0.45 per minute for calls within Cuba and CUC$2.45 to CUC$5.85 for international calls. To rent a phone in Cuba costs CUC$6 plus a CUC$3 per day activation fee. You'll also need to pay a CUC$100 deposit. Charges after this amount to around CUC$0.35 per minute. For up-to-date costs and information see www.etecsa.cu

Phone Codes

It's complicated!

➡ To call Cuba from abroad, dial your international access code, Cuba's country code (53), the city or area code (minus the '0,' which is used when dialing domestically between provinces), and the local number.

➡ To call internationally from Cuba, dial Cuba's international access code (119), the country code, the area code and the number. To the US, you just dial 119, then 1, the area code and the number.

➡ To call cell phone to cell phone just dial the eight-digit number (which always starts with a '5').

➡ To call cell phone to landline dial '0' + provincial code + local number.

➡ To call landline to cell phone dial '01' (or '0' if in Havana) followed by the eight-digit cell phone number.

➡ To call landline to landline dial '01' + provincial code + local number (or just '0' when calling to or from Havana).

Phonecards

Etecsa is where you buy phonecards, use the internet and make international calls. Blue public Etecsa phones accepting magnetized or computer-chip cards are everywhere. The cards are sold in convertibles (CUC$10, CUC$20 and CUC$50), and in Cuban pesos (five and 10 pesos). You can call nationally with either, but you can call internationally only with convertible cards.

You will also see coin-operated phone booths good for *moneda nacional* (Cuban pesos) only.

Phone Rates

Local calls cost approximately five centavos per minute, while interprovincial calls cost from 35 centavos to one peso per minute (note that only the peso coins with the star work in pay phones). Since most coin phones don't return change, common courtesy means that you should push the 'R' button so that the next person in line can make their call with your remaining money.

International calls made with a card cost from CUC$2 per minute to the US and Canada and CUC$5 to Europe and Oceania. Calls placed through an operator cost slightly more.

Hotels with three stars and up usually offer slightly pricier international phone rates.

Tourist Information

Cuba's official tourist information bureau is called **Infotur** (www.infotur.cu). It has offices in all the main provincial towns and desks in most of the bigger hotels and airports. Travel agencies, such as Cubanacán, Cubatur and Ecotur can usually supply some general information.

Travelers with Disabilities

Cuba's inclusive culture extends to disabled travelers, and while facilities may be lacking, the generous nature of Cubans generally compensates. Sight-impaired travelers will be helped across streets and given priority in lines. The same holds true for travelers in wheelchairs, who will find the few ramps ridiculously steep and will have trouble in colonial parts of town where sidewalks are narrow and streets are cobblestoned. Elevators are often out of order. Etecsa phone centers have telephone equipment for the hearing-impaired, and TV programs are broadcast with closed captioning.

Visas & Tourist Cards

Regular tourists who plan to spend up to two months in Cuba do not need visas. Instead, you get a *tarjeta de turista* (tourist card), valid for 30 days, which can be extended once you're in Cuba (Canadians get 90 days plus the option of a 90-day extension). Those going 'air only' usually buy the tourist card from the travel agency or airline office that sells them the plane ticket – but check ahead. Package tourists receive their card with their other travel documents.

You are usually not allowed to board a plane to Cuba without this card, but if by some chance you are, you should be able to buy one at Aeropuerto Internacional José Martí in Havana – although this is a hassle (and risk) best avoided. Once in Havana, tourist-card extensions or replacements cost another CUC$25. You cannot leave Cuba without presenting your tourist card, so don't lose it. You are not permitted entry to Cuba without an onward ticket. Note that Cubans don't stamp your passport on either entry or exit; instead they stamp your tourist card.

Fill out the tourist card clearly and carefully, as the custom guys are particularly fussy about crossing out and illegibility.

Business travelers and journalists need visas. Applications should be made through a consulate at least three weeks in advance (longer if you apply through a consulate in a country other than your own).

Visitors with visas or anyone who has stayed in Cuba longer than 90 days must apply for an exit permit from an immigration office. The Cuban consulate in London issues official visas (£32 plus two photos). They take two weeks to process, and the name of an official contact in Cuba is necessary.

Extensions

For most travelers, obtaining an extension once in Cuba is easy: you just go to the *inmigración* (immigration office) and present your documents and CUC$25 in stamps. Obtain these stamps from a branch of Bandec or Banco Financiero Internacional beforehand. You'll only receive an additional 30 days after your original 30 days (apart from Canadians who get an additional 90 days after their original 90), but you can exit and re-enter the country for 24 hours and start over again (some travel agencies in Havana have special deals for this type of trip). Attend to extensions at least a few business days before your visa is due to expire and never attempt travel around Cuba with an expired visa.

Cuban Immigration Offices

Nearly all provincial towns have an immigration office (where you can extend your visa), though the staff rarely speak English and aren't always overly helpful. Try to avoid Havana's office if you can, as it gets ridiculously crowded. Hours are normally 8am to 7pm Monday, Wednesday and Friday, 8am to 5pm Tuesday, 8am-noon Thursday and Saturday. Immigration office branches are as follows:

Baracoa (Antonio Maceo No 48)

Bayamo (Carretera Central Km 2) In a big complex 200m south of the Hotel Sierra Maestra.

Camagüey (Calle 3 No 156, btwn Calles 8 & 10, Reparto Vista Hermosa,)

Ciego de Ávila (cnr Delgado & Independencia)

Cienfuegos (☑43-52-10-17; Av 46, btwn Calles 29 & 31)

Guantánamo (Calle 1 Oeste, btwn Calles 14 & 15 Norte) Directly behind Hotel Guantánamo.

Guardalavaca (☑24-43-02-27, 24-43-02-26) In the police station at the entrance to the resort. Head here for visa extensions.

Havana (Calle 17 No 203, btwn Calles J & K, Vedado)

Holguín (Calle Fomento No 256 cnr Peralejo) Arrive early – it gets crowded here.

Las Tunas (Av Camilo Cienfuegos, Reparto Buenavista) Northeast of the train station.

Sancti Spíritus (☑41-32-47-29; Independencia Norte No 107)

Santa Clara (cnr Av Sandino & Sexta) Three blocks east of Estadio Sandino.

Santiago de Cuba (☑22-65-75-07, Centro de Negocios, cnr Av Jesús Menéndez & José A Saco) Stamps for visa extensions are sold at the Banco de Crédito y Comercio at Felix Peña No 614 on Parque Céspedes.

Trinidad (Julio Cueva Díaz) Off Paseo Agramonte.

Varadero (cnr Av 1 & Calle 39)

Volunteering

There are a number of bodies offering volunteer work in Cuba, though it is always best to organize things in your home country first. Just turning up in Havana and volunteering can be difficult, if not impossible. Take a look at the following:

Canada-Cuba Farmer to Farmer Project (www.farmertofarmer.ca) Vancouver-based sustainable agriculture organization.

Canada World Youth (www.cwy-jcm.org) Head office in Montreal, Canada.

Cuban Solidarity Campaign (www.cuba-solidarity.org) Head office in London, UK.

Pastors for Peace (www.ifconews.org) Collects donations across the US to take to Cuba.

Witness for Peace (www. witnessforpeace.org) Looking for Spanish-speakers with a two-year commitment.

Weights & Measures

Cuba uses the metric system, except in some fruit and vegetable markets where the imperial system takes over.

Women Travelers

In terms of physical safety, Cuba is a dream destination for women travelers. Most streets can be walked alone at night, violent crime is rare and the chivalrous part of machismo means you'll never step into oncoming traffic. But machismo cuts both ways, protecting on one side and pursuing – relentlessly – on the other. Cuban women are used to *piropos* (the whistles, kissing sounds and compliments constantly ringing in their ears), and might even reply with their own if they're feeling frisky. For foreign women, however, it can feel like an invasion.

Ignoring *piropos* is the first step. But sometimes ignoring isn't enough. Learn some rejoinders in Spanish so you can shut men up. *No me moleste* (don't bother me), *está bueno ya* (all right already) or *que falta respeto* (how disrespectful) are good ones, as is the withering 'don't you dare' stare that is also part of the Cuban woman's arsenal. Wearing plain, modest clothes might help lessen unwanted attention; topless sunbathing is out. An absent husband, invented or not, seldom has any effect. If you go to a disco, be very clear with Cuban dance partners what you are and are not interested in.

Transportation

GETTING THERE & AWAY

Entering the Country

Whether It's your first or 50th time, descending low into José Martí International Airport, over rust-red tobacco fields, is an exciting and unforgettable experience. Fortunately, entry procedures are relatively straightforward, and with an excess of 2.7 million visitors a year, immigration officials are used to dealing with foreign arrivals.

Outside Cuba, the capital city is called Havana, and this is how travel agents, airlines and other professionals will refer to it. Within Cuba, it's almost always called La Habana.

For the sake of consistency, we have used the former spelling throughout.

Flights, tours and rail tickets can be booked online at lonelyplanet.com/bookings.

Air

Airports

Cuba has 10 international airports. The largest by far is **José Martí** in Havana. The only other sizeable airport is **Juan Gualberto Gómez** in Varadero.

Charter flights for legally sanctioned Cuban-Americans currently fly into four Cuban airports from Miami and New York.

Airlines

In Havana most airline offices are situated in one of two clusters: the **Airline Building** (Calle 23 No 64) in Vedado, or in the **Miramar Trade Center** (Map p134; Av 3, btwn Calles 76 & 80) in Playa.

Cubana (www.cubana.cu), the national carrier, operates regular flights to Bogotá,

Buenos Aires, Mexico City, Cancún, Caracas, Madrid, Moscow, Paris, Toronto, Montreal, Rome, San José (Costa Rica) and Santo Domingo (Dominican Republic). Its modern fleet flies major routes and its airfares are usually among the cheapest. However, overbooking and delays are nagging problems. The airline has a zero-tolerance attitude toward overweight luggage, charging stiffly for every kilogram above the 20kg baggage allowance. In terms of safety, Cubana had back-to-back crashes in December 1999, with 39 fatalities, but it hasn't had any incidents since. You might want to check the latest at www.airsafe.com.

AFRICA

Direct flights from Africa originate in Luanda, Angola. From all other African countries you'll need to connect in London, Paris, Madrid, Amsterdam or Rome.

TAAG (www.taag.com) Weekly flights from Luanda to Havana.

ASIA & AUSTRALIA

There are no direct flights to Cuba from Asia or Australia. Travelers can connect through Europe, Canada, the US or Mexico.

CANADA

Flights from Canada serve 10 Cuban airports from 22 Canadian cities. Toronto and

---

DOCUMENTS REQUIRED ON ENTRY

➡ Passport valid for at least one month beyond your departure date.

➡ Cuba 'tourist card' filled out correctly.

➡ Proof of travel medical insurance (random checks at airport).

➡ Evidence of sufficient funds for the duration of your stay.

➡ Return air ticket.

AIR TRAVEL WARNINGS

Some embassies – most notably the British – recommend against internal air travel in Cuba due to safety concerns. In November 2010, a French-Italian-manufactured twin-propeller plane operated by Cuban company Aerocaribbean crashed in Sancti Spíritus province en route from Santiago de Cuba to Havana, killing all 68 people on board. At the time of writing the causes of the crash were still being investigated.

Montreal are the main hubs. Other cities are served by direct charter flights. **A Nash Travel** (www.anashtravel. com), based in Toronto, can sort out any flight/holiday queries.

Air Canada (www.aircanada. com) Flies to Havana, Cayo Coco, Cayo Largo del Sur, Holguín, Santa Clara and Varadero.

Air Transat (www.airtransat. com) Flies to Camagüey, Cayo Coco, Holguín, Santa Clara and Varadero.

CanJet (www.canjet.com) Flies to Camagüey, Cayo Coco, Cayo Largo del Sur, Holguín, Santa Clara, Santiago de Cuba and Varadero.

Hola Sun (www.holasunholi days.ca) Cuba holiday specialist operating flights into nine Cuban airports.

Sunwing (www.flysunwing. com) Flies to Cayo Coco, Camagüey, Cienfuegos, Manzanillo, Holguín, Santiago de Cuba, Varadero and Havana.

Westjet (www.westjet.com) Flies to Cayo Coco, Holguín, Santa Clara and Varadero.

CARIBBEAN

Cubana and subsidiary **Aerocaribbean** (www.fly-aerocaribbean.com) are the main airlines. The other three are listed below.

Air Caraibes Airlines (www. aircaraibes.com) Direct flights from Pointe-a-Pitre on the French island of Guadeloupe to Havana.

Bahamasair (www.bahamas air.com) Nassau in the Bahamas to Havana.

Cayman Airways (www. caymanairways.com) Grand Cayman to Havana.

EUROPE

Regular flights to Cuba depart from Belgium, France, Germany, Italy, Russia, Spain, Switzerland and the Netherlands.

Aeroflot (www.aeroflot.ru) Moscow to Havana, twice weekly.

Air Berlin (www.airberlin. com) Dusseldorf, Munich and Berlin to Havana.

Air Europa (www.aireuropa. com) Twice weekly flights from Madrid to Havana.

Air France (www.airfrance. com) Daily flights from Paris-Charles de Gaulle to Havana.

Air Italy (www.alitalia.com) Milan to Varadero.

Arkefly (www.arkefly.nl) Amsterdam to Varadero.

Blue Panorama (www. blue-panorama.com) Milan and Rome to Cayo Largo del Sur, Santa Clara, Santiago, Varadero and Havana.

Condor (www.condor.com) Frankfurt to Holguín, Varadero and Havana.

Edelwiess (www.edelweissair. ch) From Zurich to Holguín and Varadero.

Iberia (www.iberia.com) Daily flights between Madrid and Havana.

Jetairfly (www.jetairfly.com) Charter flights from Brussels to Varadero.

Neos (www.neosair.it) Charter linking Milan with Cayo Largo del Sur, Holguín and Varadero.

Transaero (www.transaero. com) Seasonal charter from St Petersburg and Moscow to Varadero.

MEXICO

Mexico City and Cancún are good places to connect with a wide number of US cities.

Interjet (www.interjet.com. mx) Flights from Mexico City and Monterrey to Havana.

SOUTH & CENTRAL AMERICA

Conviasa (www.conviasa. aero) Weekly flights from Caracas, Venezuela, to Havana.

INTERNAL FLIGHTS FROM HAVANA

DESTINATION	FREQUENCY	DURATION (HRS)
Baracoa	1 weekly	2½ hr
Bayamo	2 weekly	2 hr
Camagüey	daily	1½ hr
Cayo Coco	daily	1¼ hr
Cayo Largo del Sur	daily	40 min
Ciego de Ávila	1 weekly	1¼ hr
Guantánamo	5 weekly	2½ hr
Holguín	2-3 daily	1½ hr
Isla de la Juventud	2 daily	40 min
Manzanillo	1 weekly	2 hr
Moa	1 weekly	3 hr
Santiago de Cuba	2-3 daily	2¼ hr

Copa Airlines (www.copaair. com) Daily flights from Bogotá, in Columbia, and Panama City to Havana.

Lan Peru (www.lan.com) Weekly flights from Lima to Havana.

Taca Airlines (www.taca. com) Daily flights from San José, in Costa Rica, and Lima, in Peru, to Havana.

UK

Thomas Cook (www.thomas cook.com) Charter flights from London and Manchester to Holguín, Cayo Coco, Santa Clara and Varadero.

Thomson (www.thomson. so.uk) Charters from London and Manchester to Holguín, Santa Clara and Varadero.

Virgin Atlantic (www.virgin-atlantic.com) Twice weekly flights from London Gatwick to Havana.

UNITED STATES

Since the Obama administration loosened travel restrictions for Cuban-Americans in 2009, a handful of regular charters from the US now fly to Cuba from Miami and New York. All flights to Havana's José Martí International Airport land at Terminal 2, rather than at Terminal 3, the main international portal.

Marazul (www.marazul charters.com) is a good resource for up-to-date flight schedules and bookings

American Eagle (www. aa.com) Miami to Havana, Camagüey, Cienfuegos and Santiago de Cuba.

Miami Air International (www.miamiair.com) Charter links between Miami, and Havana and Cienfuegos.

Sky King (www.flyskyking. net) Charter from Miami and New York to Havana and Camagüey.

Tickets

Since Americans can't buy tickets to Cuba inside the US and can't use US-based travel agents, a host of businesses in Mexico, Canada and the Caribbean specialize in air-only deals. These agencies sometimes won't sell you the first leg of your trip to the 'gateway' country for fear of embargo-related repercussions. When booking online, or if an agency requires financial acrobatics to steer clear of US embargo laws (which sometimes happens), be sure to confirm details, take contact names and clarify the procedure. You will need a Cuban tourist card and these agencies should be able to arrange that for you. Except during peak holiday seasons, you can usually just arrive in Mexico, the Bahamas or whatever gateway country you are traveling through and buy your round-trip ticket to Cuba once you get there.

Sea
Cruises

Thanks to the US embargo, which prohibits vessels calling at Cuban ports from visiting the US for six months, few cruise ships include Cuba on their itineraries. Canadian company **Cuba Cruise** (www.yourcubacruise. com) runs an interesting circumnavigation of Cuba calling in at Havana, Cayo Coco, Holguín, Santiago, Montego Bay (Jamaica) and Cienfuegos. Trips run twice weekly December to March. Prices start at approximately US$600. Another new option is with **Tropicana Cruises** (www.tropicanacruises.com), which as offices in London and St Petersburg and offer a similar circumnavigation package stopping in Havana, Cayo Saetía, Santiago, Ocho Rios (Jamaica), Trinidad and Nueva Gerona.

Private Yacht

If you have your own private yacht or cruiser, Cuba has seven international entry ports equipped with customs facilities:

➡ Marina Hemingway (Havana)

➡ Marina Dásena (Varadero)

➡ Marina Cienfuegos

➡ Marina Cayo Guillermo

➡ Marina Santiago de Cuba

➡ Puerto de Vita (near Guardalavaca in Holguín province)

➡ Cayo Largo del Sur

→ Cabo San Antonio (far western tip of Pinar del Río province)

Boat owners should communicate with the Cuban coast guard on VHF 16 and 68 or the tourist network 19A. There are no scheduled ferry services to Cuba.

Tours

Cuba is popular on the organized-tour circuit, especially in the realm of soft adventure. There are also specialist tours focusing on culture, the environment, adventure, cycling, bird-watching, architecture, hiking, you name it...

Cuban Adventures (www.cubagrouptour.com) Australian-based company specializing in Cuba travel, running small tours with mainly local guides.

Explore (www.explore.co.uk) Eleven different trips including a hiking-focused 'revolutionary trails' excursion that ascends Pico Turquino.

Exodus (www.exodus.co.uk) British-based adventure-travel company offering over half a dozen regular Cuba trips, including family travel and a two-week cycling excursion.

GETTING AROUND

Air

Cubana de Aviación (www.cubana.cu) and its regional carrier Aerocaribbean have flights between Havana and 11 regional airports. There are no internal connections between the airports except via Havana.

One-way flights are half the price of round-trip flights

and weight restrictions are strict (especially on Aerocaribbean's smaller planes). You can purchase tickets at most hotel tour desks and travel agencies for the same price as at the airline offices, which are often chaotic.

Aerogaviota (www.aerogaviota.com; Av 47 No 2814, btwn Calles 28 & 34, Playa, Havana) runs more expensive charter flights to La Coloma and Cayo Levisa (Pinar del Río province), Nueva Gerona, Cayo Largo del Sur, Varadero, Cayo las Brujas, Cayo Coco, Playa Santa Lucía and Santiago de Cuba.

Bicycle

Cuba is a cyclist's paradise, with bike lanes, bike workshops and drivers accustomed to sharing the road countrywide. Spare parts are difficult to find – you should bring important spares with you. Still, Cubans are grand masters at improvised repair, and though specific parts may not be available, something can surely be jury-rigged. *Poncheros* (puncture repair stalls) fix flat tires and provide air; every small town has one.

Helmets are unheard of in Cuba except at upscale resorts, so you should bring your own. A lock is imperative, as bicycle theft is rampant. *Parqueos* are bicycle parking lots located wherever crowds congregate (eg markets, bus terminals, downtown etc); they cost one peso.

Throughout the country, the 1m-wide strip of road to the extreme right is reserved for bicycles, even on highways. It's illegal to ride on sidewalks and against traffic on one-way streets and you'll be ticketed if caught. Road lighting is deplorable, so avoid riding after dark (over one-third of vehicle accidents in Cuba involve bicycles); carry lights with you just in case.

TOURS FROM THE US

The Bush administration clamped down on organized legal travel between the United States and Cuba in 2003. However, the Obama administration reversed the order in January 2011. Legal tours are trickling back in.

Americans traveling to Cuba are still subject to Treasury laws; see the **Department of the Treasury** (www.treas.gov) website for details (type the word 'Cuba' into the site search engine).

Marazul Charters Inc (www.marazulcharters.com) Has been facilitating travel to Cuba for over 30 years and can help place you on legal sponsored trips. The company can also book tickets on their own charter flights direct from Miami to Havana or Camagüey.

Center for Cuban Studies (www.cubaupdate.org) A nonprofit educational institution located in New York that helps people involved in professional, humanitarian or religious work arrange trips to Cuba.

Global Exchange (www.globalexchange.org) An NGO based in San Francisco that promotes human rights and social and economic justice around the world. Its Cuba arm organizes eco-exchanges exploring Cuba's sustainable development.

Witness for Peace (www.witnessforpeace.org;) This US-based organization focuses on Latin America, and America's relationship with it. It organizes research trips to Cuba in tandem with Marazul Charters.

Air Routes

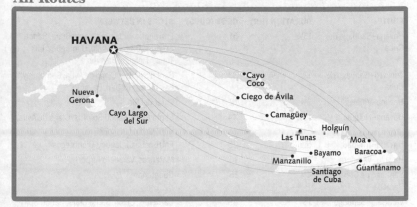

Trains with *coches de equipaje* or *bagones* (baggage carriages) should take bikes for around CUC$10 per trip. These compartments are guarded, but take your panniers with you and check over the bike when you arrive at your destination. Víazul buses also take bikes.

Purchase

Limited selection and high prices make buying a bike in Cuba through official channels unattractive. Better to ask around and strike a deal with an individual to buy their *chivo* (Cuban slang for bike) and trade it or resell it when you leave. With some earnest bargaining, you can get one for around CUC$30, although the more you pay, the less your bones are likely to shake. Despite the obvious cost savings, bringing your own bike is still the best bet by far.

Rental

Official bike rental places are scant in Cuba, though, with the private economy taking off so rapidly, this could have changed by the time you read this. You can usually procure something roadworthy for between CUC$3 per hour or CUC$15 per day. Bikes are usually included as a perk in all-inclusive resort

packages, but beware of bad brakes and zero gears.

Bus

Bus travel is a dependable way of getting around Cuba, at least in the more popular areas. **Víazul** (www.viazul.com) is the main long-distance bus company available to non-Cubans, with punctual, (over) air-conditioned coaches going to destinations of interest to travelers. Víazul charges for tickets in convertibles, and you can be confident you'll get where you're going on these buses – and on time. Buses schedule regular stops for lunch/dinner and always carry two drivers. They have daily departures, but are becoming increasingly busy. Reserve ahead on the more popular routes.

Conectando run by Cubanacán is a newer option set up to relieve some of Víazul's overcrowding. The pros are that they run between city center hotels and can be booked head of time at Infotur and Cubanacán offices. The cons are that the schedules aren't as reliable or extensive as Víazul. Check ahead that your bus is running.

Many of the popular tourist areas now have 'bus tours,' hop-on/hop-off buses that link all the main sights

in a given area and charge CUC$5 for an all-day ticket. The services are run by government transport agency **Transtur** (☎7-831-7333). Havana and Varadero both have open-topped double-decker buses. Smaller minibuses are used in Viñales, Trinidad, Cayo Coco, Guardalavaca, Cayo Santa María and Baracoa (seasonal).

Cubans travel over shorter distances in provincial buses. These buses sell tickets in pesos and are a lot less comfortable and reliable than Víazul. They leave from the provincial bus stations in each province. Schedules and prices are usually chalked up on a board inside the terminal.

Reservations

Reservations with Víazul are advisable during peak travel periods (June to August, Christmas and Easter) and on popular routes (Havana–Trinidad, Trinidad–Santa Clara, and Santiago de Cuba–Baracoa). You can usually put your name down on a list a day or two beforehand. The buses have become popular with Cuban-Americans visiting the island in the wake of the lifting of travel restrictions in 2009.

The Víazul bus out of Baracoa is almost always booked, so reserve a seat on

VÍAZUL BUS ROUTES

ROUTE	DURATION (HR)	COST (CUC$)	STOPS IN BETWEEN
Havana–Santiago de Cuba	15½	51	Entronque de Jagüey, Santa Clara, Sancti Spíritus, Ciego de Ávila, Camagüey, Las Tunas, Holguín, Bayamo
Trinidad–Santiago de Cuba	12	33	Sancti Spíritus, Ciego de Ávila, Camagüey, Las Tunas, Holguín, Bayamo
Havana–Viñales	3¼	12	Pinar del Río
Havana–Holguín	10½	44	Santa Clara, Sancti Spíritus, Ciego de Ávila, Camagüey, Las Tunas
Havana–Trinidad	5½	25	Entronque de Jagüey, Cienfuegos
Havana–Varadero	3	10	Matanzas, Varadero Airport
Santiago de Cuba–Baracoa	4¾	15	Guantánamo
Varadero–Santiago de Cuba	16	49	Cárdenas, Colón, Santa Clara, Sancti Spíritus, Ciego de Ávila, Camagüey, Las Tunas, Holguín, Bayamo
Trinidad–Varadero	6	20	Cárdenas, Colón, Entronque de Jagüey, Cienfuegos

this service when you arrive. It is now possible to make reservations online at www.viazul.com.

Car

Renting a car in Cuba is easy, but once you've factored in gas, insurance, hire fees etc, it isn't cheap. Bank on paying CUC$70 per day minimum, even for a small car. It's actually cheaper to hire a taxi for distances of under 150km (at the time of writing taxis were charging CUC$0.50 per kilometer for inter-city routes).

Driver's License

Your home license is sufficient to rent and drive a car in Cuba.

Gas

Gas sold in convertibles (as opposed to peso gas) is widely available in stations all over the country (the north coast west of Havana being the notable exception). Gas stations are often open 24 hours and may have a small parts store on site. Gas is sold by the liter and comes in *regular* (CUC$1.20 per liter) and *especial* (CUC$1.40 per liter) varieties. Rental cars are advised to use *especial*. All gas stations have efficient pump attendants, usually in the form of *trabajadores sociales* (students in the process of studying for a degree).

Spare Parts

While you cannot count on spare parts per se to be available, Cubans have decades of experience keeping old wrecks on the road without factory parts and you'll see them do amazing things with cardboard, string, rubber and clothes hangers to keep a car mobile.

If you need air in your tires or you have a puncture, use a gas station or visit the local *ponchero* (puncture repair stall). They often don't have measures, so make sure they don't overinflate them.

Insurance

Rental cars come with a recommended CUC$15 to CUC$30 per day insurance, which covers everything but theft of the radio (which you'll need to put in the trunk of the car at night). You can choose to decline the insurance, but then the refundable deposit you must leave upon renting the car (in cash if you don't have a credit card issued by a non-US bank) soars from CUC$250 to CUC$500. If you do have an accident, you must get a copy of the *denuncia* (police report) to be eligible for the insurance coverage, a process which can take all day. If the police determine that you are the party responsible for the accident, say *adiós* to your deposit.

Rental

Renting a car in Cuba is straightforward. You'll need your passport, driver's license and a refundable deposit of between CUC$250 and CUC$800 (in cash or non-US credit card). You can rent a car in one city and drop it off in another for a reasonable fee, which is handy. If you're on a tight budget, ask about diesel cars – some agencies stock a few and you'll save bundles in gas money considering a liter of non-diesel is CUC$1.20 while a liter of *petróleo* (diesel) is CUC$0.65. Note that there are very few rental cars with automatic transmission.

If you want to rent a car for three days or fewer, it will come with limited kilometers, while contracts for three days or more come with unlimited kilometers. In Cuba, you pay for the first tank of gas when you rent the car (CUC$1.40 per liter) and return it empty (a suicidal policy that sees many tight-fisted tourists running out of gas a kilometer or so from the drop-off point). Just to make it worse, you will not be refunded for any gas left in the tank. Petty theft of mirrors, antennas, taillights etc is common, so it's worth it to pay someone a convertible or two to watch your car for the night. If you lose your rental contract or keys you'll pay a CUC$50 penalty. Drivers under 25 pay a CUC$5 fee, while additional drivers on the same contract pay a CUC$3 per day surcharge.

Check over the car carefully with the rental agent before driving into the sunset, as you'll be responsible for any damage or missing parts. Make sure there is a spare tire of the correct size, a jack and a lug wrench. Check that there are seatbelts and that all the doors lock properly.

We have received many letters about poor or non-existent customer service, bogus spare tires, forgotten reservations and other car-rental problems. Reservations are only accepted 15 days in advance and are still not guaranteed. While agents are usually accommodating, you might end up paying more than you planned or having to wait for hours until someone returns a car. The more Spanish you speak and the friendlier you are, the more likely problems will be resolved to everyone's satisfaction (tips to the agent might help). As with most Cuban travel, always have a Plan B.

Road Conditions

Driving here isn't just a different ballpark, it's a different sport. The first problem is that there are no signs – almost anywhere. Major junctions and turnoffs to important resorts or cities are often not indicated at all. Not only is this distracting, it's also incredibly time-consuming. The lack of signage also extends to highway instructions. Often a one-way street is not clearly indicated or a speed limit not highlighted, which can cause problems with the police (who won't understand your inability to telepathically absorb the road rules), and road markings are nonexistent everywhere.

The Autopista, Vía Blanca and Carretera Central are generally in a good state, but be prepared for roads suddenly deteriorating into chunks of asphalt and unexpected railroad crossings everywhere else (especially in the Oriente). Rail crossings are particularly problematic, as there are hundreds of them and there are never any safety gates. Beware: however overgrown the rails may look, you can pretty much assume that the line is still in use. Cuban trains, rather like its cars, defy all normal logic when it comes to mechanics.

While motorized traffic is refreshingly light, bicycles, pedestrians, oxcarts, horse carriages and livestock are a different matter. Many old cars and trucks lack rearview mirrors, and traffic-unaware children run out of all kinds of nooks and crannies. Stay alert, drive with caution and use your horn when passing or on blind curves.

Driving at night is not recommended due to variable roads, drunk drivers, crossing cows and poor lighting. Drunk-driving remains a troublesome problem despite a government educational campaign. Late night in Havana is particularly dangerous, as it seems there's a passing lane, cruising lane and drunk lane.

Traffic lights are often busted or hard to pick out and right-of-way rules are thrown to the wind. Take extra care.

Road Rules

Cubans drive how they want, where they want. It seems chaotic at first, but it has its rhythm. Seatbelts are supposedly required and maximum speed limits are technically 50km/h in the city, 90km/h on highways and 100km/h on the Autopista, but some cars can't even go that fast and those that can go faster still.

RENT A CAR AND DRIVER

Sure, there's not a lot of traffic on the roads, but driving in Cuba isn't as easy as many people think, especially when you factor in teetering bicyclists, baseball-chasing children, galloping horses, pedestrians with limited or no peripheral vision, and – worst of all – a serious lack of signposts. To avoid hassle, you can hire both a comfortable, modern car and a driver with a growing number of companies, most notably **Car Rental Cuba** (www.carrental-cuba.com; Lorda No 56, Santa Clara) whose drivers are skilled, punctual, bilingual and friendly. The company has a head office in Santa Clara, but operates all over the country. You'll pay a daily fee along with a per-kilometer rate, but the driver and car will be at your disposal 24/7.

With so few cars on the road, it's hard not to put the pedal to the floor and just fly. Unexpected potholes are a hazard, however, and watch out for police. There are some clever speed traps, particularly along the Autopista. Speeding tickets start at CUC$30 and are noted on your car contract; the fine is deducted from your deposit when you return the car. When pulled over by the police, you're expected to get out of the car and walk over to them with your paperwork. An oncoming car flashing its lights means a hazard up ahead (and usually the police).

The Cuban transport crisis means there are a lot of people waiting for rides by the side of the road. Giving a *botella* (a lift) to local hitchhikers has advantages aside from altruism. With a Cuban passenger you'll never get lost, you'll learn about secret spots, and you'll meet some great people. There are always risks associated with picking up hitchhikers; giving lifts to older people or families may reduce the risk factor. In the provinces, people waiting for rides are systematically queued by the *amarillos* (roadside traffic organizers), and they'll hustle the most needy folks into your car, usually an elderly couple or a pregnant woman.

Ferry

The most important ferry services for travelers are the catamaran from Surgidero de Batabanó to Nueva Gerona, **Isla de la Juventud** (☎7-878-1841), and passenger ferry from Havana to Regla and **Casablanca** (☎7-867-3726). These ferries are generally safe, though in 1997 two hydrofoils crashed en route to Isla de la Juventud. In both 1994 and 2003, the Regla/Casablanca ferry was hijacked by Cubans trying to make their way to Florida. The 2003 incident involved tourists, so you can expect tight security.

Hitchhiking

The transport crisis, culture of solidarity and low crime levels make Cuba a popular hitchhiking destination. Here, hitchhiking is more like ride-sharing, and it's legally enforced. Traffic lights, railroad crossings and country crossroads are regular stops for people seeking rides. In the provinces and on the outskirts of Havana, the *amarillos* (official state-paid traffic supervisors, so-named for their mustard yellow uniforms) organize and prioritize ride seekers, and you're welcome to jump in line. Rides cost five to 20 pesos depending on distance. Travelers hitching rides will want a good map and some Spanish skills. Expect to wait two or three hours for rides in some cases. Hitchhiking is never entirely safe in any country in the world, and we don't recommend it. Travelers who decide to hitchhike should understand that they are taking a small but potentially serious risk. People who do choose to hitchhike will be safer if they travel in pairs and let someone know where they are planning to go.

Local Transportation

Bici-taxi

Bici-taxis are big pedal-powered tricycles with a double seat behind the driver and are common in Havana, Camagüey, Holguín and a few other cities. In Havana they'll insist on a CUC$1 minimum fare (Cubans pay five or 10 pesos). Some bici-taxistas ask ridiculous amounts. The fare should be clearly understood before you hop aboard. By law, bici-taxis aren't allowed to take tourists (who are expected to use regular taxis), and they're taking a risk by carrying foreigners. Bici-taxi rules are more lax in the provinces and you should be able to get one for five pesos.

Boat

Some towns, such as Havana, Cienfuegos, Gibara and Santiago de Cuba, have local ferry services.

Bus

Very crowded, very steamy, very challenging, very Cuban – *guaguas* (local buses) are useful in bigger cities. Buses work fixed routes, stopping at *paradas* (bus stops) that always have a line, even if it doesn't look like it. You have to shout out *¿el último?* to find out who was the last in line when you showed up as Cuban queues aren't lines in the normal sense of the word. Instead, people just hang around in a disorganized fashion in the vicinity of the bus stop.

Buses cost from 40 centavos to one peso. Havana and Santiago de Cuba have recently been kitted out with brand new fleets of Chinese-made metro buses. You must always walk as far back in the bus as you can and exit through the rear. Make room to pass by saying *permiso*, always wear your pack in front and watch your wallet.

Colectivo & Máquina

Colectivos are taxis running on fixed, long-distance routes, leaving when full. They are generally pre-1959 American cars that belch diesel fumes and can squash in at least three people across the front seat. State-owned taxis that charge in convertibles and hang around bus stations are faster and usually cheaper than the bus.

Horse Carriage

Many provincial cities have *coches de caballo* (horse carriages) that trot on fixed routes, often between train and bus stations and city centers. Prices in *moneda nacional* cost around one peso.

Taxi

Car taxis are metered and cost CUC$1 to start and CUC$1 per kilometer in cities. Taxi drivers are in the habit of offering foreigners a flat, off-meter rate that usually works out very close to what you'll pay with the meter. The difference is that with the meter, the money goes to the state to be divided up; without the meter it goes into the driver's pocket.

Tours

Of the many tourist agencies in Cuba, the following are the most useful:

Cubamar Viajes (7-833-2523, 7-833-2524; www. cubamarviajes.cu) Rents out campismo cabins and mobile homes (caravans).

Cubanacán (7-873-2686; www.cubanacan.cu) General tour agency that also has divisions called Cubanacán Náutica (scuba diving, boating and fishing) and Turismo Y Salud (surgery, spas and rehabilitation).

Cubatur (7-835-4155; www. cubtur.cu)

Ecotur (7-204-5188; www. ecoturcuba.co.cu)

Gaviota (204-4411; www. gaviota-grupo.com)

Havanatur (7-835-3720; www.havanatur.cu) Works with Marazul Tours in the US.

Paradiso (7-832-9538/9; paradis@paradiso.artex.com. cu) Multiday cultural and art tours.

San Cristóbal Agencia de Viajes (7-861-9171; www. viajessancristobal.cu)

Train

Public railways operated by Ferrocarriles de Cuba serve all of the provincial capitals and are a great way to experience Cuba, if you have time and patience. While train travel is safe, the departure information provided is purely theoretical. Getting a ticket is usually no problem, as there's a quota for tourists paying in convertibles.

Foreigners must pay for their tickets in cash, but prices are reasonable and the carriages, though old and worn, are fairly comfortable. The toilets are foul – bring toilet paper. Watch your luggage on overnight trips and bring some of your own food. Only the Tren Francés has snack facilities, although vendors often come through the train selling coffee (you supply the cup).

A regularly updated précis of Cuban train times, types and nuances is available on the website **The Man in Seat Sixty-one** (www.seat61. com), run by Mark Smith in the UK. The website covers train travel across the globe, but has a decent printed rundown on Cuba's main train services.

Train Stations

Cuban train stations, despite their occasionally grandiose facades, are invariably dingy, chaotic places with little visible train information. Departure times are displayed on black chalkboards or hand-written notices, there are no electronic or printed time tables. Always check train info two to three days before your intended travel.

Classes

Trains are either *especial* (air-conditioned, faster trains with fewer departures), *regular* (slowish trains with daily departures) or *lecheros* (milk trains that stop at every little town on the line). Trains on major routes such as Havana–Santiago de Cuba will be *especial* or *regular* trains.

Costs

Regular trains cost under CUC$3 per 100km, while *especial* trains cost closer to

CUBA'S TRAIN SERVICES FROM HAVANA

The following information is liable to change or cancellation. Always check ahead.

DESTINATION	TRAIN NO	FREQUENCY	COST (CUC$)
Bayamo	5	every 3rd day	26
Camagüey	1, 3, 5, 15	daily	19–41
Cienfuegos	19	every other day	11
Guantánamo	15	every 3rd day	32
Manzanillo	28	every 3rd day	32
Matanzas	3, 5, 7, 15	daily	3
Morón	29	daily	24
Pinar del Río	71	every other day	6.50
Sancti Spíritus	7	every other day	13.50
Santa Clara	1, 3, 5, 7, 9, 15	daily	10–21
Santiago de Cuba	1, 5	2 days out of 3	30–62

THE TREN FRANCÉS

Cuba's best and fastest train is the Tren Francés, which runs between Havana and Santiago de Cuba in both directions every third day (1st/2nd class CUC$62/50, 15½ hours, 861km). Train No 1 leaves Havana at 6.27pm, passing Santa Clara and Camagüey, before reaching Santiago de Cuba at 9am. Train 2 leaves Santiago de Cuba at 9pm and reaches Havana at 12.15pm. The trains use second-hand French carriages (hence the name), which formerly operated on the Paris–Brussels–Amsterdam European route. They were bought by the Cubans in 2001. The carriages are relatively comfortable, if a little worn, with frigid air-conditioning, a limited cafe, a purser (one per carriage) and decidedly dingy toilets. As with many things in Cuba, it's not so much the quality of the carriages that's the problem, but their upkeep – or lack thereof. The Tren Francés has two classes, *primera* amd *primera especial*. The latter is worth the extra CUC$12 investment.

some more frequently. There are also smaller trains linking Las Tunas and Holguín, Holguín and Santiago de Cuba, Santa Clara and Nuevitas, Cienfuegos and Sancti Spíritus, and Santa Clara and Caibarién.

The Hershey Train is the only electric railway in Cuba and was built by the Hershey Chocolate Company in the early years of the 20th century; it's a fun way to get between Havana and Matanzas.

Truck

Camiónes (trucks) are a cheap, fast way to travel within or between provinces. Every city has a provincial and municipal bus stop with *camión* departures. They run on a (loose) schedule and you'll need to take your place in line by asking for *el último* to your destination; you pay as you board. A truck from Santiago de Cuba to Guantánamo costs five pesos (CUC$0.20), while the same trip on a Víazul bus costs CUC$6.

Camión traveling is hot, crowded and uncomfortable, but is a great way to meet local people, fast; a little Spanish will go a long way.

Sometimes terminal staff tell foreigners they're prohibited from traveling on trucks. As with anything in Cuba, never take 'no' as your final answer. Crying poor, striking up a conversation with the driver, appealing to other passengers for aid etc usually helps.

CUC$5.50 per 100km. The Hershey Train is priced like the *regular* trains.

Reservations

In most train stations, you just go to the ticket window and buy a ticket. In Havana, there's a separate waiting room and ticket window for passengers paying in convertibles in La Coubre train station. Be prepared to show your passport when purchasing tickets. It's always wise to check beforehand at the station for current departures because things change.

Rail Network

Cuba's train network is comprehensive, running almost the full length of the main island from Guane in Pinar del Río province to Caimanera, just south of the city of Guantánamo. There are also several branch lines heading out north and south and linking up places such as Manzanillo, Nuevitas, Morón and Cienfuegos. Baracoa is one of the few cities without a train connection. Other trainless enclaves are the Isla de la Juventud, the far west of Pinar del Río province and the northern keys. Trinidad has been detached from the main rail network since a storm brought down a bridge in 1992, though it has a small branch line that runs along the Valle del los Ingenios.

Services

Many additional local trains operate at least daily and

Language

Spanish pronunciation is pretty straightforward – Spanish spelling is phonetically consistent, meaning that there's a clear and consistent relationship between what you see in writing and how it's pronounced. Also, most Latin American Spanish sounds are pronounced the same as their English counterparts. Note though that the kh in our pronunciation guides is a throaty sound (like the 'ch' in the Scottish *loch*), v and b are similar to the English 'b' (but softer, between a 'v' and a 'b'), and r is strongly rolled. If you read our colored pronunciation guides as if they were English, you'll be understood just fine. The stressed syllables are in italics.

Spanish nouns are marked for gender (masculine or feminine). Endings for adjectives also change to agree with the gender of the noun they modify. Where necessary, both forms are given for the phrases in this chapter, separated by a slash and with the masculine form first, eg *perdido/a* (m/f).

Spanish has two words for the English 'you': an informal (*tú*) and polite form (*Usted*) which are accompanied by a different form of the verb. When talking to people familiar to you or younger than you, use the informal form of 'you', *tú*, rather than the polite form *Usted*. In all other cases use the polite form. The polite form is used in the phrases provided in this chapter; where both options are given, they are indicated by the abbreviations 'pol' and 'inf'.

WANT MORE?

For in-depth language information and handy phrases, check out Lonely Planet's *Latin American Spanish Phrasebook*. You'll find it at **shop.lonelyplanet. com**, or you can buy Lonely Planet's iPhone phrasebooks at the Apple App Store.

BASICS

Hello.	Hola.	o·la
Goodbye.	Adiós.	a·dyos
How are you?	¿Qué tal?	ke tal
Fine, thanks.	Bien, gracias.	byen gra·syas
Excuse me.	Perdón.	per·don
Sorry.	Lo siento.	lo syen·to
Yes./No.	Sí./No.	see/no
Please.	Por favor.	por fa·vor
Thank you.	Gracias.	gra·syas
You're welcome.	De nada.	de na·da

My name is ...
Me llamo ...   me ya·mo ...

What's your name?
¿Cómo se llama Usted? ko·mo se ya·ma oo·ste (pol)
¿Cómo te llamas? ko·mo te ya·mas (inf)

Do you speak English?
¿Habla inglés? a·bla een·gles (pol)
¿Hablas inglés? a·blas een·gles (inf)

I don't understand.
Yo no entiendo.   yo no en·tyen·do

ACCOMMODATIONS

I'd like to book a room.
Quisiera reservar una   kee·sye·ra re·ser·var oo·na
habitación.   a·bee·ta·syon

How much is it per night/person?
¿Cuánto cuesta por   kwan·to kwes·ta por
noche/persona?   no·che/per·so·na

Does it include breakfast?
¿Incluye el desayuno?   een·kloo·ye el de·sa·yoo·no

campsite	terreno de cámping	te·re·no de kam·peeng
hotel	hotel	o·tel
guesthouse	pensión	pen·syon
youth hostel	albergue juvenil	al·ber·ge khoo·ve·neel

I'd like a ... room.	Quisiera una habitación ...	kee·sye·ra oo·na a·bee·ta·syon ...
single	individual	een·dee·vee·dwal
double	doble	do·ble

air-con	aire acondicionado	ai·re a·kon·dee·syo·na·do
bathroom	baño	ba·nyo
bed	cama	ka·ma
window	ventana	ven·ta·na

DIRECTIONS

Where's ...?
¿Dónde está ...?   don·de es·ta ...

What's the address?
¿Cuál es la dirección?   kwal es la dee·rek·syon

Could you please write it down?
¿Puede escribirlo, por favor?   pwe·de es·kree·beer·lo por fa·vor

Can you show me (on the map)?
¿Me lo puede indicar (en el mapa)?   me lo pwe·de een·dee·kar (en el ma·pa)

at the corner	en la esquina	en la es·kee·na
at the traffic lights	en el semáforo	en el se·ma·fo·ro
behind ...	detrás de ...	de·tras de ...
far	lejos	le·khos
in front of ...	enfrente de ...	en·fren·te de ...
left	izquierda	ees·kyer·da
near	cerca	ser·ka
next to ...	al lado de ...	al la·do de ...
opposite ...	frente a ...	fren·te a ...
right	derecha	de·re·cha
straight ahead	todo recto	to·do rek·to

EATING & DRINKING

What would you recommend?
¿Qué recomienda?   ke re·ko·myen·da

What's in that dish?
¿Que lleva ese plato?   ke ye·va e·se pla·to

I don't eat ...
No como ...   no ko·mo ...

That was delicious!
¡Estaba buenísimo!   es·ta·ba bwe·nee·see·mo

Please bring the bill.
Por favor nos trae la cuenta.   por fa·vor nos tra·e la kwen·ta

Cheers!
¡Salud!   sa·loo

KEY PATTERNS

To get by in Spanish, mix and match these simple patterns with words of your choice:

When's (the next flight)?
¿Cuándo sale (el próximo vuelo)?   kwan·do sa·le (el prok·see·mo vwe·lo)

Where's (the station)?
¿Dónde está (la estación)?   don·de es·ta (la es·ta·syon)

Where can I (buy a ticket)?
¿Dónde puedo (comprar un billete)?   don·de pwe·do (kom·prar oon bee·ye·te)

Do you have (a map)?
¿Tiene (un mapa)?   tye·ne (oon ma·pa)

Is there (a toilet)?
¿Hay (servicios)?   ai (ser·vee·syos)

I'd like (a coffee).
Quisiera (un café).   kee·sye·ra (oon ka·fe)

I'd like (to hire a car).
Quisiera (alquilar un coche).   kee·sye·ra (al·kee·lar oon ko·che)

Can I (enter)?
¿Se puede (entrar)?   se pwe·de (en·trar)

Could you please (help me)?
¿Puede (ayudarme), por favor?   pwe·de (a·yoo·dar·me) por fa·vor

Do I have to (get a visa)?
¿Necesito (obtener un visado)?   ne·se·see·to (ob·te·ner oon vee·sa·do)

I'd like to book a table for ...	Quisiera reservar una mesa para ...	kee·sye·ra re·ser·var oo·na me·sa pa·ra ...
(eight) o'clock	las (ocho)	las (o·cho)
(two) people	(dos) personas	(dos) per·so·nas

Key Words

appetisers	aperitivos	a·pe·ree·tee·vos
bottle	botella	bo·te·ya
bowl	bol	bol
breakfast	desayuno	de·sa·yoo·no
children's menu	menú infantil	me·noo een·fan·teel
(too) cold	(muy) frío	(mooy) free·o
dinner	cena	se·na
food	comida	ko·mee·da
fork	tenedor	te·ne·dor
glass	vaso	va·so

highchair	trona	tro·na
hot (warm)	caliente	kal·yen·te
knife	cuchillo	koo·chee·yo
lunch	comida	ko·mee·da
main course	segundo plato	se·goon·do pla·to
market	mercado	mer·ka·do
menu (in English)	menú (en inglés)	me·noo (en een·gles)
plate	plato	pla·to
restaurant	restaurante	res·tow·ran·te
spoon	cuchara	koo·cha·ra
vegetarian food	comida vegetariana	ko·mee·da ve·khe·ta·rya·na
with/without	con/sin	kon/seen

Meat & Fish

beef	carne de vaca	kar·ne de va·ka
chicken	pollo	po·yo
duck	pato	pa·to
fish	pescado	pes·ka·do
lamb	cordero	kor·de·ro
pork	cerdo	ser·do
turkey	pavo	pa·vo
veal	ternera	ter·ne·ra

Fruit & Vegetables

apple	manzana	man·sa·na
apricot	albaricoque	al·ba·ree·ko·ke
artichoke	alcachofa	al·ka·cho·fa
asparagus	espárragos	es·pa·ra·gos
banana	plátano	pla·ta·no
beans	judías	khoo·dee·as
beetroot	remolacha	re·mo·la·cha
cabbage	col	kol
carrot	zanahoria	sa·na·o·rya
celery	apio	a·pyo
cherry	cereza	se·re·sa
corn	maíz	ma·ees
cucumber	pepino	pe·pee·no
fruit	fruta	froo·ta
grape	uvas	oo·vas
lemon	limón	lee·mon
lentils	lentejas	len·te·khas
lettuce	lechuga	le·choo·ga
mushroom	champiñón	cham·pee·nyon
nuts	nueces	nwe·ses
onion	cebolla	se·bo·ya

orange	naranja	na·ran·kha
peach	melocotón	me·lo·ko·ton
peas	guisantes	gee·san·tes
(red/green) pepper	pimiento (rojo/verde)	pee·myen·to (ro·kho/ver·de)
pineapple	piña	pee·nya
plum	ciruela	seer·we·la
potato	patata	pa·ta·ta
pumpkin	calabaza	ka·la·ba·sa
spinach	espinacas	es·pee·na·kas
strawberry	fresa	fre·sa
tomato	tomate	to·ma·te
vegetable	verdura	ver·doo·ra
watermelon	sandía	san·dee·a

Other

bread	pan	pan
butter	mantequilla	man·te·kee·ya
cheese	queso	ke·so
egg	huevo	we·vo
honey	miel	myel
jam	mermelada	mer·me·la·da
oil	aceite	a·sey·te
pasta	pasta	pas·ta
pepper	pimienta	pee·myen·ta
rice	arroz	a·ros
salt	sal	sal
sugar	azúcar	a·soo·kar
vinegar	vinagre	vee·na·gre

Drinks

beer	cerveza	ser·ve·sa
coffee	café	ka·fe
(orange) juice	zumo (de naranja)	soo·mo (de na·ran·kha)
milk	leche	le·che
tea	té	te

Signs

Abierto	Open
Cerrado	Closed
Entrada	Entrance
Hombres/Varones	Men
Mujeres/Damas	Women
Prohibido	Prohibited
Salida	Exit
Servicios/Baños	Toilets

LANGUAGE EATING & DRINKING

(mineral) water	agua (mineral)	a·gwa (mee·ne·ral)
(red/white) wine	vino (tinto/ blanco)	vee·no (teen·to/ blan·ko)

EMERGENCIES

Help!	¡Socorro!	so·ko·ro
Go away!	¡Vete!	ve·te

Call ...!	¡Llame a ...!	ya·me a ...
a doctor	un médico	oon me·dee·ko
the police	la policía	la po·lee·see·a

I'm lost.
Estoy perdido/a.   es·toy per·dee·do/a (m/f)

I'm ill.
Estoy enfermo/a.   es·toy en·fer·mo/a (m/f)

I'm allergic to (antibiotics).
Soy alérgico/a a   soy a·ler·khee·ko/a a
(los antibióticos).   (los an·tee·byo·tee·kos) (m/f)

Where are the toilets?
¿Dónde están   don·de es·tan
los servicios?   los ser·vee·syos

SHOPPING & SERVICES

I'd like to buy ...
Quisiera comprar ...   kee·sye·ra kom·prar ...

I'm just looking.
Sólo estoy mirando.   so·lo es·toy mee·ran·do

May I look at it?
¿Puedo verlo?   pwe·do ver·lo

I don't like it.
No me gusta.   no me goos·ta

How much is it?
¿Cuánto cuesta?   kwan·to kwes·ta

That's too expensive.
Es muy caro.   es mooy ka·ro

Can you lower the price?
¿Podría bajar un   po·dree·a ba·khar oon
poco el precio?   po·ko el pre·syo

There's a mistake in the bill.
Hay un error   ai oon e·ror
en la cuenta.   en la kwen·ta

Question Words		
How?	¿Cómo?	ko·mo
What?	¿Qué?	ke
When?	¿Cuándo?	kwan·do
Where?	¿Dónde?	don·de
Who?	¿Quién?	kyen
Why?	¿Por qué?	por ke

ATM	cajero automático	ka·khe·ro ow·to·ma·tee·ko
credit card	tarjeta de crédito	tar·khe·ta de kre·dee·to
internet cafe	cibercafé	see·ber·ka·fe
post office	correos	ko·re·os
tourist office	oficina de turismo	o·fee·see·na de too·rees·mo

TIME & DATES

What time is it?	¿Qué hora es?	ke o·ra es
It's (10) o'clock.	Son (las diez).	son (las dyes)
It's half past (one).	Es (la una) y media.	es (la oo·na) ee me·dya

morning	mañana	ma·nya·na
afternoon	tarde	tar·de
evening	noche	no·che
yesterday	ayer	a·yer
today	hoy	oy
tomorrow	mañana	ma·nya·na

Monday	lunes	loo·nes
Tuesday	martes	mar·tes
Wednesday	miércoles	myer·ko·les
Thursday	jueves	khwe·ves
Friday	viernes	vyer·nes
Saturday	sábado	sa·ba·do
Sunday	domingo	do·meen·go

January	enero	e·ne·ro
February	febrero	fe·bre·ro
March	marzo	mar·so
April	abril	a·breel
May	mayo	ma·yo
June	junio	khoon·yo
July	julio	khool·yo
August	agosto	a·gos·to
September	septiembre	sep·tyem·bre
October	octubre	ok·too·bre
November	noviembre	no·vyem·bre
December	diciembre	dee·syem·bre

TRANSPORTATION

Public Transportation

boat	barco	bar·ko
bus	autobús	ow·to·boos
plane	avión	a·vyon
train	tren	tren

LANGUAGE TRANSPORTATION

Numbers

1	uno	oo·no
2	dos	dos
3	tres	tres
4	cuatro	kwa·tro
5	cinco	seen·ko
6	seis	seys
7	siete	sye·te
8	ocho	o·cho
9	nueve	nwe·ve
10	diez	dyes
20	veinte	veyn·te
30	treinta	treyn·ta
40	cuarenta	kwa·ren·ta
50	cincuenta	seen·kwen·ta
60	sesenta	se·sen·ta
70	setenta	se·ten·ta
80	ochenta	o·chen·ta
90	noventa	no·ven·ta
100	cien	syen
1000	mil	meel

first	primero	pree·me·ro
last	último	ool·tee·mo
next	próximo	prok·see·mo

I want to go to ...
Quisiera ir a ... — kee·sye·ra eer a ...

Does it stop at ...?
¿Para en ...? — pa·ra en ...

What stop is this?
¿Cuál es esta parada? — kwal es es·ta pa·ra·da

What time does it arrive/leave?
¿A qué hora llega/sale? — a ke o·ra ye·ga/sa·le

Please tell me when we get to ...
¿Puede avisarme cuando lleguemos a ...? — pwe·de a·vee·sar·me kwan·do ye·ge·mos a ...

I want to get off here.
Quiero bajarme aquí. — kye·ro ba·khar·me a·kee

a ... ticket	un billete de ...	oon bee·ye·te de ...
1st-class	primera clase	pree·me·ra kla·se
2nd-class	segunda clase	se·goon·da kla·se
one-way	ida	ee·da
return	ida y vuelta	ee·da ee vwel·ta

airport	aeropuerto	a·e·ro·pwer·to
aisle seat	asiento de pasillo	a·syen·to de pa·see·yo
bus stop	parada de autobuses	pa·ra·da de ow·to·boo·ses
cancelled	cancelado	kan·se·la·do
delayed	retrasado	re·tra·sa·do
platform	plataforma	pla·ta·for·ma
ticket office	taquilla	ta·kee·ya
timetable	horario	o·ra·ryo
train station	estación de trenes	es·ta·syon de tre·nes
window seat	asiento junto a la ventana	a·syen·to khoon·to a la ven·ta·na

Driving & Cycling

I'd like to hire a ...	Quisiera alquilar ...	kee·sye·ra al·kee·lar ...
4WD	un todo-terreno	oon to·do te·re·no
bicycle	una bicicleta	oo·na bee·see·kle·ta
car	un coche	oon ko·che
motorcycle	una moto	oo·na mo·to

child seat	asiento de seguridad para niños	a·syen·to de se·goo·ree·da pa·ra nee·nyos
diesel	petróleo	pet·ro·le·o
helmet	casco	kas·ko
hitchhike	hacer botella	a·ser bo·te·ya
mechanic	mecánico	me·ka·nee·ko
petrol/gas	gasolina	ga·so·lee·na
service station	gasolinera	ga·so·lee·ne·ra
truck	camion	ka·myon

Is this the road to ...?
¿Se va a ... por esta carretera? — se va a ... por es·ta ka·re·te·ra

(How long) Can I park here?
¿(Por cuánto tiempo) Puedo aparcar aquí? — (por kwan·to tyem·po) pwe·do a·par·kar a·kee

The car has broken down (at ...).
El coche se ha averiado (en ...). — el ko·che se a a·ve·rya·do (en ...)

I have a flat tyre.
Tengo un pinchazo. — ten·go oon peen·cha·so

I've run out of petrol.
Me he quedado sin gasolina. — me e ke·da·do seen ga·so·lee·na

GLOSSARY

altos – upstairs apartment; caps when in an address

agropecuario – vegetable market; also sells rice, fruit

amarillo – a roadside traffic organizer in a yellow uniform

americano/a – in Cuba this means a citizen of any Western hemisphere country (from Canada to Argentina); a citizen of the US is called a *norteamericano/a* or *estado- unidense*; also gringo/a and yuma

Arawak – linguistically related Indian tribes that inhabited most of the Caribbean islands and northern South America

Autopista – the national highway that has four, six or eight lanes depending on the region

babalawo – a *Santería* priest; also *babalao*; see also *santero*

bahía – bay

bailes – dances

barbuda – name given to Castro's rebel army; literally 'bearded one'

barrio – neighborhood

bici-taxi – bicycle taxi

bodega – stores distributing ration-card products

bohío – thatched hut

bolero – a romantic love song

botella – hitchhiking; literally 'bottle'

cabaña – cabin, hut

cabildo – a town council during the colonial era; also an association of tribes in Cuban religions of African origin

cacique – chief; originally used to describe an Indian chief and today used to designate a petty tyrant

Cadeca – exchange booth

cafetal – coffee plantation

caliente – hot

calle – street

camión – truck

campesinos – people who live in the *campo*

campismo – national network of 82 camping installations, not all of which are open to foreigners

casa particular – private house

that lets out rooms to foreigners (and sometimes Cubans); all legal casas must display a green triangle on the door

casco histórico – historic center of a city (eg Trinidad, Santiago de Cuba)

CDR – Comités de Defensa de la Revolución; neighborhood-watch bodies originally formed in 1960 to consolidate grassroots support for the Revolution; they now play a decisive role in health, education, social, recycling and voluntary labor campaigns

chachachá – cha-cha; dance music in 4/4 meter derived from the rumba and mambo

Changó – the *Santería* deity signifying war and fire, twinned with Santa Barbara in Catholicism

chivo – Cuban slang for 'bike'

cimarrón – a runaway slave

claves – rhythm sticks used by musicians

coches de caballo – horse carriages

Cohiba – native Indian name for a smoking implement; one of Cuba's top brands of cigar

colectivo – collective taxi that takes on as many passengers as possible; usually a classic American car

comida criolla – Creole food

compañero/a – companion or partner, with revolutionary connotations (ie 'comrade')

congrí – rice flecked with black beans

conseguir – to get, obtain

convertibles – convertible pesos

coppelia – Cuban ice creamery

criollo – Creole; Spaniard born in the Americas

Cubanacán – soon after landing in Cuba, Christopher Columbus visited a Taíno village the Indians called Cubanacán (meaning 'in the center of the island'); a large Cuban tourism company uses the name

danzón – a traditional Cuban ballroom dance colored with African influences, pioneered in Matanzas during the late 19th century

décima – the rhyming, eight-

syllable verse that provides the lyrics for Cuban son

duende – spirit/charm; used in flamenco to describe the ultimate climax to the music

El Líder Máximo – Maximum Leader; title often used to describe Fidel Castro

el último – literally 'the last'; this term is key to mastering Cuban queues (you must 'take' *el último* when joining a line and 'give it up' when someone new arrives)

entronque – crossroads in rural areas

finca – farm

Gitmo – American slang for Guantánamo US Naval Base

Granma – the yacht that carried Fidel and his companions from Mexico to Cuba in 1956 to launch the Revolution; in 1975 the name was adopted for the province where the Granma arrived; also name of Cuba's leading daily newspaper

guajiros – country folk

guarapo – fresh sugarcane juice

habanero/a – someone from Havana

herbero – seller of herbs, natural medicines and concocter of remedies; typically a wealth of knowledge on natural cures

ingenio – an antiquated term for a sugar mill; see central

inmigración – immigration office

jardín – garden

jinetera – a female tout; a woman who attaches herself to male foreigners

jinetero – a male tout who hustles tourists; literally 'jockey'

M-26-7 – the '26th of July Movement,' Fidel Castro's revolutionary organization, was named for the abortive assault on the Moncada army barracks in Santiago de Cuba on July 26, 1953

maqueta – scale model

máquina – private peso taxi

mercado – market

mirador – lookout or viewpoint

mogote – a limestone monolith found at Viñales

Moncada – a former army barracks in Santiago de Cuba named for General Guillermo Moncada (1848-95), a hero of the Wars of Independence

moneda nacional – abbreviated to MN; Cuban pesos

mudéjar – Iberian Peninsula's Moorish-influenced style in architecture and decoration that lasted from the 12th to 16th centuries and combined elements of Islamic and Christian art

nueva trova – philosophical folk/guitar music popularized in the late '60s and early '70s by Silvio Rodríguez and Pablo Milanés

Operación Milagros – the unofficial name given to a pioneering medical program hatched between Cuba and Venezuela in 2004 that offers free eye treatment for impoverished Venezuelans in Cuban hospitals

Oriente – the region comprised of Las Tunas, Holguín, Granma, Santiago de Cuba and Guantánamo provinces; literally 'the east'

orisha – a Santería deity

paladar – a privately owned restaurant

parada – bus stop

parque – park

PCC – Partido Comunista de Cuba; Cuba's only political party, formed in October 1965 by merging cadres from the Partido Socialista Popular (the pre-1959 Communist Party) and veterans of the guerrilla campaign

peña – musical performance or get-together in any genre: son, rap, rock, poetry etc; see also esquina

período especial – the 'Special Period in Time of Peace' (Cuba's economic reality post-1991)

pregón – a singsong manner of selling fruits, vegetables, brooms, whatever; often comic, they are belted out by pregoneros/as

puente – bridge

quinciñera – Cuban rite of passage for girls turning 15 (quince), whereby they dress up like brides, have their photos taken in gorgeous natural or architectural settings and then have a big party with lots of food and dancing

ranchón – rural farm/restaurant

reggaetón – Cuban hip-hop

Regla de Ocha – set of related religious beliefs popularly known as Santería

resolver – to resolve or fix a problematic situation; along with el último, this is among the most indispensable words in Cuban vocabulary

río – river

salsa – Cuban music based on son

salsero – salsa singer

Santería – Afro-Cuban religion resulting from the syncretization of the Yoruba religion of West Africa and Spanish Catholicism

santero – a priest of Santería; see also babalawo

santiagüero – someone from Santiago de Cuba

s/n – sin número; indicates an address that has no street number

son – Cuba's basic form of popular music that jelled from African and Spanish elements in the late 19th century

Taíno – a settled, Arawak-speaking tribe that inhabited much of Cuba prior to the Spanish conquest; the word itself means 'we the good people'

tambores – Santería drumming ritual

telepunto – Etecsa (Cuban state-run telecommunications company) telephone and internet shop/call center

temporada alta/baja – high/low season

Behind the Scenes

SEND US YOUR FEEDBACK

We love to hear from travellers – your comments keep us on our toes and help make our books better. Our well-travelled team reads every word on what you loved or loathed about this book. Although we cannot reply individually to postal submissions, we always guarantee that your feedback goes straight to the appropriate authors, in time for the next edition. Each person who sends us information is thanked in the next edition – the most useful submissions are rewarded with a selection of digital PDF chapters.

Visit **lonelyplanet.com/contact** to submit your updates and suggestions or to ask for help. Our award-winning website also features inspirational travel stories, news and discussions.

Note: We may edit, reproduce and incorporate your comments in Lonely Planet products such as guidebooks, websites and digital products, so let us know if you don't want your comments reproduced or your name acknowledged. For a copy of our privacy policy visit lonelyplanet.com/privacy.

OUR READERS

Many thanks to the travelers who used the last edition and wrote to us with helpful hints, useful advice and interesting anecdotes:

Alejandro Meyer, Alex Boladeras, Ana Richardson, Andrew Butchers, Anna Austin, Anne Finmans, Arie van Oosterwijk, Birgitt Ettl, Caridad Gonzalez Fernandez, Carol Henshaw, Caroline Kassell, Caroline Vandermeeren, Cathy Johnson, Claire Jessup, Clara Lange, Clare Lahiff, Claudia Sigge, Claudia Tavani, Claudia Zeiske, Clive Andrew Hepworth, Conners Brown, David Dimasi, David Torrance, Dorothea Koschmieder, Elaine Bevan, Elisabeth Roth, Erik Futtrup, Garrick Larkin, Gaylen Armstrong, Gerry Willms, Gill Pursey, Hannah van Meurs, Hanzer Lamora, Harley Goldberg, Hassan Shojania, Helena Reis, Howard Hopkins, Isabel von Au, Jean Linden, Jiri Navratil, Johan Rochel, John Varley, Jon Carrodus, Jonathan Montagu, Jose Antonio Alvarez Fernandez, Julia Roth, Kateřina Sobotová, Kay Rogers, Kirsten Friis, Koen Volleberg, Krista Klassen, Laura Drisaldi, Laura Jutglar Martínez, Laura van Eerten, Liam Robertson, Lorraine Meltzer, Malin Larsson & Sara Sigfridsson, Marcel de Vries, Marilyn Hicks, Mark Adam, Marleen Wieldraaijer, Martijn Grijpstra, Martin Zettersten, Maryline Jumeau, Mercedes Meyer, Michael Tesch, Mick Hansen, Micki Honkanen, Mike Dudley-Jones, Mirenda Clifford, Molly Walker, Myriam El Hadj Ali, Natalie Howell, Ole Hemmer-Hansen, Olga Gomez, Paolo Nardi, Patrick Neumann, Pavel Bandakov, Peter Lancefield, Petra van de Bovenkamp, Philip Eastaff, Piet Peters, Rachel Bristow, Rafael Villalón Almeida, Raphael Jibib, Richard Bains, Robert James, Roberto Gasperi, Rocco Baldinger, Sabine Gerull, Sabine van den Bergh, Sally McCarty, Sara Liviero, Sean Kelly, Stephanie Mitterschiffthaler & Pierluigi Maglio, Stephanie Schiest'l, Sylvester Jønsson, Sylvia Ringeling, Therese Hackr, Tjeerd Havinga, Wey Roger, Yair Lev, Zoe Porter, Zvika Rimalt,

AUTHOR THANKS

Brendan Sainsbury

Muchas gracias to all my Cuban amigos; in particular Carlos Sarimento for his fantastic company and driving skills, Julio Munoz for teaching my son how to ride a horse, Angel Rodriguez for his humor and insights, and Julio and Elsa Roque for their indispensible help in Havana. Special mentions also to Yoan and Yarelis Reyes in Viñales, Hector in Sancti Spíritus, Ramberto in Nueva Gerona, Joel and Mayra in Matanzas, and Luis Miguel in Havana.

Luke Waterson

Thank you to the spare-parts merchants, renegade mechanics, taxi drivers, dilapidated 1950s cars and out-of-the-blue hitches that made the wheels of my trip, and the wheels of every trip in Cuba, go smoothly with little more than gaffer tape and a bit of determination. Special thanks too to Maité and Idolka in

Morón, the indefatigable Rafael in Camagüey, Guido and Anley in Bayamo, Jorge in Holguín and, *por supuesto,* the ever-lovely Gisel and Nilson out east.

Classification', Hydrology and Earth System Sciences, 11, 1633¬44.

Cover photograph: Old Chevrolet parked in front of a Che Guevara mural in Havana, Cuba, Frederic Soltan/Corbis ©

ACKNOWLEDGMENTS

Climate map data adapted from Peel MC, Finlayson BL & McMahon TA (2007) 'Updated World Map of the Köppen-Geiger Climate

THIS BOOK

This 7th edition of Lonely Planet's *Cuba* guidebook was researched and written by Brendan Sainsbury (co-ordinating author) and Luke Waterson. The last edition was also researched and written by Brendan Sainsbury and Luke Waterson. The 5th edition was researched and written by Brendan Sainsbury as sole author.

This guidebook was commissioned in Lonely Planet's Oakland office, and produced by the following:

Commissioning Editor Catherine Craddock-Carrillo

Coordinating Editor Kate Whitfield

Senior Cartographers Mark Griffiths, Alison Lyall

Coordinating Layout Designer Joseph Spanti

Managing Editors Bruce Evans, Brigitte Ellemor

Managing Layout Designer Chris Girdler

Assisting Editors Penny Cordner, Adrienne Costanzo, Kate Kiely, Anne Mulvaney, Joanne Newell, Kristin Odijk, Erin Richards, Helen Yeates

Assisting Cartographers Jeff Cameron, Corey Hutchison, Rachel Imeson, Jennifer Johnston, Anthony Phelan

Cover Research Naomi Parker

Internal Image Research Kylie McLaughlin

Language Content Branislava Vladisavljevic

Thanks to Ryan Evans, Larissa Frost, Genesys India, Jouve India, Catherine Naghten, Karyn Noble, Trent Paton, Kerrianne Southway, Gerard Walker

Index

Map Legend

Sights

- Beach
- Bird Sanctuary
- Buddhist
- Castle/Palace
- Christian
- Confucian
- Hindu
- Islamic
- Jain
- Jewish
- Monument
- Museum/Gallery/Historic Building
- Ruin
- Sento Hot Baths/Onsen
- Shinto
- Sikh
- Taoist
- Winery/Vineyard
- Zoo/Wildlife Sanctuary
- Other Sight

Activities, Courses & Tours

- Bodysurfing
- Diving/Snorkelling
- Canoeing/Kayaking
- Course/Tour
- Skiing
- Snorkelling
- Surfing
- Swimming/Pool
- Walking
- Windsurfing
- Other Activity

Sleeping

- Sleeping
- Camping

Eating

- Eating

Drinking & Nightlife

- Drinking & Nightlife
- Cafe

Entertainment

- Entertainment

Shopping

- Shopping

Information

- Bank
- Embassy/Consulate
- Hospital/Medical
- Internet
- Police
- Post Office
- Telephone
- Toilet
- Tourist Information
- Other Information

Geographic

- Beach
- Hut/Shelter
- Lighthouse
- Lookout
- Mountain/Volcano
- Oasis
- Park
- Pass
- Picnic Area
- Waterfall

Population

- Capital (National)
- Capital (State/Province)
- City/Large Town
- Town/Village

Transport

- Airport
- Border crossing
- Bus
- Cable car/Funicular
- Cycling
- Ferry
- Metro station
- Monorail
- Parking
- Petrol station
- Subway station
- Taxi
- Train station/Railway
- Tram
- Underground station
- Other Transport

Note: Not all symbols displayed above appear on the maps in this book

Routes

- Tollway
- Freeway
- Primary
- Secondary
- Tertiary
- Lane
- Unsealed road
- Road under construction
- Plaza/Mall
- Steps
- Tunnel
- Pedestrian overpass
- Walking Tour
- Walking Tour detour
- Path/Walking Trail

Boundaries

- International
- State/Province
- Disputed
- Regional/Suburb
- Marine Park
- Cliff
- Wall

Hydrography

- River, Creek
- Intermittent River
- Canal
- Water
- Dry/Salt/Intermittent Lake
- Reef

Areas

- Airport/Runway
- Beach/Desert
- Cemetery (Christian)
- Cemetery (Other)
- Glacier
- Mudflat
- Park/Forest
- Sight (Building)
- Sportsground
- Swamp/Mangrove

OUR STORY

A beat-up old car, a few dollars in the pocket and a sense of adventure. In 1972 that's all Tony and Maureen Wheeler needed for the trip of a lifetime – across Europe and Asia overland to Australia. It took several months, and at the end – broke but inspired – they sat at their kitchen table writing and stapling together their first travel guide, *Across Asia on the Cheap*. Within a week they'd sold 1500 copies. Lonely Planet was born.

Today, Lonely Planet has offices in Melbourne, London and Oakland, with more than 600 staff and writers. We share Tony's belief that 'a great guidebook should do three things: inform, educate and amuse'.

OUR WRITERS

Brendan Sainsbury

Coordinating Author, Havana, Artemisa & Mayabeque, Isla de la Juventud, Pinar del Río, Matanzas, Cienfuegos, Villa Clara, Sancti Spíritus Born and bred in Hampshire, England, Brendan first visited Cuba in 1997 as a curious traveler aided by the first edition of this guidebook. He has been back 16 times in the years since, both as a travel guide and a writer, but never again as a tourist. This is his fifth Cuba-related guidebook, though he has covered numerous other countries for Lonely Planet, including Angola, Italy and the USA. Cuba remains a favorite haunt and he lists Havana (along with London, and Granada in Spain) as one of his top world cities. When not writing or traveling, Brendan enjoys following the fortunes of Southampton football club, listening to old Clash records and running ridiculous distances across deserts. Brendan also wrote the Plan Your Trip, Understand and Survival Guide chapters.

Read more about Brendan at
lonelyplanet.com/members/brendansainsbury

Luke Waterson

Ciego de Ávila, Camagüey, Las Tunas, Holguín, Granma, Santiago de Cuba, Guantánamo Was it when the church accidentally caught fire in Bayamo during fireworks commemorating, er, when Bayamo caught fire? Breaking down (again) by the most belching of Moa's nickel mines? Spying the world's smallest frog (yep, officially)? Or the endlessly incredible seafood, coffee, and cigars? Such are candidates for Luke's funniest/most serendipitous moments on research returning for this edition of Lonely Planet Cuba. Writing mainly on way-off-the-beaten-track places in Latin America (which he's spent 10 years travelling across), Luke is also, as a helpless caffeine addict, author of whimsical coffee blog BrewingRevolution.com.

Read more about Luke at
lonelyplanet.com/members/lukewaterson

Published by Lonely Planet Publications Pty Ltd
ABN 36 005 607 983
7th edition – Oct 2013
ISBN 978 1 74220 422 2
© Lonely Planet 2013   Photographs © as indicated 2013
10 9 8 7 6 5 4 3 2
Printed in China